Systems Analysis and Design:

Hoffer/George/Valacich, *Modern Systems Analysis and Design 3/e*

Marakas, *Systems Analysis and Design: An Active Approach*

Valacich/George/Hoffer, *Essentials of Systems Analysis & Design 2/e*

Kendall & Kendall, *Systems Analysis and Design 5/e*

Telecommunications, Networking and Business Data Communications:

Stamper & Case, *Business Data Communications 6/e*

Panko, *Business Data Networks and Telecommunications 4/e*

Security:

Panko, *Corporate Computer and Network Security*

Other Titles:

Awad & Ghaziri, *Knowledge Management*

Marakas, *Decision Support Systems in the 21st Century 2/e*

Marakas, *Modern Data Warehousing, Mining, and Visualization: Core Concepts*

Turban & Aronson, *Decision Support Systems and Intelligent Systems 6/e*

Database
Processing

Database Processing
Fundamentals, Design & Implementation

Ninth Edition

David M. Kroenke
University of Washington

PEARSON
Prentice Hall

Prentice Hall
Upper Saddle River, NJ 07458

Library of Congress Cataloging-in-Publication Data

Kroenke, David.
  Database processing / David Kroenke.— 9th ed.
    p. cm.
  ISBN 0-13-101514-1
  1. Database management.   I. Title.
  QA76.9.D3 K7365 2002
  005.74—dc21

                                                    2002153328

Executive Editor, MIS: David Alexander
Publisher: Natalie E. Anderson
Editorial Assistant: Maat Van Uitert
Senior Marketing Manager: Sharon K. Turkovich
Production Editor: Vanessa Nuttry
Manufacturing Buyer: Natacha St. Hill Moore
Designer: Patricia Smythe
Cover Design/Illustration: Jerry McDaniel
Manager, Print Production: Vincent Scelta
Text Printer/Binder: Quebecor World
Executive Editor, MIS: Bob Horan
Editorial Project Manager: Kyle Hannon
Media Project Manager: Joan Waxman
Managing Editor (Production): Gail Steier de Acevedo
Permissions Supervisor: Suzanne Grappi
Design Manager: Maria Lange
Interior Design: Heather Peres
Line Art (interior): ElectraGraphics, Inc.
Cover Printer: Phoenix Color
Composition/Full-Service Project Management: Impressions Book & Journal Services, Inc.

Credits and acknowledgments borrowed from other sources and reproduced, with permission, in this textbook appear on appropriate page within text.

Microsoft® and Windows® are registered trademarks of the Microsoft Corporation in the U.S.A. and other countries. Screen shots and icons reprinted with permission from the Microsoft Corporation. This book is not sponsored or endorsed by or affiliated with the Microsoft Corporation.

Pearson Education LTD.
Pearson Education Singapore, Pte. Ltd
Pearson Education, Canada, Ltd
Pearson Education–Japan
Pearson Education Australia PTY, Limited
Pearson Education North Asia Ltd
Pearson Educación de Mexico, S.A. de C.V.
Pearson Education Malaysia, Pte. Ltd

10 9 8 7 6 5 4 3 2 1

ISBN 0-13-101514-1

Brief Contents

Contents

Preface

Databases are everywhere. They provide core functionality for client-server applications, for legacy organizational applications, and for both business-to-consumer and business-to-business e-commerce applications. They are also used on millions of desktops. Because of this popularity, database processing has become the most important topic in the information systems curriculum. Knowledge of database design, development, administration, and access technology is critical for the success of every information systems graduate.

Unfortunately, increased popularity has not meant increased competency. Many students (as well as professionals) have been deceived by the simplicity of creating a small databases using products such as Microsoft Access. With this background, they believe they know sufficient database technology to create databases that have more complicated structure and greater processing complexity. The result is often a mess: databases that are hard to use, barely meet system requirements, and are difficult to redesign.

The situation is similar to that for teaching computer programming. Having learned the syntax of a language, students think they can build complicated applications without learning program design skills as well. The importance of program design becomes apparent only as the programs become larger and more complex.

► CHANGES IN DATABASE PROCESSING FROM THE EIGHTH EDITION

The increased importance of database technology along with the disturbing prevalence of poorly designed databases caused me to reflect seriously on the organization of this text. The result is the most extensive revision in nine editions.

Deeper Discussions of Data Modeling and Database Design

To begin, I decided that the text needed a deeper discussion of both data modeling and database design. With that decision, I realized that presenting two data modeling techniques in parallel is not the best method for teaching novices. Students need greater understanding of one technique and much more practice applying it. Consequently, I de-emphasized the semantic object model by placing it in an appendix and deepened the discussion of the entity-relationship model. In this edition, you will find two chapters on E-R modeling. Also, to facilitate students' learning of data modeling, those chapters conclude with pages and pages of data modeling questions and projects. For students to gain data modeling proficiency, I believe it is essential for them to answer those questions and work those projects.

One of the challenges of going deeper into the E-R model is that there is no generally accepted version of it. As discussed in Chapter 2, there is the classic E-R model, the Information Processing version, the national standard IDEF1X version, and the version that has been incorporated into UML. To take the E-R model discussion deeper, I had to decide which of these versions to use. The decision process is explained in Chapter 2; the gist of the decision is that although I believe the UML version will ultimately be the most important, at present, the IDEF1X version is more useful because it is found in popular data modeling tools such as Visio and ERWin. Thus, the bulk of the discussion in Chapters 2, 3, and 5 uses IDEF1X. The UML version is presented, however, at the end of Chapter 2.

With a deeper discussion of data modeling, the database design chapters can delve more deeply as well. This edition includes two chapters on database design. Chapter 5 describes the transformation of data models into database designs, and Chapter 8 presents database redesign. The discussion in Chapter 5 now includes much more than "where to put the foreign key." In particular, referential integrity actions are discussed at length. Additionally, more advanced topics, such as the design for recursive relationships and designs for binary constraints on ternary relationships, are also discussed. Chapter 5 concludes with more than 80 questions and projects, as well as tasks for both the FiredUp and Twigs running cases.

Upon graduation, few students will begin by designing a database from scratch. Rather, most students are more likely to work first on database redesign projects. Consequently, I added a new chapter that addresses this important topic. This new chapter appears after the chapters on SQL because SQL is required to understand and to accomplish database redesign. As a side benefit, redesign requires the use of correlated subqueries and EXISTS/NOT EXISTS, and this new topic provides realistic examples of their use.

Extended SQL Coverage

In addition to expanding the coverage of data modeling and database design, I have also expanded the SQL coverage in this edition. Chapter 6 discusses basic SQL for both data definition and data manipulation. Data definition SQL is important because graphical design tools cannot be used programmatically, and they become tedious to use repetitively. Chapter 6 presents basic DML for the SQL-92 standard, and includes two formats of join as well as a discussion of inner and outer joins.

Chapter 7 introduces a sample database for View Ridge Galleries; this database is used extensively in the chapters that follow. Chapter 7 then builds on the SQL from Chapter 6 and describes the use of SQL in database applications. SQL views are discussed extensively, as well as techniques for embedding SQL in applications. Also, Chapter 7 includes discussions of the use of SQL in triggers and stored procedures.

Chapter 8 then shows the use of SQL for database redesign. As stated, this chapter will give the students a realistic understanding of the use and need for more complicated SQL statements.

XML and ADO.NET

A third major change in this edition occurs in Chapter 13. This chapter presents a complete rewrite of the XML discussion from the eighth edition, and it includes a new discussion of ADO.NET. Regardless of one's opinion about Microsoft, ADO.NET datasets are a major innovation and are exceedingly important for XML Web services. With ADO.NET, the developer can create a full relational database in memory that is disconnected from any external database managed by Oracle, DB2, SQL Server or other DBMS product. Such a database can be managed by applications written in any of the .NET languages such as C#, C++, or VB.NET.

Chapter 13 uses VB.NET to create an ASP.NET application that creates a dataset and produces table, XML, and XML schema views of that dataset. To reduce the heavy Microsoft presence, this application shows the use of ADO.NET in conjunction with Oracle.

Balanced Coverage of Oracle 9i and SQL Server 2000

With the exception of ADO.NET, I have balanced equally the discussions of Oracle and SQL Server. Chapter 7 shows pseudo-triggers and pseudo-stored procedures that have both an Oracle and SQL Sever flavor. Chapter 9 introduces multi-user DBMS with a balanced discussion of Oracle and SQL Server features. Chapter 10 (using Oracle) and Chapter 11 (using SQL Server) have the same outline and depth of coverage. The same stored procedures and triggers are illustrated in both chapters. Chapter 12 shows ASP applications that drive both Oracle and SQL Server databases. Because SQL Server does not provide object-oriented functionality like Oracle does, Chapter 16 has a definite Oracle flavor.

You can order this text bound with either Oracle or SQL Server. The text has been designed so that you can use either product with equal success.

▶ ORGANIZATION OF THE TEXT

Chapter 1 introduces database processing using the framework of why, what, how. The need for database processing is illustrated by describing the problems of managing non-normalized data in a spreadsheet. Then, the components of a database system are described and a summary of the database development process is presented. Chapter 1 concludes with a brief history of database processing.

Chapters 2 and 3 discuss data modeling using the entity-relationship model. Chapter 2 describes E-R tools, including the traditional E-R model, IDEF1X, and UML, and then illustrates techniques for using these tools. Chapter 3 extends the data modeling discussion by explaining the data-modeling process, presenting modeling examples of illustrative forms and reports, and demonstrating the development of a data model for a small university.

Chapters 4 and 5 consider database design. Chapter 4 introduces the relational model and describes normalization. Chapter 5 then shows how to transform entity-relationship data models into relational designs. As stated, this chapter goes deeper than just describing where to place the foreign keys. Referential integrity rules and actions are discussed in detail.

The next three chapters present SQL. Chapter 6 introduces SQL, and describes and illustrates SQL for data definition and data manipulation. Chapter 7 then shows the use of SQL in applications and includes discussions on views, embedded SQL, triggers, and stored procedures. Chapter 8 then addresses database redesign. The chapter begins by discussing correlated subqueries and EXISTS/NOT EXISTS. Then, the process for performing database redesign is described and categories of redesign activities are discussed.

The chapters in Part IV have a common structure. Chapter 9 introduces data administration and database administration, and discusses the challenges of managing a large, multi-user database. Chapter 10 then follows the outline of Chapter 9 to present features and functions of Oracle 9i, including the use of stored procedures and triggers. Chapter 11 parallels the discussion in Chapter 10, and describes features and functions of SQL Sever 2000.

Chapter 12, 13, and 14 concern the processing of databases from applications. Chapter 12 discusses ODBC, OLE DB, and ADO; and shows the use of VBScript for invoking ADO from ASP pages. The database and stored procedures developed in Chapters 10 and 11 are used for illustrating Oracle and SQL Server processing from ASP. Chapter 13 introduces XML and XML Schema, and explains their importance for database processing. The second half of Chapter 13 illustrates SELECT...FOR XML statements, and explains and demonstrates the use of ADO.NET for creating and processing datasets. The capability of datasets to provide table, XML, and XML Schema views of the same data is illustrated.

Chapter 14 shows database processing using open-source software. The role of JDBC and the use of Java and Java Server Pages are described, and a database is developed using MySQL for the View Ridge Gallery—the same example used for Oracle and SQL Server in Chapters 10 and 11. Students should be able to gain the gist of the discussion, even if they are not Java programmers. Students who know Java should find this chapter easy to read.

Chapters 15 and 16 conclude the text. Chapter 15 addresses enterprise database processing and discusses OLAP. Chapter 16 presents concepts and techniques for object-oriented databases. The use of Oracle facilities for object-relational databases is discussed.

Two appendices are included. Appendix A presents basic data structures. Appendix B presents the semantic object model, and shows how such models can be transformed into relational database designs. This appendix includes all of the conceptual material on this model from the eighth edition of this text; only examples have been removed. The instructor's manual includes a discussion of the experiences I have had over the years, including several critical mistakes, while attempting to introduce the semantic object model to industry.

▶ SUPPLEMENTS

Instructor's Resource CD-ROM (0-13-140241-2)

Most of the support materials described in the following section are available for adopters on the Instructor's Resource CD-ROM. The CD includes the Instructor's Resource Manual, Test Item File, TestGen, PowerPoint slides, and the helpful lecture tool "Image Library."

Image Library (on the Instructor's Resource CD-ROM)

The Image Library is an impressive resource to help instructors create vibrant lecture presentations. Nearly every figure in the text is provided and organized by chapter for convenience. These images and lecture notes can be easily imported into Microsoft PowerPoint to create new presentations or to add to existing ones.

Instructor's Manual (on the Instructor's Resource CD-ROM)

The Instructor's Manual, by Glenn T. Smith of James Madison University, not only features the answers to Group 1 and 2 questions, Fired Up Projects, and Twigs Tree Trimming Service Projects; but also contains teaching objectives and teaching suggestions. This supplement and the corresponding solution files can be downloaded from the secure faculty section of the Kroenke Web site, and is also available on the Instructor's Resource CD-ROM.

Test Item File (on the Instructor's Resource CD-ROM)

The Test Item File, by David J. Auer of Western Washington University, is a comprehensive collection of true–false, multiple-choice, fill-in-the-blank, and essay questions. The questions are rated by difficulty level, and the answers are referenced by page number. An electronic version of the Test Item File and TestGen, a computerized test bank, are available on the Instructor's Resource CD-ROM.

PowerPoint Slides (on the Web and Instructor's Resource CD-ROM)

Electronic color slides, by Ranida Boonthanom of Florida State University, are available in Microsoft PowerPoint, Version 2000. The slides illuminate and build on key concepts in the text. Both students and faculty can download the PowerPoint slides from the Web site, and they are also provided on the Instructor's Resource CD-ROM.

Companion Web Site (www.prenhall.com/kroenke)

There is a dedicated Web site for the text that provides a dynamic complement to the text. The site includes an Interactive Study Guide, created by Carol Buse of Amarillo College, for students, select text figures with computer code, and Tabledesigner software which allows you to create semantic object models and transform those models into Microsoft Access or other databases.

▶ ACKNOWLEDGMENTS

First, I want to thank the reviewers of the eighth edition who provided helpful and insightful guidance during the process of creating this major revision:

Karen Dowling, Arizona State University
Richard Heath, St. Cloud State University
Vicki Jonathan, Portland Community College
Brian Mackie, Northern Illinois University
Matt McGowan, Bradley University
Claire McInerney, Rutgers University
Chang Miao, Northwestern University
Marty Murray, Portland Community College
David Palzer, Clover Park Technical College
David Petrie, University of Redlands
Linda Preece, Southern Illinois University
Kevin Roberts, Devry University
Asharif Shirani, San Jose State University
Eileen Sikkema, University of Washington
Bob Spear, University of Maryland
Sharon Tuttle, Humboldt State University
Diane Walz, University of Texas at San Antonio
Peter Wolcott, University of Nebraska Omaha

In addition, I thank Donald Nilson of the Microsoft Corporation for extensive discussions with me regarding the purpose and functionality of ADO.NET. Also, I wish to thank Harry A. Sparks of Sparks Consulting (and an adjunct professor at Webster University in St. Louis) for suggestions on how to improve the security discussion in Chapter 9. I also thank Marcia Williams at Bellevue Community College and all of the attendees in my classes at the Educator to Educator Conference in Bellevue, Washington, in the summer of 2002.

I believe this edition of *Database Processing* is the best edition ever. In large measure that is due to the time and attention of Bob Horan, my editor at Prentice Hall. I sincerely thank Bob for his enthusiasm and for his wise guidance and direction. Also, I thank Kyle Hannon of Prentice Hall who, in spite of an incredibly busy schedule, always does a great job on myriads of editorial tasks. Thanks also to Vanessa Nuttry in production at Prentice Hall. Vanessa has managed the production of three of my books, and I am sincerely grateful to her for her dedication and professionalism in all of these projects. Finally, I thank Lynda, my wife, for her love, patience, and understanding.

David Kroenke
Seattle, Washington

David M. Kroenke

David M. Kroenke is one of the pioneers in database technology. In 1971, while working at the Pentagon, he programmed one of the world's first DBMS products. In 1974, Grace Hopper appointed him to the CODAYSL EUF committee; and in 1977, he worked as a consultant for Fred Brooks at IBM. He helped to start the Microrim Corporation, where he led the development of the R:base family of DBMS products. In a 1991 article, Wayne Ratliff credited one of Kroenke's textbooks for giving him the idea for the development of d:base. In 1989, Kroenke consulted with Microsoft on the project that lead to the development of Microsoft Access. He is also the father of the semantic object model, a data model that many believe is superior to the entity-relationship model.

Kroenke is the author of five computer textbooks; his text *Database Processing* was first published in 1977, and is currently in its ninth edition. In 1990 and 1991, he was the Hanson Professor of Management Science at the University of Washington. In that same year the International Association for Computer Information Systems named him Computer Educator of the Year. Most recently, Kroenke has been teaching at the University of Washington. He holds a B.S. degree in economics from the U.S. Air Force Academy, an M.S. in management science from the University of Southern California, and a Ph.D. from Colorado State University, where he studied linear models under Franklin Graybill.

CHAPTER 1

Introduction to Database Processing

Database processing has always been an important topic in the study of information systems. In recent years, however, the explosion of the Internet and the dramatic development of new technology for the Internet have made knowledge of database technology one of the hottest career paths. Database technology enables Internet applications to step beyond the simple brochure publishing that characterized early applications. At the same time, Internet technology provides a standardized and readily accessible means of publishing database content to users. None of these new developments takes away from the need for classical database applications that were vital to business interests prior to the rise of the Internet. They simply amplify the importance of database knowledge.

Many students find this subject enjoyable and interesting, even though it can be challenging. Database design and development involve both art and engineering. Understanding user requirements and translating them into effective database designs is an artistic process. Transforming those designs into physical databases with functionally complete, high-performance applications is an engineering process. Both aspects are full of challenging and enjoyable intellectual puzzles.

Because of the immense need for database technology, the skills you develop and the knowledge you gain in this course will be in great demand. The goal of this text is to provide a solid foundation in the fundamentals of database technology so that you can begin a successful career in this field if you choose to do so.

In this chapter, we will address the why, what, and how of database processing. We will discuss why databases are used, tell you what the components of database systems are, and summarize how database systems are developed. We will conclude this chapter with a sketch of the history of database processing.

WHY USE A DATABASE?

The purpose of a database is to help people and organizations keep track of things. On the surface, that sounds like a modest goal, and you might be wondering why we need complicated technology and a whole course devoted to such a subject. Most of us just make a list when we need to keep track of something. I have a list of things to do this week, a list of things to buy at the grocery store, a list of expenses for tax reporting, and so forth. Why not do the same for information systems?

In the very early stages of information technology, lists were used—punched on cards and written on computer tape. Over time, however, it became clear that quite a few problems developed with such lists. In the next section, we will discuss those problems and then we will describe how databases are constructed to solve them.

Problems of Lists

Consider the list shown in Figure 1-1, which is a list used by Lakeview Equipment Rentals. Lakeview rents construction equipment such as backhoes and cranes to construction contractors. Figure 1-1 shows just a small portion of its rental activity, but even this small example illustrates a number of important problems with lists.

FIGURE 1-1

Lakeview Equipment Example List

Lakeview Equipment Rentals									
Job	**Contractor**	**Phone**	**Equipment Type**	**Equipment Number**	**Daily Rate**	**Start Date**	**End Date**	**Days**	**Charge**
Sea View Bldg	KH Services	213.444.1181	Backhoe	10400	$750	6/17/2002	6/19/2002	3	$2,250
Highland Center	Comstock, Inc	232.492.3383	Backhoe	10400	$750	6/24/2002	6/24/2002	1	$750
Sea View Bldg	KH Services	213.444.1181	Medium Crane	335	$350	6/17/2002	7/3/2002	17	$5,950
Long Plaza	KH Services	213.444.1181	Backhoe	10020	$650	7/1/2002	7/3/2002	3	$1,950
Sea View Bldg	KH Services	213.444.1181	Scaffolding		$135	6/15/2002			
Highland Center	Comstock, Inc	232.492.3383	Medium Crane	335	$400	7/1/2002	7/8/2002	8	$3,200
Village Square	RB Partnership	508.555.3233	Backhoe	10020	$750	7/8/2002	7/11/2002	4	$3,000

For one, what happens if a contractor changes its phone number? Suppose, for example, that KH Services changes its number to 213.444.9988. To keep this list accurate, we need to make changes in four lines. If we do not make the change in all four lines, we'll have inconsistent data, and we won't know which number is the correct one. Further, suppose this list has rental activity for a whole quarter or year. There might be hundreds or thousands of rows in the list. To record the changed phone number, we would need to search the list and make the correct change for every row that has KH Services. This process is both time-consuming and error-prone.

A related problem occurs when we delete data from such a list. Say RB Partnership decides not to rent the back hoe, so we delete the last line. In the process of that deletion, not only do we lose data about the rental, but we also lose the phone number for RB Partnership, we lose the fact that RB Partnership is working on a project named Village Square, and we lose the fact that they had agreed to rent the back hoe at a daily rate of $750. Most likely, we only wanted to remove the data about the date of the rental.

In a similar vein, what do we do when we have some (but not all) of the data? Maybe we know that University Swaging has a phone number of 206.555.8989 and that it is working on a job called Center Street Bridge Renewal. We want to record that data, but where does it go in this list? As yet, this company has not rented from us.

Another problem concerns data inconsistencies. We could make a simple keying mistake in the contractor name and accidentally have a KJ Services as well as a KH services. Users of the list will wonder whether we have a new customer or whether it is a mistake. Such errors could not occur if we chose a contractor from a list of existing contractors.

Some inconsistencies are more subtle. Examine the fourth and last rows. They each refer to the rental of a backhoe with the Equipment Number of 10020. In row four, the daily rate is $650, but in the last row, it is $750. Now, is this an inconsistency due to a keying mistake, or do rental rates vary from one rental to another? Or, maybe rental rates vary from contractor to contractor. In that case, KH Services has negotiated a price of $650 for that back hoe, and RB Partnership has negotiated a price of $750. If this latter case is correct, then we have to make sure that every time we enter the combination of KH Services and back hoe number 10020, we also enter the price of $650.

Still another problem concerns missing data. There is no value for End Date in the rental of the scaffolding. Is this a keying mistake or does it mean something else? It could mean that the rental is not yet over or that KH Services wants to keep the scaffolding for an indeterminate period.

Problems of Shared Data

Other problems with using a list come to light when you consider that this data must be shared among many people at Lakeview Equipment Rentals. Lakeview wants everyone to have access to contractor names and phone numbers from a common data source. That way, if there's a change in a phone number, that change need only be made in the common source for everyone in the company to have it. Otherwise, employees have to update that data item many times on many computers.

If the contractor data is shared, however, other problems develop. Accounting wants to keep track of contractor invoices, amounts due, and payments. Sales wants to keep track of contractor contacts, meetings, and requests. Customer support wants to know what problems have developed for specific contractors and what has been done to solve those problems. And those departments don't necessarily want to share all of that data with each other. To improve accounting controls, the accounting department does not want anyone outside of accounting to have access to the invoice and payment data. To protect the privacy of its customers, the support department does not want everyone at Lakeview to know what problems its customers are having. So, the departments want to share some, but not all, of their data.

There are other problems with using lists, but you get the idea. We need a more robust way of storing data.

Databases as Groups of Related Tables

One serious problem with lists like the one in Figure 1-1 is that they contain data about many different themes. Remember your eighth-grade English teacher? He or she said a paragraph should have a single theme. If you have a paragraph with two or more themes, you should break it up into different paragraphs, each with a single theme. That is the essence of a process called **normalization**, which we will investigate in depth in Chapter 4.

Examine the list in Figure 1-1. How many themes are there? There is one for jobs, one for contractors, one for equipment, and one for rentals. Figure 1-2 shows the results of breaking the list up into these separate components. Each of these components is a table of data, so we will refer to them as *tables*.

When the list is broken up into four tables, many of the problems we discussed earlier disappear. If KH Services changes its phone number to 213.444.9988, we just make that change once, in the CONTRACTOR table. If we want to delete a rental, we just delete a row from the RENTAL table; we will not lose any data about jobs, contractors, or equipment. If we want to add data for a new customer, we just add that data to the CONTRACTOR table.

With regard to data inconsistencies, we can design our database application so that when someone needs to record a new rental, they just pick from a list of choices in the CONTRACTOR table. That way, they cannot make a keying mistake. This, by the way, will also give us a way to control the acceptance of new customers; we can make it so that only certain people, maybe those in accounting, can add new rows to the CONTRACTOR table.

What about the inconsistent rental rate in Figure 1-1? For me, this is where the fun begins. In Figure 1-2, Daily Rate is placed into the EQUIPMENT table. This means that a piece of equipment should rent for the same rate for all customers. The design of these tables implies that statement. Now, is that correct? It depends on the business rules and customs at Lakeview. It is correct if the users at Lakeview say that's what they do. If, however, the rate is negotiated separately for every rental, Daily Rate should be placed in the RENTAL table. If every contractor negotiates its own rate, a new table must be constructed.

The point here is not to solve this particular problem. The point is that table design must reflect the practices and policies of the organization that uses it. We will spend a good deal of time and effort in this text addressing this very issue.

FIGURE 1-2

Lakeview Equipment Data in Tables

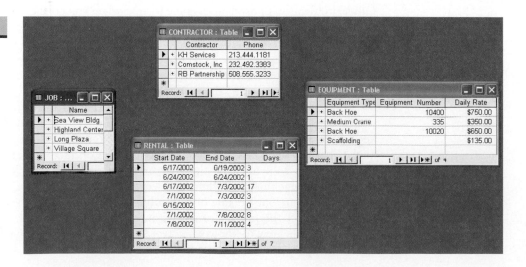

FIGURE 1-3

CONTRACTOR Table with Additional Data

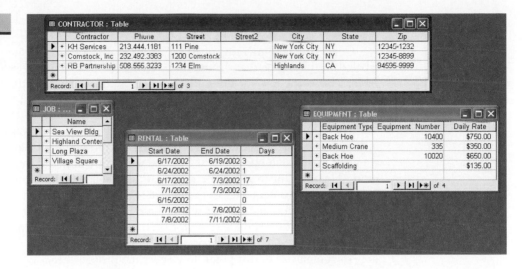

Breaking the tables up also enables us to add more data about each theme than appear in the list in Figure 1-1. Figure 1-3, for example, shows additional data for contractors. If necessary, we can develop our database applications so that only authorized personnel will be able to view this additional data.

Expressing Relationships

By now, you must be really frustrated with a burning question. The data in Figure 1-2 or 1-3 are fine, but where are the relationships? How do I know which contractor rented which equipment for which job on which dates? It's not possible to tell from the data in either of these figures what relates to what.

Here again, we have come to one of the fundamental questions in database processing. We will address that question in Chapters 5 and 8 when we discuss database design. For now, consider Figure 1-4, which shows one way of relating these tables.

We have given each row an arbitrary unique identifier, labeled ID, in each of the tables in Figure 1-4. This identifier has no meaning to the users at Lakeview; its purpose

FIGURE 1-4

Lakeview Tables with Relationships

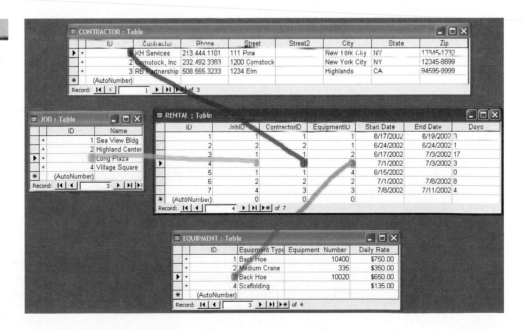

is just to give a unique identity to each row of each table. We can use the values of ID to represent a connection to a RENTAL row.

Consider the fourth row of RENTAL in Figure 1-4. The value of 3 in the column labeled JobID means that this rental is for the job having an ID value of 3 in the JOB table. This is the row for Long Plaza, which is consistent with the data in Figure 1-1. Similarly, this rental is for the contractor having an ID of 1 (KH Services) and for the equipment having an ID of 3 (back hoe number 10020).

The list in Figure 1-1 shows a column labeled Charge, but no such column appears in Figure 1-4. The reason for this is that we can compute the Charge column whenever we need it. Thus, in our database, Charge will be a computed rather than a stored column. This may or may not be a good design, again depending on the policies at Lakeview. One consequence of this design is that if a value of Daily Rate in RENTAL is changed, then all of the charges will be based on the new rate when they are next computed. We may thus show a value for Charge that is different from what the customer was charged at the time. Again, we will discuss issues like this in chapters to come.

To summarize to this point, to correct the problems that occur with a list like the one in Figure 1-1, we break the list up into four tables, each table having its own theme. Then, we relate the tables using a unique identifier. As you will learn, the unique identifier is called a key column, or simply **key**. A key that represents a relationship such as JobID in RENTAL is called a **foreign key**. We will use those terms many times in the discussions to follow.

Joining Tables Together

"Aha," you are saying, "but where's my list?" Figure 1-4 might be great from the standpoint of the database design, but the users at Lakeview, at least some of them, will want to see a list like the one with which we started. Where is it?

Chapters 6 through 8 discuss a language, really a data sublanguage, called **Structured Query Language,** or **SQL** (pronounced SEE-QUEL), that is used to manipulate tables like the one in Figure 1-4. SQL is an industry standard that is supported by all major database management system (DBMS) products. The following SQL statement was used in Access to join the tables together to display a list like that in Figure 1-1.

```
SELECT JOB.Name, CONTRACTOR.Contractor, CONTRACTOR.Phone,
        EQUIPMENT.[Equipment Type], EQUIPMENT.[Equipment Number],
        EQUIPMENT.[Daily Rate], RENTAL.[Start Date], RENTAL.[End Date],
        RENTAL.Days, [Daily Rate]*[Days] AS Charge
FROM   JOB, EQUIPMENT, CONTRACTOR, RENTAL
WHERE CONTRACTOR.ID = RENTAL.ContractorID
AND    EQUIPMENT.ID = RENTAL.EquipmentID
AND    JOB.ID = RENTAL.JobID;
```

The result of this statement is the table shown in Figure 1-5. This table contains the list, corrected for errors, with which we started.

Examine the preceding SQL statement to determine its general structure, but do not be concerned about understanding its particulars. By the time you finish this text, you will easily be able to write statements like this and others of greater complexity.

FIGURE 1-5

Original List Constructed from Tables

Job	Contractor	Phone	Equipment Type	Equipment Number	Daily Rate	Start Date	End Date	Days	Charge
Sea View Bldg	KH Services	213.444.1181	Back Hoe	10400	$750.00	6/17/2002	6/19/2002	3	$2,250.00
Highland Center	Comstock, Inc	232.492.3383	Back Hoe	10400	$750.00	6/24/2002	6/24/2002	1	$750.00
Sea View Bldg	KH Services	213.444.1181	Medium Crane	335	$350.00	6/17/2002	7/3/2002	17	$5,950.00
Long Plaza	KH Services	213.444.1181	Back Hoe	10020	$650.00	7/1/2002	7/3/2002	3	$1,950.00
Sea View Bldg	KH Services	213.444.1181	Scaffolding		$135.00	6/15/2002		0	$0.00
Highland Center	Comstock, Inc	232.492.3383	Medium Crane	335	$350.00	7/1/2002	7/8/2002	8	$2,800.00
Village Square	RB Partnership	508.555.3233	Back Hoe	10020	$650.00	7/8/2002	7/11/2002	4	$2,600.00

Record: 1 of 7

WHAT IS A DATABASE PROCESSING SYSTEM?

Figure 1-6 shows the four basic elements of a database. Starting from the left, users employ the database system to perform their jobs. They input new data, modify existing data, and delete data. They also read data in a variety of ways: through forms, via queries, and by producing reports. The next component, a database application, is a set of one or more computer programs that serves as an intermediary between the user and the DBMS, a program that processes the database. The application produces forms, queries, and reports; sends and receives data to and from the user; and transforms user actions into requests for data management activity by the DBMS.

The purpose of the DBMS is to receive requests from applications and to translate those requests into reads and writes on the database files. In most cases, the DBMS receives SQL statements and translates those statements into instructions to the computer's operating system to read and write data in the database files. Now, consider the functions of the application program and the DBMS in more detail.

Functions of Application Programs

Figure 1-7 lists the functions of database applications and the DBMS. First, the application program creates and processes forms. In the case of a Web-based application, for

FIGURE 1-6

Components of a Database System

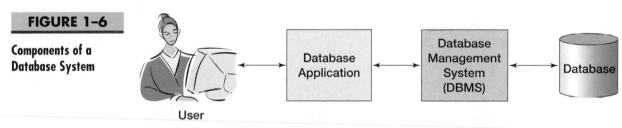

User

FIGURE 1-7

Functions and Content of Database Processing Components

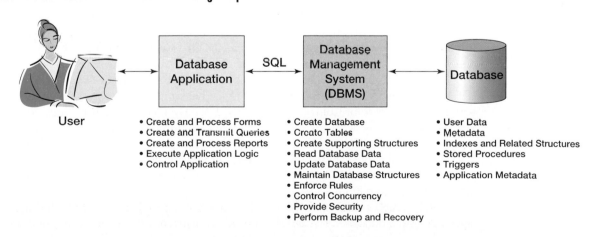

User

- Create and Process Forms
- Create and Transmit Queries
- Create and Process Reports
- Execute Application Logic
- Control Application

- Create Database
- Create Tables
- Create Supporting Structures
- Read Database Data
- Update Database Data
- Maintain Database Structures
- Enforce Rules
- Control Concurrency
- Provide Security
- Perform Backup and Recovery

- User Data
- Metadata
- Indexes and Related Structures
- Stored Procedures
- Triggers
- Application Metadata

example, the application program generates HTML and other Web-form constructs that cause the form to be displayed on the user's computer. When the user fills out the form and sends the data back, the application program then determines which tables of data need to be modified and sends requests to the DBMS to cause needed modifications. If errors occur in this process, the application program receives the errors and generates an appropriate message to the user or takes some other action.

The second function of the application program shown in Figure 1-7 is to create and transmit queries. Here, the application program first generates a query request to the DBMS. Such requests are almost always expressed in SQL. Once the query has been processed, the results are formatted and then transmitted to the user. The third function is similar to the second. The application program first queries the DBMS for data (again using SQL) and then formats the results of the query in the form of a report.

In addition to forms, queries, and reports, the application program also takes other action to update the database in accordance with application-specific logic. For example, in an order entry application, suppose a user requests 10 units of a particular item. Further, suppose that when the application program queries the database (via the DBMS), it finds only 8 items in stock. What should happen? It depends on the logic of that particular application. Perhaps no items should be removed from inventory and the user should be notified, or perhaps the 8 items should be removed and 2 more placed on back order. Or perhaps some other action should be taken. Whatever the case, it is the job of the application program to execute the appropriate logic.

The last function for application programs listed in Figure 1-7 is to control the application. There are two ways in which this is done. First, the application needs to be written so that only logical options are presented to the user. The application may generate a menu with user choices. If so, it needs to ensure that only appropriate choices are available. Second, the application needs to control data activities with the DBMS. The application may direct the DBMS, for example, to make a certain set of data changes as a unit. The DBMS may be told to either make all of these changes or make none of them.

Functions of the DBMS

Whereas application programs are often written by companies that use them, the DBMS is almost always licensed as a commercial product. Commercial DBMS products include Oracle from the Oracle Corporation, DB2 from the IBM Corporation, and Access and SQL Server from Microsoft. There are dozens of other DBMS products, but these four have the lion's share of the market.

Functions of the DBMS product are listed in Figure 1-7. The DBMS is used to create the database itself, to create tables, and to create other supporting structures such as indexes.

The next two functions of the DBMS are to read and update database data. To do this, the DBMS receives SQL and other requests and transforms those requests into actions on the database. Another DBMS function is to maintain all of the database structures. For example, it may be necessary to change the format of a table or other supporting structure from time to time. Developers use the DBMS to make such changes.

With most DBMS products, it is possible to declare rules about data values for the DBMS to enforce. For example, in Figure 1-4, what would happen if a user mistakenly entered a value of 4 for ContractorID in the RENTAL table? There is no such contractor, and such a value will cause numerous errors. To prevent this situation, it is possible to declare to the DBMS that any value of ContractorID in the RENTAL table must already be a value of ID in the CONTRACTOR table. If no such value exists, the insert or update request is to be disallowed. Such rules, called **referential integrity constraints**, are enforced by the DBMS.

The last three functions of the DBMS listed in Figure 1-7 have to do with the management of the database. The DBMS controls concurrency by ensuring that one user's work does not inappropriately interfere with another user's work. This important (and complicated) function will be discussed in Chapter 9. Also, the DBMS contains a security system that is used to ensure that only authorized users perform authorized activities against the database. Users can be prevented from seeing certain data and their actions can be constrained to making only certain data changes on specified data.

Finally, the database, as a centralized repository of data, is a valuable organizational asset. Consider, for example, the value of the book database to a company such as Amazon.com. Because the database is so important, steps need to be taken to ensure that no data will be lost in the event of errors, hardware problems, or natural catastrophes. The DBMS provides facilities for backing up database data and recovering it from backups when necessary.

Definition and Components of the Database

In Figure 1-7, the rightmost component of a database system is the database itself. Before continuing, we need to define the term *database* more specifically and describe its components as well.

In the most general case, *a database is a self-describing collection of related records*. For all relational databases (almost all databases today, and the only type we consider in this book), we can modify this definition to say *a database is a self-describing collection of related tables*.

The key terms in this definition are *self-describing* and *related tables*. You already have a good idea of what we mean by *related tables*. JOB, CONTRACTOR, EQUIPMENT, and RENTAL are examples of related tables. We will add to your understanding of this term in Chapters 5 and 8.

By *self-describing*, we mean that a description of the structure of the database is contained within the database itself. Because this is so, we can always determine the contents of a database just by looking inside it. We don't have to look anyplace else. This situation is akin to that of your campus library. You can tell what's in the library by examining the card catalog that resides within the library itself.

Data about the structure of a database is called **metadata**. Examples of metadata are the names of tables, the names of columns and the tables to which they belong; properties of tables and columns; and so forth.

Figure 1-8 shows example metadata for the Lakeview database described earlier. A table named SYSTABLES contains data about each of the tables in the database, and a second table named SYSCOLUMNS contains data about each of the columns and the relationship of the column to the tables. This figure is just an example of metadata; tables like this exist within databases processed by products such as Oracle, SQL Server, or DB2, but they are more complicated. Note, however, that the metadata itself is carried in tables. This means that knowledgeable personnel can use SQL to query the metadata, just as they query user data.

All DBMS vendors provide a set of tools for displaying the structure of their databases. For example, Figure 1-9 shows the use of the Describe command in an Oracle database. As shown, this command lists the names and properties of columns in a table.

According to Figure 1-7, the database contains user data and metadata, as just described. A database also has indexes and other structures that exist to improve database performance. We'll say more about such structures as we proceed. For now, just understand that an index is like the index at the back of the book. Instead of showing where certain topics can be found in the book, however, it shows where certain records can be found in a table. For example, one might construct an index on EquipmentID in RENTAL. This index could be used to quickly locate all rows in RENTAL that have a particular value of ID.

A **stored procedure** is a program that is stored within the database. Some stored procedures are utility programs for the database. For example, Lakeview might have a stored procedure that removes and backs up all rental data that is more than a year old, as long as all payments for that rental data have been received. Such a stored procedure

FIGURE 1-8

Example Metadata

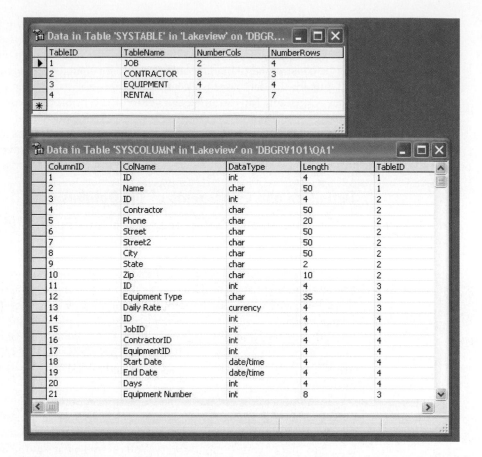

FIGURE 1-9

Use of Oracle Describe Command

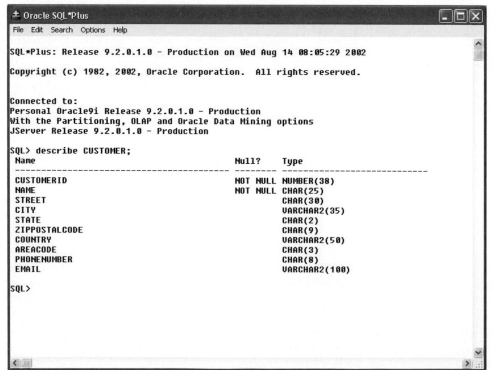

may need to check many tables in the database and execute complicated logic. Other stored procedures implement portions of application logic. An example is a stored procedure for generating back orders.

A **trigger** is a procedure that is executed when a particular data activity occurs. Lakeview might have a CustomerCheck trigger that ensures that a customer is in good credit standing before any new RENTAL data can be stored for that customer. Whenever an attempt is made to add a row to the RENTAL table, the DBMS will load and process the trigger before making the update. In this case, the trigger will disallow the insertion of a new row if the credit is bad. Like stored procedures, triggers are stored in the database. Stored procedures and triggers are written either in a language that is unique to the DBMS, or they are written in a general-purpose language such as Java. You will learn about stored procedures and triggers in Chapters 10 and 11.

Finally, some databases contain application metadata; this is simply data that describe application elements such as forms and reports. Microsoft Access, for example, carries application metadata as part of its databases.

Three Example Database Systems

Database technology can be used in a wide array of applications. On one .end of the continuum, a researcher might use database technology to track the results of experiments in his or her lab. In such a database there might be only a few tables, and each table would have, at most, several hundred rows. The researcher would be the only user of this application.

At the other end of the continuum there are enormous databases that support international organizations. Such databases have hundreds of tables with millions of rows of data and support thousands of concurrent users. These databases are in use 24 hours a day, seven days a week. Just making a backup of such a database is a difficult task.

This section illustrates three different database applications: one used by an individual, one used by a small business, and a third used by a large governmental agency.

Mary Richards Housepainting   Mary Richards is a professional housepainter who owns and operates a small company consisting of herself, another professional painter, and part-time painters when needed. Mary has been in business for 10 years and has earned a reputation as a high-quality painter who works for a reasonable rate. Mary gets most of her work through repeat business and from word-of-mouth referrals. In addition to homeowners, Mary gets work from building contractors and professional interior designers.

Customers remember Mary far better than she remembers them. Indeed, sometimes she is embarrassed when a customer calls and says something like, "Hi Mary, this is John Maples. You painted my house three years ago." Mary knows she is supposed to remember the caller and the work she did for him, but because she paints more than 50 houses a year, it is difficult for her to do so. This situation becomes worse when the customer says something like, "My neighbor likes the job you did on our house and wants something similar done to her house."

In order to help her memory and to keep better track of her business records, Mary had a consultant develop a database and database application that she uses on her personal computer. The database stores records regarding customers, jobs, and referral sources in the form of tables, as shown in the example in Figure 1-10.

As stated, the DBMS stores and retrieves data in these tables. Unfortunately, when such data are in the form of tables, they are not very useful to Mary. Rather, she wants to know how customers and jobs and referrals relate to one another—for example, what jobs she has done for a particular customer or what customers have been referred by a particular person.

To provide this capability, Mary's consultant created a database application that processes data-entry forms and produces reports. Consider the example form in Figure

FIGURE 1-10

Tables of Data for Mary Richards Housepainting

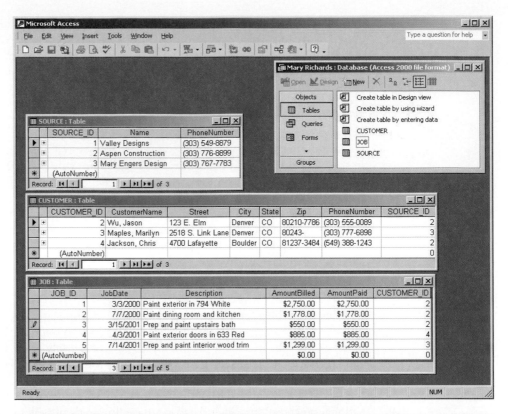

FIGURE 1-11

Example Data-Entry Form for Mary Richards Housepainting

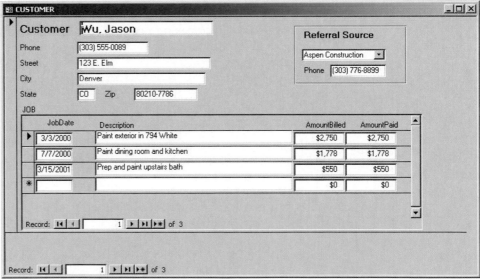

1-11. Here, Mary keys in data about customers—such as name, phone number, and address. She also links the customer to a particular referral source and keys in data about jobs performed for the customer. This data can then be displayed in reports like the one shown in Figure 1-12. Other uses of the database include recording bid estimates, tracking referral sources, and producing mailing labels for the direct sales literature Mary sends out from time to time.

The database application and the DBMS process the form and store the data that are entered into the table shown in Figure 1-10. Similarly, the application and DBMS extract data from the table to create a report like the one shown in Figure 1-12.

Consider again the data in Figure 1-10, and notice how the rows in the tables cross-reference one another. Each JOB contains the Customer_ID of the CUSTOMER who

FIGURE 1-12

Example Report for Mary Richards Housepainting

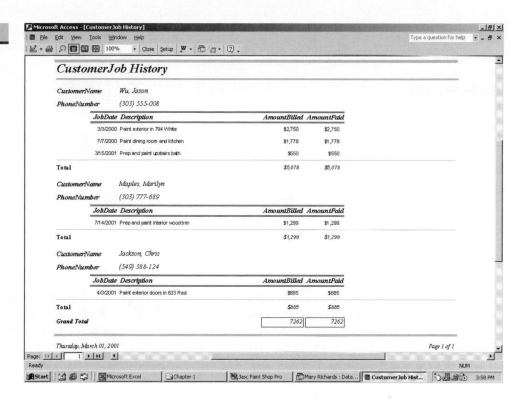

purchased that JOB, and each CUSTOMER contains the Source_ID of the person who referred that customer. These references are used to combine the data to produce forms and reports like those shown in Figures 1-11 and 1-12.

As you can imagine, Mary is unlikely to know how to design the tables in Figure 1-10, how to use a DBMS to create those tables, or how to develop the application to create the forms and reports. But by the time you have finished this course, you should know how to use database technology to create this database and its application. You should also know how to design and manipulate tables to create forms and reports of greater complexity.

Treble Clef Music Mary Richards' database is called a **single-user** database because only one user accesses the database at a given time. In some cases, this limitation is too restrictive; multiple people need to access the database simultaneously from multiple computers. Such **multi-user** databases are more complicated because the DBMS and the application must keep one user's work from interfering with another's.

Treble Clef Music uses a database application to keep track of the musical instruments it rents out. It needs a multi-user database application because several salespeople may need to rent musical instruments at the same time during busy periods. Also, the store manager needs to access the rental database to determine when to order more instruments of a given type. She does not want to interrupt the rental process when she does this.

The Treble Clef store has a local area network that connects several personal computers to a server computer that holds the rental database, as shown in Figure 1-13. Each clerk has access to a database application that has the three forms illustrated in Figure 1-14. The Customer form is used to maintain customer data, the Rental Agreement form is used to track the instruments that have been rented and whether or not they have been returned, and the Instrument Data form is used to show instrument data and rental history.

To understand the problems that must be overcome in a multi-user database, consider what happens when two customers attempt to rent the same B-flat clarinet at the same time. The DBMS and the application programs must somehow detect that this situation is occurring and inform the clerks that they must choose a different instrument.

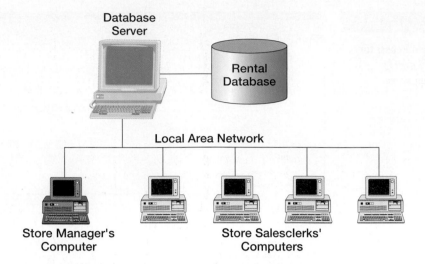

State Licensing and Vehicle Registration Bureau   Now, consider an even larger application of database technology: a state licensing and auto registration bureau. It has 52 centers that conduct drivers' tests, and issue and renew drivers' licenses; and it also has 37 offices that sell vehicle registrations.

The personnel in these offices access a database to perform their jobs. Before people can be issued (or can renew) their driver's licenses, their records in the database are checked for traffic violations, accidents, or arrests. These data are used to determine whether the license can be renewed and, if so, whether it should carry any limitations. Similarly, personnel in the auto registration department access the database to determine whether an auto has been registered before; if so, to whom it is registered and whether there are any outstanding matters that should prohibit the registration.

This database system has hundreds of users, including not only the license and registration personnel, but also the people in the state department of revenue and in law enforcement. Components of this system are shown in Figure 1-15.

Notice that the applications are written in different languages and probably in different periods of time. Also, Oracle is processing two different databases on behalf of these applications. Because of the importance of these applications, the system must be available 24 hours a day, seven days a week. This level of availability makes simple tasks such as backup very challenging.

Large organizational databases such as the licensing and registration bureau were the first applications of database technology. These systems have been in existence for 20 or 30 years, and have been modified to meet changing requirements over that period. Other examples of organizational databases concern account processing at banks and financial institutions, production and material supply systems at large manufacturers, medical-records processing at hospitals and insurance companies, and governmental agencies.

Today, many organizations are adapting their organizational database applications to enable customers to access and even to change their own data over the Internet. If you work for a large organization, you may be assigned to such a project.

Comparison of Database Applications   These examples represent a sampling of the uses of database technology. Hundreds of thousands of databases are like the one used by Mary Richards Housepainting: single-user databases with a relatively small amount of data—say, fewer than 10 megabytes. The forms and reports for these databases are generally simple and straightforward.

Other databases are similar to the one used by Treble Clef Music; they have more than one user, but usually fewer than 20 or 30 users altogether. They contain a moderate amount of data—say, 50 or 100 megabytes. The forms and reports need to be complex enough to support several different business functions.

FIGURE 1–14

Three Forms Used by
Treble Clef Music
(a) Customer Form;
(b) Rental Agreement
Form and
(c) Instrument Data
Form

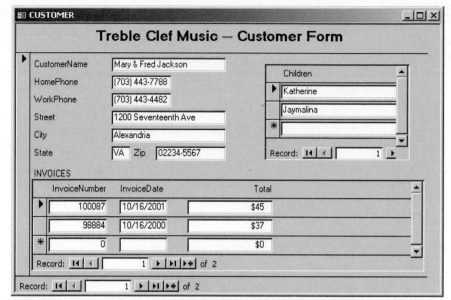

(a)

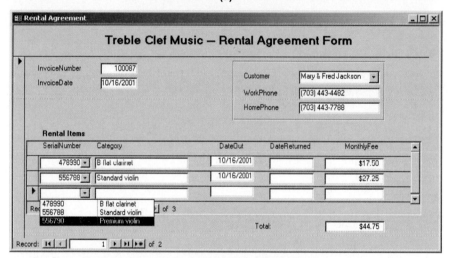

(b)

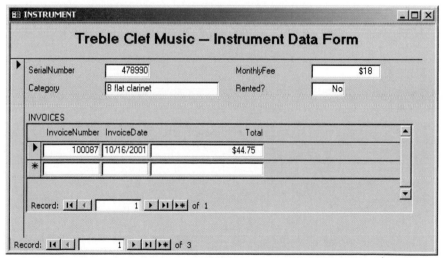

(c)

FIGURE 1–15

Organizational Database System

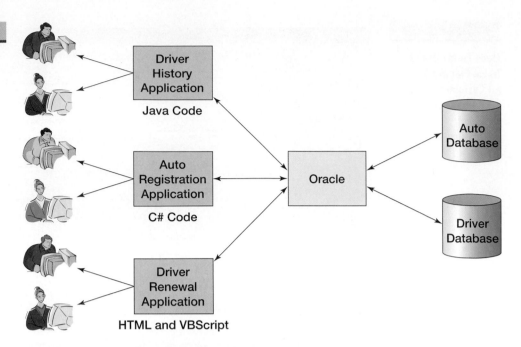

The largest databases are like those in the auto registration case, which have hundreds of users and trillions of bytes of data. Many different applications are in use, with each application having its own forms and reports. The characteristics of these types of databases are summarized in Figure 1-16.

When you finish this book, you should be able to design and create databases and database applications such as those used by Mary Richards and Treble Clef. You will probably not be able to create one as large and complicated as the vehicle registration database, but you will be able to serve as an effective member of a team that does design and create such a database. You should also be able to create a small to medium database using Internet technology.

HOW TO BUILD A DATABASE SYSTEM

The process for building a database system is essentially the same as the process for building any other information system. As shown in Figure 1-17, there are three basic phases: requirements, design, and implementation. Most of this book addresses the center column, although we will consider the design and implementation of queries and application code in some chapters. Primarily, however, we will be concerned with the development of the database component.

FIGURE 1–16

Characteristics of Different Types of Databases

Type	Example	Typical Number of Concurrent Users	Typical Size of Database
Personal	Mary Richards Housepainting	1	<10 Megabytes
Workgroup	Treble Clef Music	<25	<100 Megabytes
Organizational	Licensing and Registration	Hundreds to Thousands	>1 Trillion Bytes, possibly several databases

FIGURE 1-17

Summary of Database Development Phases

Development Phase	Database	Application
Requirements	Build data model Specify data items Define constraints and rules	Determine application requirements
Design	Tables Relationships Indexes Constraints Stored procedures and triggers	Forms Reports Queries Application code
Implementation	Create tables Create relationships Create constraints Write stored procedures and triggers Fill database Test	Create forms Create reports Create queries Write application code Test

Requirements Phase

During the requirements phase, a data model is developed; data item types, lengths, and other properties are determined; and constraints and rules on data constructs are defined.

A data model is a logical representation of the structure of the database. Data modeling is very important because the design of the database and all of its structures depend on the data model. If the data model is incorrect, the result will be waste, aggravation, delays, and frustration. Because of its importance, the next two chapters will describe data modeling in detail.

Figure 1-18 shows an example of a data model diagram for Lakeview Rentals. This figure is an example of an **entity-relationship diagram**, a means of expressing data models that has become the industry standard. In this figure, JOB, CONTRACTOR, RENTAL, and EQUIPMENT are entities. The diamonds represent relationships between those entities. You can ignore the rest of the details for now; you just need to know that such diagrams exist for documenting data models.

As you will learn, during the requirements phase, it is necessary to define data item properties such as data type, maximum length, whether values are required, and so forth. Also, constraints on data item values and rules on the processing of data need to be defined. An example of a data constraint is the following: The value of Equipment

FIGURE 1-18

Entity-Relationship Diagram for Lakeview Rentals

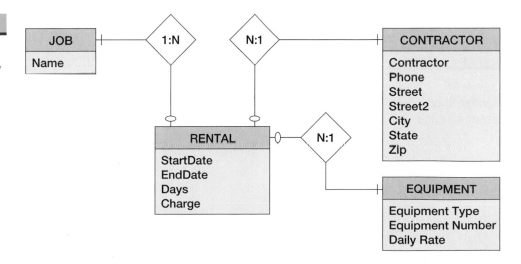

Type must be one of ['Backhoe', 'Small Crane', 'Medium Crane', 'Large Crane', 'Scaffolding']. We will address constraints and rules in the next two chapters.

Design Phase

During the design phase, the data model is transformed into tables and relationships. Figure 1-19 shows an example data structure diagram, a diagram used to show tables and their relationships. In this diagram, the line between EQUIPMENT and RENTAL represents a relationship. The fork in the line adjacent to RENTAL means that a given row in the EQUIPMENT table can relate to many rows of RENTAL table. We will use these and similar diagrams to express database designs in Chapters 5 and 8. You will learn the meaning of the other elements of this figure in those later chapters.

The need for indexes is determined during the database design phase, and sometimes the characteristics of the indexes are specified as well (we say *sometimes* because not all DBMS products allow this specification). Constraint enforcement mechanisms, stored procedures, and triggers are all designed. You will learn about these in Chapters 10-12.

Implementation Phase

As listed in Figure 1-17, tables and relationships are created during the implementation phase. Two common ways are used to create tables: via SQL and via a graphical design tool. Figure 1-20(a) shows SQL statements for creating the EQUIPMENT and RENTAL tables and for defining the relationship between them. Such SQL statements can be input to the database to define the tables and relationship. Figure 1-20(b) shows a different technique, in which a graphical design tool is used to define the CONTRAC-TOR table in SQL Server. Most DBMS products allow either technique to be used. Similarly, with most DBMS products, data constraints can be specified in either SQL or via graphical tools. You will learn how to write SQL for these purposes in Chapters 7 and 8.

During implementation, stored procedures and triggers are written and tested. You will learn how to do this for Oracle in Chapter 10 and for SQL Server in Chapter 11. Finally, the database is filled with data and the system is tested.

In truth, few information systems are ever finished. Normally, by the time the database and its applications have been completed, there will be a need to modify them to meet new requirements that have developed during implementation. Such modifications also go through these same three phases (requirements, design, and implementation), but they do so in the context of an existing database and applications. Changing existing databases can be very difficult and challenging, and accordingly we will discuss this process, called **database redesign**, in Chapter 8.

FIGURE 1-19

Example Data Structure Diagram for Lakeview Rentals

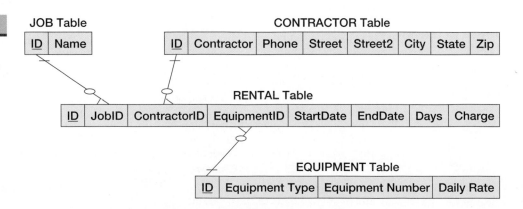

FIGURE 1-20

(a) Creating Tables with Text Commands and (b) Creating Tables with Graphical Tools

```
CREATE TABLE EQUIPMENT(
    ID                  Int           Primary Key,
    EquipmentType       Char (35)     Not Null,
    EquipmentNumber     Char (25)     Not Null,
    DailyRate           Number (6,2));

CREATE TABLE RENTAL(
    ID                  Int           Primary Key,
    JobID               Int           Not Null,
    ContractorID        Int           Not Null,
    EquipmentID         Int           Not Null,
    StartDate           Char (12)     Not Null,
    EndDate             Char (12),
    Days                SmallInt,
    Charge              Number (8,2));

ALTER TABLE RENTAL ADD CONSTRAINT EquipmentFK
    FOREIGN KEY (EquipmentID) REFERENCES RENTAL;
```
(a)

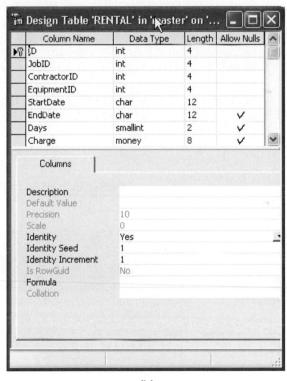

(b)

Application Development

Application development proceeds in parallel with database development. This text is devoted to database processing, so we will not address application development very much. Chapter 7 will discuss the use of SQL in applications; Chapters 10 and 11 will describe the coding of stored procedures and triggers. For the most part, however, we will leave the third column of Figure 1-17 to your systems development class.

Before turning to data modeling, we will conclude this chapter with a brief sketch of the history of database processing.

▶ BRIEF HISTORY OF DATABASE PROCESSING

Figure 1-21 summarizes the development of database technology. Until the mid-1960s, almost all computer data storage was on magnetic tape. Because tape could be processed only sequentially, data had to be maintained in the form of lists (or sequential files, as they were called). As you learned at the start of this chapter, however, there are significant problems with maintaining all but the simplest data in this format.

Early Database Models

With the commercial success of disk storage in the mid-1960s, it became possible to have non-sequential, or direct, access to records. At that point, databases were designed that eliminated the problems of sequential file processing. Two competing architectures or models were initially successful. IBM developed and promoted **DL/I**, or **Data Language One**, which modeled database data in the form of hierarchies or trees (see Figure 1-22(a)). This model, which was developed in conjunction with the manufacturing industry, was easily used for maintaining data such as bills of materials and parts lists, but was not truly general-purpose. Representing non-hierarchical network data (see Figure 1-22(b)) was cumbersome.

Consequently, CODASYL, the group that developed the standards for the COBOL language, created a model in the 1970s called the **DBTG (Data Base Task Group) Model**. The DBTG model could readily represent both hierarchies and networks. This model was at one time proposed as a national standard, but was never adopted primarily because of its complexity. It was, however, the basis of a number of commercially successful DBMS products in the 1970s and 1980s. Cullinane Corporation's product IDMS was the most successful.

FIGURE 1–21

Summary of the History of Database Processing

Timeframe	Technology	Remarks
Pre–1968	File Processing	Predecessor of database processing. Data maintained in lists. Processing characteristics determined by common use of magnetic tape medium.
1968–1980	Hierarchical and network models	Era of non-relational database processing. Prominent hierarchical data model was DL/I, part of IBM's first DBMS called IMS. Prominent network data model was CODASYL DBTG model; IDMS was most popular network DBMS.
1980 to present	Relational data model	Relational data model, first published in 1970; began to see commercial application in 1980. IBM endorsed it with DB2; other vendors followed by modifying their DBMS products or by creating new ones. Oracle achieved prominence. SQL became standard relational language.
1982	First microcomputer DBMS products	Ashton-Tate developed dBase products; Microrim created R:Base; Borland followed with Paradox.
1985	Interest in object-oriented DBMS (OODBMS) develops	With advent of object-oriented programming, OODBMS were proposed. Little success commercially, primarily because advantages did not justify the cost of converting billions of bytes of organizations' data to new format. Under development today.
1991	Microsoft ships Access	Personal DBMS created as element of Windows. Gradually supplanted all other personal DBMS products.
1995	First Internet database applications	Databases become key component of Internet applications. Popularity of the Internet greatly increases need and demand for database expertise.
1997	XML applied to database processing	Use of XML solves long-standing database problems. Major vendors begin to integrate XML into DBMS products.

FIGURE 1–22

(a) Example Hierarchy: University Organization and (b) Example Network: Classes and Students

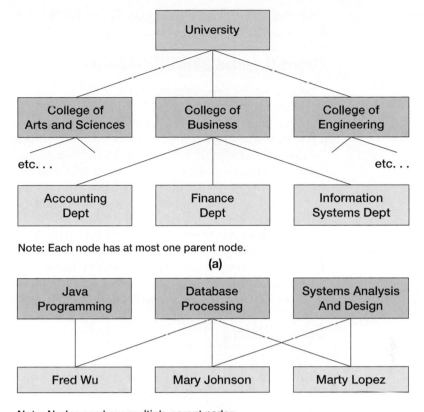

Note: Each node has at most one parent node.

(a)

Note: Nodes can have multiple parent nodes.

(b)

The Relational Model

The relational model, which represents data in the format shown in Figure 1-4, was first proposed by E.F. Codd in 1970. Codd worked for IBM and after 10 years of research, development, and corporate lobbying, he and others convinced IBM to develop DBMS products based on the relational model. The most famous of these products is DB2, a DBMS that is still actively used today.

Meanwhile, other corporations (such as Oracle, Ingres, Sybase, and Informix) developed DBMS products based on the relational model. SQL Server was developed by Sybase and sold to Microsoft in the late 1980s. Today, DB2, Oracle, and SQL Server are the most prominent commercial DBMS products.

Personal Computer DBMS Products

With the advent of the microcomputer, it became possible to have personal databases; as a result, a number of personal DBMS products were developed. The most successful of these was dBase, a product marketed by the Ashton-Tate Corporation. Other early personal DBMS products were R:base from the Microrim Corporation and Paradox from Borland.

Because there was plenty of computing power available on personal computers, personal DBMS products were able to provide more graphical user interfaces. Over time, the influence of these products changed the interfaces of larger organizational DBMS products as well. Figure 1-20 illustrates this point. The technology behind Figure 1-20(a) was developed for the character-based interfaces that were common with DBMS products prior to the personal computer. Figure 1-20(b) shows an example of the graphical interfaces that emerged from microcomputer DBMS products.

Object Oriented DBMS (OODBMS)

Object-oriented programming began to be used in the mid-1980s and it lead to the development of object-oriented DBMS products. The goal of these products was to be able to store object-oriented programming objects (such as those in C++ or Java) in a database without having to transform them into relational format.

To date, OODBMS have not been a commercial success. Their use requires organizations to transform their databases from relational to OODBMS format. Also, most large organizations have older applications that are not based on object-oriented programming. Somehow, the programs in these applications would need to be accommodated by the new OODBMS. Thus, the high cost of migrating existing databases and information systems from relational DBMS to OODMBS has prohibited their wide use.

Object-relational DBMS products, such as Oracle 8i and 9i, have been developed that allow both relational and object views of data on the same database. They are beginning to have commercial success, but nothing like that of pure-relational DBMS products. We will examine object-relational DBMS processing in Chapter 16.

Recent History

In 1991, Microsoft shipped Access and it supplanted all other personal DBMS products within a few years. This was possible in part because Access was integrated into the Microsoft Office suite, and Microsoft was able to use its marketing clout as well as its Windows monopoly to overwhelm other products. But in fairness to Microsoft, Access is a superb product. To a large extent, it dominated the market because it is an easy-to-use and powerful DBMS.

As everyone knows, Internet usage exploded in the mid-1990s. What most people do not know is that this phenomenon dramatically increased the value and importance of database technology and expertise. As early static Web pages gave way to dynamic Web sites, as companies such as Amazon.com became successful, and as major organizations began to use the Internet to publish their data, more and more sites became dependent on databases. That trend continues today.

Finally, recent years have seen the introduction and use of XML, which is a technology that originated to support Web sites, but has since been extended to provide important solutions to database problems. We will discuss XML in depth in Chapter 13. For now, just realize that the integration of database technology and XML is the leading edge of the database field today and will be important for many years in the future.

SUMMARY

Although database processing has always been an important topic, the advent of the Internet has made this topic one of the hottest career paths. The skills you develop and the knowledge you gain will be in great demand.

The purpose of a database is to help people and organizations keep track of things. Although lists can be used for this purpose, they have many problems. They are difficult to change without inconsistencies, deletions from lists may have unintended consequences, and partial data is difficult to record. Additionally, it is easy to create data inconsistencies when entering data. Finally, different parts of an organization want to maintain some data in common and some data privately. This is difficult to accomplish when using lists.

Databases consist of groups of related tables. In most cases, each table contains data about a single theme. Maintaining data in this way solves the problems described for lists. Relationships among tables are represented in different ways; in this chapter, relationships were represented by giving each row a unique ID and using that ID to relate a row in one table to a row in a second table. A **key** is a column that identifies a unique row; a **foreign key** is a column in one table that is a unique identifier in a second table. Foreign keys are used to represent relationships. Tables can be combined by using SQL, which is an industry standard language for processing tables.

A database system consists of four basic elements: users, database applications, the DBMS, and the database. Users employ the database system to perform their jobs. Applications produce forms, queries, and reports; execute application logic; and control processing. The DBMS creates, processes, and administers the database. A database is a self-describing collection of integrated records. It contains user data, metadata, indexes, stored procedures, triggers, and application metadata. A stored procedure is a program that processes a portion of the database that is stored within the database. A trigger is a procedure that is invoked when a specified action occurs. Figure 1-7 summarizes the functions of database components.

Database technology can be used in a wide array of applications. Some databases are used by a single individual, some are used by workgroups, and others are used by large organizations. Figure 1-16 summarizes some of the characteristics of these different types of databases.

Like all information systems, database systems are developed using a process of three phases: requirements, design, and implementation. During the requirements phase, a data model, or logical representation of the structure of the database, is developed. Data models are important because the design of the database and applications are derived from it. An entity-relationship diagram is a tool used to represent a data model.

The data model is transformed into tables and relationships during the design phase. Indexes, constraints, stored procedures, and triggers are also designed. Data structure diagrams are sometimes used to document tables and their relationships. During implementation, tables, relationships, and constraints are created, stored procedures and triggers are written, the database is filled, and systems are tested. Today, tables and related constructs can be created using either SQL or via graphical tools that are part of the DBMS.

Application development occurs in parallel with database development. Most of this text is devoted to database development, but the design and construction of queries and some application code will be considered in later chapters. Significant events in the history of database processing are shown in Figure 1-21.

GROUP I QUESTIONS

1.1 Why is database processing more important today than ever?

1.2 State the purpose of a database.

1.3 Summarize problems that can occur when using a list to keep track of something.

1.4 Based on your answer to question 1.3, when do you think it is appropriate to use a list to keep track of something?

Use the following list when answering questions 1.5 to 1.9:

Adviser	Adviser Phone	Student	Major	Dept Head
Jones	221.2345	Parks	Accounting	Greene
Kwail	223.4444	Stein	Info Systems	Masters
Rosenbloom	281.3944	Johnson	Accounting	Greene
Rosenbloom	281.3944	Gonzales	Accounting	Greene
Jones	221.2345	Rickey	Accounting	Greene

1.5 Describe problems that can occur when an adviser changes his or her phone number.

1.6 Suppose student Stein drops out of school, and the second row is deleted. Describe the side effects of this deletion.

1.7 How do we use this list to record the fact that Smith is the department head of the computer science department?

1.8 Suppose the entry in the last row, last column is changed from Greene to Abernathy. What problems will then occur in interpreting this list?

1.9 Change this list to a set of three interrelated tables. Use the technique shown in Figure 1-4 for representing relationships.

1.10 Explain how none of the problems encountered in questions 1.5 to 1.8 can occur with the tables developed in your answer to question 1.9.

1.11 Using the SQL statement on page 6 as an example, guess at a similar statement for joining together the tables in your answer to question 1.9. If any of your column names have spaces in them, put the column names in brackets [ ]. Because there is no computation in your result, you will not need an expression like [Daily Rate]*[Days] As Charge in your answer.

1.12 Name the four components of a database system.

1.13 List the functions of a database application.

1.14 What does DBMS stand for? List the functions of a DBMS.

1.15 Define the term *database.*

1.16 List the contents of a database.

1.17 What is metadata? Give an example.

1.18 What is the difference between a stored procedure and a trigger?

1.19 Explain the differences between personal, workgroup, and organizational databases.

1.20 Summarize the tasks in the requirements phase of the development on a database system.

1.21 What is a data model? Why are such models important?

1.22 Summarize the tasks in the design phase of the development on a database system.

1.23 Summarize the tasks in the implementation phase of the development on a database system.

1.24 Name two data models that preceded the relational model.

1.25 Describe the disadvantages of the two data models in your answer to question 1.24.

1.26 Who first proposed the relational model?

1.27 How did personal DBMS products influence the development of organizational DBMS products?

1.28 Name three early personal DBMS products.

1.29 What is the purpose of an OODBMS?

1.30 Why have OODBMS not been commercially successful?

1.31 What is an object relational DBMS?

1.32 What technology is at the leading edge of the database field today?

GROUP II QUESTIONS

1.33 Suppose that the New Orleans Wooden Boat Society (a fictitious organization) publishes a monthly newsletter for which it charges $35 per year. Assume they keep the following data in the form of list in a spreadsheet:

Name, Street, ApartmentNo, City, State, Zip, StartDate, EndDate, AmountPaid

What problems are likely to occur when maintaining this data as a list?

1.34 Suppose that a subscriber who has received the newsletter for three years changes his or her address. Should the address data be changed on all subscriptions, or on only the current subscription? Why or why not?

1.35 Break the list in question 1.33 into two tables, one for SUBSCRIBER and one for SUBSCRIPTION. Relate the tables using Figure 1-4 as an example. How does this arrangement fix the problems you identified in question 1.33? How does this arrangement affect your answer to question 1.34? Make an argument that this two-table design is not an improvement over the spreadsheet, and is thus unnecessary.

1.36 Suppose that the society decides to have two publications: a shop guide that is published quarterly (Winter, Spring, Summer, Fall), and the newsletter that is published monthly. Assume that the cost of the shop guide is $15 per year, and the cost of the newsletter is $35 per year. Assume that the society keeps the following data:

Name, Street, ApartmentNo, City, State, Zip, Publication, StartDate, EndDate, AmountPaid

What problems are likely to occur when maintaining this data as a list?

1.37 Break the list in question 1.36 into two tables: one for SUBSCRIBER and one for SUBSCRIPTION. Relate the tables using Figure 1-4 as an example. How does this arrangement fix the problems you identified in question 1.36? Explain why it is easier to make the argument that this two-table design is an improvement over the spreadsheet.

1.38 Suppose that the cost of the shop guide is $15 per year, and the cost of the newsletter is $35 per year, but the cost of both is $40 per year. Does this situation affect the design of your tables for question 1.37? Why or why not? How should the society handle this situation?

1.39 Just about anyone with computer skills in the society can create and process a list in a spreadsheet. Developing a database and database application, however, requires specialized knowledge and skills. If the society asked you to help them determine whether the cost and trouble of a database were worthwhile, how would you proceed? What questions would you ask? What sort of an analysis would you do?

FIREDUP PROJECT QUESTIONS

FiredUp, Inc., is a small business owned by Curt and Julie Robards. Based in Brisbane, Australia, FiredUp manufactures and sells a lightweight camping stove called the FiredNow. Curt, who previously worked as an aerospace engineer, invented a patented burning nozzle that enables the stove to stay lit in very high winds—up to 90 miles per hour. Julie, an industrial designer by training, developed an elegant folding design that is small, lightweight, easy to set up, and very stable. The Robards manufacture the stove in their garage, and they sell it directly to their customers over the Internet, via fax, and via postal mail.

The owners of FiredUp need to keep track of the stoves they have sold, in case they should ever need to contact their users regarding product failures or other product-liability matters. Accordingly, they include a product registration form with each of their stoves. The form contains the following data:

PurchaserName, StreetAddress, ApartmentNumber, City, State/Province, Zip/PostalCode, Country, EmailAddress, PhoneNumber, DateOfPurchase, SerialNumber

A. Assume that FiredUp stores this data as a list in a spreadsheet. Describe five potential problems they can have when storing the data in this manner.

B. Assume that instead of a spreadsheet, they decide to create a personal database with the following tables:

CUSTOMER (PurchaserName, StreetAddress, ApartmentNumber, City, State/Province, Zip/PostalCode, Country, EmailAddress, PhoneNumber)

and

PURCHASE (DateOfPurchase, SerialNumber)

1. Construct a table of sample data that conforms to the CUSTOMER structure. Include at least four rows in your table. For this question and the following questions, just list the data using a word processor.

2. Which of the columns of the CUSTOMER table can be used as a key (a column that identifies to identify a unique row of the table)?

3. Construct a table of data that conforms to the PURCHASE structure. Include at least four rows in your table.

4. Which of the columns of the PURCHASE table can be used as a key of PURCHASE?

5. Using the tables defined previously, there is no way to relate a particular customer to his or her stove. One way to do that is to add SerialNumber of PURCHASE to CUSTOMER. The CUSTOMER table then appears as follows:

CUSTOMER (PurchaserName, StreetAddress, ApartmentNumber, City, State/Province, Zip/PostalCode, Country, EmailAddress, PhoneNumber, SerialNumber)

Copy your sample CUSTOMER data and add the SerialNumber column to it. Call this new table CUSTOMER1

6. An alternative technique for representing the relationship of the two tables is to place EmailAddress of CUSTOMER in PURCHASE. The PURCHASE table then appears as follows:

PURCHASE (DateOfPurchase, SerialNumber, EmailAddress)

Copy your sample PURCHASE data and add the EmailAddress column to it. Call this new table PURCHASE1.

7. You now have three possible database structures:

DB1: CUSTOMER1 with PURCHASE

DB2: CUSTOMER with PURCHASE1

DB3: CUSTOMER1 with PURCHASE1

a. Under what circumstances would you recommend the structure in DB1?

b. Under what circumstances would you recommend the structure in DB2?

c. Under what circumstances would you recommend the structure in DB3?

TWIGS TREE TRIMMING SERVICE

Samantha Green owns and operates Twigs Tree Trimming Service. Samantha graduated from the forestry program and worked for a large landscape design firm that performs tree trimming and removal. After several years of experience, she bought her own truck, stump grinder, and other equipment and then opened her own business in St. Louis, Missouri.

Although many of her jobs are one-time operations to remove a tree or stump, others are recurring: trimming a tree or groups of trees every year or every other year. When business is slow, she calls former clients to remind them of her service and of the need to trim their trees on a regular basis.

Samantha keeps the following data about each of her jobs:

OwnerName, Phone, Street Address, City, State, Zip, DateOfService, Description, AmountBilled, AmountPaid, DateOfPayment.

A. Assume that Samantha stores this data as a list in a spreadsheet. Describe five potential problems Samantha can have when storing the data in this manner.

B. Assume that instead of a spreadsheet, Samantha decides to create a personal database with the following tables:

CUSTOMER (OwnerName, Phone, Street Address, City, State, Zip)

and

SERVICE (DateOfService, Description, AmountBilled, AmountPaid, DateOfPayment)

1. Construct a table of sample data that conforms to the CUSTOMER structure. Include at least four rows in your table. For this question and the following questions, just list the data using a word processor.

2. Which of the columns of the CUSTOMER table can be used as a key (a column that identifies a unique row of the table)?

3. Construct a table of data that conforms to the SERVICE structure. Include at least four rows in your table.

4. Explain why none of the columns in the SERVICE table can be used as a key.

5. Add an ID column to SERVICE similar to that for the tables in Figure 1-4. Modify your example data to include the ID column.

6. Using the tables defined previously, there is no way to relate a particular customer to his or her service. One way to do that is to add ID of SERVICE to CUSTOMER. The CUSTOMER table then appears as follows:

CUSTOMER (OwnerName, Phone, Street Address, City, State, Zip, ServiceID)

Copy your sample CUSTOMER data, and add the ServiceID column to it. Call this new table CUSTOMER1.

7. An alternative technique for representing the relationship of the two tables is to place Phone of CUSTOMER in SERVICE. The SERVICE table then appears as follows:

SERVICE (DateOfService, Description, AmountBilled, AmountPaid, DateOfPayment, Phone)

Copy your sample SERVICE data, and add the Phone column to it. Call this new table SERVICE1.

8. You now have three possible database structures:

DB1: CUSTOMER1 with SERVICE

DB2: CUSTOMER with SERVICE1 and

DB3: CUSTOMER1 with SERVICE1

a. Under what circumstances would you recommend the structure in DB1?

b. Under what circumstances would you recommend the structure in DB2?

c. Under what circumstances would you recommend the structure in DB3?

PART I

Entity-Relationship Data Modeling

The two chapters in this part discuss data modeling tools, techniques, processes, and examples. Chapter 2 introduces the entity-relationship data model and discusses variants of that model that you are likely to encounter in your career. In this chapter, you will learn the components of data modeling tools. Chapter 3 then outlines data modeling processes and uses those processes with the tools from Chapter 2 to present numerous data modeling examples.

The best way to learn data modeling is to do it, and you are encouraged to work the problems and examples at the end of these chapters. You will learn even more if you obtain a data modeling product and use it to create your own data models. Instructions for doing that are presented in Chapter 2, page 56.

Entity-Relationship Data Modeling: Tools and Techniques

This chapter describes data modeling tools and techniques. We begin with a description of the ANSI/SPARC three schema model. We will use that model to understand the role and use of data modeling. Next, we will describe the entity-relationship data model as it was originally proposed. As you will see, there are good reasons to understand the model in that form. Then, we will investigate the more recent IDEFX1 version of the entity-relationship model, which is the version that is most common in today's industry. Finally, you will learn how the entity-relationship model has been incorporated into UML, an object-oriented programming methodology.

Once you understand these models and tools, you will learn how to use them in the next chapter.

► ANSI/SPARC THREE SCHEMA MODEL

The American National Standards Institute/Standards Planning and Requirements Committee (ANSI/SPARC) three schema model was first published in 1975[1]. Even though this is an old model, it provides an excellent framework to describe the role and purpose of data modeling.

Let's begin by defining **schema**. A schema is a representation of something. Blueprints for a house are one type of schema; a flowchart or object diagram is another type of schema. The three schemas in this model are used to make three different representations of a database.

External, Conceptual, and Internal Schemas

As shown in Figure 2-1, the three schemas are the external schema, the conceptual schema, and the internal schema. The **external schema**, sometimes called the **user view**, is a representation of how users view the database. For all but the simplest databases, an external schema portrays just a portion of the database. For example, in the Lakeview database in Chapter 1, an external schema for salespeople might contain data from only the CONTRACTOR and RENTAL tables.

A **conceptual schema** is a complete logical view of the database that contains a description of all the data and relationships in the database. The conceptual schema is logical, in that it is independent of any particular means of storing the data. A conceptual schema can be stored in a database, but it can also be stored in a file cabinet, or represented by a series of linked spreadsheets or in some other fashion.

One conceptual schema will usually have many different external schemas based upon it. At Lakeview, there might be one external schema for sales, one for marketing, one for operations, and so forth.

An **internal schema** is a representation of a conceptual schema as physically stored using a particular product and/or technique. The description of a set of tables, keys, foreign keys, indexes, and other physical structures is an internal schema. A conceptual schema can be represented by many different internal schemas. We could create an internal schema for a conceptual schema to be processed by Oracle, and a different one for the same conceptual schema to be stored by DB2. Those two internal schemas could be very similar or very different. For our purposes, as long as they accurately represent

FIGURE 2-1

Three Schema Model

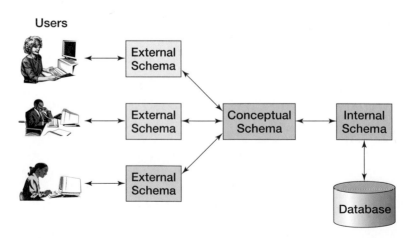

---

[1] Rosen, Bruce and Margaret Law. *Guide to Data Administration*. Gaithersburg, MD: U.S. Dept of Commerce, National Institute of Standards and Technology, 1989 (this is the date the document was placed on microfiche).

the conceptual schema, those differences are unimportant. (Of course, when it comes to processing efficiency, we may greatly prefer one internal schema over another one.)

Constructing a Conceptual Schema

Why is all of this important? When building a data model, our job is to construct a conceptual schema. Users, however, will not communicate with us in terms of this schema. They will discuss the data as they need it for their jobs, which will be their particular view (one external schema) of the data. Our job will be to work backward from the users' external schemas and construct a conceptual schema that will support all of those users' views.

Similarly, when creating a conceptual schema, it is vitally important not to confuse the conceptual schema with the internal schema. We do not want to mix the logical view of the data with the physical view. If we do, we may find that the characteristics of the DBMS will constrain and influence our thinking about the conceptual model. In this case, we may miss something important in the user's world—or, even worse, cause the characteristics of a DBMS to constrain what the users can do. Such constraints allow the tail to wag the dog. We do not want the characteristics of DBMS indexes to determine how salespeople can sell!

Of course, after we have a conceptual schema, we may find that we have to compromise it to store it effectively in an internal schema. But, at least we will have recorded what the users really wanted before we do this, and we will know we are compromising. It may be that later, with more thinking or expertise, we can find a way to support the conceptual schema that the users want. Or, perhaps a new product or product feature will come along that will allow us to support the conceptual view that is really wanted.

So, when creating conceptual models, endeavor to forget about physical structures and elements of the internal schema. Instead, focus on what is needed to provide users the external views that they need to perform their jobs.

Over the years, a number of different techniques, concepts, and symbols have been developed for documenting conceptual models. The most popular are based on the entity-relationship model, and we will consider them in this and the next chapter. A different technique, called the semantic object model, is described in Appendix B.

The Saga of Bruce and Zelda

To clarify the three schema model, consider the case of Bruce and Zelda. Bruce is a biologist who studies rivers; he investigates pollution and looks for evidence of PCBs and other chemicals. Several times a year, he visits rivers and counts fish because such counts are an important factor in assessing river health. To record his results, he uses a data entry form like the one shown in Figure 2-2. He locates the form data for the river he is studying and records the fish counts in a table within that form.

Zelda, a zoologist, studies fish. Her results are used by federal and state agencies to determine allowable limits for fishing, to close certain species from the catch, and to assess the health of various fish species. To record data that are important to her, Zelda uses a form like that shown in Figure 2-3. She first accesses data for the fish species that she is studying and then records the results for the rivers on which she finds the fish.

Bruce and Zelda work at the same university, and one day that university decides to create a single database containing all fish and river data. To create this database, someone schedules a meeting with Bruce and Zelda.

The meeting goes something like this: Zelda starts by saying, "Bruce, I've looked at the way you record your data (Figure 2-2), and you have it backward. We need to first access the fish species and then we can record the counts on the various rivers where the fish swim."

Bruce responds, "Zelda, I believe fish formaldehyde has gotten to your brain. That's not the way to do it at all. We first need to access the river data and then record the

FIGURE 2-2

Bruce's External View

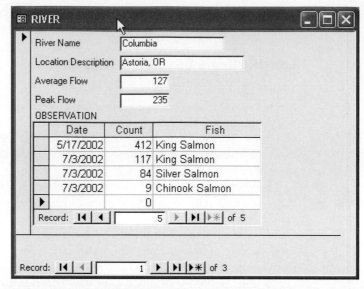

FIGURE 2-3

Zelda's External View

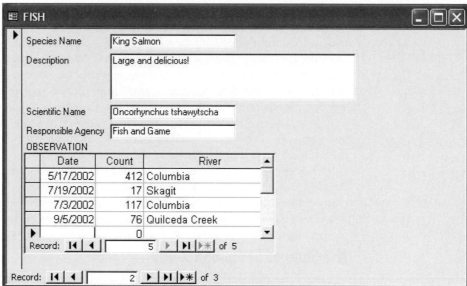

counts of the fish we find in that river. It would take me hours if I had to record my data the way you do (Figure 2-3)."

Warming up to the challenge, Zelda answers, "*Au contraire*, Bruce, it's you—too many PCBs have reduced your thinking skills. If we record the data *your* way…" And so it will go, each claiming that his or her view is the correct one. Believe it or not, thousands (maybe millions) of hours have been spent in meetings just like this. The problem, of course, is that Bruce and Zelda have two very different perspectives on the same data.

About this time, along comes Conrad the conceptualizer. Conrad looks at the forms in Figures 2-2 and 2-3 and thinks, "These forms represent two different ways of viewing the same data; two different external schemas. I wonder if there is a way to reconcile them into one conceptual schema?"

So, Conrad constructs the conceptual schema shown in Figure 2-4. Recall that a conceptual schema is the complete logical view of the data. As such, it will contain many other elements than shown here, but this example will do for a start.

The schema in Figure 2-4 shows three different groups of data: one for FISH, one for RIVER, and a third for OBSERVATION. The lines represent relationships. Note that RIVER is related to possibly many OBSERVATIONs and FISH is also related to possibly many OBSERVATIONs.

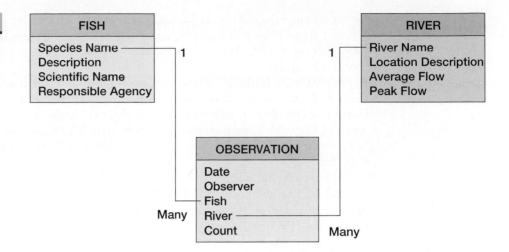

FIGURE 2–4

Conceptual Schema for Observation Database

Now, to support Bruce's view of the data, one would first access the RIVER data, find all related instances (possibly many) of OBSERVATION, and from there obtain any FISH data if any besides Fish (Species Name) is needed in Bruce's view. To support Zelda's view of the data, one would first access the FISH data; then the related instances (possibly many) of OBSERVATION; and then any RIVER data, if any besides River (River Name) is needed. Thus, both external schemas can be supported from the same conceptual schema.

The conceptual schema in Figure 2-4 is fine as far as it goes, but we must record much more detail to build a real database. Consequently, we will describe tools and techniques for representing such conceptual schemas in useful ways in the rest of this chapter.

Before we do, however, we can finish this story. Conrad takes the conceptual schema to Olive, an Oracle oracle. Olive uses this schema to create an internal schema, or database design, for an Oracle database. She will design tables, define keys and foreign keys, create indexes, and allocate tables to physical storage groups and make other internal schema design decisions. She will then implement her design, creating the database and all of its structures. We will describe the design and implementation process throughout this text, in Chapters 4, 5, 8, 10, and 11.

▶ THE ENTITY-RELATIONSHIP MODEL AND ITS VARIANTS

The **Entity Relationship (E-R) model** is a set of concepts and graphical symbols that can be used to create conceptual schemas. The E-R model was first published by Peter Chen in 1976[2]. In this paper, Chen set out the basic elements. Subtypes (discussed later) were added to the E-R model to create the **extended E-R model**[3], and today it is the extended E-R model that most people mean when they use the term **E-R model**.

Versions of the E-R Model

The fundamental ideas of the extended E-R model have been widely adopted by data modeling and database professionals, and today almost all data modeling projects use

[2] Peter P. Chen. "The Entity-Relationship Model—Towards a Unified View of Data," ACM Transactions on Database Systems, January 1976, pp. 9–36.

[3] T.J. Teorey, D. Yang, and J. P. Fry, "A Logical Design Methodology for Relational Databases Using the Extended Entity-Relationship Model," *ACM Computing Surveys*, June 1986, pp. 197–222.

some version of the E-R model. Unfortunately, however, there are a number of different versions in use. One of them, called **Information Engineering**, or **IE**, was developed by James Martin in 1990. This version has the least use in industry today, and we will not consider it further.

In 1993, the National Institute of Standards and Technology announced another version of the E-R model as a national standard. This version is called **IDEF1X**, or **Integrated Definition 1, Extended**[4]. This standard incorporates the basic ideas of the E-R model, but uses different graphical symbols. IDEF1X includes facilities for developing both conceptual and internal schemas and provides a methodology for translating one to the other.

Meanwhile, to add further complication, a new object-oriented development methodology called the **Unified Modeling Language (UML)** adopted the E-R model, but introduced its own symbols while putting an object-oriented programming spin on the model.

To summarize, we have the original E-R model, the extended E-R model, the IE version, the IDEF1X national standard version, and the UML version. We can decry this situation as absurd (and it is), but calling it absurd will not change it. The question is what are we going to do about it?

Choosing an E-R Version to Use

It is tempting to throw up our hands and say, "With all these versions, let's just focus on the extended E-R model and learn the others later, if necessary." The problem with this approach is that when IDEF1X became a national standard, companies that sold data modeling tools had to conform to IDEF1X in order to sell to the government. Such a large market could not be ignored, so most of today's popular data modeling products, such as ERWin and Visio, use IDEF1X. This means that IDEF1X is the E-R version you are most likely to encounter, even more so than the extended E-R model.

At the same time, with the growing popularity of object-oriented systems development and object-oriented programming, the use of UML is on the rise. But UML was designed primarily to model processes and programs, and many people believe that it is not quite ready for prime time as a data modeling tool. It needs more development before it will have the maturity of the IDEF1X or IE models. Also, if you are not familiar with object-oriented concepts, UML will seem strange.

In truth, given these circumstances, whatever we do will be frustrating. Nonetheless, here is our approach: You need to know the classic extended E-R model because its concepts and symbols are the basis for all the versions and because it is so widely known in industry. Unfortunately, you also need to know the IDEF1X model because when you work with a data modeling tool, IDEF1X is the version you are most likely to encounter. Finally, you should at least be familiar with the symbols used in the UML version.

So, this chapter will first present the extended E-R model in its classic version. Then, we will describe the IDEF1X version of the E-R model, which not only uses different symbols, but also classifies relationships differently. Finally, we will survey the use of E-R in UML in the last section of this chapter.

Throughout the rest of this text, we will use either the extended E-R model or the IDEF1X version of the E-R model. Although this will add complications to the discussion from time to time, there is no way around it without leaving you ill-prepared for data modeling tasks in your future career.

[4] *Integrated Definition for Information Modeling (IDEF1X)*. Federal Information Processing Standards Publication 184, 1993.

▶ THE EXTENDED E-R MODEL

The basic elements of all versions of the E-R model are entities, attributes, and relationships. Consider each in turn.

Entities

An *entity* is something that can be identified in the users' work environment; something that the users want to track. Example entities are EMPLOYEE Mary Doe, CUSTOMER 12345, SALES-ORDER 1000, SALESPERSON John Smith, and PRODUCT A4200. Entities of a given type are grouped into **entity classes**. Thus, the EMPLOYEE entity class is the collection of all EMPLOYEE entities. In this text, entity classes are printed in capital letters.

It is important to understand the differences between an entity class and an entity instance. An *entity class* is a collection of entities and is described by the structure or format of the entities in that class. An *entity instance* of an entity class is the representation of a particular entity, such as CUSTOMER 12345; it is described by the values of attributes of the entity. There are usually many instances of an entity in an entity class. For example, within the class CUSTOMER, there are many instances—one for each customer represented in the database. An entity class and two of its instances are shown in Figure 2-5.

Attributes

Entities have **attributes** that describe the entity's characteristics. Examples of attributes are EmployeeName, DateOfHire, and JobSkillCode. In this text, attributes are printed in both uppercase and lowercase letters. The E-R model assumes that all instances of a given entity class have the same attributes.

The original E-R model definition includes both composite and multi-value attributes. An example of a composite attribute is Address, which consists of the group of attributes {Street, City, State/Province, Zip/PostalCode}. An example of a multi-value attribute is ContactName in CUSTOMER, in which more than one person's name is associated with a given Customer. An attribute can be both multi-value and composite; for example, the composite attribute Phone {AreaCode, Number} could be multi-value

---

FIGURE 2-5

CUSTOMER: An Example of an Entity

CUSTOMER
entity contains:
   CustNumber
   CustName
   Address
   City
   State
   Zip
   ContactName
   PhoneNumber

Two instances of CUSTOMER:

12345 Ajax Manufacturing 123 Elm St Memphis TN 32455 P. Schwartz 223-5567	67890 Jefferson Dance Club 345-10th Avenue Boston MA 01234 Frita Bellingsley 210-8896

to allow for multiple phone numbers. Most versions of the E-R model ignore single-value composite attributes. They require multi-value attributes (whether composite or not) to be transformed into entities as will be shown later.

Identifiers

Entity instances have **identifiers**, which are attributes that name, or identify, entity instances. For example, EMPLOYEE instances can be identified by SocialSecurityNumber, EmployeeNumber, or EmployeeName. EMPLOYEE instances are not likely to be identified by attributes such as Salary or DateOfHire because these attributes are not normally used in a naming role. Similarly, CUSTOMERs can be identified by CustomerNumber or CustomerName, and SALES-ORDERs can be identified by OrderNumber.

The identifier of an entity instance consists of one or more of the entity's attributes. An identifier may be either **unique** or **non-unique**. If it is unique, its value will identify one and only one entity instance. If it is non-unique, the value will identify a set of instances. EmployeeNumber is most likely a unique identifier, whereas EmployeeName is most likely a non-unique identifier (there may be many John Smiths, for example).

Identifiers that consist of two or more attributes are called *composite identifiers.* Examples are {AreaCode, LocalNumber}, {ProjectName, TaskName}, and {FirstName, LastName, DateOfHire}.

Relationships

Entities can be associated with one another in relationships. The E-R model contains both relationship classes and relationship instances.[5] Relationship classes are associations among entity classes, and relationship instances are associations among entity instances. Relationships can have attributes.

A relationship class can involve many entity classes. The number of entity classes in the relationship is the **degree** of the relationship. In Figure 2-6(a), the SP-ORDER relationship is of degree 2 because it involves two entity classes: SALESPERSON and ORDER. The PARENT relationship in Figure 2-6(b) is of degree 3 because it involves three entity classes: MOTHER, FATHER, and CHILD. Relationships of degree 2 are very common and are often referred to by the term **binary relationships**.

Three Types of Binary Relationships   Figure 2-7 shows the three types of binary relationships. In a 1:1 (read "one-to-one") relationship, a single-entity instance of one type is related to a single-entity instance of another type. In Figure 2-7(a), the AUTO-ASSIGNMENT relationship associates a single EMPLOYEE with a single AUTO. According to this diagram, no employee has more than one automobile assigned, and no automobile is assigned to more than one employee.

FIGURE 2-6	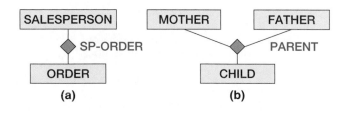
Relationships of Different Degrees (a) Example Relationship of Degree 2 and (b) Example Relationship of Degree 3	

---

[5] For brevity, we sometimes drop the word *instance* when the context makes it clear that an instance rather than an entity class is involved.

FIGURE 2-7

Three Types of Binary Relationships (a) 1:1 Binary Relationship; (b) 1:N Binary Relationship and (c) N:M Binary Relationship

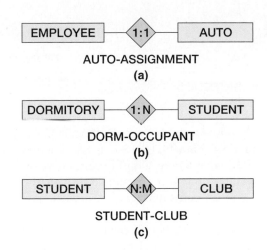

Figure 2-7(b) shows the second type of relationship, 1:N (read "one to N" or "one to many"). In this relationship, called the DORM-OCCUPANT relationship, a single instance of DORMITORY relates to many instances of STUDENT. According to this sketch, a dormitory has many students, but a student has only one dormitory.

The positions of the 1 and the N are significant. The 1 is close to the line connecting DORMITORY, which means that the 1 refers to the DORMITORY side of the relationship, and the N is close to the line connecting STUDENT, which means that the N refers to the STUDENT side of the relationship. If the 1 and the N were reversed and the relationship were written N:1, a DORMITORY would have one STUDENT and a STUDENT would have many DORMITORIES. Of course, this is not the case.

Figure 2-7(c) shows the third type of binary relationship, N:M (read "N to M" or "many to many"). This relationship is named STUDENT-CLUB, and it relates instances of STUDENT to instances of CLUB. A student can join more than one club and a club can have many students as members.

The numbers inside the relationship diamond show the maximum number of entities that can occur on one side of the relationship. Such constraints are called the relationship's **maximum cardinality.** The relationship in Figure 2-7(b), for example, is said to have a maximum cardinality of 1:N. But the cardinalities are not restricted to the values shown here. It is possible, for example, for the maximum cardinality to be other than 1 and N. The relationship between BASKETBALL-TEAM and PLAYER, for example, could be 1:5, indicating that a basketball team has at most five players.

Relationships of the types shown in Figure 2-7 are sometimes called **HAS-A relationships**. This term is used because an entity *has a* relationship with another entity. For example, an EMPLOYEE has an AUTO; a STUDENT has a DORMITORY; and a CLUB has STUDENTs.

Entity-Relationship Diagrams   The sketches in Figure 2-7 are called **entity-relationship** or **E-R diagrams**. In both the original and extended E-R models, entity classes are shown by rectangles, relationships are shown by diamonds, and the maximum cardinality of the relationship is shown inside the diamond. The name of the entity is shown inside the rectangle, and the name of the relationship is shown near the diamond. Other E-R versions use different symbols, as you will see.

As stated, the maximum cardinality indicates the maximum number of entities that can be involved in a relationship. The diagrams do not indicate the minimum. For example, Figure 2-7(b) shows that a student is related to a maximum of one dormitory, but it does not show whether a student *must be* related to a dormitory.

Several different ways are used to show **minimum cardinality.** One way to show it, as illustrated in Figure 2-8, is to place a hash mark across the relationship line to indicate that an entity must exist in the relationship and to place an oval across the relationship line to indicate that there may or may not be an entity in the relationship. Accordingly,

FIGURE 2–8

Relationship with
Minimum Cardinality
Shown

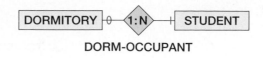

DORM-OCCUPANT

Figure 2-8 shows that a DORMITORY must have a relationship with at least one STUDENT, but a STUDENT is not required to have a relationship with a DORMITORY. The complete relationship restrictions are that a DORMITORY has a minimum cardinality of one and a maximum cardinality of many STUDENT entities. A STUDENT has a minimum cardinality of zero and a maximum cardinality of one DORMITORY entity.

A relationship may exist among entities of the same class. For example, the relationship ROOMS-WITH can be defined on the entity STUDENT. Figure 2-9(a) shows such a relationship, and Figure 2-9(b) shows instances of entities that conform to this relationship. Relationships among entities of a single class are sometimes called *recursive relationships.*

Showing Attributes in Entity-Relationship Diagrams   In some versions of E-R diagrams, the attributes are shown in ellipses and are connected to the entity or relationship to which they belong. Figure 2-10 shows the DORMITORY and STUDENT entities and the DORM-OCCUPANT relationship with the attributes. As shown, DORMITORY has DormName, Location, and NumberOfRooms attributes, and STUDENT has StudentNumber, StudentName, and StudentYear attributes. The relationship DORM-OCCUPANT has the attribute Rent, which shows the amount of rent paid by a particular student in a particular dorm.

If an entity has many attributes, listing them in this way on the E-R diagram may make the diagram cluttered and difficult to interpret. Other E-R versions show attributes differently as you will see.

FIGURE 2–9

Recursive Relationship
(a) E-R Diagram and
(b) Sample Data

FIGURE 2–10

Showing Attributes in
an Entity-Relationship
Diagram

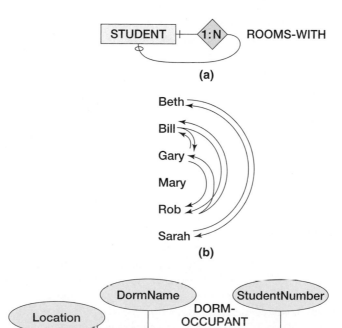

Weak Entities

The entity-relationship model defines a special type of entity called a **weak entity**. Weak entities are those that cannot exist in the database unless another type of entity also exists in the database. An entity that is not weak is called a **strong entity.**

To understand weak entities, consider a human resource database with EMPLOYEE and DEPENDENT entity classes. Suppose the business has a rule that an EMPLOYEE instance *can exist* without having a relationship to any DEPENDENT entity, but a DEPENDENT entity *cannot exist* without having a relationship to a particular EMPLOYEE entity. In such a case, DEPENDENT is a weak entity. This means that DEPENDENT data can be stored in the database only if the DEPENDENT has a relationship with an EMPLOYEE entity.

As shown in Figure 2-11(a), weak entities are signified by rounding the corners of the entity rectangle. In addition, the relationship on which the entity depends for its existence is shown in a diamond with rounded corners. In some E-R diagrams (not shown here), weak entities are depicted by using a double line for the boundary of the weak entity rectangle and double diamonds for the relationship on which the entity depends.

The E-R model includes a special type of weak entity called an **ID-dependent entity**. This type of entity is one in which the identifier of one entity includes the identifier of another entity. Consider the entities BUILDING and APARTMENT. Suppose the identifier of BUILDING is BuildingName, and the identifier of APARTMENT is the composite identifier {BuildingName, ApartmentNumber}. Because the identifier of APARTMENT contains the identifier of BUILDING (BuildingName), we say APARTMENT is ID-dependent on BUILDING. Contrast Figure 2-11(b) with Figure 2-11(a). Another way to think of this is that both logically and physically an APARTMENT cannot exist unless a BUILDING exists.

ID-dependent entities are common. Another example is the entity VERSION in the relationship between PRODUCT and VERSION, where PRODUCT is a software product and VERSION is a release of that software product. The identifier of PRODUCT is ProductName, and the identifier of VERSION is {ProductName, ReleaseNumber}. A third example is EDITION in the relationship between TEXTBOOK and EDITION. The identifier of TEXTBOOK is Title and the identifier of EDITION is {Title, EditionNumber}.

Unfortunately, there is an ambiguity hidden in the definition of weak entity, and this ambiguity is interpreted differently by different versions of the E-R model and by different modeling products. The ambiguity is this: In a strict sense, if a weak entity is defined as any entity whose presence in the database depends on another entity, then any entity that participates in a relationship having a minimum cardinality of 1 to a second entity is a weak entity. Thus, in an academic database, if a STUDENT must have an ADVISER, STUDENT is a weak entity because a STUDENT entity cannot be stored without an

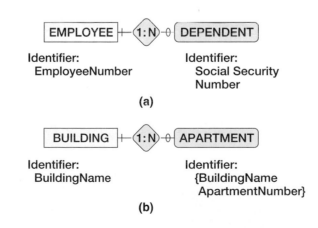

FIGURE 2-11

**Weak Entities
(a) Weak, but Not ID-Dependent and (b) ID-Dependent**

ADVISER. This interpretation, however, seems too broad to some people. A STUDENT is not physically dependent on an ADVISER (unlike APARTMENTs and BUILDINGs), and a STUDENT is not logically dependent on an ADVISER (in spite of how it might appear to either the student or the adviser!), so a STUDENT should be considered a strong entity.

To avoid such situations, some people interpret the definition of a weak entity more narrowly. To be a weak entity, an entity must *logically* depend on another entity. According to this definition, both DEPENDENT and APARTMENT would be considered weak entities, but STUDENT would not. A DEPENDENT cannot be a dependent unless it has someone to depend on, and an APARTMENT cannot exist without a BUILDING to reside in. A STUDENT, however, can logically exist without an ADVISER, even if a business rule requires it.

To illustrate this interpretation, consider several examples. Suppose a data model includes the relationship between an ORDER and a SALESPERSON (Figure 2-12(a)). Although we might say that an ORDER must have a SALESPERSON, it does not necessarily require one for its existence (the ORDER could be a cash sale in which the salesperson is not recorded). Hence, the minimum cardinality of 1 arises from a business rule, not from logical necessity. Thus, ORDER requires a SALESPERSON but is not existence-dependent on it, and ORDER would be considered a strong entity.

Now, however, consider the relationship of PATIENT and PRESCRIPTION in Figure 2-12(b). Here, a PRESCRIPTION cannot logically exist without a PATIENT. Thus, not only is the minimum cardinality 1, but also the PRESCRIPTION is existence-dependent on PATIENT. PRESCRIPTION is thus a weak entity. Finally, consider ASSIGNMENT in Figure 2-12(c), in which the identifier of ASSIGNMENT contains the identifier of PROJECT. Here, not only does ASSIGNMENT have a minimum cardinality of 1, and not only is ASSIGNMENT existence-dependent on PROJECT, but it is also ID-dependent on PROJECT because its key includes the key of another entity. Thus, ASSIGNMENT is a weak entity.

In this text, we will resolve this ambiguity by defining weak entities as those that must logically depend on another entity. Therefore, not all entities that have a minimum cardinality of 1 in relationship to another entity are weak; only those that are logically dependent are termed weak. This definition also implies that all ID-dependent entities are weak. Additionally, every weak entity has a minimum cardinality of 1 on the entity on which it depends, but every entity that has a minimum cardinality of 1 need not necessarily be weak.

Representing Multi-Value Attributes with ID-Dependent Entities

Multi-value attributes are represented in E-R-models by creating a new ID-dependent entity to represent the multi-value attribute and constructing a one-to-many relationship to it. For example, Figure 2-13(a) shows the representation of the multi-value attribute ContactName in CUSTOMER. A new ID-dependent entity called CONTACTNAME is

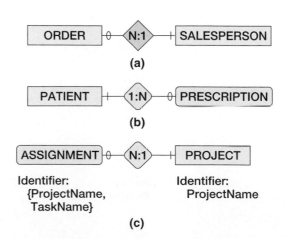

(a)

(b)

Identifier:
{ProjectName,
TaskName}

Identifier:
ProjectName

(c)

FIGURE 2-13

Representing Multi-Value Attributes with Weak Entities

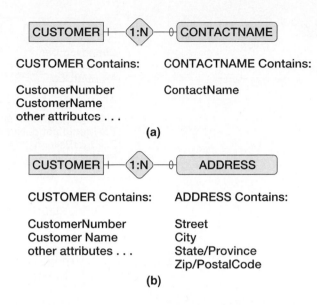

FIGURE 2-13

Representing Multi-Value Attributes with Weak Entities

created with a single attribute ContactName. The relationship between CUSTOMER and CONTACTNAME is one-to-many. The constructed entity must be ID-dependent because it must contain the identifier of the entity that had the multi-value attribute.

Figure 2-13(b) shows the representation of the multi-value composite attribute Address. The new weak entity ADDRESS contains all of the attributes of the composite: namely, Street, City, State/Province, and Zip/PostalCode.

Subtype Entities

A **subtype entity** is an entity that represents a special case of another entity, called its **supertype**. For example, the supertype entity STUDENT could be modeled to have subtypes of GRADUATE_STUDENT and UNDERGRADUATE_STUDENT. Or, STUDENT could be modeled to have subtypes BUSINESS_MAJOR, SCIENCE_MAJOR, LIBERAL_ARTS_MAJOR, and so forth.

The relationship between a supertype and its subtypes is sometimes called an **IS-A** relationship. A GRADUATE_STUDENT is a STUDENT; a SCIENCE_MAJOR is a STUDENT. Compare this to the relationships we described previously, say the relationship between an ORDER and SALESPERSON. It does not make sense to say an ORDER is a SALESPERSON; that is not true. Rather, an ORDER has a SALESPERSON.

Thus, a supertype and its subtypes represent different aspects of the same entity. STUDENT Mary Jones and GRADUATE_STUDENT Mary Jones are the same entity, but we are just viewing them differently. For example, consider CLIENT with attributes ClientNumber, ClientName, and AmountDue. Suppose that a CLIENT can be an individual, a partnership, or a corporation; and that additional data are to be stored, depending on the type. Assume that these additional data are as follows:

INDIVIDUAL-CLIENT:

Address, SocialSecurityNumber

PARTNERSHIP-CLIENT:

ManagingPartnerName, Address, TaxIdentificationNumber

CORPORATE-CLIENT:

ContactPerson, Phone, TaxIdentificationNumber

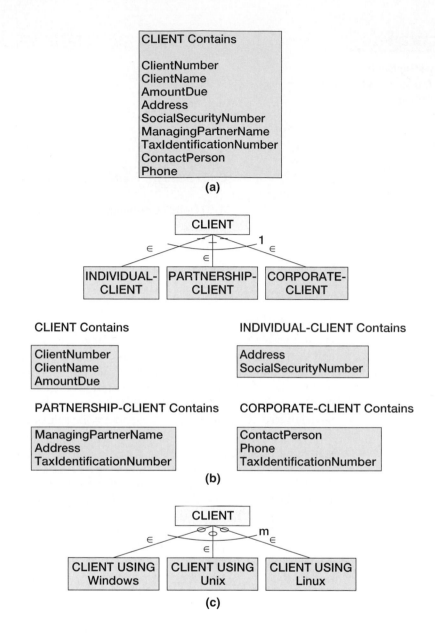

Subtype Entities
(a) CLIENT Without
Subtype Entities;
(b) CLIENT with
Subtype Entities and
(c) Non-Exclusive
Subtypes with
Optional Supertype

One possibility is to allocate all of these attributes to the entity CLIENT, as shown in Figure 2-14(a). In this case, some of the attributes are not applicable. ManagingPartnerName has no meaning for an individual or corporate client, so it cannot have a value.

A closer-fitting model would instead define three subtype entities, as shown in Figure 2-14(b). Here, the INDIVIDUAL-CLIENT, PARTNERSHIP-CLIENT, and CORPORATE-CLIENT entities are shown as subtypes of CLIENT. CLIENT, in turn, is a supertype of the INDIVIDUAL-CLIENT, PARTNERSHIP-CLIENT, and CORPORATE-CLIENT entities.

The ∈ next to the relationship lines indicates that INDIVIDUAL-CLIENT, PARTNERSHIP-CLIENT, and CORPORATE-CLIENT are subtypes of CLIENT. Each subtype entity must belong to the supertype CLIENT. The curved line with a 1 next to it indicates that a CLIENT entity must belong to one and only one subtype. It means that the subtypes are exclusive and one of them is required.

Entities with an IS-A relationship should have the same identifier because they represent different aspects of the same thing. In this case, that identifier is Client Number.

Contrast this situation with the HAS-A relationships shown in Figure 2-7, in which the entities represent aspects of different things and thus have different identifiers.

Generalization hierarchies have a special characteristic called **inheritance**, which means that the entities in subtypes inherit attributes of the supertype. PARTNERSHIP-CLIENT, for example, inherits ClientNumber, ClientName and AmountDue from CLIENT.

The reasons for using subtypes in data modeling differ from the reasons for using them in object-oriented programming. In fact, the major reason to use them in a data model is to avoid situations in which some attributes are required to be null. For example, in Figure 2-14(a), if SocialSecurityNumber has a value, the last four attributes must be null. The situation can be more obvious in medical applications—asking a male patient for the number of his pregnancies, for example. Null values are discussed in greater detail in Chapter 5.

Example E-R Diagram

Figure 2-15 is an example E-R diagram that contains all of the elements of the E-R model that we have been discussing. It shows the entities and relationships for an engineering consulting company that analyzes the construction and condition of houses and other buildings and facilities.

There is an entity class for the company's employees. Because some EMPLOYEEs are ENGINEERs, there is a subtype relationship between EMPLOYEE and ENGINEER. Every ENGINEER must be an EMPLOYEE; ENGINEER has a 1:1 relationship to TRUCK; and each TRUCK must be assigned to an ENGINEER, but not all ENGINEERs have a TRUCK.

ENGINEERs provide SERVICEs to CLIENTs. An ENGINEER can provide from zero to many services, but a given SERVICE must be provided by an ENGINEER and can be provided by only that ENGINEER. CLIENTs have many SERVICEs and a SERVICE can be requested by many CLIENTs. A CLIENT must have purchased at least one SERVICE, but SERVICE need not have any CLIENTs. The CLIENT-SERVICE relationship has an attribute Fee, which shows the amount that a particular client paid for a particular service. (Other attributes of entities and relationships are not shown in this diagram.)

Sometimes, CLIENTs refer one another, which is indicated by the recursive relationship REFERRED-BY. A given CLIENT can refer one or more other CLIENTs. A CLIENT may or may not have been referred by another client, but a CLIENT can be referred by only one other CLIENT.

FIGURE 2-15

Example Entity-Relationship Diagram

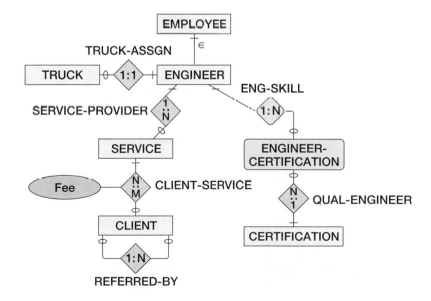

The ENGINEER-CERTIFICATION entity shows that a given ENGINEER has completed the education and testing required to earn a particular certificate. An ENGINEER may have earned many CERTIFICATIONs. ENGINEER-CERTIFICATION's existence is dependent on ENGINEER through the relationship ENG-SKILL. CERTIFICATION is the entity that describes a particular certification.

▶ THE IDEF1X STANDARD

As stated, **IDEF1X (Integrated Definition 1, Extended)** version of the E-R model was announced as a national standard in 1993. The standard was based on earlier work done for the U.S. military in the mid-1980s. IFEF1X is based on the E-R model, but extends that model to support the creation of both conceptual and internal schemas. It assumes that a relational database is to be created.

IDEF1X includes entities, relationships, and attributes, but it tightens the meaning of these terms and qualifies them with more specific terminology. In addition, IDEF1X includes the definition of **domains**, a component not present in the extended E-R model. Finally, IDEF1X changed the E-R graphical symbols, eliminating the diamond and adding new symbols for categories, a version of generalization hierarchies and subtypes. Differences between the extended E-R model and the IDEF1X model are summarized in Figure 2-16.

IDEF1X Entities

IDEF1X entities are the same as entities in the extended E-R model. They represent something that the users want to track—something about which users want to keep data. Like the extended E-R model, entities are shown with either square or rounded corners, although the meaning of entities with rounded corners is slightly different in IDEF1X, as you will learn when we discuss identifying relationships.

Entities can be shown with no attributes (Figure 2-17(a)), with just primary key attributes (Figure 2-17(b)), or with all of their attributes (Figure 2-17(c)). We will define primary and other types of key in detail in Chapter 4. For now, just think of the primary

---

FIGURE 2-16

Correspondence of Terms between the Extended E-R Model and the IDEF1X Version of the E-R Model

Extended E-R Model Term	Corresponding IDEF1X E-R Version Term	Remarks
Entity	Entity	Same
Attribute	Attribute	Same
Relationship	Relationship	Same
1:1 and 1:N Relationships	Non-Identifying Connection Relationship	Connection relationship is the same as HAS-A relationship
N:M Relationship	Non-specific Relationship	
ID-Dependent Relationship	Identifying Connection Relationship	
Weak entity, but not ID-dependent	None	
Supertype Entity	Generic Entity	Generic entity has an IS-A relationship to a category cluster
Subtype Entity	Category Entity	Category entities are mutually exclusive in their category cluster
None	Domain	

FIGURE 2–17

Levels of Detail in IDEF1X Models: (a) Entities Only; (b) Entities and Primary Keys and (c) Entities and Attributes

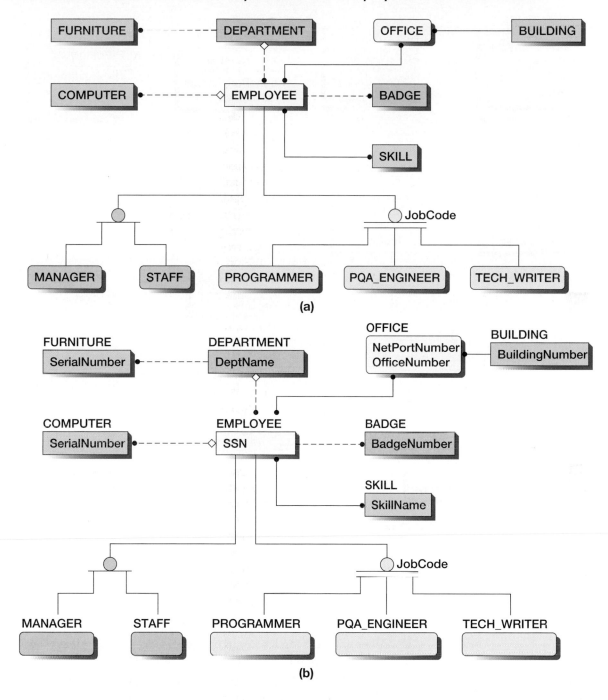

key as the principal unique identifier of the entity. When all attributes are shown, the entity is divided into two sections: the top section contains the primary key attribute(s) and the lower section contains all other attributes.

Recall from Figure 1-4 in Chapter 1 that relationships are created in the relational model by placing a key of one table into a second table. When placed into the second table, that key referred to as a **foreign key**. The process of creating foreign keys and the rules that surround their placement are the subjects of database design. Such keys are part of the internal schema.

FIGURE 2-17

(continued)

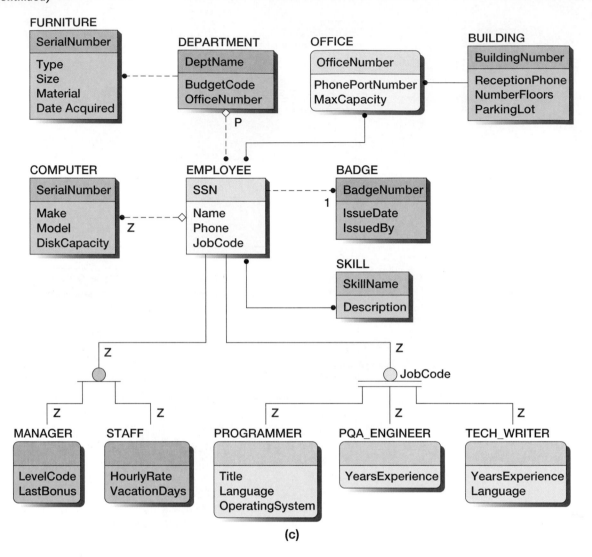

(c)

Because modeling tools based on IDEF1X can be used for both conceptual and internal schema modeling, they have facilities for showing foreign key placement. Most of the time, during conceptual data modeling, the display of foreign keys is distracting. Data modeling tools allow you to turn off the display of foreign keys and you may want to do this. The one exception is when modeling identifying relationships. As you will see below, for such relationships, the foreign key of one entity is part of the primary key of a second entity. With such entities, it is useful to display foreign keys. Other than that, ignore foreign keys during conceptual design. You will learn more about them when we discuss database design in Chapter 5.

IDEF1X Relationships

Figure 2-18 lists the four types of IDEF1X relationships. Although the terminology is awkward, it is very specific—just what you would expect from a national standard. We will consider each type in turn.

Non-Identifying Connection Relationships **Non-identifying connection relationships** are 1:1 or 1:N relationships between two non-ID-dependent (hence

FIGURE 2–18

IDEF1X Relationship Types

- Non-Identifying Connection Relationships
- Identifying Connection Relationships
- Non-Specific Relationships
- Categorization Relationships

FIGURE 2–19

Non-Identifying Connection Relationships

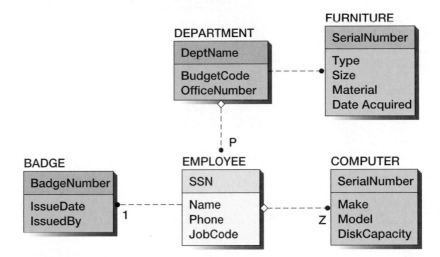

non-identifying) entities. Connection relationships are the same as what are called HAS-A relationships in the extended E-R model.

Figure 2-19 shows examples of non-identifying connection relationships. According to the standard, non-identifying relationships are represented with a dashed line. Furthermore, in IDEF1X, connection relationships are always drawn from a parent to a child entity. In the case of 1:N relationships, the parent is the entity on the 1 side of the relationship. For 1:1 relationships, either entity can be considered the parent, but IDEF1X forces you to pick one of the entities for that role. As shown in Figure 2-19, a filled-in circle is placed on the relationship line adjacent to the child entity in an IDEF1X entity-relationship diagram.

In IDEF1X, the default cardinality of a non-identifying connection relationship is one-to-many, with a mandatory parent and an optional child. Such relationships are shown by a dashed line with a filled circle by the child, and no other notation. Thus, in Figure 2-19, the relationship from DEPARTMENT to FURNITURE is 1:N, no DEPARTMENT is required to have any FURNITURE, and every FURNITURE entity must be assigned to a DEPARTMENT.

If the relationship cardinality is different from this default, additional notation is added to the diagram. If the child is required, a P is placed near the circle, indicating that one or more child entities are required (the P stands for *positive*, as in positive number). If the parent is optional, a diamond is added to the line, adjacent to the parent. In Figure 2-19, the relationship from DEPARTMENT to EMPLOYEE is 1:N, a DEPARTMENT must have at least one EMPLOYEE, and an EMPLOYEE is not required to be related to a DEPARTMENT.

1:1 relationships are denoted by adding notation near the circle on the relationship line. A 1 indicates that exactly one child is required; a Z indicates that zero or one children are allowed. Thus, in Figure 2-19, an EMPLOYEE is connected to exactly one BADGE entity, and is also connected to zero or one COMPUTER entities. The diamond indicates that a COMPUTER need not be related to an EMPLOYEE. Because there is no diamond on the EMPLOYEE side of the BADGE:EMPLOYEE relationship, a BADGE must be connected to an EMPLOYEE.

Identifying Connection Relationships Identifying connection relationships are the same as ID-dependent relationships in the extended E-R model.

FIGURE 2-20

Identifying Connection
Relationship

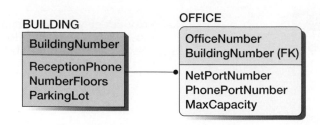

The identifier of the parent is always part of the identifier of the child. In Figure 2-20, a BUILDING entity is the parent of an ID-dependent relationship to the OFFICE entity. Note the identifier of BUILDING, BuildingNumber, is part of the identifier of OFFICE. The notation (FK) means that this attribute is a foreign key of another entity (here BUILDING). Identifying relationships are portrayed with solid lines, and child entities in identifying relationships are shown with rounded corners.

In this example, there is no additional notation by the filled-in circle, so the default cardinality is assumed. Thus, a BUILDING may be connected to zero, one, or many OFFICEs. If a 1, Z, or P were placed by the circle, a BUILDING would connect to at most 1, to zero or 1, or to 1 or more OFFICE entities, respectively. There can never be a diamond on the parent side of an identifying relationship because children in identifying relationships always require a parent.

There is an important difference between weak entities in the extended E-R model and identifying relationships in the IDEF1X model. As stated earlier, a weak entity is an entity that is logically dependent on another entity. It may be an ID-dependent entity or it may have an identifier of its own, but it is logically dependent on another entity. DEPENDENT in Figure 2-11 is a weak entity, but it has its own identifier, different from that of EMPLOYEE.

While IDEF1X allows for weak entities that are not identifying, it provides no special notation for such entities. The minimum cardinality for the parent in such relationships is 1, but no other means exists for documenting the fact that they are logically dependent on their parent.

To state this in different terms, in the extended E-R model, we distinguished between an entity that is logically dependent on another entity (DEPENDENT on EMPLOYEE) and an independent entity that just happens to have a required parent. DEPENDENT logically requires an EMPLOYEE because logically one cannot be a dependent without having someone to depend upon. STUDENTs, who may be required to have an ADVISER, are not logically dependent on an ADVISER. IDEF1X admits this distinction, but provides no notation for documenting it.

The bottom line is that in the extended E-R model, rounded corners signify weak entities, which may be either ID-dependent or just logically dependent. In the IDEF1X model, however, rounded corners signify ID-dependent entities only. There is no way in IDEF1X to document a weak entity that is not an ID-dependent entity.

Non-Specific Relationships A non-specific IDEF1X relationship is simply a many-to-many relationship. Non-specific relationships are shown with a filled-in circle on each end of the solid relationship line, as shown in Figure 2-21(a). In IDEF1X, there is no way to set minimum cardinalities of a non-specific relationship.

IDEF1X treats many-to-many relationships as poor stepchildren of non-identifying connection relationships. This is done because such relationships have no direct expression in the relational model. As you will learn in Chapter 5, such relationships must be converted to two 1:N relationships before they can be processed in a relational database.

To some people, this is a glaring fault in IDEF1X because it confounds conceptual schema ideas with internal schema ideas. These people would say that one should be able to fully document an M:N relationship, including minimum cardinalities, in the conceptual model. What happens to that relationship later in designing the internal schema should not be a factor in conceptual design.

FIGURE 2-21

Non-Specific
Relationships
(a) Model with N:M
Relationship and
(b) Model Showing
Missing Entity

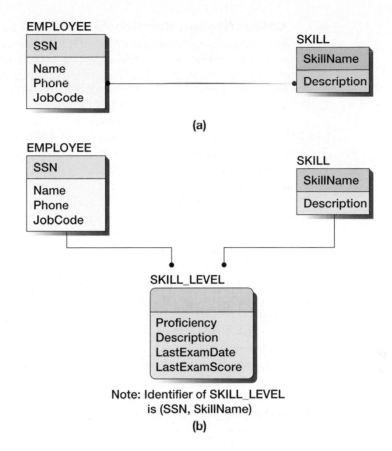

(a)

SKILL_LEVEL

Proficiency
Description
LastExamDate
LastExamScore

Note: Identifier of SKILL_LEVEL
is (SSN, SkillName)

(b)

To other people, N:M relationships do not really exist. They only appear to exist because something has been left out of the model. Consider the N:M relationship between EMPLOYEE and SKILL shown in Figure 2-21(a). In most cases, an organization wants to know not just what skills employees have, but also how proficient they are at those skills. Thus, there is a missing entity. If we add SKILL_LEVEL to the model (Figure 2-21(b)), we can see that the N:M relationships has been transformed into two 1:N relationships. The primary key of SKILL_LEVEL will be a composite of the keys of EMPLOYEE and SKILL or (SSN, SkillName).

Consider the relationship between STUDENT and CLASS. A student can take many classes and a class can have many students. Thus, this appears to be an N:M relationship. But students also receive grades. If we add GRADE to this model, then what appeared as an N:M relationship between STUDENT and CLASS becomes a 1:N relationship between STUDENT and GRADE and a second 1:N relationship between CLASS and GRADE. To those who think this way, calling N:M relationships non-specific is exactly right.

But what of a relationship like the N:M relationship that represents the interests that students have in rock groups? A STUDENT is interested in many ROCK_GROUPs and a ROCK_GROUP has many STUDENTs interested in it. Where is the missing entity here? The album that got someone interested? The first rock concert they attended of that group? These additional entities seem contrived and artificial.

Or, what about an N:M relationship between EMPLOYEE and OFFICE? What are the missing data here? The date that someone was assigned to an office? Their physical location in the office? These entities also seem contrived.

You will need to form your own opinion on this matter. Be careful, though, because some people have very strong beliefs about it. Your professor may be one!

Categorization Relationships   Categorization relationships are a specialization of generalization/subtype relationships in the extended E-R model. Specifically, a categorization relationship is a relationship between a **generic entity** and another entity called a **category entity**. Category entities are grouped into **categorization clusters**. For example, in Figure 2-22, EMPLOYEE is generic entity, PROGRAMMER, PQA_ENGINEER, and TECH_WRITER are category entities, and the category cluster, represented by the filled-in circle over two horizontal lines, is the collection of PROGRAMMER, PQA_ENGINEER, and TECH_WRITER.

Categorization relationships are IS-A relationships. A programmer is an employee, for example. Because they are IS-A relationships, the primary key of the category entities is the same as the category key of the generic entity. In this case, the primary key of PROGRAMMER, PQA_ENGINEER, and TECH_WRITER is SSN. Because this is so, category entities are shown without primary keys.

In IDEF1X, the entities in a category cluster are mutually exclusive. In Figure 2-22, an EMPLOYEE can be a PROGRAMMER, a PQA_ENGINEER, *or* a TECH_WRITER. An employee cannot be two or more of these.

Category clusters may have a **discriminator**, which is an attribute of the generic entity that indicates the type of the EMPLOYEE. In Figure 2-22, JobCode is the discriminator. The means the value of JobCode can be used to determine whether the EMPLOYEE is a PROGRAMMER, PQA_ENGINEER, or TECH_WRITER. The means by which this is done is not specified in the conceptual model; we are simply recoding here that it can be done. Some category clusters do not have a discriminator; the determination of category entity is left unspecified.

There are two types of category clusters: complete and incomplete. In a **complete category cluster**, every possible type of category for the cluster is shown. Complete category clusters are denoted by two horizontal lines, with a gap in-between. The category cluster in Figure 2-22 is complete. Because this cluster is complete, all the categories of EMPLOYEE are shown; there is no missing category. Hence, every EMPLOYEE can be categorized as one of PROGRAMMER, PQA_ENGINEER, or TECH_WRITER.

(You may be saying, "Wait a minute. Of course, there are other types of employees. What about accountants, for example?" The point is that *according to this model* there are no other types of employee. Maybe this model is used only in a software development group in which there are no other employee types. Or, maybe this model is in error. Whatever the case, however, there are no other types of employees according to this model.)

FIGURE 2–22

Categorization Relationship

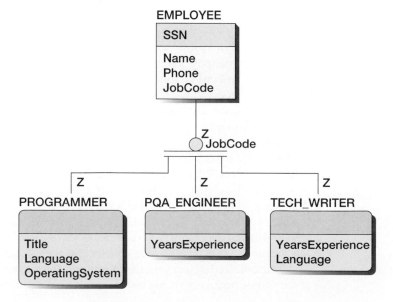

All category entities are existence-dependent on the generic category, so the minimum cardinality from the category entity to the generic entity is one. Because this is always true, that cardinality is not shown in the diagram.

According to the IDEF1X standard, the cardinalities of the relationships from the generic entity to the category entities are always zero or one. The Z on the line between the generic entity and the cluster symbol indicates that an EMPLOYEE may or may not have one of the category entities. The Z on the lines to the category entities show that the generic entity may or may not be one of those types.

Many people find this use of the Z notation puzzling, if not wrong. As stated, categories in a cluster are mutually exclusive. Thus, after an entity has a relationship to one category entity, the cardinality of the relationship to the other entities in that cluster is zero. Additionally, the Z on the line between the generic entity and the cluster symbol indicates that a generic entity may or may not have a category entity. For complete clusters, the Z should be a 1 in some cases, indicating that the generic entity must have a relationship to a category entity. There is no way to specify a 1 in the IDEF1X model for this case.

Figure 2-23 shows a second category cluster that consists of MANAGER and STAFF category entities. This cluster is incomplete, which is indicated by placing the category cluster circle on top of a single line, there is no gap between horizontal lines. This means that a least one category is missing. An employee might be a PART_TIME employee, for example. Again, all the cardinalities are marked as Z.

We stated that within category clusters, category entities are mutually exclusive. This does not mean, however, that an entity cannot have a relationship to two or more category entities in different clusters. Thus, as shown in Figure 2-23, an EMPLOYEE can be a MANAGER and also PROGRAMMER. An EMPLOYEE cannot, however, be both a MANAGER and STAFF.

As you can see, the IDEF1X model adds structure to the generalization/subtype relationships in the extended E-R model. By further defining these concepts, the IDEF1X model makes them more meaningful and hence more useful.

Relationship Names   In IDEF1X, non-category relationships can be named. Normally, a name consists of a verb or verb phrase expressed from the standpoint of the

FIGURE 2-23

Incomplete and Complete Category Clusters

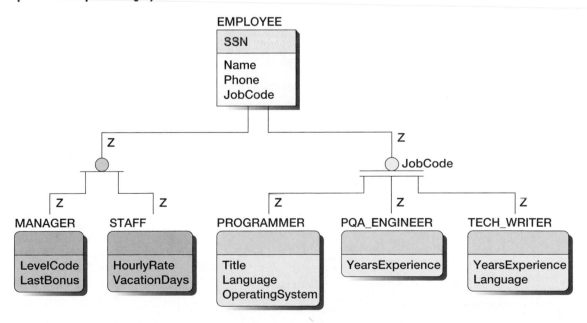

parent in the relationship, followed by a slash, and followed by the verb phrase expressed from the standpoint of the child. (You can pick either entity to be the parent in an N:M relationship.) Thus, in Figure 2-24, EMPLOYEE *Uses* a COMPUTER, and a COMPUTER is *Used By* an EMPLOYEE. Similarly, an EMPLOYEE *Occupies* an OFFICE, and an OFFICE is *Occupied By* an EMPLOYEE. Normally, the verb phrase from the child's view is the passive form of the verb phrase from the parent's view. Sometimes this is awkward, however, and a different verb is used. Thus, a BUILDING *Contains* an OFFICE, but an OFFICE is *Located In* a BUILDING.

Because of this repetitive pattern, relationship names are often predictable and therefore not informative. They can be helpful, however, when the relationship between two entities is ambiguous. In Figure 2-25, there are two relationships between CUSTOMER and SALE. One relationship is used to document that a customer can buy something; a second is used to document that a customer can sell something.

Relationship names need to be unique only among relationships between the same two entities. In Figure 2-25, the relationship between SALESPERSON and SALE has the same name as one of the relationships between CUSTOMER and SALE. This is not a problem. The two relationships between CUSTOMER and SALE, however, must have different names.

FIGURE 2-24

IDEF1X Model Showing Relationship Names

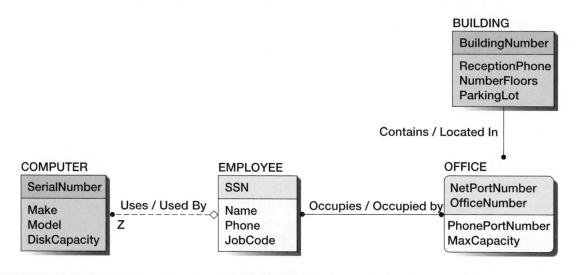

FIGURE 2-25

Using Names for Multiple Relationships between the Two Entities

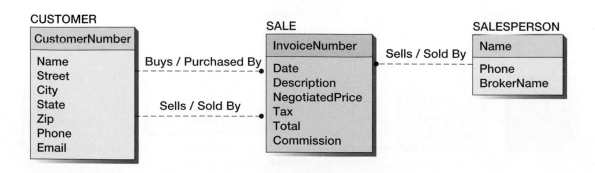

Domains

IDEF1X introduced the concept of domains to the extended E-R model. A **domain** is a named set of values that an attribute can have. A domain can consist of a specific list of values, or it can be defined more generally, for example, as a set of strings of maximum length 50. As an example of the former, a university could have a domain called DEPARTMENT_NAMES that consists of the names of all official departments at that university. The domain would be defined by enumerating that list: {'Accounting', 'Biology', 'Chemistry', 'Computer Science', 'Information Systems', 'Management', 'Physics'} As an example of the latter, the domain STUDENT_NAMES could be defined as any character string of length less than 75.

Domains Reduce Ambiguity Domains are both important and useful. For example, notice that both PROGRAMMER and TECH_WRITER in Figure 2-23 have an attribute named Language. Without domains, these attribute names are ambiguous. Do they refer to the same thing or not? It might be that Language for PROGRAMMER is a computer language, whereas Language for TECH_WRITER is a human language. Or, they may both be a computer language. This ambiguity can be eliminated by specifying the domain upon which each of these attributes is based.

We can define the domain COMPUTER_LANGUAGE to be the list {'C#', 'C++', 'Java', 'VisualBasic', 'VisualBasic.Net'} and the domain HUMAN_LANGUAGE to be {'Canadian French', 'France French', 'Spanish', 'UK English', 'US English'}. If we now say that Language of PROGRAMMER is based on the COMPUTER_LANGUAGE domain and Language of TECH_WRITER is based on the HUMAN_LANGUAGE domain, there will never be any ambiguity between these two attributes.

Furthermore, named domains eliminate ambiguity from attributes whose values look similar, but are not the same. In Figure 2-23, suppose that staff employees can accrue only 30 days of vacation. Further, suppose that employees are assumed to never work more than 30 years. In that case, the attributes STAFF.VacationDays, PQA_ENGINEER.YearsExperience, and TECH_WRITER.YearsExperience will all have values from 0 to 30. (In this notation, we identify attributes by appending the entity name to the attribute name with a period in-between.) Without domain specification, we cannot tell whether these values refer to the same thing or not.

Suppose we define a domain VACATION_DAYS as integers from 0 to 30, and a second domain EXPERIENCE as integers from 0 to 30. Now, we can state that the attribute STAFF.VacationDays is based on the VACATION_DAYS domain; the attributes PQA_ENGINEER.YearsExperience and TECH_WRITER.YearsExperience are based on the EXPERIENCE domain.

Domains Are Practically Useful Domains not only reduce ambiguity, they are also practically useful. Suppose that in a model of a university database we have an attribute called CampusAddress that is used in many different entities. It could be used in STUDENT, PROFESSOR, DEPARTMENT, LAB, and so forth. Further suppose that we base all of these CampusAddress attributes on the same domain, called CAMPUS_ADDRESS, and define that domain as all values of the pattern BBB-NNN, in which BBB is a list of building codes and NNN is a list of room numbers. When we define the domain in this way, all of the attributes in the model will inherit this definition.

Now, suppose that as we build our model, we discover that some room numbers have four digits. Without a domain definition, we would need to find all of the attributes in the model that use a campus address and change them to have NNNN for room number. With domains, we simply change the domain definition, and all of the attributes based on the domain will inherit the change. This not only reduces work, it eliminates errors that are difficult to find and hard to fix when they are found.

Another practical use for domains is to assess whether two attributes that are named differently are referring to the same thing. For example, an entity named DEPARTMENT might have an attribute named BudgetCode and a second entity named PROJECT may have an attribute named ExpenseCategory. Using domains, we can readily check to determine whether these two attributes are based on the same domain. Without domains, it would be difficult to know. Even if attribute values look similar, they may have different meanings.

Base Domains and Typed Domains   IDEF1X defines two types of domains. A **base domain** is a domain having a data type and possibly a value list or range definition. The default data types are Character, Numeric, and Boolean. The specification allows users to define additional data types such as Date, Time, Currency, and so forth. A value list is a set of values like that described for the COMPUTER_LANGUAGE domain, and a range definition is like that described for the EXPERIENCE domain.

A **type domain** is a subset of a base domain or a subset of another type domain. Figure 2-26 illustrates type domains based on the DEPARTMENT_NAMES domain. Type domains allow the definition of domain hierarchies that can be used for greater specificity.

IDEF1X and Data Modeling Products

There are a number of data modeling software products on the market. All of the diagrams shown for IDEF1X were drawn with a tool called ERWin, a product licensed by Computer Associates. Microsoft Visio has a database template that can be used to create either extended E-R models or IDEF1X models. ERWin is purpose-built for data modeling and as such is easier to use than Visio. You can download a trial version of ERWin from the site **www.ca.com**; follow the links to the download section of its site. You can also obtain a trial 60-day license of Visio from **www.microsoft.com**. Designer/2000 is a third product for creating E-R models that is available from Oracle. If you are using Oracle in your class, your instructor may have already obtained this product for you.

You are strongly advised to obtain access to one of these products or to a similar product and to work the exercises at the end of this chapter and the next. The most effective way to learn data modeling is to do it!

FIGURE 2-26

Example of Domain Hierarchy

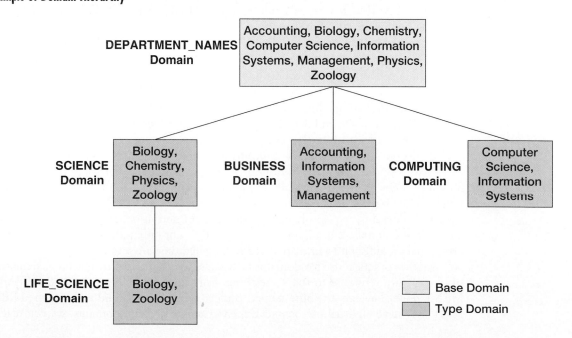

UML-STYLE ENTITY-RELATIONSHIP DIAGRAMS

The Unified Modeling Language (UML) is a set of structures and techniques for modeling and designing object-oriented programs (OOP) and applications. UML is both a methodology for developing OOP systems and a set of tools to support the development of such systems. UML has received prominence via the Object Management Group, an organization that has been developing OOP models, technology, and standards since the 1980s. It has also begun to receive widespread use among OOP practitioners. UML is the basis of the object-oriented design tools from IBM.

Because it is an application development methodology, UML is a subject for a course on systems development and is of limited concern to us. You may, however, encounter UML-style entity-relationship diagrams, so you should be familiar with their style.

UML Entities and Relationships

Figure 2-27 shows the UML representation of the designs in Figure 2-7. Each entity is represented by an **entity class**, which is shown as a rectangle with three segments. The top segment shows the name of the entity and other data that we will discuss. The second segment lists the names of the attributes in the entity, and the third documents constraints and lists methods (program procedures) that belong to the entity.

FIGURE 2–27

(a) UML Representation of a 1:1 Relationship; (b) UML Representation of a 1:N Relationship and (c) UML Representation of an N:M Relationship

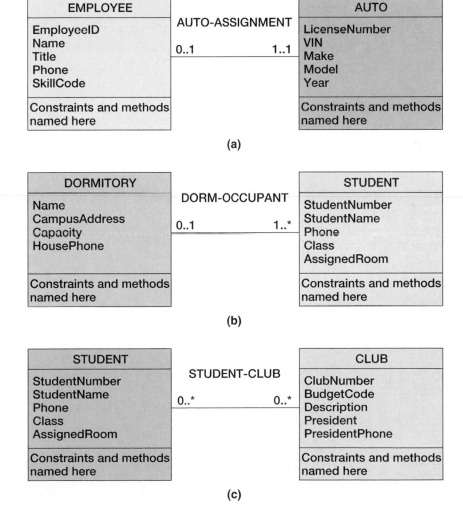

Relationships are shown with a line between two entities. Cardinalities are represented in the format *x..y,* where *x* is the minimum required and *y* is the maximum allowed. Thus, 0..1 means that no entity is required and at most one is allowed. An asterisk represents an unlimited number. Thus, 1..* means that one is required and an unlimited number is allowed. Examine Figures 2-27(a)–(c) for examples of 1:1, 1:N, and N:M maximum cardinality relationships.

Representation of Weak Entities Figure 2-28 shows the UML representation of weak entities. A filled-in diamond is placed on the line to the parent of the weak entity (the entity on which the weak entity depends). In Figure 2-28(a), PRESCRIPTION is the weak entity and PATIENT is the parent entity. All weak entities have a parent, so the cardinality on their side of the weak relationship is always 1..1. Because this is so, the cardinality on the parent entity is shown simply as 1.

Figure 2-28(a) shows a weak entity that is not an ID-dependent entity. It is denoted by the expression <non-identifying> on the PATIENT-PRESCRIPTION relationship. Figure 2-28(b) shows a weak entity that is ID-dependent. It is denoted with the label <identifying>.

Representation of Subtypes UML represents subtypes as shown in Figure 2-29. In this figure, INDIVIDUAL, PARTNERSHIP, and CORPORATE subtypes of CLIENT are allowed. According to this figure, a given CLIENT could be one, two, or three of these subtypes. For this situation, it does not make sense; a CLIENT should be one and only one of these types. The current version of UML does not provide a means to document exclusivity. Such notation can be added to a UML diagram, however.

Figure 2-30 presents a UML version of the entity-relationship diagram, shown previously as Figure 2-15. Because the relationship between SERVICE and CLIENT has an attribute—Fee—a separate entity CLIENT-SERVICE has been defined to carry that attribute. This is standard practice when using UML tools. Also note the representation of the recursive relationship REFERRED-BY.

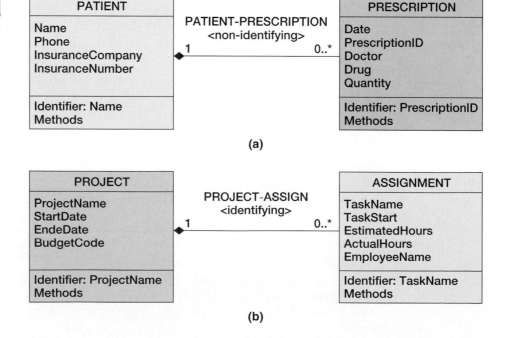

FIGURE 2-28

UML Representation of Weak Entities (a) Non-ID-Dependent Weak Entity and (b) ID-Dependent Weak Entity

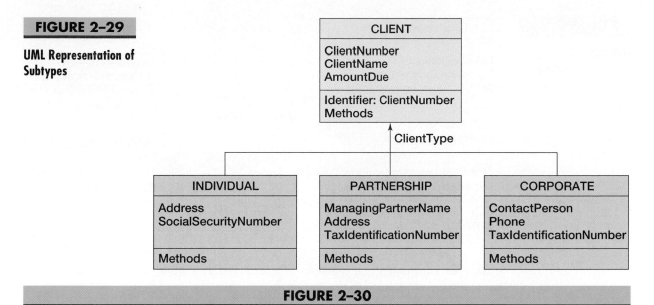

FIGURE 2–29

UML Representation of Subtypes

FIGURE 2–30

UML Version of E-R Diagram in Figure 3-11

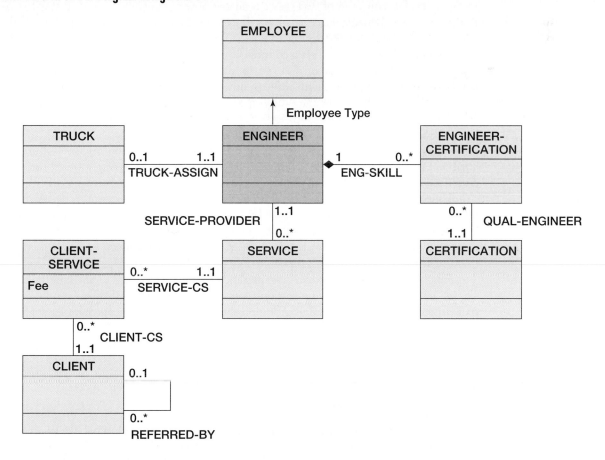

OOP Constructs Introduced by UML

Because UML is an object-oriented technology, several OOP constructs have been added to UML entity classes. We will touch on these ideas here and develop them further in Chapter 16. First, the classes of all entities that are to be stored in the database are labeled with the keyword <Persistent>. This simply means that data should continue to

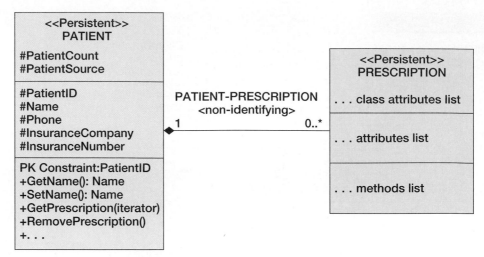

FIGURE 2-31

**UML Entity Classes
with OOP Constructs**

exist, even if the object that processes it is destroyed. In simpler terms, it means that the entity class is to be stored in the database.

Next, UML entity classes allow for **class attributes**. Such attributes differ from entity attributes because they pertain to the class of all entities of a given type. Thus, in Figure 2-31, PatientCount of PATIENT is an attribute of the collection of all PATIENTs in the database. PatientSource is an attribute that documents the source of all of the PATIENTs in the database.

As you will learn, such class attributes have no place to reside when using the relational model. Instead, in some cases, attributes like PatientCount are not stored in the database but are computed at run-time. In other cases, a new entity is introduced to contain the class attributes. For the entity in Figure 2-31, a new entity called PATIENT-SOURCE can be defined to hold both PatientCount and PatientSource attributes. In this case, all of the entities in PATIENT are connected to PATIENT-SOURCE.

A third new feature is that UML uses object-oriented notation for the visibility of attributes and methods. Attributes preceded by a + are public, those with a # are protected, and those with a – are private. In Figure 2-31, Name in PATIENT is a protected attribute.

These terms arise from the discipline of object-oriented programming. A *public* attribute can be accessed and changed by any method of any object. A public method can be invoked by any method of any object. *Protected* means that the attribute or method is accessible only by methods of this class or of its subclasses, and *private* means that the attribute or method is accessible only by methods of this class.

Finally, UML entities specify constraints and methods in the third segment of the entity classes. In Figure 2-31, a primary key constraint is placed on PatientID. This simply means that PatientID is a unique identifier. Additionally, Figure 2-31 documents that GetName() is to be created to provide public access (note the + in front of GetName) to the Name attribute; SetName() is to be used to set its value and the method GetPrescription() can be used to iterate over the set of Prescription entities related to this PATIENT entity.

The Role of UML In Database Processing Today

The ideas illustrated in Figure 2-31 lie in the murky water where database processing and object thinking merge. Such object-oriented notation doesn't fit with the practices and procedures of commercial database processing today. The notion that an entity attribute can be hidden in an object doesn't make sense unless only object-oriented programs are processing the database; even then, those programs must process the data in conformance with that policy. This is never done except for special-purpose, object-oriented DBMS (OODBMS) products and applications.

Instead, most commercial DBMS products have features that allow all types of programs to access the database and process any data for which they have security authority.

Moreover, with facilities like SQL, there is no way to limit access to attribute values to a single object.

So, the bottom line is that you should know how to interpret UML-style entity relationship diagrams. They can be used for database design just as extended E-R diagrams can. At present, however, the object-oriented notation they introduce is of limited practical value. See Chapter 16 for more information on this topic.

SUMMARY

The ANSI/SPARC three schema model provides perspective on the role of data modeling and database development. It defines three schema types: external, conceptual, and internal. A schema is a representation; an external schema is a representation of the way a user views database data. External schemas normally show just a portion of the database. A conceptual schema is a complete logical view, and an internal schema is a representation of a conceptual schema as physically stored using a particular product and/or technique. One conceptual schema will normally have many different external schemas based upon it. A conceptual schema can be represented by many internal schemas, depending on the product and technique to be used.

Users communicate with database developers in terms of external schemas; developers work backward to construct a conceptual schema that will support the users' external views. It is vitally important not to confuse the conceptual schema with the internal schema. The conceptual schema should represent a logical view, not compromised by the nature or limitations of the DBMS to be used.

The entity-relationship model was proposed by Peter Chen in 1975; it and its variants can be used to model conceptual schemas. The original E-R model was extended to include subtypes by Teorey and others to form the extended E-R model, which is what most people mean by the term *E-R model* today. In 1993, the National Institute of Standards and Technology announced a data modeling standard called the Integrated Definition for Information Modeling (IDEF1X). This standard incorporates a version of the extended E-R model, but it uses different symbols and adds facilities for modeling internal schemas. A number of data modeling products are based upon the IDEF1X model, but they add their own twists to that model as well. The object modeling community has developed a methodology called the Unified Modeling Language (UML), which also has incorporated a version of the E-R model.

The basic elements of all versions of the E-R model are entities, attributes, and relationships. An entity is an identifiable thing that users want to track. Entities of a given type are grouped into entity classes. Entities have attributes that describe the entities' characteristics. An identifier is an attribute that names or identifies entity instances. A unique identifier names a single instance in an entity class; a non-unique identifier names multiple instances in an entity class.

A relationship is an association among entities. Relationship classes are associations among entities; relationship instances are associations among entity instances. A relationship class that involves only two entity classes is called a binary relationship. In practice, most relationships are binary.

The three types of binary relationships are 1:1, 1:N, and N:M; the numbers refer to the maximum cardinality of the relationship. In traditional E-R diagrams, entities are represented as rectangles with square or rounded corners, and relationships are represented by diamonds. Relationships have a minimum cardinality, which defines the minimum number of entity instances that must exist on side of a relationship instance. Typical minimum cardinalities are 0 or 1, but other values are possible.

In the extended E-R model, a weak entity is an entity that cannot exist in a database without the presence of a second entity. A weak entity can be either an ID-dependent entity or an entity whose existence logically depends on a second entity. An ID-dependent entity is an entity whose identifier contains the identifier of a second entity. Weak entities are represented by diamonds and rectangles with rounded corners. Multi-valued attributes and multi-valued attribute groups can be represented by weak, ID-dependent entities.

A subtype entity represents a special case of another entity called a supertype. The relationship between a supertype and its subtypes is an IS-A relationship because all instances of a supertype and its subtypes refer to the same thing. Subtypes are used in database processing when values are inappropriate for some entity instances.

IDEF1X incorporates the extended E-R model, but the meanings of some terms are different, and the concept of domains is added to the model. IDEF1X can be used to document both conceptual and internal schemas. This chapter considered only its use for conceptual schema modeling.

In IDEF1X, entities are shown in rectangles. If attributes are shown, the primary key attribute(s) is shown in the top section of the rectangle and all non-primary key attributes are shown in the bottom section. Foreign keys can be shown in an IDEF1X E-R diagram, but such a display is normally inappropriate for conceptual schema modeling.

There are four types of IDEF1X relationships: non-identifying connection relationships, identifying connection relationships, non-specific relationships, and categorization relationships. Non-identifying relationships are the same as 1:1 and 1:N HAS-A relationships in the extended E-R model. In an IDEF1X diagram, non-identifying connection relationships are shown with a dashed line having a filled-in circle by the child entity. Optional parents are shown with a diamond next to them on the line. If there is no notation on the child side of the line, the child-side cardinality is 0, 1, or more. A P denotes a cardinality of 1 or more, a Z denotes 0 or 1, and a 1 denotes exactly 1 child is required.

Identifying connection relationships are the same as ID-dependent relationships in the extended E-R model. Such relationships are represented by a solid line with a filled-in circle by the child entity. Allowable child-side cardinalities are 0, 1, or more; 0 or 1; or 1. The parent is always required. IDEF1X does not provide a means to model weak entities that are not ID-dependent. Thus, although entities with rounded corners in the extended E-R model represent weak entities; entities with rounded corners in IDEF1X represent only ID-dependent entities.

Non-specific IDEF1X relationships are used to represent M:N relationships. Some people argue that M:N relationships do not truly exist; there is always an entity missing when it appears that there is an M:N relationship. Others argue that they do exist and should have better representation in the IDEF1X model.

Categorization relationships are IS-A relationships. They consist of a generic entity, one or more category entities, and a category cluster. The categories in a cluster are mutually exclusive. In a complete category, all possible subtypes are shown; in an incomplete category, some subtypes are missing. A discriminator is an attribute of the generic entity that can be used to determine the entity's category. An entity may have more than one category cluster and may have a relationship to more than one category entity, as long as each such entity is from a different category.

In IDEF1X, relationships can be named. Normally, the name is a verb phrase expressed from the parent's perspective, a slash, and a verb phrase from the child's perspective. Relationship names are important when two entities have more than one relationship to each other.

IDEF1X introduced the concept of domain to the E-R model. A domain is a named set of values that an attribute can have. Domains reduce ambiguity between attributes having the same name that may or may not refer to the same thing. They also reduce ambiguity among attributes that have the same values, but may or may not be the same. Domains are practically useful because they enable attributes to inherit their characteristics from a common domain. If a characteristic changes, the domain can be changed and all attributes based on that domain will inherit the change. A base domain is a domain having a data type and possibly a value list or range definition. A type domain is a subset of a base domain or a subset of another type domain.

There are a number of products that support the construction of IDEF1X models. ERWin, Visio, and Designer\2000 are three examples.

Unified Modeling Language (UML) is a set of structures and techniques for modeling and designing object-oriented programs. UML is an application development methodology and is the subject for a course on systems analysis. UML includes a version of the E-R model, however, for modeling databases.

UML entities, relationships, and attributes are very similar to those for the extended E-R model. The primary difference is in notation and also that object-oriented programming constructs have been added to entities and attributes. UML supports weak entities.

GROUP I QUESTIONS

2.1 Explain the word *schema* in your own words.

2.2 Name and explain the purpose of the three schemas in the ANSI/SPARC three schema model.

2.3 Explain a circumstance under which an organization could have three different external schemas for the same conceptual schema.

2.4 Describe how external schemas can be used to devise a conceptual schema.

2.5 Why is it important not to confuse the conceptual schema with the internal schema?

2.6 What was the problem between Bruce and Zelda? Do you think they can ever agree on a single way of viewing the data?

2.7 What is the difference between the E-R model and the extended E-R model?

2.8 Why is IDEF1X important?

2.9 Why is UML important?

2.10 Define *entity* and give an example.

2.11 Explain the difference between an entity class and an entity instance.

2.12 Define *attribute* and give examples for the entity you described in question 2.10.

2.13 Explain what a composite identifier is and give an example.

2.14 Which attribute defined in your answer to question 2.12 identifies the entity?

2.15 Define *relationship* and give an example.

2.16 Explain the difference between a *relationship class* and a *relationship instance*.

2.17 Define *degree of relationship*. Give an example, other than the one in this text, of a relationship greater than degree 2.

2.18 List and give an example of the three types of binary relationships. Draw an E-R diagram for each.

2.19 Define the terms *maximum cardinality* and *minimum cardinality*.

2.20 Name and sketch the symbols used in the extended E-R model entity-relationship diagrams for (a) entity, (b) relationship, (c) weak entity and its relationship, (d) recursive relationship, and (e) subtype entity.

2.21 Give an example E-R diagram for the entities DEPARTMENT and EMPLOYEE, which have a 1:N relationship. Assume that a DEPARTMENT does not need to have any EMPLOYEE, but that every EMPLOYEE does have a DEPARTMENT.

2.22 Give an example of a recursive relationship and show it in an E-R diagram.

2.23 Define the term *weak entity* and give an example other than the one in this text.

2.24 Explain the ambiguity in the definition of the term *weak entity*. Explain how this term is interpreted for the extended E-R model. Give examples other than those in this text of each type of weak entity.

2.25 Define the term *ID-dependent entity* and give an example other than one in this text.

2.26 Show how to use an ID-dependent entity to represent the multi-value attribute Skill in an EMPLOYEE entity. Indicate both the maximum and minimum cardinalities on both sides of the relationship. Use extended E-R symbols.

2.27 Show how to use an ID-dependent entity to represent the multi-value composite attribute Phone that contains the single-value attributes AreaCode, PhoneNumber. Assume that Phone appears in an entity called SALESPERSON. Indicate both the maximum and minimum cardinalities on both sides of the relationship. Use extended E-R symbols.

2.28 Describe subtype entities and give an example other than those in this text.

2.29 Explain the statement "In database processing, subtypes are used when values are inappropriate for some attributes of some entity instances." Show how this statement applies to your answer to question 2.28.

2.30 Explain the difference between a HAS-A relationship and an IS-A relationship, and give an example of each.

2.31 Define *primary key*.

2.32 What is a foreign key and why are such keys inappropriate in a conceptual model?

2.33 What are non-identifying connection relationships?

2.34 Give an example of a non-identifying connection relationship.

2.35 Explain the meaning of a filled-in circle, a diamond, the letter P, the letter Z, and the number 1 in an IDEF1X E-R diagram.

2.36 What is the default cardinality of a non-identifying connection relationship?

2.37 How do identifying connection relationships relate to the extended E-R model?

2.38 What is the difference between a weak entity in the extended E-R model and an identifying connection relationship in the IDEF1X model?

2.39 How does the IDEF1X model represent a weak entity that is not ID-dependent?

2.40 How are N:M relationships represented in an IDEF1X model?

2.41 Make the argument that N:M relationships do not exist. Give examples other than the ones in this text in your answer.

2.42 Make the argument that N:M relationships do exist. Give examples other than the ones in this text in your answer.

2.43 Of the two arguments in your answers to question 2.41 and 2.42, which do you believe? Why?

2.44 Explain the terms *generic entity*, *category entity*, and *categorization cluster*. Give an example of each.

2.45 What is the role of a discriminator in a category relationship?

2.46 Explain the difference between a complete category cluster and an incomplete category cluster.

2.47 Explain why the Z notation with complete category clusters is puzzling.

2.48 Explain the circumstances under which an entity instance may have a relationship to two or more category entity instances.

2.49 What are the differences between a categorization relationship in the IDEF1X model and subtypes/supertypes in the extended E-R model?

2.50 Explain the normal way that relationships are named.

2.51 When are relationship names particularly useful?

2.52 What is a domain?

2.53 Explain two ways that domains reduce ambiguity.

2.54 Describe how domains are practically useful.

2.55 Define *base domain*.

2.56 Define *type domain*.

GROUP II QUESTIONS

Use the STUDENT ACTIVITY IDEF1X diagram in Figure 2-32 to answer the following questions:

2.57 Consider the relationship between STUDENT and EQUIPMENT:

   A. What type is this relationship?

   B. What are the maximum cardinalities?

   C. What are the minimum cardinalities?

   D. Describe any cardinality changes that you think should be made. Justify your changes.

   E. Give an appropriate name for this relationship.

2.58 Consider the relationship between EQUIPMENT and COURSE:

   A. What type is this relationship?

   B. What are the maximum cardinalities?

   C. What are the minimum cardinalities?

   D. Describe any cardinality changes that you think should be made. Justify your changes.

   E. Give an appropriate name for this relationship.

2.59 In Figure 2-32, COURSE describes a course such as Beginning Kayaking or Intermediate Scuba; CLASS describes a particular offering of a course, such as the class Beginning Kayaking offered on January 7, 2003. For the relationship between COURSE and CLASS:

   A. What type is this relationship? Is this the correct type for this relationship?

   B. What are the maximum cardinalities?

   C. What are the minimum cardinalities?

   D. Describe any cardinality changes that you think should be made. Justify your changes.

   E. Give an appropriate name for this relationship.

FIGURE 2-32

IDEF1X Diagram

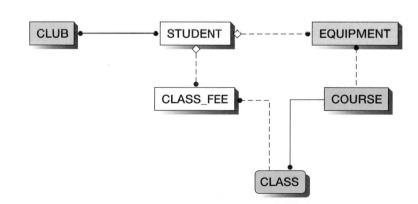

2.60 Consider the relationship between CLASS_FEE and CLASS:

    A. What type is this relationship?

    B. What are the maximum cardinalities?

    C. What are the minimum cardinalities?

    D. Describe any cardinality changes that you think should be made. Justify your changes.

    E. Give an appropriate name for this relationship.

2.61 Consider the relationship between CLASS_FEE and STUDENT:

    A. What type is this relationship?

    B. What are the maximum cardinalities?

    C. What are the minimum cardinalities?

    D. Describe any cardinality changes that you think should be made. Justify your changes.

    E. Give an appropriate name for this relationship.

2.62 Consider the relationship between STUDENT and CLUB:

    A. What type is this relationship?

    B. Describe a possible new entity that would change this relationship into two non-identifying connection relationships. Specify appropriate cardinalities for your new relationships.

    C. Do you think the design in your answer to question B is a better design than the relationship shown in this figure?

2.63 Add a new entity called INSTRUCTOR. Create a new relationship between INSTRUCTOR and COURSE and a new relationship between INSTRUCTOR and EQUIPMENT.

    A. Justify the type of relationships you have chosen.

    B. Specify cardinalities for your new relationships.

    C. Name your new relationships.

    D. Redraw the diagram in Figure 2-32 to show your new relationships. Place all cardinalities from your answers to questions 2.57 to 2.62 on this diagram.

2.64 Modify your answer in question 2.63 to make INSTRUCTOR and CLUB_OFFICER category entities of STUDENT.

    A. Should you use a complete or an incomplete category cluster? Explain your answer.

    B. Name and describe an attribute that could be used as a discriminator for this category cluster.

    C. Redraw the diagram in your answer to question 2.63 to show your new relationships.

Use the EMPLOYEE TRIP IDEF1X diagram in Figure 2-33 to answer the following questions:

2.65 Consider the relationship between EMLOYEE and TRIP:

    A. What type is this relationship?

    B. What are the maximum cardinalities?

    C. What are the minimum cardinalities?

    D. Describe any cardinality changes that you think should be made. Justify your changes.

    E. Give an appropriate name for this relationship.

FIGURE 2–33

IDEF1X Diagram

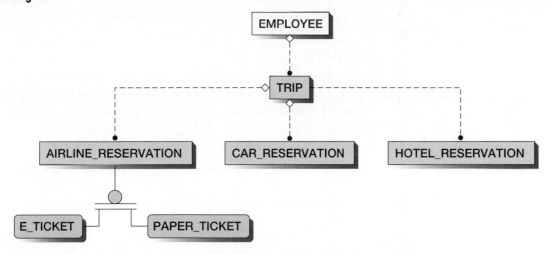

2.66 Consider the relationship between TRIP and AIRLINE_RESERVATION:

   A. What type is this relationship?

   B. What are the maximum cardinalities?

   C. What are the minimum cardinalities?

   D. Describe any cardinality changes that you think should be made. Justify your changes.

   E. Give an appropriate name for this relationship.

2.67 Consider the relationship between TRIP and CAR_RESERVATION:

   A. What type is this relationship?

   B. What are the maximum cardinalities?

   C. What are the minimum cardinalities?

   D. Describe any cardinality changes that you think should be made. Justify your changes.

   E. Give an appropriate name for this relationship.

2.68 Consider the relationship between TRIP and HOTEL_RESERVATION:

   A. What type is this relationship?

   B. What are the maximum cardinalities?

   C. What are the minimum cardinalities?

   D. Describe any cardinality changes that you think should be made. Justify your changes.

   E. Give an appropriate name for this relationship.

2.69 Consider the relationships among AIRLINE_RESERVATION, E_TICKET, and PAPER_TICKET:

   A. What type is this relationship?

   B. What are the maximum cardinalities?

   C. What are the minimum cardinalities?

   D. Is this a complete or an incomplete category cluster? Should it be a different type of category cluster?

   E. Give an example discriminator for this relationship.

2.70 Add a new entity called EXPENSE_REPORT. Create a new relationship between EMPLOYEE and EXPENSE_REPORT and a new relationship between TRIP and EXPENSE_REPORT.

A. Justify the type of relationships you have chosen.

B. Specify cardinalities for your new relationships.

C. Name your new relationships.

D. Redraw the diagram in Figure 2-33 to show your new relationships.

2.71 Modify your answer in question 2.70 to make BUSINESS and PERSONAL category entities of TRIP. Assume that there can be no relationship between EXPENSE_REPORT and PERSONAL.

A. Should you use a complete or an incomplete category cluster?

B. Name and describe an attribute that could be used as a discriminator for this category cluster.

C. Redraw the diagram in your answer to question 2.70 to show your new relationships.

Figure 2-34 shows an IDEF1X version of the conceptual schema for the saga of Bruce and Zelda. Use it when answering the following questions:

2.72 Consider the relationship between FISH and OBSERVATION:

A. What type is this relationship?

B. What are the maximum cardinalities?

C. What are the minimum cardinalities?

D. Describe any cardinality changes that you think should be made. Justify your changes.

E. Give an appropriate name for this relationship.

2.73 Consider the relationship between RIVER and OBSERVATION:

A. What type is this relationship?

B. What are the maximum cardinalities?

C. What are the minimum cardinalities?

D. Describe any cardinality changes that you think should be made. Justify your changes.

E. Give an appropriate name for this relationship.

2.74 Add a new entity called RIVER_SITE as a child entity in an identifying connection relationship to RIVER. Remove the relationship between RIVER and OBSERVATION and place a new relationship between OBSERVATION and RIVER_SITE.

A. Define and justify cardinalities between RIVER and RIVER_SITE.

B. Define and justify cardinalities between RIVER_SITE and OBSERVATION.

C. Name your new relationships.

D. Redraw Figure 2-34 given your new design.

FIGURE 2-34

IDEF1X Diagram for the Saga of Bruce and Zelda

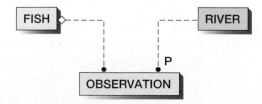

2.75 Add a new entity called OBSERVER to your answer to question 2.74. Create a relationship between OBSERVATION and OBSERVER. Also, add a category cluster to OBSERVER with two categories: PROFESSIONAL and VOLUNTEER.

    A. What type of relationship is appropriate? Justify your answer.

    B. Define and justify cardinalities between OBSERVER and OBSERVATION. Name this relationship.

    C. What type of category cluster is appropriate?

    D. Redraw your answer to question 2.74 given your new design.

2.76 Create a new entity called CLASS. Construct a relationship between VOLUNTEER and CLASS.

    A. What type of relationship is appropriate? Justify your answer.

    B. Redraw your answer to question 2.75 given your new relationship.

    C. Create another entity called CLASS_OFFERING, which represents a particular offering of a particular class. Add and remove relationships as appropriate. For each new relationship, give the type, give the cardinalities, and name the relationship.

    D. Redraw your answer to question 2.75 given your new design.

2.77 The Public Affairs Office at Highline University receives requests for speakers on particular topics. To be able to respond to such request, that office wants to build a database. In particular, it wants to keep track of topics, speakers, speeches, and organizations to which someone from Highline has spoken.

    A. Make a list of possible entities for the Speaker database.

    B. Create an IDEF1X E-R diagram showing only entities (like Figure 2-34). Assume that there is an M:N relationship between SPEAKER and TOPIC.

    C. For each relationship in your diagram, specify the relationship type, and the minimum and maximum cardinality on both parent and child. Name each relationship.

    D. Repeat questions B and C, but add an entity to your diagram so that there will be no N:M relationship.

    E. Do you prefer the design in question B and C or the design in question D? Justify your preference.

2.78 The Metropolitan Housing Agency (MHA) is a non-profit organization that advocates the development and improvement of low-income housing. The MHA operates in a metropolitan area of approximately 2.2 million people in a midwestern city. The MHA maintains data about the location, availability, and condition of low-income housing in 11 different census tracts in the metropolitan area. Within the boundaries of these tracts are approximately 250 different buildings that provide low-income housing. On average, each building contains 25 apartments or other units.

The MHA keeps data about each census tract, including geographic boundaries, median income of the population, elected officials, principal businesses, principal investors involved in attributes in that tract, and other demographic and economic data. It also maintains a limited amount of data about crime. For each building, the MHA stores the name, address, size, owner(s)'s name and address, mortgagor(s)'s name and address, renovations and repairs, and availability of facilities for handicapped people. In addition, the MHA keeps a list of each of the units within each building, including the type of unit, size, number of bedrooms, number of baths, kitchen and dining facilities, location in the building, and any special remarks. The MHA wants to maintain data regarding the average occupancy rates for each unit, but to date it has been unable to collect or store such data. The MHA does, however, keep data about whether a given unit is occupied.

The MHA serves as an information clearinghouse and offers three basic services. First, it works with politicians, lobbyists, and advocacy groups to support legislation that encourages the development of low-income housing through tax incentives, developmental zoning preferences, and other legislative inducements. To accomplish this, the MHA provides information about low-income housing to state, county, and city governments. Second, through speeches, seminars, displays at conventions, and other public relations activities, the MHA officials strive to raise the community's consciousness about the need for low-income housing. Finally, the MHA provides information about the availability of low-income housing to other agencies that work with the low-income and homeless populations.

A. Make a list of possible entities for a database to support MHA's information needs.

B. Construct an IDEF1X entity-relationships diagram for the entities in question A.

C. Name each relationship and ensure that you have correctly defined the minimum and maximum cardinalities.

Note: You may find that as you answer question B, you will add, remove, or change some of the entities in your answer to question A. This is normal and very typical of the data modeling process. Just keep working back and forth until you have an IDEF1X E-R diagram that you believe is correct.

FIREDUP PROJECT QUESTIONS

Consider the situation of FiredUp, which was discussed at the end of Chapter 1. Assume that FiredUp has now developed a line of three different stoves: FiredNow, FiredAlways, and FiredAtCamp. Further, assume that the owners are selling spare parts for each of their stoves and that they also are making stove repairs. Some repairs are at no charge because they are within the stove warranty period; other repairs are made at a charge for parts only; and still others are made for parts and labor. FiredUp wants to keep track of all of these data. When asked for further details, the owners made the following list:

CUSTOMER: Name, StreetAddress, ApartmentNumber, City, State/Province, Zip/PostalCode, Country, EmailAddress, PhoneNumber

STOVE: SerialNumber, Type, ManufactureDate, InspectorInitials

INVOICE: InvoiceNumber, Date, Customer with a list of items and prices that were sold, TotalPrice

REPAIR: RepairNumber, Customer, Stove, Description with a list of items that were used in the repair and the charge for them (if any), TotalAmount of the repair

PART: Number, Description, Cost, SalesPrice

A. Create an extended E-R entity-relationship diagram of a database for FiredUp. Set the minimum and maximum cardinality of the relationships among entities, as you think is appropriate. Explain your rationale for each cardinality value. Use weak entities as appropriate. Do not use subtypes. Name any ID-dependent entities, if any.

B.   Modify the entity-relationship diagram in your answer to question A by representing INVOICE and REPAIR with appropriate subtypes. Under what circumstances is this design better than the one in your answer to question A?

C.   Transform your answer to question B to an IDEF1X diagram. Make changes to subtypes and weak entity relationships as appropriate.

D.   Suppose that FiredUp wants to keep track of home, fax, and cell phone numbers as well as multiple e-mail addresses for each of its customers. Modify your model in A to allow for multiple values of PhoneNumber and EmailAddress. You can use either the extended E-R diagram or the IDEF1X diagram, depending on which you prefer.

E.   Suppose that FiredUp develops different versions of the same stove product. Thus, it develops a FiredNow Version 1 and a FiredNow Version 2, and so on. Although FiredUp could consider each version of a stove to be a new product, it does not want to do that. Modify your entity-relationship diagram from question D as necessary to account for this situation. You can use either extended E-R or IDEF1X format, depending on which you prefer.

TWIGS TREE TRIMMING SERVICE PROJECT QUESTIONS

Consider the situation of Samantha Green, who owns and operates Twigs Tree Trimming Service, described at the end of Chapter 1. Although many of her jobs are one-time operations to remove a tree or stump, others are recurring: trimming a tree or groups of trees every year or every other year. When business is slow, she calls former clients to remind them of her service and of the need to trim their trees on a regular basis.

Samantha grinds the branches and trunks that she cuts into small chips using a chip grinder that she tows behind her truck. The chips are thrown into the back of her truck as they are ground. For years, Samantha took these chips to the recycling center, but recently she discovered that she could sell these chips to nurseries and organizations for use as mulch. Even more recently, she discovered that some of her own tree trimming customers want to buy chips as well. (Yes, it is possible that customers could pay her to cut a tree and grind the branches, and repurchase their own chips as mulch some time later. Samantha's response to that was, "I love America!")

Samantha keeps the following data:

OWNER OwnerName, Phone, Street, City, State, Zip

RECURRING_SERVICE MonthsBetweenService, Description, ServiceFee

SERVICE DateOfService, Description, AmountBilled, AmountPaid, DateOfPayment

CHIP_DELIVERY CustomerName, Phone, Street, City State, Zip, DateDelivered, LoadSize, AmountBilled, AmountPaid

A.   To begin, assume that all jobs are recurring. Create an IDEF1X E-R diagram for OWNER, RECURRING_SERVICE, and SERVICE. Model the relationship between RECURRING_SERVICE and SERVICE as an ID-dependent entity. State the type of all relationships, give the minimum and maximum cardinalities, and name each relationship.

B.   Now, assume that no jobs are recurring. That is, remove RECURRING_SERVICE and model SERVICE as a strong entity. Create an IDEF1X model: state the type of all relationships, give the cardinalities, and name each relationship.

C. Combine your answers to questions A and B by naming the entity for services that are recurring as RECURRING_SERVICE, naming the entity for services that are non-recurring as NON_RECURRING_SERVICE, and creating a new generic entity called SERVICE that has RECURRING_SERVICE and NON_RECURRING_SERVICE as category entities. Create an IDEF1X model: state the type of all relationships, give the cardinalities, and name each relationship.

D. Add an entity called CHIP_DELIVERY to your model in question C. To begin, assume that none of Samantha's trimming customers ever buy chips. Create a new entity called CHIP_CUSTOMER for chip deliveries. Create an IDEF1X model: state the type of all relationships, give the cardinalities, and name each relationship.

E. Answer question D, but assume that some of her trimming customers can also buy chips. Use category entities to model the types of customers similar to that in question C. Create an IDEF1X model: state the type of all relationships, give the cardinalities, and name each relationship.

CHAPTER 3

Entity-Relationship Data Modeling
Process and Examples

This chapter describes a process for creating data models. Because this process is so important, we will take three different perspectives. First, we will describe the steps necessary to create a data model. Then, we will examine sample forms and reports and see how to construct a data model from them. Finally, we will consider a case of data model development for a university. Each of these perspectives sheds light on the other perspectives. Consequently, the best way to study this chapter is to read it two or three times. All the sections fit together as a single topic or structure.

As stated in Chapter 2, after you understand the underlying concepts, the next step is to apply those concepts by creating data models from examples. Therefore, you should answer the questions and work the projects at the end of the chapter. If possible, use one of the data modeling products described in Chapter 2.

▶ A DATA MODELING PROCESS

Figure 3-1 lists steps in the data modeling process. The first step is to plan the project. Major tasks in this step are obtaining project authorization and budget; building the project team; planning the team's activities; establishing tools, techniques, and standards so that team members will produce consistent results; and defining the project's scope.

Scope definition is particularly important for data modeling because in most organizations everything is related to something else. For example, entities in the sales organization will have relationships to entities in the credit department, which will have relationships to entities in customer relations management, which will have relationships to entities in operations, and so forth. Without a clear delineation of the scope and boundary of the project, data modeling activities can spiral out of control. This means, of course, that some relationships will be unspecified or ignored at the boundaries of the project.

Determining System Requirements

The next step in the data modeling project is to determine system requirements, especially those that concern the database. This broad and important topic requires several chapters of its own in a systems development text. Here, we will simply discuss common sources for data modeling requirements. You will learn more about techniques for obtaining these requirements in your systems development class.

User Interviews and Observations of User Activity Figure 3-2 lists the most common sources of requirements. User interviews and observations of user activities are extremely valuable sources of requirements, but they are the most difficult sources to use well. Users are notorious for seeming to want everything, yet they are also notorious for forgetting important requirements. A user at the start of an accounting period will often forget requirements at the end of the accounting period, and so forth. Again, responding to these challenges is beyond the scope of a database book, but it is important knowledge to gain from your systems text.

As far as data modeling is concerned, the goal of a user interview is to learn of potential entities and their relationships to one another. It is also important to obtain source documents, such as existing forms and reports, which indicate entities and their relationships and also provide lists of potential attributes. Recall from the saga of Bruce and Zelda that users view data from different perspectives, and they also use different names for the same thing and the same name for different things. The goal in an interview is to obtain an accurate description of that user's or user group's perspective or external view(s) of the data.

Keep the possibility of terminology differences in mind when interviewing users. CUSTOMER_HISTORY in accounting may be a very different thing from CUSTOMER_HISTORY in sales. Thinking that you already know what CUSTOMER_HISTORY means because you understand the accounting version of it is risky when you interview the sales department.

Results from user interviews and observations will be documented as notes, sketches, data element definitions, and so forth. Team members should create consistent documentation and record their results into a consolidated repository.

Forms and Reports Forms and reports are an excellent (often the best) source of data modeling requirements. Existing documents can be analyzed to determine how data is currently viewed and processed, and new documents indicate either changes in data views or the need for additional data to be maintained. Examples of filled-in forms and reports should be made part of the requirements repository. These documents can be used for subsequent data model development and later data model validation. We will show many examples of the creation of data models from forms and reports in the next section.

FIGURE 3-1

Steps in the Data
Modeling Process

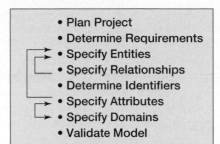

- Plan Project
- Determine Requirements
- Specify Entities
- Specify Relationships
- Determine Identifiers
- Specify Attributes
- Specify Domains
- Validate Model

FIGURE 3-2

Sources for Database
Requirements

- User Interviews
- User Activity Observations
- Existing Forms and Reports
- New Forms and Reports
- Existing Manual Files
- Existing Computer Files/Databases
- Formally Defined Interfaces (XML)
- Domain Expertise

Existing Files   Existing files are another excellent source of requirements. Some files are manual; users will say something like, "I keep a list of product codes in a notebook or in a card file." Photocopies of such lists or cards should be made part of the requirements documentation. Sometimes, users will have existing computer files in the form of spreadsheets or personal databases. These, too, are excellent sources of information for data modeling, and copies of such files or file extracts should also be obtained.

For larger databases, data modeling products such as ERWin and Visio can be used to **reverse engineer** an existing database to create a data model. The models created in this manner are based on internal schemas and are not conceptual in nature. They're more like an integrated view of the tables in the database. They are complete (like conceptual schemas), but they are not logical (unlike conceptual schemas); instead, they are representations of physical structures.

Today, few large databases are constructed from scratch. Instead, many projects consist of modifications to existing databases. Reverse engineering is an important tool for such projects. We will address this topic in detail in Chapter 8, "Database Redesign." We must wait until then to discuss it because you need to know SQL to understand the discussion.

Formal Interfaces   A formal interface is a standardized external view. Such interfaces are created by governmental agencies, industry groups, and large enterprises to facilitate interorganizational data transfer. Sometimes, new databases systems are required to receive data from or publish data to such an interface. If so, the interface is a good source of data requirements.

Formal interfaces have been around for many years, but the need for interorganizational standards increased with the advent of the Internet. Additionally, the use of XML makes the publication and use of such standards much easier. Almost every business profession or major industry category has (or is in the process of developing) XML standards.

We will discuss XML in Chapter 13; in that chapter, you will see the close relationship between database processing and XML. Both SQL Server and Oracle, for example, can get or put data in the form of XML.

You can expect the use of formal interfaces to increase in the future, and the need to support such interfaces will become an ever more important source of data model requirements.

Domain Experts   Domain experts are individuals who have deep knowledge of a particular problem area. A company such as 3M, for example, has domain experts in adhesives, abrasives, safety products, safety standards, and so forth. Such experts are usually found in staff offices. Consequently, they are unlikely to be users of a new database system, but they can provide important background information about the business domain.

For example, in a company such as 3M, there may be thousands upon thousands of abrasive products. In this situation, there may be dozens of different ways to develop subtypes/supertype relationships or category clusters. Domain experts can be invaluable for sorting through the myriad of data modeling choices, eliminating many possibilities on the basis of their knowledge.

Using domain experts, however, has a downside. Nothing is more dangerous in a development project than a group of "experts" sitting around a table saying, "If I were a user, I'd want…" No one but a user knows what data users want or the form(s) in which they need it. So, although domain expertise can shed light on a particular project, the primary focus for requirements determination must be the users themselves.

The result of the requirements determination will be a repository of notes, diagrams, forms, reports, files, etc. that can be used to develop the data model.

Specifying Entities

Given the results of the requirements work, the team is ready to create the data model. Figure 3-1 lists the specification of entities, relationships, attributes, and domains as separate sequential steps. In truth, these specifications are often done in repetitive parallel fashion. While analyzing forms or reports, for example, both entities and relationships will be discovered. The contents of the forms or reports also give rise to the definition of attributes. So, although we will describe these specifications separately, realize they are often done together and iteratively.

An entity is something that the users want to track, something the users want to keep data about. Entities are often physical things such as OFFICE or PRODUCT, but they can also be logical concepts such as ORDER, TRANSACTION, or CONTRACT. Entities are identifiable; you can tell one from another. They are also things that are readily described by nouns rather than characteristics that are readily described by adjectives. Consider the following user statement:

"First, I take the orders and sort them by shipping weight."

In this statement, the thing being processed is an ORDER (a noun). One of the characteristics of an order—its shipping weight (an adjective)—is being used to perform some action (sort). Thus, ShippingWeight is likely an attribute.

Other user statements give can rise to ambiguity, however. Consider the following:

"First, I take today's orders and sort them by shipping weight."

The words *today's orders* could imply that the entity ORDER has an attribute like OrderDate and that attribute is being used to select from the set of all orders. Or, this statement might mean that there is a need for a subtype or category entity. It might be necessary to model, for example, the generic entity ORDER and the category entities ORDER_TODAY, ORDER_PAST_WEEK, and ORDER_PAST_MONTH. Both are possibilities, and further study of other interviews, forms, reports and other requirements will be needed to determine which of these is the better model. In some cases, both designs are carried forward in the data model (that is, both subtypes and OrderDate are put into the data model) and the one that is incorrect is removed as the process continues.

Statements of the form "x of y" such as "phone of customer," "region of salesperson," and "PCB level of river" almost always indicate that the word after *of* is an entity. In these examples, CUSTOMER, SALESPERSON, and RIVER are all entities.

Frequently, such statements indicate that the word before the *of* is an attribute, but it can also indicate the need for a second entity. In the previous statements, *phone* and *PCB level* are likely to be attributes, but *region* can either be an attribute or another entity.

We will show later in this chapter how to use forms and reports to extract entities, relationships, and attributes. For now, realize that the result of this data modeling activity will be a list of entities such as that shown in Figure 3-3. As the project progresses, this list will be modified many times. Some of the entities in the list will be found to be synonyms of one another; some entities will be removed because they are found to be irrelevant, and others will be added.

The list in Figure 3-3 is part of a data modeling project for a small plant and garden nursery. This figure shows the initial set of entities as well as the final set after the data modeling project was finished. During the project, the team determined that DELIVERY and GIFT-CERTIFICATE were unnecessary as entities, so they were removed. The entities PLANT and FURNITURE were different subtypes of a missing entity PRODUCT. After PRODUCT was defined, the team examined the requirements and decided there was insufficient need for PLANT and FURNITURE subtypes, so those entities were removed. Also, the team discovered that INVOICE and ORDER were synonyms, and the term ORDER was adopted as the preferred term to use. There were missing entities SUPPLIER and SUPPLIER_RETURN, and these were added. Finally, the team decided to define the term PURCHASE for a purchase by a CUSTOMER and to define the term ORDER for a purchase by the nursery to a SUPPLIER.

This last comment indicates the need to define the meaning and use of entities during the requirements phase. Figure 3-4 shows the definitions used at Padden Creek.

FIGURE 3-3

Entity Lists for Padden Creek Gardens;
(a) Initial Entity List and (b) Final Entity List

(a)
PLANT
PURCHASE
CUSTOMER
ORDER
DELIVERY
BUYER
GIFT-CERTIFICATE
RETURN
INVOICE
FURNITURE

(b)
PRODUCT
PURCHASE
CUSTOMER
SUPPLIER
ORDER
RETURN
SUPPLIER_RETURN

FIGURE 3-4

Entity Descriptions

Entity	Description
PRODUCT	A product that is ordered from suppliers and purchased by customers. Products are identified by name of plant or product type, not by individual item. Thus, a product is "*Poeneia, Rosetta,*" or "Festive Planter," not a particular peony or plantor.
PURCHASE	A record of items purchased by a customer. Many purchases are written as cash sales and do not include identifying customer information. The record of credit card purchases has the credit card receipt stapled to it, but there is no goal to track customer credit card data. The identifying customer data is recorded for purchases over $150 and for purchases by frequent buyers.
CUSTOMER	Someone who buys from Padden Creek. Identifying data is kept only for certain customers.
SUPPLIER	A vendor of plants, furniture, or other items to Padden Creek.
ORDER	An order of products from a supplier.
RETURN	A record of the return of a product to us by a customer.
SUPPLIER_RETURN	A record of the return of a product to a supplier by us.

Specifying Relationships

A data model includes the specification of all relationships between entities. This specification includes the identity of the parent and child entities, the relationship type, the minimum and maximum cardinalities, and the name of the relationships. Entities and their relationships are normally documented by using extended E-R diagrams, IDEF1X diagrams, UML diagrams, or some other standardized technique.

Two approaches are used for finding relationships. One is to examine every combination of two entities and determine whether a relationship might exist. If so, the next step is to examine all requirements to determine the cardinalities and other characteristics of the relationship. The second technique is to process all requirements documents and find all relationships indicated in those documents. Sometimes, a combination of the two approaches is used.

To examine all combinations of two entities, a table with the names of all entities in the rows and columns can be constructed—like the one shown in Figure 3-5. Then, each pair of entities is considered in turn and a Y or yes is placed in the cell if a relationship might exist between the two entities. In the first row of Figure 3-5, for example, the CUSTOMER entity is compared to every other entity for the Padden Creek database. Here, CUSTOMER is possibly related to PURCHASE and SUPPLIER.

There is no such thing as a one-way relationship. If CUSTOMER has a relationship to PURCHASE, then PURCHASE has a relationship to CUSTOMER. Thus, if the table in Figure 3-5 is filled out correctly, it should be symmetrical. It is possible, however, that applications will use a relationship in one direction and never in another. For example, it is possible that applications access the ORDER entity and use it to find all related SUPPLIERs, but no application ever accesses the SUPPLIER entity and uses it to find an ORDER. In this case, the potential relationship diagram would be asymmetrical. Such situations are rare, however.

After the possibility of a relationship has been determined, the data modeling team investigates all sources of requirements to determine whether the relationship exists in fact. If so, the relationship is documented; otherwise, the Y is taken from the relationship grid.

If the data model is large (suppose there are 50 different entities), using such a diagram is unwieldy. There will be 50 x 50 -50 or 2,250 comparisons made. This is a long, boring, labor-intensive process that is probably not worth the cost. Instead, the team will

FIGURE 3-5

Potential Relationship Diagram

	CUSTOMER	ORDER	PRODUCT	PURCHASE	RETURN	SUPPLIER	SUPPLIER_RETURN
CUSTOMER	X			Y	Y		
ORDER		X	Y			Y	
PRODUCT		Y	X	Y	Y		Y
PURCHASE	Y		Y	X			
RETURN	Y		Y		X		
SUPPLIER		Y				X	Y
SUPPLIER_RETURN			Y			Y	X

Y   → Yes, there is a possible direct relationship
Blank → Relationship is unlikely

rely on an analysis of forms, reports, and other requirements to determine all relationships. We will show how to do that in the discussion beginning on page 83.

Determining Identifiers

Every true entity has an identifier, which is an attribute or group of attributes that uniquely identifies an entity instance. If it appears that an entity has no identifier, then either attributes are missing or it is not a true entity. For example, consider the candidate entity SHIPPING_MODE with attributes {Vendor, Date, Cost}. None of these attributes is a good identifier of SHIPPING_MODE. Vendor might be an identifier of a VENDOR entity, but not of SHIPPING_MODE. Perhaps there is an attribute like ShipmentType that is missing or perhaps these attributes really belong to a different entity such as ORDER.

Of course, ID-dependent entities contain only a portion of their identifier. APARTMENT, for example, has the identifier {BuildingName, ApartmentNumber}, but only ApartmentNumber will belong to APARTMENT. The BuildingName attribute will belong to BUILDING, the parent of APARTMENT in the ID-dependent relationship. Thus, when it is difficult to find a proper identifier for an entity that has been classified as non-ID-dependent, it is sometimes worthwhile to consider whether the entity is ID-dependent on another entity. It might be that the parent entity is even missing from the model.

Entities that have the same identifier should be examined closely. It may be that the two entities are synonyms for one another. Or, it may be that they are subtypes or categories of a common entity. For example, in a vehicle licensing application, the entities CAR, TRUCK, BOAT, TRAILER, and AIRPLANE may all have the identifier LicenseNumber. In this case, they are probably all subtypes or categories of a generalized entity like TAXABLE_VEHICLE.

In some rare cases, however, two entities are truly different but happen to have the same identifier. EMPLOYEE and BADGE, for example, may both have the identifier EmployeeID. Or, BADGE could be considered to be ID-dependent on EMPLOYEE, with the full identifier of BADGE being {EmployeeID, IssueDate}. Sometimes, the decision among such alternatives must be made on aesthetic grounds.

Specifying Attributes and Domains

The next two steps are to specify attributes and domains. Normally, this is done by finding attributes on forms, reports, existing files, and the like and then adding them to entities. Each time an attribute is added, the team looks to determine whether it has already defined a domain on which that attribute can be defined. If so, the attribute is based upon that domain. If not, a new domain is defined.

Initially, every attribute will require the definition of a new domain. As the work progresses and more domains are defined, however, attributes will be found that arise from already defined domains.

After all attributes have been defined, it is a good idea to look through the domains to determine whether some domains are the same, or some domains are types of other domains. After this has been done, the team should make a second pass through the attributes to determine whether any domain adjustments need be made.

Data modeling products provide a variety of tools for documenting domains. With some, you can define the domain and create attributes based upon the domain by dragging the domain into an entity. By default, the name of the attribute will be the name of the domain (this default name can be changed if necessary).

Domain Property Inheritance   Chapter 2 discussed some of the practical advantages of using domains. Principally, these advantages occur because the properties of the domain are inherited by all attributes based on that domain. When the domain properties change, all the attribute properties change as well. For example, if the data type of a domain is changed, all attributes based on that domain will inherit the new data type.

Other inheritable domain properties are the domain definition and notes about the domain. These may sound trivial, but they are quite useful. For example, a note that says that the domain PartCode is based on a definition as established in 2001 might be important. Having every attribute based on PartCode inherit that note will save work and confusion.

Domains also have initial value and value constraint properties. The initial value property specifies the value to be given to any new instance of an attribute based on the domain; the constraint property describes limitations on the values of attributes based on the domain. For example, the PartCode domain could be given an initial value property of "P0000" and a constraint property that specifies that values are to begin with a P or Z and followed by four decimal digits. Both of these properties will be inherited by all attributes based on the domain.

Using Domains to Enforce Data Standards   Of course, it is possible to ignore domains and define every attribute as unique and independent from all others. In essence, this is what is done with products such as Microsoft Access. The developer sets properties of each of the table's columns, one at a time. No concept of domain is ever used.

In organizations, this practice can lead to incompatible data types and incompatible systems. For example, if PartCode is defined as numeric between 10000 and 99999 in one system, but as character in the pattern *xxnnnnn*, where xx is the letters "PC" and *nnnnn* is a decimal number greater or equal to 10000, it will be difficult to integrate the two systems. Part codes that should match will appear not to match, so it will be necessary to write special-purpose program code to convert one part code scheme to the other. This situation is doubly frustrating because they really are using the same part code; they are simply expressing that code differently.

To prevent such incompatibility, some organizations develop a data dictionary of standardized domains and properties. These domains and properties are imported into data modeling tools and are used to create attributes in the data model. In this way, every data modeling project will be working with the same standardized components. Of course, some models will require the definition of new domains; however, the goal is to do this only when an existing domain will not do. This is one of the functions of the data administrator that we will discuss further in Chapter 9.

Attributes Suggesting Missing Entities and Relationships   The specification of attributes sometimes suggests the addition of additional entities or relationships to the model. In particular, attributes that are names of something other than the entity in which they reside can suggest the need for an additional entity or relationship.

For example, in a SALESPERSON entity, an attribute such as Region suggests that there may be a need for a new entity named REGION. If so, the Region attribute is replaced by the relationship between SALESPERSON and REGION. Similarly, an entity PART with an attribute Category suggests the need for a CATEGORY entity with a relationship to PART. Attributes whose name includes the word *name* are particularly suspect in this regard. In an ORDER document, an attribute like ShippingCompanyName suggests the need for an entity SHIPPING_COMPANY with a relationship to ORDER.

Because of this phenomenon, once all attributes have been specified for all entities, the team should review the model looking for attributes that may suggest such missing entities. Of course, even though the entity exists in principle, this does not necessarily mean that the entity should be added to the model. It may be that even though it would be possible to define a SHIPPING_COMPANY entity, there is no need to have such an entity in the data model. Or, it may be that the definition of such an entity lies outside the scope of the project. In that case, keeping an attribute named ShippingCompany, for example, may be the best way to cut the model from continuing on across the organization.

Validate Model

The last step in the data modeling process is to validate the data model. This is perhaps the most important step because if the data model is incorrect, then the database design will be incorrect. Forms, reports, and other application elements will then either be wrong, or their design will conflict with the design of the database and it will be very difficult and expensive to construct them. Furthermore, changing the data model at this stage is simply a matter of modifying E-R diagrams. Changing the database after it has been implemented can be complicated and difficult, as you will learn in Chapter 8. As the machinists say, "The best way to solve a problem is not to have it in the first place."

What Makes a Data Model Wrong?   One very important question that is often overlooked because its answer seems obvious is "What makes a data model wrong?" It is tempting to say that data models should model the real world, and that a data model is wrong if it does not fit reality. The problem with this answer is that data models do not model reality. This very important point is difficult to understand; but if you can understand it, you will save many hours in your life and be a much better member of a data modeling team.

The German philosopher Immanuel Kant was the first to write that what we perceive of reality is completely determined by the nature of our minds and our perceptive apparatus. By analogy, a computer has an instruction set; that instruction set limits the computational capability of that computer. Humans also have "an instruction set" in the apparatus in our brains. That instruction set limits what we know and how we think. Kant defined the world as we perceive and know it as the *phenomenal* world. The world of things as they are in and of themselves, as things would be if we were not here to perceive them, the essence of things, he called the *noumenal* world. As humans, we can never know anything about that world.

All of this goes to say that we can never justify any model because it is a better representation of the "real world." None of us knows anything about the "real world." Our human apparatus does not allow us to know about it.

But you're probably saying, "Wait a minute, some models are closer to what people refer to when they use the term *real world* than are other models. A model of a FIRE_TRUCK that included attributes such as NumberOfSails or LastPromotionDate would be a very poor model because fire trucks don't have sails or get promoted."

To respond to that question, we first have to say that humans make models of the noumenal world, given the mental apparatus that we have. Throughout human history, the best human models have been those that most effectively help our species to survive. That's all we can say. We cannot say they are the most accurate representation of the noumenal world because we know nothing about that world. We can say only that they work well enough that humans can think and communicate in a fashion that has, so far, facilitated human species survival.

Now, taking this into the world of computing, a data model is a model not of reality, but of a model of a human model, which in turn is a model of whatever-is-out-there. A data model of a FIRE_TRUCK is a model of the model that humans make of fire trucks.

If you're following this discussion, you're probably saying, "Hold it, there are hundreds of different human models of a fire truck. Someone who has seen only pictures of a fire truck has one model, someone whose home has been saved by a fire truck has another model, and someone who has spent 30 years as a firefighter has yet another model. Which model should we base our model on?"

Now, that question leads us in the right direction, and it is a question that we can answer. We need to construct a data model that is the best model of the mental model that is in the minds of the users of the system. Period. We need to know whether a model accurately reflects how the users think about their world.

I personally have wasted dozens if not hundreds of hours in meetings in which one person was attempting to justify his or her data model by saying "it's a better model of reality." Of course, anyone who happens to have different life experiences and who thinks differently will have a different "model of reality" and will take exception to this statement. This argument is especially troublesome when it is between two data modelers who are trying to justify not two different external schemas (for which there might be resolution, as in the case of Bruce and Zelda), but rather two different versions of the same conceptual schema. As you know, there can only be one conceptual schema.

To summarize, no one creates a data model that is an accurate model of reality. Instead, humans make mental models of reality that more or less work for survival. Data modelers, in turn, make models of human models. The only relevant question when evaluating a data model is the following: "How well does it fit the mental models of the people who are going to use the system?" The person who is doing the data modeling may think the model under construction is a weird way of viewing the world, but that is not the point. The only valid point is: Does it fit how the users view their world?

Now that you understand this, you will never ever make this statement: "My model is a better model of reality." It cannot be anything of the sort.

Data Model Evaluation Methods

The most common way of evaluating a data model is through a series of reviews. First, the data modeling group conducts design reviews among its own members. Sometimes, a group of team members who have created one part of the data model present their results to a second group of team members who constructed a different part. During these reviews, the data model is evaluated against system requirements. Of course, if the requirements are vague, the review can be only cursory. This is one more reason why comprehensive requirements are so important.

During the reviews, the team ensures that the data model incorporates all user descriptions of the data needs. Any data needs defined from observations of users must be supported in the data model. Additionally, the team ensures that it will be possible to construct an external schema to support every form and report in the requirements. If external interfaces are to be supported, the reviewing team examines the data model to ensure that all such interfaces can be met. During the team review, questions about the requirements are often generated. These questions need to be documented for clarification during the user reviews.

After the data model is corrected to remove any problems discovered during the team review, a second round of reviews is conducted with the users themselves. Usually one or two key users from each group that will use the new system are involved in these reviews. Any questions that developed during the team review are answered during the user review. Also, there are sometimes aspects of the data model that were decided by artistic judgment rather than absolute requirement. There may, for example, be several different ways of accomplishing the same goal. If so, sometimes the users are asked to comment upon the various alternatives that could be used.

If possible, the best way to conduct user interviews is to teach the users the meaning of the E-R symbols being used and then to ask users to review and comment upon the data model in diagram format. Although these symbols may be new, many users are able to understand them and use them effectively.

In some cases, however, users will be unable or unwilling to review the data model in E-R diagram format. In that case, mockups of forms and reports need to be constructed that manifest design choices made in the data model. For example, an example order form that has space for only one salesperson manifests the fact that the relationship from order to salesperson has a maximum cardinality of one. If the users ask,

"Where do I put the second salesperson?" it is likely that the maximum cardinality from order to salesperson is greater than one.

This idea can be taken even further by constructing prototypes of forms and reports. Such prototypes can, however, be expensive to produce, and often they are done for only the most critical aspects of the data model.

Model validation is a complicated subject and we could devote several chapters to it. However, the best way to learn data modeling and model validation is to work with seasoned and experienced data modelers on actual projects. In this area, there is no substitute for first-hand experience.

The result of the validation phase is a data model that both team members and users believe is sufficiently robust to meet the requirements for the new system. The data model can then be used to design the database and other components.

▶ CONSTRUCTING DATA MODELS FROM FORMS AND REPORTS

This section demonstrates the construction of data models from forms and reports. We will use the IDEF1X notation here, but any modeling technique could be used as well. Your goal should be to understand how to interpret user documents and create the entities and relationships necessary to support them.

Single Entity

Figure 3-6(a) shows a report based on a single entity, EQUIPMENT. We know it is a single entity report because all of the attributes arise from a single theme, or idea. The entity EQUIPMENT is shown in Figure 3-6(b).

Single entities that have no relationships to other entities are rare. They do occur, but you should take a second look when you find such entities. Sometimes, such an entity participates in a relationship that is evident in a different form or report. For example, a report about projects might show equipment used on that project. If so, EQUIPMENT would be revised to include that relationship. You will see examples of evolving entities and relationships in the last section of this chapter.

FIGURE 3-6

**Single Entity
(a) Report Showing
Need for Single Entity
and (b) Entity for the
Report in (a)**

EQUIPMENT TAG:
  EquipmentNumber: 100   Description: Desk
  AcquisitionDate: 2/27/2002 PurchaseCost: $350.00

EQUIPMENT TAG:
  EquipmentNumber: 200   Description: Lamp
  AcquisitionDate: 3/1/2002 PurchaseCost: $39.95

(a)

EQUIPMENT

EquipmentNumber

Description
AcquisitionDate
PurchaseCost

(b)

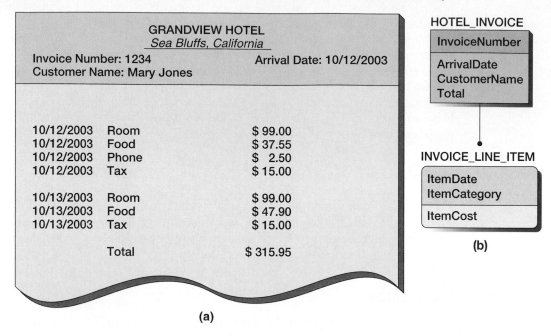

FIGURE 3-7

Identifying Connection Relationships (a) Sample Invoice and (b) Identifying Connection Relationship

(a)

(b)

Identifying Connection Relationships

The hotel invoice in Figure 3-7(a) is an example of a report that contains repeating elements. Here, the group {Date, Category, Cost} repeats several times within an invoice. Such a repeating group indicates that the base entity (call it HOTEL_INVOICE) has a relationship with many instances of a second entity (call it INVOICE_LINE_ITEM).

But what is the type of relationship between HOTEL_INVOICE and INVOICE_LINE_ITEM? It is a connection relationship, but is it identifying or non-identifying? A group like {10/12/2002, Room, $99.00} has no meaning outside the hotel bill. By itself, it is just data with no context. Therefore, the relationship is identifying, as shown in Figure 3-7(b). Notice, too, that a composite identifier (ItemDate, ItemCategory) is needed to uniquely identify an INVOICE_LINE_ITEM within the context of a particular HOTEL_INVOICE.

From the report in Figure 3-7(a), we cannot determine the minimum cardinality between HOTEL_INVOICE and INVOICE_LINE_ITEM. It could be either 0-to-many or 1-to-many. This is an example of a question to be resolved by users. Do they start an invoice before there are line items or not? In this case, suppose the answer to that question is yes. Thus, the minimum cardinality is zero, as indicated in Figure 3-7(b). (If the minimum cardinality were 1, there would be a P next to the filled-in circle.)

In the other direction (from INVOICE_LINE-ITEM to HOTEL_INVOICE), the minimum cardinality is 1 because every ID-dependent entity must have a parent entity.

Figure 3-8(a) shows a second version of a hotel invoice in which there are two repeating elements: one for the line item data and a second for the customer name. Because these groups are independent of one another, two different relationships are used to represent them. Figure 3-8(b) shows two identifying connection relationships for these two repeating groups.

Contrast Figure 3-8 with Figure 3-9. Here, INVOICE_THREE_LINE_ITEM is an ID-dependent entity that contains a second ID-dependent entity within it (SUB_LINE_ITEM). In Figure 3-9(b), the second identifying connection relationship is thus between INVOICE_THREE_LINE_ITEM and SUB_LINE_ITEM.

FIGURE 3-8

Hotel Invoice with Two
Repeating Groups
(a) Sample Invoice and
(b) Two Identifying
Connection
Relationships

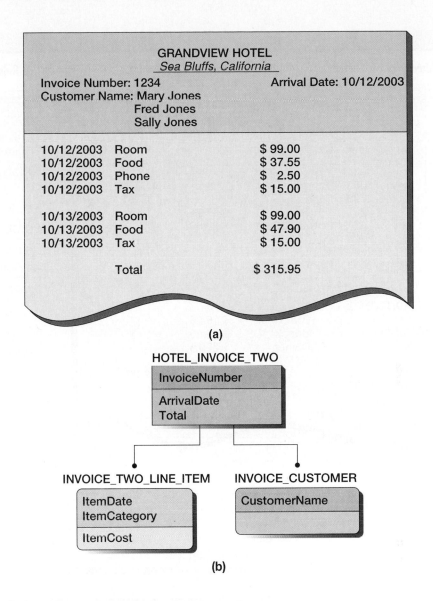

GRANDVIEW HOTEL
Sea Bluffs, California

Invoice Number: 1234   Arrival Date: 10/12/2003
Customer Name: Mary Jones
                       Fred Jones
                       Sally Jones

10/12/2003	Room	$ 99.00
10/12/2003	Food	$ 37.55
10/12/2003	Phone	$ 2.50
10/12/2003	Tax	$ 15.00
10/13/2003	Room	$ 99.00
10/13/2003	Food	$ 47.90
10/13/2003	Tax	$ 15.00
	Total	$ 315.95

(a)

HOTEL_INVOICE_TWO
InvoiceNumber
ArrivalDate
Total

INVOICE_TWO_LINE_ITEM
ItemDate
ItemCategory
ItemCost

INVOICE_CUSTOMER
CustomerName

(b)

Non-Identifying Connection Relationships

Figures 3-10 and 3-11 show examples of non-identifying connection relationships. In Figure 3-10(a), there is space for one employee name in the Employee assignment field, and there is space for one auto in the Auto assigned field. Thus, these forms imply that the maximum cardinality between VEHICLE and EMPLOYEE is 1:1. The entities and relationships are shown in Figure 3-10(b).

We cannot determine the minimum cardinalities from the forms in Figure 3-10(a). Instead, it is necessary to ask the users what they are. One possibility is shown in Figure 3-10(b), where a VEHICLE must be assigned to an EMPLOYEE, but an EMPLOYEE need not have a VEHICLE.

Figure 3-11(a) shows a situation that often occurs in practice. The DORMITORY OCCUPANCY REPORT shows a relationship between a dormitory and the students who live there. The Student Data Form, however, does not show any relationship from student to dorm. The CampusAddress attribute hints of that relationship, but a campus address can be something other than a dormitory name. Sometimes, there is not even a hint of one side of the relationship.

As stated earlier, there is no such thing as a one-way relationship. If A is related to B, then B is related to A; it cannot be otherwise. So, when you find two entities that have a

FIGURE 3–9

Hotel Invoice with Nested Groups (a) Sample Invoice and (b) Nested Identifying Connection Relationships

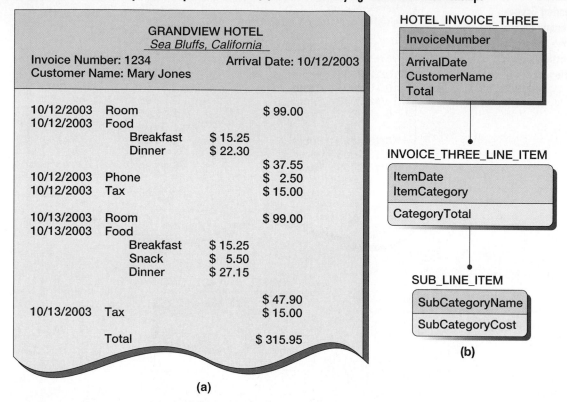

GRANDVIEW HOTEL
Sea Bluffs, California

Invoice Number: 1234   Arrival Date: 10/12/2003
Customer Name: Mary Jones

10/12/2003	Room		$ 99.00
10/12/2003	Food		
	Breakfast	$ 15.25	
	Dinner	$ 22.30	
			$ 37.55
10/12/2003	Phone		$ 2.50
10/12/2003	Tax		$ 15.00
10/13/2003	Room		$ 99.00
10/13/2003	Food		
	Breakfast	$ 15.25	
	Snack	$ 5.50	
	Dinner	$ 27.15	
			$ 47.90
10/13/2003	Tax		$ 15.00
	Total		$ 315.95

(a)

HOTEL_INVOICE_THREE

InvoiceNumber

ArrivalDate
CustomerName
Total

INVOICE_THREE_LINE_ITEM

ItemDate
ItemCategory

CategoryTotal

SUB_LINE_ITEM

SubCategoryName

SubCategoryCost

(b)

FIGURE 3–10

1:1 Non-Identifying Connection Relationship (a) Sample Forms and (b) Non-identifying Relationship

VEHICLE DATA			
License number	Serial number		
Make	Type	Year	Color
Employee assignment			

EMPLOYEE WORK DATA			
Employee name		Employee ID	
MailStop		Division	Phone
Pay code	Skill code	Hire date	Auto assigned

(a)

VEHICLE

LicenseNumber

SerialNumber
Make
Type
Year
Color

EMPLOYEE

EmployeeID

EmployeeName
MailStop
Division
Phone
PayCode
SkillCode
HireDate

1

(b)

FIGURE 3-11

1:N Non-identifying
Connection
Relationship
(a) Sample Forms;
(b) Non-identifying
Relationship and
(c) Using Relationship
for Resident Assistant

DORMITORY OCCUPANCY REPORT		
Dormitory	Resident Assistant	Phone
Ingersoll	Sarah and Allen French	3-5567

Student name	Student Number	Class
Adams, Elizabeth	710	SO
Baker, Rex	104	FR
Baker, Brydie	744	JN
Charles, Stewart	319	SO
Scott, Sally	447	SO
Taylor, Lynne	810	FR

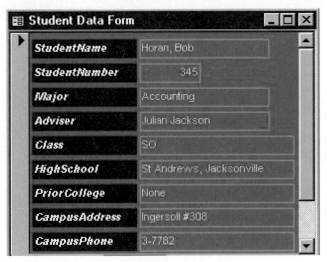

Student Data Form	
StudentName	Horan, Bob
StudentNumber	345
Major	Accounting
Adviser	Julian Jackson
Class	SO
HighSchool	St Andrews, Jacksonville
PriorCollege	None
CampusAddress	Ingersoll #308
CampusPhone	3-7782

(a)

relationship in one direction, look for evidence of that relationship in the other direction. If you can find no form or report showing both sides of the relationship, you need to learn the cardinalities of the missing side of the relationship from the users. Figure 3-11(b) shows that DORM is related to 0-to-many STUDENTS and a STUDENT may or may not live in one DORM.

Figure 3-11(a) presents an interesting modeling dilemma. Notice that Resident Assistant is part of the dormitory data. A resident assistant, however, is a student. Therefore, rather than placing the attribute ResidentAssistant in DORMITORY, an alternative is to create a second relationship between DORMITORY and STUDENT that represents the Resident Assistant field. This alternative is shown in Figure 3-11(c).

However, there is a problem with this design, too. The data in the DORMITORY OCCUPANCY report shows Sarah and Allen French as the assistants. This is couple, not a student. Does this mean there is a need for an entity COUPLE as well as STUDENT? And does it mean there needs to be relationships between DORMITORY and COUPLE as well as DORMITORY and STUDENT? All of this can be done, but the question arises: Is it worth it? One can argue that there is no need to represent Resident Assistant with such precision and that the field Resident Assistant is more of a note than a relationship to a specific student or couple.

This dilemma is a great example of the decisions that must be made when data modeling. There is no clear answer; the decision must be made on aesthetic grounds rather than engineering principles. The best that can be done is to discuss this matter with the users, but they are unlikely to understand the nuances involved, and even less likely to

FIGURE 3-11

(continued)

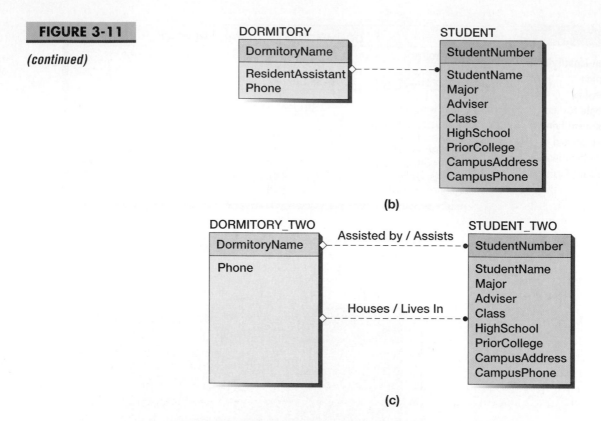

(b)

(c)

FIGURE 3-12

N:M Relationship (a) Sample Forms and (b) Non-Specific Relationship

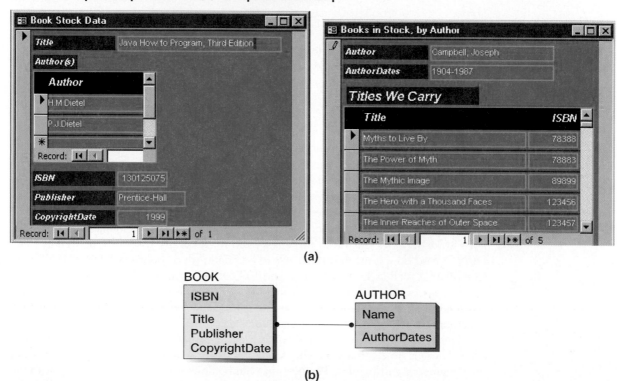

(a)

(b)

care. There is a good chance that both approaches have disadvantages; this might be a choose-your-regrets design decision.

Non-Specific (N:M) Relationships

Figure 3-12(a) shows an example of two forms from a bookstore that indicate the need for an N:M relationship. A BOOK relates to many AUTHORs and an AUTHOR relates to many BOOKS. The corresponding IDEF1X diagram appears in Figure 3-12(b).

Recall from Chapter 2 that some people think that non-specific relationships do not exist. They think there is always some missing entity that will transform the N:M relationship into two 1:N relationships. This bookstore example provides a counter-example to that argument. Although we can think of missing entities, all such entities are forced. There is no natural intermediate entity between the AUTHOR and BOOK entities. Hence, in this case, the relationship needs to be left as an N:M or non-specific relationship in the data model. We will see what to do with it during the discussion of database design in Chapter 5.

Now, consider a second N:M relationship that arises at an architectural firm. Suppose that user interviews indicate the need for an ARCHITECT entity and a PROJECT entity. Assume that the data modeling team uses a diagram like that shown in Figure 3-5 to identify potential relationships. By doing so, they determine that an architect may be assigned many projects and that a project may have many architects assigned to it. Thus, the relationship from ARCHITECT to PROJECT must be N:M.

Later in the project, however, the team encounters the Project Assignment Report found in Figure 3-13(a). This report reveals the need for a missing entity: ASSIGNMENT. As shown in Figure 3-13(b), ASSIGNMENT has two identifying connection relationships: one to PROJECT and the second to ARCHITECT. The team determines from user interviews that every ARCHITECT has at least one ASSIGNMENT, but that there can be some PROJECTs with no ASSIGNMENT. The appropriate minimum cardinalities are shown.

ASSIGNMENT has no identifier of its own. As is typical for entities having two dependent relationships, the identifier of ASSIGNMENT will be the composite of the two identifiers that it inherits from PROJECT and ARCHITECT.

Figure 3-14 shows a third design that involves flights, pilots, and airplanes. In this case, there is a strong entity called FLIGHT that has two connection relationships, one to AIRPLANE and the second to PILOT. The differences between Figure 3-13(b) and Figure 3-14(b) is that FLIGHT has an identifier of its own, namely FlightNumber, and the relationships that FLIGHT has are non-identifying.

Consider the diagrams in Figures 3-12(b), 3-13(b), and 3-14(b) as a group. They show a continuum of possible N:M relationships. In Figure 3-12(b), BOOK and AUTHOR have no intervening entity and their relationship is modeled as N:M. It is not transformed into anything else. In Figure 3-13(b), the relationship between PROJECT and ARCHITECT first appears as N:M, but later an intervening entity called ASSIGNMENT is found that causes the N:M relationship to be transformed into two identifying 1:N relationships. In Figure 3-14(b), a pattern similar to that in Figure 3-13(b) exists, but FLIGHT is a strong rather than an ID-dependent entity. In theory, AIRPLANE and PILOT could have an N:M relationship. However, that relationship never arises because the strong entity FLIGHT is present.

FIGURE 3–13

Assignment
Relationship
(a) Assignment Report
and (b) Two Identifying
Connection
Relationships

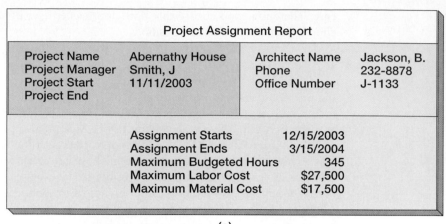

(a)

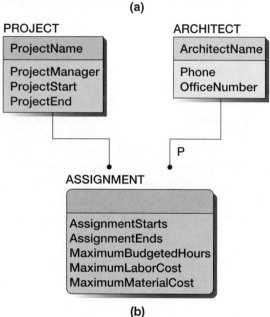

(b)

Subtype and Category Entities

Subtype and category entities arise in several ways during a data modeling project[1]. Sometimes, the data modeling team realizes that several entities are logically the same thing. At the Padden Creek Gardens, for example, the team realized that PLANT and FURNITURE were both variations on a generic entity PRODUCT (refer to Figure 3-3). Other times, the team analyzes an identifying relationship and finds that there is no identifier in the ID-dependent entity other than the identifier of the parent. In such cases, the entity is a category entity (or subtype) rather than an ID-dependent entity.

---

[1] Subtypes are part of the extended E-R model, and category entities are part of the IDEF1X model. They are slightly different, as you learned in Chapter 2 (category entities are always mutually exclusive in category clusters). Here, this difference is unimportant and we use the two terms synonymously.

FIGURE 3-14

Need for Strong FLIGHT Entity (a) Sample Documents and (b) Two Non-identifying Relationships

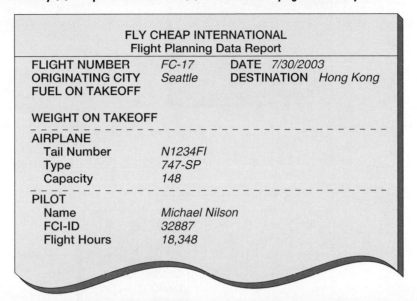

FLY CHEAP INTERNATIONAL
Flight Planning Data Report

FLIGHT NUMBER	*FC-17*	DATE	*7/30/2003*
ORIGINATING CITY	*Seattle*	DESTINATION	*Hong Kong*
FUEL ON TAKEOFF			

WEIGHT ON TAKEOFF

AIRPLANE
   Tail Number   *N1234FI*
   Type   *747-SP*
   Capacity   *148*

PILOT
   Name   *Michael Nilson*
   FCI-ID   *32887*
   Flight Hours   *18,348*

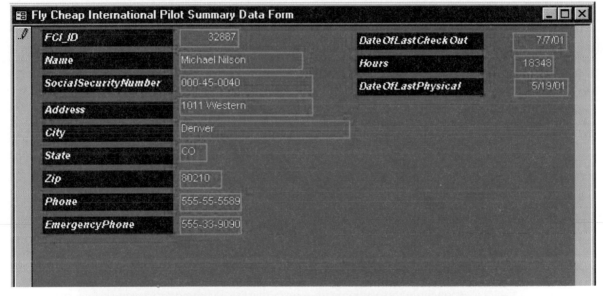

Fly Cheap International Pilot Summary Data Form

FCI_ID	32887	Date Of Last Check Out	7/7/01
Name	Michael Nilson	Hours	18348
SocialSecurityNumber	000-45-0040	Date Of Last Physical	5/19/01
Address	1011 Western		
City	Denver		
State	CO		
Zip	80210		
Phone	555-55-5589		
EmergencyPhone	555-33-9090		

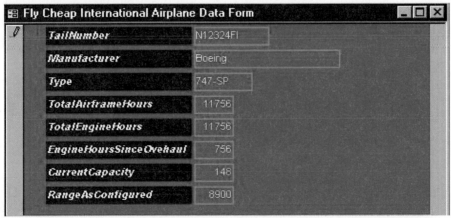

Fly Cheap International Airplane Data Form

TailNumber	N12324FI
Manufacturer	Boeing
Type	747-SP
TotalAirframeHours	11756
TotalEngineHours	11756
EngineHoursSinceOverhaul	756
CurrentCapacity	148
RangeAsConfigured	8900

(a)

FIGURE 3-14

(*continued*)

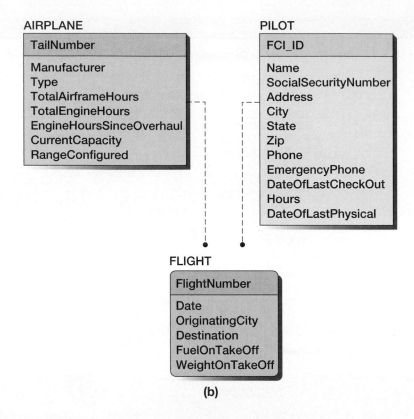

(b)

Sometimes, the forms themselves provide hints that subtypes or categories are needed. In Figure 3-15(a), the shaded portions of the form indicate that there are two different types of resident fishing licenses. When you encounter forms with shading or boxes or other characteristics that imply different types of something, think about subtypes or categories.

Figures 3-15(b) and 3-15(c) show two different versions of an IDEF1X model. In the second, a strong entity VESSEL is defined as a separate entity from COMMERCIAL_LICENSE. Observe that category entities (or subtypes) may not only have different attributes, but they may also have different relationships to other entities.

Deciding between the designs in these two figures involves an aesthetic judgment. They both could be considered correct. The decision probably comes down to whether or not there are other needs for the VESSEL entity. If not, the design in Figure 3-15(b) is used.

SALES_ORDER Model

We conclude this section with a form that is so common that you should know how to model it as part of your general knowledge. Also, it illustrates a form that gives rise to several entities at once.

Figure 3-16(a) shows a Sales Order Form. If you look at the design of the form, the heavy lines imply the need for different entities. There is the entity for the form itself, which is SALES_ORDER, then a heavy line, then data for CUSTOMER, then a heavy line, and then data for SALESPERSON. The grid is a multi-value group, which gives rise to the dependent entity ORDER_LINE_ITEM. If you examine this line item, you see that it contains some data that pertain to the order itself (quantity and extended price) and other data that pertain to items in general. Thus, there is a need for a separate ITEM entity.

Figure 3-16(b) shows the results of these observations. Notice that ORDER_LINE_ITEM is dependent on both SALES_ORDER and ITEM. The identifier of ORDER_LINE_ITEM is the composite (SalesOrderNumber, ItemNumber). This means that an item may appear just once on a given SALES_ORDER. Also notice that ItemPrice is placed in both ITEM and ORDER_LINE_ITEM. ITEM.ItemPrice is

FIGURE 3–15

Example Category Relationship (a) Form Suggesting Need for Categories (Subtypes); (b) Category Cluster with Two Categories and (c) One Category Has Additional Relationship

Resident Fishing License 2003 Season *State of xxxxx*		License No: 03-1123432
Name:		
Street:		
City:	State:	Zip:

For Use by Commercial Fishers Only	For Use by Sport Fishers Only
Vessel Number:	Number Years at this Address:
Vessel Name:	Prior Year License Number:
Vessel Type:	
Tax ID:	

(a)

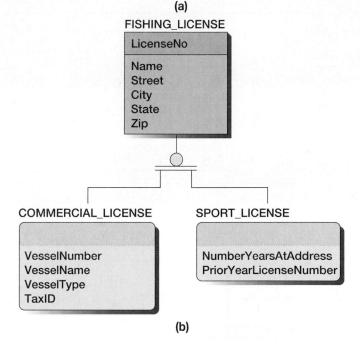

(b)

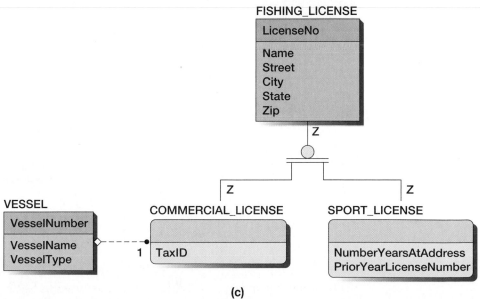

(c)

FIGURE 3-16

Sales Order Example (a) Sample Document; (b) LINE_ITEM with Two Identifying Relationships and (c) LINE_ITEM with One Identifying Relationship

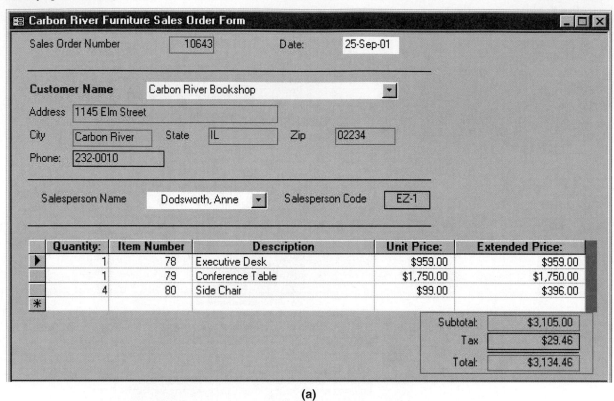

(a)

(b)

FIGURE 3-16

(*continued*)

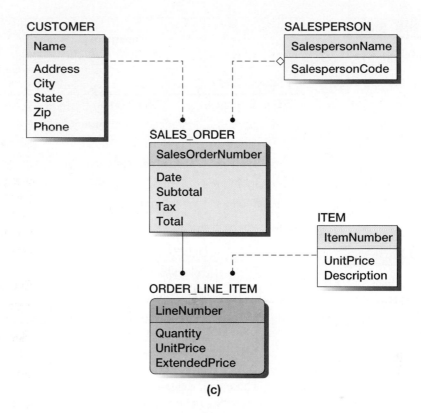

(c)

the current price of an item; ORDER_LINE_ITEM.ItemPrice is the price of the item at the time the sale was made. The two values are the same when the sale order is created, but they may vary over time.

Figure 3-16(c) shows an alternative design that allows an item to appear more than once on a given order. Here, the identifying relationship between ITEM and ORDER_LINE_ITEM is replaced by a non-identifying relationship. To give ORDER_LINE_ITEM an identifier, a new attribute LineNumber is created. The full identifier of ORDER_LINE_ITEM becomes (SalesOrderNumber, LineNumber). This second design is better if an item may occur on more than one line-item in the same order.

You have now seen examples of the common types of data model entities and relationships. In the next section, we will show how the data model is developed when modeling a sequence of related forms and reports.

DEVELOPING A DATA MODEL: AN EXAMPLE

Suppose the administration at a hypothetical university named Highline University wants to create a database to track colleges, departments, faculty, and students. To do this, a data modeling team collects a series of reports as part of its requirements determination. In the next sections, we will analyze these reports to produce a data model.

The College Report

The example report in Figure 3-17 is about a college—specifically, the College of Business. This example is one instance of this report; Highline University has similar reports about other colleges, such as the College of Engineering or the College of Social Sciences. The data modeling team needs to gather enough examples to form a representative sample of all the college reports. Here, assume the report in Figure 3-17 is representative.

Examining the report, we find data specific to the college—such as the name, dean, telephone number, and campus address—and also facts about each department within

FIGURE 3-17

Sample College Report

College of Business		
Mary B. Jefferson, Dean		
Phone: 232-1187		Campus Address: Business Building, Room 100	
Department	Chairperson	Phone	Total Majors
Accounting	Jackson, Seymour P.	232-1841	318
Finance	HeuTeng, Susan	232-1414	211
Info Systems	Brammer, Nathaniel D.	236-0011	247
Management	Tuttle, Christine A.	236-9988	184
Production	Barnes, Jack T.	236-1184	212

FIGURE 3-18

Data Model from College Report

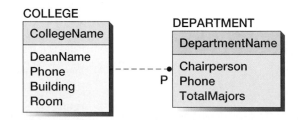

the college. These data suggest the data model should have COLLEGE and DEPART-MENT entities with a relationship between them, as shown in Figure 3-18.

The relationship in Figure 3-18 is non-identifying. You may be wondering how to tell when to use an identifying relationship and when to use a non-identifying relation-ship. The question to ask is, "Does the child entity (DEPARTMENT in this case) have an obvious identifier that does not include the identifier of the parent?" If so, the child entity is a strong entity and a non-identifying relationship is appropriate. Here, DEPARTMENT has the obvious identifier DepartmentName, so it is a strong entity with a non-identifying relationship to COLLEGE.

We cannot tell from the report in Figure 3-17 whether a department can belong to many colleges. To answer this question, we need to ask the users or look for other forms or reports to give us the answer. Here, assume we know from the users that a department belongs to just one college and the relationship is thus 1:N from COLLEGE to DEPARTMENT. The report in Figure 3-17 does not show us the minimum cardinalities, either. Again, assume we learn from the users that a college must have at least one department, and a department must be assigned to at least one college.

The Department/Professor Report

The Department Report shown in Figure 3-19 contains departmental data along with a list of the professors who are assigned to that department. Note that this report contains data concerning the department's campus address. Because these data do not appear in the entity in Figure 3-18, we need to add them to the DEPARTMENT entity, as shown in Figure 3-20(a). This is typical of the data modeling process. That is, entities and rela-tionships are adjusted as additional forms, reports, and other requirements are analyzed.

Figure 3-20(a) shows the relationship between DEPARTMENT and PROFES-SOR as non-specific. This was done because a professor might have a joint appoint-ment. The data modeling team must further investigate the requirements to determine whether joint appointments are allowed. If not, the relationship can be redefined as a non-identifying connection type, as shown in Figure 3-20(b).

Another possibility is that the team will find a form, report, or other requirement that concerns the combination of a department with a professor. At Highline, suppose

FIGURE 3-19

Sample Department Report

Information Systems Department
College of Business
Chairperson: Brammer, Nathaniel D
Phone: 236-0011
Campus Address: Social Science Building, Room 213

Professor	Office	Phone
Jones, Paul D.	Social Science, 219	232-7713
Parks, Mary B	Social Science, 308	232-5791
Wu, Elizabeth	Social Science, 207	232-9112

the team finds a report that describes the title and employment terms for each professor in each department. Figure 3-20(c) shows an entity for such a report, named APPOINTMENT. Notice that APPOINTMENT is ID-dependent on both DEPARTMENT and PROFESSOR. This means the identifier of APPOINTMENT is the composite of the identifiers of DEPARTMENT and PROFESSOR, or (DepartmentName, ProfessorName). We will use this model of the department/professor relationship for the rest of this discussion.

A chairperson is a professor, so another improvement on the model is to remove the Chairperson data from DEPARTMENT and replace it with a chairperson relationship. This was done in Figure 3-20(d): In the Chairs/Chaired By relationship, the PROFESSOR is the parent entity. A professor can be a chair of zero one departments and a department must have exactly one professor as chair.

With the Chairs/Chaired By relationship, the attribute Chairperson is no longer needed in DEPARTMENT, so it is removed. Normally, a chairperson has his or her office in the department office; if this is the case, Phone, Building, and Room in DEPARTMENT duplicate Phone, Building, and OfficeNumber in PROFESSOR. Consequently, it might be possible to remove Phone, Building, and Room from DEPARTMENT. On the other hand, a professor may have a different Phone from the official department phone, and the professor may also have an office outside of the department's office. Because of this possibility, we will leave Phone, Building, and Room in DEPARTMENT.

FIGURE 3-20

Alternative Models for the DEPARTMENT/ PROFESSOR Relationship (a) Model with Non-Specific Relationship; (b) Model with Non-Identifying Relationship; (c) Model with APPOINTMENT Entity and (d) Model with Department Chair Expressed as Relationship

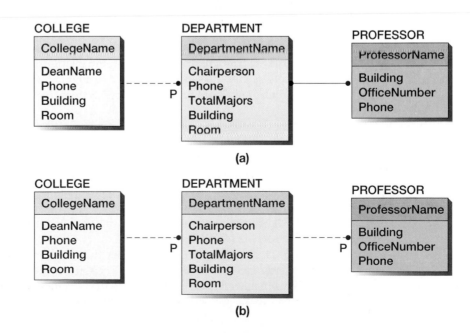

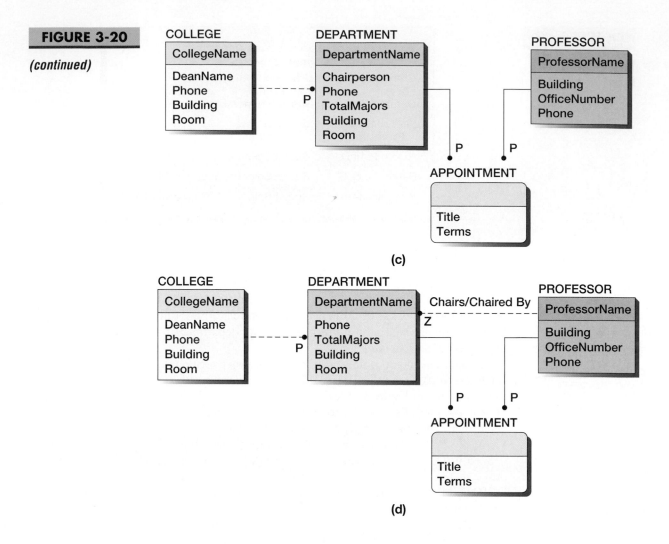

FIGURE 3-20

(continued)

(c)

(d)

The Department / Major Report

Figure 3-21 shows a report of a department and the students who major in that department. This report indicates the need for a new object called STUDENT; because students are not ID-dependent on departments, the relationship between DEPARTMENT and STUDENT is non-identifying, as shown in Figure 3-22. Using the contents of this report as a guide, attributes StudentNumber, StudentName, and Phone are added to STUDENT.

There are two subtleties in this interpretation of the report in Figure 3-21. First, observe that Major's Name was changed to StudentName when the attribute was placed in STUDENT. This was done because StudentName is more generic. Major's Name has no meaning outside the context of the Major relationship. Additionally, the heading of the report in Figure 3-21 possesses a potential ambiguity. Is the phone number shown for the department to be a value of DEPARTMENT.Phone or a value of PROFESSOR.Phone? The team needs to investigate this further with the users. Most likely, it is a value of DEPARTMENT.Phone.

Figure 3-23 shows the acceptance letter that Highline sends to its incoming students. This letter can be considered to be a report for the purposes of data modeling. The data items that need to be represented in the data model are shown in boldface type.

FIGURE 3–21

Second Department Report

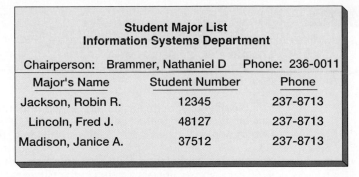

Student Major List Information Systems Department		
Chairperson: Brammer, Nathaniel D Phone: 236-0011		
Major's Name	Student Number	Phone
Jackson, Robin R.	12345	237-8713
Lincoln, Fred J.	48127	237-8713
Madison, Janice A.	37512	237-8713

FIGURE 3–22

Model with STUDENT Entity

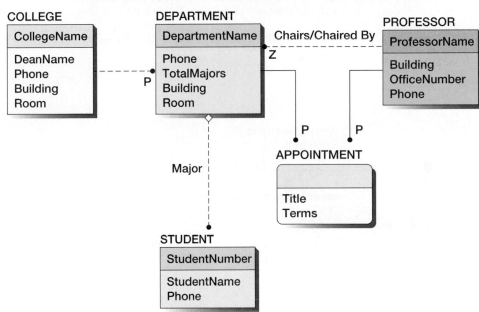

In addition to data concerning the student, this letter also contains data regarding the student's major department as well as data about the student's adviser.

We can use this letter to add an Advises/Advised relationship to the data model. However, which entity should be the parent of this relationship? Because an adviser is a professor, it is tempting to make PROFESSOR the parent. But a professor is acting as an adviser within the context of a particular department. Therefore, in Figure 3-24, we made APPOINTMENT the parent of ADVISER. To produce the report in Figure 3-23, the professor's data can be retrieved by accessing the related APPOINTMENT entity and then accessing that entity's PROFESSOR parent. This decision is not cut-and-dried, however. One can make a strong argument that the parent of the relationship should be PROFESSOR.

According to this data model, a student has at most one major and at most one adviser. These constraints cannot be determined from any of the reports shown. It might be that a student can have multiple majors, but that the student in this particular instance had only one major. The data modeling team needs to check out these assumptions with the users.

The acceptance letter uses the title *Mr.* in the salutation. Therefore, a new attribute called Title is added to STUDENT. Observe that this Title is different from that in APPOINTMENT. This difference can be determined by examining the domains for the attributes, as described in the next section. The acceptance letter also shows the need to add new home address attributes to STUDENT.

Mr. Fred Parks
123 Elm Street
Los Angeles, CA 98002

Dear **Mr. Parks:**

You have been admitted as a major in the **Accounting** Department at Highline University, starting in the Fall Semester, 2003. The office of the Accounting Department is located in the **Business** Building, Room **210**.

Your adviser is professor **Elizabeth Johnson**, whose telephone number is **232-8740** and whose office is located in the **Business** building, Room **227**. Please schedule an appointment with your adviser as soon as you arrive on campus.

Congratulations and welcome to Highline University!

Sincerely,

Jan P. Smathers
President

JPS/rkp

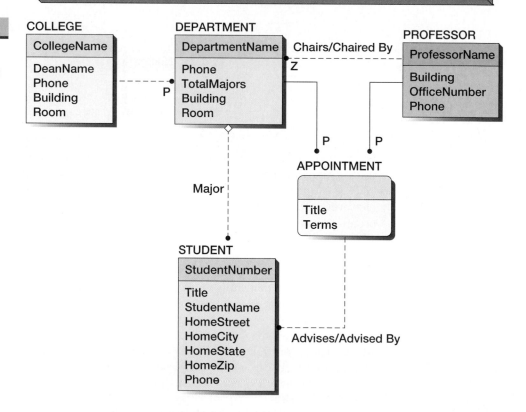

The acceptance letter reveals a problem. The name of the student is Fred Parks, but we have allocated only one attribute StudentName in STUDENT. It is difficult to reliably disentangle first and last names from a single attribute, so a better model is to have two attributes: StudentFirstName and StudentLastName. Similarly, note that the adviser in this letter is Elizabeth Johnson. So far, all professor names have been in the format

Johnson, Elizabeth. To accommodate both forms of name, ProfessorName in PROFESSOR must be changed to the two attributes ProfessorFirstName, ProfessorLastName. A similar change is necessary for DeanName. These changes are shown in Figure 3-25, which is the final form of this data model.

This section should give you a feel for a real data modeling project. Forms and reports are examined in sequence, and the data model is adjusted as necessary to accommodate the knowledge gained from each new form or report. It is very typical to revise the data model many times throughout the data modeling process.

Domains

Although the IDEF1X standard does include the concept of domains, it did not specify any standard way of documenting or displaying them. Hence, the way in which domains are specified depends upon the data modeling tool used. Each tool uses a slightly different means.

Figure 3-26(a) shows domains for the Highline University data model defined in the data modeling product ERWin. Examine the String domain, for example, and you can see that a type domain named Address has been defined on String. The type domains City, State, Street, and Zip have been created as a type domains under Address.

ERWin allows the definition of a wide range of domain characteristics. The Domain Dictionary is shown in Figure 3-26(b). In this example, properties of the BuildingName domain are displayed. In the top dialog box, you can see that the data type is Char(25), which means a fixed character data length of 25 bytes. BuildingName has a list of valid values that it can have. The name BuildingNameList is shown in the Valid drop-down list box. Clicking on the … causes the Validation Rules dialog box to be displayed. You

---

FIGURE 3–25

Final Data Model

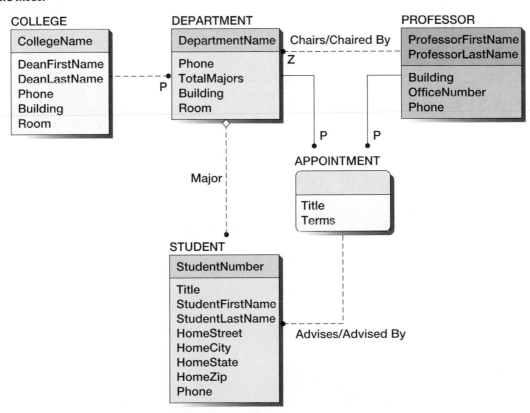

FIGURE 3-26

Representing Domains in ERWIN (a) Hierarchical Domains and (b) Building Name Domain Definition

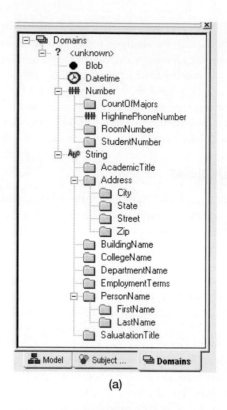

(a)

can see in this dialog box that the BuildingNameList domain has a validation rule specifying the list of valid values.

One use for domains is shown in Figure 3-27. This is the same as Figure 3-25, except that domain names have been appended to the attribute names. In COLLEGE, for example, the attribute DeanFirstName is based on the domain FirstName. As shown in the hand-drawn black circles, the domain BuildingName is used by three attributes. If the data modeler were to change one of the properties of the BuildingName domain (for example, add another building name to the domain list), that change would be inherited by all three of these attributes. This display can also be used to identify different-named attributes that are based on the same domain.

Similarly, it is possible to determine from this display that attributes having the same name are actually different. For example, the attributes Title (in the hand-drawn red circles) are different because they are based on different domains. STUDENT.Title is based on the domain SalutationTitles, whereas APPOINTMENT.Title is based on the domain AcademicTitle.

There are many more features for processing domains in ERWin and in other data modeling products as well. From this example, you can see how they are used and why they are important.

This concludes the discussion of data modeling using the entity-relationship model. As mentioned at the start of this chapter, you probably will benefit from reading the material a second or third time.

We will next turn to the topic of database design. In Chapter 4, we will define important terms in the relational model and discuss the process of normalization. Then we will bring all of this together in Chapter 5 to show how to use data models to create relational database designs.

FIGURE 3-26

(continued)

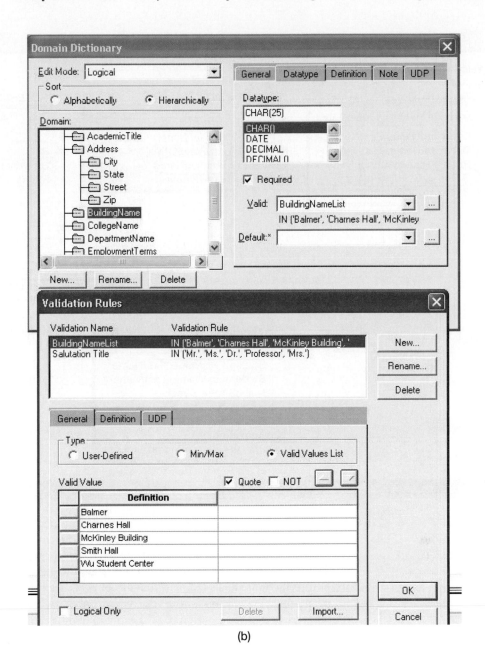

(b)

FIGURE 3-27

Model with Domain Names

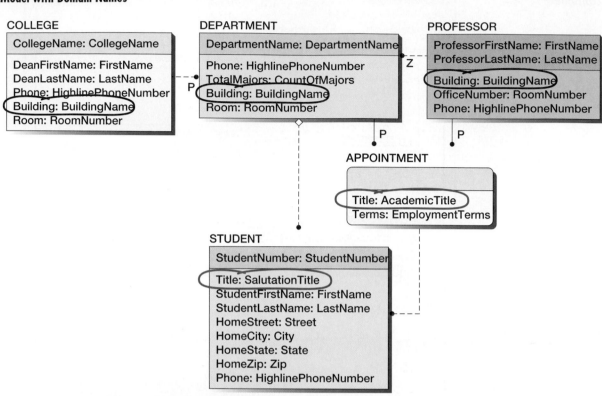

SUMMARY

The first step in the data modeling process is to plan the project, which includes obtaining project authorization, forming the team, developing standards, and planning activities. System requirements are then specified. Users are interviewed and observed, sample forms and reports are obtained, existing and new file formats are examined, formal interfaces are analyzed, and domain experts are interviewed. The result of the requirements specification is a repository of notes, documents, file structures, and other materials that can be used to create the data model.

After the project has been planned and the requirements have been specified, data modeling can begin. Figure 3-1 lists the data modeling steps: specify entities, specify relationships, determine identifiers, specify attributes, and specify domains. In truth, the process is never sequential. The specification of relationships indicates the need for new entities, the specification of attributes indicates the need for new domains, and so forth. Normally, the elements of the data model are created in parallel.

Entities are something the users want to track. They can be identified by analyzing user statements and observations and by studying forms, reports, and other requirements documents. The entities in a data model are dynamic; as the project progresses, entities will be added, dropped, and modified many times.

Relationships can be specified either by considering a possible relationship between every entity and every other entity (refer to Figure 3-5) or by analyzing requirements. There is no such thing as a one-way relationship; relationships always exist in both directions. It may be that for a particular application, however, only one direction of the relationship is ever used. If so, relationship cardinalities for the unused direction need to be obtained from user interviews.

Every true entity has an identifier. If there is difficulty specifying an identifier, then usually there is something wrong with the entity. Maybe it should be part of a different entity, maybe it is a subtype or category, or maybe it needs one or more identifying relationships. Problems with identifiers are opportunities to correct the data model.

Attributes are normally specified by analyzing forms, reports, file structures, and the like. Every time an attribute is added to the data model, the domain list is examined to determine whether there is already a domain for that type of attribute. If not, a new domain is created. Domains are useful because attributes inherit their properties from domains, so changing a domain property changes all of the properties of attributes based on it. Domains can also be used to enforce data standards. Some attributes suggest missing entities and relationships. Attributes whose names include the word *name* are particularly likely to do this.

After the data model is complete, it is validated. No data model is a model of reality; nothing can model reality. Instead, a data model is a model of humans' models. A data model is wrong if it does not accurately reflect the ways the users think about their world.

Data models are validated through a series of reviews. Normally, a team review is followed by user reviews. The data model can often be communicated to users in terms of the E-R model, but sometimes mockups and prototypes are necessary to communicate features of the data model.

The balance of the chapter showed how to use forms and reports to construct data models, and it illustrated the data modeling process for a simple database at a hypothetical university.

GROUP I QUESTIONS

3.1 List the steps in the data modeling process.

3.2 Describe tasks to be accomplished during the planning step.

3.3 List common sources of requirements.

3.4 Explain how user interviews and observations can be used to develop components of a data model.

3.5 Why is it important to clarify terms during user interviews?

3.6 How can forms and reports be used to develop components of the data model?

3.7 How can existing files be used to develop components of the data model?

3.8 What does the term *reverse engineer* mean in the context of data models?

3.9 Explain how formal interfaces can be used to obtain requirements.

3.10 Why is the use of formal interfaces increasing?

3.11 Describe a domain expert and explain advantages and disadvantages of using domain experts in requirements specification.

3.12 In the following statement, what is probably an entity and what is probably an attribute?

I group the student applications by date

3.13 In the following phrase, what is probably an entity and what is probably an attribute? Can two entities be referenced here? If so, what are they?

I use the department name of professor…

3.14 Explain why the list of entities is likely to change as the data modeling project proceeds.

3.15 Why is it important to define the meaning and use of entities?

3.16 What elements comprise the definition of a relationship?

3.17 Describe two ways to find relationships.

3.18 Explain in your own words why there is no such thing as a one-way relationship.

3.19 Is it possible that only one direction of a relationship is used in an application? Why or why not?

3.20 Give an example of an entity that has no obvious identifier. What should be done with the entity?

3.21 Give an example, other than the one in this text, of two different entities that have the same identifier.

3.22 Explain the relationship of an attribute and a domain.

3.23 How are domains created?

3.24 Explain the advantage of domain property inheritance.

3.25 How can domains be used to enforce organizational data standards?

3.26 Give an example of two attributes that suggest the need for a new entity. Choose one whose name includes the word *name* and one whose name does not include *name*.

3.27 Why is it important to validate the data model?

3.28 Explain what is wrong with this statement: "My data model is a better model of reality than your data model."

3.29 If someone made the statement in question 3.28 to you, how would you respond?

3.30 Explain the following statement: "We cannot say that human models are an accurate representation of the real world because we know nothing about that world. We can only say that those models work well enough that humans can think and communicate in a fashion that has, so far, facilitated human species survival."

3.31 What is the sole criterion for evaluating a data model?

3.32 Explain how a team review of a data model is conducted.

3.33 Explain how a user review of a data model is conducted.

3.34 Explain how to use a mockup to demonstrate to users the consequences of maximum cardinality between two entities.

GROUP II QUESTIONS

Answer the following questions using IDEF1X notation:

3.35 Examine the subscription form shown in Figure 3-28. Using the structure of this form, do the following:

A. Create a single entity model. Specify the identifier and attributes.

B. Create a model with two entities, one for customer and a second for subscription. Specify identifiers, attributes, relationship name, type, and cardinalities.

C. Under what conditions do you prefer the model in A to that in B?

D. Under what conditions do you prefer the model in B to that in A?

3.36 Consider the traffic citation shown in Figure 3-29. The rounded corners on this form provide graphical hints about the boundaries of entities represented here.

FIGURE 3-28

Subscription Form

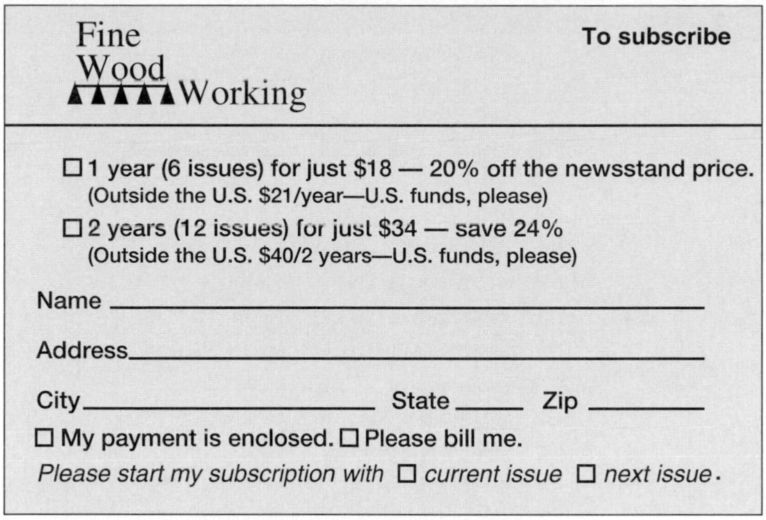

Fine
Wood
▲▲▲▲▲Working

To subscribe

☐ 1 year (6 issues) for just $18 — 20% off the newsstand price.
(Outside the U.S. $21/year—U.S. funds, please)

☐ 2 years (12 issues) for just $34 — save 24%
(Outside the U.S. $40/2 years—U.S. funds, please)

Name _____

Address_____

City_____ State _____ Zip _____

☐ My payment is enclosed. ☐ Please bill me.

Please start my subscription with ☐ *current issue* ☐ *next issue .*

FIGURE 3-29

Traffic Citation

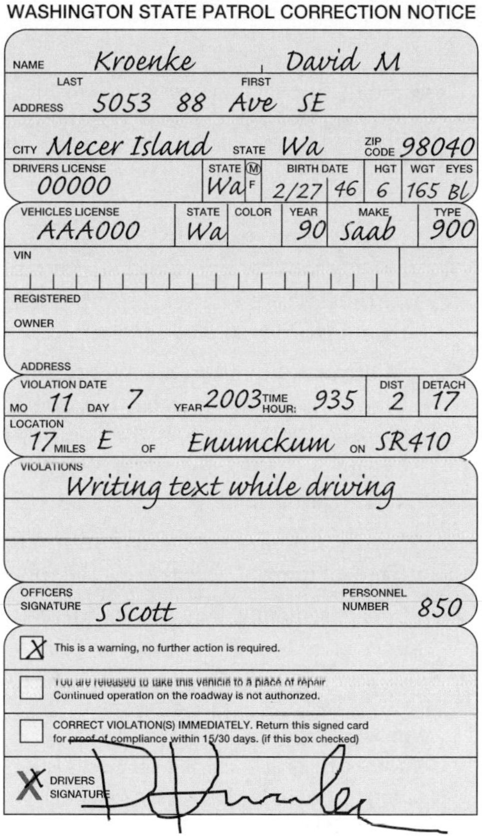

WASHINGTON STATE PATROL CORRECTION NOTICE

NAME	*Kroenke*	*David M*
LAST	FIRST	

ADDRESS *5053 88 Ave SE*

CITY *Mecer Island* STATE *Wa* ZIP CODE *98040*

DRIVERS LICENSE	STATE	☒M	BIRTH DATE	HGT	WGT	EYES
00000	*Wa*	F	*2/27 46*	*6*	*165*	*Bl*

VEHICLES LICENSE	STATE	COLOR	YEAR	MAKE	TYPE
AAA000	*Wa*		*90*	*Saab*	*900*

VIN | | | | | | | | | | | | | | | | |

REGISTERED

OWNER

ADDRESS

VIOLATION DATE				TIME HOUR:	DIST	DETACH
MO *11* DAY *7* YEAR *2003*				*935*	*2*	*17*

LOCATION
17 MILES *E* OF *Enumckum* ON *SR410*

VIOLATIONS
Writing text while driving

OFFICERS SIGNATURE	*S Scott*	PERSONNEL NUMBER	*850*

☒ This is a warning, no further action is required.

☐ You are released to take this vehicle to a place of repair
Continued operation on the roadway is not authorized.

☐ CORRECT VIOLATION(S) IMMEDIATELY. Return this signed card
for proof of compliance within 15/30 days. (if this box checked)

☒ DRIVERS
SIGNATURE

A. Create a data model with five entities. Use the data items on the form to specify identifiers and attributes for those entities.

B. Specify relationships among the entities. Name the relationship and give its type and cardinalities. Indicate which cardinalities can be inferred from data on the form and which need to be checked out with systems users.

FIGURE 3-30

Email List

☐	From	Subject	Date ↓	Size
☐	WDA2259@sailmail.com	Big Wind	5/13/2002	3 KB
☐	WDA2259@sailmail.com	Update	5/12/2002	4 KB
☐	WDA2259@sailmail.com	Re: Saturday Am	5/11/2002	4 KB
☐	WDA2259@sailmail.com	Re: Weather window!	5/10/2002	4 KB
☐	WDA2259@sailmail.com	Re: Howdy!	5/10/2002	3 KB
☐	WDA2259@sailmail.com	Still here	5/9/2002	3 KB
☐	WDA2259@sailmail.com	Re: Turle Bay	5/8/2002	4 KB
☐	WDA2259@sailmail.com	Turle Bay	5/8/2002	4 KB
☐	WDA2259@sailmail.com	Re: Hi	5/6/2002	3 KB
☐	WDA2259@sailmail.com	Sunday, Santa Maria	5/5/2002	3 KB
☐	Ki6yu@aol.com	Cabo, Thurs. Noon	5/2/2002	2 KB
☐	WDA2259@sailmail.com	turbo	5/1/2002	3 KB
☐	WDA2259@sailmail.com	on our way	4/28/2002	3 KB
☐	Tom Cooper	RE: Hola!	4/26/2002	3 KB
☐	Tom Cooper	RE: Hola!	4/24/2002	2 KB
☐	Tom Cooper	RE: Hola!	4/23/2002	3 KB

3.37 Examine the list of email messages in Figure 3-30. Using the structure and example data items in this list, do the following:

A. Create a single entity data model for this list. Specify the identifier and all attributes.

B. Modify your answer to A to include entities SENDER and SUBJECT. Specify the identifiers and attributes of entities and the type and cardinalities of relationships. Explain which cardinalities can be inferred from Figure 3-30 and which need to be checked out with users.

C. There are two different styles of email address in the From column in Figure 3-30. One style has the true email address; the second style (Tom Cooper, for example) is the name of an entry in the user's email dictionary. Create two categories of SENDER for these two styles. Specify identifiers and attributes.

3.38 Examine the list of stock quotations in Figure 3-31. Using the structure and example data items in this list, do the following:

A. Create a single entity data model for this list. Specify the identifier and attributes.

FIGURE 3-31

Stock Quotations

Symbol	Name	Last	Change	% Chg
$COMPX	Nasdaq Combined Composite Index	1,400.74 ▼	-4.87	-0.35%
$INDU	Dow Jones Industrial Average Index	9,255.10 ▼	-19.80	-0.21%
$INX	S&P 500 INDEX	971.14 ▼	-5.84	-0.60%
ALTR	Altera Corporation	13.45 ▼	-0.450	-3.24%
AMZN	Amazon.com, Inc.	15.62 ▲	+0.680	+4.55%
CSCO	Cisco Systems, Inc.	13.39 ▼	-0.280	-2.05%
DELL	Dell Computer Corporation	24.58 ▼	-0.170	-0.69%
ENGCX	Enterprise Growth C	14.60 ▼	-0.210	-1.42%
INTC	Intel Corporation	18.12 ▼	-0.380	-2.05%
JNJ	Johnson & Johnson	53.29 ▼	-0.290	-0.54%
KO	Coca-Cola Company	56.70 ▼	-0.580	-1.01%
MSFT	Microsoft Corporation	53.96 ▲	+1.040	+1.97%
NKE	NIKE, Inc.	57.34 ▲	+0.580	+1.02%

B. Modify your answer to A to include the entities COMPANY and INDEX. Specify the identifier and attributes of the entities and the type and cardinalities for relationships. Explain which cardinalities can be inferred from Figure 3-31 and which need to be checked out with users.

C. The list in Figure 3-31 is for a quotation on a particular day at a particular time of day. Suppose that the list were changed to show closing daily prices for each of these stocks and that it includes a new column: QuoteDate. Modify your model in B appropriately.

D. Change your model in C to include the tracking of a portfolio. Assume the portfolio has an owner name, phone, email address, and a list of stocks held. The list includes the identity of the stock and the number of shares held. Specify all additional entities, their identifiers and attributes, and the type and cardinality of all relationships.

E. Change your answer to question D to keep track of portfolio stock purchases and sales in a portfolio. Specify entities, their identifiers and attributes, and the type and cardinality of all relationships.

3.39 Figure 3-32 shows the specifications for single stage air compressor products. Notice that there are two categories of products for different Air Performance characteristics: the A models at 125 (pounds per square inch of pressure), and the E models at 150 (pounds per square inch of pressure). Using the structure and example data items in this list, do the following:

A. Create a category cluster to represent these compressors. The generic entity will have attributes for all single stage compressors, and the category entities will have attributes for products having the two different types of Air Performance. Assume there might be additional products with different types of Air Performance. Specify the entities, identifiers, attributes, relationships, type of category cluster, and possible determinant.

FIGURE 3-32

Air Compressor Specifications

| | | | Air Performance | | | | | | | Dimensions | | |
| | | | A @ 125 | | | E @ 150 | | | Approx Ship Weight | | | |
HP	Model	Tank Gal	Pump RPM	CFM Disp	DEL'D Air	Pump RPM	CFM Disp	DEL'D Air		L	W	H
1/2	F12A-17	17	680	3.4	2.2	590	2.9	1.6	135	37	14	25
3/4	F34A-17	17	1000	5.0	3.1	950	4.7	2.3	140	37	14	25
3/4	F34A-30	30	1080	5.3	3.1	950	4.7	2.3	160	38	16	31
1	K1A-30	30	560	6.2	4.0	500	5.7	3.1	190	38	16	34
1 1/2	K15A-30	30	870	9.8	6.2	860	9.7	5.8	205	49	20	34
1 1/2	K15A-60	60	870	9.8	6.2	860	9.7	5.8	315	38	16	34
2	K2A-30	30	1140	13.1	8.0	1060	12.0	7.0	205	49	20	39
2	K2A-60	60	1140	13.1	8.0	1060	12.0	7.0	315	48	20	34
2	GC2A-30	30	480	13.1	9.1	460	12.4	7.9	270	38	16	36
2	GC2A-60	60	480	13.1	9.1	460	12.4	7.9	370	49	20	41
3	GC3A-60	60	770	21.0	14.0	740	19.9	12.3	200	38	10	30
5	GC5A-60	60	770	21.0	14.0	740	19.9	12.3	388	49	20	41
5	GC5A-60	60	1020	27.8	17.8	910	24.6	15.0	410	49	20	41
5	GC5A-80	80	1020	27.8	17.8	910	24.6	15.0	450	62	20	41
5	J5A-80	60	780	28.7	19.0	770	28.6	18.0	570	49	23	43
5	J5A-80	80	780	28.7	19.0	770	28.6	18.0	610	63	23	43

Single Stage
Set 95 to 150 PSI also available, substitute "E" for "A" in model number. i.e., K15A-30 make K15E-30

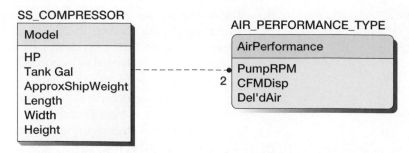

FIGURE 3-33

Alternative Model for Compressor Data

B. Figure 3-33 shows a different model for the compressor data. Explain the entities, their type, the relationship, its type, and its cardinality. How well do you think this model fits the data shown in Figure 3-32?

C. Compare your answer in question A to the model in Figure 3-33. What are the essential differences in the two models? Which do you think is better?

D. Suppose you had the job of explaining the differences in these two models to a highly motivated, intelligent end user. How would you accomplish this?

3.40 Figure 3-34 shows a listing of movie times at theaters in Seattle. Using this data as an example, do the following:

A. Create a model to represent this report using the entities MOVIE, THEATER, and SHOW_TIME. Assume that theaters may be showing movies other than this one. Although this report is for a particular day, your data model should allow for movie times on different days as well. Specify the

FIGURE 3-34

Movie Time Listing

Movie
Men in Black II
Even Tommy Lee Jones at his funniest can't save Will Smith or this goofy alien flick from sequel-itis.

Local Theaters and Showtimes

40 miles from the center of Seattle, WA <u>Change Area</u>
Tue, Jul 9 <u>Wed</u> <u>Thu</u> <u>Fri</u> <u>Sat</u>

Displaying 1 - 32 results, sorted by distance.

AMC Pacific Place 11 (0.5 miles)
600 Pine St, Seattle (206) 652-2404
Showtimes: 11:00 am, 12:00 pm, 12:45 pm, 1:30 pm, 2:30 pm, 3:15 pm, 4:00 pm, 5:00 pm, 5:45 pm, 6:30 pm, 7:30 pm, 8:30 pm, 9:00 pm, 10:00 pm, 10:45 pm

Neptune Theatre (3.9 miles)
1303 NE 45th, Seattle (206) 633-5545
Showtimes: 11:20 am, 1:30 pm, 3:40 pm, 5:50 pm, 8:00 pm, 10:10 pm

Regal Bellevue Galleria 11 (6.2 miles)
500 106th Ave NE, Bellevue (425) 451-7161
Showtimes: 11:00 am, 11:30 am, 1:00 pm, 1:30 pm, 3:00 pm, 3:30 pm, 5:05 pm, 5:35 pm, 7:10 pm, 7:40 pm, 9:20 pm, 9:50 pm

LCE Oak Tree Cinema (6.6 miles)
10006 Aurora Ave N., Seattle (206) 527-1748
Showtimes: 11:45 am, 2:15 pm, 4:45 pm, 7:15 pm, 9:45 pm

LCE Factoria Cinemas 8 (7.8 miles)
3505 Factoria Blvd SE, Bellevue (425) 641-9206
Showtimes: 12:00 pm, 1:00 pm, 2:15 pm, 3:15 pm, 4:30 pm, 5:45 pm, 7:30 pm, 8:15 pm, 9:45 pm, 10:30 pm

Kirkland Parkplace Cinema (8 miles)
404 Parkplace Ctr, Kirkland (425) 827-9000
Showtimes: 12:15 pm, 2:30 pm, 4:45 pm, 7:20 pm, 9:35 pm

identifier of the entities and their attributes. Name the relationships, describe the relationships' type, and indicate relationship cardinality. Explain which cardinalities you can logically deduce from Figure 3-34 and which need to be checked out with users. Assume that distance is an attribute of THEATER.

B. This report was prepared for a user who is located near downtown Seattle. Suppose that it is necessary to produce this same report for these theaters, but for a user located in a suburb such as Bellevue, Renton, Redmond, and Tacoma (these are suburbs of Seattle). In this case, distance cannot be an attribute of THEATER. Change your answer in A for this situation. Specify the identifier of entities and their attributes. Name the relationships, describe the relationships' type, and indicate relationship cardinality.

C. Now, suppose that you want to make this data model national. Change your answer to question B so that it can be used for other metropolitan areas. Change your answer in A for this situation. Specify the identifier of entities and their attributes. Name the relationships, describe the relationships' type, and indicate relationship cardinality.

D. Modify your answer to question C to include the leading cast members. Assume that the role of a cast member is not to be modeled. Specify the identifier of new entities and their attributes. Name new relationships, describe their relationships' type, and indicate their cardinality.

E. Modify your answer to question D to include the leading cast members. Assume that the role of a cast member is to be modeled. Specify the identifier of new entities and their attributes. Name new relationships, describe their relationships' type, and indicate their cardinality.

3.41 Consider the three reports in Figure 3-35. The data are samples of data that would appear in the reports like these.

A. Make a list of as many potential entities as these reports suggest to you.

B. Examine your list to determine whether any entities are synonyms. If so, consolidate your list.

C. Construct an IDEF1X diagram showing relationships among your entities. Name each relationship and specify cardinalities. Indicate which cardinalities you can justify on the basis of these reports and which you will need to check out with the users.

3.42 Consider the CD cover in Figure 3-36.

A. Specify identifiers and attributes for the entities CD, ARTIST, ROLE, and SONG.

B. Construct an IDEF1X diagram showing relationships among these three entities. Name each relationship and specify its type and cardinalities. Indicate which cardinalities you can justify on the basis of the CD cover and which you will need to check out with the users.

C. Consider a CD that does not involve a musical, so there is no need for ROLE. There is, however, a need for an entity SONG_WRITER. Create an IDEF1X diagram for CD, ARTIST, SONG, and SONG_WRITER. Assume that an ARTIST can either be a group or an individual. Assume that some artists record individually and as part of a group.

D. Combine the models you developed in your answers to questions B and C. Create new entities if necessary, but strive to keep your model as simple as possible. Specify identifiers and attributes of new entities, name new relationships, and indicate their cardinalities.

FIGURE 3-35

Cereal Product Reports

NUTRITION INFORMATION
SERVING SIZE: 1 OZ. (28.4 g, ABOUT 1 CUP)
SERVINGS PER PACKAGE: 13

	CEREAL	WITH ½ CUP VITAMINS A & D SKIM MILK
CALORIES	110	150*
PROTEIN	2 g	6g
CARBOHYDRATE	25 g	31g
FAT	0 g	0g*
CHOLESTEROL	0 mg	0mg*
SODIUM	290 mg	350mg
POTASSIUM	35 mg	240mg

PERCENTAGE OF U.S. RECOMMENDED DAILY ALLOWANCES (U.S. RDA)

PROTEIN	2	10
VITAMIN A	25	30
VITAMIN C	25	25
THIAMIN	35	40
RIBOFLAVIN	35	45
NIACIN	35	35
CALCIUM	**	15
IRON	10	10
VITAMIN D	10	25
VITAMIN B₆	35	35
FOLIC ACID	35	35
PHOSPHORUS	4	15
MAGNESIUM	2	6
ZINC	2	6
COPPER	2	4

*WHOLE MILK SUPPLIES AN ADDITIONAL 30 CALORIES, 4 g FAT, AND 15 mg CHOLESTEROL.
**CONTAINS LESS THAN 2% OF THE U.S. RDA OF THIS NUTRIENT.

INGREDIENTS: RICE, SUGAR, SALT, CORN SYRUP, MALT FLAVORING.

VITAMINS AND IRON: VITAMIN C (SODIUM ASCORBATE AND ASCORBIC ACID), NIACINAMIDE, IRON, VITAMIN B₆ (PYRIDOXINE HYDROCHLORIDE), VITAMIN A (PALMITATE), VITAMIN B₂ (RIBOFLAVIN), VITAMIN B₁ (THIAMIN HYDROCHLORIDE), FOLIC ACID, AND VITAMIN D.
TO KEEP THIS CEREAL FRESH, BHT HAS BEEN ADDED TO THE PACKAGING.

FDA REPORT #6272
Date: 06/30/2003
Issuer: Kellogg's Corporation
Report Title: Product Summary by Ingredient

Corn	Corn Flakes
	Krispix
	Nutrigrain (Corn)
Corn syrup	Rice Krispies
	Frosted Flakes
	Sugar Pops
Malt	Rice Krispies
	Sugar Smacks
Wheat	Sugar Smacks
	Nutrigrain (Wheat)

(a)

SUPPLIERS LIST
Date: 06/30/2003

Ingredient	Supplier	Price
Corn	Wilson	2.80
	J. Perkins	2.72
	Pollack	2.83
	McKay	2.80
Wheat	Adams	1.19
	Kroner	1.19
	Schmidt	1.22
Barley	Wilson	0.85
	Pollack	0.84

(b)

FIGURE 3-36

CD Cover

West Side Story
Based on a conception of Jerome Robbins

Book by ARTHUR LAURENTS
Music by LEONARD BERNSTEIN
Lyrics by STEPHEN SONDHEIM

Entire Original Production Directed
and Choreographed by JEROME ROBBINS

Originally produced on Broadway by Robert E. Griffith and Harold S. Prince
by arrangement with Roger L. Stevens
Orchestration by Leonard Bernstein with Sid Ramin and Irwin Kostal

HIGHLIGHTS FROM THE COMPLETE RECORDING

Maria . . . . KIRI TE KANAWA
Tony . . . . JOSE CARRERAS
Anita . . . . TATIANA TROYANOS
Riff . . . . KURT OLLMAN
and MARILYN HORNE singing "Somewhere"

Rosalia . . . . Louise Edeiken	Diesel . . . . Marty Nelson
Consuela . . . . Stella Zambalis	Baby John . . . . . Stephen Bogardus
Fancisca . . . . Angelina Reaux	A-rab . . . . Peter Thom
Action . . . . David Livingston	Snowboy . . . . Todd Lester
Bernardo . . . Richard Harrell	

1	**Jet Song** (Riff, Action, Baby John, A-rab, Chorus)		[3'13]
2	**Something's Coming** (Tony)		[2'33]
3	**Maria** (Tony)		[2'56]
4	**Tonight** (Maria, Tony)		[5'27]
5	**America** (Anita, Rosalia, Chorus)		[4'47]
6	**Cool** (Riff, Chorus)		[4'37]
7	**One Hand, One Heart** (Tony, Maria)		[5'38]
8	**Tonight** (Ensemble) (Entire Cast)		[3'40]
9	**I Feel Pretty** (Maria, Chorus)		[3'22]
10	**Somewhere** (A Girl)		[2'34]
11	**Gee OFicer Krupke** (Action, Snowboy, Diesel, A-rab, Baby John, Chorus)		[4'18]
12	**A Boy Like That** (Anita, Maria)		[2'05]
13	**I Have a Love** (Maria, Anita)		[3'30]
14	**Taunting Scene** (Orchestra)		[1'21]
15	**Finale** (Maria, Tony)		[2'40]

MODELING PROBLEMS

3.43 The Jefferson Dance Club teaches social dancing and offers both private and group lessons. Jefferson charges $45 per hour per student (or couple) for a private lesson and charges $6 per hour per student for a group lesson. Private lessons are offered six days per week (from noon until 10 p.m.). Group lessons are offered in the evenings.

Jefferson employs two types of instructors: full-time salaried instructors and part-time instructors. The full-time instructors are paid a fixed amount per week, and the part-time instructors are paid either a set amount for an evening or a set amount for teaching a particular class.

In addition to the lessons, Jefferson sponsors two weekly social dances featuring recorded music. The admission charge is $5 per person. The Friday night dance is the more popular and averages around 80 people; the Sunday night dance attracts about 30 attendees. The purpose of the dances is to give the students a place in which to practice their skills. No food or drinks are served.

Jefferson wants to develop an information system to keep track of students and the classes they have taken. Jefferson's managers also want to know how many and which types of lessons each teacher has taught and to compute the average revenue generated per lesson for each of their instructors.

Suppose Jefferson has hired you to construct a database for them. To do this, you decide to create a data model. You know you will need to interview users and gather forms, reports, and other requirements. Before you do this, however, you decide to construct a trial data model. You are hoping that this model will help you determine specific questions that you will need to ask Jefferson personnel.

A. To construct such a trial model, read through the preceding description and pick out all of the important nouns. From these nouns, construct a list of potential entities.

B. Review the list you made in A and eliminate any synonyms. Also, identify entities that are subtypes or category entities. Name a likely identifier for each entity. Eliminate any hard-to-justify entities.

C. This description does not provide sufficient data for you to specify attributes of the entities you have identified. Therefore, create an IDEF1X diagram that shows only entities and relationships. Name each relationship and specify its type and cardinalities. Justify the decisions you make.

D. Now, examine your model and make a list of questions that you would need to ask in order to create an accurate data model.

E. Do you think the process of creating a trial data model before interviewing users is a good idea? What are the advantages? What are the disadvantages?

3.44 San Juan Sailboat Charters is an agent that leases sailboats to customers for a fee. San Juan does not own any sailboats; it leases boats on behalf of the owners who wish to earn income when they are not using their boats. San Juan charges a fee for its service. San Juan specializes in boats that can be used for multi-day or weekly charters—the smallest sailboat in its inventory is 28 feet and the largest is 51 feet.

Each sailboat is fully equipped at the time it is leased. Most of the equipment is provided by the owners, but some is added by San Juan. The owner-provided equipment includes what is fixed on the boat, such as radios, compasses, depth indicators and other instrumentation, stoves, and refrigerators. Other owner-provided equipment is not installed as part of the boat. Such equipment includes sails; lines; anchors; dinghies; life preservers; and (in the cabin) dishes, silverware, cooking utensils, bedding, and the like. San Juan provides consumable equipment, (which can also be considered supplies) such as charts, navigation books, tide and current tables, soap, dishtowels, toilet paper, and similar items.

An important part of San Juan's responsibilities is keeping track of the equipment on the boat. Much of it is expensive, and some of it, particularly what is not attached to the boat, can easily be lost or stolen. Customers are responsible for all equipment during the period of their charter. San Juan likes to keep accurate records of its customers and the charters, not only for marketing but also for recording the trips that customers have taken. Some itineraries and weather conditions are more dangerous than others, so San Juan likes to know which customers have what experience.

Most of San Juan's business is bare-boat chartering, which means that no skipper or other crew is provided. In some cases, however, customers request the services of a skipper or other crew member, so San Juan hires such personnel on a part-time basis.

Sailboats often need maintenance. San Juan is required by its contracts with the boat owners to keep accurate records of all maintenance activities and costs, including normal activities (for example, cleaning or engine-oil changes) and unscheduled repairs. In some cases, repairs are necessary during a charter. A boat engine, for example, might fail while the boat is far away from San Juan's facility. In this case, the customers radio the San Juan dispatcher, who determines the best facility to make the repair and sends the facility's personnel to the disabled boat. To make these decisions, the dispatchers need information about repair facilities as well as past histories of repair quality and costs.

Suppose that San Juan has hired you to construct a database for them. To do this, you decide to create a data model. You know you will need to interview users and gather forms, reports, and other requirements. Before you do this, however, you decide to construct a trial data model. You are hoping that this model will help you determine specific questions that you will need to ask Jefferson personnel.

A. To construct such a trial model, read through the preceding description and pick out all of the important nouns. From these nouns, construct a list of potential entities.

B. Review the list you made in A and eliminate any synonyms. Also, identify entities that are subtypes or category entities. Name a likely identifier for each entity. Eliminate any hard-to-justify entities.

C. This description does not provide sufficient data for you to specify attributes of the entities you have identified. Therefore, create an IDEF1X diagram that shows only entities and relationships. Name each relationship and specify its type and cardinalities. Justify the decisions you make.

D. Now, examine your model and make a list of questions that you would need to ask in order to create an accurate data model.

E. Do you think the process of creating a trial data model before interviewing users is a good idea? What are the advantages? What are the disadvantages?

FIREDUP PROJECT QUESTIONS

Review the FiredUp Project Questions at the end of Chapter 2 and answer the questions there if you have not already done so.

A.   Consider the data modeling steps in Figure 3-1 in the context of FiredUp's business. Without having access to the personnel at FiredUp, it is not possible to plan a data modeling project. Instead, make a list of questions that you would need to have answered in order to be able to plan a data modeling project.

B.   With regard to requirements determination, consider the sources of requirements in Figure 3-2. Describe how you think each of these types of requirements might apply to FiredUp. How would you document the results of your requirements documentation?

C.   Consider your answer to FiredUp question E, Chapter 2. How would you go about validating this model? Make a list of questions that you would ask FiredUp personnel. In what ways could you use mockups? In what ways could you use prototypes?

TWIGS TREE TRIMMING SERVICE

Review the Twigs Service Project Questions at the end of Chapter 2 and answer the questions there if you have not already done so.

A.   Consider the data modeling steps in Figure 3-1 in the context of Twigs business. Without having access to Samantha and other personnel (if any) at Twigs, it is not possible to plan a data modeling project. Instead, make a list of questions that you would need to have answered in order to be able to plan a data modeling project.

B.   With regard to requirements determination, consider the sources of requirements in Figure 3-2. Describe how you think each of these types of requirements might apply to Twigs. How would you document results of your requirements documentation?

C.   Consider your answer to Twigs question E, Chapter 2. How would you go about validating this model? Make a list of questions that you would ask Samantha. In what ways could you use mockups? In what ways could you use prototypes?

PART II

DATABASE DESIGN

The chapters in Part II discuss database design. Chapter 4 presents the relational model and normalization. The relational model is important because it is the standard in which most database designs are expressed; it is also the foundation of most of today's DBMS products. Normalization is important because it is a technique for checking the quality of a relational design. Given the groundwork in Chapter 4, we then consider the process of transforming entity-relationship data models into DBMS-independent relational designs in Chapter 5.

CHAPTER 4

The Relational Model and Normalization

The relational model is the industry-standard way to store and process database data. In this chapter, we will discuss the basic terms and concepts of this model. We will also describe normalization, which is a technique for transforming relations that have undesirable characteristics into those that do not have those characteristics. In Chapters 6 through 8, we will describe SQL, a language for defining and processing relations.

The relational model was first proposed by E.F. Codd in a landmark 1970 paper.[1] Initially, the relational model was considered by the industry to be "too theoretical" and too slow and cumbersome for high-speed transaction processing. This objection was gradually overcome, and by the 1980s, thanks to products such as DB2 and Oracle, large relational databases were in use for high-volume transaction processing.

We will begin this chapter with definitions of some key terms.

---

[1] E.F. Codd, "A Relational Model of Data for Large Shared Databanks," *Communications of the ACM*, June, 1970, pp. 377–387.

▶ RELATIONS

Chapter 1 stated that relational DBMS products store data in the form of tables. Actually, this is not quite correct. They store data in the form of relations, which are a special type of table. Specifically, a **relation** is a two-dimensional table that has the characteristics listed in Figure 4-1. First, each row in the table holds data that pertain to some entity or a portion of some entity. Second, each column of the table contains data that represent an attribute of the entity. Thus, in an EMPLOYEE relation, each row contains data about a particular employee, and each column contains data that represent an attribute of that employee—such as Name, Phone, or EmailAddress.

In addition, to be a relation, the cells of the table must hold a single value; no repeating elements are allowed in a cell. Also, all of the entries in any column must be of the same kind. For example, if the third column in the first row of a table contains EmployeeNumber, the third column in all other rows must contain EmployeeNumber as well. Further, each column has a unique name, and the order of the columns in the table is unimportant. Similarly, the order of the rows is unimportant. Finally, no two rows in a table may be identical.

Sample Relation and Two Non-relations

Figure 4-2 shows a sample EMPLOYEE table. Consider this table in light of the characteristics shown in Figure 4-1. First, each row is about an EMPLOYEE entity and each column represents an attribute of employees, so those two conditions are met. There is only one value per cell, and all entries in a column are of the same kind. Column names are unique, and we could change the order of either the columns or the rows and not lose any information. Finally, no two rows are identical. Because this table has all the characteristics listed in Figure 4-1, we can classify it as a relation.

Figures 4-3(a) and 4-3(b) show two tables that are not relations. The EMPLOYEE table in Figure 4-3(a) is not a relation because the Phone column has cells with multiple entries. Tom Caruthers has three values for phone, and Richard Bandalone has two. Multiple entries per cell are not allowed in a relation.

FIGURE 4–1

Characteristics of a Relation

- Rows contain data about an entity
- Columns contain data about attributes of the entity
- Cells of the table hold a single value
- All entries in a column are of the same kind
- Each column has a unique name
- The order of the columns is unimportant
- The order of the rows is unimportant
- No two rows may be identical

FIGURE 4–2

Sample Relation

EmployeeNumber	FirstName	LastName	Department	Email	Phone
100	Jerry	Johnson	Accounting	JJ@somewhere.com	236-9987
200	Mary	Abernathy	Finance	MA@somewhere.com	444-8898
300	Liz	Smathers	Finance	LS@somewhere.com	777-0098
400	Tom	Caruthers	Accounting	TC@somewhere.com	236-9987
500	Tom	Jackson	Production	TJ@somewhere.com	444-9980
600	Eleanore	Caldera	Legal	EC@somewhere.com	767-0900
700	Richard	Bandalone	Legal	RB@somewhere.com	767-0900

FIGURE 4–3

Tables but Not Relations (a) Order of Rows is Important and (b) Multiple Entries per Cell

EmployeeNumber	FirstName	LastName	Department	Email	Phone
100	Jerry	Johnson	Accounting	JJ@somewhere.com	236-9987
200	Mary	Abernathy	Finance	MA@somewhere.com	444-8898
300	Liz	Smathers	Finance	LS@somewhere.com	777-0098
400	Tom	Caruthers	Accounting	TC@somewhere.com	236-9987, 266-9987, 555-7171
500	Tom	Jackson	Production	TJ@somewhere.com	444-9980
600	Eleanore	Caldera	Legal	EC@somewhere.com	767-0900
700	Richard	Bandalone	Legal	RB@somewhere.com	767-0900, 767-0011

(a)

EmployeeNumber	FirstName	LastName	Department	Email	Phone
100	Jerry	Johnson	Accounting	JJ@somewhere.com	236-9987
200	Mary	Abernathy	Finance	MA@somewhere.com	444-8898
300	Liz	Smathers	Finance	LS@somewhere.com	777-0098
400	Tom	Caruthers	Accounting	TC@somewhere.com	236-9987
				Fax:	266-9987
				Home:	555-7171
500	Tom	Jackson	Production	TJ@somewhere.com	444-9980
600	Eleanore	Caldera	Legal	EC@somewhere.com	767-0900
				Fax:	236-9987
				Home:	555-7171
700	Richard	Bandalone	Legal	RB@somewhere.com	767-0900

(b)

The table in Figure 4-3(b) is not a relation for two reasons. First, the order of the rows is *not* unimportant. The row under Tom Caruthers contains his fax phone number. If we rearrange the rows, we may lose track of the correspondence between his name and data and his fax phone number. The second reason is that not all values in the Email column are of the same kind. Some of the values are email addresses and others are types of phone numbers.

Note, by the way, that although we can have at most one value in a cell, that value can vary in length. Figure 4-4 shows the table shown in Figure 4-2 with a variable length

FIGURE 4–4

Relation with Variable Length Attribute

EmployeeNumber	FirstName	LastName	Department	Email	Phone	Comment
100	Jerry	Johnson	Accounting	JJ@somewhere.com	236-9987	Joined the Accounting Department in March after completing his MBA at night. Will sit for CPA exam this fall.
200	Mary	Abernathy	Finance	MA@somewhere.com	444-8898	
300	Liz	Smathers	Finance	LS@somewhere.com	777-0098	
400	Tom	Caruthers	Accounting	TC@somewhere.com	236-9987	
500	Tom	Jackson	Production	TJ@somewhere.com	444-9980	
600	Eleanore	Caldera	Legal	EC@somewhere.com	767-0900	
700	Richard	Bandalone	Legal	RB@somewhere.com	767-0900	Is a full-time consultant to legal on a retainer basis.

Comment attribute. Even though this Comment is lengthy and varies in length from row to row, there is still only one Comment per cell. Thus, the table in Figure 4-4 is a relation.

A Note on Terminology

In the database world, people generally use the terms *table* and *relation* interchangeably. Accordingly, from now on we will do the same in this book. Thus, any time we use the term *table,* we mean a table that meets the characteristics listed in Figure 4-1. Keep in mind, however, that strictly speaking there are tables that are not relations.

Sometimes, especially in traditional data processing, people will use the term *file* or *datafile* instead of relation. When they do so, they will use the term *record* for row and the term *field* for column. To further complicate the issue, database theoreticians sometimes use yet another set of terms: they call a relation a *relation*, a column an *attribute*, and a row a *tuple* (rhymes with "couple"). To make things even more confusing, people often mix up these sets of terms. It is typical to hear someone refer to a relation that has rows and fields. As long as you know what is intended, this mixing is not important.

Before we move on, there is one other source of confusion to discuss. According to Figure 4-1, a table that has duplicate rows is not a relation. In practice, however, this condition is often ignored. Particularly when we manipulate relations with the SQL, we may end up with a table that has duplicate rows. To make that table into a relation, we should eliminate the duplicates. On a large table, however, checking for duplication can be very time-consuming. Therefore, the default behavior for DBMS products is not to check for duplicate rows. Hence, in practice, there may be tables with duplicate rows that are still called relations. You will see examples of this situation in Chapter 6.

▶ *TYPES* OF KEYS

A **key** is one or more columns of a relation that identifies a row. A key can be unique or non-unique. For example, for the relation in Figure 4-2, EmployeeNumber is a **unique key** because a value of EmployeeNumber identifies a unique row. Thus, a query to display all EMPLOYEEs having an EmployeeNumber of 200 produce a single row. On the other hand, Department is a **non-unique** key. It is a key because it is used to identify a row, but it is non-unique because a value of Department identifies potentially more than one row. Thus, a query to display all rows having a Department value of 'Accounting' produces several rows.

From the data in Figure 4-2, it appears that EmployeeNumber, LastName, and Email are all unique identifiers. In deciding if this is true, however, it is not sufficient simply to examine sample data. Rather, the developers must ask the users or other subject matter experts whether or not a certain column is unique. The column LastName is a good example. It may turn out that our sample data just happens to have unique values for LastName. In general, the users may say that LastName is not always unique in the EMPLOYEE relation.

Composite Keys

Suppose the users say that LastName is not unique in general, but that the combination of LastName and Department is unique. Somehow, the users know that there will never be two Johnsons, for example, in the Accounting department. If that were the case, then we could say that the combination (LastName, Department) is a unique key. A key that contains two or more attributes is called a **composite key**.

It might turn out that users say that the combination (LastName, Department) is not unique, but that the combination (FirstName, LastName, Department) is unique. Such a key is a composite key with three attributes.

Primary and Candidate Keys

Now, suppose the users tell us that EmployeeNumber is a unique key, that Email is a unique key, and that the combination (FirstName, LastName, Department) is a unique key. As you will learn in the next chapter, when designing a database, we choose one of the unique identifiers to be the **primary key**. The other unique keys are referred to as **candidate keys** because they are candidates to be the primary key.

The primary key is important not only because it can be used to identify unique rows, but also because it is used to represent rows in relationships. (You saw an example of the use of ID keys for Lakeview Equipment Rentals in Chapter 1.) Additionally, many DBMS products use values of the primary key to organize storage for the relation. They also build indexes and other special structures to make it easy (and fast) to use a primary key value to locate a row in physical storage.

Sometimes, relations are denoted by showing the name of the relation followed by the columns of the relation in parentheses. The primary key of the relation is underlined. Thus, the following expression denotes a relation named CUSTOMER, having CustomerID, Name, Email, Phone, and Balance columns:

CUSTOMER (<u>CustomerID</u>, Name, Email, Phone, Balance)

The primary key of the relation is CustomerID. There may also be candidate keys, but they are not shown with this notation.

Functional Dependencies

To understand functional dependency, let's make a short excursion into the world of algebra. Suppose you are buying boxes of cookies and someone tells you that each box costs $4. With this fact, you can compute the cost of several boxes with the formula:

CookieCost = NumberOfBoxes x $5

A more general way to express the relationship between CookieCost and NumberOfBoxes is to say that CookieCost depends upon NumberOfBoxes. Such a statement tells us the character of the relationship of CookieCost and NumberOfBoxes, even though it doesn't give us the formula. More formally, we can say that CookieCost is functionally dependent on NumberOfBoxes. Such a statement can be written as follows:

NumberOfBoxes → CookieCost

This expression can also be read as "NumberOfBoxes determines CookieCost." The variable on the left NumberOfBoxes in this example is called the **determinant**.

Using another example, we can compute the extended price of a part order by multiplying the quantity of the item times its unit price, or the following:

ExtendedPrice = Quantity * UnitPrice

In this case, we say that ExtendedPrice is functionally dependent on Quantity and UnitPrice.

Or the following:

(Quantity, UnitPrice) → ExtendedPrice

In this case, the composite (Quantity, UnitPrice) is the determinant of ExtendedPrice.

Now, let's expand these ideas a bit. Suppose you know that a sack contains red, blue, or yellow objects. Further, suppose you know that the red objects weigh five pounds, the blue objects weigh three pounds, and the yellow objects weigh seven pounds. If a friend looks into the sack, sees an object, and tells you the color of the object, you can tell her the weight of the object. We can formalize this the same way we did previously:

ObjectColor → Weight

Thus, "Weight is functionally dependent on ObjectColor," or "ObjectColor determines Weight." The relationship here does not involve an equation, but this functional dependency is still true. Given a value for ObjectColor, you can determine the object's weight.

If we also know that the red objects are balls, the blue objects are cubes, and the yellow objects are cubes, we can also say the following:

ObjectColor → Shape

Thus, ObjectColor determines shape. We can put these two together to state the following:

ObjectColor → (Weight, Shape)

Thus, ObjectColor determines Weight and Shape.

A way to represent these facts is to put them into a table as follows:

ObjectColor	Weight	Shape
Red	5	Ball
Blue	3	Cube
Yellow	7	Cube

This table meets all of the conditions shown in Figure 4-1, so we can refer to it as a relation. It has a primary key of ObjectColor. We can express this relation as follows:

OBJECT (ObjectColor, Weight, Shape)

Now, you may be thinking that we have just performed some trick or sleight-of-hand to arrive at a relation, but in truth, one can make the argument that the only reason for having relations is to store instances of functional dependencies. When we have a relation like the following:

PLANT (ItemNumber, VarietyName, Cost, Price)

We are simply storing facts that express the functional dependency:

ItemNumber → (VarietyName, Cost, Price)

Functional Dependencies with Composite Groups Composite groups, such as (Quantity, Price), can occur on either side of a functional dependency. The meaning of the group, however, is different, depending on which side it appears. For example,

OrderNumber → (CustomerNumber, ItemNumber, Quantity)

means that, given a value of OrderNumber, we can determine the values of CustomerNumber, ItemNumber, and Quantity. We can also write this expression as three separate expressions:

OrderNumber → CustomerNumber

OrderNumber→ ItemNumber

OrderNumber → Quantity

On the other hand, the following expression:

(CustomerNumber, ItemNumber, Quantity) → Price

means that given values for CustomerNumber, ItemNumber, Quantity, we can determine Price. Notice that we cannot split this determinant into pieces. For example, it is *not* true that if

(CustomerNumber, ItemNumber, Quantity) → Price

then

CustomerNumber → Price

We need all three parts of the determinant to obtain the value of Price.

Difference between Primary Key and Determinant   Before we move on, it is important for you to understand that although a primary key is always a determinant, a determinant is not necessarily a primary key. Consider the following relation

HOUSING (SID, DormName, Fee)

where SID is the identifier of a student, DormName is the name of a dormitory and Fee is the rental cost of living in that dormitory. Assume all students in a particular dorm pay the same Fee.

Because SID is a primary key, we know that SID → (DormName, Fee). Thus, SID is both a primary key and a determinant. Also, because all students in a particular dorm pay the same fee, we know that DormName→ Fee. Thus, DormName is a determinant, but it is not a primary key.

▶ NORMALIZATION

Unfortunately, not all relations are equally desirable. A table that meets the minimum definition of a relation may not have an effective or appropriate structure. For some relations, changing the data can have undesirable consequences, called **modification anomalies**. Anomalies can be eliminated by redefining the relation into two or more relations. In most circumstances, the redefined, or **normalized**, relations are preferred.

Modification Anomalies

Consider the Activity relation in Figure 4-5. If we delete the tuple for Student 100, we will lose not only the fact that Student 100 is a skier but also the fact that skiing costs $200. This is called a **deletion anomaly**; that is, by deleting the facts about one entity (that Student 100 is a skier), we inadvertently delete facts about another entity (that skiing costs $200). With one deletion, we lose facts about two entities.

FIGURE 4-5

Activity Relation

ACTIVITY (SID, Activity, Fee)
Sample Data

SID	Activity	Fee
100	Skiing	200
150	Swimming	50
175	Squash	50
200	Swimming	50

The same relation can be used to illustrate an **insertion anomaly**. Suppose we want to store the fact that scuba diving costs $175, but we cannot enter this data into the ACTIVITY relation until a student takes up scuba diving. This restriction seems silly. Why should we have to wait until someone takes the activity before we can record its price? This restriction is called an insertion anomaly. We cannot insert a fact about one entity until we have an additional fact about another entity.

The relation in Figure 4-5 can be used for some applications, but it obviously has problems. We can eliminate both the deletion and the insertion anomalies by dividing the ACTIVITY relation into two relations, each dealing with a different theme. For example, we can put the SID and Activity attributes into one relation (we will call the new relation STU-ACT for student activity), and we can put the Activity and Fee attributes into a relation called ACT-COST (for activity cost). Figure 4-6 shows the same sample data stored in these two new relations.

Now, if we delete Student 100 from STU-ACT, we do not lose the fact that skiing costs $200. Furthermore, we can add scuba diving and its fee to the ACT-COST relation, even before anyone enrolls. Thus, the deletion and the insertion anomalies have been eliminated.

Separating one relation into two relations has a disadvantage, however. Suppose a student tries to sign up for a nonexistent activity. For instance, Student 250 wants to enroll in racquetball. We can insert this new tuple in STU-ACT (the row would contain 250, Racquetball), but should we? Should a student be allowed to enroll in an activity that is not in the relation ACT-COST? Put another way, should the system somehow prevent student rows from being added if the value of the ACTIVITY is not in the ACT-COST table? The answer to this question lies with the users' requirements. If the action should be prohibited, this constraint (a type of business rule) must be documented as part of the schema design. Later in implementation, the constraint will be defined to the DBMS if the product in use provides such constraint checking. If not, the constraint must be enforced by application programs.

Suppose the user specifies that activities can exist before any student enrolls in them, but no student may enroll in an activity that does not have a fee assigned to it (that is, no activities that are not in the ACT-COST table). We can document this constraint in any of several ways in the database design: Activity in STU-ACT is a subset of Activity in ACT-COST, or STU-ACT [Activity] is a subset of ACT-COST [Activity], or STU-ACT [Activity] ⊆ ACT-COST [Activity].

According to this notation, the brackets [ ] denote a column of data that is extracted from a relation. These expressions simply mean that the values in the Activity attribute

FIGURE 4-6

The Division of ACTIVITY into Two Relations

STU-ACT (SID, Activity)

SID	Activity
100	Skiing
150	Swimming
175	Squash
200	Swimming

ACT-COST (Activity, Fee)

Activity	Fee
Skiing	200
Swimming	50
Squash	50

of STU-ACT must exist in the Activity attribute of ACT-COST. It also means that before we allow an Activity to be entered into STU-ACT, we must check to make sure that it is already present in ACT-COST. Constraints like this are called **referential integrity constraints**.

Essence of Normalization

The anomalies in the ACTIVITY relation shown in Figure 4-5 can be stated in the following intuitive way: Problems occur because ACTIVITY contains facts about two different themes:

> Students who participate in each activity
> How much each activity costs

When we add a new row, we must add data about two themes at once; when we delete a row, we are forced to delete data about two themes at once.

The essence of the normalization process is the following: Every normalized relation should have a single theme. Any relation having two or more themes should be broken up into two or more relations, each of which has a single theme. When we find a relation with modification anomalies, we eliminate them by splitting the relation into two or more separate ones, each containing a single theme.

Every time we break up a relation, however, we may create referential integrity constraints. Hence, remember to check for such constraints every time you break a relation into two or more.

In the remainder of this chapter, you will learn many rules about normalization. All of these rules are special cases of the process just described.

Classes of Relations

Relations can be classified by the types of modification anomalies to which they are vulnerable. In the 1970s, relational theorists chipped away at these types. Someone would find an anomaly, classify it, and think of a way to prevent it. Each time this happened, the criteria for designing relations improved. These classes of relations and the techniques for preventing anomalies are called **normal forms**. Depending on its structure, a relation may be in first normal form, second normal form, or some other normal form.

As shown in Figure 4-7, these normal forms are nested. That is, a relation in second normal form is also in first normal form, and a relation in 5NF (fifth normal form) is also in 4NF, BCNF, 3NF, 2NF, and 1NF.

These normal forms were helpful, but they had a serious limitation. No theory guaranteed that any of them would eliminate all anomalies; each form could eliminate just certain ones. This changed in 1981, however, when R. Fagin defined a new normal form called **domain/key normal form (DK/NF)**. In an important paper, Fagin showed that a

FIGURE 4–7

Relationship of Normal Forms

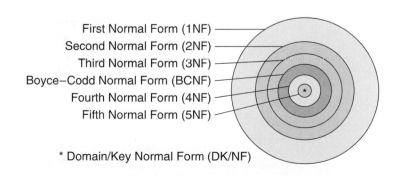

First Normal Form (1NF)
Second Normal Form (2NF)
Third Normal Form (3NF)
Boyce–Codd Normal Form (BCNF)
Fourth Normal Form (4NF)
Fifth Normal Form (5NF)

* Domain/Key Normal Form (DK/NF)

relation in DK/NF is free of all modification anomalies, regardless of their type.[2] He also showed that any relation that is free of modification anomalies must be in DK/NF.

Until DK/NF was defined, it was necessary for relational database theorists to continue looking for more and more anomalies and more and more normal forms. Fagin's proof, however, simplified the situation. If we can put a relation in DK/NF, we can be sure that it will have no anomalies. The trick is knowing how to put relations in DK/NF.

▶ FIRST THROUGH FIFTH NORMAL FORMS

Any table of data that meets the definition of a relation is said to be in **first normal form**. Remember that for a table to be a relation, it must have the characteristics listed in Figure 4-1.

The relation shown in Figure 4-5 is in first normal form. As we have seen, however, relations in first normal form may have modification anomalies. To eliminate those anomalies, we split the relation into two or more relations. When we do this, the new relations are in some other normal form—just which one depends on the anomalies we have eliminated, as well as the ones to which the new relations are vulnerable.

Second Normal Form

To understand second normal form, consider the ACTIVITIES relation illustrated in Figure 4-8. This relation has modification anomalies similar to the ones we examined earlier. If we delete the tuple for Student 175, we will lose the fact that squash costs $50. Also, we cannot enter an activity until a student signs up for it. Thus, the relation suffers from both deletion and insertion anomalies.

The problem with this relation is that it has a dependency involving only part of the key. The key is the composite (SID, Activity), but the relation contains a dependency, Activity → Fee. The determinant of this dependency (Activity) is only part of the key (SID, Activity). In this case, we say that Fee is *partially dependent* on the key of the table. There would be no modification anomalies if Fee were dependent on all of the key. To eliminate the anomalies, we must separate the relation into two relations.

This example leads to the definition of second normal form: *A relation is in second normal form if all its non-key attributes are dependent on all of the key*. According to this definition, if a relation has a single attribute as its key, it is automatically in second normal form. Because the key is only one attribute, by default every non-key attribute is dependent on all of the key; there can be no partial dependencies. Thus, second normal is of concern only in relations that have composite keys.

FIGURE 4–8

ACTIVITIES Relation

ACTIVITIES (<u>SID</u>, <u>Activity</u>, Fee)

SID	Activity	Fee
100	Skiing	200
100	Golf	65
150	Swimming	50
175	Squash	50
175	Swimming	50
200	Swimming	50
200	Golf	65

[2] R. Fagin, "A Normal Form for Relational Databases That Is Based on Domains and Keys," *ACM Transactions on Database Systems*, September 1981, pp. 387–414.

ACTIVITIES can be decomposed to form two relations in second normal form. The relations are the same as those shown in Figure 4-6: namely, STU-ACT and ACT-COST. We know the new relations are in second normal form because they both have single-attribute keys.

Third Normal Form

Relations in second normal form can also have anomalies. Consider the HOUSING relation in Figure 4-9(a). The key is SID, and the functional dependencies are SID → Dorm and Dorm → Fee. These dependencies arise because each student lives in only one dormitory and each dormitory charges only one fee. Everyone living in Randolph Hall, for example, pays $3,200 per quarter.

Since SID determines Dorm and Dorm determines Fee, then indirectly SID → Fee. An arrangement of functional dependencies like this is called a **transitive dependency** because SID determines Fee through the attribute Dorm.

The key of HOUSING is SID (both Dorm and Fee are determined by SID), and hence the relation is in second normal form. Despite this, however, HOUSING has anomalies because of the transitive dependency.

What happens if we delete the second tuple shown in Figure 4-10(a)? We lose not only the fact that Student 150 lives in Ingersoll Hall, but also the fact that it costs $3,100 to live there. This is a deletion anomaly. And how can we record the fact that the Fee for Carrigg Hall is $3,500? We cannot record it until a student decides to move in. This is an insertion anomaly.

To eliminate the anomalies from a relation in second normal form, the transitive dependency must be removed, which leads to a definition of third normal form: *A relation is in third normal form if it is in second normal form and has no transitive dependencies.*

The HOUSING relation can be divided into two relations in third normal form. This has been done for the relations STU-HOUSING (SID, Dorm) and BLDG-FEE (Dorm, Fee) in Figure 4-9(b).

HOUSING (<u>SID</u>, Dorm, Fee)
Key: SID
Functional
dependencies: Dorm → Fee
SID → Dorm → Fee

SID	Dorm	Fee
100	Randolph	3200
150	Ingersoll	3100
200	Randolph	3200
250	Pitkin	3100
300	Randolph	3200

(a)

STU-HOUSING (<u>SID</u>, Dorm)

SID	Dorm
100	Randolph
150	Ingersoll
200	Randolph
250	Pitkin
300	Randolph

BLDG-FEE (<u>Dorm</u>, Fee)

Dorm	Fee
Randolph	3200
Ingersoll	3100
Pitkin	3100

(b)

FIGURE 4–10

Boyce–Codd Normal Form (a) Relation in Third Normal Form, but Not in Boyce–Codd Normal Form and (b) Relations in Boyce–Codd Normal Form

ADVISER (SID, Major, Fname)

Key (candidate): (SID, Fname)

Functional dependencies: Fname→Major

SID	Major	Fname
100	Math	Cauchy
150	Psychology	Jung
200	Math	Riemann
250	Math	Cauchy
300	Psychology	Perls
300	Math	Riemann

(a)

STU-ADV (SID, Fname)

SID	Fname
100	Cauchy
150	Jung
200	Riemann
250	Cauchy
300	Perls
300	Riemann

ADV-SUBJ (Fname, Subject)

Fname	Subject
Cauchy	Math
Jung	Psychology
Riemann	Math
Perls	Psychology

(b)

The ACTIVITY relation shown in Figure 4-5 also has a transitive dependency. In ACTIVITY, SID determines Activity and Activity determines Fee. Therefore, ACTIVITY is not in third normal form. Decomposing ACTIVITY into the relations STU-ACT (SID, Activity) and ACT-COST (Activity, Fee) eliminates the anomalies.

Boyce–Codd Normal Form

Unfortunately, even relations in third normal form can have anomalies. Consider the ADVISER relation in Figure 4-10(a). Suppose the requirements underlying this relation are that a student (SID) can have one or more majors (Major), a major can have several faculty members (Fname) as advisers, and a faculty member (Fname) advises in only one major area. Also assume no two faculty members have the same name.

Because students can have several majors, SID does not determine Major. Moreover, because students can have several advisers, SID also does not determine Fname. Thus, SID by itself cannot be a key.

The combination (SID, Major) determines Fname, and the combination (SID, Fname) determines Major. Hence, either of the combinations can be a key. As stated, two or more attributes or attribute collections that can be a key are called candidate keys. Whichever of the candidates is selected to be *the* key is called the primary key.

In addition to the candidate keys, there is another functional dependency to consider: Fname determines Major (any faculty member advises in only one major. Therefore, given the Fname, we can determine the Major). Thus, Fname is a determinant.

By definition, ADVISER is in first normal form. It is also in second normal form because it has no non-key attribute (all attributes are part of at least one key). And it also is in third normal form because it has no transitive dependencies. Despite all this, however, it has modification anomalies.

Suppose Student 300 drops out of school. If we delete Student 300's tuple, we lose the fact that Perls advises in psychology. This is a deletion anomaly. Similarly, how can we store the fact that Keynes advises in economics? We cannot store it until a student majors in economics. This is an insertion anomaly.

Situations like this lead to the definition of Boyce–Codd normal form (BCNF): *A relation is in BCNF if every determinant is a candidate key.* ADVISER is not in BCNF because the determinant, Fname, is not a candidate key.

As with the other examples, ADVISER can be decomposed into two relations having no anomalies. For example, the relations STU-ADV (SID, Fname) and ADV-SUBJ (Fname, Subject) have no anomalies.

Relations in BCNF have no anomalies in regard to functional dependencies and this seemed to put the issue of modification anomalies to rest. It was soon discovered, however, that anomalies can arise from situations other than functional dependencies.

Fourth Normal Form

Consider the STUDENT relation in Figure 4-11, showing the relationship among students, majors, and activities. Suppose that students can enroll in several different majors and participate in several different activities. Because this is so, the only key is the combination of attributes (SID, Major, Activity). Student 100 majors in music and accounting, and she also participates in swimming and tennis. Student 150 majors only in math and participates in jogging.

What is the relationship between SID and Major? It is not a functional dependency because students can have several majors. A single value of SID can have many values of Major. Also, a single value of SID can have many values of Activity.

This attribute dependency is called a **multi-value dependency**. Multi-value dependencies lead to modification anomalies. To begin, note the data redundancy in Figure 4-11. Student 100 has four records, each of which shows one of her majors paired with one of her activities. If the data were stored with fewer rows—say, there were only two rows, one for music and swimming and one for accounting and tennis—the implications would be misleading. It would *appear* that Student 100 swam only when she was a music major and played tennis only when she was an accounting major. But this interpretation is illogical. Her majors and her activities are completely independent of each other. So to prevent such a misleading conclusion, we store all the combinations of majors and activities.

Suppose that because Student 100 decides to sign up for skiing, we add the tuple [100, MUSIC, SKIING], as shown in Figure 4-12(a). The relation at this point implies that Student 100 skis as a music major, but not as an accounting major. In order to keep the data consistent, we must add one row for each of her majors paired with skiing. Thus, we must also add the row [100, ACCOUNTING, SKIING], as illustrated in Figure 4-12(b). This is an update anomaly—too much updating needs to be done to make a simple change in the data.

FIGURE 4-11

Relation with Multi-Value Dependencies

STUDENT (<u>SID</u>, <u>Major</u>, <u>Activity</u>)

Multi-value dependencies: SID $\rightarrow\!\!\rightarrow$ Major
SID $\rightarrow\!\!\rightarrow$ Activity

SID	Major	Activity
100	Music	Swimming
100	Accounting	Swimming
100	Music	Tennis
100	Accounting	Tennis
150	Math	Jogging

FIGURE 4–12

FIGURE 4–12

STUDENT Relations with Insertion Anomalies (a) Insertion of a Single Tuple and (b) Insertion of Two Tuples

STUDENT (<u>SID</u>, <u>Major</u>, <u>Activity</u>)

SID	Major	Activity
100	Music	Skiing
100	Music	Swimming
100	Accounting	Swimming
100	Music	Tennis
100	Accounting	Tennis
150	Math	Jogging

(a)

SID	Major	Activity
100	Music	Skiing
100	Accounting	Skiing
100	Music	Swimming
100	Accounting	Swimming
100	Music	Tennis
100	Accounting	Tennis
150	Math	Jogging

(b)

In general, a multi-value dependency exists when a relation has at least three attributes, two of them are multi-value, and their values depend on only the third attribute. In other words, in a relation R (A, B, C), a multi-value dependency exists if A determines multiple values of B, A determines multiple values of C, and B and C are independent of each other. As we saw in the previous example, SID determines multiple values of Major and SID determines multiple values of Activity, but Major and Activity are independent of each other.

Refer to Figure 4-11. Notice how multi-value dependencies are written: SID $\rightarrow\rightarrow$ Major, and SID $\rightarrow\rightarrow$ Activity. This is read as follows: "SID multi-determines Major, and SID multi-determines Activity." This relation is in BCNF (2-NF because it is all key; 3NF because it has no transitive dependencies; and BCNF because it has no non-key determinants). However, as we have seen, it has anomalies: If a student adds a major, we must enter a row for the new major, paired with each of the student's activities. The same holds true if a student enrolls in a new activity. If a student drops a major, we must delete each of his rows containing that major. If he participates in four activities, there are four rows containing the major he has dropped, and each of them must be deleted.

To eliminate these anomalies, we must eliminate the multi-value dependency. We do this by creating two relations, each one storing data for only one of the multi-value attributes. The resulting relations do not have anomalies. They are STU-MAJOR (SID, Major) and STU-ACT (SID, Activity), as seen in Figure 4-13.

From these observations, we define fourth normal form in the following way: *A relation is in fourth normal form if it is in BCNF and has no multi-value dependencies.* After

FIGURE 4–13

Elimination of Multi-Value Dependency

STU-MAJOR (<u>SID</u>, <u>Major</u>)

SID	Major
100	Music
100	Accounting
150	Math

STU-ACT (<u>SID</u>, <u>Activity</u>)

SID	Activity
100	Skiing
100	Swimming
100	Tennis
150	Jogging

we have discussed domain/key normal form later in this chapter, we will return to describe multi-value dependencies in another more intuitive way.

Fifth Normal Form

Fifth normal form concerns dependencies that are rather obscure. It has to do with relations that can be divided into subrelations, as we have been doing, but then cannot be reconstructed. The condition under which this situation arises has no clear intuitive meaning. We do not know what the consequences of such dependencies are or even if they have any practical consequences. For more information about fifth normal form, refer to *SQL for Smarties*, pp. 34, 35.[3]

▶ DOMAIN/KEY NORMAL FORM

Each of the normal forms we have discussed was identified by researchers who found anomalies with some relations that were in a lower normal form: Noticing modification anomalies with relations in second normal form led to the definition of third normal form, and so on. Although each normal form solved some of the problems that had been identified with the previous one, no one could know what problems had not yet been identified. With each step, progress was made toward a well-structured database design, but no one could guarantee that no more anomalies would be found. In this section, we study a normal form that guarantees that there will be no anomalies of any type. When we put relations into that form, we know that even the obscure anomalies associated with fifth normal form cannot occur.

In 1981, Fagin published an important paper in which he defined domain/key normal form (DK/NF).[4] He showed that a relation in DK/NF has no modification anomalies and that a relation having no modification anomalies must be in DK/NF. This finding establishes a bound on the definition of normal forms, so no higher normal form is needed—at least in order to eliminate modification anomalies.

Equally important, DK/NF involves only the concepts of key and domain—concepts that are fundamental and close to the heart of database practitioners. They are readily supported by DBMS products (or could be, at least). In a sense, Fagin's work formalized and justified what many practitioners believed intuitively, but were unable to express precisely.

Definition

In concept, DK/NF is quite simple: A relation is in DK/NF if every constraint on the relation is a logical consequence of the definition of keys and domains. Consider the important terms in this definition: constraint, key, and domain.

Constraint in this definition is intended to be very broad. Fagin defines a constraint as any rule governing static values of attributes that is precise enough so that we can ascertain whether or not it is true. Edit rules, intrarelation and interrelation constraints, functional dependencies, and multi-value dependencies are examples of such constraints. Fagin expressly excludes constraints pertaining to changes in data values or time-dependent constraints. For example, the rule "Salesperson salary in the current period can never be less than salary in the prior period" is excluded from Fagin's definition of constraint. Except for time-dependent constraints, Fagin's definition is both broad and inclusive.

---

[3] Celko, Joe. SQL for Smarties, Second Edition. *San Francisco: Morgan Kaufman, 2000.*
[4] Fagin, pp. 387–414.

A **key** is a unique identifier of a row, as we have already defined. The third significant term in the definition of DK/NF is **domain**. In Chapter 2, we defined domain as a named set of possible attribute values. Fagin's proof says a domain constraint has been satisfied if attribute values meet the restrictions of the domain definition.

Informally, a relation is in DK/NF if enforcing key and domain restrictions causes all of the constraints to be met. Moreover, because relations in DK/NF cannot have modification anomalies, the DBMS can prohibit them by enforcing key and domain restrictions.

Unfortunately, there is no known algorithm for converting a relation to DK/NF, nor is it even known which relations can be converted to DK/NF. Finding or designing DK/NF relations is more art than a science.

In spite of this, DK/NF is an exceedingly useful design objective in the practical world of database design. If we can define relations so that constraints on them are logical consequences of domains and keys, there will be no modification anomalies. For many designs, this objective can be accomplished. When it cannot, the constraints must be built into the logic of application programs that process the database.

The following three examples illustrate DK/NF.

Example 1 of Domain/Key Normal Form

Consider the STUDENT relation in Figure 4-14, which contains attributes SID, GradeLevel, Dorm, and Fee. Dorm is the dorm in which the student lives, and Fee is the amount the student pays to live in that dorm.

SID functionally determines the other three attributes, so SID is a key. Assume we also know from the requirements definition that Dorm → Fee and that SIDs must not begin with 1. If we can express these constraints as logical consequences of domain and key definitions, we can be certain, according to Fagin's theorem, that there will be no modification anomalies. For this example, it will be easy.

To enforce the constraint that student numbers not begin with 1, we simply define the domain for student numbers to incorporate this constraint (see Figure 4-15). Enforcing the domain restriction guarantees that this constraint will be met.

Next, we need to make the functional dependency Dorm → Fee a logical consequence of keys. If Dorm were a key attribute, Dorm → Fee would be a logical consequence of a key. Therefore, the question becomes how to make Dorm a key. It cannot be

FIGURE 4-14

Example 1 of DK/NF

STUDENT (<u>SID</u>, GradeLevel, Dorm, Fee)

Key: SID

Constraints: Dorm → Fee
 SID must not begin with digit 1

FIGURE 4-15

Domain Key Definition for Example 1

Domain Definitions:

Attribute	Domain Name	Values
SID	StudentID	4 decimal digits, first digit not 1
GradeLevel	StudentYear	{'FR', 'SO', 'JR', 'SN', 'GR'}
Dorm	BuildingNames	Char(4)
Fee	StudentFees	Any currency value

Relation and Key Definitions:

STUDENT (<u>SID</u>, GradeLevel, Dorm)

BLDG-FEE (<u>Dorm</u>, Fee)

a key in STUDENT because more than one student lives in the same dorm, but it can be a key of its own relation. Thus, we define the relation BLDG-FEE with Dorm and Fee as its attributes. Dorm is the key of this relation. Having defined this new relation, we can remove Fee from STUDENT. The final domain and relation definitions for this example appear in Figure 4-15.

This is the same result we obtained when converting a relation from 2NF to 3NF to remove transitive dependencies. In this case, however, the process was simpler and the result more robust. It was simpler because we did not need to know that we were eliminating a transitive dependency. We simply needed to find creative ways to make all the constraints logical consequences of domain and key definitions. The result was more robust because when converting the relation to 3NF, we knew only that it had fewer anomalies than when it was in 2NF. By converting the relation to DK/NF, we know that the relations have no modification anomalies whatsoever.

Example 2 of Domain/Key Normal Form

The next more complicated example involves the relation shown in Figure 4-16. The PROFESSOR relation contains data about professors, the classes they teach, and the students they advise. FID (for Faculty ID) and Fname uniquely identify a professor. SID uniquely identifies a student, but Sname does not necessarily identify a SID. Professors can teach several classes and advise several students, but a student is advised by only one professor. FIDs start with a 1, but SIDs must not start with a 1.

These statements can be expressed more precisely by the functional and multi-value dependencies shown in Figure 4-16. FID and Fname functionally determine each other (in essence, they are equivalent). FID and Fname multi-determine Class and SID. SID functionally determines FID and Fname. SID determines Sname.

In more complex examples such as this one, it is helpful to consider DK/NF from a more intuitive light. Remember that the essence of normalization is that every relation should have a single theme. Considered from this perspective, there are three themes in PROFESSOR. One is the correspondence between FIDs and Fnames; the second concerns the classes that a professor teaches; and the third concerns the identification number, name, and adviser of a given student.

Figure 4-17 shows three relations that reflect these themes. The FACULTY relation represents the equivalence of FID and Fname. FID is the key and Fname is an alternative key, which means that both attributes are unique to the relation. Because both are keys, the functional dependencies FID → Fname and Fname → FID are logical consequences of keys.

The PREPARATION relation contains the correspondence of faculty and classes; it shows the classes that a professor is prepared to teach. The key is the combination (Fname, Class). Both attributes are required in the key because a professor may teach several classes, and a class may be taught by several professors. Finally, STUDENT represents the student and adviser names for a particular SID. Observe that each of these relations has a

FIGURE 4–16

Example 2 of DK/NF

PROFESSOR (<u>FID</u>, Fname, <u>Class</u>, <u>SID</u>, Sname)

Constraints:
FID → Fname
Fname → FID
FID → → Class | SID
Fname → → Class | SID
SID → FID
SID → Fname
SID → Sname
FID must start with 1; SID must not start with 1

FIGURE 4–17

**Domain Key Definition
for Example 2**

Domain Definitions:

Attribute	Domain Name	Values
FID	FacultyID	4 decimal digits, first digit is 1
Fname	PersonNames	Char(50)
Class	ClassNames	Char(10); values {list of valid course names}
SID	StudentID	4 decimal digits, first digit is not 1
Sname	PersonNames	Char(50)

Relation and Key Definitions:

FACULTY (<u>FID</u>, Fname)

Candidate key: Fname

PREPARATION (<u>Fname</u>, <u>Class</u>)

STUDENT (<u>SID</u>, Sname, Fname)

single theme. These relations express all of the constraints of Figure 4-16 as a logical consequence of domains and key definitions. These relations are, therefore, in DK/NF.

Note that separating the PREPARATION theme from the STUDENT theme has eliminated the multi-value dependencies. When we examined fourth normal form, we found that in order to eliminate multi-value dependencies, we had to separate the multi-value attributes into different relations. Our approach here is to break a relation with several themes into several relations, each with one theme. In doing that, we eliminated a multi-value dependency. In fact, we arrived at the same solution using both approaches.

Example 3 of Domain/Key Normal Form

The next example concerns a situation that was not addressed by any of the other normal forms, but occurs frequently in practice. This relation has a constraint among data values within a tuple that is neither a functional dependency nor a multi-value dependency.

Consider the constraints in the relation STU-ADVISER illustrated in Figure 4-18. This relation contains information about a student and his or her adviser. SID determines Sname, FID, Fname, and GradFacultyStatus, so it is therefore the key. FID and Fname identify a unique faculty member and are equivalent to each other, as in Example 2. Both FID and Fname determine GradFacultyStatus. Finally, the new type of constraint is that only members of the graduate faculty are allowed to advise graduate students.

FIGURE 4–18

Example 3 of DK/NF

STU-ADVISER (SID, Sname, FID, Fname, GradFacultyStatus)

Key: SID

Constraints: FID $\twoheadrightarrow$ Fname
Fname $\twoheadrightarrow$ FID
FID and Fname $\twoheadrightarrow$ GradFacultyStatus
Only graduate faculty can advise graduate students
FID begins with 1
SID must not begin with 1
SID of graduate student begins with 9
GradFacultyStatus = $\begin{cases} 0 \text{ for undergraduate faculty} \\ 1 \text{ for graduate faculty} \end{cases}$

The domain restrictions are that SID must not begin with a 1, SID must begin with a 9 for graduate students, FID must begin with a 1, and GradFacultyStatus is 0 for undergraduate faculty and 1 for graduate faculty. With these domain definitions, the constraint that graduate students must be advised by graduate faculty can be expressed as a constraint on row values. Specifically, if the SID starts with 9, the value of GradFacultyStatus must be 1.

To put this relation in DK/NF, we proceed as in Example 2. What are the basic themes of this relation? There is one regarding faculty personnel that relates FID, Fname, and GradFacultyStatus. Because FID and Fname determine GradFacultyStatus, either of these attributes can be the key, and this relation is in DK/NF (see Figure 4-19).

Now, consider the data regarding students and advisers. Although it may first appear that there is only one theme, that of advising, the constraint that only graduate faculty can advise graduate students implies otherwise. Actually, there are two themes: graduate advising and undergraduate advising. Thus, Figure 4-19 contains a G_ADV relation for graduate students and a UG_ADV relation for undergraduates. Look at the domain definitions: GSID starts with a 9, Gfname is the Fname of a FACULTY tuple with GradFacultyStatus equal to 1, and UGSID must not begin with 1 or 9. All the constraints described in Figure 4-18 are implied by the key and domain definitions shown in Figure 4-19. These relations are therefore in DK/NF and have no modification anomalies.

To summarize the discussion of normalization, Figure 4-20 lists the normal forms and presents the defining characteristic of each.

FIGURE 4–19

Doman Key Definition for Example 3

Domain Definitions:

Attribute	Domain Name	Values
FID	FacultyID	4 decimal digits, first digit is 1
Fname	PersonNames	Char(50)
GradFacultyStatus	FacultyStatus	Values {0, 1}
GSID	GradStudentID	4 decimal digits, first digit is 9
UGSID	UnderGradStudentID	4 decimal digits, first digit is not 1 and not 9
Sname	PersonNames	Char(50)
Gfname	PersonNames	Values {FACULTY.Fname where GradFacultyStatus = 1 }

Relation and Key Definitions:

FACULTY (<u>FID</u>, Fname, GradFacultyStatus)

    Candidate key: Fname

G_ADV (<u>GSID</u>, Sname, Gfname)

UG_ADV (<u>UGSID</u>, Sname, Fname)

FIGURE 4–20

Summary of Normal Forms

Form	Defining Characteristic
1NF	Any relation
2NF	All nonkey attributes are dependent on all of each key.
3NF	There are no transitive dependencies.
BCNF	Every determinant is a candidate key.
4NF	There are no multi-valued dependencies.
5NF	Not described in this discussion.
DK/NF	All constraints on relations are logical consequences of domains and keys.

▶ THE SYNTHESIS OF RELATIONS

In the previous section, we approached relational design from an analytical perspective. The questions we asked were these: "Given a relation, is it in good form? Does it have modification anomalies?" In this section, we look at relational design from a different perspective—a synthetic one. From this perspective, we ask, "Given a set of attributes with certain functional dependencies, what relations should we form?"

First, observe that two attributes (A and B, for example) can be related in three ways:

1. They determine each other:
    A → B and B → A
    Hence, A and B have a one-to-one attribute relationship.
2. One determines the other.
    A → B, but B not → A
    Hence, A and B have a many-to-one relationship.
3. They are functionally unrelated.
    A not → B and B not → A
    Hence, A and B have a many-to-many attribute relationship.

One-to-One Attribute Relationships

If A determines B and B determines A, the values of the attributes have a one-to-one relationship. This must be because if A determines B, the relationship between A and B is many-to-one. It is also true, however, that if B determines A, the relationship between B and A must be many-to-one. For both statements to be true at the same time, the relationship between A and B must actually be one-to-one (which is a special case of many-to-one), and the relationship between B and A is also actually one-to-one. Therefore, the relationship is one-to-one.

This case is illustrated by FID and Fname in Examples 2 and 3 in the previous section on domain/key normal form. Each of these attributes uniquely identifies a faculty person. Consequently, one value of FID corresponds to exactly one value of Fname, and vice versa.

Three equivalent statements can be drawn from the example of FID and Fname:

> If two attributes functionally determine each other, the relationship of their data values is one-to-one.
> If two attributes uniquely identify the same entity, the relationship of their data values is one-to-one.
> If two attributes have a one-to-one relationship, they functionally determine each other.

When creating a database with attributes that have a one-to-one relationship, the two attributes must occur together in at least one relation. Other attributes that are functionally determined by these (an attribute that is functionally determined by one of them is functionally determined by the other as well) may also reside in this same relation.

Consider FACULTY (FID, Fname, GradFacultyStatus) in Example 3 in the previous section. FID and Fname determine each other. GradFacultyStatus can also occur in this relation because it is determined by FID and Fname. Attributes that are not functionally determined by these attributes may not occur in a relation with them. Consider the relations FACULTY and PREPARATION in Example 2, in which both FID and Fname occur in FACULTY, but Class (from PREPARATION) may not. Class can have multiple values for a faculty member, so Class is not dependent on FID or Fname. If we added Class to the FACULTY relation, the key of FACULTY would need to be either (FID, Class) or (Fname, Class). In this case, however, FACULTY would not be in

DK/NF because the dependencies between FID and Fname would not be logically implied by either of the possible keys.

These statements are summarized in the first column of Figure 4-21, and the record definition rules are listed in Figure 4-22. If A and B have a one-to-one relationship, they can reside in the same relation, say R. A determines B and B determines A. The key of the relation can be either A or B. A new attribute, C, can be added to R if either A or B functionally determines C.

Attributes having a one-to-one relationship must exist together in at least one relation in order to establish their equivalence (FID of 198, for example, refers to Professor Heart). It is generally undesirable to have them occur together in more than one relation, however, because this causes needless data duplication. Often, one or both of the two attributes occur in other relations. In Example 2, Fname occurs in both PREPARATION and STUDENT. Although it is possible to place Fname in PREPARATION and

FIGURE 4-21

Summary of Three Types of Attribute Relationships

Type of Attribute Relationship

	One to One	Many to One	Many to Many
Relation Definition*	R(A,B)	S(C,D)	T(E,F)
Dependencies	A → B B → A	C → D D ↛ C	E ↛ F F ↛ E
Key	Either A or B	C	(E,F)
Rule for Adding Another Attribute	Either A or B → C	C → E	(E,F) → G

* The letters used in these relation definitions match those used in Figure 4-22.

FIGURE 4-22

Summary of Rules for Constructing Relations

Concerning One-to-One Attribute Relationships

- Attributes that have a one-to-one relationship must occur together in at least one relation. Call the relation *R* and the attributes *A* and *B*.
- Either *A* or *B* must be the key of *R*.
- An attribute can be added to *R* if it is functionally determined by *A* or *B*.
- An attribute that is not functionally determined by *A* or *B* cannot be added to *R*.
- *A* and *B* must occur together in *R*, but should not occur together in other relations.
- Either *A* or *B* should be consistently used to represent the pair in relations other than *R*.

Concerning Many-to-One Attribute Relationships

- Attributes that have a many-to-one relationship can exist in a relation together. Assume *C* determines *D* in relation *S*.
- *C* must be the key of *S*.
- An attribute can be added to *S* if it is determined by *C*.
- An attribute that is not determined by *C* cannot be added to *S*.

Concerning Many-to-Many Attribute Relationships

- Attributes that have a many-to-many relationship can exist in a relation together. Assume two such attributes, *E* and *F*, reside together in relation *T*.
- The key of *T* must be (*E*, *F*).
- An attribute can be added to *T* if it is determined by the combination (*E*, *F*).
- An attribute may not be added to *T* if it is not determined by the combination (*E*, *F*).
- If adding a new attribute, *G*, expands the key to (*E*, *F*, *G*), then the theme of the relation has been changed. Either *G* does not belong in *T* or the name of *T* must be changed to reflect the new theme.

FID in STUDENT, this generally is bad practice because when attributes are paired in this way, one of them should be selected to represent the pair in all other relations. Fname was selected in Example 2.

Many-to-One Attribute Relationships

If attribute A determines B, but B does not determine A, the relationship among their data values is many-to-one. In the adviser relationship in Example 2, SID determines FID. Many students (SID) are advised by a faculty member (FID), but each student is advised by only one faculty member. This then is a many-to-one relationship.

For a relation to be in DK/NF, all constraints must be implied by keys, so every determinant must be a key. If A, B, and C are in the same relation, and if A determines B, then A must be the key (meaning it also determines C). If instead (A, B) determines C, (A, B) must be the key. In this latter case, no other functional dependency, such as A determines B, is allowed.

You can apply these statements to database design in the following way: If A determines B when constructing a relation, the only other attributes you can add to the relation must also be determined by A. For example, suppose you put SID and Dorm together in a relation called STUDENT. You may add any other attribute determined by SID, such as Sname, to this relation. But if the attribute Fee is determined by Dorm, you may not add it to this relation. Fee can be added only if SID → Fee.

These statements are summarized in the center column of Figure 4-21. If C and D have an N:1 relationship, they may reside together in a relation (S, for example). C will determine D, but D will not determine C. The key of S will be C. Another attribute, E, can be added to S only if C determines E.

Many-to-Many Attribute Relationships

If A does not determine B and B does not determine A, the relationship among their data values is many-to-many. In Example 2, Fname and Class have a many-to-many relationship. A professor teaches many classes and a class is taught by many professors. In a many-to-many relationship, both attributes must be a key of the relation. For instance, the key of PREPARATION in Example 2 is the combination (Fname, Class).

When constructing relations that have multiple attributes as keys, you can add new attributes that are functionally dependent on all of the key. NumberOfTimesTaught is functionally dependent on both (Fname, Class) and can be added to the relation. FacultyOffice, however, cannot be added because it would be dependent only on Fname, not on Class. If FacultyOffice needs to be stored in the database, it must be added to the relation regarding faculty, not to the relation regarding preparations.

These statements are summarized in the right column of Figure 4-21. If E and F have an M:N relationship, E does not determine F and F does not determine E. Both E and F can be put into a relation T; if this is done, the key of T will be the composite (E, F). A new attribute, G, can be added to T if it is determined by all of (E, F). It cannot be added to T if it is determined by only one of E or F.

Consider a similar example. Suppose we add Classroom Number to PREPARATION. Is ClassroomNumber functionally determined by the key of PREPARATION, (Fname, Class)? Most likely it is not because a professor could teach a particular class in many different rooms.

The composite (Fname, Class) and ClassroomNumber have an M:N relationship. Because this is so, the rules in Figure 4-21 can be applied, but with E representing (Fname, Class) and F representing ClassroomNumber. Now we can compose a new relation, T, with attributes Fname, Class, and ClassroomNumber. The key becomes (Fname, Class, ClassroomNumber). In this situation, we have created a new relation with a new theme. Consider relation T, which contains faculty names, classes, and classroom numbers. The theme of this relation is therefore no longer PREPARATION, but instead is WHO-WHAT-WHERE-TAUGHT.

Changing the theme may or may not be appropriate. If ClassroomNumber is important, the theme does need to be changed. In that case, PREPARATION is the wrong relation, and WHO-WHAT-WHERE-TAUGHT is a more suitable theme.

On the other hand, depending on user requirements, PREPARATION may be completely suitable as it is. If so, then if ClassroomNumber belongs in the database at all, it should be located in a different relation—perhaps SECTION-NUMBER, CLASS-SECTION, or some similar relation.

▶ MULTI-VALUE DEPENDENCIES, ITERATION 2

The discussion about many-to-many attribute value relationships may make the concept of multi-value dependencies easier to understand. The problem with the relation STUDENT (SID, Major, Activity) in Figure 4-11 is that it has *two* different many-to-many relationships—one between SID and Major and the other between SID and Activity. Clearly, a student's various majors have nothing to do with his or her various activities. Putting both of these many-to-many relationships in the same relation, however, makes it appear as if there is some association.

Major and Activity are independent, and there is no problem if a student has only one of each. SID functionally determines Major and Activity, and the relation is in DK/NF. In this case, both the relationships between Major and SID and Activity and SID are many-to-one.

Another way of perceiving the difficulty is to examine the key (SID, Major, Activity). Because STUDENT has many-to-many relationships, all of the attributes have to be in the key. Now what theme does this key represent? We might say the combination of a student's studies and activities. But this is not one thing; it is plural. One row of this relation describes only part of the combination, and we need all of the rows about a particular student in order to get the whole picture. *In general, a row should have all of the data about one instance of the relation's theme.* A row of Customer, for example, should have all the data we want about a particular customer.

Consider PREPARATION in Example 2 in the section on domain/key normal form. The key is (Fname, Class). The theme this represents is that a particular professor is prepared to teach a particular class. We need only one row of the relation to get all of the information we have about the combination of that professor and that class. Looking at more rows does not generate any more information about it.

As you know, the solution to the multi-value dependency constraint problem is to split the relation into two relations, each with a single theme. STU-MAJOR shows the combination of a student and a major. Everything we know about the combination is in a single row, and we will not gain more information about that combination by examining more rows.

▶ DE-NORMALIZED DESIGNS

The techniques of normalization are designed to eliminate anomalies by reducing data duplication to key values. Although this goal is usually appropriate, there are situations in which de-normalized designs are preferred. In particular, when a normalized design is unnatural, awkward, or results in unacceptable performance, a de-normalized design is better.

Normalization Unnatural

Consider the relation:

CUSTOMER (<u>CustNumber</u>, CustName, City, State, Zip)

This relation is not in domain/key normal form because it contains the functional dependency Zip → (City, State) that is not implied by CustNumber, the key. Thus, there is a constraint that is not implied by domains and keys.

Following the usual normalization procedure, we can break this relation into two relations that are in domain/key normal form:

CUSTOMER (CustNumber, CustName, Zip)

CODES (Zip, City, State)

with the referential integrity constraint that values of CUSTOMER.Zip must already exist in CODES.Zip.

These two tables are in domain/key normal form, but they most likely do not represent a better design. Every time a user wants to know a customer's city and state, a lookup in the CODES table (meaning to read the row that has the appropriate city and state data) is required. If the design were not normalized, the city and state data would be stored with the rest of the customer data and no lookup would be necessary. Further, the disadvantages of duplicating the city and state data are probably not very important.

Normalization Awkward

For another example of de-normalization, consider the following relation:

COLLEGE (CollegeName, Dean, AssistantDean)

and suppose that a college has one dean and from one to three assistant deans. In this case, the key of the table is (CollegeName, AssistantDean). This table is not in domain/key normal form because the constraint CollegeName → Dean is not a logical consequence of the table's key.

COLLEGE can be normalized into the following relation:

DEAN (CollegeName, Dean)

and the following relation:

ASSISTANT-DEAN(CollegeName, AssistantDean)

But now, whenever a database application needs to obtain data about the college, it must read at least two rows and possibly as many as four rows of data. An alternative to this design is to place all three AssistantDeans into the COLLEGE table, each in a separate attribute. The table is then the following:

COLLEGE1 (CollegeName, Dean, AssistantDean1, AssistantDean2, AssistantDean3)

COLLEGE1 is in domain/key normal form because all of its attributes are functionally dependent on the key CollegeName. But something has been lost. To see what is lost, suppose that you want to determine the names of the COLLEGEs that have an assistant dean named 'Mary Abernathy.' To do this, you have to look for this value in each of the three AssistantDean columns. Your query would appear something like this:[5]

---

[5] These statements are examples of SQL, a relational language that we will discuss in detail in Chapters 6 and 7. For now, just think of them intuitively; you will learn the format of them in that chapter.

```
SELECT      CollegeName
FROM        COLLEGE1
WHERE       AssistantDean1 = 'Mary Abernathy' OR
            AssistantDean2 = 'Mary Abernathy' OR
            AssistantDean3 = 'Mary Abernathy'
```

Using the normalized design with ASSISTANT-DEAN, you would need only to state the following:

```
SELECT      CollegeName
FROM        ASSISTANT-DEAN
WHERE       AssistantDean = 'Mary Abernathy'
```

Thus, there are three possible designs. The first design is un-normalized and duplicates dean data. The second one is normalized, but it requires processing two to four rows to obtain all of the college data; the third is normalized, but it is awkward to process.

Which design is best? It depends on the requirements, the workload, the size of the database, and so forth. If few colleges have more than one assistant dean, the first design is probably acceptable. If any college can have more than three assistant deans, the last design is infeasible. This last design also feels wrong on an aesthetic basis. There are three columns that represent the same attribute, and usually only one column is used for an attribute.

The point of this example is to show that sometimes a design team must consider criteria other than normalization.

Normalization Can Cause Poor Performance

Consider a mail order company that uses a database with the following table, which is in domain/key normal form:

ITEM   (ItemNumber, Name, Color, Description, Picture, QuantityOnHand, QuantityOnOrder, Price)

Assume this table is used to prepare the monthly catalog and to support order processing. To support catalog production, Description is a long memo field that explains the features and benefits of the product. It may be 1000 bytes or longer. Even more problematic, Picture is a jpg-style image that can be as large as 256K bytes. For purposes of creating the catalog, such large attributes are not a problem because the table is processed just once in sequence.

The order processing application, however, accesses the ITEM table thousands of times and in random order, and fast performance is very important. Assume also that the order processing application does not need Description and Price. Unfortunately, depending on the characteristics of the DBMS in use, the presence of the two large attributes Description and Picture may significantly slow retrieval and update performance.

If this is the case, the designers might decide to create a second table that contains a duplicate copy of data needed by the order processing application. They may create, for example, a table like the following with duplicate data used only by order processing:

ORDERITEM   (ItemNumber, Name, Color, QuantityOnHand, QuantityOnOrder, Price)

Now, both of these tables are normalized, so you might say this design is not really a normalization problem. But the purpose of normalization is to reduce data duplication to prevent anomalies and integrity problems. By duplicating the data, the designers are forcing multiple updates to record a single fact. This is akin to an insertion anomaly, even if the insertion occurs on two different tables.

Such a duplicate table design creates a potential for serious data integrity problems. The designers will need to develop both automated and manual controls to ensure that both copies of the data are updated in a consistent manner. Before implementing this design, the developers need to ensure that the increased performance will be worth the cost of the controls and the risk of integrity problems.

Another reason for duplicating data is to support query and reporting applications. You will see examples of such duplication by using what is called a **star schema** when we discuss OLAP processing in Chapter 15.

SUMMARY

The relational model is the industry standard for database processing today. It was first published by E. F. Codd in 1970. At first, it was deemed too theoretical, but it was used for high-volume transaction processing in organizations by the 1980s, thanks to DBMS products such as DB2 and Oracle.

A relation is a two-dimensional table that has the characteristics listed in Figure 4-1. In this book and in the database world in general, the term *table* is used synonymously with relation. Three sets of terminology are used for relational structures. *Table, row,* and *column* are most commonly used, but *file* (or *datafile*), *record,* and *field* are sometimes used in traditional data processing. Theorists also use *relation, tuple,* and *attribute* for the same three constructs. Sometimes, these terms are mixed and matched. Strictly speaking, a relation may not have duplicate rows; sometimes this condition is relaxed, however, because eliminating duplicates can be a time-consuming process.

A key is one or more columns of a relation that is used to identify a row. A unique key identifies a single row; a non-unique key identifies several rows. A composite key is a key having two or more attributes. A relation has one primary key, which must be a unique key. A relation may also have additional unique keys, which are called candidate keys. A primary key is used to represent the table in relationships, and many DBMS products use values of the primary key to organize table storage. Also, an index is normally constructed to give fast access by primary key values.

A functional dependency occurs when the value of one attribute (or set of attributes) determines the value of a second attribute (or set of attributes). The attribute on the left side of the functional dependency is called the determinant. One way to view the purpose of a relation is to say that the relation exists to store instances of functional dependencies. Another way to define a primary (and candidate key) is to say that such a key is an attribute that functionally determines all of the other attributes in a relation.

When updated, some relations suffer from undesirable consequences called modification anomalies. A deletion anomaly occurs when the deletion of a row loses information about two or more entities. An insertion anomaly occurs when the relational structure forces the addition of facts about two entities at the same time. Anomalies can be removed by splitting the relation into two or more relations.

There are many types of modification anomalies. Relations can be classified by the types of anomaly that they eliminate. Such classifications are called normal forms.

By definition, every relation is in first normal form. A relation is in second normal form if all non-key attributes are dependent on all of the key. A relation is in third normal form if it is in second normal form and has no transitive dependencies. A relation is in Boyce–Codd normal form if every determinant is a candidate key. A relation is in fourth normal form if it is in Boyce–Codd normal form and has no multi-value dependencies. The definition of fifth normal form is intuitively obscure, so we did not define it.

A relation is in domain/key normal form if every constraint on the relation is a logical consequence of the definition of domains and keys. A constraint is any constraint on the static values of attributes whose truth can be evaluated. A domain is a named set of values that an attribute can have.

In addition to normalization, which is a process of analyzing relations, it is also possible to construct well-formed relations by synthesis, according to the relationship between attribute values. If two attributes functionally determine each other, they have a one-to-one relationship. If one attribute functionally determines the other, but not the reverse, the attributes have a many-to-one relationship. If neither attribute determines the other, they have a many-to-many relationship. These facts can be used when constructing relations, as summarized in Figure 4-22.

In some cases, normalization is not desirable. Whenever a table is split into two or more tables, extra processing is required when the tables are later rejoined. Also, referential integrity constraints need to be enforced. If the cost of the extra processing of the two tables and their integrity constraint is greater than the benefit of avoiding modification anomalies, normalization is not recommended. In some cases, creating repeating columns is preferred to the standard normalization techniques; and in other cases, controlled redundancy is used to improve performance.

GROUP I QUESTIONS

4.1 What restrictions must be placed on a table for it to be considered a relation?

4.2 Define the following terms: *relation, tuple, attribute, file, record, field, table, row, column.*

4.3 Define *functional dependency.* Give an example of two attributes that have a functional dependency and give an example of two attributes that do not have a functional dependency.

4.4 If SID functionally determines Activity, does this mean that only one value of SID can exist in the relation? Why or why not?

4.5 Define *determinant.*

4.6 Give an example of a relation having a functional dependency in which the determinant has two or more attributes.

4.7 Define *key.*

4.8 If SID is a key of a relation, is it a determinant? Can a given value of SID occur more than once in the relation?

4.9 What is a deletion anomaly? Give an example other than one in this text.

4.10 What is an insertion anomaly? Give an example other than one in this text.

4.11 Explain the relationship of first, second, third, Boyce–Codd, fourth, fifth, and domain/key normal forms.

4.12 Define *second normal form.* Give an example of a relation in 1NF, but not in 2NF. Transform the relation into relations in 2NF.

4.13 Define *third normal form.* Give an example of a relation in 2NF, but not in 3NF. Transform the relation into relations in 3NF.

4.14 Define *BCNF.* Give an example of a relation in 3NF, but not in BCNF. Transform the relation into relations in BCNF.

4.15 Define *multi-value dependency.* Give an example.

4.16 Why are multi-value dependencies not a problem in relations with only two attributes?

4.17 Define *fourth normal form.* Give an example of a relation in BCNF, but not in 4NF. Transform the relation into relations in 4NF.

4.18 Define *domain/key normal form.* Why is it important?

4.19 Transform the following relation into DK/NF. Make and state the appropriate assumptions about functional dependencies and domains.

EQUIPMENT (Manufacturer, Model, AcquisitionDate, BuyerName, BuyerPhone, PlantLocation, City, State, ZIP)

4.20 Transform the following relation into DK/NF. Make and state the appropriate assumptions about functional dependencies and domains.

INVOICE (Number, CustomerName, CustomerNumber, CustomerAddress, ItemNumber, ItemPrice, ItemQuantity, SalespersonNumber, SalespersonName, Subtotal, Tax, TotalDue)

4.21 Answer question 4.20 again, but this time add attribute CustomerTaxStatus (0 if nonexempt, 1 if exempt). Also, add the constraint that there will be no tax if CustomerTaxStatus = 1.

4.22 Give an example, other than one in this text, in which you would judge normalization to be not worthwhile. Show the relations and justify your design.

4.23 Explain two situations in which database designers might intentionally choose to create data duplication. What is the risk of such designs?

GROUP II QUESTIONS

4.24 Consider the following relation definition and sample data:

PROJECT Relation

ProjectID	EmployeeName	EmployeeSalary
100A	Jones	64K
100A	Smith	51K
100B	Smith	51K
200A	Jones	64K
200B	Jones	64K
200C	Parks	28K
200C	Smith	51K
200D	Parks	28K

PROJECT (ProjectID, EmployeeName, EmployeeSalary)

Where ProjectID is the name of a work project

EmployeeName is the name of an employee who works on that project

EmployeeSalary is the salary of the employee whose name is EmployeeName

Assuming that all of the functional dependencies and constraints are apparent in this data, which of the following statements is true?

A. ProjectID → EmployeeName

B. ProjectID → EmployeeSalary

C. (ProjectID, EmployeeName) → EmployeeSalary

D. EmployeeName → EmployeeSalary

E. EmployeeSalary → ProjectID

F. EmployeeSalary → (ProjectID, EmployeeName)

Answer these questions:

G. What is the key of PROJECT?

H. Are all non-key attributes (if any) dependent on all of the key?

I. In what normal form is PROJECT?

J. Describe two modification anomalies from which PROJECT suffers.

K. Is ProjectID a determinant?

L. Is EmployeeName a determinant?

M. Is (ProjectID, EmployeeName) a determinant?

N. Is EmployeeSalary a determinant?

O. Does this relation contain a partial-key problem? If so, what is it?

P. Redesign this relation to eliminate the modification anomalies.

4.25 Consider the following relation definition and sample data:

PROJECT-HOURS Relation

EmployeeName	ProjectID	TaskID	Phone	TotalHours
Don	100A	B-1	12345	12
Don	100A	P-1	12345	12
Don	200B	B-1	12345	12
Don	200B	P-1	12345	12
Pam	100A	C-1	67890	26
Pam	200A	C-1	67890	26
Pam	200D	C-1	67890	26

PROJECT-HOURS (EmployeeName, ProjectID, TaskID, Phone, TotalHours)

Where EmployeeName is the name of an employee

ProjectID is the name of a project

TaskID is the name standard work task

Phone is the employee's telephone number

TotalHours is the hours worked by the employee on this project

Assuming that all of the functional dependencies and constraints are apparent in this data, which of the following statements is true?

A. EmployeeName → ProjectID

B. EmployeeName →→ ProjectID

C. EmployeeName → TaskID

D. EmployeeName →→ TaskID

E. EmployeeName → Phone

F. EmployeeName → TotalHours

G. (EmployeeName, ProjectID) → TotalHours

H. (EmployeeName, Phone) → TaskID

I. ProjectID → TaskID

J. TaskID → ProjectID

Answer these questions:

K. What are all of the determinants?

L. Does this relation contain a partial-key problem? If so, what is it?

M. Does this relation contain a multi-value dependency? If so, what are the unrelated attributes?

N. What is the deletion anomaly that this relation contains?

O. How many themes does this relation have?

P. Redesign this relation to eliminate the modification anomalies. How many relations did you use? How many themes does each of your new relations contain?

4.26 Consider the following domain, relation, and key definitions:

Domain Definitions

EmployeeName	in	Names values CHAR(20)
PhoneNumber	in	Phones values DEC(5)
EquipmentName	in	ENames values CHAR(10)
Location	in	Places values CHAR(7)
Cost	in	Money values CURRENCY
Date	in	Dates values YYMMDD
Time	in	Times values HHMM where HH between 00 and 23 and MM between 00 and 59

Definitions of Relation, Key, and Constraint

EMPLOYEE (EmployeeName, PhoneNumber)
   Key: EmployeeName
   Constraints: EmployeeName → PhoneNumber
EQUIPMENT (EquipmentName, Location, Cost)
   Key: EquipmentName
   Constraints: EquipmentName → Location
          EquipmentName → Cost
APPOINTMENT (Date, Time, EquipmentName, EmployeeName)
   Key: (Date, Time, EquipmentName)
   Constraints: (Date, Time, EquipmentName) → EmployeeName

A. Modify the definitions to enforce this constraint: An employee may not sign up for more than one equipment appointment.

B. Define nighttime to refer to the hours between 2100 and 0500. Add an attribute Employee Type whose value is 1 if the employee works during nighttime. Change this design to enforce the constraint that only employees who work at night can schedule nighttime appointments.

FIREDUP PROJECT QUESTIONS

FiredUp hired a team of database designers (who should have been fired!) to create the following relations for a database to keep track of their stove, repair, and customer data. See the projects at the end of Chapters 1 through 3 to review their needs. For each of the following relations, specify candidate keys, functional dependencies, and multi-valued dependencies (if any). Justify these specifications unless they are obvious. Given your specifications about keys and so on, what normal form does each relation have? Transform each relation into two or more relations that are in domain/key normal form. Indicate the primary key of each table, candidate keys, foreign keys; and specify any referential integrity constraints.

In answering these questions, assume the following:

> Stove type and version determine tank capacity.
> A stove can be repaired many times, but never more than once on a given day.
> Each stove repair has its own repair invoice.
> A stove can be registered to different users, but never at the same time.
> A stove has many component parts and each component part can be used on many stoves. Thus, FiredUp maintains records about part types, such as *burner valve,* and not about particular parts such as burner valve number 41734 manufactured on 12 December 2003.

A. PRODUCT1 (SerialNumber, Type, VersionNumber, TankCapacity, DateOfManufacture, InspectorInitials)

B. PRODUCT2 (SerialNumber, Type, TankCapacity, RepairDate, RepairInvoiceNumber, RepairCost)

C. REPAIR1 (RepairInvoiceNumber, RepairDate, RepairCost, RepairEmployeeName, RepairEmployeePhone)

D. REPAIR2 (RepairInvoiceNumber, RepairDate, RepairCost, RepairEmployeeName, RepairEmployeePhone, SerialNumber, Type, TankCapacity)

E. REPAIR3 (RepairDate, RepairCost, SerialNumber, DateOfManufacture)

F. STOVE1 (SerialNumber, RepairInvoiceNumber, ComponentPartNumber)

G. STOVE2 (SerialNumber, RepairInvoiceNumber, RegisteredOwnerID)

Assume there is a need to record the owner of a stove, even if it has never been repaired.

H. Given the assumptions of this case, the relations and attributes in items A–G and your knowledge of small business, construct a set of domain/key relations for FiredUp. Indicate primary keys, foreign keys, and referential integrity constraints.

TWIGS TREE TRIMMING SERVICE PROJECT QUESTIONS

Samantha hired a team of database designers who created the following relations for a database to keep track of her customer, service, chip, and related data. See the projects at the end of Chapters 1 through 3 to review her needs. For each of the following relations, specify candidate keys, functional dependencies, and multi-valued dependencies (if any). Justify these specifications unless they are obvious. Given your specifications about keys, etc., what normal form does each relation have? Transform each relation into two or more relations that are in domain/key normal form. Indicate the primary key of each table, candidate keys, foreign keys; and specify any referential integrity constraints. In answering these questions, assume the following:

> Customers can request multiple services, but only one service on a given day.
> Samantha creates one invoice for all services performed for a customer on a given day, but customers sometimes make partial payments on a given invoice.
> A given tree species can receive multiple types of service and is also susceptible to multiple diseases.
> A customer owns only one property.
> Customers do move, but they leave their trees behind. When they move, they may or may not change their phone numbers. Either way, Samantha wants to continue to track the customers.
> Customers can have multiple services and multiple chip deliveries.

A. CUSTOMER1 (Name, Phone, Street, City, State, Zip, AppointmentDate, ServiceRequested)

B. CUSTOMER2 (Name, Phone, Street, City, State, Zip, AppointmentDate, ServiceRequested, InvoiceNumber, AmountBilled, DatePaid, AmountPaid)

C. TREE (Customer, Street, City, State, Zip, LocationOnProperty, Species, ApproxAge, ServiceDate, ServiceDescription)

D. SPECIES (SpeciesName, Disease, ServiceType)

E. RECURRING_SERVICE (CustomerName, Phone, ServiceDescription, ServiceInterval, LastServiceDate)

F. CHIP_DELIVERY_REQUEST (CustomerName, Phone, DateOfRequest, DateOfDelivery)

CHAPTER 5

Database Design

This chapter discusses the transformation of entity-relationship data models into relational database designs. As you will see, the data model and other system requirements are input to the design process. Entities are transformed into tables, keys are defined, relationships are represented, and processing constraints are defined. The result is a relational database design that consists of relations, keys, and referential integrity constraints and actions.

We begin with an overview of this process.

▶ THE DATABASE DESIGN PROCESS

Figure 5-1 shows the components in the database design process. The data model and other systems requirements are used as a starting point. In all but the simplest cases, the data model will have been produced using a data modeling tool such as ERWin or Visio, and will exist in the format of a data file. Additional requirements, such as business rules or processing constraints, are documented in manual form outside of the data model.

The first step in building a database design is to create tables and columns from the data model entities and attributes

Creating Tables and Columns from Entities and Attributes

To transform an entity-relationship model into a relational database design, each entity is represented as a table. All attributes of the entity become columns of that table. By default, the identifier of the entity will become the primary key of the new table. Thus, the BUILDING entity in Figure 5-2(a) is transformed into the BUILDING relation or table in Figure 5-2(b). The identifier of the BUILDING entity, BuildingName, becomes the primary key of the BUILDING table.

FIGURE 5-1

Elements of Database Design

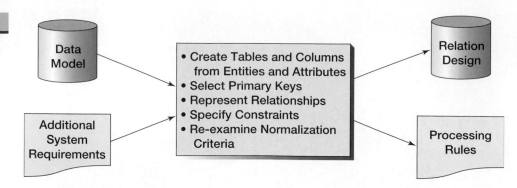

The diagrams in Figure 5-2 were drawn using ERWin. Notice the key symbol on BuildingName; this indicates that BuildingName is the primary key of the BUILDING table.

Unfortunately, the shape of the entity diagrams and the shape of the table diagrams are very similar. In this text, we distinguish between the two by shading the boxes that represent entities and not shading the boxes that represent tables. Still, these shapes are still very similar. Sometimes, designers use a diagram like that in Figure 5-2(c) to represent tables. In such tables, primary key attributes are shown underlined.

One of the important properties of an attribute is whether or not it is required. Some people believe this determination is part of the data model. If so, this decision would have been made during the data modeling stage. Others believe this determination should be made during the design phase. Either way, it must be done before the database design is complete. All primary keys are required. Foreign keys may or may not be required, as you will see. For other attributes, the system requirements determine whether or not an attribute value is required.

FIGURE 5-2

Transforming an Entity to a Table (a) BULDING Entity; (b) BUILDING Table and (c) Alternative Table Diagram

BUILDING

BuildingName
Street
City
State
Zip
Type
ManagerName

(a)

BUILDING

🔑 BuildingName: NOT NULL
Street: NULL
City: NOT NULL
State: NULL
Zip: NULL
Type: NULL
ManagerName: NULL

(b)

<u>BuildingName</u>	Street	City	State	Zip	Type	ManagerName

(c)

Figure 5-2(b) shows the words NULL or NOT NULL after each attribute. NULL means an attribute value is not required; NOT NULL means it is required. In this example, the database designers have determined from system requirements that only BuildingName and City are required. In Figure 5-2(c), required attributes are shown in bold typeface.

Selecting the Primary Key

The selection of the primary key is important. Most DBMS products build indexes on the primary key columns so that key values can be used to organize physical storage and to facilitate searching and sorting using primary key values. Further, as you will see, the values of primary keys are copied into other relations to represent relationships. For these reasons, an ideal primary key is short (so that it takes little storage and is fast to process), numeric (easy to index), and seldom changing (because key values may be placed in many different relations, all of which need to be changed when the key value is updated). Thus, a 32-bit integer part number is an ideal primary key.

As noted in Chapter 2, some tables may have more than one identifier. If so, it is important to choose the best of them for the primary key. For example, Figure 5-3 shows a DEPARTMENT table with DepartmentName as the identifier and with two candidate keys: BudgetCode and the composite {Building, Room}. In IDEF1X terminology, candidate keys are called **alternate keys**. The notation AK$n.m$ means the attribute is part of the nth alternate key, and the mth attribute in that key. Thus, the Building attribute is part of alternate key number 2 and is the first attribute in that key group.

During design, the team needs to review each table and primary key. If there are alternate identifiers, they should be evaluated and the best one chosen as the table's primary key. If the entity has no identifier, then an attribute needs to be selected as the identifier, or a surrogate key should be defined, as described in the following.

Given the criteria of short, numeric, and seldom-changing, the attribute BudgetCode in Figure 5-3 is probably the best choice for primary key. One could make the argument, however, that DepartmentName would be a better primary key because it is more natural to the users. Anyone can look at the value 'Accounting' and know what it means. Few people, however, can look at BudgetCode 10445 and know that it represents the accounting department. Therefore, as long as department names are reasonably short, DepartmentName could also be selected as the primary key.

Consider, however, the relation TREE shown in Figure 5-4(a). Assume this table is used by a tree trimming or spraying service. The primary key is the composite (Street, City, State, Zip, Location) where Location is a description of where the tree is located on the property. This key will be very long and will consequently be difficult to index. Additionally, consider what happens if this relation is a parent in a relationship.

For example, consider the ID-dependent table TREE_SERVICE shown in Figure 5-4(b). By definition, for an identifying relationship, the primary key of the child includes the primary key of the parent. In this example, the huge primary key of TREE is placed in TREE_SERVICE. Now there are two problematic keys: one in TREE and one in TREE_SERVICE. In situations like these, designers often use surrogate keys.

FIGURE 5–3

Table with Alternate Keys

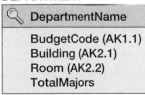

DEPARTMENT

🔑	DepartmentName
	BudgetCode (AK1.1)
	Building (AK2.1)
	Room (AK2.2)
	TotalMajors

FIGURE 5-4

Need for Surrogate
Keys (a) Table with
Large Primary Key;
(b) Migration of Large
Primary Key to Second
Table and (c) Design
Using Surrogate Keys

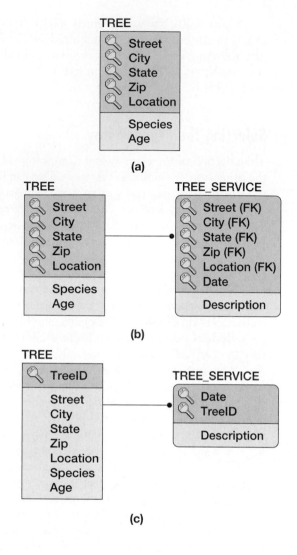

(a)

(b)

(c)

Surrogate Keys

A *surrogate key* is a unique, DBMS-supplied identifier used as the primary key of a relation. The values of a surrogate key have no meaning to the users and are normally hidden on forms and reports. The DBMS does not allow the value of a surrogate key to be changed.

Each DBMS product has its own way of defining surrogate keys. Figure 5-5 shows the definition of a surrogate key using SQL Server. The Identity Seed is the starting number for the surrogate key. The first row inserted into the TREE table receives this value. The Identity Increment is the amount to be added to the current surrogate key value to obtain the next surrogate key value. For the example in Figure 5-5, the first row will receive the value of 100 for TreeID, the second row will receive the value 110, and so forth. We will show how to define surrogate keys using Oracle in Chapter 10.

Surrogate keys are short, numeric, and can never change. Thus, they are ideal keys. Further, they add the minimum amount of overhead when used as foreign keys. Contrast the design for the TREE and TREE_SERVICE relations in Figures 5-6(b) and 5-6(c). Using the surrogate key saves potentially hundreds of bytes of storage *per row* in TREE_SERVICE.

Although surrogate keys have advantages, they also have two important disadvantages. First, foreign keys that are based on surrogate keys have no meaning to the users. To see why this is a problem, suppose an EMPLOYEE table contains the foreign key

FIGURE 5-5

Defining a Surrogate
Key in SQL Server

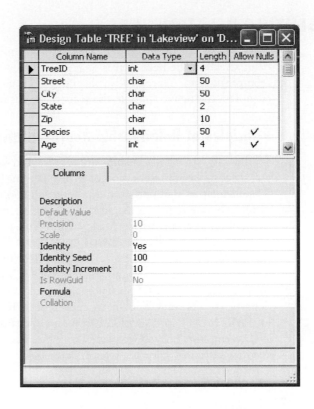

DeptID, which corresponds to the surrogate key ID in DEPARTMENT. A DeptID value of, say, 1150 means nothing to the users. To find the name of the department, the DEPARTMENT row with an ID value of 1150 needs to be read from the database.

Contrast this with the situation if DepartmentName is used as the primary key of DEPARTMENT and as the foreign key in EMPLOYEE. Reading a row of EMPLOYEE will obtain a value for DepartmentName. If name is all the user needs to know about the employee's department, no second read is required.

The second disadvantage of surrogate keys arises when data is shared among different databases. Suppose, for example, a company maintains three different SALES databases, one for each of three different product lines. Assume that each of these databases has a table called SALES_ORDER that has a surrogate key called ID. The DBMS assigns values to ID so that they are unique within a particular database. It does not, however, assign ID values so they are unique across the three different databases. Thus, it is possible for two different SALE_ORDER rows, in two different databases, to have the same value of ID.

This is not a problem until data from the different databases are merged. When that happens, to prevent duplicates, ID values will need to be changed. However, if ID values are changed, then possibly foreign key values will need to be changed as well, and the result is a mess, or at least much work to prevent a mess.

It is, of course, possible to construct a scheme using different surrogate key seeds to ensure that the three databases always have different values of ID. This requires careful management and procedures, however, and the possibility of duplication still exists.

One final note: Some database designers take the position that, for consistency, if one table has a surrogate key, all of the tables in the database should have a surrogate key. Others think such a policy is too rigid; after all, there are good data keys such as ProductID, and if one exists, it should be used instead of a surrogate key.

▶ REPRESENTING RELATIONSHIPS

After a table has been created for each entity and after the primary key of the table has been selected, the next step is to represent relationships. For the relational model, all relationships are expressed by placing the primary key of one table into a second table. As noted, the new column in the second table is referred to as a *foreign key*.

Principles of Relationship Representation

The specific ways relationships are represented depend on the type of relationship. We will discuss the representation of each type, but before we do, you need to understand three principles that pertain to the representation of all relationship types: preservation of referential integrity constraints, specification of referential integrity actions, and representation of minimum cardinality. Consider each in turn.

Preserving Referential Integrity Constraints

Whenever we create a foreign key, we also create a referential integrity constraint. For example, suppose we want to represent the relationship between EMPLOYEE and DEPARTMENT. Also, suppose that a department has many employees, but an employee works in just one department. As you will learn, we represent such a 1:N relationship by placing the key of DEPARTMENT in EMPLOYEE. Assume in this case that the key of DEPARTMENT is DepartmentName, so we place DepartmentName into EMPLOYEE as a foreign key. We now have the following referential integrity constraint:

EMPLOYEE.DepartmentName must exist in DEPARTMENT.DepartmentName.

When we create the relationship, we can instruct the DBMS to enforce this constraint. (You will see how to do this using SQL in the next chapter.) If we do this, then whenever a new EMPLOYEE row is created, the DBMS determines whether the value of EMPLOYEE.DepartmentName is present as one of the values of DEPARTMENT.DepartmentName. If not, the insertion is disallowed. Similarly, whenever the value of the EMPLOYEE.DepartmentName is updated, the DBMS determines whether the updated value is present as one of the values of DEPARTMENT.DepartmentName. If not, the update is disallowed. Deletions of a child row do not impact this constraint, so are not considered.

On the parent side, if the parent's primary key is changed to a new value, the referential integrity constraint will be violated for any child rows that it has. Therefore, by default, the DBMS disallows the update of a primary key if the row has children. Thus, if the Bookkeeping department changes its name to Accounting, the update is disallowed if the Bookkeeping department has any employees.

Similarly, if a parent row is deleted, the value of the foreign key for any of that parent's child rows violates this constraint. Therefore, no parent can be deleted if it has children. Instead, the children must first be deleted and then the parent can be deleted. Insertions of a new parent row cannot influence the referential integrity constraint, so they are not considered. These default rules for referential integrity enforcement are summarized in Figure 5-6.

FIGURE 5-6

Default Rules for Enforcing Referential Integrity

Action on Parent	Insert new row	Insert always OK.
	Update primary key	Disallow update if parent row has child rows.
	Delete row	Disallow deletion if parent row has child rows.
Action on Child	Insert new row	Disallow insert if foreign key in new row does not match a primary key value in the parent table.
	Update foreign key	Disallow update if updated foreign key does not match a primary key value in the parent table.
	Delete existing row	Delete always OK.

Specifying Referential Integrity Actions   For some databases, the default referential integrity enforcement behavior just described is too strong. For example, an application might have the policy that parent rows are to be created for child rows when necessary. In the DEPARTMENT/EMPLOYEE example, if an EMPLOYEE row is inserted for a nonexistent department, a new DEPARTMENT row is to be created as well.

If there is such a policy, it overrides the default referential integrity enforcement rules and it must be defined during database design. Later, during implementation, the policy will be programmed into triggers, as you will learn in Chapter 7.

Such policies are described in **referential integrity actions**. For every relationship, there are six possible actions: three for the child and three for the parent. They are *insert*, *update*, and *delete* on the child; and *insert*, *update*, and *delete* on the parent. As we define a relationship, we need always to think about the need for any of these referential integrity actions.

Two referential integrity overrides are particularly common. They concern update and deletion on the parent side of a relationship. Considering updates, the default behavior is not to allow an update of a primary key value if the row has any related child rows. Another possibility, however, is to automatically change the value of the foreign key in all related child rows to the new value.

For example, when the Bookkeeping department changes its name to Accounting, it is possible to change the value of Bookkeeping to Accounting in all related child rows as well. In that way, the relationships among the rows are maintained, and the referential integrity constraint is also preserved. Such a policy is called **cascading updates**. During database design, if we want this behavior, we need to define it as a referential integrity action on updates.

Similarly, considering deletions, rather than disallow the deletion of parent rows that have children, the DBMS can instead automatically delete all related child rows. This action, too, preserves the referential integrity constraint. This behavior is called **cascading deletions**. Again, if we want this behavior, we need to define it during database design as a referential integrity action on a delete of a parent.

Enforcing Minimum Cardinality   A third important principle concerns a difference in the way we enforce minimum cardinality for child and parent rows. If a child row is required to have a parent, we need only declare the foreign key column to be required. If this is done, the DBMS never allows the foreign key to have a null value, so the child row always has a parent row.

If, however, the child is required, there is no convenient way to ensure that a parent always has a child. Instead, we must define referential integrity actions for this constraint, and during implementation we must write trigger code to enforce those actions.

Consider the actions required on the child side of the relationship. If the minimum cardinality on the child is one, at least one child row must be connected to the parent. This means the last child in the relationship cannot leave the parent. In our example, if a DEPARTMENT is required to have at least one row in EMPLOYEE, we cannot allow a deletion of an EMPLOYEE row if that row is the only employee in that department. Similarly, we cannot allow an update of EMPLOYEE.DepartmentName if the employee is the only employee in that department.

Now, consider the required child constraint from the standpoint of the parent. Whenever we insert a new parent, we must also obtain a child to relate to that parent. This can be done by creating a new child row or by moving an existing child row to the parent.

Unfortunately, DBMS products do not have features to enforce these constraints. Instead, the database development team must document them as referential integrity actions on the update and deletion of a child and on insert of the parent. Thus, whenever you see a required child in any relationship, realize that you will need to create such referential integrity actions.

FIGURE 5–7

Correspondence of
Relationship
Terminology

Extended E-R Relationship Type	IDEF1X Relationship Type	Comment
ID-dependent	Identifying Connection	
1:1, 1:N Has-A	Non-identifying Connection	In IDEF1X, parent / child terminology is forced on 1:1 relationships.
N:M Has-A	Non-specific	
Supertype/Subtype	Generic/Category	Categories are always mutually exclusive in their cluster. No similar constraint in extended E-R.
Weak, non-ID-dependent	None	Implemented using referential integrity actions.

With this background, we can now describe the representation of each type of relationship. Figure 5-7 summarizes relationship types and shows the correspondence of terms used between the extended E-R model and the IDEF1X model. In the next sections, we will consider each of these types, starting with ID-dependent and working down the rows to conclude with Weak, non-ID-dependent.

Representing ID-Dependent Relationships

For ID-dependent relationships (called *Identifying Connection Relationships* in the IDEF1X model), all that is necessary is to place the key of the parent relation as a new column in the child relation. By definition, for ID-dependent relationships, that new column becomes part of the child's primary key. Thus, in Figure 5-8(a), the key of BUILD-ING, which is BuildingName, is added to APARTMENT, as shown in Figure 5-8(b). The primary key of APARTMENT becomes the composite {BuildingName, ApartmentNumber}. Of course, if the primary key of the parent is a composite, all elements of that composite key are added to the child as noted for the TREE relation in Figure 5-4.

BuildingName in APARTMENT is a foreign key. For ID-dependent relationships, the column that is a foreign key is also part of the primary key. Thus, BuildingName is both a foreign key and is also part of the primary key in APARTMENT. BuildingName is a primary key only in BUILDING, however.

Referential Integrity Actions After we have placed the foreign key, the next step is to determine the need for any possible referential integrity actions. As described previously, these actions may be required either to alter the default referential integrity enforcement rules or to enforce the need for a required child. Considering the former, the definition of the ID-dependent relationship creates the following referential integrity constraint:

APARTMENT.BuildingName must exist in BUILDING.BuildingName

Now do we need to define referential integrity actions to override the default enforcement behavior on this constraint? On the child side, the default behavior is fine. We want to disallow the insert of a new row in APARTMENT if BuildingName does not match an existing BUILDING.BuildingName, and we want to disallow an update under the same conditions.

From the parent side, however, we probably want to allow updates to cascade. If, for some reason, a building name is changed, there is no reason to disallow the change, and it makes sense to allow that change to cascade to the children.

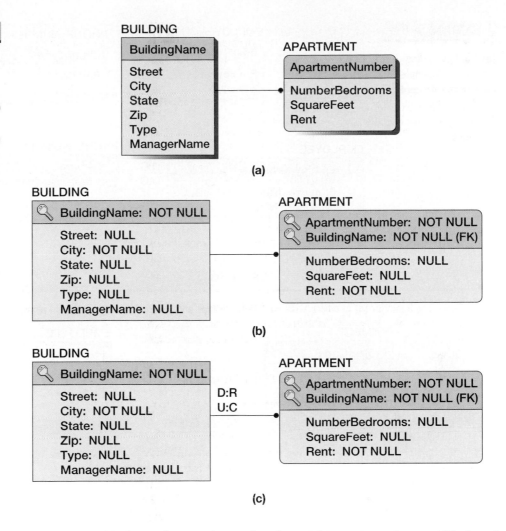

FIGURE 5-8

Representation of ID-dependent Relationships (a) ID-dependent Relationship Example; (b) Relationship Design for Example in (a) and (c) Specifying Referential Integrity Actions

Figure 5-8(c) shows the way that such referential integrity actions are displayed using ERWin. The U:C is an abbreviation for Update : Cascade. Thus, according to this design, changes to BuildingName will be allowed and such changes will cascade to the apartments in that building.

The D:R on the BUILDING side of the relationship is an abbreviation for Delete:Restrict. This specification means do not allow deletions of buildings that are related to apartment records. Because this is the default behavior, there is no need to specify this referential integrity action. It is shown here only to emphasize that deletions will not cascade.

Guidelines on Cascading Deletions with ID-dependent Relationships   Cascading updates are not much of a problem; data values are simply updated to keep child rows consistent with parent rows. Cascading deletions can be a different matter, however, especially if the child participates in relationships with other entities. In this section, we will consider guidelines for making this decision.

As a general rule, if the ID-dependent entity is representing multi-value attributes, such as the multi-value phone numbers in Figure 5-9(a), cascading deletions are appropriate. After all, it makes little sense to disallow a deletion just because an employee has multiple phone numbers. Figure 5-9(b) shows the appropriate referential integrity actions.

On the other hand, if the ID-dependent entity is not just a multivalue attribute, the decision about cascading deletions requires careful consideration of requirements. For example, consider ASSIGNMENT in Figure 5-10(a). If an employee's data is deleted, is there justification for removing that employee's assignment data? Similarly, if a project is

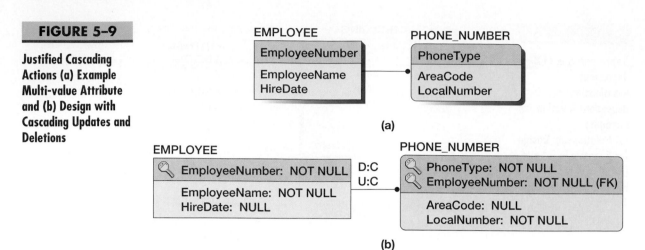

FIGURE 5-9

Justified Cascading Actions (a) Example Multi-value Attribute and (b) Design with Cascading Updates and Deletions

(a)

(b)

FIGURE 5-10

Mixed Cascading Behavior (a) Example with Two Relationships and (b) No Cascading Deletion from **EMPLOYEE**

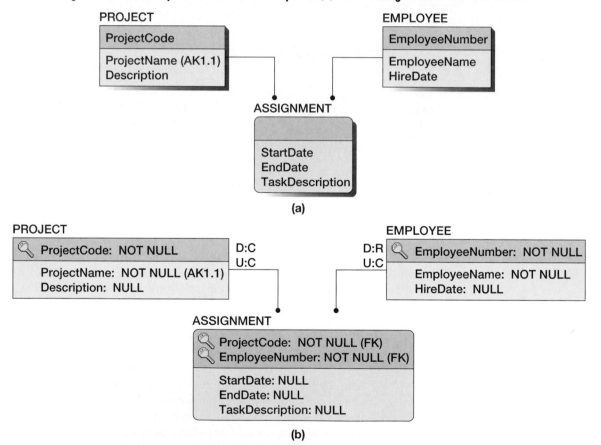

(a)

(b)

deleted, is there justification for deleting that project's assignments? One can make a good argument for either of these alternatives, and the only way to resolve them is to check requirements or to ask the users.

Figure 5-10(b) documents the decision that the deletion of a project can cause cascading deletions of ASSIGNMENT, but that the deletion of an employee cannot. The justification in this case is that if the project is deleted, assignments are unimportant. On the other hand, if an employee is deleted, someone else must take over that employee's assignments. Thus, the application will be written to first reassign the to-be-deleted employee's assignments by creating new assignments for a different employee, then deleting the assignments for the first employee, and then deleting the row for that employee.

Representing ID-Dependent Relationships Using Surrogate Keys If the parent in an ID-dependent relationship has a surrogate key as its primary key, but the child has a data key, the design rule explained previously will work fine. Just use the parent's surrogate key as a primary key. For example, for the BUILDING/APARTMENT case, suppose the primary key of BUILDING is BuildingID, a surrogate key, and the local identifier of APARTMENT is ApartmentNumber. In this case, the primary key of APARTMENT will be {BuildingID, ApartmentNumber) with the following referential integrity constraint:

APARTMENT.BuildingID must exist in BUILDING.BuildingID

Although this design strategy works, it does not create the best design. The composite {BuildingID, ApartmentNumber} is a mixture of a surrogate key with a data key, and it will have no meaning to the users. Because this is so, there is no advantage to using ApartmentNumber as part of the key. Rather, the primary key of APARTMENT should be a pure surrogate key, named something like ApartmentID.

In this case, BuildingID will need to be placed in the APARTMENT table as a foreign key, but it will not be part of APARTMENT's primary key. The relations are:

BUILDING (<u>BuildingID</u>, BuildingName, Street, … other non-key attributes)

APARTMENT (<u>ApartmentID</u>, *BuildingID*, ApartmentNumber, … other non-key attributes)

with referential integrity constraint

APARTMENT.BuildingID must exist in BUILDING.BuildingID

Primary keys are underlined and the foreign key is shown in italics.

Whenever the parent in an ID-dependent relationship has a surrogate key, this situation will develop. Therefore, we can generalize as follows: Whenever any parent of an ID-dependent relationship has a surrogate key, the child should have a surrogate key as well.

Notice, too, that by using surrogate keys in the child table, the relationship type has changed. In the preceding example, APARTMENT with a surrogate key of ApartmentID is no longer an ID-dependent table. It now has a key of its own, and thus is not ID-dependent. This is neither an advantage nor a disadvantage, you should simply be aware that by using surrogate keys in this way, you have transformed the ID-dependent relationship into a 1:N non-identifying relationship.

Representing 1:1 and 1:N HAS-A Relationships

According to the extended E-R model, there are three types of HAS-A relationships: 1:1, 1:N, N:M. We will describe the representation of the first two of these three types in this section. N:M HAS-A relationships will be discussed in the next section. Recall from Figure 5-7 and from Chapter 2 that in the IDEF1X model, 1:1 and 1:N HAS-A relationships are called *Non-identifying connection relationships*, and N:M relationships are called *non-specific relationships*. Thus, in IDEF1X terms, this section will describe the representation of non-identifying connection relationships.

Representing One-to-One Relationships Figure 5-11 shows a 1:1 relationship expressed in extended E-R notation, and Figure 5-12(a) and Figure 5-13(a) show the IDEF1X notation. In all of these figures, an auto is required to be related to exactly one employee, but an employee has zero or one autos assigned.

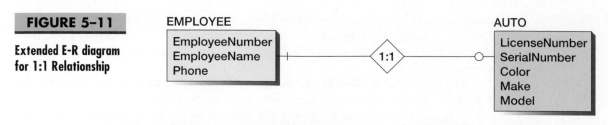

FIGURE 5–12

1:1 with EMPLOYEE Considered as Parent (a) IDEF1X Model; (b) Table Design and (c) Referential Integrity Actions

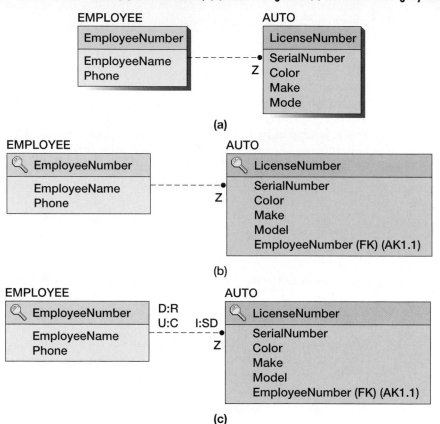

To represent a 1:1 relationship, we place the key of one table into the other. Here, we can place the key of EMPLOYEE into AUTO, or we can place the key of AUTO into EMPLOYEE. For performance reasons, one choice may be preferred to the other, but either strategy works for the purpose of representing the 1:1 relationship.

Because the relationship is 1:1, only one child row can have a given value of the foreign key. For example, if AUTO has the foreign key EmployeeNumber, a given EmployeeNumber may appear only once in AUTO. Thus, EmployeeNumber must be defined as UNIQUE in AUTO. Alternatively, if EMPLOYEE has the foreign key LicenseNumber, a given LicenseNumber may appear only once in EMPLOYEE. Thus, LicenseNumber must be defined as UNIQUE in EMPLOYEE.

The Design with EMPLOYEE as Parent The IDEF1X model imposes structure on the representation of 1:1 relationships. Recall that in IDEF1X, every connection relationship has a parent entity and a child entity. For 1:1 relationships, the choice is forced; either entity could be considered the parent or the child. Figure 5-12 shows the model and corresponding database design if we consider EMPLOYEE as the parent and AUTO as the child. We will consider the opposite case in Figure 5-13.

The key of a parent entity is always placed into the child. Thus, in Figure 5-12(b), we place EmployeeNumber in AUTO. Because this is a 1:1 relationship, EmployeeNumber must be defined as unique. Using ERWin, the tool used to make these diagrams, the only way to make a column unique is to define it as an alternate key. This has been done in Figure 5-12(b). As you interpret this figure, however, realize that EmployeeNum is meant only to be unique. Semantically, it is not an alternate key for AUTO.

When we create a foreign key, we also create a referential integrity constraint. In Figure 5-12(b), the constraint is the following:

AUTO.EmployeeNumber must exist in EMPLOYEE.EmployeeNumber.

Whenever we have such a constraint, we must consider referential integrity actions. As shown in Figure 5-12(c), from the EMPLOYEE side of the relationship, we will restrict deletions and we will cascade updates. There is no need to show an insertion referential integrity action because an EMPLOYEE does not require an AUTO. We can insert the EMPLOYEE without considering its relationship to AUTO.

From the AUTO side of the relationship, because an employee need not have a relationship to an auto, we can delete autos and reassign them without any restriction. Therefore, there is no delete or update referential integrity action declared for AUTO. However, the minimum cardinality from AUTO to EMPLOYEE is one, meaning an AUTO must have an EMPLOYEE. Therefore, AUTO.EmployeeNumber cannot be not null. Because it is required, we need to specify an action for connecting an EMPLOYEE to an AUTO when a new AUTO row is created. Here, that action is defined as SD (for set default). This means that we will write a trigger to follow a default policy for selecting the EMPLOYEE to relate to the new AUTO row. At this point, we need not document that default policy; here we are just recording the need for such a policy.

The Design with AUTO as Parent   Figure 5-13 shows the model and design if AUTO is chosen to be the parent. In this design, the foreign key, LicenseNumber, is placed in EMPLOYEE. Because an EMPLOYEE is not required to have an AUTO, EMPLOYEE.LicenseNumber can be NULL, as shown in Figure 5-13(b). Also, notice that EMPLOYEE.LicenseNumber is shown as an alternate key. Again, this is done because the relationship is 1:1 and we need to ensure that a given value of LicenseNumber appears only once in EMPLOYEE. Defining it as an alternate key ensures that its values will be unique.

The referential integrity constraint for this design is as follows:

EMPLOYEE.LicenseNumber must exist in AUTO.LicenseNumber

Referential integrity actions for this relationship are shown in Figure 5-13(c). The actions are more complicated here than for the design in Figure 5-12(c) because AUTO has a required child. As noted before, the only way to enforce such a constraint is to define referential integrity actions.

Starting on the AUTO side of the relationship, if an auto is deleted, the action on the LicenseNumber foreign key is SN, or SET to NULL. This makes sense because the data model does not require an EMPLOYEE to have an AUTO. If the AUTO row is deleted, the employee loses the auto, but no constraint is violated in the process.

When a new AUTO is inserted, the action is specified as Set Default. This action means we will need to write a trigger to follow a default policy for assigning the AUTO to an EMPLOYEE. We must do this because an AUTO must have an EMPLOYEE according to the data model. Finally, if the LicenseNumber in AUTO is changed, the change should cascade to EMPLOYEE.LicenseNumber. This is done to be able to give autos new license numbers without violating the constraint and while preserving the existing relationship.

FIGURE 5-13

1:1 with AUTO Considered as Parent (a) IDEF1X Model; (b) Table Design and (c) Referential Integrity Actions

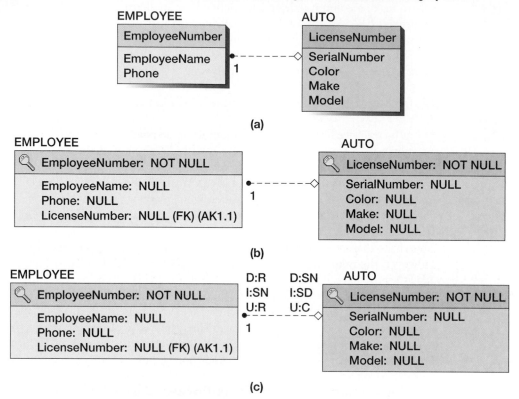

(a)

(b)

(c)

From the EMPLOYEE side, deletions are restricted. If an EMPLOYEE has a relationship to an AUTO, then that EMPLOYEE cannot be deleted. The AUTO must first be deleted or reassigned to another EMPLOYEE. When a new EMPLOYEE row is inserted, the LicenseNumber foreign key is to be set to NULL. Null values are allowed because EMPLOYEEs need not have a relationship to an AUTO.

Finally, updates to LicenseNumber are restricted. In this case, "restricted" does not necessarily mean "cannot be changed." If the current value of LicenseNumber is null, it can be changed to a valid LicenseNumber. However, once LicenseNumber obtains a non-null value, it cannot be changed until the current auto is either deleted or assigned to a different employee. These rules need to be documented as part of the database design.

Take some time to compare the designs in Figure 5-12 and 5-13. Be sure you understand why AUTO.EmployeeNumber in Figure 5-12(b) cannot be null, but EMPLOYEE.LicenseNumber in Figure 5-13(b) can be null. Also, be sure to understand the differences in referential integrity actions between the two designs. If you understand these two designs, you are well on your way to learning how to design relational databases.

Representing One-to-Many Relationships The representation of one-to-many relationships is similar to that for a one-to-one relationship. In this case, however, the choice of parent entity is not arbitrary. Instead, the parent entity is always the entity on the one side of the one-to-many relationship.

Figure 5-14(a) shows three entities with two 1:N relationships. A DEPARTMENT has from zero to many items of FURNITURE, and an item of FURNITURE must be assigned to exactly one DEPARTMENT. Additionally, a DEPARTMENT has

FIGURE 5-14

Two Example 1:N Relationships (a) IDEF1X Model and (b) Table Design

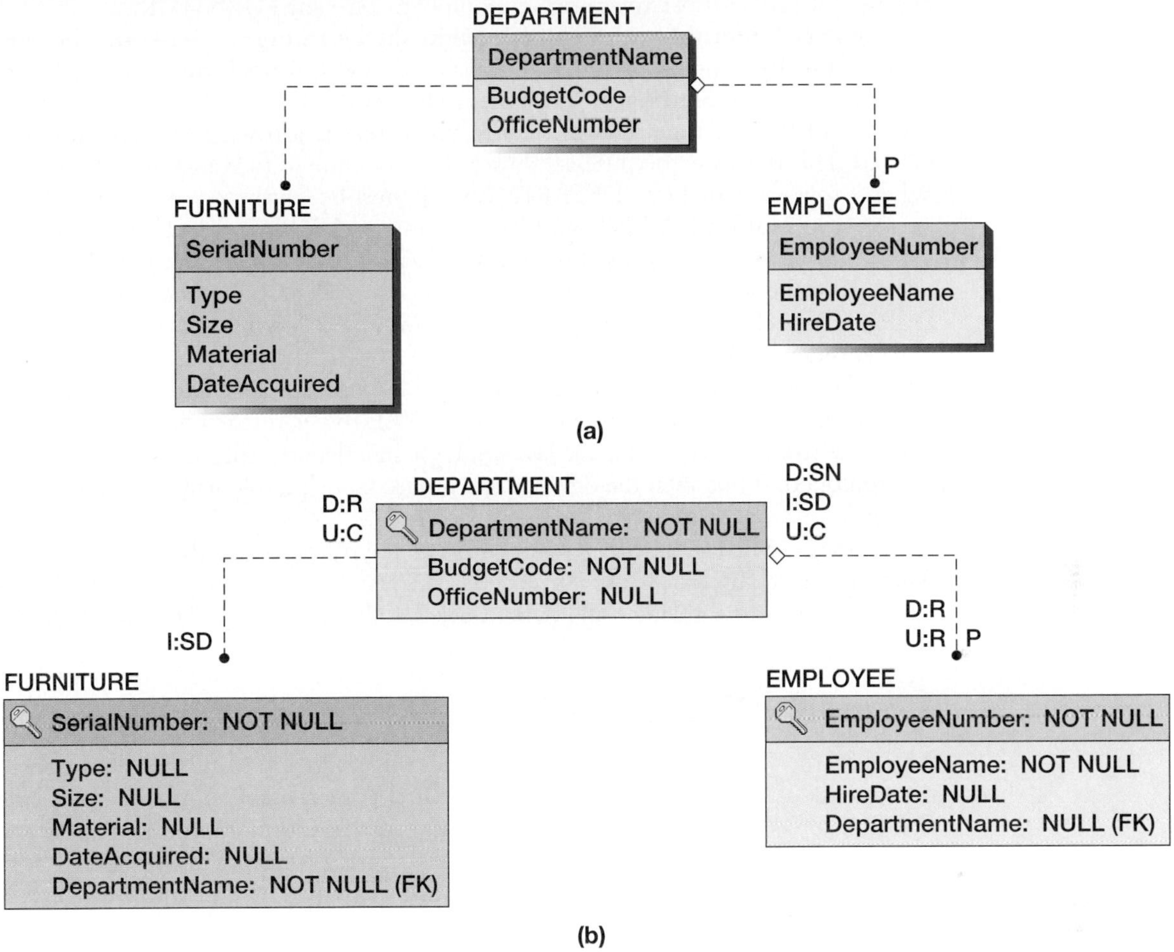

DEPARTMENT

DepartmentName
BudgetCode
OfficeNumber

FURNITURE

SerialNumber
Type
Size
Material
DateAcquired

P

EMPLOYEE

EmployeeNumber
EmployeeName
HireDate

(a)

D:R
U:C

DEPARTMENT

D:SN
I:SD
U:C

🔑 DepartmentName: NOT NULL
BudgetCode: NOT NULL
OfficeNumber: NULL

D:R
U:R P

I:SD

FURNITURE

🔑 SerialNumber: NOT NULL
Type: NULL
Size: NULL
Material: NULL
DateAcquired: NULL
DepartmentName: NOT NULL (FK)

EMPLOYEE

🔑 EmployeeNumber: NOT NULL
EmployeeName: NOT NULL
HireDate: NULL
DepartmentName: NULL (FK)

(b)

from one to many EMPLOYEEs, and an EMPLOYEE is assigned to zero or one DEPARTMENTs.

To represent a 1:N relationship, we place the primary key of the parent into the child. Thus, in Figure 5-14(b), we place DepartmentName into FURNITURE for the first relationship, and DepartmentName into EMPLOYEE for the second relationship. Notice that DepartmentName in FURNITURE is NOT NULL, indicating that an item of furniture must be assigned to a department. On the other hand, DepartmentName in EMPLOYEE could be null, indicating that an employee may or may not be assigned to a department.

Now, consider the referential integrity actions. For the first relationship, a row can be inserted in DEPARTMENT without any referential integrity action because departments are not required to have any furniture. A DEPARTMENT row cannot be deleted, however, if it has any FURNITURE because furniture is required to have a relationship to DEPARTMENT. Finally, if the value of DepartmentName is updated, that change is to cascade to FURNITURE.DepartmentName.

Considering referential integrity actions from the perspective of FURNITURE, when a new row is inserted into FURNTIURE, the rule is SD or set default. This setting means to use the default policy in assigning furniture to a department; this rule is necessary because furniture must belong to a department. The default policy might be to add furniture to the Warehouse Department, for example, when it is first placed into the database.

When rows in FURNITURE are updated or deleted, no action need be taken because DEPARTMENT rows are not required to have any FURNITURE.

Now, consider the second relationship shown in Figure 5-14(b). The referential integrity actions are more complicated here because this relationship has a required child. Starting on the parent side of the relationship, the foreign key EMPLOYEE.DepartmentName is to be set to null if a row in DEPARTMENT is deleted. This is allowed because employees are not required to belong to a department. When a row is inserted into DEPARTMENT, it must be connected to an EMPLOYEE because every DEPARTMENT must have at least one EMPLOYEE. Here, the referential integrity action is to connect to an EMPLOYEE using the default policy. A trigger will need to be written to handle this case. Finally, if DepartmentName is updated in DEPARTMENT, that update is to cascade to EMPLOYEE.DepartmentName.

Considering the relationship from the EMPLOYEE perspective, nothing need be done when a new EMPLOYEE row is inserted because employees are not required to have departments. The deletion of an EMPLOYEE row is restricted. Here, this means that if the row to be deleted is the last employee in a department, the deletion needs to be prohibited. If not, then the deletion can proceed. Such a rule will be enforced using triggers.

Updates of EMPLOYEE.DepartmentName are restricted for the same reason that deletions are restricted. If the employee is the last employee in the department, an update of DepartmentName will not be allowed. Otherwise, the update can be allowed.

Representing N:M Relationships

As you learned in Chapter 2, there is a difference regarding N:M relationships between the extended E-R model and the IDEF1X version of the E-R model. In particular, IDEF1X refers to N:M relationships as non-specific relationships and favors the position that such relationships do not truly exist. Instead, according to IDEF1X, the appearance of an N:M relationship is only an indication that an entity is missing. In this section, we will explore this difference further.

First, however, consider the basis of the problem. Suppose we have an N:M relationship between the entities AUTHOR and BOOK. The relationship is N:M because one author may write many books and because one book may have been written by many authors. Figure 5-15(a) shows sample data for this relationship. The lines mean that there is a relationship between one entity instance and another. For example, the first author, Jones, wrote both books 150 and 410.

If we try to represent this relationship using the same strategy as for 1:N relationships, we will have a problem. For example, the design in Figure 5-15(b) attempts to represent this relationship by placing the key of AUTHOR in BOOK. The problem here is that we have no place to store the ID of the second author of any book. For example, in the second row of the BOOK table, we want to place the AuthorIDs 10 and 30, but there is no place to put the 30 because by the definition of a relation, only one value can be placed in each cell.

The solution to this problem is to create a third table, called an **intersection table,** that represents the relationship of a book with an author. Figure 5-15(c) shows an intersection table for the sample data in this figure. This table contains the primary keys of the two tables having the N:M relationship. Figure 5-16(a) shows the IDEF1X representation of an N:M relationship, and Figure 5-16(b) shows the intersection table (here labeled AUTHOR_BOOK_INT).

Intersection tables always consist of the keys of the two tables they relate. Therefore, they are always ID-dependent and they always have two ID-dependent relationships like

FIGURE 5–15

Representing N:M Relationships (a) Example N:M Relationship; (b) Incorrect Design and (c) Design with Intersection Table

AUTHOR Table

AuthorID	Name	Other Data...
10	Jones	
20	Smith	
30	Wu	
40	Green	

BOOK Table

ISBN	Title	Other Data...
100	A	
150	B	
300	C	
410	D	

(a)

AUTHOR Table

AuthorID	Name	Other Data...
10	Jones	
20	Smith	
30	Wu	
40	Green	

BOOK Table

ISBN	Title	Other Data...	AuthorID
100	A		20
150	B		10 ?
300	C		
410	D		

(b)

those shown in Figure 5-16(b). Further, the creation of an intersection table creates two referential integrity constraints. In the case of Figure 5-16(b), they are as follows:

AUTHOR_BOOK_INT.AuthorID must exist in AUTHOR.AuthorID

and

AUTHOR_BOOK_INT.ISBN must exist in BOOK.ISBN

Notice, too, that the minimum cardinality from the intersection table back to the parents is always 1. Like all ID-dependent relationships, rows in the intersection table must have parents or they make no sense.

Finally, consider the minimum cardinality from the parent tables to the intersection table. If an author must write a book to be in the database, the minimum cardinality of the relationship from AUTHOR to AUTHOR_BOOK_INT is one. If a book must have an author, the minimum cardinality of from BOOK to AUTHOR_BOOK_INT must also be one. In Figure 5-16(b), the *P* indicates that a BOOK must have at least one AUTHOR, but an AUTHOR need not have any BOOKs.

The referential integrity actions shown in Figure 5-16(b) are straightforward. Consider first the AUTHOR to AUTHOR_BOOK_INT relationship. An AUTHOR can be inserted

FIGURE 5-15

(continued)

AUTHOR Table

AuthorID	Name	Other Data...
10	Jones	
20	Smith	
30	Wu	
40	Green	

BOOK Table

ISBN	Title	Other Data...
100	A	
150	B	
300	C	
410	D	

Intersection Table

AuthorID	ISBN
10	150
10	410
20	100
30	150
30	410
40	300

(c)

FIGURE 5–16

N:M Relationship Example (a) Non-specific Relationship and (b) Design with Intersection Table

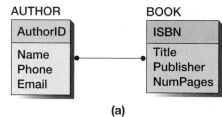

(a)

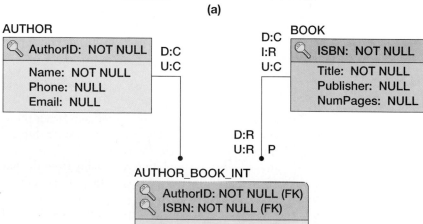

(b)

without special processing, and both deletions and updates of AuthorID should cascade to the intersection table. The intersection table has no restrictions on inserts, updates, or deletions beyond the default behavior for enforcing referential integrity.

Considering the BOOK to AUTHOR_BOOK_INT relationship, the actions are more complicated because BOOK has a required child. First, deletions and updates on BOOK.ISBN should cascade to the intersection table. Inserts on BOOK are restricted because a BOOK must have at least one author. Trigger code will need to be written to ensure the constraint is fulfilled.

From the intersection-table-side of its relationship to BOOK, insertions are not limited beyond the default referential integrity checking. Both updates and deletions are restricted, however, because a BOOK must have at least one child. Thus, the intersection row that represents the only author for a book may not be updated nor deleted.

To summarize, when you have an N:M relationship, convert it into two ID-dependent relationships by defining an intersection table. Two referential integrity constraints will be created. As with all ID-dependent relationships, the child must have a parent, so the minimum cardinality from the child to the parent is always one. The minimum cardinality from the parent to the intersection table may be zero, one, or more, depending on the system requirements. Referential integrity actions need to be specified in accordance with the principles already described.

N:M Relationships Suggesting Missing Entities

As stated in Chapter 2, IDEF1X views N:M has-a relationships with suspicion. According to that model, the apparent need for an N:M relationship suggests a missing entity. For example, examine the N:M relationship between SALESPERSON and SALES_ORDER in Figure 5-17(a). The underlying assumption here is that one or more salespeople are responsible for generating a SALES_ORDER. This model is appropriate for sales teams that sell large items such as airplanes or major medical equipment. So, a salesperson can generate many orders, and an order can be generated by many salespeople.

SALES_ORDER contains the attribute TotalCommission. The presence of this attribute suggests the question, "How is the commission to be divided?" This question, in turn, suggests the model in Figure 5-17(b). Note this is a model (shaded boxes) and not a relational design. The entity SALESPERSON_SHARE is ID-dependent on both SALESPERSON and SALES_ORDER, and it carries the attribute CommissionPercent. The relational design for this model is shown in Figure 5-17(c).

Now, compare Figure 5-16(b) with Figure 5-17(c). The only difference between the two is that SALESPERSON_SHARE has a non-key attribute and AUTHOR_BOOK_INT does not. Otherwise, the structures are identical.

For this reason, tools based on the IDEF1X model want you to convert all N:M relationships by creating an ID-dependent entity between the two entities in the N:M relationship. That is why IDEF1X calls N:M relationships "non-specific." They are non-specific because they have not yet been transformed into two ID-dependent relationships.

If, as in the case of AUTHOR and BOOK, there is no non-key attribute for the created entity, the IDEF1X proponents say, "No problem." Just create an entity for the N:M relationship that is ID-dependent on both AUTHOR and BOOK and that has no non-key attributes. As you can see, that strategy is the same thing as creating an intersection table, so you have the same answer as with the extended E-R model, but it is dressed in different words.

In summary, IDEF1X views N:M relationships skeptically and asks the designer to question whether some connecting entity is missing. If so, that entity will be ID-dependent on both of its parents. If no such missing entity is found, just create the connecting entity with no non-key attributes.

One can take the posture of either the extended E-R model or that of IDEF1X, and arrive in the same place. You can say, "Of course, there are N:M relationships," model them as such, and create intersection tables when you design your database. Or, you can

FIGURE 5–17

N:M Relationship with Missing Entity (a) Non-Specific Relationship; (b) Model with Missing Entity and (c) Design without Intersection Table

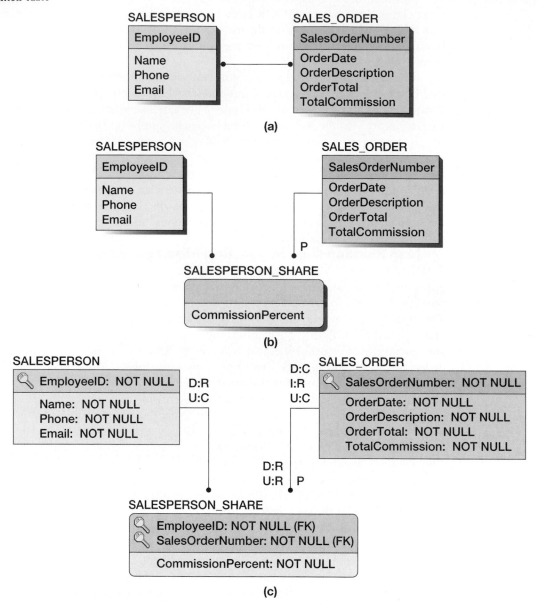

say, "No, such relationships exist" and look for the missing entity; if one is not found, force the definition of an entity that is ID-dependent on both parents. You will create the same set of relations and relationships, regardless of which flavor you choose.

Some would say the IDEF1X approach is better because it forces the designer to think again about the possibility of a connecting entity. Others would say that good data modelers will have done that, anyway. You can make your own assessment.

Representing Subtype and Category Relationships

Before describing the representation of subtype and category entities, it is helpful to review the discussion about them in Chapter 2. Subtypes and supertypes in the extended

E-R model are less restrictive than generic and category entities in IDEF1X. Therefore, if you know how to represent generic and category entities, you also know how to represent the simpler supertype and subtypes of the extended E-R model. Hence, in this section we will primarily focus on IDEF1X concepts.

Review of Supertype/Subtype and Generic/Category Entities

As explained in Chapter 2, subtypes are entities that represent different subclasses of an entity called a supertype. A PET, for example, could be a FISH, CAT, or a DOG. In this example, PET is the supertype; and FISH, CAT, and DOG are the subtypes.

IDEF1X extends this concept by adding the concept of a category cluster. Figure 5-18(a) shows a portion of an IDEF1X diagram developed in Chapter 2. The EMPLOYEE entity is the generic entity and it has two category clusters. MANAGER

FIGURE 5-18

Category Representation (a) Model with Two Category Clusters; (b) Foreign Keys in Category Tables and (c) Referential Integrity Actions

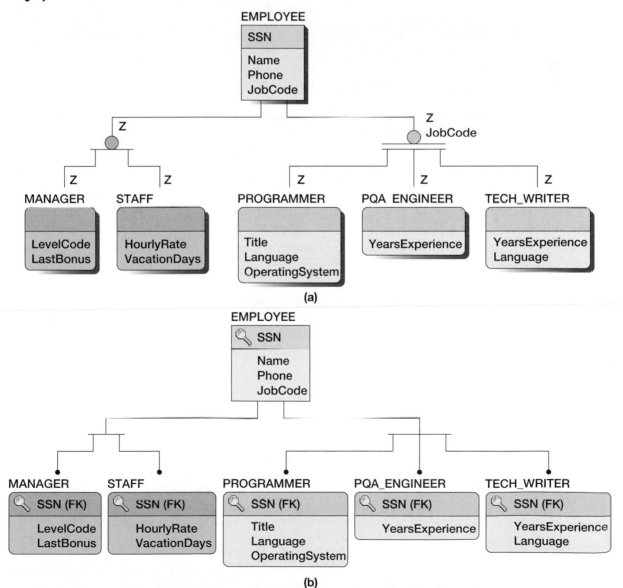

and STAFF are in one cluster; and PROGRAMMER, PQA_ENGINEER, and TECH_WRITER are in a second cluster.

In terms of the extended E-R model, EMPLOYEE is the supertype; and MANAGER, STAFF, PROGRAMMER, PQA_ENGINEER, and TECH_WRITER are subtypes. However, IDEF1X adds not only the idea of a category cluster, but also the constraint that category entities are mutually exclusive within their cluster. Thus, an EMPLOYEE can be either MANAGER or STAFF, but not both.

In IDEF1X, category clusters can be complete or incomplete. If complete, every possible type of a cluster is present within the cluster. Thus, the generic entity must be one of the entities in the cluster. If incomplete, at least one type is missing from the cluster, and there is the possibility that the generic entity will not be of any of the types.

According to the notation in Figure 5-18(a), the MANAGER/STAFF cluster is incomplete (denoted by the single line under the cluster circle); some employees are neither managers nor staff members. They might be part time employees, for example. The second cluster, however, is complete (denoted by the double line under the cluster circle). An EMPLOYEE must be a PROGRAMMER, PQA_ENGINEER, or TECH_WRITER.

Finally, some clusters have a discriminator, which is an attribute of the generic entity that determines which category entity the generic entity is. In Figure 5-18, JobCode can be used to determine whether an EMPLOYEE is a PROGRAMMER, PQA ENGINEER, or TECH_WRITER. The model does not say how to interpret JobCode to make this determination; it just indicates that such a determination is possible.

Relations and Keys for Category Entities   Now, given all of this, the representation of category entities is straightforward. Represent each category with a table and define the primary key of that table to be the same as the primary key of the generic entity. In doing this, the primary key of the category will also be a foreign key. Finally, define referential integrity constraints to ensure that the key values of the tables representing category entities are present as key values in the table representing the generic entity.

Figure 5-18(b) shows such a design for the model in Figure 5-18(a), in which SSN, the primary key of EMPLOYEE, has been placed as the primary key of each of the category entities. Notice that SSN is placed in the primary key location of the category entities, and that it is marked as a foreign key as well.

The following referential integrity constraints will also be defined:

MANAGER.SSN exists in EMPLOYEE.SSN

STAFF.SSN exists in EMPLOYEE.SSN

PROGRAMMER.SSN exists in EMPLOYEE.SSN

PQA_ENGINEER.SSN exists in EMPLOYEE.SSN

TECH_WRITER.SSN exists in EMPLOYEE.SSN

An identical strategy is used to represent subtypes.

Referential Integrity Actions   Figure 5-18(c) shows referential integrity actions for each of the generic/category relationships. In all cases, updates or deletions of EMPLOYEE should cascade. This makes sense: If the SSN changes for the employee, that change should be propagated to all categories of that employee. Similarly, if the employee is removed from the database, all categories of that employee should be removed as well.

In all cases, insertion of new category entities is restricted. Because categories are mutually exclusive in their clusters, a new row cannot be inserted unless that entity is not represented in any other category entity in that cluster. This means that before a new row can be inserted in, say, MANAGER, the STAFF table must be checked to ensure that the employee does have a STAFF category. If so, that STAFF row needs to be deleted before the new row can be added to MANAGER.

FIGURE 5-18

(continued)

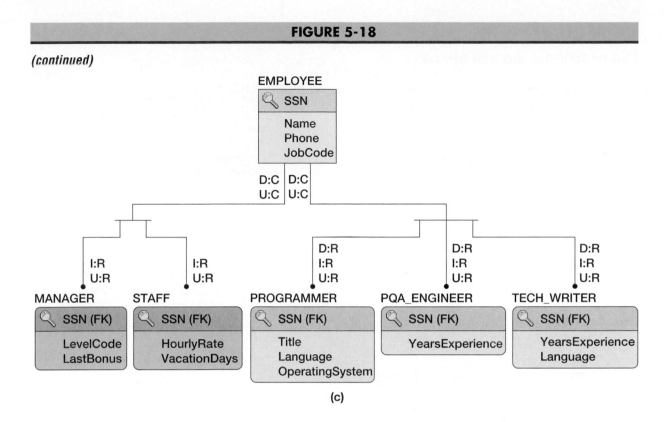

(c)

Figure 5-18(c) shows the updating of all category clusters to be restricted as well. In truth, updating an SSN in a category should never occur at all. Doing so is like saying that the record that did apply to Jones now applies to Smith. This is not sensible, and such updating should always be prohibited.

Finally, notice that deletions are also restricted for PROGRAMMER, PQA_ENGINEER, and TECH_WRITER. This is because the cluster of those categories is complete; an EMPLOYEE must be one of those types. If the deletion is allowed, it can be allowed only if one of the other types is inserted. This action would occur if an employee switched from, say, a PQA_Engineer to a PROGRAMMER. Finally, because the second cluster is complete, when a new row is inserted in EMPLOYEE, a new row must also be inserted in one of PROGRAMMER, PQA_ENGINEER, or TECH_WRITER. This is not called out in Figure 5-18(b), but it is a requirement.

DBMS products provide no support for the processing of category clusters. All of the referential integrity actions described here for them must be implemented in triggers.

Representing Weak, but Not ID-dependent Relationships

The extended E-R model allows for weak entities that are not ID-dependent. Such non-ID-dependent entities logically depend on the existence of another entity in the database. An example of such an entity is DEPENDENT, where a DEPENDENT entity represents data about an employee's dependents. In this case, an EMPLOYEE has a 1:N relationship to DEPENDENT, and a DEPENDENT can exist only if there is a corresponding EMPLOYEE row.

The design for such entities is the same as for any other 1:N relationship except that particular referential integrity actions are required. Consider the design in Figure 5-19. The foreign key of EMPLOYEE, EmployeeNumber, has been placed into DEPENDENT with the referential integrity constraint.

DEPENDENT.EmployeeNumber must exist in EMPLOYEE.EmployeeNumber.

FIGURE 5-19

Weak but Not ID-Dependent Entity Table Design

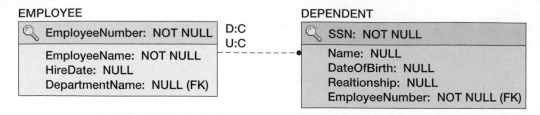

Because DEPENDENT logically requires an EMPLOYEE, deletions and updates of EMPLOYEE must cascade. In fact, these two referential integrity actions are always required for the parents of such weak entities. Additionally, the foreign key for such entities is always required, or NOT NULL. Given the referential integrity constraint, insertions and updates of the foreign key value will be restricted to existing employees, so no further child referential integrity action is needed.

With these required referential integrity actions, the representation of such weak entities is just the same as any other 1:N relationship.

Relationship Examples

In this section we will consider three examples from the data models that were developed in Chapter 3.

Nested ID-dependent Relationships   Figure 5-20(a) shows the data model for the third hotel invoice example (shown in Figure 3-9(b)). This invoice has a multi-valued group contained within a multi-valued group, and hence has two ID-dependent entities—one as a child of the other.

To represent each of the ID-dependent relationships, we place the key of the parent into the child as both a foreign key and as part of the child's primary key. The table for the nested ID-dependent relation will have the key of its parent, which includes the key of its grandparent, as shown in Figure 5-20(b). Notice that both deletions and updates

FIGURE 5-20

Design with Nested ID-Dependent Entities (a) Example Entities and (b) Table Design

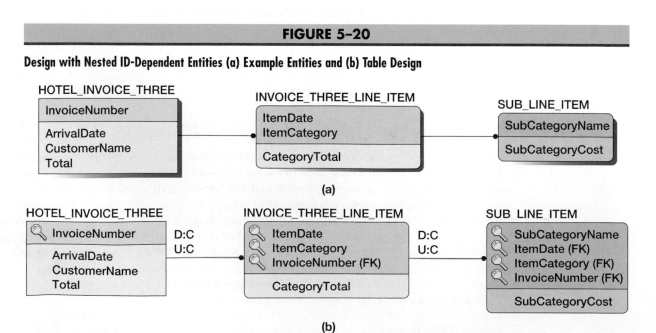

are to cascade from the parent, as is typical for ID-dependent relationships. The process would be extended for ID-dependent entities nested even more deeply.

Obviously, given the size of the nested table keys, this design could be improved by using surrogate keys.

Multiple Relationships between the Same Two Entities   Figure 5-21(a) shows the data model for the second data model of students and dormitories (Figure 3-11(b)). In this model, there are two relationships between DORMITORY_TWO and STUDENT_TWO. One relationship is for students who assist in the dorm and the other is for students who live in the dorm. Each of these relationships is represented by its own foreign key, as shown in Figure 5-21(b). The attribute named DormitoryNameLivedIn is the foreign for the Houses_Lives_In relationship, and the attributed named DormitoryNameAssistsIn is the foreign key for the Assisted_by_Assists relationship.

The referential integrity actions for this design are typical for relationships having a required child. However, the Assisted_by_Assists relationship is 1:1, and the Houses_Lives_In relationship is 1:N, so the actions are slightly different between the two. For example, a delete of STUDENT_TWO can never be allowed for the first relationship, but can be allowed for all but the last child on the second relationship.

Design for Highline University Data Model   Figure 5-22(a) shows the final data model for Highline University considered in Chapter 3 (Figure 3-25). The relational design, shown in Figure 5-22(b), is a straightforward application of the design principles described in this chapter.

There are multiple foreign keys in both DEPARTMENT and STUDENT. In DEPARTMENT, CollegeName is a foreign key to COLLEGE, and professor name (first

---

FIGURE 5-21

Design with Two Relationships between Two Entities (a) Example Entities and (b) Table Design

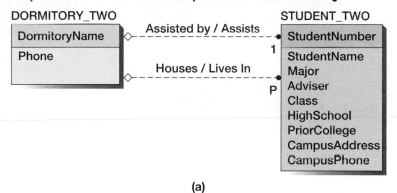

(a)

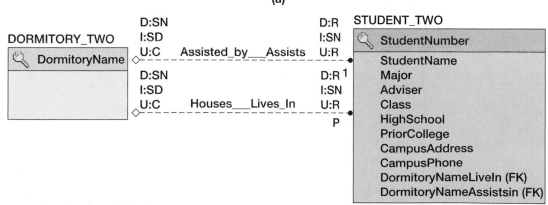

(b)

FIGURE 5-22

Highline University Example (a) Highline University Data Model and (b) Database Design for Highline University

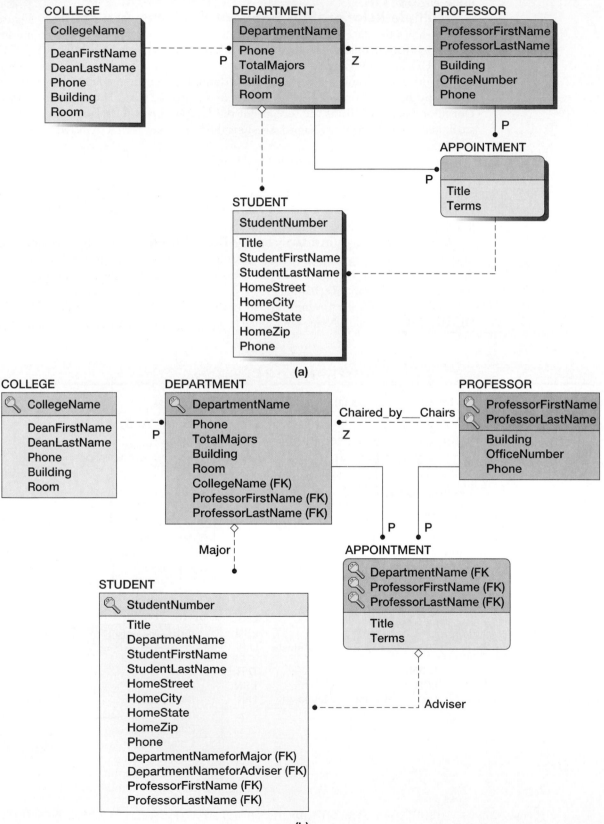

(a)

(b)

and last) is a foreign key back to the PROFESSOR. This latter foreign key is for the Chairs_Chaired_by relationship, and should be marked as AK1.1 (not shown in figure).

In STUDENT, DepartmentNameforMajor is the foreign key for the Major relationships. DepartmentNameforAdviser is a portion of the key of APPOINTMENT that is used to represent the Adviser relationship. The other elements of that foreign key are ProfessorFirstName and ProfessorLastName.

Referential integrity actions are also a straightforward application of the concepts presented in this chapter. We will leave their specification as exercise 5.82.

▶ SPECIAL SITUATIONS

We conclude this chapter with a discussion of three special topics: the representation of recursive relationships, the problems of binary constraints on ternary relationships, and the ambiguity of null values.

Representation of Recursive Relationships

A **recursive relationship** is a relationship among entities of the same class. Recursive relationships are not fundamentally different from other HAS-A relationships and can be represented using the same techniques. As with non-recursive HAS-A relationships, there are three types of recursive relationships: 1:1, 1:N, and N:M; Figure 5-23 shows an example of each.

Consider first the SPONSORED BY relationship. As a 1:1 relationship, one person can sponsor another person, and each person is sponsored by no more than one person. Figure 5-24(a) shows sample data for this relationship.

To represent 1:1 recursive relationships, we take an approach that is nearly identical to that for regular 1:1 relationships: We can place the key of the person being sponsored in the row of the sponsor, or we can place the key of the sponsor in the row of the person being sponsored. Figure 5-24(b) shows the first alternative, and Figure 5-24(c) shows the second. Both work, so the choice depends on performance issues. Because the recursive relationship is 1:1, the foreign key must be defined as UNIQUE.

This technique is identical to that for non-recursive 1:1 relationships, except that both the child and parent rows reside in the same relation. You can think of the process as follows: Pretend that the relationship is between two different relations. Determine where the key goes and then combine the two relations into a single one.

To represent 1:N recursive relationships, consider the REFERRED_BY relationship shown in Figure 5-25. Sample data is shown in Figure 5-25(a). When this data is placed in a relation, one row represents the referrer, and the other rows represent those who have been referred. The referrer row takes the role of the parent, and the referred rows take the role of the child. As with all 1:N relationships, we place the key of the parent in the child. In Figure 5-25(b), we place the number of the referrer in all the rows that have been referred.

Now, consider M:N recursive relationships. The TREATED TREATED BY relationship in Figure 5-26 represents the situation in which doctors give treatments to each

FIGURE 5-23

Example Recursive Relationships

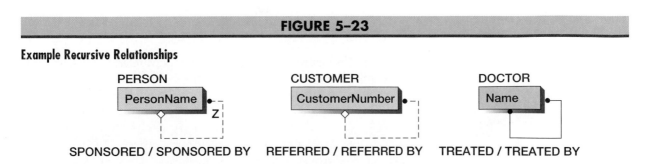

SPONSORED / SPONSORED BY   REFERRED / REFERRED BY   TREATED / TREATED BY

Example of a 1:1 Recursive Relationship (a) Sample Data for 1:1 Recursive Relationship; (b) First Alternative for Representing a 1:1 Recursive Relationship and (c) Second Alternative for Representing a 1:1 Recursive Relationship

Person

Jones
Smith
Parks

Myrtle
Pines

(a)

PERSON1 Relation

Person	PersonSponsored
Jones	Smith
Smith	Parks
Parks	null
Myrtle	Pines
Pines	null

Referential integrity constraint:
PersonSponsored in PERSON1
must exist in Person in PERSON1

(b)

PERSON2 Relation

Person	PersonSponsoredBy
Jones	null
Smith	Jones
Parks	Smith
Myrtle	null
Pines	Myrtle

Referential integrity constraint:
PersonSponsoredBy PERSON2
must exist in Person in PERSON2

(c)

Example of a 1:N Recursive Relationship (a) Sample Data for the REFERRED_BY Relationship and (b) Representing a 1:N Recursive Relationship by Means of a Relation

Customer Number	Referred These Customers
100	200, 400
300	500
400	600, 700

(a)

CUSTOMER Relation

CustomerNumber	CustomerData	ReferredBy
100	. . .	null
200	. . .	100
300	. . .	null
400	. . .	100
500	. . .	300
600	. . .	400
700	. . .	400

Referential integrity constraint:
ReferredBy in CUSTOMER must exist in
CustomerNumber in CUSTOMER

(b)

other. Sample data is shown in Figure 5-26(a). As with other N:M relationships, we must create an intersection table that shows pairs of related rows. The name of the doctor in the first column is the one who provided the treatment, and the name of the doctor in the second column is the one who received the treatment. This structure is shown in Figure 5-26(b).

FIGURE 5–26

Example of an M:N
Recursive Relationship
(a) Sample Data for
the TREATED-BY
Relationship and
(b) Representing an
M:N Recursive
Relationship by Means
of Relations

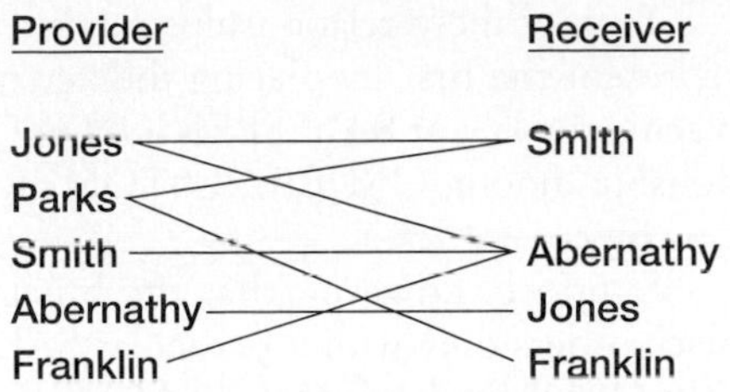

Provider   Receiver

Jones ———————— Smith
Parks ————————
Smith ———————— Abernathy
Abernathy ——————— Jones
Franklin ———————— Franklin

(a)

DOCTOR relation

Name	Other Attributes
Jones	. . .
Parks	. . .
Smith	. . .
Abernathy	. . .
O'Leary	. . .
Franklin	. . .

TREATMENT-INTERSECTION relation

Physician	Patient
Jones	Smith
Parks	Smith
Smith	Abernathy
Abernathy	Jones
Parks	Franklin
Franklin	Abernathy
Jones	Abernathy

Referential integrity constraints:
    Physician in TREATMENT-INTERSECTION
    must exist in Name in DOCTOR

    Patient in TREATMENT-INTERSECTION
    must exist in Name in DOCTOR

(b)

Recursive relationships are thus represented in the same way as are other relationships. The rows of the tables take two different roles, however. Some are parent rows, and others are child rows. If a key is supposed to be a parent key and if the row has no parent, its value will be null. If a key is supposed to be a child key and the row has no child, its value will be null.

Representing Ternary and Higher-Order Relationships

Ternary relationships are represented using the techniques described in this chapter, but there is often a special constraint that needs to be documented as a business rule. To illustrate this constraint, consider the entities ORDER, CUSTOMER, and SALESPERSON.

Assume an ORDER has a single CUSTOMER, but a CUSTOMER can have many ORDERs. Hence, that relationship is binary N:1. Similarly, suppose the ORDER has just one SALESPERSON, and a SALESPERSON has many ORDERs. That relationship is also binary N:1.

Both of these relationships can be represented using the techniques described. We represent the first by placing the key of CUSTOMER in ORDER and the second by placing the key of SALESPERSON in ORDER. Thus, we have treated the ternary relationship among ORDER:CUSTOMER:SALESPERSON as two separate binary relationships.

Suppose, however, that the business has the rule that each CUSTOMER can place orders only with a particular SALESPERSON. In this case, the ternary relationship ORDER:CUSTOMER:SALESPERSON is constrained by an additional binary N:1 relationship between CUSTOMER and SALESPERSON. To represent the constraint (called a MUST constraint), we need to add the key of SALESPERSON to CUSTOMER. The three relations will be as follows:

ORDER (<u>OrderNumber,</u> nonkey data attributes, *CustomerNumber, SalespersonNumber*)

CUSTOMER (<u>CustomerNumber,</u> nonkey data attributes, *SalespersonNumber*)

SALESPERSON (<u>SalespersonNumber,</u> nonkey data attributes)

The constraint that a particular CUSTOMER is sold to by a particular SALESPERSON means that only certain values of CustomerNumber and SalespersonNumber can exist together in ORDER. Unfortunately, there is no way to express this constraint by using the relational model. It must be documented in the design, however, and enforced either by triggers or by application programs. See Figure 5-27(a).

Other types of such binary constraints are MUST NOT and MUST COVER constraints. In a MUST NOT constraint, the binary relationship indicates combinations that are not allowed to occur in the ternary relationship. For example, the ternary relationship PRESCRIPTION:DRUG:CUSTOMER can be constrained by a binary relationship in the ALLERGY table that indicates drugs that a customer is not allowed to take. See Figure 5-27(b).

In a MUST COVER constraint, the binary relationship indicates all combinations that must appear in the ternary relationship. For example, consider the relationship AUTO:REPAIR:TASK. Suppose that a given repair consists of a number of TASKs, all of which must be performed for the REPAIR to be successful. In this case, in the relation AUTO-REPAIR, when a given auto has a given REPAIR, then all of the TASKs for that repair must appear as rows in that relation. See Figure 5-27(c).

None of the three types of binary constraints discussed here can be represented in the relational design. Instead, all the relationships must be treated as a combination of binary relationships. The constraints, however, must be documented as part of the design and implemented in triggers or application programs.

Null values

A **null value** is an attribute value that has never been supplied. The problem of null values is that they are ambiguous. A null value can mean (a) the value is unknown, (b) the value is not appropriate, or (c) the value is known to be blank. For example, consider the attribute DeceasedDate in a CUSTOMER relation. What does a null value for DeceasedDate mean? It could mean the users don't know whether the customer is alive or not, or it could mean that the users know the customer is a corporation and DeceasedDate is inappropriate, or it could mean that the users know both that the customer is a person and that she is alive.

FIGURE 5–27

Examples of Binary Constraints on Ternary Relationships (a) MUST; (b) MUST NOT and (c) MUST COVER

SALESPERSON Table

SalespersonNumber	Other nonkey data
10	
20	
30	

CUSTOMER Table

CustomerNumber	Other nonkey data	SalespersonNumber
1000		10
2000		20
3000		30

← Binary MUST Constraint ⌝

ORDER Table

OrderNumber	Other nonkey data	SalespersonNumber	CustomerNumber
100		10	1000
200		20	2000
300		10	1000
400		30	3000
500			2000

Only 20 is allowed here ⌝

(a)

DRUG Table

DrugNumber	Other nonkey data
10	
20	
30	
45	
70	
90	

ALLERGY Table

CustomerNumber	DrugNumber	Other nonkey data
1000	10	
1000	20	
2000	20	
2000	45	
3000	30	
3000	45	
3000	70	

⌞ Binary MUST NOT Constraint ⌝

PRESCRIPTION Table

PrescriptionNumber	Other nonkey data	DrugNumber	CustomerNumber
100		45	1000
200		10	2000
300		70	1000
400		20	3000
500			2000

Neither 20 nor 45 can appear here ⌝

(b)

FIGURE 5-27

(continued)

REPAIR Table

RepairNumber	Other nonkey data
10	
20	
30	
40	

TASK Table

TaskNumber	Other nonkey data	*RepairNumber*
1001		10
1002		10
1003		10
2001		20
2002		20
3001		30
4001		40

← Binary MUST COVER Constraint ⤵

AUTO-REPAIR Table

InvoiceNumber	RepairNumber	TaskNumber	Other nonkey data
100	10	1001	
200	10	1002	
300	10	1003	
400	20	2001	
500	20		

2002 must appear here⤴

(c)

There are several ways of eliminating these ambiguities. The first is not to allow them. Define the attribute as required. This is fine as long as the attribute truly is required in the minds of the users. The users, however, will be aggravated to be forced to provide a value of CustomerColorPreference if such a value is inessential to their business function.

In Chapter 3, we discussed how to eliminate value-inappropriate nulls using subtypes. Defining MALE-PATIENT and FEMALE-PATIENT as subtypes of PATIENT will eliminate males from having to provide number of pregnancies, and females from being asked the condition of their prostate. This solution, however, is expensive in that it forces the definition of two new tables and requires them to be joined together to have all of the PATIENT data.

Yet a third solution is to define each attribute as having an initial value that is recognized as blank. A text attribute, for example, could be given the initial value (*unknown*). Users could subsequently give it the value (*not appropriate*) when the value is known to be inappropriate. This will be more effective if such choices appear in drop-down text boxes. Although this solution works for text attributes, it leaves the problem for numeric, date, currency, and other nontext attributes. Of course, a solution for them is to model them as text data so that the value of (*unknown*) and (*not appropriate*) can be entered. In that case, however, you have to write your own editing code to ensure that valid numbers, dates, or currency are entered. You'll also have to cast the values in program code before performing numeric or date operations on them.

Sometimes, the best solution is to do nothing about null values. If the users can deal with the ambiguity or if the solution is more costly than it is worth, just document the fact that the problem exists and move on. Also, see the next chapter for more information about the consequences of null values in join operations.

SUMMARY

The data model and other written requirements are the starting points for creating a database design. Each entity in the data model is transformed into a relation. The attributes of the entity become columns of the table. The identifier of the entity becomes the primary key. The table design needs to specify whether or not attributes are allowed to have null values.

The ideal primary key is short, numeric, and seldom changing. If the initial primary key does not have these characteristics, the designers need to select a different key from alternate keys, if possible. If not, a surrogate key should be used.

A surrogate key is a unique DBMS-supplied identifier used as the primary key of a relation. DBMS products vary in the way that surrogate keys are defined. With SQL Server, the Identity Seed is the starting value of the surrogate key, and the Identity Increment is the amount to be added to the current key value to obtain the next key value.

Surrogate keys have two important disadvantages. First, they have no meaning to the users. Whereas a foreign key based on a data key can supply user information (such as DepartmentName), a surrogate key used the same way provides no user information. Second, surrogate key values may be duplicated when data from different databases is merged together. This duplication may necessitate changing surrogate key values and foreign key values as well.

For consistency, some database designers believe that if one table has a surrogate key, then all tables should have surrogate keys. Others believe that surrogate keys should be used only when no good data key is available.

Relationships are represented by placing the primary key of a table into a related table as a foreign key. The way this is done depends on the type of relationship. In all cases, however, creating a foreign key creates a referential integrity constraint.

The default rules for preserving a referential integrity constraint are summarized in Figure 5-6. Updates and deletions on the primary key of the parent are disallowed if the parent row has any child rows. Insertions and updates of the foreign key in the child are disallowed if the new foreign key value does not match a value already present in the primary key column of the parent.

Referential integrity actions can be defined to modify the default behavior for preserving referential integrity constraints. Two common modifications are to allow updates and deletions on the parent to cascade to the child. Other actions can be defined as well.

There is a difference in the way that required parents and required children are represented in a database design. A required parent can be specified by making the foreign key value NOT NULL. A required child can be represented only by creating appropriate update and delete referential integrity actions on the child and appropriate insert referential integrity actions on the parent.

For ID-dependent (identifying connection in IDEF1X) relationships, the primary key of the parent is placed in the child as both a foreign key and as also part of the primary key. The child must have a parent, so the foreign key value is required. Additionally, updates and deletions from the parent can be cascaded in an ID-dependent relationship.

For 1:1 and 1:N HAS-A relationships (non-identifying connection relationships in IDEF1X), the key of one table is placed in the other as a foreign key, but not as a primary key. For 1:1 relationships, the key of either table can be placed in the second table. Because the relationship is 1:1, the foreign key must be made unique.

IDEF1X forces one of the two tables in a 1:1 relationship to be called the parent; the key of this table is placed in the second table. The foreign key will be not null if the system requirements indicate that the parent is required. If the child is required, referential integrity actions need to be specified for this constraint.

For 1:N relationships, the primary of the parent table is placed into the child table. If system requirements indicate that the parent is required, the foreign key will be not null. If the child is required, additional referential integrity actions will need to be specified for this constraint.

In the extended E-R model, a third table called an intersection table must be created to represent N:M relationships. This third table contains the primary keys of the tables having the N:M relationship. The intersection table will have two ID-dependent relationships to the entities in the N:M relationship.

The IDEF1X model views N:M relationships with suspicion; such relationships are termed non-specific relationships. Such relationships suggest that an entity is missing. When this is so, the missing entity is normally ID-dependent on the entities having the apparent N:M relationship. With the IDEF1X philosophy, even if the third entity has no non-key attribute, it still is needed to transpose the N:M non-specific relationship into two identifying connection relationships. At bottom, it does not matter which philosophy you choose; you will finish with the same design.

The intersection table (or equivalently the ID-dependent entity) will always require both parents, so the foreign keys will always be non-null. The minimum cardinality from the original entities to the intersection table is determined from the system requirements. The referential integrity actions from the parents to the intersection table will normally be delete cascade and update cascade. Other referential integrity actions depend on the system requirements.

Subtypes (from the extended E-R model) and categories (from the IDEF1X model) are represented by placing the primary key of the supertype (or generic) entity into the subtype (or category entity). The only difference between the extended E-R approach and the IDEF1X approach is that IDEF1X has category clusters that place constraints on category entities. Specifically, category entities are mutually exclusive in the categories; and for complete categories, the generic entity will have to have exactly one category entity in that cluster. These constraints are enforced by properly specifying referential integrity actions.

Weak, non ID-dependent entities are defined in the extended E-R model. These entities are modeled with 1:1 or 1:N HAS-A relationships. The only difference is that referential integrity actions need to be specified to ensure that when the parent is deleted, the weak entity is deleted as well. Also, a default policy needs to be instituted that ensures that new weak entities have a parent with which to connect.

A recursive relationship occurs when an entity has a relationship to itself. There are three types: 1:1, 1:N, and N:M. These types are represented the same as non- recursive relationships. For 1:1 and 1:N recursive relationships, add a foreign key to the relation that represents the entity. For N:M recursive relationships, add a new intersection table that represents the N:M relationship.

Ternary and higher-order relationships can be treated as combinations of binary relationships. When this is done, however, any binary constraints on the ternary relationship must also be represented in the design. Three types of such constraints occur: MUST, MUST NOT, and MUST COVER. Because it is not possible to enforce the constraint via relational design, these constraints must be documented as business rules and enforced in application programs or triggers.

A null value is an attribute value that has not been supplied. Such values are ambiguous and have three possible interpretations: the value is unknown, the value is inappropriate, or the value is known to be blank. Inappropriate nulls can be avoided by defining subtype or category entities. Other possibilities are to force attribute values through the use of not null or by supplying initial values. Nulls can also be ignored if the attendant ambiguity is not a problem to the users.

GROUP I QUESTIONS

5.1 Describe the inputs to the database design process.

5.2 Name the major tasks in developing a database design.

5.3 Describe the process for transforming an entity into a relation.

5.4 How are entities and relations distinguished in the diagrams in this chapter?

5.5 How do you determine if an attribute is required?

5.6 Besides their role in identifying rows, why are primary keys important?

5.7 Describe the characteristics of an ideal primary key.

5.8 Define alternate key and explain the notation *AKn.m*.

5.9 Describe a situation, other than the one in this chapter, in which an alternate key might be chosen as the primary key because it is more natural.

5.10 Define surrogate key.

5.11 Describe a situation that begs for a surrogate key.

5.12 Define the terms Identity Seed and Identity Increment, and explain their uses.

5.13 Explain two disadvantages of surrogate keys.

5.14 Do you think that if one relation has a surrogate key, all relations in that database should have a surrogate key? Explain why or why not.

5.15 Explain referential integrity constraint and give an example of one.

5.16 Describe the default rules for enforcing referential integrity constraints.

5.17 Explain how referential integrity actions can be used to override the default referential integrity constraints.

5.18 Explain the terms *cascading updates* and *cascading deletions*.

5.19 Describe the way in which a required parent constraint is implemented.

5.20 Describe the way in which a required child constraint is implemented.

5.21 What is the difference between an ID-dependent relationship and an identifying connection relationship?

5.22 How are ID-dependent relationships expressed in the relational model?

5.23 Give an example of two entities having an ID-dependent relationship and show how those entities are expressed using relations. State the referential integrity constraint that results. Use an example other than one in this text.

5.24 In your answer to question 5.23, is the foreign key NULL or NOT NULL? Explain your answer.

5.25 Are cascading updates appropriate for your answer in question 5.23?

5.26 Are cascading deletions appropriate for your answer in question 5.23?

5.27 If deletions are prohibited on the parent row in an ID-dependent relationship, how can the parent row data ever be removed from the database?

5.28 Summarize guidelines for using cascading deletions on ID-dependent relationships.

5.29 If the parent of an ID-dependent relationship has a surrogate key, should the child have one as well? Why or why not?

5.30 Give an example of a 1:1 HAS-A relationship other than the ones in this text. Construct the relationship so that one entity is required and the other is optional.

5.31 For your answer to question 5.30, show two ways to represent the 1:1 relationship. Specify any unique and any required columns.

5.32 What structure does IDEF1X impose upon 1:1 relationships?

5.33 Show two ways to model your answer to question 5.30 using IDEF1X.

5.34 Show the relations that result when you represent the relationships in your answers to question 5.33.

5.35 Specify referential integrity constraints for your answers to question 5.33.

5.36 Specify referential integrity actions for your answers to question 5.33. Justify your decisions.

5.37 In a 1:N relationship, which entity is the parent and which is the child?

5.38 State a general rule for foreign key placement when representing 1:N relationships.

5.39 Give an example of two entities having a 1:N relationship other than ones in this text. Specify minimum cardinalities that you think are appropriate for your example.

5.40 Represent your answer to question 5.39 with relations.

5.41 State the referential integrity constraint in your answer to question 5.40.

5.42 State appropriate referential integrity actions for your answer to question 5.40. Justify your decisions.

5.43 Why does the strategy for representing 1:N relationships not work for representing N:M relationships?

5.44 What is an intersection table? Why is it necessary for N:M relationships?

5.45 Give an example of two entities having an N:M relationship other than the ones in this text.

5.46 Show how to represent the entities in your answer to question 5.45 using an intersection table. Specify minimum cardinalities. Which of these cardinalities are determined by system requirements and which are determined by nature of intersection tables?

5.47 State the referential integrity constraints in your answer to question 5.46.

5.48 State referential integrity actions in your answer to question 5.46. Justify your decisions.

5.49 Explain why the model in Figure 5-17(a) suggests a missing entity.

5.50 Explain the difference between Figures 5-16(b) and 5-17(c). How does the ID-dependent entity in Figure 5-17(c) differ from an intersection table?

5.51 Explain the IDEF1X philosophy regarding N:M relationships.

5.52 Explain the differences in philosophy on N:M relationships between the extended E-R model and the IDEF1X model. Which do you think is the better philosophy?

5.53 What is the difference between supertype/subtype and generic/category entities?

5.54 Give an example of an entity with two category clusters. Use an example other than ones in this text. Make one of your category clusters complete and the other incomplete.

5.55 Show how to represent your answer to question 5.54 with relations.

5.56 State referential integrity constraints for your answer to question 5.55.

5.57 Explain how the rule that category entities be mutually exclusive in their subtypes influences referential integrity actions.

5.58 Explain how referential integrity actions differ between complete and incomplete category clusters.

5.59 Specify referential integrity actions for your answer to question 5.55.

5.60 Explain how weak but not ID-dependent entities can be represented. State required referential integrity actions.

5.61 Give an example of a weak but not ID-dependent entity other than ones in this text.

5.62 Show how to model your answer to question 5.61 using relations. State the referential integrity constraint and referential integrity actions.

5.63 Suppose an entity A has two different 1:N relationships to an entity B. Explain how the relationships will be represented.

5.64 Give examples of the three types of recursive relationships other than ones in this text.

5.65 Using your answer to question 5.64, show how to represent a 1:1 recursive relationship.

5.66 Using your answer to question 5.64, show how to represent a 1:N recursive relationship.

5.67 Using your answer to question 5.64, show how to represent an N:M recursive relationship.

5.68 Give an example, other than one in this text, of a ternary relationship that is constrained by a binary relationship.

5.69 Explain the differences between MUST, MUST NOT, and MUST COVER binary relationship constraints.

5.70 What are three possible interpretations of null values?

5.71 Explain how the definition of subtype or category entities can eliminate the possibility of value-inappropriate nulls.

GROUP II QUESTIONS

5.72 Answer question 3.35 if you have not already done so. Create a database design for the model in your answer to question 3.35(b). Your design should include a specification of tables, attributes, primary and foreign keys, referential integrity constraints, and referential integrity actions.

5.73 Answer question 3.36 if you have not already done so. Create a database design for your model. Your design should include a specification of tables, attributes, primary and foreign keys, referential integrity constraints, and referential integrity actions.

5.74 Answer question 3.37 if you have not already done so. Create a database design for your answer to question 3.37(c). Your design should include a specification of tables, attributes, primary and foreign keys, referential integrity constraints, and referential integrity actions.

5.75 Answer question 3.38 if you have not already done so. Create a database design for each of the different models in your answers to questions A through E. Your design should include a specification of tables, attributes, primary and foreign keys, referential integrity constraints, and referential integrity actions.

5.76 Answer question 3.39 if you have not already done so. Create a database design for the model in your answer to question A and a second design for the model in Figure 3-33. Your design should include a specification of tables, attributes, primary and foreign keys, referential integrity constraints, and referential integrity actions.

5.77 Answer question 3.40, part E, if you have not already done so. Create a database design for your model. Your design should include a specification of tables, attributes, primary and foreign keys, referential integrity constraints, and referential integrity actions.

5.78 Answer question 3.41, part C, if you have not already done so. Create a database design for your model. Your design should include a specification of tables, attributes, primary and foreign keys, referential integrity constraints, and referential integrity actions.

5.79 Answer question 3.42, part D, if you have not already done so. Create a database design for your model. Your design should include a specification of tables, attributes, primary and foreign keys, referential integrity constraints, and referential integrity actions.

5.80 Answer question 3.43, part C, if you have not already done so. Create a database design for your model. You will not be able to specify non-key attributes. Instead, just specify tables, keys, referential integrity constraints, and referential integrity actions.

5.81 Answer question 3.44, part C, if you have not already done so. Create a database design for your model. You will not be able to specify non-key attributes. Instead, just specify tables, keys, referential integrity constraints, and referential integrity actions.

5.82 Consider the database design for Highline University shown in Figure 5-22(b). Use the principles described in this chapter to specify the referential integrity constraints for each of the relationships in this model.

FIREDUP PROJECT QUESTIONS

If you have not already done so, answer question D of the FiredUp Project questions at the end of Chapter 2 (pages 70-71).

Create a database design for your model. Your design should include a specification of tables, attributes, primary and foreign keys, referential integrity constraints, and referential integrity actions.

TWIGS TREE TRIMMING SERVICE PROJECT QUESTIONS

If you have not already done so, answer questions C and E of the Twigs Project Questions end of Chapter 2 (pages 71-72).

A. Create a database design for your answer to question C. Your design should include a specification of tables, attributes, primary and foreign keys, referential integrity constraints, and referential integrity actions.

B. Create a database design for your answer to question E. Your design should include a specification of tables, attributes, primary and foreign keys, referential integrity constraints, and referential integrity actions.

PART III

Structured Query Language

The three chapters in this part address Structured Query Language, or SQL. Chapter 6 introduces the topic and explains basic SQL statements for creating database structures as well as for querying and manipulating database data. Then, Chapter 7 shows SQL in the context of an application. It discusses SQL views and illustrates the use of SQL statements in application programs, triggers and stored procedures.

Chapter 8 concludes this part with a discussion of database redesign. Here, you will learn to use SQL to modify existing database structures. This chapter also presents two more advanced SQL statements: correlated subqueries and EXISTS/NOT EXISTS. These statements are useful not only for traditional queries, but also for examining database content prior to redesign transformations.

CHAPTER 6

Introduction to Structured Query Language (SQL)

This chapter introduces **Structured Query Language** or **SQL**. SQL is not a complete programming language, but rather is a *data sublanguage*. It consists only of language statements for defining and processing a database. To obtain a full programming language, SQL statements must be embedded in scripting languages such as VBScript or in programming languages such as Java or C#. SQL statements can also be used in stored procedures and triggers, and they can be submitted interactively using a DBMS-supplied command prompt. You will learn more about embedding SQL in programming languages and about its use in stored procedures and triggers in the next chapter. In this chapter, we will focus on the syntax of SQL statements and their use from a command prompt.

SQL was developed by the IBM Corporation in the late 1970s and was endorsed as a national standard by the American National Standards Institute (ANSI) in 1992. The version presented here is based on that standard, sometimes referred to as SQL-92. A later version, SQL3, incorporates some object-oriented concepts. This later version has received little attention from commercial DBMS vendors and at present is unimportant for practical database processing. We will consider it briefly in Chapter 16.

The SQL-92 standard is large and comprehensive. None of the major DBMS products, such as DB2, Oracle, or SQL Server, implement the full standard. In this chapter, we will focus on the commonly supported SQL-92 statements. Statements that are particular to Oracle and SQL Server will be discussed in Chapters 10 and 11, respectively.

SQL is text-oriented. It was developed long before graphical user interfaces and requires only a text processor. Today, of course, SQL Server, Oracle, DB2, and other DBMS products provide graphical tools for doing many of the tasks that are performed using SQL. But the key phrase in that last sentence is "many of." You cannot do everything with graphical tools that you can do with SQL; furthermore, you must use SQL to generate SQL statements dynamically in program code.

SQL can be used to define database structures, to query database data, and to update database data. The data definition commands are sometimes referred to as **DDL (data definition language)** and the query and update commands are sometimes called **DML (data manipulation language)**. We will discuss each of these in turn. First, however, we describe a sample database that will be used for illustration.

▶ SAMPLE DATABASE

Figure 6-1 shows a data model and database design for the sample database we will use in this chapter. In this model, a PROJECT is related to one or more ASSIGNMENTs, and an EMPLOYEE is related to zero or more ASSIGNMENTs. ASSIGNMENT is ID-dependent on both PROJECT and EMPLOYEE. Note the foreign key for the EMPLOYEE/ASSIGNMENT relationship is named EmployeeNumber rather than EmployeeID. It still references EmployeeID, however. The two referential integrity constraints are

ASSIGNMENT.ProjectID must exist in PROJECT.ProjectID

and

ASSIGNMENT.EmployeeID must exist in EMPLOYEE.EmployeeNumber

Observe the referential integrity actions in Figure 6-1(b). Both deletions and updates cascade from PROJECT to ASSIGNMENT, but only updates cascade from EMPLOYEE to ASSIGNMENT. Deletions of EMPLOYEE are restricted. If an employee has no assignments, the employee row can be deleted. Otherwise, an employee's existing assignments need to deleted or transferred to another employee before the row for that employee can be deleted.

Because a project must have at least one assignment, inserts to PROJECT are restricted. This means that a related ASSIGNMENT row must be created when a new PROJECT row is created. You will learn how to use triggers for this purpose in Chapter 7.

With regard to actions on ASSIGNMENT, the update of ProjectID is restricted. After an assignment has been made to a particular project, it cannot be moved to another project. Also, the last ASSIGNMENT for a project cannot be deleted. There are no such restrictions on the EMPLOYEE/ASSIGNMENT relationship.

Sample data for these relations are shown in Figure 6-2.

FIGURE 6-1

Example Database (a) Data Model and (b) Database Design

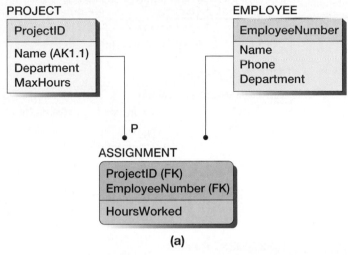

(a)

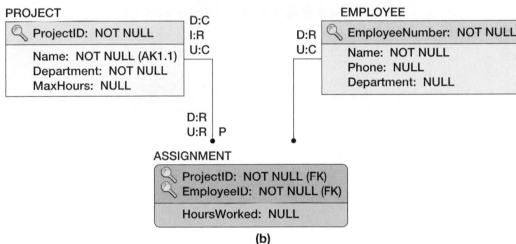

(b)

▶ SQL FOR DATA DEFINITION

The SQL language can be used to create and modify database structures. This chapter discusses only the initial creation of database structures. SQL for the modification of existing database structures is presented in Chapter 8. Tables are created using the SQL CREATE TABLE statement. Sometimes, the ALTER statement is used in conjunction with CREATE TABLE to specify primary and foreign keys, as you will learn.

The CREATE TABLE Statement

The basic function of this statement is to name a new table and describe its columns and their data types. In addition, the CREATE TABLE statement can be used to define both primary and alternate keys; to define foreign keys with some referential integrity actions; and to specify constraints on columns, the table, and column values.

To start, consider the simple example in Figure 6-3. The name of the table is PROJECT, and the definition of four columns is shown enclosed in parentheses. Each column definition has three parts: the *name* of the column, its *data type*, and optional column *constraints*. Like all SQL statements, the SQL CREATE statement is terminated with a semi-colon.

FIGURE 6–2

Sample Data for
PROJECT, EMPLOYEE,
and ASSIGNMENT
Relations

PROJECT Relation

ProjectID	Name	Department	MaxHours
1000	Q3 Portfolio Analysis	Finance	75.0
1200	Q3 Tax Prep	Accounting	145.0
1400	Q4 Product Plan	Marketing	138.0
1500	Q4 Portfolio Analysis	Finance	110.0

EMPLOYEE Relation

EmployeeNumber	Name	Phone	Department
100	Mary Jacobs	285-8879	Accounting
200	Kenji Numoto	287-0098	Marketing
300	Heather Jones	287-9981	Finance
400	Rosalie Jackson	285-1273	Accounting
500	James Nestor		Info Systems
600	Richard Wu	287-0123	Info Systems
700	Kim Sung	287-3222	Marketing

ASSIGNMENT Relation

ProjectID	EmployeeNum	HoursWorked
1000	100	17.50
1000	300	12.50
1000	400	8.00
1000	500	20.25
1200	100	45.75
1600	400	70.50
1200	600	40.50
1400	200	75.00
1400	700	20.25
1400	500	25.25

FIGURE 6–3

Basic CREATE TABLE
Statement

```
CREATE TABLE PROJECT (
    ProjectID       Integer         Primary Key,
    Name            Char(25)        Unique Not Null,
    Department      VarChar(100)    Null,
    MaxHours        Numeric(6,1)    Default 100);
```

There are five types of SQL constraints: PRIMARY KEY, NULL/NOT NULL, UNIQUE, FOREIGN KEY, and CHECK. We will explain the first four of these in this chapter. CHECK constraints will be discussed in Chapter 7.

In Figure 6-3, the column ProjectID is of type *Integer* and has the property *Primary Key*. The next column, Name, is of type character (signified by *Char*) and is 25 characters in length. Because it is an alternate key, the keywords *Unique Not Null* have been added to its description. These keywords mean that Name values are unique in the PROJECT table and that a value for Name is required.

In SQL, primary keys may never have null values. That is why ProjectID can be defined as Primary Key without any null specification. The keywords *Primary Key* imply that ProjectID will have no nulls. Unique columns, however, can have null values. If the keyword *Unique* were specified without *Not Null*, Name could have null values. That specification is unacceptable here, however, because Name is defined as an alternate key in the database design.

The third column, Department, is of type *VarChar(100)* and has the property *Null*. VarChar means variable-length character. Thus, Department contains character data values that vary in length from row to row; and the maximum length of a Department value is 100 characters. *Null* signifies that null values are allowed.

As implied, Char values are fixed-length. The Char(25) definition for Name means that twenty-five characters will be stored for every value of Name, regardless of the length of the value entered. Names will be padded with blanks to fill the 25 spaces where necessary. VarChar values vary in length. If a Department value has only four characters, only four characters will be stored.

Given the advantage of VarChar, why not use it all the time? The answer to this question is that extra processing is required for VarChar columns. A few extra bytes are required to store the length of the value, and the DBMS must go to some trouble to arrange variable length values in memory and on disk. Vendors of DBMS products usually provide guidelines for when to use which type. See the documentation of your DBMS product.

The fourth column of PROJECT has the data type Numeric (6,1). This data type means that MaxHours values consist of six decimal numbers with one number assumed to the right of the decimal point. (The decimal point is not stored and does not count as one of the five.) Thus, the stored value 123456 would be displayed by the DBMS as 12345.6. No column property is assigned to MaxHours, so it is given the default property of Null. The keyword *Default* is used to specify that 100 is to be supplied as the initial value of MaxHours when a new PROJECT row is created.

The four data types illustrated in Figure 6-3 are the basic SQL data types. There are many more in the SQL-92 standard, however, and DBMS vendors have added other data types to their products. Figures 6-4(a) and (b) show some of the data types supported by Microsoft SQL Server and by Oracle.

Defining Primary and Foreign Keys with the ALTER Statement

After a table has been defined, its structure, properties, or constraints can be changed using the ALTER statement. In this chapter, we will show how to use the ALTER statement to create both primary and foreign keys.

For example, Figure 6-5 shows an alternative way to define a primary key by first defining the table and then modifying that definition using the ALTER statement. The EMPLOYEE table is defined with all of its columns, and none of them are defined as primary key. Once the table is defined, the ALTER TABLE then defines a new constraint, called EmployeePK, that specifies EmployeeNumber as the primary key.

The name of the constraint is up to the table designer. Usually, however, database projects have naming standards that should be followed. Here, we are using the standard that constraints defining primary keys be named by appending the name of the table to the letters PK. Other developers (and your professor) will have different standards, however.

In Figure 6-5, compare the way that the primary key is defined for PROJECT and EMPLOYEE. Both ways are correct. The only difference is that the database designer specified the name of the primary key constraint for EMPLOYEE. The primary key constraint of PROJECT will also have a name, but it will be a name chosen by the DBMS. This will likely be some horribly long unintelligible name like SYSTEM_CON-STRAINT_PRIMARY_KEY_WCY8690, or worse. Thus, the second method is generally preferred to the first.

(All constraints are stored in the database metadata. As you will see in Chapters 10 and 11, you can access that metadata using the SQL language. We will not address that topic here because the way this is done varies from DBMS to DBMS. In all cases, however, having an easily recognized name that conforms to a data standard will ease data administration tasks.)

The definition of the third table in Figure 6-5 shows yet another way of defining the primary key. Here, the constraint is placed within the CREATE statement, after all of the columns have been defined. Using this technique, the developer can choose the name of

FIGURE 6–4

SQL Data Types in
DBMS Products
(a) Common Data
Types in SQL Server
(b) Common Data
Types in Oracle

Data Type	Description
Binary	Binary, length 0 to 8000 bytes.
Char	Character, length 0 to 8000 bytes.
Datetime	8-byte datetime. Range from January 1, 1753, through December 31, 9999, with an accuracy of three-hundredths of a second.
Image	Variable length binary data. Maximum length 2,147,483,647 bytes.
Integer	4-byte integer. Value range from -2,147,483,648 through 2,147,483,647.
Money	8-byte money. Range from -922,337,203,685,477.5808 through +922,337,203,685,477.5807, with accuracy to a ten-thousandth of a monetary unit.
Numeric	Decimal – can set precision and scale. Range $-10^{38}+1$ through $10^{38}-1$.
Smalldatetime	4-byte datetime. Range from January 1, 1900, through June 6, 2079, with an accuracy of one minute.
Smallint	2-byte integer. Range from -32,768 through 32,767.
Smallmoney	4-byte money, Range from 214,748.3648 through +214,748.3647, with accuracy to a ten-thousandth of a monetary unit.
Text	Variable length text, maximum length 2,147,483,647 characters.
Tinyint	1-byte integer. Range from 0 through 255.
Varchar	Variable-length character, length 0 to 8000 bytes.

(a)

Data Type	Description
BLOB	Binary large object. Up to 4 gigabytes in length.
CHAR(n)	Fixed length character field of length *n*. Maximum 2,000 characters.
DATE	7-byte field containing both date and time.
INTEGER	Whole number of length 38.
NUMBER(n,d)	Numeric field of length *n*, d places to the right of the decimal
VARCHAR(n) or VARCHAR2(n)	Variable length character field up to *n* characters long. Maximum value of *n* = 4,000

(b)

the constraint, and he or she can specify it at table definition time without using ALTER. Most developers prefer this third method of defining the primary key.

Note, too, that a composite key is defined by listing the attribute names within parentheses. The primary key of ASSIGNMENT is (ProjectID, EmployeeNum). Composite primary keys cannot be defined using the method that was used for the PROJECT table.

The ALTER statement can also be used to define foreign keys, as shown in Figure 6-5. In the next-to-last statement, the constraint EmployeeFK is defined. This constraint indicates that EmployeeNum is a foreign key that references EMPLOYEE.EmployeeNumber. Observe the names of the primary and foreign key columns need not be the same. Also note that the naming standard here is to append the name of the table the foreign key references to the letters *FK*.

When defining foreign keys, the developer can also indicate update and delete referential integrity actions. As explained in Chapter 5, the default behavior for preserving referential integrity constraints is to allow no change to the primary key if related child rows exist and to disallow any deletion if related child rows exist.

Referential integrity actions can be specified using the ON UPDATE and ON DELETE expressions. In Figure 6-5, the referential integrity action of constraint EmployeeFK specifies cascading updates with the keywords ON UPDATE CASCADE.

```
CREATE TABLE PROJECT (
        ProjectID               Integer             Primary Key,
        Name                    Char(25)            Unique Not Null,
        Department              VarChar(100)        Null,
        MaxHours                Numeric(6,1)        Default 100);

CREATE TABLE EMPLOYEE (
        EmployeeNumber          Integer             Not Null,
        Name                    Char(25)            Not Null,
        Phone                   Char(8),
        Department              VarChar(100));

ALTER TABLE EMPLOYEE
        ADD CONSTRAINT EmployeePK PRIMARY KEY (EmployeeNumber);

CREATE TABLE ASSIGNMENT (
        ProjectID       Integer         Not Null,
        EmployeeNum     Integer         Not Null,
        HoursWorked     Numeric (5,2)   DEFAULT 10,
        CONSTRAINT AssignmentPK PRIMARY KEY (ProjectID, EmployeeNum));

ALTER TABLE ASSIGNMENT
        ADD CONSTRAINT EmployeeFK
        FOREIGN KEY (EmployeeNum) REFERENCES EMPLOYEE (EmployeeNumber)
                ON UPDATE CASCADE
                ON DELETE NO ACTION;

ALTER TABLE ASSIGNMENT
        ADD CONSTRAINT ProjectFK
        FOREIGN KEY (ProjectID) REFERENCES PROJECT (ProjectID)
                ON UPDATE CASCADE
                ON DELETE CASCADE;
```

Further, the referential integrity action of EmployeeFK for deletions specifies ON DELETE NO ACTION. This latter specification is unnecessary, by the way, because NO ACTION is the default. It is shown here so that you know that it exists and can be used for documentation purposes.

The constraint ProjectFK defines the ProjectID foreign key. Note that both cascading updates and cascading deletions are defined for it.

Both ON UPDATE CASCADE and ON DELETE CASCADE are part of the SQL-92 standard. Not all DBMS products support them, however. In particular, Oracle allows ON DELETE CASCADE, but does not support ON UPDATE CASCADE. With Oracle, cascading deletion referential integrity action must be implemented by the developer in triggers.

Figure 6-6 shows a different version of Figure 6-5 that uses no ALTER statements. Instead, all constraints are defined within the CREATE statement. Notice the two different ways of defining the foreign key constraints in ASSIGNMENT. One of them defines the constraint within the ProjectID column definition, and the second defines the constraint after the columns have all been defined. With neither of them, however, does the developer name the constraints. Instead, the DBMS will name them.

Preferred Use of CREATE

Figures 6-5 and 6-6 show different techniques and options for defining tables. All other things being equal, I prefer the options that allow the developer to name constraints. I also prefer to minimize use of ALTER so as to keep table definitions within the

FIGURE 6-6

Varieties of SQL
CREATE TABLE
Statements

```
CREATE TABLE PROJECT (
    ProjectID        Integer          Primary Key,
    Name             Char(25)         Unique Not Null,
    Department       VarChar(100)     Null,
    MaxHours         Numeric(6,1)     Default 100);

CREATE TABLE EMPLOYEE (
    EmployeeNumber           Integer         Not Null,
    Name                     Char(25)        Not Null,
    Phone                    Char(8),
    Department               VarChar(100),
    CONSTRAINT EmployeePK PRIMARY KEY (EmployeeNumber));

CREATE TABLE ASSIGNMENT (
    ProjectID                Integer         Not Null
            FOREIGN KEY  REFERENCES PROJECT (ProjectID),
    EmployeeNum              Integer         Not Null,
    HoursWorked              Numeric (5,2)   Default 10,
    CONSTRAINT AssignmentPK PRIMARY KEY (ProjectID, EmployeeNum),
    FOREIGN KEY (EmployeeNum) REFERENCES EMPLOYEE (EmployeeNumber));
```

CREATE statement as much as possible. Figure 6-7 shows CREATE TABLE statements that follow these guidelines. Note, too, that the closing parenthesis of each CREATE TABLE statement is dropped to a separate line for clarity.

The statements in Figure 6-7 and those in Figures 6-5 and 6-6 all result in the same design. The statements in Figure 6-7 just seem more aesthetically pleasing to me. The choice among these alternative techniques is simply a matter of style.

As with style in every discipline, opinions vary. Check with your professor to see if he or she has a different opinion from that expressed here. Over time, you will develop your own preferences, and the teams on which you work will likely have their own SQL coding standards as well.

Submitting SQL to the DBMS

After you have developed a text file with SQL statements like those shown in Figure 6-7, you then submit them to the DBMS. The means by which this is done vary from DBMS to DBMS. With Oracle, you can use a tool called SQL*Plus, which is a text-based command window, or you can use the Oracle Enterprise Manager Console, which provides a graphical user interface for this purpose. With SQL Server, you can use a tool called the Query Analyzer or you can submit SQL within the Visual Studio.NET tool. We will discuss these options in Chapters 10 and 11.

DROP Statements

There are many other SQL DDL statements and options. One of the most useful is DROP TABLE. It is, however, also one of the most dangerous because this statement drops the table's structure **along with all of the table's data**.

If you want to drop a table named CUSTOMER and all of its data, issue the following statement:

DROP TABLE CUSTOMER;

The DROP TABLE statement does not work if the table contains or could contain values needed to fulfill referential integrity constraints. PROJECT, for example, could contain values of ProjectID needed by the foreign key constraint ProjectFK. An attempt to issue the statement DROP TABLE PROJECT will fail and an error message will be generated.

FIGURE 6-7

Recommended Style of CREATE TABLE Statements

```
CREATE TABLE PROJECT (
      ProjectID               Integer         Not Null,
      Name                    Char(25)        Unique Not Null,
      Department              VarChar(100)    Null,
      MaxHours                Numeric(6,1)    Default 100
      CONSTRAINT ProjectPK  PRIMARY KEY (ProjectID));

CREATE TABLE EMPLOYEE (
      EmployeeNumber          Integer         Not Null,
      Name                    Char(25)        Not Null,
      Phone                   Char(8),
      Department              VarChar(100),
      CONSTRAINT EmployeePK PRIMARY KEY (EmployeeNumber));

CREATE TABLE ASSIGNMENT (
      ProjectID               Integer     Not Null,
      EmployeeNum             Integer     Not Null,
      HoursWorked             Numeric (5,2) DEFAULT 10,
      CONSTRAINT AssignmentPK PRIMARY KEY (ProjectID, EmployeeNum),
      CONSTRAINT EmployeeFK FOREIGN KEY
            (EmployeeNum) REFERENCES EMPLOYEE (EmployeeNumber)
                  ON UPDATE CASCADE
                  ON DELETE NO ACTION,
      CONSTRAINT ProjectFK FOREIGN KEY
            (ProjectID) REFERENCES PROJECT (ProjectID)
                  ON UPDATE CASCADE
                  ON DELETE CASCADE);
```

If you want to drop the PROJECT table, you need first either to delete the foreign key constraint ProjectFK or drop the ASSIGNMENT table altogether. You can drop the constraint with the following:

ALTER TABLE ASSIGNMENT DROP CONSTRAINT ProjectFK;

Or, you can drop the ASSIGNMENT table with the following:

DROP TABLE ASSIGNMENT;

After either of these, you can then drop the PROJECT table.

In Chapter 8, we will consider additional uses for the SQL ALTER statement, including its use when changing the structure of tables that have data. For now, we will consider SQL data manipulation language.

▶ SQL FOR RELATIONAL QUERY

After tables have been defined, you can add data to them, modify data values, and delete data. You can also query data in a multitude of ways. SQL statements for these activities will be easier to learn if we begin with query statements. After that, we will show SQL for adding, modifying, and deleting data.

For the following, assume that the sample data shown in Figure 6-2 has already been entered into the database.

Reading Specified Columns from a Single Table

The following SQL statement will query (read) three of the four columns of the PROJECT table:

SELECT   Name, Department, MaxHours

FROM   PROJECT;

Notice that the names of the columns to be queried follow the keyword SELECT, and the name of the relation to use follows the keyword FROM. The result of this statement using the data in the PROJECT table in Figure 6-1 is the following:

Q3 Portfolio Analysis	Finance	75.0
Q3 Tax Prep	Accounting	145.0
Q4 Product Plan	Marketing	138.0
Q4 Portfolio Analysis	Finance	110.0

The result of a SQL SELECT statement is a relation. This is always true for SELECT statements. They start with one or more relations, manipulate them in some way, and then produce a relation. Even if the result of the manipulation is a single number, that number is considered to be a relation with one row and one column.

The order of the column names after the keyword SELECT determines the order of columns in the resulting table. Thus, if we change the order of columns in the SELECT statement above to the following:

SELECT   Name, MaxHours, Department

FROM   PROJECT;

The result will be:

Q3 Portfolio Analysis	75.0	Finance
Q3 Tax Prep	145.0	Accounting
Q4 Product Plan	138.0	Marketing
Q4 Portfolio Analysis	110.0	Finance

The next SQL statement obtains just the Department column from the PROJECT table:

SELECT   Department

FROM   PROJECT;

The result is:

Finance
Accounting
Marketing
Finance

Notice that the first and last rows of this table are duplicates. According to the definition of relation in Chapter 4, however, duplicate rows are prohibited. However, the process of checking for and eliminating duplicate rows is time-consuming. Therefore, by default, DBMS products do not check for duplication. Thus, in practice, duplicate rows do occur.

If the developer wants the DBMS to check for and eliminate duplicate rows, he or she must use the DISTINCT keyword, as follows:

SELECT   DISTINCT Department

FROM   PROJECT;

The result of this statement is:

| Finance |
| Accounting |
| Marketing |

The duplicate row has been eliminated as desired.

Reading Specified Rows from a Single Table

All of the preceding SQL statements selected certain columns for all rows of a table. SQL statements can also be used for the reverse; that is, they can be used to select all of the columns for certain rows. For example, the following SQL statement obtains all of the columns of the PROJECT table for projects sponsored by the Finance department:

SELECT   ProjectID, Name, Department, MaxHours

FROM   PROJECT

WHERE   Department = 'Finance';

The result is:

| 1000 | Q3 Portfolio Analysis | Finance | 75.0 |
| 1500 | Q4 Portfolio Analysis | Finance | 110.0 |

A second way to specify all of the columns of a table is to use the special character * after the keyword SELECT. The following SQL statement is equivalent to the previous one:

SELECT   *

FROM   PROJECT

WHERE   Department = 'Finance';

The result is a table of all of the columns of PROJECT for rows having Department of Finance:

| 1000 | Q3 Portfolio Analysis | Finance | 75.0 |
| 1500 | Q4 Portfolio Analysis | Finance | 110.0 |

The pattern SELECT/FROM/WHERE is the fundamental pattern of SQL SELECT statements. Many different conditions can be placed in a WHERE clause. For example, the following query selects all columns from PROJECT where the MaxHours column is greater than 100:

SELECT   *

FROM   PROJECT

WHERE   MaxHours > 100;

The result is:

1200	Q3 Tax Prep	Accounting	145.0
1400	Q4 Product Plan	Marketing	138.0
1500	Q4 Portfolio Analysis	Finance	110.0

Notice that when the column data type is Char or VarChar, comparison values must be placed in single quotes. If the column is Integer or Numeric, no quotes are necessary. Thus, we use the notation Department = 'Finance' for a WHERE condition of the VarChar column Department, but we use the notation MaxHours = 100 for the Numeric column MaxHours.

(By the way, values placed in quotations are case-sensitive. WHERE Department = 'Finance' and WHERE Department = 'FINANCE' are *not* the same.)

More than one condition can be placed in a WHERE clause by using the keyword AND as follows:

```
SELECT      *
FROM        PROJECT
WHERE       Department = 'Finance' AND MaxHours > 100;
```

The result of this statement is:

1500	Q4 Portfolio Analysis	Finance	110.0

Reading Specified Columns and Specified Rows from a Single Table

We can combine the techniques shown previously to select some columns and some rows from a table. For example, to obtain just the Name and Department of employees in the Accounting department, we use the following:

```
SELECT      Name, Department
FROM        EMPLOYEE
WHERE       Department = 'Accounting';
```

The result is:

Mary Jacobs	Accounting
Rosalie Jackson	Accounting

Another form of the WHERE clause is to specify that a column should have one of a set of values by using the IN keyword as follows:

```
SELECT      Name, Phone, Department
FROM        EMPLOYEE
WHERE       Department IN ('Accounting', 'Finance', 'Marketing');
```

The result is:

Mary Jacobs	285-8879	Accounting
Kenji Numoto	287-0098	Marketing
Heather Jones	287-9981	Finance
Rosalie Jackson	285-1273	Accounting
Kim Sung	287-3222	Marketing

In this result, a row is displayed if it has a Department value equal to any of 'Accounting' or 'Finance' or 'Marketing'.

To select rows that do not have a Department with any of these values, we use NOT IN:

SELECT   Name, Phone, Department

FROM   EMPLOYEE

WHERE   Department NOT IN ('Accounting', 'Finance', 'Marketing');

The result of this query is as follows:

James Nestor		Info Systems
Richard Wu	287-0123	Info Systems

Notice the essential difference between IN and NOT IN. When using IN, the column may equal *any* one of the values in the list. When using NOT IN, the column must not be equal to *all* of the values in the list.

Ranges, Wildcards and Nulls in WHERE Clauses

WHERE clauses can also refer to ranges and partial values. The keyword BETWEEN is used for ranges. For example, the following statement

SELECT   Name, Department

FROM   EMPLOYEE

WHERE   EmployeeNumber BETWEEN 200 AND 500;

obtains the following result:

Kenji Numoto	Marketing
Heather Jones	Finance
Rosalie Jackson	Accounting
James Nestor	Info Systems

This statement is equivalent to the following:

SELECT   Name, Department

FROM   EMPLOYEE

WHERE   EmployeeNumber >= 200

         AND   EmployeeNumber <= 500;

Thus, the end values of BETWEEN (here 200 and 500) are included in the selected range.

The keyword LIKE is used in SQL expression to select on partial values. The underscore symbol _ represents a single unspecified character. It can be used to find values that fit a pattern, as in the following:

SELECT   *

FROM   PROJECT

WHERE   Name LIKE 'Q_ Portfolio Analysis';

The underscore means that any character can occur in that spot. The result of this statement is:

1000	Q3 Portfolio Analysis	Finance	75.0
1500	Q4 Portfolio Analysis	Finance	110.0

To find all employees who have a phone that begins with '285', we can use four underscores to represent any last four digits, as follows:

```
SELECT      *
FROM        EMPLOYEE
WHERE       Phone LIKE '285-____';
```

The result is:

100	Mary Jacobs	285-8879	Accounting
400	Rosalie Jackson	285-1273	Accounting

The percent sign symbol (%) is used to represent a series of one or more unspecified characters. Another way to write the query for employees having a phone number starting with '285' is the following:

```
SELECT      *
FROM        EMPLOYEE
WHERE       Phone LIKE '285%';
```

The result is the same as previously.

If we want to find all the employees who work in Departments that end in *ing*, we could use the % character as follows:

```
SELECT      *
FROM        EMPLOYEE
WHERE       Department LIKE '%ing';
```

The result is:

100	Mary Jacobs	285-8879	Accounting
200	Kenji Numoto	287-0098	Marketing
400	Rosalie Jackson	285-1273	Accounting
700	Kim Sung	287-3222	Marketing

By the way, Microsoft Access uses different symbols than the SQL-92 standard. Access uses a question mark (?) instead of an underscore and an asterisk (*) instead of a percent sign.

The keyword IS NULL can be used in a WHERE clause to search for null values. The following SQL finds the names and departments of all employees having a null value for phone:

```
SELECT      Name, Department
FROM        EMPLOYEE
WHERE       Phone IS NULL;
```

The result of this query is:

James Nestor	Info Systems

Sorting the Results

The order of rows in the results of a SELECT statement is arbitrary. If this is undesirable, the ORDER BY phrase can be used to sort the rows. For example, the following displays the names and departments of all employees sorted by Department:

```
SELECT      Name, Department
FROM        EMPLOYEE
ORDER BY    Department;
```

The result is:

Mary Jacobs	Accounting
Rosalie Jackson	Accounting
Heather Jones	Finance
James Nestor	Info Systems
Richard Wu	Info Systems
Kenji Numoto	Marketing
Kim Sung	Marketing

By default, SQL sorts in ascending order. The keywords ASC and DESC can be used to specify ascending and descending when necessary. Thus, to sort employees in descending order by Department, use the following:

```
SELECT      Name, Department
FROM        EMPLOYEE
ORDER BY    Department DESC;
```

The result is:

Kenji Numoto	Marketing
Kim Sung	Marketing
Richard Wu	Info Systems
James Nestor	Info Systems
Heather Jones	Finance
Rosalie Jackson	Accounting
Mary Jacobs	Accounting

Two or more columns may also be used for sorting purposes. To sort the employee names and departments first in descending value of Department and then within Department by ascending value of Name, we would specify the following:

```
SELECT      Name, Department
FROM        EMPLOYEE
ORDER BY    Department DESC, Name ASC;
```

The result is:

Kenji Numoto	Marketing
Kim Sung	Marketing
James Nestor	Info Systems
Richard Wu	Info Systems
Heather Jones	Finance
Mary Jacobs	Accounting
Rosalie Jackson	Accounting

SQL Built-in Functions

SQL includes five built-in functions: COUNT, SUM, AVG, MAX, and MIN. These functions operate on the results of a SELECT statement. COUNT works regardless of column data type; but SUM, AVG, MAX, and MIN operate only on integer, numeric, and other number-based columns.

COUNT and SUM sound similar but are different. COUNT counts the number of rows in the result; SUM totals the values in a numeric column. Thus, the following SQL statement counts the number of rows in the PROJECT table:

SELECT   COUNT(*)

FROM   PROJECT;

The result of this statement is the following relation:

4

As stated earlier, the result of a SQL SELECT statement is always a relation. If, as is the case here, the result is a single number, that number is considered to be a relation with a single row and a single column.

Consider the following two SELECT statements:

SELECT   COUNT (Department)

FROM   PROJECT;

and

SELECT   COUNT (DISTINCT Department)

FROM   PROJECT;

The result of the first statement is the relation:

4

Whereas the result of the second is:

3

The difference in answers occurs because duplicate rows were eliminated in the count in the second SELECT.

Another example of the use of built-in functions is the following:

SELECT   MIN(MaxHours), MAX(MaxHours), SUM(MaxHours)

FROM   PROJECT

WHERE   ProjectID < 1500;

The result is:

| 75.00 | 145.00 | 358.00 |

Except as shown with GROUP BY below, column names cannot be mixed with built-in functions. Thus, the following is NOT ALLOWED:

```
SELECT          Name, SUM(MaxHours)
FROM            PROJECT
WHERE           ProjectID < 1500;
```

Also, DBMS products vary in the ways in which built-in functions can be used. In SQL-92 and in most products, built-in functions cannot be used in WHERE clauses. Thus, a WHERE clause such as the following is not normally allowed:

```
WHERE           MaxHours < AVG(MaxHours)
```

Built-in Functions and Grouping

To increase the utility of built-in functions, they can be applied to groups of rows of data. For example, the following statement counts the number of employees in each department:

```
SELECT          Department, Count(*)
FROM            EMPLOYEE
GROUP BY        Department;
```

The result is:

Accounting	2
Finance	1
Info Systems	2
Marketing	2

The GROUP BY keyword tells the DBMS to sort the table by the named column and then to apply the built-in function to groups of rows having the same value of the named column. When GROUP BY is used, the name of the grouping column and built-in functions may appear in the SELECT phrase. This is the only time that a column and a built-in function can appear together.

We can further restrict the results by applying conditions to the groups that are formed. For example, if we want to consider only groups with more than two members, we could specify the following:

```
SELECT          Department, Count(*)
FROM            EMPLOYEE
GROUP BY        Department
HAVING          COUNT(*) > 1;
```

The result of this SQL statement is as follows:

Accounting	2
Info Systems	2
Marketing	2

It is possible to add WHERE clauses when using GROUP BY. There is an ambiguity when this is done, however. If the WHERE condition is applied before the groups are formed, we will obtain one result. On the other hand, if the WHERE condition is applied after the groups are formed, we get a different result. To resolve this ambiguity, the SQL standard specifies that when WHERE and GROUP BY occur together, the WHERE condition will be applied first. For example, consider the following statement:

SELECT	Department, Count(*)
FROM	EMPLOYEE
WHERE	EmployeeNumber < 600
GROUP BY	Department
HAVING	COUNT(*) > 1;

In this expression, first the WHERE clause is applied to select employees with an EmployeeNumber less than 600. Then, the groups are formed, and finally the HAVING condition is applied. The result is the following:

Accounting	2

Querying Multiple Tables with Subqueries

The queries we have considered so far have involved data from a single table. There are times, however, when more than one table must be processed to obtain the desired information. For example, suppose we want to know the names of all employees who have worked more than 40 hours on any single assignment. The names of employees are stored in the EMPLOYEE table, but the hours they have worked are stored in the ASSIGNMENT table.

If we knew that employees 100 and 500 have worked more than 40 hours on an assignment, we could obtain their names with the following expression:

SELECT	DISTINCT Name
FROM	EMPLOYEE
WHERE	EmployeeNumber IN (100, 500);

According to the problem description, however, we are not given the employee numbers. We can, however, obtain the appropriate employee numbers with the following:

SELECT	EmployeeNum
FROM	ASSIGNMENT
WHERE	HoursWorked > 40;

The result is:

100
400
600
200

Now, we can combine these two SQL statements using what is called a **subquery**, as follows:

SELECT	DISTINCT Name
FROM	EMPLOYEE
WHERE	EmployeeNumber IN

```
(SELECT        EmployeeNum
FROM           ASSIGNMENT
WHERE          HoursWorked > 40);
```

The result of this expression is:

| Kenji Numoto |
| Mary Jacobs |
| Richard Wu |
| Rosalie Jackson |

These are indeed the names of the employees who have worked more than 40 hours on any single assignment.

Subqueries can be extended to include three, four, or even more levels. Suppose, for example, we need to know the names of employees who have worked more than 40 hours on a project sponsored by the Accounting department.

We can obtain the ProjectIDs of projects sponsored by accounting with the following:

```
SELECT        ProjectID
FROM          PROJECT
WHERE         Department = 'Accounting';
```

We can obtain the EmployeeNums of employees working more than 40 hours on those projects with the following:

```
SELECT        EmployeeNum
FROM          ASSIGNMENT
WHERE         HoursWorked > 40
    AND       ProjectID IN
              (SELECT        ProjectID
              FROM           PROJECT
              WHERE          Department = 'Accounting');
```

Finally, we can obtain the names of the employees in the above SQL statement with the following:

```
SELECT        DISTINCT Name
FROM          EMPLOYEE
WHERE         EmployeeNumber IN
              (SELECT        EmployeeNum
              FROM           ASSIGNMENT
              WHERE          HoursWorked > 40
                  AND        ProjectID IN
                             (SELECT        ProjectID
                             FROM           PROJECT
                             WHERE          Department = 'Accounting'));
```

The result is:

| Mary Jacobs |
| Richard Wu |
| Rosalie Jackson |

Querying Multiple Tables with Joins

Subqueries are effective for processing multiple tables as long as the results (the columns in the SELECT phrase) come from a single table. If we need to display data from two or more tables, however, subqueries won't work. We need to use a **join** operation instead.

The basic idea of a join is to form a new relation by connecting the contents of two or more other relations. Consider the following example:

SELECT	Name, HoursWorked
FROM	EMPLOYEE, ASSIGNMENT
WHERE	EmployeeNumber = EmployeeNum;

The meaning of this statement is to create a new table having the two columns Name and HoursWorked. Those columns are to be taken from the EMPLOYEE and ASSIGNMENT tables under the condition that EmployeeNumber (in EMPLOYEE) equals EmployeeNum (in ASSIGNMENT).

You can think of the operation as follows: Start with the first row in EMPLOYEE. Using the value of EmployeeNumber in this first row (100 for the data in Figure 6-1), examine the rows in ASSIGNMENT. When you find a row in ASSIGNMENT where EmployeeNum is also equal to 100, join Name of the first row of EMPLOYEE with HoursWorked from the row you just found in ASSIGNMENT.

For the data in Figure 6-1, the first row of ASSIGNMENT has EmployeeNum equal to 100, so we join Name from the first row of EMPLOYEE with HoursWorked from the first row in ASSIGNMENT to form the first row of the join:

| Mary Jacobs | 17.5 |

Now, still using the EmployeeNumber value of 100, look for a second row in ASSIGN-MENT that has EmployeeNum equal to 100. For our data, the fifth row of ASSIGNMENT has such a value. So, join the Name from the first row of EMPLOYEE to the HoursWorked in the fifth row of ASSIGNMENT to obtain the second row of the join, as follows:

| Mary Jacobs | 17.50 |
| Mary Jacobs | 45.75 |

Continue in this way, looking for matches for the EmployeeNumber value of 100. There are no more in our sample data, so now move to the second row of EMPLOYEE, obtain the new value of EmployeeNumber of 200, and begin searching for matches for it in the rows of ASSIGNMENT. In this case, the eighth row has such a match, so we take Name and HoursWorked and add them to our result to obtain:

Mary Jacobs	17.50
Mary Jacobs	45.75
Kenji Numoto	75.00

We continue in this way until all rows of EMPLOYEE have been examined. The final result will be:

Mary Jacobs	17.50
Mary Jacobs	45.75
Kenji Numoto	75.00
Heather Jones	12.50
Rosalie Jackson	8.00
Rosalie Jackson	70.50
James Nestor	20.25
James Nestor	25.25
Richard Wu	40.50
Kim Sung	20.25

Processing the Joined Table This joined table can be processed like any other table. For example, we can group the rows of the join by employee and sum the hours they worked. The SQL for such a query is the following:

SELECT   Name, SUM(HoursWorked)
FROM   EMPLOYEE, ASSIGNMENT
WHERE   EmployeeNumber = EmployeeNum
GROUP BY   Name;

The result of this query is:

Heather Jones	12.50
James Nestor	45.50
Kenji Numoto	75.00
Kim Sung	20.25
Mary Jacobs	63.25
Richard Wu	40.50
Rosalie Jackson	78.50

Or, we can apply a WHERE clause during the process of creating the join as follows:

SELECT   Name, HoursWorked
FROM   EMPLOYEE, ASSIGNMENT
WHERE   EmployeeNumber = EmployeeNum
       AND   HoursWorked > 40;

The result of this join is:

Mary Jacobs	45.75
Rosalie Jackson	70.50
Richard Wu	40.50
Kenji Numoto	75.00

A join is just another table, so all of the earlier SQL SELECT commands are available to it.

Now, suppose that we want to join PROJECTs to ASSIGNMENTs. We can use the same SQL statement structure as before, except for one complication. There are two columns named ProjectID: one is in the PROJECT table and one is in the ASSIGNMENT table. We can eliminate the ambiguity in these names by appending the name of the table to the column name, as we have done before. Thus, we will refer to the ProjectID in the PROJECT table as PROJECT.ProjectID and refer to the ProjectID in the ASSIGNMENT table as ASSIGNMENT.ProjectID. Using this nomenclature, a join of the PROJECT and ASSIGNMENT tables is as follows:

SELECT	Name, HoursWorked
FROM	PROJECT, ASSIGNMENT
WHERE	PROJECT.ProjectID = ASSIGNMENT.ProjectID;

The result of this expression is the following:

Q3 Portfolio Analysis	17.50
Q3 Portfolio Analysis	12.50
Q3 Portfolio Analysis	8.00
Q3 Portfolio Analysis	20.25
Q3 Tax Prep	45.75
Q3 Tax Prep	70.50
Q3 Tax Prep	40.50
Q4 Product Plan	75.00
Q4 Product Plan	20.25
Q4 Product Plan	25.25

The results shown here are correct, but there is a surprising result. What happened to the project named Q4 Portfolio Analysis? It does not appear in the join results because there was no match for its ProjectID value of 1500 in the ASSIGNMENT table. There is nothing wrong with this result; you just need to be aware that unmatched rows will not appear in the result of a join.

Joining Three Tables We will consider the disappearing row problem further, but before we do, consider the need for joining three tables together. Suppose, for example, we want to know the Name of each project, the HoursWorked on that project, and the Name of the Employee who worked those hours. To obtain this result, we need to join all three tables together, as follows:

SELECT	PROJECT.Name, HoursWorked, EMPLOYEE.Name
FROM	PROJECT, ASSIGNMENT, EMPLOYEE
WHERE	PROJECT.ProjectID = ASSIGNMENT.ProjectID
AND	EMPLOYEE.EmployeeNumber = ASSIGNMENT.EmployeeNum;

The result of this join is the following:

Q3 Portfolio Analysis	17.50	Mary Jacobs
Q3 Portfolio Analysis	12.50	Heather Jones
Q3 Portfolio Analysis	8.00	Rosalie Jackson
Q3 Portfolio Analysis	20.25	James Nestor
Q3 Tax Prep	45.75	Mary Jacobs
Q3 Tax Prep	70.50	Rosalie Jackson
Q3 Tax Prep	40.50	Richard Wu
Q4 Product Plan	75.00	Kenji Numoto
Q4 Product Plan	20.25	Kim Sung
Q4 Product Plan	25.25	James Nestor

Alternate Join Syntax SQL-92 introduced an alternative join syntax that has become very popular because it is easier to interpret. This syntax substitutes the words JOIN and ON for WHERE, as follows:

```
SELECT        Name, HoursWorked
FROM          EMPLOYEE JOIN ASSIGNMENT
    ON        EMPLOYEE.EmployeeNumber = ASSIGNMENT.EmployeeNum;
```

The results of this are:

Mary Jacobs	17.50
Mary Jacobs	45.75
Kenji Numoto	75.00
Heather Jones	12.50
Rosalie Jackson	8.00
Rosalie Jackson	70.50
James Nestor	20.25
James Nestor	25.25
Richard Wu	40.50
Kim Sung	20.25

In addition, it is possible to improve the readability of a join by using aliases for table names. The expression FROM EMPLOYEE E will assign the alias E to the EMPLOYEE table. Using this syntax the join above is the following:

```
SELECT        Name, HoursWorked
FROM          EMPLOYEE AS E JOIN ASSIGNMENT AS A
    ON        E.EmployeeNumber = A.EmployeeNum;
```

A join of three tables is expressed by adding the third join to the end of this join, as follows:

```
SELECT        P.Name, HoursWorked, E.Name
FROM          PROJECT P JOIN ASSIGNMENT A
    ON        P.ProjectID = A.ProjectID
    JOIN    EMPLOYEE E
    ON        A.EmployeeNum = E.EmployeeNumber;
```

Observe that when you need to qualify a column name in the first line of the SELECT, the alias must be used as the qualifier rather than the table name. Thus, the preceding SELECT uses P.Name and not PROJECT.Name. Also note that the keyword AS can be omitted, if desired.

As queries become more complicated, this format is easier to interpret and it is the format we will use for all of the joins in Chapters 7 and 8. You should know both formats, however, because both are used in industry.

Comparison of SQL Subquery and Join

A join can be used as an alternative way of expressing many subqueries. For example, we used a subquery to find the names of employee who have worked more than 40 hours on a project. We can also use a join to express this query:

```
SELECT        DISTINCT Name
FROM          EMPLOYEE JOIN ASSIGNMENT
    ON        EMPLOYEE.EmployeeNumber = ASSIGNMENT.EmployeeNum
    AND    HoursWorked > 40;
```

Although join expressions can substitute for many subquery expressions, they cannot substitute for all of them. For instance, joins cannot substitute for correlated subqueries nor for queries that involve EXISTS and NOT EXISTS (discussed in Chapter 8).

Similarly, subqueries cannot be substituted for all joins. When using a join, the displayed columns may come from any of the joined tables. When using a subquery, however, the displayed columns may come from only the table named in the FROM expression in the first SELECT. For example, in the following subquery, only columns from the EMPLOYEE number may appear in the result:

```
SELECT        DISTINCT Name
FROM          EMPLOYEE
WHERE         EmployeeNumber IN
                (SELECT       EmployeeNum
                FROM          ASSIGNMENT
                WHERE         ProjectID IN
                    (SELECT       ProjectID
                    FROM          PROJECT
                    WHERE         Department = 'Accounting'));
```

If we want to include ASSIGNMENT.HoursWorked and PROJECT.Name, we must use a join:

```
SELECT        EMPLOYEE.Name, HoursWorked, PROJECT.Name
FROM          EMPLOYEE, ASSIGNMENT, PROJECT
WHERE         EMPLOYEE.EmployeeNumber = ASSIGNMENT.EmployeeNum
    AND       ASSIGNMENT.ProjectID = PROJECT.ProjectID;
```

Or, using the alternate join format:

```
SELECT        EMPLOYEE.Name, HoursWorked, PROJECT.Name
FROM          EMPLOYEE JOIN ASSIGNMENT
    ON        EMPLOYEE.EmployeeNumber = ASSIGNMENT.EmployeeNum
    JOIN    PROJECT
    ON        ASSIGNMENT.ProjectID = PROJECT.ProjectID;
```

Outer Joins

In an earlier example, we saw that data can be lost when performing a join. In particular, if a row has a value that does not match the WHERE clause condition, that row will not be included in the join result. Project 'Q4 Portfolio Analysis' was lost in a previous join because there was no row in ASSIGNMENT that matched its ProjectID value. This loss is not always desirable, so a special type of join called an **outer join** was created to avoid it.

If we wish to construct the join so that every row on the table on the left hand side is included in the results even though the row may not have a match, we must use the following join syntax:

SELECT   Name, HoursWorked

FROM   PROJECT LEFT JOIN ASSIGNMENT

       ON   PROJECT.ProjectID = ASSIGNMENT.ProjectID;

The meaning of this join is to append rows of PROJECT to those of ASSIGN-MENT, as described previously, except that if any row in the table on the left side of the JOIN keyword (here, it is PROJECT) has no match, include it in the results anyway. For the sample data in Figure 6-2, the result of this query is:

Q3 Portfolio Analysis	17.50
Q3 Portfolio Analysis	12.50
Q3 Portfolio Analysis	8.00
Q3 Portfolio Analysis	20.25
Q3 Tax Prep	45.75
Q3 Tax Prep	70.50
Q3 Tax Prep	40.50
Q4 Product Plan	75.00
Q4 Product Plan	20.25
Q4 Product Plan	25.25
Q4 Portfolio Analysis	Null

Notice that the last row of this table appends 'Q4 Portfolio Analysis' to a null value.

Right outer joins operate similarly, except that rows in the table on the right side of the FROM clause are included:

SELECT   Name, HoursWorked

FROM   PROJECT RIGHT JOIN ASSIGNMENT

       ON   PROJECT.ProjectID = ASSIGNMENT.ProjectID;

Outer joins can be nested. For example, we can join all three tables together with the following nested outer joins:

SELECT   PROJECT.Name, HoursWorked, EMPLOYEE.Name

FROM   ((PROJECT LEFT JOIN ASSIGNMENT

       ON   PROJECT.ProjectID = ASSIGNMENT.ProjectID)

                LEFT   JOIN EMPLOYEE

                       ON   EMPLOYEE.EmployeeNumber =
                                Assignment.EmployeeNum);

The result of this join is:

Q3 Portfolio Analysis	17.50	Mary Jacobs
Q3 Portfolio Analysis	12.50	Heather Jones
Q3 Portfolio Analysis	8.00	Rosalie Jackson
Q3 Portfolio Analysis	20.25	James Nestor
Q3 Tax Prep	45.75	Mary Jacobs
Q3 Tax Prep	70.50	Rosalie Jackson
Q3 Tax Prep	40.50	Richard Wu
Q4 Product Plan	75.00	Kenji Numoto
Q4 Product Plan	20.25	Kim Sung
Q4 Product Plan	25.25	James Nestor
Q4 Portfolio Analysis	Null	Null

▶ SQL FOR DATA MODIFICATION

There are three data modification operations: insert, modify, and delete. We will consider SQL for each of these in turn.

Inserting Data

Data can be added to a relation using the SQL INSERT command. There are two forms of this command, depending on whether or not data for all of the columns is supplied. If data for all columns is supplied, the following INSERT can be used:

INSERT INTO PROJECT VALUES (1600, 'Q4 Tax Prep', 'Accounting', 100);

Observe that Integer and Numeric values are not enclosed in quotes, but that Char and VarChar values are.

If data for some columns are missing, the names of the columns for which data is provided must be listed. For example, the following adds a new row with values for Name and ProjectID and nulls for Department and MaxHours:

INSERT INTO PROJECT (Name, ProjectID) VALUES ('Q1+ Tax Prep', 1700);

Note, however, the default of MaxHours was set to 100 in the CREATE TABLE statement for PROJECT, so even though no MaxHours value was provided in the INSERT statement, the DBMS will set it to 100. Department will be stored as a null value.

There are several additional points to make regarding the second version of the INSERT command. First, the order of the column names must match the order of the values. In the previous example, the order of the column names is Name, ProjectID, so the order of the values must also be Name, ProjectID. (By the way, this is not the order of the columns in the table.) Second, for the insert to work, values for all NOT NULL columns must be provided.

Third, with either version of INSERT, if the primary key is a surrogate key, no value needs to be provided for it; the DBMS provides it automatically. Hence, if ProjectID is a surrogate key, we can insert a row as follows:

INSERT INTO PROJECT VALUES ('Q4 Tax Prep', 'Accounting', 100);

The value for ProjectID will be provided by the DBMS. As an aside, if you're using Oracle, this is slightly different, as you will learn in Chapter 10.

Finally, for bulk inserts from a second table, it is possible to use a select statement to provide the values. For example, the following SQL copies the values of Name and EmployeeNumber from table EMPLOYEE to a second table named EMPLOYEE1:

INSERT INTO EMPLOYEE1 (Name, EmployeeNumber)

SELECT Name, EmployeeNumber

FROM EMPLOYEE;

Notice in this case that the keyword VALUES is not included in the INSERT statement.

Modifying Data

The values of existing data can be modified using the SQL UPDATE command. This is a powerful command, however, that needs to be used with care. Consider the following example:

UPDATE   EMPLOYEE

SET   Phone = '287-1435'

WHERE   Name = 'James Nestor';

This command sets the value of the Phone column in the row for 'James Nestor' to '287-1435'.

Now, consider the need for care when using this command. Suppose that while intending to make this update, you make an error and forget to include the WHERE clause. Thus, you submit the following to the DBMS:

UPDATE   EMPLOYEE

SET   Phone = '287-1435';

After this command has executed, the EMPLOYEE relation appears as follows:

100	Mary Jacobs	287-1435	Accounting
200	Kenji Numoto	287-1435	Marketing
300	Heather Jones	287-1435	Finance
400	Rosalie Jackson	287-1435	Accounting
500	James Nestor	287-1435	Info Systems
600	Richard Wu	287-1435	Info Systems
700	Kim Sung	287-1435	Marketing

This is clearly not what you intended. If you were to do this at your new job where there might be, say, 10,000 rows in the EMPLOYEE table, you'd most likely have a sinking feeling in the pit of your stomach (as you update your resume…).

So, the message here is: UPDATE is powerful and easy to use, but is also capable of causing disasters.

UPDATE can also be used to modify more than one column value at a time. The following SQL illustrates this:

UPDATE   EMPLOYEE

SET   Phone = '285-0091', Department = 'Production'

WHERE   EmployeeNumber = 200;

This command changes the values of both Phone and Department for the indicated employee.

Deleting Data

You can eliminate rows with the SQL DELETE command. The same warnings pertain to DELETE, however, as the warnings given for UPDATE. It is deceptively simple to use and very easy to apply in unintended ways. The following deletes all projects sponsored by the Accounting department:

```
DELETE
FROM        PROJECT
WHERE       Department = 'Accounting';
```

Given the ON DELETE CASCADE referential integrity constraint, this delete operation not only removes PROJECT rows, it also removes any related ASSIGNMENT ROWS. For the data in Figure 6-1, this delete operation removes the fifth and seventh rows of the ASSIGNMENT table.

As with UPDATE, if you forget to include the WHERE clause, disaster will ensue. For example, the following deletes all of the rows in PROJECT (and, because of the CASCADE DELETE constraint, all of the related ASSIGNMENT rows as well):

```
DELETE
FROM        PROJECT;
```

This truly would be a disaster!

Observe how the referential integrity actions differ between PROJECT and EMPLOYEE. If we try to process the following command, the delete operation will fail because rows in ASSIGNMENT depend on the value of 100 in EMPLOYEE:

```
DELETE
FROM        EMPLOYEE
WHERE       EmployeeNumber = 100;
```

If you want to delete the row for this employee, you must first reassign or delete the rows in ASSIGNMENT.

SUMMARY

Structured Query Language, or SQL, is a data sublanguage that has constructs for defining and processing a database. It can be used stand-alone within a DBMS command processing window, it can be embedded in triggers and stored procedures, or it can be used in scripting languages such as VBScript or programming languages such as Java and C#.

SQL was developed by IBM and was endorsed as a national standard by ANSI in 1992. A later version, SQL3, has not gained acceptance in industry and is not considered here. Modern DBMS products provide graphical facilities for accomplishing many of the tasks that SQL does. Use of SQL is mandatory for dynamically creating SQL statements from programs.

The CREATE TABLE statement is used for creating relations. Each column is described with three parts: the column name, data type, and optional constraints. There are five types of constraints: PRIMARY KEY, UNIQUE, NULL/NOT NULL, FOR-

EIGN KEY, and CHECK. (CHECK constraints will be described in the next chapter.) The default constraint is NULL.

Primary keys may never have null values, and the constraint PRIMARY KEY includes NOT NULL. Columns with UNIQUE constraints may have null values. If a column is to be both UNIQUE and NOT NULL, both constraints must be specified.

Standard data types are Char, VarChar, Integer, and Numeric; they have been supplemented by DBMS vendors. VarChar allows for varying character lengths, but requires additional processing than for fixed length Char data types. (See your DBMS product documentation for guidance about when to use which one.) Figure 6-4 shows some of the additional data types for SQL Server and Oracle.

Constraints can be defined within the CREATE TABLE statement, or they can be added to the table after it is created by using the ALTER table statement. Some forms of constraint definition allow the developer to name the constraint and some forms do not. In the latter, the DBMS names the constraint with a long and not particularly meaningful name. In this text, we will use forms of CREATE TABLE and ALTER that always allow the developer to name the constraint. Additionally, if possible, the constraint will be defined within the CREATE TABLE statement. Figure 6-7 shows the preferred method for defining tables and constraints.

Tables (and their data) may be removed from the database using DROP TABLE. Constraints may be removed using the ALTER TABLE DROP CONSTRAINT command.

The basic format of the SQL SELECT command is SELECT (column names or *), FROM (table names, separated by commas, if there are more than one), WHERE (conditions). SELECT can be used to obtain specific columns, specific rows, or both.

Conditions after the WHERE clause require quotes around values for Char and VarChar columns, but no quotes for Integer and Numeric columns. Compound conditions can be specified with AND. Sets of values can be used with IN (match any in the set) or NOT IN (not match all in the set). The wildcards _ and % can be used with LIKE to specify a single unknown character or multiple unknown characters, respectively. IS NULL can be used to test for null values.

Results can be sorted using the ORDER BY command. The five SQL built-in functions are COUNT, SUM, MAX, MIN, and AVG. Groups can be created using GROUP BY, and groups can be limited using HAVING. If both WHERE and HAVING keywords occur in a SQL statement, WHERE is applied before HAVING.

Multiple tables can be queried by using either subqueries or joins. If all of the result data comes from a single table, subqueries can be used. If results come from two or more tables, joins must be used. Rows that do not match the join conditions will not appear in the result. Outer joins can be used to ensure that all rows from a table appear in the result.

Data can be added using the INSERT command; it can be modified using UPDATE, and it can be deleted using DELETE. Both UPDATE and DELETE can easily cause disasters, so they must be used with great care.

REVIEW QUESTIONS

6.1 What does SQL stand for?

6.2 What is a data sublanguage?

6.3 Explain the importance of SQL-92.

6.4 Why is it important to learn SQL?

6.5 In your own words, describe the meanings of the phrases ON UPDATE CASCADE and ON DELETE CASCADE.

Use the following tables for your answers to questions 6.6–6.9:

EMPLOYEE (<u>EmployeeID</u>, Name, Phone, Email)

COMPUTER (<u>SerialNumber</u>, Make, Model, *EmployeeID*)

(See Figure 6-8 for sample data.)

6.6 Code a CREATE TABLE command to create the EMPLOYEE table. Justify your choices of column data types and constraints.

6.7 Code a CREATE TABLE command to create the COMPUTER table. Justify your choices of column constraints. Should EmployeeID be null or not null?

6.8 Create a referential integrity constraint on COMPUTER.EmployeeID. Assume that deletions should not cascade, but that updates should cascade.

6.9 Code the required SQL statements for the following alternative version of the COMPUTER table:

COMPUTER1 (<u>SerialNumber</u>, Make, Model, <u>*EmployeeID*</u>)

6.10 Is COMPUTER or COMPUTER1 a better design? Explain your rationale.

6.11 Code SQL to remove the EMPLOYEE table from the database. Assume that the referential integrity constraint is to be removed.

6.12 Code SQL to remove the EMPLOYEE table from the database. Assume that the COMPUTER table is to be removed, also.

For questions 6.13–6.42, use the EMPLOYEE and COMPUTER tables. Assume that EmployeeID and ComputerID are surrogate keys.

6.13 Write a SQL statement to display all columns of all rows of COMPUTER. Do not use the * notation.

6.14 Write a SQL statement to display all columns of all rows of COMPUTER. Use the * notation.

6.15 Write SQL to display the Make and Model of all COMPUTERs.

6.16 Write SQL to display the ComputerID, Make, and Model of all COMPUTERs having the Make 'Dell'.

6.17 Write SQL to display the Make column of COMPUTER.

6.18 Write SQL to display the Make column of COMPUTER (do not show duplicates).

FIGURE 6-8

Sample EMPLOYEE and COMPUTER Data

EMPLOYEE

EmployeeID	Name	Phone	Email
100	Mary Smathers	206.555.1234	MS@somewhere.com
200	Tran Chau	213.555.1299	TC@somewhere.com
300	Kai Choi	312.555.3344	KC@somewhere.com
400	Bryan Jackson	222.555.8858	BJ@somewhere.com

COMPUTER

SerialNumber	Make	Model	EmployeeID
1000	Compaq	4000	400
2000	Toshiba	200	200
2500	Compaq	4000	300
7000	Dell	4100	300
8000	Dell	8100	300

6.19 Write SQL to display the Make and Model of all computers having the type 'Dell' and the Model 4100.

6.20 Write SQL to display the SerialNumber, Make, and Model of all computers that are not of Type Dell or IBM.

6.21 Write SQL to display the SerialNumber, Make, and Model for all computers having a four-character Make starting with D.

6.22 Write SQL to display the Name and Email address of all employees who have an email address ending with 'somewhere.com'. Assume that email account names can be any number of characters.

6.23 Write SQL to display the SerialNumber of any computer that has a null value for Model.

6.24 Write SQL to display the Make and Model of all computers sorted by EmployeeID.

6.25 Write SQL to display the Make and Model of all computers sorted by Make in ascending order and by Model in descending order within Make.

6.26 Write SQL to count the number of computers.

6.27 Write SQL to count the number of distinct Makes.

6.28 For the following table, write SQL to display the minimum, maximum, and average Weight of computers.

COMPUTER2 (<u>SerialNumber</u>, Make, Model, Weight, *OwnerID*)

6.29 For the COMPUTER2 table, write SQL to group the data by Make and display the average Weight per make.

6.30 Answer question 6.29, but consider only Makes for which there are five or more computers in the database.

6.31 Answer question 6.30, but do not consider any computer having the Make 'Dell'.

6.32 Using the tables in Figure 6-8, write SQL to display Name and Email of any employees with Dell computers. Use a subquery.

6.33 Using the tables in Figure 6-8, write SQL to display Name and Email of any employees with Dell computers with the Model 4100. Use a join.

6.34 Suppose that the following new table is added to the database:

MANUFACTURER (<u>Name</u>, City, State)

Assume that Make of COMPUTER is a foreign key in Name of MANUFAC-TURER. Code SQL to display the Name and Email of any employee with a computer that was made by a manufacturer in Atlanta. Use subquery format.

6.35 Answer question 6.34, but use joins in the standard SELECT FROM WHERE format.

6.36 Answer question 6.34, but use joins in the JOIN ON format.

6.37 Answer question 6.34, but include employees, regardless of whether they have a computer.

6.38 Code SQL to add three new rows to the COMPUTER table. Assume that SerialNumber is a surrogate key and the DBMS will provide a value for it. Otherwise, assume you have all of the data.

6.39 Code SQL to add three new rows to the EMPLOYEE table. Assume that EmployeeID is a surrogate key and the DBMS will provide a value for it. Also assume that you have values for Name and Phone and that Email is Null.

6.40 Code SQL to change the values of 'Compaq' in Make of COMPUTER to 'HP'.

6.41 Explain what will happen if you leave the WHERE clause off your answer to question 6.40.

6.42 Code SQL to delete all rows of COMPUTERs of Model 'Desktop'. What will happen if you forget to code the WHERE clause in this statement?

EXERCISES

6.43 Write SQL statements to create the tables for a relational design of the data model shown in Figure 5-17(c). Use the format of statements shown in Figure 6-7. Define foreign keys and set cascading behavior in accordance with the referential integrity actions shown there. Which of the referential integrity actions cannot be implemented using foreign key constraints?

6.44 Use SQL INSERT statements to add data to the tables you created in question 6.43. Ensure that you have at least three salespeople, three sales orders, and seven records of salesperson share.

6.45 Using the tables from your answers to questions 6.43 and 6.44, write SQL statements for the following questions. Where joins are required, use the JOIN ON format of join; use aliases for table names in join statements.

A. Show the Names and Phone numbers of SALESPEOPLE who have a null Email address. Explain why the query should find no such rows.

B. Show the Names of SALESPEOPLE and the total and average of OrderTotal of all orders in which they have participated.

C. For each order, show the SalesOrderNumber and sum of CommissionPercent.

D. Show the SalesOrderNumber and Name of SALESPERSON for orders in which more than two salespeople have participated.

E. Same as B, but include all salespeople, regardless of whether they have any SALESPERSON_SHARE data.

F. It is possible to perform calculations in SELECT statements. Thus, the following displays the product of columns A and B as a new column C:

```
SELECT   A, B, (A*B) as C
FROM     TABLE1;
```

Using this structure, code a SQL statement to list the Names of SalesPeople and the amount of commission they have received on each order in which they have participated.

6.46 Write SQL statements to create the tables shown in Figure 5-20(b). Drop the word THREE from the first two tables; it adds no value here. Thus, the first table should be named HOTEL_INVOICE. Use the format of statements shown in Figure 6-7. Define foreign keys and set cascading behavior in accordance with the referential integrity actions shown there. Are there referential integrity actions that cannot be implemented using foreign key constraints?

6.47 Use SQL INSERT statements to add data to the tables you created in Question 6.46. Ensure that you have at least three HOTEL_INVOICE rows, six INVOICE_LINE_ITEM rows, and twelve SUB_LINE_ITEM rows. Two invoices should be for the same customer. Also, at least one of your invoices should have no INVOICE_LINE_ITEM rows, and at least one of your INVOICE_LINE_ITEM rows should have no SUB_LINE_ITEM rows.

6.48 Using the tables from your answers to questions 6.46 and 6.47, write SQL statements for the following questions. Use subqueries except where joins are required. For joins, use the JOIN ON format and use aliases for table names in join statements.

A. Show the InvoiceNumber, CustomerName for all invoices having a CategoryTotal greater than 100.

B. Suppose that you want to show the InvoiceNumber, CustomerName, and sum of CategoryTotal for each invoice. A subquery will not work. Explain why.

C. Construct a join to show the InvoiceNumber, CustomerName, and sum of CategoryTotal for each invoice.

D. Construct a join to show the CustomerName and sum of CategoryTotal for each customer.

E. Construct a join to show the CategoryTotal and sum of SubCategoryCost for each line item.

F. Explain why you cannot construct a join to show the InvoiceNumber, CustomerName, sum of CategoryTotal, and sum of SubCategoryCost for each invoice.

FIREDUP PROJECT QUESTIONS

Assume that FiredUp has created a database with the following tables:

CUSTOMER (CustomerSK, Name, Phone, EmailAddress)

STOVE (SerialNumber, Type, Version, DateOfManufacture)

REGISTRATION (*CustomerSK*, *SerialNumber*, *Date*)

STOVE_REPAIR (RepairInvoiceNumber, *SerialNumber*, Date, Description, Cost, *CustomerSK*)

Code SQL for the following. Assume that all dates are in the format *mmddyyyy.*

A. Show all of the data in each of the four FiredUp tables.

B. List the Versions of all stoves.

C. List the Versions of all stoves of the type 'Fired Now'.

D. List the SerialNumber and Date of all registrations in the year 2002.

E. List the SerialNumber and Date of all registrations in February. Use the underscore (_) wildcard.

F. List the SerialNumber and Date of all registrations in February. Use the percent (%) wildcard.

G. List the names and email addresses of all customers who have an email address.

H. List the names of all customers who do not have an EmailAddress; present the results in descending sorted order of Name.

I. Determine the maximum cost of a stove repair.

J. Determine the average cost of a stove repair.

K. Count all stoves.

L. Count all stoves of each type and display the Type and count.

M. List the name and email addresses of all customers who have had a stove repair that cost more than $50. Use a subquery.

N. List the names and email addresses of all customers who have registered a stove of the type 'FiredNow'. Use a subquery.

O. List the names and email addresses of all customers who have had a stove repair that cost more than $50. Use join with the JOIN ON syntax.

P. List the names and email addresses of all customers who have registered a stove of type 'FiredNow'. Use join with the JOIN ON syntax.

Q. List the names, email addresses, and registration date of all customer registrations.

R. Show the names and email addresses of all customers who have registered a stove, and who have had the stove repaired.

S. Show the names and email addresses of all customers who have registered a stove, but who have not had any stove repaired.

TWIGS TREE TRIMMING SERVICE PROJECT QUESTIONS

Assume that Twigs has created a database with the following tables:

OWNER (<u>OwnerName</u>, Phone, Street, City, State, Zip)

SERVICE (<u>DateOfService</u>, <u>OwnerName</u>, Description, AmountBilled, AmountPaid, DateOfPayment)

CHIP_DELIVERY (<u>CustomerName</u>, <u>DateDelivered</u>, LoadSize, AmountBilled, AmountPaid, DateOfPayment)

Code SQL for the following. Assume that SERVICE.OwnerName and CHIP_DELIVERY.CustomerName are foreign keys to OWNER.OwnerName. Also assume that all dates are in the format *mmddyyyy*.

A. Show all of the data in each of the three Twigs tables.

B. List the Cities of all owners.

C. List the Cities of all owners without duplicates.

D. List the OwnerName and DateOfService for all services performed in year 2002.

E. List the CustomerName and DateDelivered for all chip deliveries paid for in February. Use the underscore (_) wildcard.

F. Same as question E, but use the percent (%) wildcard.

G. List the names and cities of all owners who have a phone number.

H. List the names of all owners who do not have a phone number and present the results in descending sorted order of CustomerName.

I. Determine the maximum amount billed for a service.

J. Determine the average load size of a chip delivery.

K. Count all chip deliveries.

L. Count all chip deliveries for each owner and display the CustomerName and count.

M. List the names and phone numbers of all owners who have service with a non-null AmountBilled and a null AmountPaid. Use a subquery.

N. List the names and LoadSize of all owners who have a chip delivery and who also have a service with a non-null AmountBilled and a null AmountPaid. Use a subquery.

O. Same as M, but use join with the JOIN ON syntax.

P. Same as N, but use join with the JOIN ON syntax.

Q. Show the names and phone numbers of all owners who have had both a service and a chip delivery.

R. Show the names and phone numbers of all owners who have had a chip delivery, but not a service.

CHAPTER 7

Using SQL in Applications

I n Chapter 6, you learned the syntax of basic SQL statements, but those statements were presented in isolation.
In this chapter, we consider SQL in the context of applications, in the setting of a business. We begin by summa-
rizing the information needs at a small, hypothetical art
gallery named View Ridge Gallery. From that summary, we
build a data model and then transform that data model into
a relational database design. We will use this example not
only in this chapter, but in many other chapters to follow.

Given this example, we then describe the syntax for
SQL CHECK constraints and for the SQL CREATE VIEW
statement. Next, we discuss two important issues that need
to be addressed when embedding SQL in application
code. We then describe triggers for validity checking, for
computing default values, for updating views, and for
implementing referential integrity actions. Finally, we will
illustrate the use of SQL in stored procedures and discuss
the use of SQL in application code.

▶ VIEW RIDGE GALLERY

View Ridge Gallery is a small art gallery that sells contemporary European and North American fine art, including lithographs, original paintings, and photographs. All of the lithographs and photos are signed and numbered, and most of the art is priced between $5,000 and $50,000. View Ridge has been in business for 30 years, has one owner who works full-time; three salespeople; and two workers who make frames, hang art in the gallery, and prepare art works for shipment.

View Ridge holds openings and other gallery events to attract customers to the gallery. Art is also placed on display in local companies and restaurants and in other public places. View Ridge owns all of the art that it sells; it holds no items on a consignment basis.

Application Requirements

The requirements for the View Ridge application are summarized in Figure 7-1. First, both the owner and the salespeople want to keep track of their customers' names, addresses, phone numbers, and email addresses. They also want to know which artists have appeal to which customers. The salespeople use this information to determine whom to contact when new art arrives and to create personal verbal and email communications with their customers.

When the gallery purchases new art, data about the artist, work, and the date acquired and acquisition price are recorded. Occasionally, the gallery also repurchases art from a customer and resells it, so a work may appear in the gallery multiple times. When art is repurchased, the artist and work data is not re-entered, but the most recent acquisition date and price is recorded. In addition, when art is sold, the purchase date, sales price, and identity of the purchasing customer are stored in the database.

Salespeople want to examine past purchase data so they can devote more time to the most active buyers. They also sometimes use the purchase records to identify the location of art they have sold in the past.

For marketing purposes, View Ridge wants its database application to provide a list of artists and works that have appeared in the gallery. The owner also wants to be able to determine how fast an artist's work sells and at what sales margins. Finally, database application should display current inventory on a Web page that customers can access via the Internet.

View Ridge Data Model

Figure 7-2(a) shows an IDEF1X data model for the View Ridge database. There are two strong entities, CUSTOMER and ARTIST. In addition, the entity WORK is ID-dependent on ARTIST, and the entity TRANSACTION is ID-dependent on WORK. There is also a non-identifying connection relationship from CUSTOMER to WORK.

An artist may be recorded in the database even if none of his or her works have appeared in the gallery. This is done to record customer preferences for artists whose works might appear in the future. Thus, an artist may have from zero to many works.

The identifier of WORK is the composite (Title, Copy) because, in the case of lithographs and photos, there may be many copies of a given title. Also, the requirements

FIGURE 7-1

Summary of View Ridge Requirements

- Track customers and their artist interests
- Record gallery's purchases
- Record customers' art purchases
- List the artists and works that have appeared in the gallery
- Report how fast an artist's works have sold and at what margin
- Show current inventory in a Web page

FIGURE 7–2

View Ridge Database with Data Keys (a) Data Model and (b) Database Design

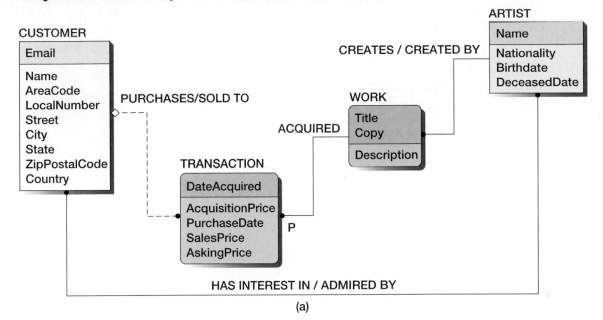

(a)

indicate that a work may appear in the gallery many times, so there is a need for potentially many TRANSACTION entities for each WORK. Each time a work appears in the gallery, the acquisition date and price must be recorded. Thus, there must be at least one TRANSACTION row for each WORK.

A customer may purchase many works; this is recorded in the 1:N relationship from CUSTOMER to TRANSACTION. Note that this relationship is optional in both directions. Finally, there is a N:M relationship between CUSTOMERs and ARTISTs. This is a real N:M relationship; the team searched in vain for a missing connecting entity.

Database Design with Data Keys A database design for the data model in Figure 7-2(a) is shown in Figure 7-2(b). This design uses data keys, and as you can tell, every primary key except ARTIST.Name has problems. The keys for WORK and TRANSACTION are huge and the key for CUSTOMER is doubtful; many customers may not have an email address. Because of these problems, this design cries out for surrogate keys.

Surrogate Key Data Model The data model for a surrogate key database is shown in Figure 7-3(a). Notice that the two ID-dependent relationships have been changed to non-identifying relationships. This was done because there is no need to carry composite, ID-dependent keys in WORK and TRANSACTION once ARTIST has a surrogate key. The need for changes like this was described in Chapter 5, page 161.

Notice that ARTIST.Name has been defined as an alternate key. This will ensure that artists are not duplicated in the database. Similarly, (Title, Copy) is defined as an alternate key so that a given work cannot be recorded in the databases more than once.

Surrogate Key Database Design The database design for the surrogate key data model is shown in Figure 7-3(b). This is the design we will use in this chapter and in the chapters to come. All keys are shown as surrogates in the format IDENTITY (n, m). The first number is the identity seed and the second number is the identity increment. All keys are to be incremented by 1, but each has a different starting value.

The foreign key placement is a straightforward application of the techniques described in Chapter 5. TRANSACTION.CustomerID can have null values; this specification allows the creation of a TRANSACTION row before any customer has purchased the work. All other foreign keys are required.

FIGURE 7-2

(continued)

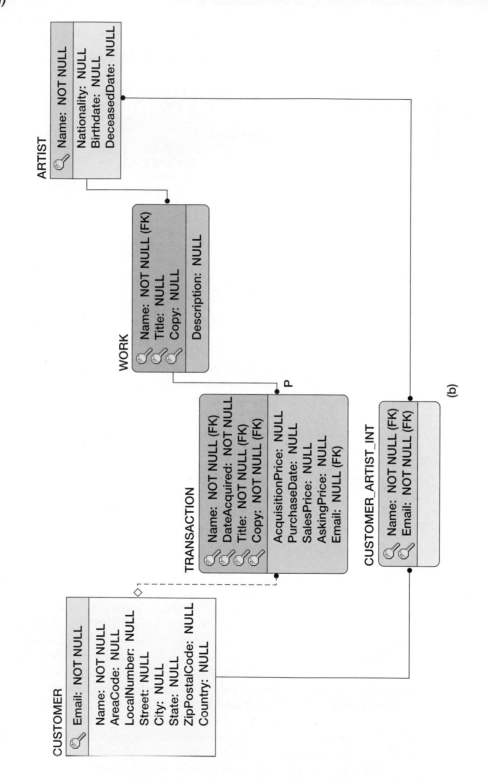

FIGURE 7-3

View Ridge Database with Surrogate Keys (a) Data Model and (b) Database Design

(a)

Referential Integrity Actions on Parent Tables Deletions cascade from CUSTOMER and ARTIST to CUSTOMER_ARTIST_INT. This makes sense; when a customer or artist is removed from the database, there is no need to record preferences. No other deletions cascade. If a CUSTOMER has a TRANSACTION, the CUSTOMER cannot be deleted. If an ARTIST has a WORK, the WORK cannot be deleted. If a WORK has a TRANSACTION, the WORK cannot be deleted.

This last statement poses a potential problem. Whenever a WORK is inserted, a related TRANSACTION row must be created for it to hold the DateAcquired and AcquisitionPrice. Therefore, all WORKs will have at least one TRANSACTION. Using the preceding deletion rule, however, no TRANSACTION can be deleted that has a WORK. Therefore, it will be impossible to delete a WORK, even if it has never been sold.

It is possible that the gallery wants never to delete a WORK that has been added to the database. Another possibility is that if a WORK has only been in the gallery once, and if it did not sell (the CustomerID of its TRANSACTION is null), the WORK can be deleted. For this application, we assume the latter. We will need to use a trigger to handle the deletion, as shown later in this chapter.

Considering update and insert referential integrity actions, all parent-to-child updates are shown as cascading. In truth, this rule is unnecessary because no surrogate key values can change. Finally, the only insert referential integrity actions from the parent side of the relationships are the normal referential integrity constraints. For example, WORK.ArtistID must exist in ARTIST.ArtistID. All such constraints will be enforced by the DBMS and we need only define them in the schema.

Referential Integrity Actions on Child Tables Considering referential integrity actions from the child side, all updates are restricted. For CUSTOMER_ARTIST_INT, WORK, and TRANSACTION.WorkID, there should never be a reason to change a foreign key value; and restricted means never allow an update to any of them. For TRANSACTION.CustomerID, there is a need to update CustomerID when the work is sold. After that, however, CustomerID should never be changed. Thus, if CustomerID is null, it can be updated; otherwise, it cannot be updated. This rule, too, will need to be implemented in a trigger.

FIGURE 7-3

(continued)

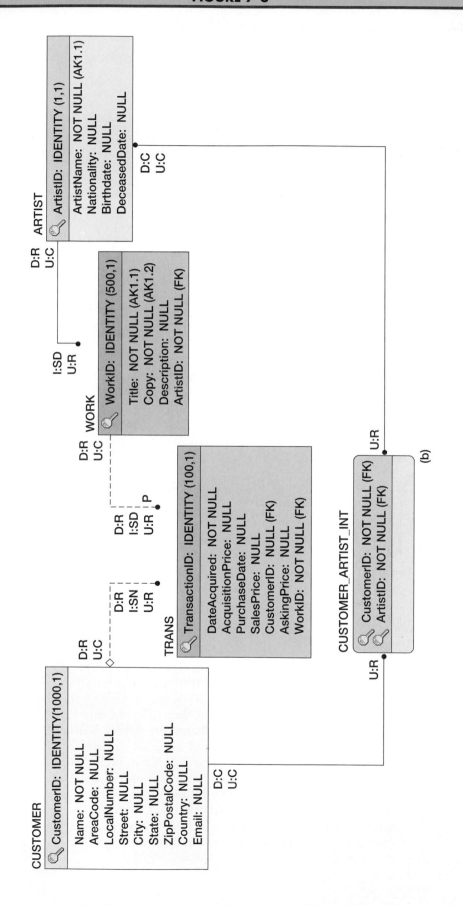

Inserts to WORK and TRANSACTION foreign keys are specified as *set default*, meaning set them to the ARTIST and WORK to which they belong. The CustomerID foreign key in TRANSACTION is *set null* on insert; no value will be provided until a customer buys the work.

Deletions of WORK and TRANSACTION from the child side are marked as restricted, but for different reasons. If TRANSACTION.CustomerID is not null, the row is never to be deleted. If it is null, it can be deleted only if TRANSACTION is the only transaction for a WORK and if WORK itself is being deleted. This pair of deletions will need to be done in a trigger, as mentioned previously. Finally, a WORK can be deleted if it is related to a single TRANSACTION having a null value of CustomerID. Rows in CUSTOMER_ARTIST_INT can be deleted either via cascading deletions or via application when a customer indicates he or she no longer has an interest in a given artist.

SQL DDL for View Ridge

The SQL for the database design in Figure 7-3(b) is shown in Figure 7-4. There are five CREATE TABLE statements for each of the five tables. The style used here is in accordance with that recommended in Figure 6-7, so the developer is able to name all constraints. Notice that TRANSACTION.CustomerID is null; all other foreign keys are required.

One note on column definitions is that the columns Birthdate and DeceasedDate in ARTIST are represented as four digit years. The users at View Ridge Gallery did not care about the particular month, day, and year of an artist's birth or death. They just wanted to know the year.

All of the SQL in Figure 7-4 was discussed in Chapter 6, with the exception of the CHECK constraints. Such constraints are used to limit the column values. Two of the most common types of check constraint are range checks and enumerated lists. An example of the former occurs in the TRANSACTION table, in which the SalesPrice column values are restricted to be greater than 1000, but less than or equal to 200,000.

An example of an enumerated list occurs in the definition of the ARTIST table. Here, constraint NationalityValues limits the column values to the elements shown in the list. This list reflects the gallery's business policy of representing only European and North American artists.

Additional types of constraints compare one column value to another. In the work table, for example, the constraint BirthValuesCheck specifies that the Birthdate must be less than DeceasedDate. A similar constraint is ValidTransDate in the TRANSACTION table definition.

Still another type of constraint limits values to a particular format. In the definition of the ARTIST table, Birthdate and DeceasedDate are required to have four decimal digits, and the first digit must be either 1 or 2. Values such as 799 or 3100 would therefore not be allowed.

According to the SQL-92 standard, CHECK constraints may not include the system date. This is unfortunate because for columns like PurchaseDate, it would be convenient to have the constraint that PurchaseDate be less than or equal to the current date. This constraint can be implemented in triggers, however.

Another possible CHECK constraint, not shown in Figure 7-4, is to specify a subquery in the constraint statement. For example, suppose that the table STATECODE has a column, ValidStateAbbreviation, which has all the valid abbreviations for state columns. The following constraint could be added to the CREATE TABLE statement for CUSTOMER:

```
CONSTRAINT ValidStateCheck CHECK (State IN
        (SELECT ValidStateAbbreviation
        FROM STATECODE
        WHERE ValidStateAbbreviation = State)),
```

FIGURE 7-4

SQL for Creating the View Ridge Database in Figure 7-3(b)

```
CREATE TABLE CUSTOMER(
        CustomerID      int             NOT NULL IDENTITY (1000,1),
        Name            char(25)        NOT NULL,
        Street          char(30)        NULL,
        City            char(35)        NULL,
        State           char(2)         NULL,
        ZipPostalCode   char(9)         NULL,
        Country         char(50)        NULL,
        AreaCode        char(3)         NULL,
        PhoneNumber     char(8)         NULL,
        Email           char(100)       NULL,

        CONSTRAINT      CustomerPK      PRIMARY KEY (CustomerID)
);

CREATE TABLE ARTIST(
        ArtistID        int             NOT NULL IDENTITY (1,1),
        Name            char(25)        NOT NULL,
        Nationality     char(30)        NULL,
        Birthdate       numeric (4)     NULL,
        DeceasedDate    numeric(4)      NULL,

        CONSTRAINT      ArtistPK        PRIMARY KEY (ArtistID),
        CONSTRAINT      ArtistAK1       UNIQUE (Name),
        CONSTRAINT      NationalityValues CHECK
                        (Nationality IN
                                ('Canadian', 'English', 'French', 'German',
                                'Mexican', 'Russian', 'Spanish', 'US')),
        CONSTRAINT      BirthValuesCheck CHECK (Birthdate < DeceasedDate),
        CONSTRAINT      ValidBirthYear CHECK (Birthdate LIKE '[1-2][0-9][0-9][0-9]'),
        CONSTRAINT      ValidDeathYear CHECK (DeceasedDate LIKE '[1-2][0-9][0-9][0-9]')
);

CREATE TABLE CUSTOMER_ARTIST_INT(
        ArtistID        int             NOT NULL,
        CustomerID      int             NOT NULL,

        CONSTRAINT      CustomerArtistPK PRIMARY KEY (ArtistID, CustomerID),
        CONSTRAINT      Customer_Artist_Int_ArtistFK FOREIGN KEY (ArtistID)
                        REFERENCES ARTIST (ArtistID)
                        ON UPDATE CASCADE
                        ON DELETE CASCADE,
        CONSTRAINT      Customer_Artist_Int_CustomerFK FOREIGN KEY (CustomerID)
                        REFERENCES CUSTOMER (CustomerID)
                        ON UPDATE CASCADE
                        ON DELETE CASCADE
);
```

Such a CHECK constraint is not implemented by all DBMS products, however. There are many other CHECK constraint possibilities defined in the SQL-92 standard, but they are also inconsistently supported by DBMS products. Search the documentation of your DBMS for the term *CHECK CONSTRAINT* to learn which options are available for the DBMS you use.

Sample Values

Figure 7-5 shows sample values for the five tables defined in Figure 7-4. We will use this data for the rest of the discussion in this chapter as well as for discussions of Oracle and SQL Server in Chapters 10 and 11.

FIGURE 7-4

(continued)

```
CREATE TABLE WORK (
        WorkID          int             NOT NULL IDENTITY (500,1),
        Title           char(25)        NOT NULL,
        Description     varchar(1000)   NULL,
        Copy            char(8)         NOT NULL,
        ArtistID        int             NOT NULL,

        CONSTRAINT  WorkPK      PRIMARY KEY (WorkID),
        CONSTRAINT  WorkAK1     UNIQUE (Title, Copy),
        CONSTRAINT  ArtistFK    FOREIGN KEY(ArtistID) REFERENCES ARTIST (ArtistID)
);

CREATE TABLE TRANSACTION (
        TransactionID    int            NOT NULL IDENTITY (100,10),
        DateAcquired     date           NOT NULL,
        AcquisitionPrice numeric(8,2)   NULL,
        PurchaseDate     date           NULL,
        SalesPrice       numeric(8,2)   NULL,
        AskingPrice      numeric(8,2)   NULL,
        CustomerID       int            NULL,
        WorkID           int            NOT NULL,

        CONSTRAINT  TransactionPK PRIMARY KEY (TransactionID),
        CONSTRAINT  SalesPriceRange
                    CHECK ((SalesPrice > 1000) AND (SalesPrice <=200000)),
        CONSTRAINT  ValidTransDate CHECK (DateAcquired <= PurchaseDate),
        CONSTRAINT  TransactionWorkFK
                    FOREIGN KEY(WorkID) REFERENCES WORK (WorkID),
        CONSTRAINT  TransactionCustomerFK
                    FOREIGN KEY(CustomerID) REFERENCES CUSTOMER (CustomerID)
);
```

▶ USING SQL VIEWS

A SQL view is a virtual table that is constructed from other tables or views. A view has no data of its own, but obtains data from tables or other views. Views are constructed from SQL SELECT statements; the only limitation on such statements is that they may not contain an ORDER BY clause[1]. Sorting order must be provided by the SELECT statement that processes the view.

For example, the following defines a view CustomerName on the CUSTOMER table:

```
CREATE VIEW      CustomerNameView AS
    SELECT       Name AS CustomerName
    FROM         CUSTOMER;
```

To obtain a list of customer names in sorted order, the view would then be processed by the following SQL statement:

```
SELECT          *
FROM            CustomerNameView
ORDER BY        CustomerName;
```

---

[1] This is according to the SQL-92 standard. ORDER BY is allowed for views in Oracle and is allowed in special circumstances by SQL Server, however. In this text, we will assume that ORDER BY is not allowed for View definition.

FIGURE 7–5

Sample View Ridge Data (a) Sample ARTIST Data; (b) Sample WORK Data; (c) Sample TRANSACTION Data; (d) Sample CUSTOMER Data and (e) Sample CUSTOMER_ARTIST_INT Data

ArtistID	Name	Nationality	Birthdate	DeceasedDate
3	Miro	Spanish	1870	1950
4	Kandinsky	Russian	1854	1900
5	Frings	US	1700	1800
6	Klee	German	1900	<NULL>
8	Moos	US	<NULL>	<NULL>
14	Tobey	US	<NULL>	<NULL>
15	Matisse	French	<NULL>	<NULL>
16	Chagall	French	<NULL>	<NULL>

(a)

TransactionID	DateAcquired	AcquisitionPrice
100	2/27/1974	8750
101	7/17/1989	28900
121	11/17/1989	4500
122	2/27/1999	8000
124	4/7/2001	38700
129	11/21/2001	6750
130	11/21/2001	21500
135	7/17/2002	47000

(c)

CustomerID	Name	Street	City	State	ZipPostalCode
1000	Jeffrey Janes	123 W. Elm St	Renton	WA	98123
1001	David Smith	813 Tumbleweed L	Loveland	CO	80345
1015	Tiffany Twilight	88 - First Avenue	Langley	WA	98114
1033	Fred Smathers	10899 - 88th Ave	Bainbridge Island	WA	98108
1034	Mary Beth Frederic	25 South Lafayette	Denver	CO	80210
1036	Selma Warning	205 Burnaby	Vancouver	BC	V0N 1B4
1037	Susan Wu	105 Locust Ave	Atlanta	GA	23224
1040	Donald G. Gray	55 Bodega Ave	Bodega Bay	CA	92114
1041	Lynda Johnson	117 C Street	Washington	DC	11345
1051	Chris Wilkens	87 Highland Drive	Olympia	WA	98008

(d)

FIGURE 7-5

FIGURE 7-5

(continued)

WorkID	Title	Description	Copy	ArtistID
505	Mystic Fabric	One of the only pr	99/135	14
506	Mi Vida	Very black, but ve	7/100	3
507	Slow Embers	From the artist's c	HC	14
525	Mystic Fabric	Some water dama	105/135	14
530	Northwest by Night	Wonderful, moody	37/50	16

(b)

PurchaseDate	SalesPrice	AskingPrice	CustomerID	WorkID
3/18/1974	18500	20000	1015	505
10/14/1989	46700	47000	1001	505
11/21/2000	9750	10000	1040	525
3/15/2000	17500	17500	1036	525
8/17/2000	73500	75000	1036	506
3/18/2002	14500	15000	1040	507
<NULL>	<NULL>	<NULL>	<NULL>	525
10/2/2002	71500	72500	1015	530

(c *continued*)

ArtistID	CustomerID
3	1036
5	1015
5	1034
5	1041
5	1051
8	1034
8	1041
14	1001
14	1015
14	1033
14	1034
14	1036
14	1040
14	1041
14	1051
16	1015

(e)

Country	AreaCode	PhoneNumber	Email
USA	206	555-1345	Customer1000@somewhere.com
USA	303	555-5434	Customer1001@somewhere.com
USA	206	555-1000	Customer1015@somewhere.com
USA	206	555-1234	Customer1033@somewhere.com
USA	303	555-1000	Customer1034@somewhere.com
Canada	253	555-1234	Customer1036@somewhere.com
USA	721	555-1234	Customer1037@somewhere.com
USA	705	555-1234	Customer1040@somewhere.com
USA	703	555-1000	<NULL>
USA	206	555-1234	<NULL>

(d *continued*)

FIGURE 7-6

CustomerNameView
Results

```
CustomerName
- - - - - - - - - - - - - - - - - -
Chris Wilkens
David Smith
Donald G. Gray
Fred Smathers
Jeffrey Janes
Lynda Johnson
Mary Beth Frederickson
Selma Warning
Susan Wu
Tiffany Twilight
No more results.
(10 row(s) returned)
```

The result for the sample data in Figure 7-5 is shown in Figure 7-6. Notice that the SELECT * expression is used on the query of CustomerNameView. As you know, the SELECT * format returns all columns. In this case, only one column is returned because CustomerNameView has only one column even though the underlying CUSTOMER table has many.

Also notice that the column CUSTOMER.Name in the original table has been renamed to CustomerName in the view. Because of this, the ORDER BY phrase in the SELECT statement must use the name CustomerName and not Name. Also, the DBMS returns results using the column name CustomerName.

Views are used for many purposes. For one, they can hide columns or rows. They can also be used to show the results of computed columns, to hide complicated SQL statements, and to provide a level of indirection between the data that applications process and the actual table data. We will show examples of each of these and then describe several other view uses as well.

Using Views to Hide Columns and Rows

Views can be used to hide columns. This is done to simplify a result or to prevent the display of sensitive data. Suppose the users at View Ridge want a list of customers and the phone numbers only. They do not want to see all of the address data nor the email data. The following statement defines a view BasicCustomerData that presents only the desired data:

```
CREATE VIEW      BasicCustomerData AS
SELECT           Name, AreaCode, PhoneNumber
FROM             CUSTOMER;
```

The results of a SELECT * on this table are shown in Figure 7-7. A similar technique can be used to hide columns such as AcquisitionPrice or SalesPrice in TRANSACTION in situations where displaying that sensitive data would be inappropriate.

Rows can also be hidden in a view by supplying a WHERE clause in the view definition. The next SQL statement defines a view of customer name and phone data for all customers with an address in Washington:

```
CREATE VIEW      BasicCustomerData_WA AS
SELECT           Name, AreaCode, PhoneNumber
FROM             CUSTOMER
WHERE            State = 'WA';
```

FIGURE 7-7

BasicCustomerData
Results

Name	AreaCode	PhoneNumber
Jeffrey Janes	206	555-1345
David Smith	303	555-5434
Tiffany Twilight	206	555-1000
Fred Smathers	206	555-1234
Mary Beth Frederickson	303	555-1000
Selma Warning	253	555-1234
Susan Wu	721	555-1234
Donald G. Gray	705	555-1234
Lynda Johnson	703	555-1000
Chris Wilkens	206	555-1234

No more results.
(10 row(s) returned)

FIGURE 7-8

BasicCustomerData_WA
Results

Name	AreaCode	PhoneNumber
Jeffrey Janes	206	555-1345
Tiffany Twilight	206	555-1000
Fred Smathers	206	555-1234
Chris Wilkens	206	555-1234

No more results.
(4 row(s) returned)

Figure 7-8 shows the contents of this view. As desired, only customers who live in Washington are shown in this view. This fact is not obvious because State is not part of the view results. This characteristic is good or bad depending on the use of the view. It is good if this view is used in a setting in which only Washington customers matter; it is bad if the view miscommunicates that these customers are the only View Ridge customers.

Using Views to Display Results of Computed Columns

Another purpose of views is to show the results of computations without requiring the user to enter computation expressions. For example, the following view combines the AreaCode and PhoneNumber columns and formats the result:

```
CREATE VIEW      CustomerPhone AS
    SELECT       Name, ('(' + AreaCode + ') ' + PhoneNumber) As Phone
    FROM         CUSTOMER;
```

When the view user enters:

```
SELECT      *
FROM        CustomerPhone;
```

the results will be displayed as in Figure 7-9[2].

Placing computations in views has two major advantages. First, it saves users of the view from having to write an expression to get the results they want (and from having to know how to do so). It also ensures that results are consistent. If each developer who

---

[2] In Oracle, the plus sign (+) must be replaced by double vertical bars (||) for string concatenation.

FIGURE 7–9

CustomerPhone Results

Name	Phone
Jeffrey Janes	(206) 555-1345
David Smith	(303) 555-5434
Tiffany Twilight	(206) 555-1000
Fred Smathers	(206) 555-1234
Mary Beth Frederickson	(303) 555-1000
Selma Warning	(253) 555-1234
Susan Wu	(721) 555-1234
Donald G. Gray	(705) 555-1234
Lynda Johnson	(703) 555-1000
Chris Wilkens	(206) 555-1234

No more results.
(10 row(s) returned)

uses a computation writes his or her own SQL expression, there is the chance that they will write it differently, possibly causing inconsistent results.

Using Views to Hide SQL Syntax

Another purpose for views is to hide SQL syntax. This can be done to save developers from having to enter a complicated statement whenever they want a particular view, or it can be done to give the benefit of more complicated SQL statements to developers who do not know SQL. Like using views for computations, this use of views also ensures consistency.

Two common view applications are to hide joins and to hide subqueries.

Hiding Joins   View Ridge salespeople need to know which customers are interested in which artists. Because the relationship from CUSTOMER to ARTIST is N:M, this relationship is carried via an intersection table. Thus, to display customer interests, two joins are necessary; one to join CUSTOMER to CUSTOMER_ARTIST_INT and another to join that result to ARTIST. The following SQL statement defines a view that constructs these joins:

```
CREATE VIEW CustomerInterests AS
        SELECT      C.Name as Customer, A.Name as Artist
        FROM        CUSTOMER C
        JOIN        CUSTOMER_ARTIST_INT CI
                    ON C.CustomerID = CI.CustomerID
                    JOIN ARTIST A
                        ON CI.ArtistID = A.ArtistID;
```

This statement is a standard two-part join. Notice the use of aliases for the table names (C for Customer, CI for CUSTOMER_ARTIST_INT, and A for ARTIST). Such aliases simplify the ON expressions. For example, C.CustomerID = CI.CustomerID is easier to write than CUSTOMER.CustomerID = CUSTOMER_ARTIST_INT.CustomerID. The use of table name aliases is optional.

Also notice the renaming of C.Name to Customer and A.Name to Artist. These column renamings are *not* optional; if they were not done, the view would have two columns with the name Name. The DBMS would not be able to distinguish one Name from the other and would generate an error message when creating the view.

The following SQL statement queries the CustomerInterests view and sorts the results by Customer:

```
SELECT      *
FROM        CustomerInterests
ORDER BY    Customer;
```

Results are displayed in Figure 7-10. Clearly, using the view is much simpler than constructing the join syntax!

Hiding Group By and Built-in Functions   Views are also used to hide Group By and built-in functions. To understand this, consider the view definition:

```
CREATE VIEW ArtistWorkNet AS
    SELECT      W.WorkID, Name, Title, Copy, AcquisitionPrice,
                SalesPrice, (SalesPrice - AcquisitionPrice) AS NetPrice
    FROM        TRANSACTION T
    JOIN        WORK W
                ON T.WorkID = W .WorkID
                JOIN ARTIST A
                    ON W.ArtistID = A.ArtistID;
```

This view joins TRANSACTION, WORK, and ARTIST and creates a computed column NetPrice. We can use SQL statements on this view and treat NetPrice as if it were a real table column. For example, to obtain the total net for each work in the gallery, we can use the following SQL:

```
SELECT      Name, Title, Copy, sum(NetPrice)as TotalNet
FROM        ArtistWorkNet
GROUP BY    Name, Title, Copy;
```

FIGURE 7-10		Name	Artist
CustomerInterests Results		Chris Wilkens	Frings
		Chris Wilkens	Tobey
		David Smith	Tobey
		Donald G. Gray	Tobey
		Fred Smathers	Tobey
		Lynda Johnson	Tobey
		Lynda Johnson	Moos
		Lynda Johnson	Frings
		Mary Beth Frederickson	Frings
		Mary Beth Frederickson	Moos
		Mary Beth Frederickson	Tobey
		Selma Warning	Tobey
		Selma Warning	Miro
		Tiffany Twilight	Chagall
		Tiffany Twilight	Frings
		Tiffany Twilight	Tobey
		No more results.	
		(16 row(s) returned)	

Name	Title	Copy	TotalNet
Chagall	Northwest by Night	37/50	24500
Miro	Mi Vida	7/100	34800
Tobey	Mystic Fabric	105/135	14750
Tobey	Mystic Fabric	99/135	27550
Tobey	Slow Embers	HC	7750

No more results.
(5 row(s) returned)

The results of this query are shown in Figure 7-11.

We can use this statement to define another view with the following statement:

CREATE VIEW WorkNet as

      SELECT   Name, Title, Copy, sum(NetPrice)as TotalNet

      FROM   ArtistWorkNet

      GROUP BY   Name, Title, Copy;

Now, to obtain the results of Figure 7-11, the view user need only enter:

SELECT   *

FROM   WorkNet;

Similarly, we can define the view ArtistNet with:

CREATE VIEW ArtistNet as

      SELECT   Name, sum(NetPrice)as TotalNet

      FROM   ArtistWorkNet

      GROUP BY   Name;

The following statement will produce the results shown in Figure 7-12:

SELECT   *

FROM   ArtistNet;

Other Uses for Views

There are three other important view uses. For one, views can provide a level of indirection between the database application and the actual tables. This indirection can be important when the source of data may change and for other reasons as explained in the next chapter. To understand this use, suppose we define the view:

Name	TotalNet
Chagall	24500
Miro	34800
Tobey	50050

No more results.
(3 row(s) returned)

```
CREATE VIEW        CustomerTable1 AS
     SELECT        *
     FROM          CUSTOMER;
```

In essence, this view assigns the alias CustomerTable1 to the CUSTOMER table. We can process the view CustomerTable1 in exactly the same ways that we can process the table CUSTOMER.

If all application code uses the name CustomerTable1, then the source of the underlying data can be changed without impacting any of the application code. Hence, at some future date, if the source of customer data is changed to a different table, say, one named NEW_CUSTOMER, then all that need be done is to redefine the CustomerTable1 view as follows:

```
CREATE VIEW        CustomerTable1 AS
     SELECT        *
     FROM          NEW_CUSTOMER;
```

All of the application code that was written against CustomerTable1 will now run without problem on the new data source.

Because of the potential need to change data sources, some organizations never expose the real tables to developers. Instead, they expose only views of the real tables as shown here. This strategy increases flexibility for future database development projects and eases database redesign tasks, as you will learn in the next chapter.

In a similar vein, sometimes views are constructed to give different sets of processing permissions to the same table. We will discuss security more in Chapters 9 through 11, but for now, understand that it is possible to limit insert, update, delete, and read permission on tables and views.

For example, an organization might define a view of CUSTOMER called CustomerRead with only read permissions on CUSTOMER and a second view of CUSTOMER called CustomerUpdate with both read and update permissions. Applications that need not update the customer data would work with CustomerRead, whereas those that need to update this data would work with CustomerUpdate.

A third reason for using views is to enable different sets of triggers to be defined for a table. Triggers are assigned to a table or a view, so each view can have its own set of triggers. Thus, there might be different processing rules for the same data that is accessed via different views.

Updating Views

Depending on how they are defined, views may or may not be updatable. The rules by which update status is determined are both complicated and DBMS-dependent. To understand why this is so, consider the following two update requests on views defined in the last section:

```
UPDATE      CustomerTable1
SET         Email = 'NewEmailAddress@somewhere.com'
WHERE       CustomerID = 1000;
```

and

```
UPDATE        ArtistNet
SET           TotalNet = 23000
WHERE         Artist = 'Tobey';
```

The first request can be processed without any problem because CustomerTable1 has a structure identical to the CUSTOMER table; it is simply an alias for that table. On the other hand, the second update request makes no sense at all. TotalNet is a sum of a computed column. Nowhere in the database is there any such column to be updated. Clearly this second update cannot be processed.

Figure 7-13 shows guidelines to determine whether a view is updatable. In general, to update a view, the DBMS must be able to associate the column(s) to be updated with a particular row in a particular underlying table. A way to approach this question is to ask yourself "What would I do if I were the DBMS and I were asked to update this view? Would the request make sense? If so, would I have sufficient data to make the update?" Clearly, if the entire table is present and there are no computed columns, the view is updatable.

If any required (NOT NULL) columns are missing from the view, the view cannot be used for inserts. Such a view may be used for updates and deletions, however, as long as the primary key (or a candidate key for some DBMS products) is present in the view. Multi-table views may be updatable on the most subordinate table if the primary key or a candidate key for that table is in the view.

All views that have an INSTEAD OF trigger defined on them are considered to be updatable. When the update request is received by the DBMS, it will call the INSTEAD OF trigger as described in the section on triggers later in this chapter.

SQL Views Are Not External Views

Before leaving the topic of views, it is very important that you understand that they are NOT the same as what we called external views in Chapter 2. A SQL view (the kind of views we are discussing in this chapter) is composed of data from a single SQL statement.

To understand the difference, examine Figure 7-3(b). Suppose that a user wants to use a data entry form that has all data for a customer. The external view needed by such a form must include all of the customer's purchases and all of the customer's artist interests. We can use a SQL view to obtain all of the purchases, or we can use a SQL view to obtain all of the artist interests, but we cannot build a SQL view that has both. The basis of the problem is that there are two separate multi-valued paths through the database schema and each requires a separate SELECT statement.

Thus, SQL views are a subset of external views. They can be used to represent some, but not all, external views. A view like the one for all customer data must be composed in an application program, as shown in the last section of this chapter. It can also be

FIGURE 7–13

Guidelines for Updating Views

> **Updatable Views:**
>
> • View based on a single table with no computed columns and all non-null columns present in the view
> • View based on any number of tables, with or without computed columns, and INSTEAD OF trigger defined for the view
>
> **Possibly Updatable Views:**
>
> • Based on a single table, primary key in view, some required columns missing from view, update and delete may be allowed. Insert is not allowed.
> • Based on multiple tables, updates may be allowed on the most subordinate table in the view if rows of that table can be uniquely identified.

materialized in the form of an XML document, as we will discuss in Chapter 13. It cannot, however, be represented as a SQL view.

▶ EMBEDDING SQL IN PROGRAM CODE

SQL statements can be embedded in triggers, stored procedures, and program code. Before we discuss those subjects, however, we need to explain in general terms how SQL statements are placed in program code.

There are two problems to be overcome. First, some means is necessary to assign the results of SQL statements to program variables. Many different techniques are used. Some involve object-oriented programs, as you will learn in Chapters 12 and 13. Others are simpler. For example, in PL/SQL, Oracle's native language, the following statement assigns the count of the number of rows in CUSTOMER the variable rowcount:

```
SELECT        Count(*) into rowcount
FROM          CUSTOMER;
```

A similar statement in SQL Server is the following:

```
SELECT        @rowcount = Count(*)
FROM          CUSTOMER
```

In either case, the number of rows in the CUSTOMER table will have been placed in the program variable *rowcount* or *@rowcount*.

The second problem to overcome concerns a paradigm mismatch between SQL and application programming languages. SQL is set-oriented; most SQL statements return a table or a set of rows. Programs, on the other hand, are element- or row-oriented. Because of this difference, a statement like the following makes no sense:

```
SELECT        Name into custName
FROM          CUSTOMER;
```

If there are 100 rows in the CUSTOMER table, there will be 100 values of Name. The program variable custName, however, is expecting to receive just one value.

To get around this problem, the results of SQL statements are treated like pseudo-files. A SQL statement is executed and returns a set of rows. A cursor is placed on the first row and is processed. Then, the cursor is moved to the next row and that row is processed, iterating in this way until all rows have been processed. The typical pattern is as follows:

```
Open SQL (SELECT * FROM CUSTOMER);
Move cursor to first row;
        While cursor not past end of table {
                Set custName= Cursor.Name;
                … other statements that use the value in custName …
                Advance cursor to next row;
        };
        … continue processing …
```

In this way, the rows of a SQL result are processed one at a time.

You will see many examples of these techniques and others like them in the chapters to follow. For now, just strive to gain an intuitive understanding of how SQL is embedded in program code.

▶ USING TRIGGERS

A **trigger** is a stored program that is attached to a table or view. The trigger code is invoked by the DBMS when an insert, update, or delete request is issued on the table or view to which the trigger is attached. Triggers for Oracle can be written in a propriety programming language called **Programming Language for SQL (PL/SQL)**, or they can be written in Java. SQL Server triggers are written in a proprietary language called **Transaction-SQL (T-SQL)**.

Oracle supports three kinds of triggers: BEFORE, INSTEAD OF, and AFTER. As you would expect, BEFORE triggers are executed before the insert, update, or deletion request is processed; INSTEAD OF triggers are executed in place of the insert, update, or deletion request; and AFTER triggers are executed after the insert, update, or deletion request has been processed. Altogether there are nine possible trigger types: BEFORE (Insert, Update, Delete), INSTEAD OF (Insert, Update, Delete), and AFTER (Insert, Update, Delete).

SQL Server supports only INSTEAD OF and AFTER triggers, so there are just six possible trigger types for it. Other DBMS products support triggers differently. See the documentation of your product to determine which trigger types it supports.

When a trigger is fired, the DBMS makes the inserted, updated, or deleted data available to the trigger code. For an insert, the DBMS supplies the values of columns for the new row. For deletions, the DBMS supplies the values of columns for the deleted row; for updates, it supplies both the new and old values.

The way the values are supplied depends on the DBMS product. For now, assume that new values are supplied by prefixing a column name with the expression :*new*. Thus, during an insert on CUSTOMER, the variable :new.Name is the value of Name for the row being inserted. For an update, :new.Name has the value of Name after the update takes place. Similarly, assume that old values are supplied by prefixing a column name with the expression :*old*. Thus, for a deletion, the variable :old.Name has the value of Name for the row being deleted. For an update, :old.Name has the value of Name prior to the requested update. (This, in fact, is the strategy used by Oracle. You will see the equivalent SQL Server strategy in Chapter 11.)

There are many applications for triggers. In this chapter, we will consider four: using triggers for validity checking, using triggers to provide default values, using triggers to update views, and using triggers to enforce referential integrity actions.

Using Triggers for Validity Checking

Suppose View Ridge has a rule that no work of art may sell for less than 90 percent of its asking price. To enforce that rule, an update trigger can be written on TRANSACTION to check AskingPrice against SalesPrice. If the rule is violated, the AskingPrice can be set back to its original value.

Two strategies can be used. One is to write a BEFORE TRIGGER that checks and resets the value of SalesPrice, if necessary, before the update is made. The second strategy is to write an AFTER TRIGGER that checks and rewrites the TRANSACTION row after the update, if necessary. Either strategy works as long as the DBMS supports BEFORE triggers (SQL Server does not). Here, we will use the second strategy.

The needed trigger code is shown in Figure 7-14. This code is close to actual Oracle code, but details unimportant to our present discussion have been left out. We will show true Oracle trigger code in Chapter 10 and true SQL Server trigger code in Chapter 11 after we have discussed the missing details. Note that comment text is placed between /* .... */.

FIGURE 7-14

Example AFTER UPDATE Trigger Checking for Valid Values

```
CREATE TRIGGER TRANSACTION_SalesPriceCheck
              AFTER UPDATE ON TRANSACTION

BEGIN
        IF :new.SalesPrice < .9 * :old.AskingPrice THEN
        /* Sales Price is too low, reset it   */

              UPDATE TRANSACTION
              SET     SalesPrice = :old.AskingPrice,
                      AskingPrice = :old.AskingPrice;

        /* Note:          the above update will cause a recursive call on this
                          trigger.  The recursion will stop the second time
                          through because SalesPrice will be = AskingPrice. */

        /*  Also should send a message to the user saying what's been
                  done     */

              END IF;
      END;
```

The logic of the trigger is straightforward. If the new SalesPrice is less than 90 percent of the old AskingPrice, the SalesPrice is reset to the AskingPrice. Notice that the new SalesPrice is compared to the old AskingPrice; if it were compared to the new AskingPrice, it would be possible for someone to change both prices at once and violate the intention of the constraint. Just in case that has occurred, the AskingPrice is set to :old.AskingPrice in the UPDATE statement.

Also, observe that this trigger will be called recursively. The update statement in the trigger will cause an update on TRANSACTION, which will cause the trigger to be called again. The second time, however, the SalesPrice will be equal to :old.AskingPrice, no more updates will be made, and the recursion will stop.

This example shows the nature of processing in a simple trigger. In the next section, we consider a trigger with slightly more complexity.

Using Triggers for Default Values

You learned in Chapter 6 how to use the DEFAULT CONSTRAINT to specify an initial value for a column. This can be used to supply simple values or results from simple expressions. If, however, the specification of a default value involves more complicated logic, a trigger needs to be used.

For example, suppose there is a policy at View Ridge Gallery to set the value of AskingPrice equal to the greater of twice the AcquisitionPrice or the sum of AcquisitionPrice plus the average net gain for sales of this art in the past. The AFTER trigger in Figure 7-15 implements this policy. Again, the code in Figure 7-15 is generic.

After declaring program variables, the trigger counts the TRANSACTION rows for this work and places the count into the variable rowcount. Because this is an AFTER trigger, the new TRANSACTION row will have been inserted and the count will be 1 if this is the first time the work has been in the gallery. If so, the new value of SalesPrice is set to twice the AcquisitionPrice.

If rowcount is greater than 1, the work has been in the gallery before. To compute the average gain for this work, we can use the view ArtistWorkNet described on page 241. The next SQL statement uses that view to compute the Sum(NetPrice) for this work. The sum is placed in the variable sumNetPrice. Notice that the WHERE clause selects only rows for this work. Next, the average is computed by dividing this sum by rowcount minus 1.

You may be wondering why we do not use Avg(NetPrice) in the SQL statement. The answer is that the default SQL average function would have counted the new row in

FIGURE 7-15

Example AFTER UPDATE Trigger-Checking to Provide a Default Value

```
CREATE TRIGGER TRANSACTION_AskingPriceInitialValue
       AFTER INSERT ON TRANSACTION

DECLARE
       rowcount as int;
       sumNetPrice as numeric (10,2);
       avgNetPrice as numeric (8,2);

BEGIN
       /* First find if work has been here before */

       SELECT      Count(*) INTO rowcount
       FROM        TRANSACTION T
       WHERE       :new.WorkID = T.WorkID;

       IF rowcount = 1 Then
               /* This is first time work has been in gallery */

               :new.AskingPrice = 2 * :new.AcquisitionPrice;

       ELSE
               IF rowcount > 1 Then
                       /* Work has been here before */

                       SELECT      Sum(NetPrice) into sumNetPrice
                       FROM        ArtistWorkNet AW
                       WHERE       AW.WorkID = :new.WorkID
                       GROUP BY    AW.WorkID;

                       avgNetPrice = sumNetPrice / (rowcount – 1);

                       /* Now choose larger   */
                       IF avgNetPrice > 2 * :new.AcquisitionPrice Then

                                       :new.AskingPrice = avgNetPrice;
                       ELSE
                                       :new.AskingPrice = 2 * :new.AcquisitionPrice;

                       END IF;
               ELSE
                       /* Error, rowcount cannot be less than 1 –
                       Do something  */
               END IF;
       END IF;
END;
```

the computation of the average. We do not want that to be done, so one is subtracted from rowcount when the average is computed.

Once the value of avgNetPrice has been computed, it is compared to twice the AcquisitionPrice, and the larger is used for the new value of AskingPrice.

Updating Views

As noted, some views can be updated by the DBMS, and some cannot. For those views the DBMS cannot update, there is sometimes logic unique to the application that can be used to update the view. In this case, the application-specific logic for updating the view is placed in an INSTEAD OF trigger.

Consider the CustomerInterests view on page 241 (Figure 7-10.) This view is constructed using two joins across the intersection table between CUSTOMER and ARTIST. Suppose that this view is used to populate a grid on a user form, and further suppose that users want to make customer name corrections on the form when necessary. If such changes are not possible, the users will say something like, "But, hey, the name is right there. Why can't I change it?" Little do they know the trials and tribulations the DBMS went through to display that data!

In general, the CustomerInterests view is not updatable. However, if the user wants to change a name that happens to be unique in the CUSTOMER table, then we can update the CUSTOMER table behind the view and then regenerate the view. In this way, we can make it appear that the view is being updated. Figure 7-16 shows an INSTEAD OF trigger that will handle this case.

The trigger logic is simple. It counts the number of rows in CUSTOMER that have CUSTOMER.Name equal to :old.Customer (recall that the view column CUSTOMER.Name is given the alias Customer). If there is more than one such row, no update is possible because the value of :old.Customer is not unique in the CUSTOMER table. If there is just one such row, then the trigger issues an update on CUSTOMER. Observe that the trigger is not updating the view; rather, it is updating the table that underlies the view. After the trigger has run, the application then needs to requery the view to obtain the new customer name.

This logic is typical for INSTEAD OF triggers. They usually involve some special case such as this one to perform some action on one or more tables that underlie the trigger.

FIGURE 7-16

Example INSTEAD OF Trigger for Updating a View

```
CREATE TRIGGER CustomerInterest_CustomerName Update
          INSTEAD OF UPDATE ON CustomerInterests

DECLARE

          rowcount     int;

BEGIN
          SELECT     Count(*) INTO rowcount
          FROM       CUSTOMER C
          WHERE      C.Name = :old.Customer;


          IF rowcount > 1 THEN
                    /* Non-unique name, cannot update */

                    /* Send message to user that there are duplicates
                    and cannot update because do not know which
                    to change.  */

          ELSE

                    /* If get here, then only one customer with this name.
                         Make the name change.  */

                    UPDATE     CUSTOMER
                    SET        CUSTOMER.Name = :new.Customer
                    WHERE      CUSTOMER.Name = :old.Customer;


END;
```

Referential Integrity Actions

Writing triggers to enforce referential integrity actions requires careful analysis and design. If the purpose of a trigger is to make an action possible (for example, removing a TRANSACTION so that a delete of WORK can proceed), an AFTER TRIGGER cannot be used because the DBMS disallows the deletion before the after trigger can be called.

Another complicating issue is that there is no mechanism for triggers to send responses back to the procedure that invoked the trigger. This is particularly serious because the work of one trigger can cause the execution of another trigger, and so forth. Thus, it is sometimes difficult to notify the user or causing program what has been done by the trigger and by any cascading triggers.

All of this means that trigger code needs to be carefully designed and written. Even more it needs to be thoroughly tested for all possible data conditions. Further, fixing errors can be difficult because the source of the problem can be hidden and hard to trace.

This section describes two simple triggers for enforcing referential integrity actions. Keep in mind, however, that real situations can be far more complicated.

Ensuring that WORK Has a TRANSACTION on Insertion

According to the View Ridge data model, every WORK row is supposed to have at least one related TRANSACTION row. For new works, this row is necessary to hold the values of DateAcquired and AcquisitionPrice.

If an application erroneously creates a WORK row without creating a TRANSACTION row, a trigger must correct the situation. There are two possibilities: either remove the recently inserted WORK row or create a default TRANSACTION row. Removing the new WORK row is a drastic action, so it seems better to create a default TRANSACTION row and relate it to the new row in WORK.

The problem with creating a default TRANSACTION is determining values for the columns in the default row. DateAcquired and WorkID are the only required columns, however, and we have the value for WorkID. So, if we place the system date as a default value of DateAcquired, we have sufficient data to create the new TRANSACTION row. We have no means for determining a default value of AcquisitionPrice, however, so it will have to be null. This means that all of the code that processes this database must be prepared to encounter a null value of AcquisitionPrice.

In a typical project, at about this time someone remembers the trigger in Figure 7-15. Look back at that trigger and you can see that a null value of AcquisitionPrice will be a problem. Either we need to change the trigger in Figure 7-15 to handle the possibility of a null value, or we need to find some way to provide a value of AcquisitionPrice for the default TRANSACTION row to be created.

From this, you can understand the nature of the decisions that need to be made when enforcing referential integrity with triggers. For now, to simplify matters, suppose we decide just to remove any new WORK row that has no related TRANSACTION. A trigger for this policy appears in Figure 7-17.

The logic is simple: Count the number of TRANSACTION rows for the new value of WorkID; if there are none, remove the newly created WORK row. By the way, a better way of accomplishing this deletion is to roll back the transaction that caused the WORK insert. That way, any other database actions that were made in conjunction with the WORK insert will be removed as well. We will describe that technique after we have discussed transaction processing in Chapter 9.

Deleting WORK and TRANSACTION Together

Recall that the referential integrity actions on the View Ridge database stipulate that a WORK can be deleted only if has been in the gallery just once and if it has not been sold. In terms of the TRANSACTION table, this means that a WORK can be deleted if it has just one TRANSACTION row and if that row has a null value of CustomerID.

```
CREATE TRIGGER WORK_TRANSACTION_Check
        AFTER INSERT ON WORK

DECLARE
        rowcount as int;

BEGIN
        /* First look for a related TRANSACTION row */

        SELECT      Count(*) INTO rowcount
        FROM        TRANSACTION T
        WHERE       :new.WorkID = T.WorkID;

        IF rowcount = 0 Then

                /* remove just added WORK */
                DELETE
                FROM WORK
                WHERE       WORK.WorkID = :new.WorkID

                /* need some way to notify what has occurred here */

        END IF;
END;
```

This rule can be encoded in an INSTEAD OF DELETE trigger on WORK. Figure 7-18 shows generic code for such a trigger. There should never be a WORK with no related TRANSACTION rows, so if rowcount is zero, an error message is generated. Next, if rowcount is 1, it is necessary to determine if TRANSACTION.CustomerID is null. The SELECT statement is used to count the appropriate rows. If nullCount is 1, the rows will be deleted. The deletions must occur in the order shown. If they are reversed, the DBMS disallows the deletion of WORK because it has a dependent TRANSACTION row.

▶ USING STORED PROCEDURES

A stored procedure is a program that performs some common action on database data and that is stored in the database. In Oracle, stored procedures can be written in PL/SQL or in Java. With SQL Server, stored procedures are written in T-SQL.

Stored procedures can receive input parameters and they can return results. Unlike triggers, which are attached to a given table or view, stored procedures are attached to the database. They can be executed by any process using the database that has permission to use the procedure.

Stored procedures are used for many purposes. Although database administrators use them to perform common administration tasks, their primary use is within database applications. They can be executed from application programs written in languages such as Java, C#, C++, or VB.Net. They can also be invoked from Web pages using VBScript or JavaScript. Ad hoc users can run them from products such as SQL*Plus in Oracle or from Query Analyzer in SQL Server. Stored procedures can also be run for either Oracle or SQL Server from the Microsoft VisualStudio.NET environment.

Advantages of Stored Procedures

The advantages of using stored procedures are listed in Figure 7-19. Unlike application code, stored procedures are never distributed to client computers. They always reside in

FIGURE 7-18

Example INSTEAD OF DELETE Trigger for Enforcing a Deletion Rule

```
CREATE TRIGGER WORK_Deletion
        INSTEAD OF DELETE ON WORK
DECLARE
        rowcount as int;
        nullCount as int;
BEGIN
        /* First check related TRANSACTION row counts*/

        SELECT      Count(*) INTO rowcount
        FROM        TRANSACTION T
        WHERE       :old.WorkID = T.WorkID;

        IF rowcount = 0 Then
                /* this should never occur -- error */
                /* write to error log and do nothing */
        ELSE
                IF rowcount = 1 THEN
                /* Check for null CustomerID  */

                        SELECT   Count(*) into nullCount
                        FROM     TRANSACTION T
                        WHERE    :old.WorkID = T.WorkID
                        AND      T.CustomerID IS NULL;

                        IF nullCount = 1 THEN
                                /* Deletions must go in this order */
                                DELETE
                                FROM TRANSACTION T
                                WHERE :old.WorkID = T.WorkID;

                                DELETE
                                FROM WORK W
                                WHERE :old.WorkID = W.WorkID;
                        END IF;
                END IF;
        END IF;
END;
```

FIGURE 7-19

Advantages of Stored Procedures

Greater security
Decreased network traffic
SQL can be optimized
Code sharing
    Less work
    Standardized processing
    Specialization among developers

the database and are processed by the DBMS on the database server computer. Thus, they are more secure than distributed application code and they also reduce network traffic. Increasingly, stored procedures are the preferred mode of processing application logic over the Internet or corporate intranets. Another advantage of stored procedures is that their SQL statements can be optimized by the DBMS compiler.

When application logic is placed in a stored procedure, many different application programmers can share that code. This sharing results not only in less work, but also in standardized processing. Further, the developers best suited for database work can create the stored procedures while other developers, say those that specialize in Web-tier programming, can do other work.

Because of these advantages, it is likely that stored procedures will see increased use in the future. Also because of these advantages, it is likely that Microsoft will change SQL Server so that stored procedures can be written in .NET languages such as VB.NET and C#. As stated, you can already write Oracle stored procedures in Java.

The Add_WORK Stored Procedure

Figure 7-20 shows a stored procedure that records the acquisition of a work at View Ridge Gallery. Again, this code is generic, but this code style is close to that in SQL Server, rather than the more Oracle-like style that was used for the trigger examples in the prior section. If you compare the examples in both sections, you can gain a sense of the differences between PL/SQL and T-SQL.

The Add_WORK procedure receives five input parameters and returns none. In a more realistic example, a return would be passed back to the caller to indicate the success or failure of the operation. That discussion takes us away from database concepts, however, so we will omit it here.

This code assumes that the value of ArtistID that is passed to it is a valid ID. To verify this assumption, the first block of statements counts the number of rows that have the given ArtistID value. If the count is zero, then the ArtistID value is invalid and the procedure writes an error message and returns.

Otherwise[3], the procedure next checks to determine whether the work has been in the gallery before. If so, the WORK table will already contain a row for this Artist, Title, and Copy. If no such row exists, the procedure creates a new WORK row. Once that has been done, it then uses a select to obtain a value for WorkID. If the work row was just created, this statement is necessary to obtain the new value of the WorkID surrogate key. If the work was not created, the select on WorkID is necessary to obtain the WorkID of the existing row.

Once a value of WorkID has been obtained, the new row is inserted into TRANS-ACTION. Notice that the system function GetDate() is used to supply a value for DateAcquired in the new row.

This procedure is presented to give you a general idea of how SQL is embedded in stored procedures. It is not complete, principally because we need to do something to ensure that either all updates are made to the database or none of them are. You will learn how we do that in Chapter 9. For now, just concentrate on how the SQL you learned in the last chapter can be used as part of a database application.

▶ USING SQL IN APPLICATION CODE

We conclude this chapter with a brief discussion of the use of SQL in application programs. Consider the Customer Purchase Form shown in Figure 7-21. The form is a materialization of an external view of the CUSTOMER data. This form shows basic customer data in the center top, a grid of artist interests on the right, and a second grid of customer purchases at the bottom of the form.

Because the data behind this form involve two different multi-value paths (one through CUSTOMER_ARTIST_INT and another through TRANSACTION), the form cannot be populated using a SQL view. Instead, separate SQL statements need to be executed to obtain the form data.

---

[3] This code does not check for more than one row having the given ArtistID. Do you see why that check is not necessary? Because ArtistID is a surrogate key, the DBMS will never allow two rows to have the same value.

FIGURE 7–20

Stored Procedure to Record the Acquisition of a Work

```
CREATE PROCEDURE Add_WORK
        (
        @ArtistID int,   /* Artist must already exist in database */
        @Title char(25),
        @Copy char(8),
        @Description varchar(1000),
        @AcquisitionPrice Numeric (6,2)
        )

/* Stored procedure to record the acquisition of a work.  If the work has never been in the
gallery before, add a new WORK row.  Otherwise, use the existing WORK row.  Add a new
TRANSACTION row for the work and set DateAcquired to the system date.  */

AS

        DECLARE @rowcount as int
        DECLARE @workID as int

/* First ensure ArtistID is valid  */
        SELECT @rowcount = Count(*)
        FROM ARTIST A
        WHERE A.ArtistID = @ArtistID

        IF @rowcount = 0
        /* No such artist!  */
                BEGIN
                        Print 'No artist with id of ' + Str(@artistID)
                        Print 'Processing terminated.'
                        RETURN
                END

/* Now see if work is in database */
        SELECT          @rowcount = Count(*)
        FROM            WORK W
        WHERE           W.ArtistID = @ArtistID and
                        W.Title = @Title and
                        W.Copy = @Copy

        IF              @rowcount = 0
                        /* Not in database, put it in */
                        INSERT INTO WORK (Title, Copy, Description, ArtistID)
                        VALUES (@Title, @Copy, @Description, @ArtistID)

/* Get work surrogate key value */
        SELECT          @workID = W.WorkID
        FROM            WORK W
        WHERE           W.ArtistID = @ArtistID and
                        W.Title = @Title and
                        W.Copy = @Copy

/* Now put TRANSACTION row into database */
        INSERT INTO TRANSACTION (DateAcquired, AcquisitionPrice, WorkID)
                VALUES (GetDate(), @AcquisitionPrice, @workID)

        RETURN
```

FIGURE 7-21

Customer Purchase
Form

FIGURE 7-21

Customer Purchase Form

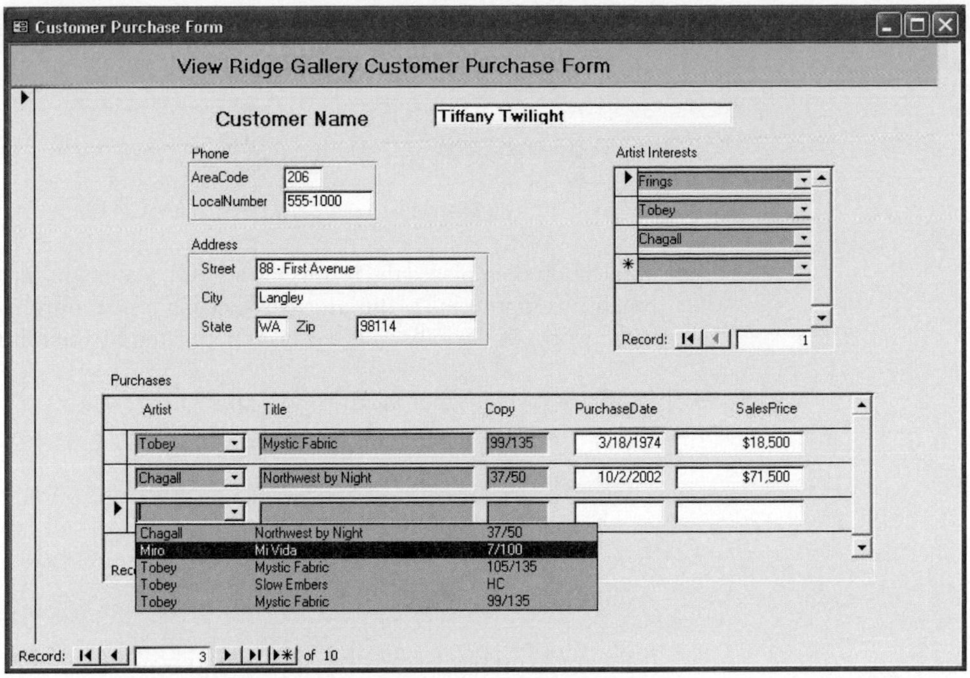

To process this form, an application program causes the appropriate SQL statements to be executed and then displays the results of the queries in the form's grid controls. The application program also processes and coordinates user actions on a form, such as populating a drop-down list box and making the appropriate changes to foreign keys to create record relationships when the user chooses and item from the list.

For the form in Figure 7-21, the Artist Interests grid is populated by joining CUSTOMER to CUSTOMER_ARTIST_INT to ARTIST as we did for the CustomerInterests view. This grid could be populated using the following SQL statement:

```
SELECT      A.Name
FROM        CUSTOMER C JOIN CUSTOMER_ARTIST_INT CA
      ON    C.CustomerID = CA.CustomerID
            JOIN ARTIST A
      ON    CA.ArtistID = A.ArtistID
WHERE       CustomerID = Form.CUSTOMER.CustomerID;
```

assuming that Form.CUSTOMER.CustomerID has the CustomerID of the customer displayed in the form (here the CustomerID for Tiffany Twilight).

Behind this form, the application program caused the preceding SQL statement (or one identical to it) to be executed and then places the results of the query in the Artist Interests grid.

Additionally, to populate the Purchases grid, another SQL statement had to be processed:

```
SELECT      A.Name, W.Title, W.Copy, W.PurchaseDate, W.SalesPrice
FROM        CUSTOMER C JOIN TRANASACTION T
      ON    C.CustomerID = T.CustomerID
```

```
               JOIN WORK W
     ON        T.WorkID = W.WorkID
               JOIN ARTIST A
     ON        W.ArtistID = A.ArtistID
WHERE          CustomerID = Form.CUSTOMER.CustomerID;
```

The application then places the results of this SQL statement into the Purchases grid.

Finally, in Figure 7-21, the user is recording a new purchase. The drop-down list shows the works in the gallery. It has been populated by the following SQL statement:

```
SELECT         A.Name, W.Title, W.Copy
FROM           TRANSACTION T JOIN WORK W
     ON        T.WorkID = W.WorkID
               JOIN ARTIST A
     ON        W.ArtistID = A.ArtistID;
```

If the user chooses a row from this combo box, the application must connect that row to the user's purchases by creating a new TRANSACTION record. Values for DatePurchased and SalesPrice need to be obtained from the form.

In truth, the form in Figure 7-21 is an Access form, and most of the SQL was generated behind the scenes by Access wizards. But at least now you know what is being done.

You can also correct the work of the wizards. For example, the generalized query that Access wrote to populate the drop-down combo box is not really appropriate because it shows all works, regardless of whether the work has already been sold. Knowing that, you can now go into the form and modify the underlying query to show only works for which TRANSACTION.CustomerID is null, or:

```
SELECT         A.Name, W.Title, W.Copy
FROM           TRANSACTION T JOIN WORK W
     ON        T.WorkID = W.WorkID
               JOIN ARTIST A
     ON        W.ArtistID = A.ArtistID
WHERE          TRANSACTION.CustomerID = Null;
```

Using this SQL, the form in Figure 7-21 would appear as shown in Figure 7-22. The only work that is available for sale is copy 105 of Mystic Fabric. Because Tiffany already owns a copy of that work, the salespeople would know to find another customer!

The particulars by which SQL code is inserted into applications depend on the language and data-manipulation methodology used. We will discuss the use of SQL in conjunction with VBScript when we discuss Web database applications in Chapter 12, and we will discuss the use of SQL with XML applications in Chapter 13. Also, Chapter 14 shows the use of SQL statements in Java in the context of Java Server Pages. These discussions will not make you a SQL application developer, but they will start you in the right direction. After completing this course, you should be able to understand how to use SQL in any language with which you work. Knowledge of that language, coupled with your knowledge of SQL, will enable you to become a successful database application developer.

FIGURE 7–22

Preferred Version of
Customer Purchase
Form

FIGURE 7–22

Preferred Version of Customer Purchase Form

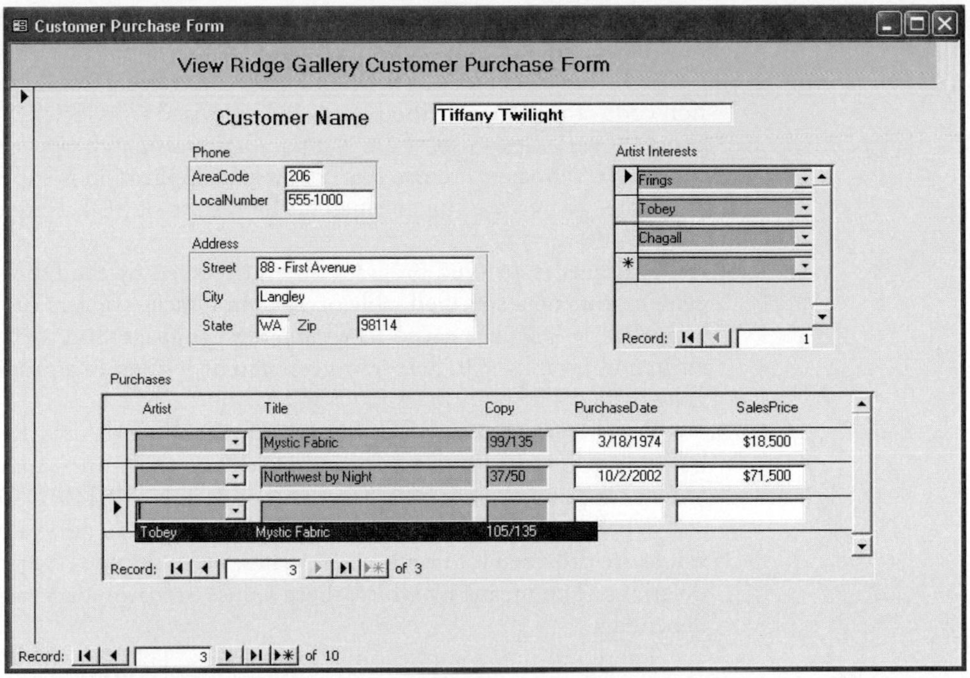

SUMMARY

This chapter builds on Chapter 6 to present the use of SQL in the context of an application for View Ridge Gallery. Application requirements for the gallery are summarized in Figure 7-1, and a data model is presented in Figures 7-2(a) and 7-2(b). The data key database design in Figure 7-2(b) has serious key problems. Consequently, the surrogate key design in Figure 7-3(b) is the design we will use in this chapter and in chapters to follow. Referential integrity actions are defined for the model, as shown in Figure 7-3(b).

CREATE TABLE statements for the surrogate database design are presented in Figure 7-4. The only new syntax in those statements is that for CHECK CONSTRAINTs. Such constraints define limits for column values. Two common uses for CHECK constraints are to specify a range of allowed values and to specify an enumerated list. Also, CHECK constraints can compare the value of one column to another, and they can be used to specify the format of column values. SQL-92 and some DBMS products also allow subqueries to be used in CHECK constraints. Sample values for the schema in Figure 7-4 are shown in Figure 7-5.

A SQL view is a virtual table that is constructed from other tables and views. SQL SELECT statements are used to define views; the only restriction is that a view definition may not include an ORDER BY clause.

Views are used to hide columns or rows, and they are also used to show the results of computed columns and to hide complicated SQL syntax like that used for joins and GROUP BY queries. Some organizations use views to provide a level of indirection between application programs and tables. Views can also be used to assign different sets of processing permissions to tables and to assign different sets of triggers as well.

The rules for determining whether a view can be updated are both complicated and DBMS-specific. Guidelines are shown in Figure 7-13. To update a view, the DBMS must be able to associate the column to be updated with a particular row in a particular table. If an INSTEAD OF UPDATE trigger is defined on a view, the DBMS will mark the view as updatable.

SQL views are a subset of the external views discussed at the start of Chapter 2. They can be used only for external views that involve one multi-valued path through the schema. External views that involve two such paths, say a view of the View Ridge database having both Purchases and Artist Interests, cannot be represented by a SQL view.

SQL can be embedded in program code in triggers, stored procedures, and application code. To do so, a method needs to be devised to associate SQL table columns with program variables. Also, there is a paradigm mismatch between SQL and programs. Most SQL statements return sets of rows; an application is expecting to work on a row at a time. To resolve this mismatch, the results of SQL statements are processed as pseudo-files.

A trigger is a stored program that is executed by the DBMS whenever a specified event occurs on a specified table or view. In Oracle, triggers can be written in a proprietary Oracle language called Programming Language/SQL (PL/SQL) and they can be written in Java. In SQL Server, triggers can be written in a proprietary SQL Server language called TRANSACT-SQL (T-SQL).

Possible triggers are BEFORE, INSTEAD OF, and AFTER. Each of these types can be declared for Insert, Update, and Delete; so there are a total of nine trigger types. Oracle supports all nine; SQL Server supports only INSTEAD OF and AFTER triggers.

When a trigger is fired, the DBMS supplies old and new values for the update. New values are provided for inserts and updates, and old values are provided for updates and deletions. The means by which these values are provided to the trigger are DBMS-dependent.

There are many applications for triggers. This chapter discussed four: validity checking (Figure 7-14), default values (Figure 7-15), updating views (Figure 7-16), and enforcing referential integrity (Figures 7-17 and 7-18).

A stored procedure is a program that is stored within the database and is compiled when used. In Oracle, stored procedures can be written in PL/SQL or Java; in SQL Server they can be written in T-SQL. Stored procedures can receive input parameters and they can return results. Unlike triggers, their scope is database-wide; they can be used by any process that has permission to use the database stored procedure.

Stored procedures can be called from programs written in standard languages such as Java or C#, or they can be written in scripting languages such as JavaScript or VBScript. They can also be called from SQL command prompt processors such as Oracles SQL-Plus or SQL Server's Query Analyzer.

Advantages of using stored procedures are summarized in Figure 7-19. An example stored procedure is shown in Figure 7-20.

SQL can also be embedded in application programs. Sometimes, several SQL statements need to be executed to populate an external view. The form in Figure 7-21, for example, needs two separate SQL statements. The application program causes the statements to be executed and then displays the results of the query in the form's grid controls. The application program would also need to process and coordinate user actions on a form, like populating a drop-down list box and making the appropriate changes to foreign keys to create record relationships.

The particulars by which SQL code is embedded in applications depend on the language and the data-manipulation methodology used. By the time you finish this course, you should be able to understand how to use SQL in conjunction with any language in which you work.

GROUP I QUESTIONS

7.1 For the data model in Figure 7-2, explain why it is appropriate to model WORK and TRANSACTION as ID-dependent entities.

7.2 Why is minimum cardinality on the relationship from ARTIST to WORK not one?

7.3 Why is the identifier of WORK the composite (Title, Copy)?

7.4   Justify the decision to make the relationship between CUSTOMER and TRANSACTION optional in both directions.

7.5   Make a list of three possible missing entities for the N:M relationship between CUSTOMER and ARTIST. Explain why (or why not) they should be included in the database design.

7.6   Explain what is wrong with the database design in Figure 7-2(b).

7.7   In the surrogate key data model in Figure 7-3(a), the WORK and TRANSACTION were changed from an ID-dependent entity to a strong entity. Why was this done?

7.8   Explain the meaning of the expression IDENTITY (4000, 5).

7.9   Summarize and justify the referential integrity actions on relationship parents for the design in Figure 7-3(b).

7.10   Describe the potential problem that exists when deleting a row in WORK or TRANSACTION.

7.11   Summarize and justify the referential integrity actions on relationship children for the design in Figure 7-3(b).

7.12   Explain the unusual characteristic of the columns BirthDate and DeceasedDate for the database design in Figure 7-4.

7.13   Give an example of a range CHECK CONSTRAINT, other than one in this chapter.

7.14   Give an example of an enumerated list CHECK CONSTRAINT, other than one in this chapter.

7.15   Give an example of a CHECK CONSTRAINT that uses two or more columns, other than one in this chapter.

7.16   Give an example of a CHECK CONSTRAINT that specifies the format of PartNumber to consist of five decimal numbers (the first of which is 5, 6, or 7; and the last of which cannot be 0).

7.17   Give an example of a CHECK CONSTRAINT that uses a subquery. Do not use the example in this chapter.

7.18   What prohibition does SQL-92 make regarding CHECK CONSTRAINTS?

7.19   In general terms, describe a SQL view.

7.20   What is the limitation on SELECT statements used in SQL views?

7.21   Code a SQL statement to create a view that shows the values of CUSTOMER.State.

7.22   Code a SQL statement to create a view that shows the unique values of CUSTOMER.State.

7.23   Code a SQL statement to create a view that shows Name, City, and State of CUSTOMER.

7.24   Code a SQL statement to create a view that shows Name, City, and State of CUSTOMER for customers in California.

7.25   Code a SQL statement to create a view that shows CUSTOMER.Name and a computed attribute called Location that combines CUSTOMER.City and CUSTOMER.State in a format like 'Chicago, IL'.

7.26   Code a SQL statement to create a view that displays the view you created in your answer to question 7.25, but shows only customers in California.

7.27   Code a SQL statement to create a view that shows ARTIST.Name, WORK.Title, and WORK.Description.

7.28 Code a SQL statement to create a view that shows CUSTOMER.Name, WORK.Title, and ARTIST.Name for all customer purchases.

7.29 Code a SQL statement to create a view that computes the NetPrice (the difference between SalesPrice and AskingPrice) for each customer purchase.

7.30 Code a SQL statement to create a view that computes the sum of NetPrice for each customer.

7.31 Code a SQL statement to create a view that computes the sum of NetPrice for each combination of customer and artist.

7.32 Describe how views are used to provide a level of indirection between application programs and tables. Why might this be important?

7.33 Explain how views can be used to improve data security.

7.34 Explain how views can be used to provide additional trigger functionality.

7.35 Give an example of a view that is clearly updatable.

7.36 Give an example of a view that is clearly not updatable.

7.37 Summarize the general idea for determining whether a view is updatable.

7.38 If a view is missing required items, what action on the view is definitely not allowed?

7.39 Explain the difference between a SQL view and an external view, as described in Chapter 2. When are they the same? When are they different?

7.40 Explain the paradigm mismatch between SQL and programming languages.

7.41 How is the mismatch in your answer to question 7.40 corrected?

7.42 Define *trigger*.

7.43 What are PL/SQL and T-SQL?

7.44 What is the relationship between a trigger and a table or view?

7.45 Name nine possible trigger types.

7.46 In general terms, explain how new and old values are made available to triggers.

7.47 Describe four possible uses for triggers.

7.48 Explain, in general terms, how to use a trigger to accomplish a deletion on WORK, given the referential integrity actions defined for the View Ridge Gallery.

7.49 What is a stored procedure? How does it differ from a trigger?

7.50 Summarize the way to invoke a stored procedure.

7.51 Summarize the key advantages of stored procedures.

7.52 Explain, in general terms, what an application program must do to materialize a form like that shown in Figure 7-20.

7.53 Can the form in Figure 7-20 be represented by a single view? Why or why not?

GROUP II QUESTIONS

Use the data model in Figure 7-23 and the related database design in Figure 7-24 to answer the following questions:

7.54 Alter the database design in Figure 7-24 to use surrogate keys. Is this design an improvement over the design in Figure 7-24? Why or why not?

7.55 Using the design in Figure 7-24, and keeping in mind the relationship cardinalities in the data model, explain the restriction on EMPLOYEE deletions to the ASSIGNMENT relationship. What does restrict mean in this context? Similarly, what do the insert and update restrictions on ASSIGNMENT in its relationship to EMPLOYEE mean?

FIGURE 7–23

Example Data Model

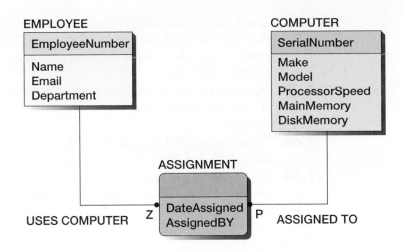

FIGURE 7–24

Database Design for Data Model in Figure 7-23

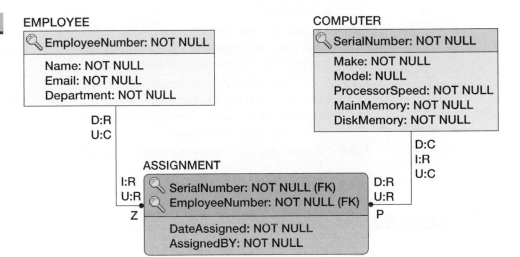

7.56 Using the design in Figure 7-24, and keeping in mind the relationship cardinalities in the data model, explain the restriction on COMPUTER insertions to the ASSIGNMENT relationship. What does restrict mean in this context? Similarly, what do the insert and update restrictions on ASSIGNMENT in its relationship to COMPUTER mean?

7.57 Code SQL CREATE TABLE statements for the database design in Figure 7-24. Write CHECK constraints to ensure that Make is one of Dell, IBM, Compaq, or other. Also, write constraints to ensure that ProcessorSpeed is between .8 and 2.5 (these are units of GHerz).

7.58 Create sample data for this database design. Your data should have at least seven EMPLOYEEs, three computers, and seven ASSIGNMENTs. Be sure to have a least one IBM computer, at least three employees in the Accounting department, and at least two ASSIGNMENTs with a value of Jones for AssignedBy.

7.59 Create an EmployeeView that has EMPLOYEE.Name and EMPLOYEE.Department. Show how to use that view to present employees sorted by name. Show the results of this view for your sample data.

7.60 Create a view AccountingEmployee that uses the view in your answer to question 7.59 for employees in the Accounting department. Show the results of this view for your sample data.

7.61 Create a view of COMPUTER named Computers that displays SerialNumber and Make and Model as one attribute named ComputerType. Place a colon and space between Model like this: Dell: 6200 Laptop. Show the results of this view for your sample data.

7.62 Create a view called ComputerMakes that shows the Make and average ProcessorSpeed for all computers. Show the results of this view for your sample data.

7.63 Create a view called ComputerUses that has all of the data of COMPUTER and ASSIGNMENT. Show the results of this view for your sample data.

7.64 Use the view from your answer to question 7.63 to create another view called ComputerUsesbyAssignee that show all data for COMPUTER and ASSIGNMENT grouped by AssignedBy. Show the results of this view for your sample data.

7.65 Use the view you created called Computers to show computer SerialNumber, ComputerType, and Employee Name. Show the results of this view for your sample data.

7.66 Explain how you would use a trigger on ASSIGNMENT to enforce the constraint that an employee has at most one computer. What type of trigger would you use? Describe the logic of such a trigger.

7.67 Explain the potential problem that exists when deleting a row in COMPUTER. How could you use a trigger to overcome this problem? What table would the trigger be based upon, what type of trigger would it be, and (in general terms) what is the logic of the trigger?

7.68 Suppose that you want to use a stored procedure to store a new row in COMPUTER. List the minimum list of parameters that need to be input to the procedure. Describe, in general terms, the logic of the stored procedure.

FIREDUP PROJECT QUESTIONS

Assume that FiredUp has created a database with the following tables:

CUSTOMER (<u>CustomerSK</u>, Name, Phone, EmailAddress)

STOVE (<u>SerialNumber</u>, Type, Version, DateOfManufacture)

REGISTRATION (*<u>CustomerSK</u>*, *<u>SerialNumber</u>*, <u>Date</u>)

STOVE_REPAIR (<u>RepairInvoiceNumber</u>, *SerialNumber*, Date, Description, TotalCost, TotalPaid, *CustomerSK*)

A. Create a view called RepairSummary that shows only RepairInvoiceNumber, TotalCost, and TotalPaid.

B. Show a SQL statement to retrieve all RepairSummary data sorted by TotalCost.

C. Create a view called RepairSummaryNet that shows RepairInvoiceNumber and the difference between TotalCost and TotalPaid as the column TotalDue.

D. Show a SQL statement to retrieve all RepairSummaryNet data sorted by TotalDue.

E. Create a view called CustomerRepair that shows CUSTOMER.Name and STOVE_REPAIR.SerialNumber, Date, Description, and TotalDue, where TotalDue is the difference between TotalCost and TotalPaid.

F. Create a view named CustomerBalance that uses the CustomerRepair view, and shows CUSTOMER.Name and the sum of TotalDue as AccountDue.

G. Suppose that FiredUp has the rule that a customer's record can be deleted only if TotalPaid is equal to TotalCost in all repair records. Explain how you would use a trigger to enforce this rule. What type of trigger would you use? On which table would you place the trigger? Show the SQL statements that you would code, but write the rest of the trigger in generic code like that shown in Figure 7-15.

H. Assume that every CUSTOMER row is required to have at least one related REGISTRATION row. Explain how you would use triggers to enforce this rule. How many triggers would you need? On which tables? On which events? Show SQL statements that you would code, but write the rest of the trigger logic in generic code like that shown in Figure 7-15.

TWIGS TREE TRIMMING SERVICE PROJECT QUESTIONS

Assume that Twigs has created a database with the following tables:

OWNER (<u>OwnerName</u>, Phone, Street, City, State, Zip)

SERVICE (<u>DateOfService</u>, <u>*OwnerName*</u>, Description, AmountBilled, AmountPaid, DateOfPayment)

CHIP_DELIVERY (<u>*CustomerName*</u>, <u>DateDelivered</u>, LoadSize, AmountBilled, AmountPaid, DateOfPayment)

A. Create a view called OwnerSummary that shows only OwnerName, Phone, and City.

B. Show a SQL statement to retrieve all OwnerSummary data sorted by OwnerName.

C. Create a view called ChipSummaryNet that shows CHIP_DELIVERY.CustomerName and CHIP_DELIVERY.DateDelivered, and the difference between AmountBilled and AmountPaid as the column TotalDue.

D. Show a SQL statement to retrieve all ChipSummaryNet data sorted by TotalDue.

E. Create a view called CustomerService that shows OWNER.OwnerName, SERVICE.DateOfService, SERVICE.Description, and TotalDue, where TotalDue is the difference between AmountBilled and AmountPaid.

F. Create a view named CustomerBalance that uses the CustomerService view, and shows OwnerName and the sum of TotalDue as AccountDue.

G. Suppose that Twigs has the rule that a customer's record can be deleted only if the customer owes no money. Thus, in every related row of SERVICE and CHIP_DELIVERY, AmountBilledTotal equals AmountPaid. Explain how you would use a trigger to enforce this rule. What type of trigger would you use? On which table would you place the trigger? Show the SQL statements that you would code, but write the rest of the trigger in generic code like that shown in Figure 7-15.

H. Assume that every OWNER row is required to have either at least one related SERVICE row, or one related CHIP_DELIVERY row. Explain how you would use triggers to enforce this rule. How many triggers would you need? On which tables? On which events? Show SQL statements that you would code, but write the rest of the trigger logic in generic code like that shown in Figure 7-15.

CHAPTER 8

Database Redesign

This chapter addresses the important topic of database redesign. So far, we have proceeded as if every database were constructed from scratch, but in truth most database design work involves redesigning existing databases. We begin this chapter with a discussion of the need for database redesign and then we will describe two important SQL statements: correlated subqueries and EXISTS. These statements play an important role when analyzing data prior to redesign. They also can be used for advanced queries and are important in their own right. After that discussion, we will turn to a variety of common database redesign tasks.

▶ THE NEED FOR DATABASE REDESIGN

You may be wondering, "Why do we have to redesign a database? If we build it correctly the first time, why would we ever need to redesign it?" There are two answers to that question. First, it is not so easy to build a database correctly the first time. Even if we can obtain all of the users' requirements, the tasks of building a correct data model and of transforming that data model into a correct database design are difficult. For large databases, the tasks are daunting and may require several stages of development. During those stages, some aspects of the database will need to be redesigned. Also, inevitably, mistakes are made that must be corrected.

The second answer to this question is the stronger and more important answer. Reflect for a moment on the relationship between information systems and the organizations that use them. It is tempting to say that they influence each other; that is, that information systems influence organizations and organizations influence information systems.

In truth, the relationship is much stronger than that. Information systems and organizations do not just influence each other; they *create* each other. When a new information system is installed, the users can behave in new ways. As the users behave in those new ways, they will want changes to the information system to accommodate their new behaviors. As those changes are made, the users will have more new behaviors, they will request more changes to the information system, and so forth in a never-ending cycle.

This circular process means that changes to an information system are not the sad consequence of a poor implementation, but rather a natural outcome of information system use. Therefore, the need for change to information systems never goes away; it neither can nor should be removed by better requirements definition, better initial design, better implementation, or anything else. Instead, change is part and parcel of information systems use. Thus, we need to plan for it. In the context of database processing, this means we need to know how to perform database redesign.

▶ ADDITIONAL SQL STATEMENTS

Database redesign is not terribly difficult if the database has no data. The serious difficulties arise when we have to change a database that has data, and when we want to make changes with minimum impact on existing data. Telling the users that the system now works the way they want, but unfortunately, all their data was lost while making the change is not acceptable to anyone.

Often, we need to know whether certain conditions or assumptions are valid in the data before we can proceed with a change. For example, we may know from user requirements that Department functionally determines BudgetCode, but we may not know whether that functional dependency is correctly represented in all the data.

Recall from Chapter 4 that if Department determines BudgetCode, every value of Department must be paired with the same value of BudgetCode. If, for example, Accounting has a BudgetCode value of 0005005 in one row, it should have that value in every row in which it appears. Similarly, if Finance has a BudgetCode of 0005007 in one row, it should have that value in all rows in which it appears. Figure 8-1 shows data that violates this assumption. In the last row, the BudgetCode for Accounting is different than for the other rows; it has too many zeroes. Examining this error, most likely someone made a keying mistake when entering BudgetCode. Such errors are typical.

Now, before we make a database change, we may need to find all such violations and correct them before proceeding. For the small table shown in Figure 8-1, we can just look at the data, but what if the EMPLOYEE table has 4,000 rows? Two SQL statements are particularly helpful in this regard: correlated subqueries and their cousin, EXISTS/NOT EXISTS. We will consider each of these in turn.

Correlated Subqueries

A correlated subquery looks very much like the subqueries we discussed in Chapter 6, but in actuality, correlated subqueries are very different. To understand the difference, consider the following subquery, which is like those in Chapter 6:

FIGURE 8-1
Table that Violates an Assumed Constraint

EmployeeNumber	Name	Department	BudgetCode
100	Jones	Accounting	0005005
200	Greene	Finance	0005007
300	Abernathy	Finance	0005007
400	Parks	Accounting	0005005
500	Kawai	Production	0005009
600	Lopez	Finance	0005007
700	Greene	Accounting	00050005

```
SELECT      A.Name
FROM        ARTIST A
WHERE       A.ArtistID IN
            (SELECT     W.ArtistID
            FROM        WORK W
            WHERE       W.Title ='Mystic Fabric');
```

The DBMS can process such subqueries from the bottom up. That is, it can first find all of the values of ArtistID in WORK, where the title is 'Mystic Fabric,' and then it can process the upper query using that set of values. There is no need to move back and forth between the two SELECT statements.

Searching for Multiple Copies of a Given Title Now, to introduce correlated subqueries, suppose that someone at View Ridge Gallery proposes that the Title column of WORK is an alternate key. If you look at the data in Figure 7-5, you can see that there are two copies of the title 'Mystic Fabric,' and therefore Title cannot be an alternate key. But, if the WORK table has a thousand or more rows, this is more difficult to determine. In that case, we want to query the WORK table to display the Title and Work of any works that share the same title.

If we were asked to write a program to perform this query, our logic would be as follows: Take the value of Title from the first row in WORK and examine all of the other rows in the table. If we find a row that has the same title as the one in the first row, we know there are duplicates, so we print the Title and Copy of the first work. We continue searching for duplicate title values until we come to the end of the WORK table.

Then, we take the value of Title in the second row and compare it to all other rows in the WORK table, printing out the Title and Copy of any duplicate works. We proceed in this way until all rows of WORK have been examined.

The following correlated subquery performs the action just described:

```
SELECT      W1.Title, W1.Copy
FROM        WORK W1
WHERE       W1.Title IN
            (SELECT     W2.Title
            FROM        WORK W2
            WHERE       W1.Title = W2.Title
            AND         W1.WorkID <> W2.WorkID);
```

The result of this query for the data in Figure 7-5 is:

| Mystic Fabric | 99/135 |
| Mystic Fabric | 105/135 |

This subquery looks deceptively similar to a regular subquery. To the surprise of many students, this subquery and the one above are drastically different. Their similarity is only superficial.

Before explaining why, first notice the notation in the correlated subquery. The WORK table is used in both the upper and the lower SELECT statements. In the upper statement, it is given the alias W1; in the lower SELECT statement, it is given the alias W2.

In essence, when we use this notation, it is as if we made two copies of the WORK table. One copy is called W1 and the second copy is called W2. In these terms, in the last two lines of the correlated subquery, values in the W1 copy of WORK are compared with values in the W2 copy.

Now, consider what makes this subquery so different. Unlike a regular subquery, the DBMS cannot run the bottom SELECT by itself, obtain a set of Titles, and then use that set to execute the upper query. The reason for this appears in the last two lines of the query:

```
WHERE        W1.Title = W2.Title
AND          W1.WorkID <> W2.WorkID);
```

In these expressions, W1.Title (from the top SELECT statement) is being compared to W2.Title (from the bottom SELECT statement). The same is true for W1.WorkID and W2.WorkID. Because of this fact, the DBMS cannot process the subquery portion independent of the upper SELECT.

Instead, the DBMS must process this statement as a subquery that is *nested* within the main query. The logic is as follows: Take the first row from W1. Using that row, evaluate the second query. To do that, for the first row in W2, compare W1.Title to W2.Title and W1.WorkID to W2.WorkID. If the titles are equal and the values of WorkID are not equal, return the value of W2.Title to the upper query. Do this for every row in W2.

Once all the rows in W2 have been evaluated for the first row in W1, move to the second row in W1 and evaluate it against all the rows in W2. Continue in this way until all rows of W1 have been compared to all rows of W2.

If this is not clear to you, write out two copies of the WORK data from Figure 7-5 on a piece of scratch paper. Label one of them W1 and the second W2 and then work through the logic as described. From this, you will see that correlated subqueries always require nested processing.

By the way, do not fall into the following common trap:

```
SELECT       W1.Title, w1.Copy
FROM         WORK W1
WHERE        W1.WorkID IN
             (SELECT     W2.WorkID
             FROM        WORK W2
             WHERE       W1.Title = W2.Title
             AND         W1.WorkID <> W2.WorkID);
```

The logic here seems correct, but it is not. No row will ever be displayed by this query, regardless of the underlying data. See if you can see why this is so before continuing.

The bottom query will indeed find all rows that have the same title and different WorkIDs. If one is found, it will produce the W2.WorkID of that row. But that value will then be compared to W1.WorkID. *These two values will always be different because of the condition* W1.WorkID <> W2.WorkID. No rows are returned because the values of the two unequal WorkIDs are used in the IN instead of the values of the two equal Titles.

Using Correlated Subqueries to Check Functional Dependencies

Correlated subqueries can be used advantageously during database redesign. As mentioned, one application is to verify functional dependencies. For example, suppose we have EMPLOYEE data like that in Figure 8-1 and we want to know whether the data conform to the functional dependency Department → BudgetCode. If so, every time a given value of Department occurs in the table, that value will be matched with the same value of BudgetCode.

The following correlated subquery will find any rows that violate this assumption:

```
SELECT      E1.Department, E1.BudgetCode
FROM        EMPLOYEE E1
WHERE       E1.Department IN
            (SELECT     E2.Department
            FROM        EMPLOYEE E2
            WHERE       E1.Department = E2.Department
            AND         E1.BudgetCode <> E2.BudgetCode);
```

The results for the data in Figure 8-1 are the following:

Accounting	0005005
Accounting	0005005
Accounting	00050005

A listing like this can readily be used to find and fix any rows that violate the functional dependency.

EXISTS and NOT EXISTS

EXISTS and NOT EXISTS are another form of correlated subquery. We can write the last correlated subquery in the form of EXISTS, as follows:

```
SELECT      E1.Department, E1.BudgetCode
FROM        EMPLOYEE E1
WHERE       EXISTS
            (SELECT      *
            FROM         EMPLOYEE E2
            WHERE        E1.Department = E2.Department
            AND    E1.BudgetCode <> E2.BudgetCode);
```

Because EXISTS is a form of a correlated subquery, the processing of the SELECT statements is nested. The first row of E1 is input to the subquery. If the subquery finds any row in E2 for which the department names are the same and the budget codes are different, then the EXISTS is true and the Department and BudgetCode for the first row are selected. Next, the second row of E1 is input to the subquery, the SELECT is processed and the EXISTS is evaluated. If true, the Department and BudgetCode of the second row are selected. This process is repeated for all of the rows in E1.

The EXISTS keyword will be true if *any* row in the subquery meets the condition. The NOT EXISTS keyword will be true only if *all* rows in the subquery fail the condition. Consequently, the double use of NOT EXISTS can be used to find rows that have some specified condition to *every* row of a table.

For example, suppose that at View Ridge the users want to know the name of any artist that every customer is interested in. We can proceed as follows. First, produce the set of all customers that are interested in a particular artist. Then, take the complement of that set, which will be the customers who are not interested in that artist. If that complement is empty, then all customers are interested in the given artist.

Before we go on, this particular NOT EXISTS pattern is famous in one guise or another among SQL practitioners. It is often used as a test of SQL knowledge in job interviews and in bragging sessions, and it can be used to advantage when assessing the desirability of certain database redesign possibilities, as you will see in the last section of this chapter. Therefore, even though this example involves some serious study, it is worth your while to understand it.

The following SQL statement implements the strategy just described:

```
SELECT      A.Name
FROM        ARTIST A
WHERE       NOT EXISTS
            (SELECT       C.CustomerID
             FROM         CUSTOMER C
             WHERE        NOT EXISTS
                (SELECT        CI.CustomerID
                 FROM          CUSTOMER_artist_int CI
                 WHERE         C.CustomerID= CI.CustomerID
                 AND     A.ArtistID = CI.ArtistID));
```

The bottom SELECT finds all of the customers that are interested in a particular artist. As you read this SELECT (the last SELECT in the query), keep in mind that this is a correlated subquery; this SELECT is nested inside the query on CUSTOMER, which is nested inside the query on ARTIST. C.CustomerID is coming from the SELECT on CUSTOMER in the middle, and A.ArtistID is coming from the SELECT on ARTIST at the top.

Now, the NOT EXISTS in the sixth line of the query will find the customers who are not interested in the given artist. If all customers are interested in the given artist, the result of the middle SELECT will be null. If the result of the middle SELECT is null, the NOT EXISTS in the third line of the query will be true and the name of that artist will be produced, just as we want.

Consider what happens for artists who do not qualify in this query. Suppose every customer except Tiffany Twilight is interested in the artist Miro. (This was not the case for the data in Figure 7-5, but assume that it were true.) Now, for the preceding query, when Miro's row is considered, the bottom SELECT will retrieve every customer except Tiffany Twilight. In this case, because of the NOT EXISTS in the sixth line of the query, the middle SELECT will produce the CustomerID for Tiffany Twilight (because her row is the only one that does not appear in the bottom SELECT). Now, because there is a result from the middle SELECT, the NOT EXISTS in the top SELECT is false and the name Miro will not be included in the output of the query. This is correct because there is a customer who is not interested in Miro.

Again, take some time to study this pattern. It is a famous one, and if you work in the database field in your career, you will certainly see it in one form or another again.

▶ ANALYZING THE EXISTING DATABASE

Before we proceed with a discussion of database redesign, reflect for moment on what this task means for a real company whose operations are dependent on the database. Suppose, for example, you work for a company like Amazon.com and further suppose that you have been tasked with an important database redesign assignment, say to change the primary key of the vendor table.

To begin, you may wonder, why would they want to do this? It could be that in the early days, when they only sold books, Amazon.com used company names for vendors. But, as Amazon.com begins to sell more types of products, company names no longer suffice. Perhaps there are too many duplicates, and they have decided to switch to an Amazon-created VendorID.

Now, what does it mean to switch primary keys? Besides adding the new data to the correct rows, what else does it mean? Clearly, if the old primary key has been used as a foreign key, all of the foreign keys need to be changed as well. So we need to know all of the relationships in which the old primary key was used. But what about views? Do any views use the old primary key? If so, they will need to be changed. And, what about triggers and stored procedures? Do any of them use the old primary key? And do not forget any existing application code that may break when the old key is removed.

Now, to create a nightmare, what happens if you get partway through the change process and something does not work correctly? Suppose you encounter unexpected data and you receive errors from the DBMS while trying to add the new primary key. Amazon.com cannot change its Web site to display "Sorry, our database is broken; come back tomorrow (we hope)!"

This nightmare brings up many topics, most of which relate to systems analysis and design. But with regard to database processing, three principles become clear. First, as carpenters say, "Measure twice and cut once." Before we attempt any structure changes to a database, we must clearly understand the current structure and contents of the database, and we must know what is dependent on what. Second, before we make any structural changes to an operational database, we must test those changes on a realistically sized test database that has all important test data cases. Finally, if at all possible, we need to create a complete backup of the operational database prior to making any structure changes. If all goes awry, the backup can be used to restore the database while problems are corrected. We will consider each of these important topics next.

Reverse Engineering

Reverse engineering is the process of reading a database schema and producing a data model from that schema. The data model produced is not truly a conceptual schema, nor is it an internal schema. It is not a conceptual schema because entities will be generated for every table; intersection tables that have no non-key data will appear as entities, for example. It is not an internal schema because it does not have all the information that an internal schema has, such as referential integrity actions. Rather, it is a thing unto itself, a table-relationship diagram that is dressed in entity-relationship clothes. In this text we will call it the **RE (reverse engineered) data model**.

Figures 8-2(a) and (b) show the RE data model produced by ERWin from a SQL Server version of the View Ridge database, as defined in Chapter 7. Figure 8-2(a) shows what ERWin calls the logical model. If you compare this to the logical model in Figure 7-3(a), you will see that ERWin came very close to capturing that model. All the relationship types are correct, and it determined that the minimum cardinality from TRANSACTION to CUSTOMER is zero.

Two problems are that it modeled the intersection table as an entity, which it is not, but that is typical for RE diagrams. Also, it did not determine that at least one TRANSACTION is required for a WORK. The cardinality on the TRANSACTION side of the WORK-TRANSACTION relationship should be shown as P. All in all, though, this is a reasonable representation of the View Ridge schema.

Figure 8-2(b) shows what ERWin calls the physical model. This model is quite accurate. The null/not null specifications are correct, the primary key identities are correct, the alternate key of ARTISTName is correct, and all foreign keys are shown correctly. The only missing items are that there is no P cardinality on TRANSACTION and none of the referential integrity actions are correct. The missing actions are not surprising

FIGURE 8-2

Reverse Engineered Data Model (a) Logical Model and (b) Physical Model

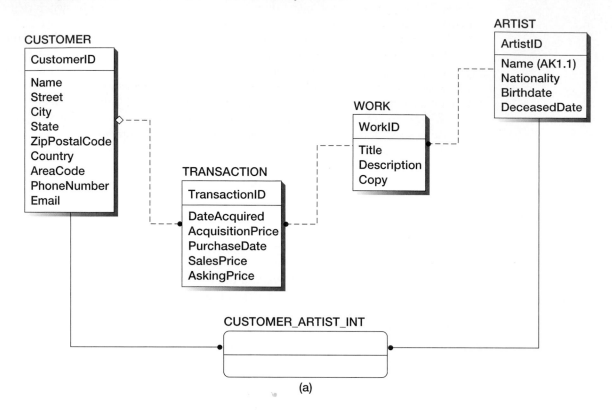

(a)

because there is no way to infer them from the data model. They will have to be supplied manually by the database redesigner.

In addition to tables and views, some data modeling products will capture constraints, triggers, and stored procedures from the database. These constructs are not interpreted, but the text of them is imported to the data model; and with some products, the relationship of the text to the items it references is also obtained. The redesign of constraints, triggers, and stored procedures is beyond the scope of our discussion here. You should realize that they, too, are part of the database, however, and are subject to redesign.

The RE data model provides a basis to begin the database redesign project. We will use it later in this chapter.

Dependency Graphs

Before making changes to database structures, it is vitally important to understand the dependencies of those structures. What is dependent on what? For example, consider changing the name of a table. Where is the table name used? In which triggers? In which stored procedures? In which relationships? Because of the need to know dependencies, many database redesign projects begin by making a **dependency graph**.

The term **graph** arises from the mathematical topic of graph theory. Dependency graphs are not graphical displays like bar charts; rather, they are diagrams that consist of nodes and arcs (or lines) that connect those nodes.

Figure 8-3(a) shows a dependency graph that was constructed by ERWin. It shows that the views BasicCustomerData and BasicCustomerData_WA are dependent on the CUSTOMER table. Figure 8-3(b) shows a similar graph for the tables ARTIST, WORK, and TRANSACTION, the view ArtistWorkNet, and views based upon it.

FIGURE 8-2

(continued)

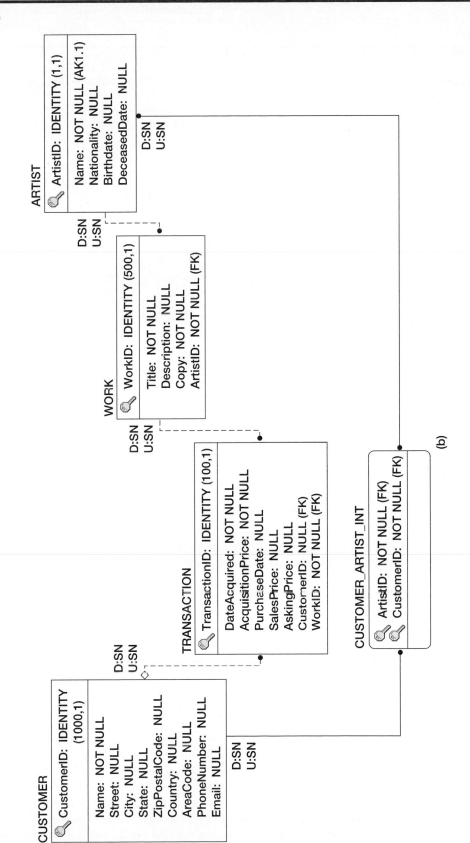

(b)

FIGURE 8-3

Fragments of a
Dependency Graph
(a) CUSTOMER and
Two Views and
(b) Sample Tables and
Views

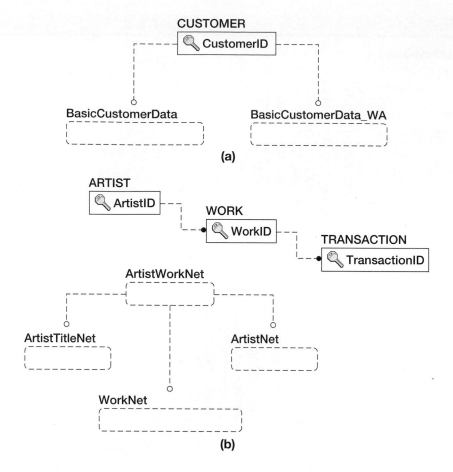

(a)

(b)

Figure 8-3(b) is another good example of reverse engineering results. It is close, but not quite correct. As mentioned, consider such results as a good starting point only. In Figure 8-3(b), the problem is that ERWin was unable to interpret the join that creates ArtistWorkNet view. Therefore, the dependency of ArtistWorkNet on (ARTIST, WORK, TRANSACTION) is not shown.

Figure 8-4 shows a partial dependency graph that was drawn using the results of the reverse engineering model, but manually interpreting views and triggers. For simplicity, this graph does not show the views of CUSTOMER, nor does it show CUSTOMER_ARTIST_INT and related structures. Also, the stored procedure Add_Work is not included, nor are the constraints.

Even this partial diagram reveals the complexity of dependencies among database constructs. You can see that it would be wise to tread lightly, for example, when changing anything in the TRANSACTION table. The consequences of such a change need to be assessed against two relationships, three triggers, and four views. Again, measure twice and cut once!

Database Backup and Test Databases

Because of the potential serious damage that can be done to a database during redesign, a complete backup of the operational database should be made prior to making any changes. Equally important, it is essential that any proposed changes be thoroughly tested. Not only must structure changes proceed successfully, but also all triggers, stored procedures, and applications must run correctly on the revised database.

Typically, there are at least three different copies of the database schema used in the redesign process. One is a small test database that can be used for initial testing. The second is a large test database, which may even be a full copy of the operational database,

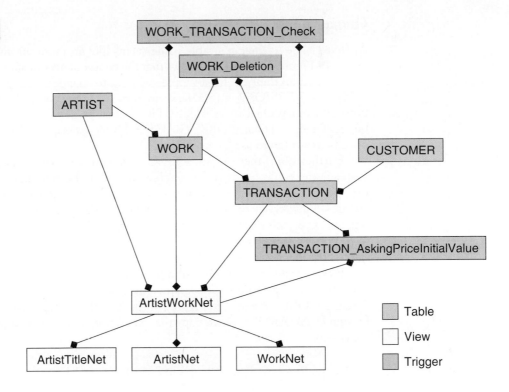

FIGURE 8–4

Example Dependency Graph (Fragment)

which is used for secondary testing. Finally, there is the operational database. Sometimes, there are several large test databases.

A means must be created to recover all test databases to their original state during the testing process. In that way, the test can be rerun as necessary against the same starting point. Depending on the facilities of the DBMS, backup and recovery or other means are used to restore the database after a test run.

Obviously, for enterprises with very large databases, it is not possible to have a test database that is a copy of the operational database. Instead, smaller test databases need to be created, but those test databases must have all the important data characteristics of the operational database; otherwise, they will not provide a realistic test environment. The construction of such test databases is itself a difficult and challenging job. In fact, there are many interesting career opportunities for developing test databases and database test suites.

Finally, for organizations that have very large databases, it may not be possible to make a complete copy of the operational database prior to making structure changes. In this case, the database is backed up in pieces and the changes are made in pieces as well. This task is very difficult and requires great knowledge and expertise. It also requires weeks or months of planning. You may participate as a junior member of a team to make such a change, but you should have years of database experience before you attempt to make structure changes to such large databases. Even then, it is a daunting task.

► CHANGING TABLE NAMES AND TABLE COLUMNS

In this section, we will consider alterations to tables names and table columns. To accomplish these changes, we will use only SQL-92 statements. Many DBMS products have features to facilitate changing structures other than SQL-92; for example, some products have graphical design tools that will simplify this process. But such features are not standardized and you should not be dependent upon them. The statements shown in this chapter will work with any common DBMS product.

Changing Table Names

At first glance, changing a table name seems like an innocent and easy operation. A review of Figure 8-4, however, shows that the consequences of such a change are greater than you would think. If, for example, we want to change the name of the table WORK to WORK_VERSION2, several tasks are necessary. The constraint that defines the relationship from WORK to TRANSACTION must be altered, ArtistWorkNet view must be redefined, and then WORK_TRANSACTION_Check and WORK_deletion triggers must be rewritten to use the new name.

Furthermore, there is no SQL-92 command to change the name of the table. Instead, the table needs to be re-created under the new name, and the old table dropped. This requirement, however, suggests a good strategy for making table name changes. First, create the new table with all attendant structures and then drop the old one once everything is working with the new table. If the table to be renamed is too large to be copied, other strategies will have to be used, but they are beyond the scope of this discussion.

First, create the table by submitting a CREATE TABLE WORK_VERSION2 statement to the DBMS. This statement can be exactly the same as the CREATE TABLE WORK statement in Figure 7-4. Include the ALTER statement that defines the foreign key to ARTIST. Next, copy the data into the new table with the following SQL statement:

INSERT INTO WORK_VERSION2 (Copy, Title, Description, ArtistID)

SELECT (Copy, Title, Description, ArtistID)

FROM WORK;

Notice that there is no VALUES expression in this INSERT command. The columns are matched by position in the column lists (here, they happen to have the same names) and values are inserted into the table.

Now all that remains to do is to define the two triggers. This can be done by copying the text of the old triggers and changing the name WORK to WORK_VERSION2.

At this point, test suites should be run against the database to verify that all changes have been made correctly. After that, stored procedures and applications that use WORK can be changed to run against the new table name[1]. If all is correct, then the foreign key constraint WorkFK and the table work can be dropped with the following:

ALTER TABLE WORK DROP CONSTRAINT WorkFK;

DROP TABLE WORK;

Clearly, there is more to changing a table name than you would think. Now, you can see why some organizations take the stand that no application or user should ever employ the true name of a table. Instead, views are described that serve as table aliases, as explained in Chapter 7. If this were done, only the views that define the aliases would need to be changed when the source table name was changed.

---

[1] Timing here is important. The WORK_VERSION2 table was created from WORK. If triggers, stored procedures, and applications continue to run against WORK while the verification of WORK_VERSION2 is underway, then WORK_VERSION2 will be out of date. Some action will need to be taken to bring it up to date before switching the stored procedures and applications over to WORK_VERSION2.

Adding and Dropping Columns

Adding null columns to a table is straightforward. For example, to add the null column DateCreated to WORK, we simply use the ALTER statement as follows:

```
ALTER TABLE WORK
       ADD COLUMN DateCreated Date NULL;
```

If there are other column constraints such as DEFAULT or UNIQUE, include them with the column definition, just as you would if the column definition were part of a CREATE TABLE statement. However, if you include a DEFAULT constraint, be aware that the default value will be applied to all new rows, but existing rows will have null values.

Suppose, for example, that you want to set the default value of DateCreated to 1/1/1900 to signify that the value has not yet been entered. In that case, you would use the ALTER statement:

```
ALTER TABLE WORK
       ADD COLUMN DateCreated Date NULL DEFAULT '1/1/1900';
```

This statement causes DateCreated for new rows in WORK to be set to 1/1/1900 by default. To set existing rows, you would need to execute the following query:

```
UPDATE WORK
       SET         DateCreated ='1/1/1900'
       WHERE       DateCreated IS NULL;
```

Adding NOT NULL Columns   To add a new NOT NULL column, first add the column as NULL. Then, use an update statement like that shown previously to give the column a value in all rows. After that, the following SQL statement can be executed to change the NULL constraint to NOT NULL for DateCreated.

```
ALTER TABLE WORK
       ALTER COLUMN DateCreated Date NOT NULL;
```

Again, however, this statement will fail if DateCreated has not been given values in all rows.

Dropping Columns   Dropping non-key columns is easy. For example, eliminating the DateCreated column from WORK can be done with the following:

```
ALTER TABLE WORK
       DROP COLUMN DateCreated;
```

To drop a foreign key column, the constraint that defines the foreign key must first be dropped. Making such a change is equivalent to dropping a relationship, and that topic is discussed later in this chapter.

To drop the primary key, the primary key constraint first needs to be dropped. To drop that, however, all foreign keys that use the primary key must first be dropped. Thus, to drop the primary key of WORK and replace it with the composite (Title, Copy, ArtistID), the following steps are necessary:

> ➤ Drop the constraint WorkFK from TRANSACTION.
> ➤ Drop the constraint WorkPK from WORK.
> ➤ Create a new constraint WorkPK using (Title, Copy, ArtistID).
> ➤ Create a new constraint WorkFK referencing (Title, Copy, ArtistID) in TRANS-ACTION.
> ➤ Drop column WorkID.

It is important to verify that all changes have been made correctly before dropping WorkID. Once it is dropped, there is no way to recover it except by restoring the WORK table from a backup.

Changing Column Data Type or Constraints

To change a column data type or to change column constraints, the column is simply redefined using the ALTER TABLE ALTER COLUMN command. However, if the column is being changed from NULL to NOT NULL, then all rows must have a value in that column for the change to succeed.

Also, some data type changes may cause data loss. Changing CHAR (50) to Date, for example, will cause loss of any text field that the DBMS cannot successfully cast as a date. Or, alternatively, the DBMS may simply refuse to make the column change. The results depend on the DBMS product in use.

Generally, converting numeric to char or varchar will succeed. Also, converting date or money or other more specific data type to char or varchar will usually succeed. Converting char or varchar back to date, money, or numeric is risky, and it may or may not be possible.

In the View Ridge schema, if Birthdate had been defined as char(4), then a risky but sensible data type change would be to modify ARTIST.Birthdate to numeric (4,0). This would be a sensible change because all of the values in this column are numeric. Recall the check constraint that was used to define Birthdate (refer to Figure 7-4). The following statement will make the change:

```
ALTER TABLE ARTIST
        ALTER COLUMN Birthdate Numeric (4,0) NULL;
ALTER TABLE ARTIST
        ADD CONSTRAINT NumericBirthYearCheck CHECK
        (Birthdate > 1900 and Birthdate < 2100);
```

The prior check constraints on BirthDate should now be deleted.

Adding and Dropping Constraints

Constraints can be added and removed using the ALTER TABLE ADD CONSTRAINT and ALTER TABLE DROP CONSTRAINT statements shown in Chapters 6 and 7. Of course, to drop a constraint, you need to know its name, which is one reason why it is better to name your own constraints rather than let the DBMS name them for you.

▶ CHANGING RELATIONSHIP CARDINALITIES AND PROPERTIES

Changing cardinalities is a common database redesign task. Sometimes, the need is to change minimum cardinalities from zero to one or from one to zero. Another common task is to change the maximum cardinality from 1:1 to 1:N or from 1:N to N:M. Another possibility, which is less common, is to decrease maximum cardinality from N:M to 1:N or from 1:N to 1:1. This latter change can only be made with loss of data, as you will see.

Changing Minimum Cardinalities

The action to be taken in changing minimum cardinalities depends on whether the change is on the parent side or the child side of the relationship.

Changing Minimum Cardinalities on the Parent Side If the change is on the parent side, meaning the child will or will not be required to have a parent, making the change is a matter of changing whether or not null values are allowed for the foreign key that represents the relationship. For example, suppose that in the 1:N relationship from EMPLOYEE to DEPARTMENT, the foreign key DepartmentNumber appears in the EMPLOYEE table. Changing whether or not an employee is required to have a department is simply a matter of changing the null status of DepartmentNumber.

If the change is from a minimum cardinality of zero to one, then the foreign key, which would have been null, must be changed to not null. Changing a column to not null can only be done if all the rows in the table have a value. In the case of a foreign key, this means that every record must already be related. If not, all records must be changed so that all have a relationship before the foreign key can be made not null. In the previous example, every employee must be related to a department before DepartmentNumber can be changed to not null.

Depending on the DBMS in use, the foreign key constraint that defines the relationship may have to be dropped before the change is made to the foreign key. Then the foreign key constraint can be re-added. The following SQL will work for the preceding example:

```
ALTER TABLE DEPARTMENT
        DROP CONSTRAINT DepartmentFK;
ALTER TABLE DEPARTMENT
        ALTER COLUMN DepartmentNumber int NOT NULL;
ALTER TABLE DEPARTMENT
        ADD CONSTRAINT DepartmentFK
            FOREIGN KEY (DepartmentNumber)
            REFERENCES DEPARTMENT (DepartmentNumber)
                ON UPDATE CASCADE;
```

Changing the minimum cardinality from one to zero is simple. Just change DepartmentNumber from NOT NULL to NULL.

Changing Minimum Cardinalities on the Child Side As noted in Chapter 7, the only way to enforce minimum cardinality different from zero on the child side of a relationship is to write triggers that enforce the constraint. So, to change the minimum cardinality from zero to one, it is necessary to write the appropriate triggers. To change the minimum cardinality from one to zero, just drop the triggers.

In the DEPARTMENT/EMPLOYEE example, to require each DEPARTMENT to have an EMPLOYEE, triggers would need to be written on INSERT of DEPARTMENT and on UPDATE and DELETE of EMPLOYEE. The trigger code in DEPARTMENT ensures that an EMPLOYEE is assigned to the new DEPARTMENT, and the trigger code in EMPLOYEE ensures that the employee being moved to a new department or the employee being deleted is not the last employee in the relationship to its parent.

This discussion assumes that the required child constraint is enforced by triggers. If the required child constraint is enforced by application programs, those programs must also be changed. This is another argument in favor of enforcing such constraints in triggers and not in application code.

Changing Maximum Cardinalities

The only difficulty when increasing cardinalities from 1:1 to 1:N or from 1:N to N:M is to preserve the existing relationships. This can be done, but it requires a bit of manipulation, as you will see. When reducing cardinalities, data will be lost. In this case, a policy must be created for deciding which relationships to lose.

Changing 1:1 to 1:N Figure 8-5 shows a 1:1 relationship between EMPLOYEE and PARKING_PERMIT. As you learned in Chapter 5, the foreign key can be placed in either table for a 1:1 relationship. Wherever it was placed, however, it must have been defined as unique to enforce the 1:1 cardinality. For the tables in Figure 8-5, the action to be taken depends on whether EMPLOYEE is to be the parent of the 1:N or whether PARKING_PERMIT is to be the parent.

If EMPLOYEE is to be the parent (employees are to have multiple parking permits), then the only change necessary is to drop the constraint that PARKING_PERMIT.EmployeeNumber is unique. The relationship will then be 1:N.

If PARKING_PERMIT is to be the parent (parking permits are to be allocated to many employees, say for a carpool), then the foreign key and appropriate values must be moved from PARKING_PERMIT to EMPLOYEE. The following SQL will accomplish this:

```
ALTER TABLE EMPLOYEE
        ADD COLUMN PermitNumber int null;
UPDATE EMPLOYEE
            SET EMPLOYEE.PermitNumber =
            (SELECT      PP.PermitNumber
            FROM         PARKING_PERMIT PP
            WHERE        PP.EmployeeNumber =
                         EMPLOYEE.EmployeeNumber);
```

FIGURE 8–5

Example 1:1 Relationships

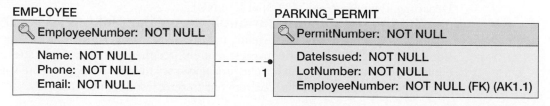

Then, a new foreign key constraint must be created to define the relationship. Once the foreign key has been moved over to EMPLOYEE, the EmployeeNumber column of PARKING_PERMIT should be dropped. Note that the new PermitNumber column in EMPLOYEE must not have a unique constraint so that multiple employees can relate to the same parking permit as required.

Changing 1:N to N:M Suppose that View Ridge Gallery decides that it wants to record multiple purchasers for a given transaction. It may be that some of its art is co-owned between a customer and a bank or a trust account, for example; or perhaps it may want to record the names of both people when a couple purchases art. For whatever reason, this change will require that the 1:N relationship between CUSTOMER and TRANSACTION be changed to a N:M relationship.

Changing a 1:N relationship is surprisingly easy[2]. Just create the new intersection table, fill it with data, and drop the old foreign key column. Figure 8-6 shows the View Ridge database design with a new intersection table to support the N:M relationship. We need to create this table and then copy the values of TransactionID and CustomerID from TRANSACTION for rows in which CustomerID is not null. First, to create the new intersection table:

FIGURE 8-6

View Ridge Database Design with New N:M Relationship

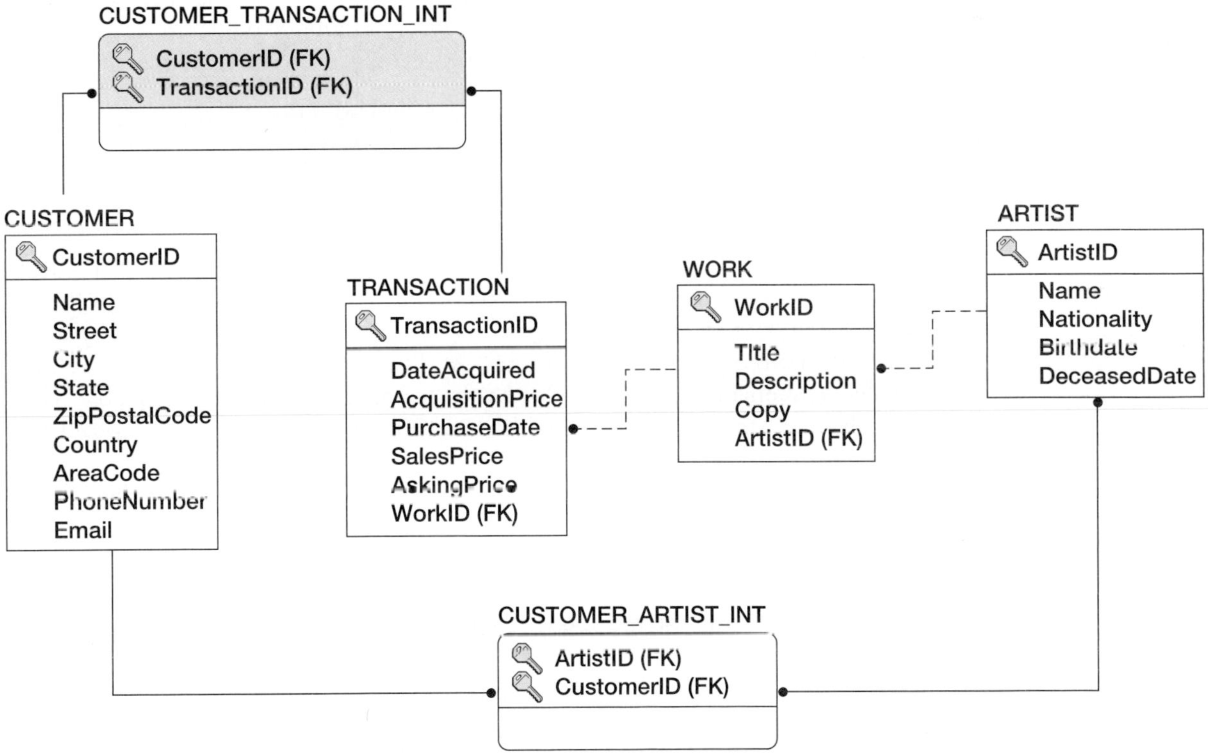

---

[2] At least making the data change is easy. Dealing with the consequences of the data change in views, triggers, stored procedures, and application code will be more difficult. All of these will need to be rewritten to join across a new intersection table. All forms and reports will also need to be changed to portray multiple customers for a transaction; this will mean changing text boxes to grids, for example. All of this work is time-consuming and hence expensive.

```
CREATE TABLE CUSTOMER_TRANSACTION_INT(
        CustomerID      int     NOT NULL,
        TransactionID   int     NOT NULL,
        CONSTRAINT CustomerTransactionPK
                PRIMARY KEY (CustomerID, TransactionID),
        CONSTRAINT Customer_Transaction_Int_TransactionFK
        FOREIGN KEY (TransactionID) REFERENCES
                TRANSACTION (TransactionID)
                        ON UPDATE CASCADE,
        CONSTRAINT Customer_Transaction_Int_CustomerFK
        FOREIGN KEY (CustomerID) REFERENCES
                CUSTOMER (CustomerID)
                        ON UPDATE CASCADE
);
```

Now, fill the table with data from the TRANSACTION table:

```
INSERT INTO CUSTOMER_TRANSACTION_INT (CustomerID,
TransactionID)
        SELECT      CustomerID, TransactionID
        FROM        TRANSACTION
        WHERE       CustomerID IS NOT NULL;
```

Before making this change, the database designers would consult a dependency graph. From that, they would determine that there is a trigger on TRANSACTION (this is not shown in the partial graph in Figure 8-4) that will need to be rewritten. That trigger ensures that the only change to TRANSACTION.CustomerID was from null to a valid value. A similar trigger will need to be written on the new intersection table. There may also be views that use the CUSTOMER and TRANSACTION tables that will need to be redesigned as well.

Once all of these changes have been made, the CustomerID column of TRANSACTION can be dropped.

Reducing Cardinalities (with Data Loss)   It is easy to make the structural changes to reduce cardinalities. To reduce an N:M relationship to 1:N, we just create a new foreign key in the relation that will be the child and fill it with data from the intersection table. To reduce a 1:N relationship to 1:1, we just make the values of the foreign key of the 1:N relationship unique and then define a unique constraint on the foreign key. In either case, the most difficult problem is deciding which data to lose.

Consider the reduction of N:M to 1:N first. Suppose, for example, that the View Ridge Gallery decides to keep just one artist interest for each customer. The relationship will then be 1:N from ARTIST to CUSTOMER. Accordingly, we add a new foreign key column ArtistID to CUSTOMER and set up a foreign key constraint to ARTIST on that customer. The following SQL will accomplish this:

```
ALTER TABLE CUSTOMER
        ADD COLUMN ArtistID int null;
ALTER TABLE CUSTOMER
        ADD CONSTRAINT ArtistInterestFK FOREIGN KEY ArtistID
        REFERENCES ARTIST (ArtistID)
            ON UPDATE CASCADE
            ON DELETE CASCADE;
```

Now which of a customer's potentially many artist interests should be preserved in the new relationship? The answer depends on the business policy at the gallery. Here, suppose we decide simply to take the first one:

```
UPDATE      CUSTOMER
SET         ArtistID =
            (SELECT      Top 1 ArtistID
            FROM         CUSTOMER_ARTIST_INT CI
            WHERE        CUSTOMER.CustomerID = CI.CustomerID);
```

The phrase Top 1 is used to return on the first qualifying row.

All views, triggers, stored procedures, and application code need to be changed to account for the new 1:N relationship. Then the constraints defined on CUSTOMER_ARTIST_INT can be dropped and finally the table CUSTOMER_ARTIST_INT can be dropped.

To change a 1:N to 1:1 relationship, we just need to remove any duplicate values of the foreign key of the relationship and then add a unique constraint on the foreign key. See question 8.57.

▶ ADDING AND DELETING RELATIONSHIPS

Adding new tables and relationships is straightforward. Just add the tables and relationships using CREATE TABLE statements with FOREIGN KEY constraints, as shown before. If an existing table has a child relationship to the new table, add a FOREIGN KEY constraint using the existing table.

For example, if a new table COUNTRY were added to the View Ridge database with primary key Name and if CUSTOMER.Country is to be used as a foreign key into the new table, a new FOREIGN KEY constraint would be defined in CUSTOMER:

```
ALTER TABLE CUSTOMER
        ADD CONSTRAINT CountryFK FOREIGN KEY Country
        REFERENCES COUNTRY (Name)
            ON UPDATE CASCADE;
```

Deleting relationships and tables is just a matter of dropping the foreign key constraints and then dropping the tables. Of course, before this is done, dependency graphs must be constructed and used to determine which views, triggers, stored procedures, and application programs will be affected by the deletions.

All of these actions are easy because they do not transform existing data. Sometimes, however, new tables and relationships arise because of the need for normalization or de-normalization. We consider these cases next.

Adding Tables and Relationships for Normalization

We began this chapter with a discussion of the EMPLOYEE table in Figure 8-1. This table, which has the format:

EMPLOYEE (<u>EmployeeNumber</u>, Name, Department, BudgetCode)

is not normalized because Department → BudgetCode, and Department is not a candidate key. You learned earlier how to use a correlated subquery to determine whether the data support the functional dependency between Department and BudgetCode. That query revealed a row whose budget code needed to be corrected. Suppose that correction has been made and we are ready to normalize the EMPLOYEE table.

Normalizing EMPLOYEE Several tasks are necessary to normalize this table: create the new DEPARTMENT table, create a 1:N relationship between DEPART-MENT and EMPLOYEE, copy the data from EMPLOYEE to DEPARTMENT, and finally, drop the BudgetCode column from EMPLOYEE.

The table and relationship creation is similar to that shown previously, and we will not consider those actions here. Assume that the new table has been defined as follows:

DEPARTMENT (<u>Name</u>, BudgetCode)

Also, assume that DepartmentName in EMPLOYEE has been defined as a foreign key on Name of DEPARTMENT.

The following SQL will copy the data from EMPLOYEE to DEPARTMENT:

INSERT INTO DEPARTMENT (Name, BudgetCode)
   SELECT   DISTINCT (DepartmentName, BudgetCode)
   FROM   EMPLOYEE;

Once views, triggers, stored procedures, and application code have been changed to use the new DEPARTMENT table, the BudgetCode column can be dropped from EMPLOYEE.

Normalizing the View Ridge WORK Table Consider the View Ridge database table WORK. It has the columns (WorkID, Title, Copy, Description, and ArtistID). There are two candidate keys: WorkID and the composite (ArtistID, Title, Copy). Suppose that the following question arises at the gallery: Is Description a description of the work itself, or is it a description of a particular copy of the work? If the former: (ArtistID, Title) → Description; if the latter: (ArtistID, Title, Copy) → Description. Furthermore, if the former is true, this table is not normalized because the constraint (ArtistID, Title) → Description is not implied by the definition of the key (ArtistID, Title, Copy).

We can use correlated subqueries to answer this question. Specifically, we can use a correlated subquery to determine whether there are any rows in which Description varies for a combination of (ArtistID, Title). If so, then the key cannot be (ArtistID, Title).

The following SQL statement will reveal any rows that have a different Description for the same combination of (ArtistID, Title):

```
SELECT        ArtistID, Title, Copy, Description
FROM          WORK W1
WHERE         W1.ArtistID IN
              (SELECT      ArtistID
               FROM        WORK W2
               WHERE       W1.Description <> W2.Description
                     AND   W1.ArtistID = W2.ArtistID
                     AND   W1.Title = W2.Title);
```

The results of this query are as follows:

| 14 | Mystic Fabric | 99/135 | One of the only privately held copies in excellent condition! |
| 14 | Mystic Fabric | 105/135 | Some water damage, but a great image! |

These results indicate that the supposition that (ArtistID, Copy) might be a candidate key is wrong. (ArtistID, Copy) does not determine a unique Description, and hence cannot be the key.

Now, we can ask whether the data supports the notion that (ArtistID, Title, Copy) can be a key. If so, there should be no rows in the following query:

```
SELECT        ArtistID, Title, Copy, Description
FROM          WORK W1
WHERE         W1.ArtistID IN
              (SELECT      ArtistID
               FROM        WORK W2
               WHERE       W1.Description <> W2.Description
                     AND   W1.ArtistID = W2.ArtistID
                     AND   W1.Title = W2.Title
                     AND   W1.Copy = W2.Copy);
```

Indeed, when we run this query, we will find that no rows are presented.

So, according to the data, (ArtistID, Title, Copy) can be the key of WORK. However, the users are the final judges on questions of the underlying functional dependencies. Suppose the users respond, "Well, we've been entering the data as if Description were for the copy and not for the title itself. But, we'd like to be able to enter a description of a title, independent of any particular copy. For example, we want to enter a description of Mystic Fabric, in general, as well as a description of each copy of Mystic Fabric that we happen to have."

Figure 8-7 shows tables for a revised View Ridge database design that supports these new requirements. Both WORK and the new table WORK_COPY contain a description column. WORK has TitleDescription and WORK_COPY has WorkDescription.

To make these changes, we are in essence normalizing WORK. We are creating a new attribute TitleDescription for which (ArtistID, Title) → TitleDescription. Hence, we need to create a table in which (ArtistID, Title) is a candidate key.

To do this, the new table WORK_COPY needs to be created using CREATE TABLE. A constraint for the relationship from WORK_COPY to WORK will need to

---

FIGURE 8-7

View Ridge Database Design with WORK_COPY Table

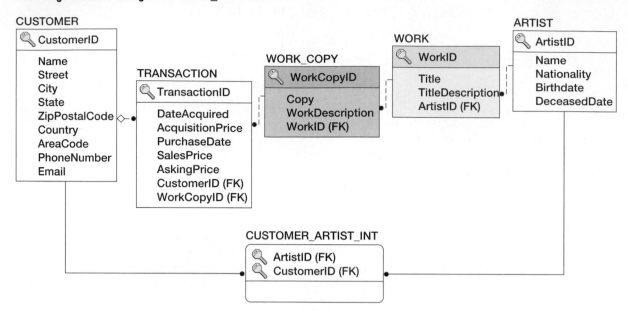

be created, too. Also, the values of Copy, Description, and WorkID need to be moved to the new table. The following SQL will accomplish the latter task:

INSERT INTO WORK_COPY (Copy, WorkDescription, WorkID)

    (SELECT   Copy, Description, WorkID

    FROM   WORK);

Once all views, triggers, stored procedures, and application code have been changed to work with the new data structures, WORK.Copy and WORK.Description columns can be dropped. Also, TitleDescription needs to be added to WORK and TRANSACTION.WorkID must be changed to TRANSACTION.WorkCopyID. Of course the foreign key data must be changed, too.

Removing Relationships for Denormalization

In some cases, it is desirable to denormalize existing data. At View Ridge Gallery, this might occur if the gallery decided that it carries only one work for an artist most of the time. In that case, combining ARTIST and WORK into one table would eliminate the relationship between those two tables and thus simplify processing. In the following, we will assume that we are working with the original View Ridge schema in Figure 7-3(b), not the schema as changed in prior sections of this chapter.

If ARTIST and WORK were combined into one table, it would have the following structure:

ARTIST_WORK (ArtistWorkID, Name, Nationality, Birthdate, DeceasedDate, Title, Copy, Description)

This table is not normalized, and the artist data will be duplicated for every work of that artist that the gallery carries. If, however, the gallery normally carried only one work per artist, this would not be a problem.

To make this change to the database, the new table would be defined using the CREATE TABLE statement. There is nothing new here, so we will not show that statement. Now the join of the existing ARTIST and WORK tables can be used to fill the new table as follows:

INSERT INTO ARTIST_WORK (Name, Nationality, Birthdate, DeceasedDate, Title, Copy Description)

SELECT	Name, Nationality, Birthdate, DeceasedDate, Title, Copy, Description
FROM	ARTIST JOIN WORK
ON	ARTIST.ArtistID = WORK.ArtistID;

Also, the TRANSACTION table would need to be changed to have its foreign key reference ARTIST_WORK rather than WORK. The SQL to fill that new foreign key with data is left as an exercise (see question 8.58). After all views, triggers, stored procedures, and application code have been changed to work with this new table, the existing WORK and ARTIST tables could be deleted.

Removing the CUSTOMER_ARTIST_INT Table   Another possibility for denormalization at View Ridge would be to remove the CUSTOMER_ARTIST_INT table. As you know, having such a table complicates all the SQL statements that use CUSTOMER and ARTIST, so there is value in removing it.

The business justification for removing the table might be that the gallery personnel believe that every customer is interested in every artist, and so the table adds no value. Or conversely, the gallery personnel may say that everyone is only interested in one or—at most—two artists, so not much is lost by eliminating the intersection table and having a single column in CUSTOMER for FavoriteArtist. This column can be a foreign key to the ARTIST table. Thus, the relationship from ARTIST to CUSTOMER becomes 1:N rather than N:M.

Checking Out the User Assumptions   You can use the SQL you have learned in this chapter to check out these assumptions. We saw a way to create a query that will show the artists for which all customers have an interest in the section on EXISTS/NOT EXISTS. For our data, there was only one such artist, so the first justification for removing the intersection table—that every customer is interested in every artist—is not true.

Suppose we want to know how many artists each customer is interested in. One simple query to determine this is as follows:

SELECT	C.Name, Count(*) as NumInterests
FROM	CUSTOMER C JOIN CUSTOMER_ARTIST_INT CI
	ON C.CustomerID = CI.CustomerID
GROUP BY	C.Name;

The result of this query for our data is the following:

Chris Wilkens	2
David Smith	1
Donald G. Gray	1
Fred Smathers	1
Jeffrey James	1
Lynda Johnson	3
Mary Beth Frederickson	3
Selma Warning	2
Susan Wu	1
Tiffany Twilight	3

If these data are typical, the data do support the assumption that having just one or two columns of favorite artists would be a workable solution.

Another way of decreasing the size of the database is to remove artists who have no customers interested in them. The following query obtains the names of artists and the count of the number of customers who are not interested in them:

SELECT A.Name, Count(*) as NumCustNotInterested

FROM ARTIST AS A, CUSTOMER AS C

WHERE EXISTS

    (SELECT C.CustomerID

    FROM CUSTOMER

    WHERE NOT EXISTS

        (SELECT CI.CustomerID

        FROM CUSTOMER_ARTIST_INT CI

        WHERE C.CustomerID= CI.CustomerID and A.ArtistID = CI.ArtistID))

  GROUP BY A.Name;

This query uses what is known as Cartesian join; notice there is no ON or WHERE condition for the two tables in the top SELECT. This type of join connects every row of artist with every row of customer. We need to do this to obtain all of the possible pairings of artist and customer; from these pairings, we select those that never appear in the intersection table.

Observe that if the first table has n rows and the second table has m rows, the Cartesian join will create $n \times m$ rows in the result. Thus, it is possible to create huge tables with this type of join, so you should use it with care.

If we define this query as a view, say as the ArtistNoInterestCount, we can left join ARTIST to this view to show all artists:

SELECT   A.Name, NumCustNotInterested

FROM   ARTIST A LEFT JOIN ArtistNoInterestCount AI

           ON A. Name = AI.Name;

The result of this query for our data is the following:

Chagall	9
Frings	6
Kandinsky	10
Klee	10
Matisse	10
Miro	9
Moos	8
Tobey	Null

Observe that Tobey has a null value for a count because all customers are interested in him. We can replace the null with a zero using the COALESCE function, as follows:

SELECT   A.Name, Coalesce (NumCustNotInterested, 0)

FROM   ARTIST A LEFT JOIN ArtistNoInterestCount AI

                ON A. Name = AI.Name;

Coalesce simply chooses the first non-null element in the arguments that are passed to it. If all are null, then the result is null as well. Here, the function will either return a non-null value of NumCustNotInterested or the value 0. The result is the following:

Chagall	9
Frings	6
Kandinsky	10
Klee	10
Matisse	10
Miro	9
Moos	8
Tobey	0

Given these results, View Ridge might decide to eliminate the intersection table. Doing so, however, will reduce your opportunity for learning how to work with an intersection table, and we will not do it. If the gallery personnel want to do so, they can eliminate it using the techniques shown earlier in this chapter.

From these examples, you can get an idea of the ways that SQL can be used to examine data prior to database redesign. Unfortunately, we will need to leave the topic of SQL and move on to other topics. If you want to learn more, read books like Celko's *SQL for Smarties* and others that discuss more advanced SQL.

▶ FORWARD ENGINEERING

It is possible to use many data modeling products to make database changes on your behalf. To do that, you first reverse engineer the database, make changes to the RE data model, and then invoke the forward engineering functionality of the data modeling tool.

We will not consider forward engineering here because it hides the SQL that you need to learn. Also, the specifics of the forward engineering process are product-dependent.

Because of the importance of making data model changes correctly, many professionals are skeptical about using an automated process for database redesign. Certainly, it is necessary to test the results thoroughly before using forward engineering on operational data. Some products will show the SQL they are about to execute for review before making the changes to the database.

Database redesign is one area in which automation may not be the best idea. Much depends on the nature of the changes to be made and the quality of the forward engineering features of the data modeling product. Given the knowledge you have gained in this chapter, you should be able to make most redesign changes writing your own SQL. There is nothing wrong with that approach!

SUMMARY

Most database design work involves redesigning existing databases. Redesign is necessary both to fix mistakes made during the initial database design and also to adapt the database to changes in system requirements. Such changes are inevitable because information systems and organizations do not just influence each other—they create each other. Thus, new information systems cause changes in systems requirements.

Correlated subqueries and EXISTS/NOT EXISTS are important SQL statements. They can be used to answer advanced queries, and they are useful during database redesign for determining whether specified data conditions exist. For example, they can be used to determine whether possible functional dependencies exist in the data.

A correlated subquery appears deceptively similar to a regular subquery. The difference is that a regular subquery can be processed from the bottom up. In a regular subquery, results from the lowest query can be determined and then used to evaluate the upper level queries. In contrast, in a correlated subquery, the processing is nested; that is, a row from an upper query statement is used in comparison with rows in a lower-level query. The key distinction of a correlated subquery is that the lower-level select statements use columns from upper-level statements.

EXISTS and NOT EXISTS are specialized forms of correlated subqueries. With them, the upper-level query produces results, depending on the existence or nonexistence of rows in lower-level queries. An EXISTS condition is true if any row in the subquery meets the specified conditions; a NOT EXISTS condition is true only if all rows in the subquery do not meet the specified condition. NOT EXISTS is useful for queries that involve conditions that must be true for all rows, such as a "customer who has purchased all products." The double use of NOT EXISTS, shown on page 270, is a famous SQL pattern that is used to test SQL knowledge.

Before redesigning a database, the existing database needs to be carefully examined to avoid making the database unusable by partially processing a database change. Measure twice and cut once is the rule. Reverse engineering is used to create a data model of the existing database. This is done to better understand the database structure before proceeding with a change. The data model produced, called a reverse engineered (RE) data model, is neither a conceptual schema nor an internal schema: It has characteristics of both. Most data modeling tools can perform reverse engineering. The RE data model almost always has missing information; such models should be carefully reviewed.

All of the elements of a database are interrelated. Dependency graphs are used to portray the dependency of one element on another. For example, a change in a table can potentially impact relationships, views, indexes, triggers, stored procedures, and application programs. These impacts need to be known and accounted for before making database changes.

A complete backup must be made to the operational database prior to any database redesign changes. Additionally, such changes must be thoroughly tested, initially on small test databases and later on larger test databases that may even be duplicates of the operational database. The redesign changes are made only after such extensive testing has been completed.

Database redesign changes can be grouped into different types. One type involves changing table names and table columns. Changing a table name has a surprising number of potential consequences. A dependency graph should be used to understand these consequences before proceeding with the change. Non-key columns are readily added and deleted. Adding a NOT NULL column must be done in three steps: first, add the column as NULL; then add data to every row; and then alter the column constraint to NOT NULL. To drop a column used as a foreign key, the foreign key constraint must first be dropped.

Column data types and constraints can be changed using the ALTER TABLE ALTER COLUMN statement. Changing the data type to char or varchar from a more specific type, such as date, is usually not a problem. Changing a data type from char or varchar to a more specific type can be a problem. In some cases, data will be lost or the DBMS may refuse the change. Constraints can be added or dropped using the ALTER TABLE ADD/DROP constraint statement. Use of this statement is easier if the developers have provided their own names for all constraints.

Changing minimum cardinalities on the parent side of a relationship is simply a matter of altering the constraint on the foreign key from NULL to NOT NULL or from NOT NULL to NULL. Changing minimum cardinalities on the child side of a relationship can be accomplished only by adding or dropping triggers that enforce the constraint.

Changing maximum cardinality from 1:1 to 1:N is simple if the foreign key resides in the correct table. In that case, just remove the unique constraint on the foreign key column. If the foreign key resides in the wrong table for this change, first move the foreign key to the other table and do not place a unique constraint on that table.

Changing a 1:N to N:M relationship requires building a new intersection table and moving the key and foreign key values to the intersection table. This aspect of the change is relatively simple. More difficult is changing all views, triggers, stored procedures, application programs, and forms and reports to use the new intersection table.

Reducing cardinalities is easy, but such changes may result in data loss. Prior to making such reductions, a policy must be determined to decide which data to keep. Changing N:M to 1:N involves creating a foreign key in the parent table and moving one value from the intersection table into that foreign key. Changing 1:N to 1:1 requires first eliminating duplicates in the foreign key and then setting a uniqueness constraint on that key. Adding and deleting relationships can be accomplished by defining new foreign key constraints or by dropping existing foreign key constraints.

Adding tables and relationships for normalization should be done in several steps. First, use correlated subqueries to determine whether the normalization assumption is justified. If not, fix the data before proceeding. Next, create a new table and move the normalized data into the new table. Then, define the appropriate foreign key.

Dropping a table and relationship for denormalization is simply a matter of defining the new columns in the table to be denormalized and then filling them with existing data. Once this has been done, the child table and relationship can be dropped.

Most data modeling tools have the capacity to perform forward engineering, which is the process of applying data model changes to an existing database. If forward engineering is used, the results should be thoroughly tested before using it on an operational database. Some tools will show the SQL that they will execute during the forward engineering process. If so, that SQL should be carefully reviewed. All in all, there is nothing wrong with writing database redesign SQL statements by hand rather than using forward engineering.

GROUP I QUESTIONS

8.1   Explain the difference between database design and database redesign.

8.2   Describe why database redesign is necessary.

8.3   Explain in your own words the following statement: "Information systems and organizations create each other." How does this relate to database redesign?

8.4   Suppose that a table contains two non-key columns: AdviserName and AdviserPhone. Further suppose that you suspect that AdviserPhone →

AdviserName. Explain how you would go about determining whether the data support this supposition.

8.5 Write a subquery, other than one in this chapter, that is not a correlated subquery.

8.6 Explain the statement that the processing of correlated subqueries is nested, whereas that of regular subqueries is not.

8.7 Write a correlated subquery, other than one in this chapter.

8.8 Explain how the query in your answer to question 8.5 differs from the query in your answer to question 8.7.

8.9 Explain what is wrong with the correlated subquery on page 268.

8.10 Write a correlated subquery to determine whether the data support the supposition in question 8.4.

8.11 Explain the meaning of the keyword EXISTS.

8.12 Answer question 8.10, but use EXISTS.

8.13 Explain a difference in the use of any and all between EXISTS and NOT EXISTS.

8.14 Explain the processing of the query on page 270.

8.15 Write a query that will display the names of any customers who are interested in all artists.

8.16 Explain how the query in your answer to question 8.15 works.

8.17 Why is it important to analyze the database before implementing database redesign tasks? What can happen if this is not done?

8.18 Explain the process of reverse engineering.

8.19 Why is the model created by reverse engineering not a conceptual schema?

8.20 What is a dependency graph? What purpose does it serve?

8.21 Explain the dependencies for WORK in the graph in Figure 8-4.

8.22 What sources are used when creating a dependency graph?

8.23 Explain two different types of test databases that should be used when testing database redesign changes.

8.24 Explain the problems that can occur when changing the name of a table.

8.25 Describe the process of changing a table name.

8.26 Considering Figure 8-4, describe the tasks that need to be accomplished to change the name of the table WORK to WORK_VERSION2.

8.27 Explain how views can simplify the process of changing a table name.

8.28 Under what conditions is the following SQL statement valid?

```
INSERT        INTO T1 (A, B)
SELECT        (C, D) FROM T2;
```

8.29 Show a SQL statement to add an integer column C1 to the table T2. Assume that C1 is NULL.

8.30 Extend your answer to question 8.29 to add C1 when C1 is to be NOT NULL.

8.31 Show a SQL statement to drop the column C1 from table T2.

8.32 Describe the process for dropping primary key C1 and making the new primary key C2.

8.33 Which data type changes are least risky?

8.34 Which data type changes are most risky?

8.35 Show a SQL statement to change a column C1 to Char(10) NOT NULL. What conditions must exist in the data for this change to be successful?

8.36 Explain how to change the minimum cardinality when a child that was required to have a parent is no longer required to have one.

8.37 Explain how to change the minimum cardinality when a child that was not required to have a parent is now required to have one. What condition must exist in the data for this change to work?

8.38 Explain how to change the minimum cardinality when a parent that was required to have a child is no longer required to have one.

8.39 Explain how to change the minimum cardinality when a parent that was not required to have a child is now required to have one.

8.40 Describe how to change the maximum cardinality from 1:1 to 1:N. Assume that the foreign key is on the side of the new child in the 1:N relationship.

8.41 Describe how to change the maximum cardinality from 1:1 to 1:N. Assume that the foreign key is on the side of the new parent in the 1:N relationship.

8.42 Assume that tables T1 and T2 have a 1:1 relationship. Assume that T2 has the foreign key. Show the SQL statements necessary to move the foreign key to T1. Make your own assumptions about the names of keys and foreign keys.

8.43 Explain how to transform a 1:N relationship into an N:M relationship.

8.44 Suppose that tables T1 and T2 have a 1:N relationship. Show the SQL statements necessary to fill an intersection T1_T2_INT. Make your own assumptions about the names of keys and foreign keys.

8.45 Explain how the reduction of maximum cardinalities causes data loss.

8.46 Using the tables in your answer to question 8.44, show the SQL statements necessary to change the relationship back to 1:N. Assume that the first row in the qualifying rows of the intersection table is to provide the foreign key. Make your own assumptions about the names of keys and foreign keys.

8.47 Using the results of your answer to question 8.46, explain what must be done to convert this relationship to 1:1. Make your own assumptions about the names of keys and foreign keys.

8.48 In general terms, what must be done to add a new relationship?

8.49 Suppose that tables T1 and T2 have a 1:N relationship, with T2 as the child. Show the SQL statements necessary to remove table T2. Make your own assumptions about the names of keys and foreign keys.

8.50 Explain the changes necessary to normalize a table that has existing data.

8.51 Assume that table T1 has two non-key columns, C1 and C2, and that it is supposed that C1→C2. Show the SQL statement necessary to normalize C1 and C2 into their own table.

8.52 In the View Ridge WORK table, explain the differences implied by the following two statements:

(ArtistID, Title) → Description

(ArtistID, Title, Copy) → Description

8.53 Explain in general terms the work necessary to denormalize two tables.

8.54 Suppose that tables T1 and T2 have a 1:N relationship. Show the SQL statements necessary to denormalize them into a single table. Make your own assumptions about the names of keys and foreign keys.

8.55 In an organization that questions the need for an intersection table, describe two different ways that correlated subqueries can be used to justify eliminating or keeping the intersection table.

8.56 What are the risks and problems of forward engineering?

GROUP II QUESTIONS

8.57 Suppose that the table EMPLOYEE has a 1:N relationship to the table PHONE_NUMBER. Further suppose that the key of EMPLOYEE is EmployeeID; and the columns of PHONE_NUMBER are PHNumber (a surrogate key), AreaCode, LocalNumber, and EmployeeID (a foreign key to EMPLOYEE). Alter this design so that EMPLOYEE has a 1:1 relationship to PHONE_NUMBER. For employees having more than one phone number, keep only the first one.

8.58 Assume that the View Ridge WORK table has been replaced by the ARTIST_WORK table, as described in this chapter. Write SQL statements to move the foreign key for the WORK/CUSTOMER relationship to the ARTIST_WORK/CUSTOMER relationship. Assume that you must add the foreign key column to ARTIST_WORK, define the relationship, and move appropriate values. When all is done, remove the CUSTOMER foreign key in WORK.

8.59 Consider the following table:

TASK (<u>EmployeeID</u>, Name, Phone, OfficeNumber, <u>ProjectName</u>, Sponsor, <u>WorkDate</u>, HoursWorked)

with the following possible functional dependencies:

EmployeeID → (Name, Phone, OfficeNumber)

ProjectName → Sponsor

A. Write SQL statements to display the values of any rows that violate these functional dependencies.

B. If no data violate these functional dependencies, can we assume they are valid? Why or why not?

C. Assume that these functional dependencies are true and that the data has been corrected, if necessary, to reflect them. Code all SQL statements necessary to redesign this table into domain/key normal form. Assume that the table does have data values that must be appropriately transformed to the new design.

8.60 Suppose that the table EMPLOYEE has a 1:N relationship to the table PHONE_NUMBER. Further suppose that the key of EMPLOYEE is EmployeeID; and the columns of PHONE_NUMBER are PHNumber (a surrogate key), AreaCode, LocalNumber, and EmployeeID (a foreign key to EMPLOYEE). Code all SQL statements necessary to redesign this database so that it has just one table. Explain the difference between the result of question 8.57 and the result of this question.

Assume that FiredUp has created a database with the following tables:

CUSTOMER (CustomerSK, Name, Phone, EmailAddress)

STOVE (SerialNumber, Type, Version, DateOfManufacture)

REGISTRATION (*CustomerSK*, *SerialNumber*, Date)

STOVE_REPAIR (RepairInvoiceNumber, *SerialNumber*, Date, Description, TotalCost, TotalPaid, *CustomerSK*)

Assume that all relationships have been defined, as implied by the foreign keys in this table list. For example, assume that foreign key constraints like REGISTRA-TION.CustomerSK is a foreign key in CUSTOMER (CustomerSK) have been defined.

A. Create a dependency graph that shows dependencies among these tables. Explain how you need to extend this graph for views and other database constructs like stored procedures.

B. Using your dependency graph, describe the tasks necessary to change the name of the REGISTRATION table to REG.

C. Write all SQL statements to make the name change described in question B.

D. Suppose that FiredUp determines that at most one REG is to be kept for each stove. Modify the design of these tables appropriately.

E. Code SQL statements necessary to redesign the database, as described in your answer to question D. For stoves that have multiple REG rows, keep the data with the latest Date.

F. Suppose that FiredUp considers changing the primary key of CUSTOMER to EmailAddress. Write correlated subqueries to display any data that indicate that this change is not justifiable.

G. Suppose that EmailAddress can be made the primary key of CUSTOMER. Make appropriate changes to the table design, assuming EmailAddress as the primary key.

H. Code all SQL statements necessary to implement the changes described in question G.

Assume Twigs has created a database with the following tables:

OWNER (OwnerName, Phone, Street, City, State, Zip)

SERVICE (DateOfService, *OwnerName*, Description, AmountBilled, AmountPaid, DateOfPayment)

CHIP_DELIVERY (*CustomerName*, DateDelivered, LoadSize, AmountBilled, AmountPaid)

Assume that all relationships have been defined as implied by the foreign keys in this table list. For example, assume that foreign key constraints like CHIP_DELIVERY.CustomerName is a foreign key in OWNER (OwnerName) have been defined.

A. Create a dependency graph that shows dependencies among these tables. Explain how you need to extend this graph for views and other database constructs like stored procedures.

B. Using your dependency graph, describe the tasks necessary to change the name of the OWNER table to CUSTOMER.

C. Write all SQL statements to make the name change described in question B.

D. Suppose that Twigs determines that some owners have more than one property. Make design changes in accordance with this new fact. Assume that Phone is an attribute of OWNER and not of PROPERTY.

E. Code SQL statements to implement your redesign recommendations in your answer to question D.

F. Suppose that Twigs considers changing the primary key of CUSTOMER to Phone. Write correlated subqueries to display any data that indicate that this change is not justifiable.

G. Suppose that Phone can be made the primary key of CUSTOMER. Make appropriate changes to the table design, assuming Phone as the primary key.

H. Code all SQL statements necessary to implement the changes described in question G.

PART IV

Multi-User Database Processing

The three chapters in Part IV describe important issues and problems of multi-user databases and illustrate responses and solutions to those issues and problems with two popular DBMS products. We begin in Chapter 9 with a description of database administration and the major tasks and techniques for multi-user database management. The next two chapters illustrate the implementation of these concepts using Oracle 9i in Chapter 10 and SQL Server 2000 in Chapter 11.

CHAPTER
9

Managing Multi-User Databases

Although multi-user databases offer great value to the organizations that create and use them, they also pose difficult problems for those same organizations. For one, multi-user databases are complicated to design and develop because they support many overlapping user views. Additionally, as discussed in the last chapter, requirements change over time, and those changes necessitate changes to the database structure and applications. Such changes must be carefully planned and controlled so that a change made for one group does not cause problems for another. In addition, when users process a database concurrently, special controls are needed to ensure that the actions of one user do not inappropriately influence the results for another. This topic is both important and complicated, as you will see.

In large organizations, processing rights and responsibilities need to be defined and enforced. What happens, for example, when an employee leaves the firm? When can his records be deleted? For the purposes of payroll processing, after the last pay period. For the purposes of quarterly reporting, at the end of the quarter. For the purposes of end-of-year tax record processing, at the end of the year. And so forth. Clearly, no department can decide unilaterally when to delete that data. Similar comments pertain to the insertion and changing of data values. For these and other reasons, security systems need to be developed that enable only authorized users to take only authorized actions at authorized times.

Databases have become key components of organizational operations and even key components of an organization's value. Unfortunately, database failures and disasters do occur. Accordingly, effective backup and recovery plans, techniques, and procedures are essential.

Finally, over time, the DBMS itself will need to be changed to improve performance to incorporate new features and releases, and to conform to changes made in the underlying operating system. All of this requires attentive management.

In order to ensure that these problems are addressed and solved, most organizations have developed an office of database administration. We begin with a description of the tasks of that office; then we describe the combination of software and manual practices and procedures that is used to perform those tasks in the rest of this chapter. In the next two chapters, we will discuss and illustrate features and functions of Oracle 9i and of SQL Server 2000, respectively, for dealing with these issues.

▶ DATABASE ADMINISTRATION

Both the terms **data administration** and **database administration** are used in industry. In some cases, the terms are considered synonymous; in other cases, they have different meanings. In this text, we use the term *data administration* to refer to a function that applies to an entire organization. The term *database administration* refers to a function that is specific to a particular database, including the applications that process that database. This chapter addresses database administration. Data administration is discussed in Chapter 15.

Databases vary considerably in size and scope: from a single-user personal database to a large interorganizational database like an airline reservation system. All of these databases have a need for database administration, although the tasks to be accomplished vary in complexity. For a personal database, for example, individuals follow simple procedures for backing up their data, and they keep minimal records for documentation. In this case, the person who uses the database also performs the DBA functions, even though he or she is probably unaware of it.

For multi-user database applications, database administration becomes both more important and more difficult. Consequently, it generally has formal recognition. For some applications, one or two people are given this function on a part-time basis. For large Internet or intranet databases, database administration responsibilities are often too time-consuming and too varied to be handled even by a single full-time person. Supporting a database with dozens or hundreds of users requires considerable time as well as both technical knowledge and diplomatic skills, and usually is handled by an office of database administration. The manager of the office is often known as the **database administrator;** in this case, the acronym **DBA** refers to either the office or the manager.

The overall responsibility of the DBA is to facilitate the development and use of the database. Usually, this means balancing the conflicting goals of protecting the database and maximizing its availability and benefit to users. The DBA is responsible for the development, operation, and maintenance of the database and its applications. Specific tasks are shown in Figure 9-1. We consider each of these tasks in the following sections.

Managing the Database Structure

Managing the database structure includes participating in the initial database design and implementation as well as controlling and managing changes to it. Ideally, the DBA is involved early in the development of the database and its applications; he or she participates in the requirements study; helps evaluate alternatives, including the DBMS to be used; and helps design the database structure. For large organizational applications, the DBA usually is a manager who supervises the work of technically oriented database design personnel.

Creating the database involves several different tasks. First, the database is created and space allocated for it and its logs. Then tables are generated, indices are created, and stored procedures and triggers are written. We will discuss examples of all of this in the next two chapters. Once the database structures are created, the database is filled with data. Most DBMS vendors provide utilities for inserting data in bulk.

Configuration Control After a database and its applications have been implemented, changes in requirements are inevitable, as described in Chapter 8. Such changes can arise from new needs, from changes in the business environment, from changes in policy, and so forth. When changes to requirements necessitate changes to the database structure, great care must be used because database structure changes seldom involve just one application.

Hence, effective database administration must include procedures and policies by which users can register their needs for changes, the entire database community can discuss the impacts of the changes, and a global decision can be made whether or not to implement proposed changes.

Because of the size and complexity of a database and its applications, changes sometimes have unexpected results. The DBA thus must be prepared to repair the database and to gather sufficient information to diagnose and correct the problem that caused the damage. The database is most vulnerable to failure after a change in its structure.

Documentation The DBA's final responsibility in managing the database structure is documentation. It is extremely important to know what changes have been made, how they were made, and when they were made. A change in the database structure may cause an error that is not revealed for six months; without proper documentation of the change, diagnosing the problem is next to impossible. Considerable work

FIGURE 9-1

Summary of Database Administration Tasks

> Managing database structure

> Controlling concurrent processing

> Managing processing rights and responsibilities

> Developing database security

> Providing for database recovery

> Managing the DBMS

> Maintaining the data repository

may be required to identify the point at which certain symptoms first appeared, and for this reason, it also is important to maintain a record of the test procedures and test runs made to verify a change. If standardized test procedures, test forms, and recordkeeping methods are used, recording the test results does not have to be time-consuming.

Although maintaining documentation is tedious and unfulfilling, the effort pays off when disaster strikes and the documentation is the difference between solving and not solving a major (and costly) problem. Today, several products are emerging that ease the burden of documentation. Many CASE tools, for example, can be used to document logical database designs. Version control software can be used to track changes. Data dictionaries provide reports and other products to read and interpret the database data structures.

Another reason for carefully documenting changes in the database structure is to use historical data properly. If, for example, marketing wants to analyze three-year-old sales data that have been in the archives for two years, it will be necessary to know what structure was current at the time the data were last active. Records that show the changes in the structure can be used to answer that question. A similar situation arises when a six-month-old backup copy of data must be used to repair a damaged database (although this should not happen, sometimes it does). The backup copy can be used to reconstruct the database to the state it was in at the time of the backup. Then, transactions and structural changes can be made in chronological order to restore the database to its current state. Figure 9-2 summarizes the DBA's responsibilities for managing the database structure.

▶ CONCURRENCY CONTROL

Concurrency control measures are taken to ensure that one user's work does not inappropriately influence another user's work. In some cases, these measures ensure that a user gets the same result when processing with other users that he or she would have received if processing alone. In other cases, it means that the user's work is influenced by other users, but in an anticipated way.

For example, in an order-entry system, a user should be able to enter an order and get the same result, regardless of whether there are no other users or hundreds of other users. On the other hand, a user who is printing a report of the most current inventory status may want to obtain in-process data changes from other users, even if there is a danger that those changes may later be cancelled.

Unfortunately, no concurrency control technique or mechanism is ideal for every circumstance. All involve trade-offs. For example, a user can obtain very strict concurrency control by locking the entire database, but no other user will be able to do anything while he or she is processing. This is strict protection, but at a high cost. As you

---

FIGURE 9–2

Summary of DBA's Responsibilities for Managing Database Structure

Participate in Database and Application Development
- Assist in requirements stage and data model creation.
- Play an active role in database design and creation.

Facilitate Changes to Database Structure
- Seek communitywide solutions.
- Assess impact on all users.
- Provide configuration control forum.
- Be prepared for problems after changes are made.
- Maintain documentation.

will see, other measures are available that are more difficult to program or enforce but that allow more throughput. Still other measures are available that maximize throughput, but for a low level of concurrency control. When designing multi-user database applications, you will need to choose among these trade-offs.

The Need for Atomic Transactions

In most database applications, users submit work in the form of **transactions**, which are also known as **logical units of work (LUWs).** A transaction (or LUW) is a series of actions to be taken on the database so that either all of them are performed successfully or none of them are performed at all, in which case the database remains unchanged. Such a transaction is sometimes called **atomic** because it is performed as a unit.

Consider the following sequence of database actions that could occur when recording a new order:

1.   Change the customer record, increasing AmountOwed.
2.   Change the salesperson record, increasing CommissionDue.
3.   Insert the new order record into the database.

Suppose that the last step failed, perhaps because of insufficient file space. Imagine the confusion if the first two changes were made, but not the third one. The customer would be billed for an order never received, and a salesperson would receive a commission on an order that was never sent to the customer. Clearly, these three actions need to be taken as a unit—either all of them should be done or none of them should be done.

Figure 9-3 compares the results of performing these activities as a series of independent steps (Figure 9-3(a)) and as an atomic transaction (Figure 9-3(b)). Notice that when the steps are carried out atomically and one fails, no changes are made in the database. Also note that the commands Start Transaction, Commit Transaction, or Rollback Transaction must be issued by the application program to mark the boundaries of the transaction logic. The particular form of these commands varies from one DBMS product to another.

Concurrent Transaction Processing   When two transactions are being processed against a database at the same time, they are termed **concurrent transactions**. Although it may appear to the users that concurrent transactions are being processed simultaneously, this cannot be true because the CPU of the machine processing the database can execute only one instruction at a time. Usually, transactions are interleaved, which means that the operating system switches CPU services among tasks so that some portion of each of them is carried out in a given interval. This switching among tasks is done so quickly that two people seated at browsers side by side, processing the same database, may believe that their two transactions are completed simultaneously; in reality, however, the two transactions are interleaved.

Figure 9-4 shows two concurrent transactions. User A's transaction reads Item 100, changes it, and rewrites it in the database. User B's transaction takes the same actions, but on Item 200. The CPU processes User A until it encounters an I/O interrupt or some other delay for User A. The operating system shifts control to User B. The CPU now processes User B until an interrupt, at which point the operating system passes control back to User A. To the users, the processing appears to be simultaneous, but actually it is interleaved, or concurrent.

Lost Update Problem   The concurrent processing illustrated in Figure 9-4 poses no problems because the users are processing different data. But suppose that both users want to process Item 100. For example, User A wants to order five units of Item 100, and User B wants to order three units of the same item.

Figure 9-5 illustrates the problem. User A reads Item 100's record into a buffer, or a section of memory. According to the record, there are 10 items in inventory. Then User B reads Item 100's record into another buffer. Again, according to the record, there are

FIGURE 9–3

Need for Transaction Processing (a) Errors Introduced without Transaction (b) Atomic Transaction Prevents Errors

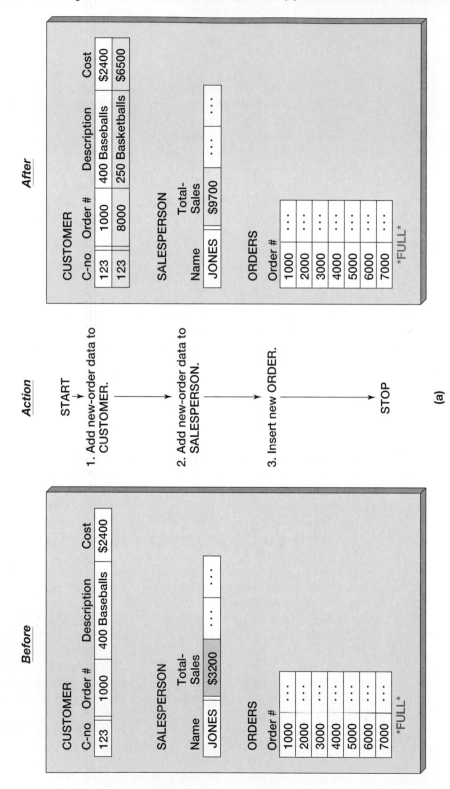

(a)

FIGURE 9-3

(continued)

Before

CUSTOMER

C-no	Order #	Description	Cost
123	1000	400 Baseballs	$2400

SALESPERSON

Name	Total-Sales		
JONES	$3200	...	...

ORDERS

Order #
1000
2000
3000
4000
5000
6000
7000
FULL

Transaction

Start Transaction
Change CUSTOMER data
Change SALESPERSON data
Insert ORDER data
If no errors then
    Commit Transactions
Else
    Rollback Transaction
End If

After

CUSTOMER

C-no	Order #	Description	Cost
123	1000	400 Baseballs	$2400

SALESPERSON

Name	Total-Sales		
JONES	$3200	...	...

ORDERS

Order #
1000
2000
3000
4000
5000
6000
7000
FULL

(b)

FIGURE 9–4

Concurrent Processing Example

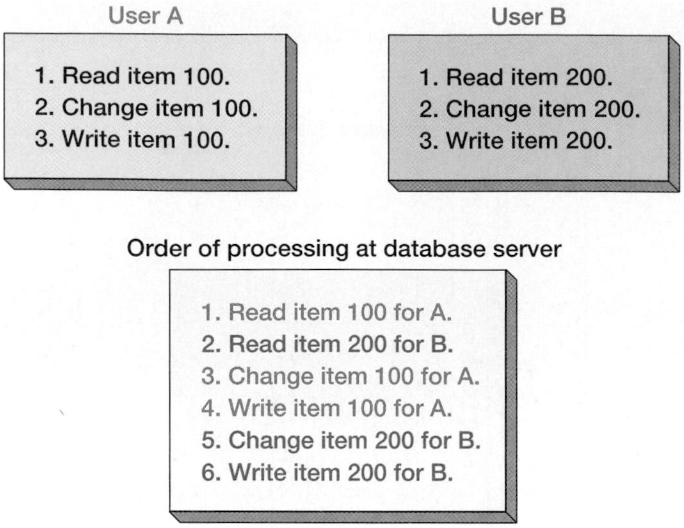

User A

1. Read item 100.
2. Change item 100.
3. Write item 100.

User B

1. Read item 200.
2. Change item 200.
3. Write item 200.

Order of processing at database server

1. Read item 100 for A.
2. Read item 200 for B.
3. Change item 100 for A.
4. Write item 100 for A.
5. Change item 200 for B.
6. Write item 200 for B.

FIGURE 9–5

Lost Update Problem

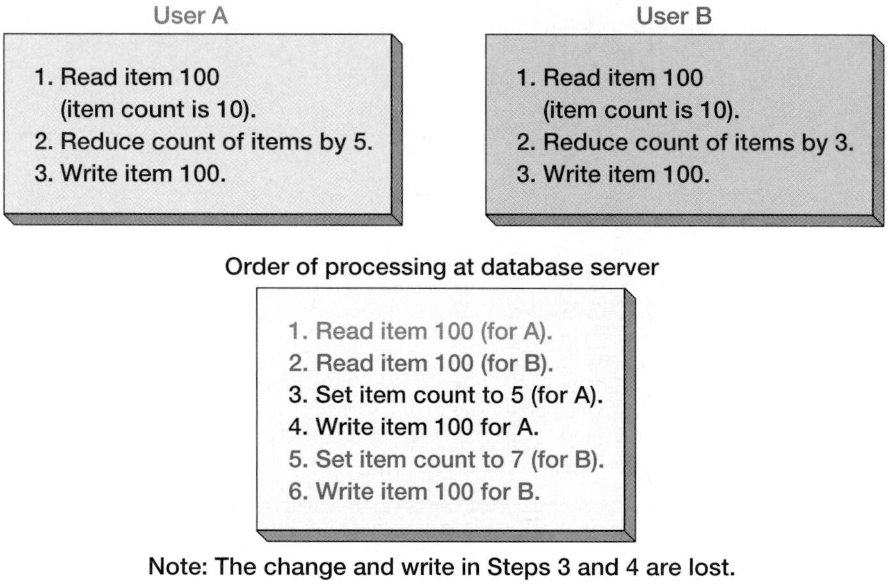

User A

1. Read item 100
   (item count is 10).
2. Reduce count of items by 5.
3. Write item 100.

User B

1. Read item 100
   (item count is 10).
2. Reduce count of items by 3.
3. Write item 100.

Order of processing at database server

1. Read item 100 (for A).
2. Read item 100 (for B).
3. Set item count to 5 (for A).
4. Write item 100 for A.
5. Set item count to 7 (for B).
6. Write item 100 for B.

Note: The change and write in Steps 3 and 4 are lost.

10 in inventory. Now User A takes five, decrements the count of items in its buffer to five, and rewrites the record for Item 100. Then User B takes three, decrements the count in its buffer to seven, and rewrites the record for Item 100. The database now shows, incorrectly, that there are seven Item 100s in inventory. To review: We started with 10 in inventory, User A took five, User B took three, and the database shows that seven are in inventory. Clearly, this is a problem.

Both users obtained data that were correct at the time they obtained them. But when User B read the record, User A already had a copy that it was about to update. This situation is called the **lost update problem** or the **concurrent update problem.** There is another similar problem, called the **inconsistent read problem.** With it, User A reads data that have been processed by a portion of a transaction from User B. As a result, User A reads incorrect data.

One remedy for the inconsistencies caused by concurrent processing is to prevent multiple applications from obtaining copies of the same record when the record is about to be changed. This remedy is called **resource locking.**

Resource Locking

The most popular way of preventing concurrent processing problems is to lock data that are retrieved for update. Figure 9-6 shows the order of processing using a **lock** command. Because of the lock, User B's transaction must wait until User A is finished with the Item 100 data. Using this strategy, User B can read Item 100's record only after User A has completed the modification. In this case, the final item count stored in the database is two, as it should be. (We started with 10, A took five, and B took three, leaving two.)

Lock Terminology   Locks can be placed either automatically by the DBMS or by a command issued to the DBMS from the application program. Locks placed by the DBMS are called **implicit locks;** those placed by command are called **explicit locks.**

In the preceding example, the locks were applied to rows of data. Not all locks are applied at this level, however. Some DBMS products lock at the page level, some at the table level, and some at the database level. The size of a lock is referred to as the **lock granularity.** Locks with large granularity are easy for the DBMS to administer, but frequently cause conflicts. Locks with small granularity are difficult to administer (there are many more details for the DBMS to track and check), but conflicts are less common.

Locks also vary by type. An **exclusive lock** locks the item from access of any type. No other transaction can read or change the data. A **shared lock** locks the item from change but not from read. That is, other transactions can read the item as long as they do not attempt to alter it.

Serializable Transactions   When two or more transactions are processed concurrently, the results in the database should be logically consistent with the results that would have been achieved had the transactions been processed in an arbitrary serial fashion. A scheme for processing concurrent transactions in this way is said to be **serializable.**

Serializability can be achieved by a number of different means. One way is to process the transaction using **two-phased locking.** With this strategy, transactions are

FIGURE 9–6

Concurrent Processing with Explicit Locks

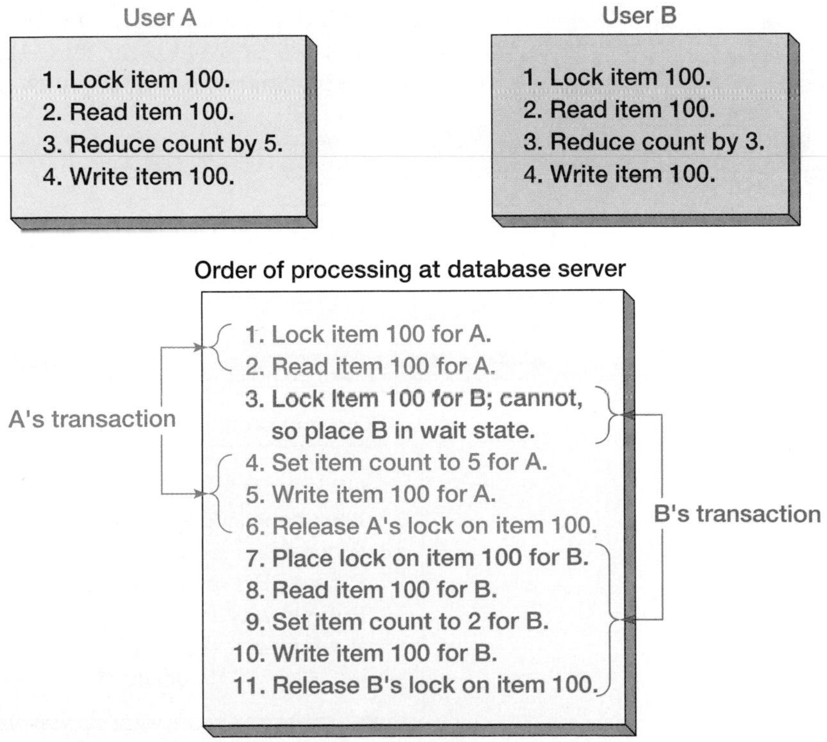

allowed to obtain locks as necessary, but once the first lock is released, no other lock can be obtained. Transactions thus have a **growing phase,** in which the locks are obtained, and a **shrinking phase,** in which the locks are released.

A special case of two-phased locking is used with a number of DBMS products. With it, locks are obtained throughout the transaction, but no lock is released until the COMMIT or ROLLBACK command is issued. This strategy is more restrictive than two-phase locking requires, but it is easier to implement.

In general, the boundaries of a transaction should correspond to the boundaries of the database view it is processing. Following the two-phase strategy, the rows of each relation in the view are locked as needed. Changes are made, but the data are not committed to the database until all of the data in the view have been processed. At this point, changes are made in the actual database, and all locks are released.

Consider an order-entry transaction that involves a view CUSTOMER-ORDER that is constructed from data in the CUSTOMER table, the SALESPERSON table, and the ORDER table. To make sure that the database will suffer no anomalies due to concurrency, the order-entry transaction issues locks on CUSTOMER, SALESPERSON, and ORDER, as needed; makes all the database changes; and then releases all its locks.

Deadlock   Although locking solves one problem, it introduces another. Consider what might happen when two users want to order two items from inventory. Suppose that User A wants to order some paper, and if she can get the paper, she wants to order some pencils. Then suppose that User B wants to order some pencils, and if he can get the pencils, he wants to order some paper. The order of processing could be that shown in Figure 9-7.

In this figure, Users A and B are locked in a condition known as **deadlock,** or sometimes as the **deadly embrace.** Each is waiting for a resource that the other person has locked. There are two common ways of solving this problem: preventing the deadlock from occurring or allowing the deadlock to occur and then breaking it.

Deadlock can be prevented in several ways. One way is to allow users to issue all lock requests at one time. Users must lock all the resources they want at once. If User A in the illustration had locked both the paper and the pencil records at the beginning, deadlock would never have taken place. A second way to prevent deadlock is to require all application programs to lock resources in the same order. Even if not all applications lock in that order, deadlock will be avoided for those that do. This philosophy could extend to an organizational programming standard, such as "Whenever processing rows

FIGURE 9-7

Deadlock

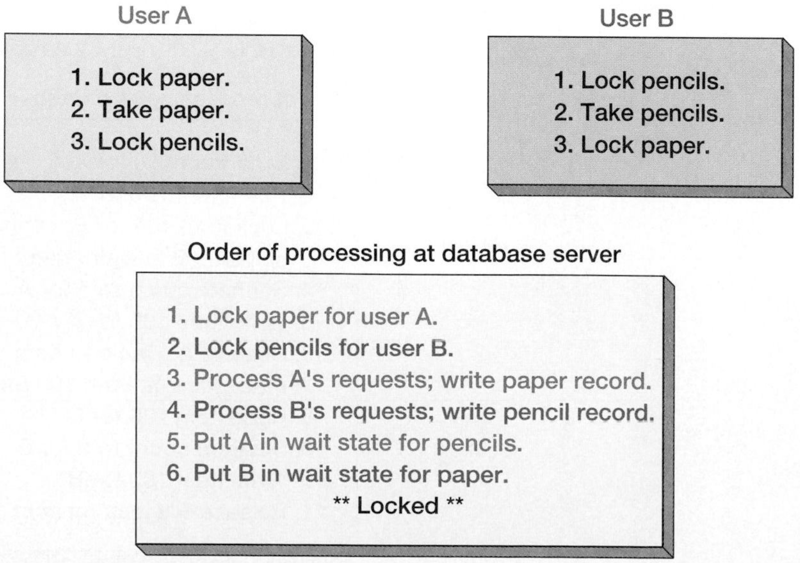

User A

1. Lock paper.
2. Take paper.
3. Lock pencils.

User B

1. Lock pencils.
2. Take pencils.
3. Lock paper.

Order of processing at database server

1. Lock paper for user A.
2. Lock pencils for user B.
3. Process A's requests; write paper record.
4. Process B's requests; write pencil record.
5. Put A in wait state for pencils.
6. Put B in wait state for paper.
               ** Locked **

from tables in a parent-child relationship, lock the parent before the child rows." This will at least reduce the likelihood of deadlock, and it might eliminate it altogether.

Almost every DBMS has algorithms for detecting deadlock. When deadlock occurs, the normal solution is to roll back one of the transactions to remove its changes from the database. You will see variants of this with Oracle and SQL Server in the next two chapters.

Optimistic versus Pessimistic Locking

Locks can be invoked in two basic styles. With **optimistic locking,** the assumption is made that no conflict will occur. Data is read, the transaction is processed, updates are issued, and then a check is made to see if conflict occurred. If not, the transaction is finished. If so, the transaction is repeated until it processes with no conflict. With **pessimistic locking,** the assumption is made that conflict will occur. First, locks are issued, the transaction is processed, and then the locks are freed.

Figure 9-8 shows an example of each style for a transaction that is reducing the quantity of the pencil row in PRODUCT by five. Figure 9-8(a) shows optimistic locking. First, the data are read and the current value of Quantity of pencils is saved in the variable OldQuantity. The transaction is then processed, and assuming that all is OK, a lock is obtained on PRODUCT. The lock might be only for the pencil row or it might be at a larger level of granularity. In any case, a SQL statement is then issued to update the pencil row with a WHERE condition that the current value of Quantity equals OldQuantity. If no other transaction has changed the Quantity of the pencil row, then this UPDATE will be successful. If another transaction has changed the Quantity of the pencil row, the UPDATE will fail and the transaction will need to be repeated.

Figure 9-8(b) shows the logic for the same transaction using pessimistic locking. Here, a lock is obtained on PRODUCT before any work is begun. Then, values are read, the transaction is processed, the UPDATE occurs, and PRODUCT is unlocked.

The advantage of optimistic locking is that the lock is obtained only after the transaction has processed. Thus, the lock is held for less time than with pessimistic locking. If the transaction is complicated or if the client is slow (due to transmission delays, the client doing other work, or the user getting a cup of coffee or shutting down without exiting the browser), the lock will be held considerably less time. This advantage will be even more important if the lock granularity lock is large—say, the entire PRODUCT table.

The disadvantage of optimistic locking is that if there is a lot of activity on the pencil row, the transaction may have to be repeated many times. Thus, transactions that involve a lot of activity on a given row (purchasing a popular stock, for example) are poorly suited for optimistic locking.

In general, the Internet is a wild and wooly place, and users are likely to take unexpected actions such as abandoning transactions in the middle. So, unless Internet users have been prequalified (by enrolling in an online brokerage stock purchase plan, for example), optimistic locking is the better choice in that environment. On intranets, however, the decision is more difficult. Optimistic locking is probably still preferred unless there is some characteristic of the application that causes substantial activity on particular rows or if application requirements make reprocessing transactions particularly undesirable.

Declaring Lock Characteristics

As you can see, concurrency control is a complicated subject; some of the decisions about lock types and strategy have to be made on the basis of trial-and-error. For this and other reasons, database application programs do not generally explicitly issue locks.

FIGURE 9-8

Optimistic and
Pessimistic Locking
(a) Optimistic Locking
and (b) Pessimistic
Locking

```
SELECT      PRODUCT.Name, PRODUCT.Quantity
FROM        PRODUCT
WHERE       PRODUCT.Name = 'Pencil'

OldQuantity = PRODUCT.Quantity

Set NewQuantity = PRODUCT.Quantity – 5

{process transaction – take exception action if NewQuantity < 0, etc.

Assuming all is OK: }

LOCK PRODUCT

UPDATE      PRODUCT
SET         PRODUCT.Quantity = NewQuantity
WHERE       PRODUCT.Name = 'Pencil'
      AND   PRODUCT.Quantity = OldQuantity

UNLOCK   PRODUCT

{check to see if update was successful;
if not, repeat transaction}
```

(a)

```
LOCK        PRODUCT

SELECT      PRODUCT.Name, PRODUCT.Quantity
FROM        PRODUCT
WHERE       PRODUCT.Name = 'Pencil'

Set NewQuantity = PRODUCT.Quantity – 5

{process transaction – take exception action if NewQuantity < 0, etc.

Assuming all is OK: }

UPDATE      PRODUCT
SET         PRODUCT.Quantity = NewQuantity
WHERE       PRODUCT.Name = 'Pencil'

UNLOCK   PRODUCT

{no need to check if update was successful}
```

(b)

Instead, they mark transaction boundaries and then declare the type of locking behavior they want the DBMS to use. In this way, if the locking behavior needs to be changed, the application need not be rewritten to place locks in different locations in the transaction. Instead, only the lock declaration need be changed.

Figure 9-9 shows the pencil transaction with transaction boundaries marked with BEGIN TRANSACTION, COMMIT TRANSACTION, and ROLLBACK TRANSACTION statements. These boundaries are the essential information that the DBMS needs in order to enforce different locking strategies. If the developer now declares (via a system parameter or similar means) that he or she wants optimistic locking, the DBMS will implicitly set the locks in the correct place for that locking style. If he or she later changes tactics and requests pessimistic locking, the DBMS will implicitly set the locks in a different place.

FIGURE 9–9

Marking Transaction Boundaries

```
BEGIN TRANSACTION:

SELECT       PRODUCT.Name, PRODUCT.Quantity
FROM         PRODUCT
WHERE        PRODUCT.Name = 'Pencil'

Old Quantity = PRODUCT.Quantity

Set NewQuantity = PRODUCT.Quantity – 5

{process transaction – take exception action if NewQuantity < 0, etc.}

UPDATE       PRODUCT
SET          PRODUCT.Quantity = NewQuantity
WHERE        PRODUCT.Name = 'Pencil'

{continue processing transaction} . . .


IF transaction has completed normally       THEN

        COMMIT TRANSACTION

ELSE

        ROLLBACK TRANSACTION

END IF

Continue processing other actions not part of this transaction . . .
```

Consistent Transactions

Sometimes, you will see the acronym ACID applied to transactions. An **ACID transaction** is one that is **a**tomic, **c**onsistent, **i**solated, and **d**urable. Atomic and durable are easy to define. As you just learned, an atomic transaction is one in which either all of the database actions occur or none of them do. A durable transaction is one for which all committed changes are permanent. The DBMS will not lose or remove such changes, even in the case of failure. If the transaction is durable, the DBMS will provide facilities to recover the changes of all committed actions when necessary.

The terms **consistent** and **isolated** are not as definitive as the terms **atomic** and **durable**. Consider the following SQL update command:

```
UPDATE       CUSTOMER
SET          AreaCode = '425'
WHERE        ZipCode = '98050'
```

Suppose that there are 500,000 rows in the CUSTOMER table and that 500 of them have ZipCode equal to '98050.' It will take some time for the DBMS to find all 500 rows. During that time, will other transactions be allowed to update the AreaCode or ZipCode fields of CUSTOMER? If the SQL statement is consistent, such updates will be disallowed. The update will apply to the set of rows as they existed at the time the SQL statement started. Such consistency is called **statement level consistency.**

Now, consider a transaction that contains two SQL update statements:

```
BEGIN TRANSACTION

UPDATE       CUSTOMER
```

```
SET          AreaCode = '425'
WHERE        ZipCode = '98050'
{other transaction work}
UPDATE       CUSTOMER
SET          Discount = 0.05
WHERE        AreaCode = '425'
{other transaction work}
COMMIT       TRANSACTION
```

Now, in this context, what does consistent mean? Statement level consistency means that each statement independently processes rows consistently, but that changes from other users to these rows might be allowed during the interval between the two SQL statements. **Transaction level consistency** means that all rows impacted by either of the SQL statements are protected from changes during the entire transaction.

Observe that transaction level consistency is so strong that, for some implementations of it, a transaction will not see its own changes. In this example, the second SQL statement may not see rows changed by the first SQL statement.

Thus, when you hear the term **consistent**, look further to determine which type of consistency is meant. Be aware as well of the potential trap of transaction level consistency.

The situation is more complicated for the term **isolated**. We consider it next.

Transaction Isolation Level

Locks prevent concurrent processes from causing lost updates, but there are other types of problems that they do not prevent. Specifically, a **dirty read** occurs when one transaction reads a changed record that has not been committed to the database. This can occur, for example, if one transaction reads a row changed by a second uncommitted transaction, and this second transaction later rolls back its changes.

Nonrepeatable reads occur when a transaction rereads data it has previously read and finds modifications or deletions caused by a committed transaction. Finally, **phantom reads** occur when a transaction rereads data and finds new rows that were inserted by a committed transaction since the prior read.

The 1992 ANSI SQL standard defines four **isolation levels,** which specify which of these problems are allowed to occur. The goal is for the application programmer to be able to declare the type of isolation level he or she wants and then to have the DBMS manage locks so as to achieve that level of isolation.

As shown in Figure 9-10, Read Uncommitted isolation level allows dirty reads, nonrepeatable reads, and phantom reads to occur. With Read Committed isolation, dirty reads are disallowed. The Repeatable Reads isolation level disallows both dirty reads and nonrepeatable reads. Serializable isolation level will not allow any of these three.

Generally, the more restrictive the level, the less the throughput, though much depends on the workload and how the application programs are written. Moreover, not all DBMS products support all of these levels. Products also vary in the manner in which they are supported and the burden they place on the application programmer. You will learn how Oracle and SQL Server support isolation levels in the next two chapters.

Cursor Type

A cursor is a pointer into a set of rows. Cursors are usually defined using SELECT statements. For example, the following statement defines a cursor named TransCursor that operates over the set of rows indicated by this SELECT statement:

FIGURE 9–10

Summary of Transaction Isolation Levels

		Isolation Level			
		Read Uncommitted	Read Committed	Repeatable Read	Serializable
Problem Type	Dirty Read	Possible	Not Possible	Not Possible	Not Possible
	Nonrepeatable Read	Possible	Possible	Not Possible	Not Possible
	Phantom Read	Possible	Possible	Possible	Not Possible

```
DECLARE CURSOR TransCursor AS
SELECT        *
FROM          TRANSACTION
WHERE         PurchasePrice > '10000'
```

When an application program opens a cursor and reads the first row, the cursor is said to be "pointing at the first row."

A transaction may open several cursors—either in sequence or at the same time. Additionally, two or more cursors may be open on the same table; either directly on the table or through a SQL view on that table. Because cursors require considerable memory, having many cursors open at the same time for, say, a thousand concurrent transactions can consume considerable memory and CPU time. One way to reduce cursor overhead is to define reduced-capability cursors and use them when a full capability cursor is not needed.

Figure 9-11 lists four cursor types used in the Windows environment (cursor types for other systems are similar). The simplest cursor is forward only. With it, the application can only move forward through the recordset. Changes made by other cursors in this transaction and by other transactions will be visible only if they occur in rows ahead of the cursor.

The next three types of cursor are called **scrollable cursors** because the application can scroll forward and backward through the recordset. A static cursor processes a snapshot of the relation that was taken when the cursor was opened. Changes made using this cursor are visible to it; changes from any other source are not visible.

Keyset cursors combine some features of static cursors with some features of dynamic cursors. When the cursor is opened, a primary key value is saved for each row in the recordset. When the application positions the cursor on a row, the DBMS uses the key value to read the current value of the row. If the application issues an update on a row that has been deleted either by a different cursor in this transaction or by a different transaction, the DBMS creates a new row with the old key value and places the updated values in the new row (assuming that all required fields are present). Inserts of new rows by other cursors in this transaction or by other transactions are not visible to a keyset cursor. Unless the isolation level of the transaction is a dirty read, only committed updates and deletions are visible to the cursor.

A dynamic cursor is a fully featured cursor. All inserts, updates, deletions, and changes in row order are visible to a dynamic cursor. As with keyset cursors, unless the isolation level of the transaction is a dirty read, only committed changes are visible.

The amount of overhead and processing required to support a cursor is different for each type. In general, the cost goes up as we move down the cursor types shown in Figure 9-11. In order to improve DBMS performance, therefore, the application developer should create cursors that are just powerful enough to do the job. It is also very

FIGURE 9-11

Summary of Cursor Types

CursorType	Description	Comments
Forward only	Application can only move forward through the recordset.	Changes made by other cursors in this transaction or in other transactions will be visible only if they occur on rows ahead of the cursor.
Static	Application sees the data as it was at the time the cursor was opened.	Changes made by this cursor are visible. Changes from other sources are not visible. Backward and forward scrolling allowed.
Keyset	When the cursor is opened, a primary key value is saved for each row in the recordset. When the application accesses a row, the key is used to fetch the current values for the row.	Updates from any source are visible. Inserts from sources outside this cursor are not visible (there is no key for them in the keyset). Inserts from this cursor appear at the bottom of the recordset. Deletions from any source are visible. Changes in row order are not visible. If the isolation level is dirty read, then committed updates and deletions are visible; otherwise only committed updates and deletions are visible.
Dynamic	Changes of any type and from any source are visible.	All inserts, updates, deletions, and changes in recordset order are visible. If the isolation level is dirty read, then uncommitted changes are visible. Otherwise, only committed changes are visible.

important to understand how a particular DBMS implements cursors and whether cursors are located on the server or on the client. In some cases, it might be better to place a dynamic cursor on the client than to have a static cursor on the server. No general rule can be stated because performance depends on the implementation used by the DBMS product and the application requirements.

A word of caution: If you do not specify the isolation level of a transaction or do not specify the type of cursors you open, the DBMS will use a default level and types. These defaults may be perfect for your application, but they also may be terrible. Thus, even though these issues can be ignored, the consequences of them cannot be avoided. Learn the capabilities of your DBMS product and use them wisely.

▶ DATABASE SECURITY

The goal of database security is to ensure that only authorized users can perform authorized activities at authorized times. This goal is difficult to achieve, and to make any progress at all, the database development team must determine the processing rights and responsibilities of all users during the project's requirements specification phase. These security requirements can then be enforced using the security features of the DBMS and additions to those features written into the application programs.

Processing Rights and Responsibilities

Consider, for example, the needs of View Ridge Gallery, discussed in Chapter 7. There are three types of users: sales personnel, management personnel, and system administrators. The sales personnel are allowed to enter new customer and transaction data, to change customer data, and to query any of the data. They are not allowed to enter new artist or work data. They are not allowed to delete any data at all.

Management personnel are allowed all of the permissions of sales personnel, plus they are allowed to enter new artist and work data, and to modify transaction data. Even though management personnel have the authority to delete data, they are not given that permission in this application. This restriction is made to prevent the possibility of accidental data loss.

The system administrator can grant processing rights to other users; and he or she can change the structure of the database elements such as tables, indices, stored procedures, and the like. Figure 9-12 summarizes these requirements.

The permissions in this table are given to types of users, or **user groups**, and not to individuals. This is typical, but not required. It would be possible to say, for example, that the user identified as "Benjamin Franklin" has certain processing rights. Note, too, that when groups are used, it is necessary to have a means for allocating users to groups. When "Mary Smith" signs on to the computer, some way needs to be available to determine which group or groups she belongs to. We will discuss this further in the next section.

In this discussion, we have used the phrase **processing rights and responsibilities**. As this phrase implies, responsibilities go with processing rights. If, for example, the manager modifies transaction data, he or she has the responsibility to ensure that these modifications do not adversely impact the gallery's operation, accounting, and so forth.

Processing responsibilities cannot be enforced by the DBMS or the database applications. Instead, they are encoded in manual procedures and explained to users during systems training. These are topics of a systems development text, and we will not consider them further here—except to reiterate that **responsibilities** go with **rights**. Such responsibilities must be documented and enforced.

According to Figure 9-1, the DBA has the task of managing processing rights and responsibilities. As this implies, these rights and responsibilities will change over time. As the database is used and as changes are made to the applications and to DBMS structure, the need for new or different rights and responsibilities will arise. The DBA is a focal point for the discussion of such changes and for their implementation.

Once processing rights have been defined, they can be implemented at many levels: operating system, network, Web server, DBMS, and application. In the next two sections, we will consider DBMS and application implementation. The others are beyond the scope of this text.

FIGURE 9-12

Processing Rights at View Ridge Gallery

	CUSTOMER	TRANSACTION	WORK	ARTIST
Sales Personnel	Insert, Change, Query	Insert, Query	Query	Query
Management Personnel	Insert, Change, Query	Insert, Change, Query	Insert, Change, Query	Insert, Change, Query
System Administrator	Grant rights, Modify Structure	Grant rights, Modify Structure	Grant rights, Modify Structure	Grant rights, Modify Structure

DBMS Security

The terminology, features, and functions of DBMS security depend on the DBMS product in use. Basically, all such products provide facilities that limit certain actions on certain objects to certain users. A general model of DBMS security is shown in Figure 9-13. A user can be assigned to one or more roles, and a role can have one or more users. Both users and roles have many permissions. Objects (used in a generic, not an OOP sense) have many permissions assigned to them. Each permission pertains to one user or role and one object.

When a user signs on to the database, the DBMS limits his or her actions to the defined permissions for that user and to the permissions for roles to which that user has been assigned. Determining whether someone actually is who they claim to be is, in general, a difficult task. All commercial DBMS products use some version of user name and password, even though such security is readily circumvented if users are careless with their identities.

Users can enter their name and password, or in some applications, the name and password is entered on behalf of the user. For example, the Windows user name and password can be directly passed to the DBMS. In other cases, an application program provides the name and password.

Internet applications usually define a group such as "Unknown Public" and assign anonymous users to that group when they sign on. In this way, companies such as Dell Computer need not enter every customer into their security system by name and password.

Models of the security systems used by Oracle and SQL Server will be discussed in Chapters 10 and 11, respectively.

DBMS Security Guidelines

Guidelines for improving security in database systems are listed in Figure 9-14. First, the DBMS must always be run behind a firewall. However, the DBA should plan security assuming that the firewall has been breached. The DBMS, the database, and all applications should be secure even if the firewall fails.

DBMS vendors, including IBM, Oracle, and Microsoft, are constantly adding product features to improve security and fixing their products to reduce vulnerability. Consequently, organizations using DBMS products should continually check the vendors' Web sites for service packs and fixes; any service packs or fixes that involve security features, functions, and processing should be installed as soon as possible.

Additionally, database features and functions that are not required by the applications should be removed or disabled from the production DBMS. For example, if TCP/IP is used to connect to the DBMS, other communications protocols should be removed. This action reduces the pathways by which unauthorized activity can reach the

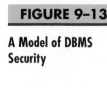

FIGURE 9-13

A Model of DBMS Security

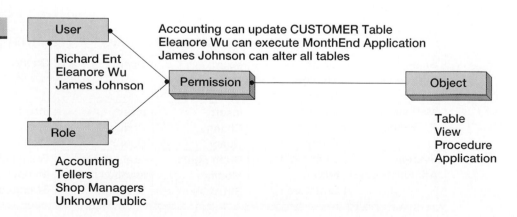

FIGURE 9–14

Summary of DBMS Security Guidelines

- Run DBMS behind a firewall, but plan as though the firewall has been breached
- Apply the latest operating system and DBMS service packs and fixes
- Use the least functionality possible
  - Support the fewest network protocols possible
  - Delete unnecessary or unused system stored procedures
  - Disable default logins and guest users, if possible
  - Unless required, never allow users to log on to the DBMS interactively
- Protect the computer that runs the DBMS
  - No user allowed to work at the computer that runs the DBMS
  - DBMS computer physically secured behind locked doors
  - Visits to the room containing the DBMS computer should be recorded in a log
- Manage accounts and passwords
  - Use a low privilege user account for the DBMS service
  - Protect database accounts with strong passwords
  - Monitor failed login attempts
  - Frequently check group and role memberships
  - Audit accounts with null passwords
  - Assign accounts the lowest privileges possible
  - Limit DBA account privileges
- Planning
  - Develop a security plan for preventing and detecting security problems
  - Create procedures for security emergencies and practice them

DBMS. Further, all DBMS products are installed with system stored procedures that provide services like starting a command file, modifying the system registry, initiating email, and the like. Any of these stored procedures that are not needed by the applications should be removed. If all users are known to the DBMS, default logins and guest user accounts should be removed as well. Finally, unless otherwise required, users should never be allowed to log on to the DBMS in interactive mode. They should always access the database via an application.

In addition, the computer that runs the DBMS must be protected. No one other than authorized DBA personnel should be allowed to work at the keyboard of the computer that runs the DBMS. That computer should be physically secured behind locked doors, and access to that facility should be controlled. Visits to the DBMS computer room should be recorded in a log.

Accounts and passwords should be assigned carefully and continually managed. The DBMS itself should run on an account that has the lowest possible operating system privileges. In that way, if an intruder were to gain control of the DBMS, the intruder would have limited authority on that local computer or network. Additionally, all accounts within the DBMS should be protected by **strong passwords**. Such passwords have at least eight characters; and contain upper- and lowercase letters, numbers, and special unprintable key combinations (certain Alt + key combinations).

The DBA should frequently check the accounts that are assigned to groups and roles to ensure that all accounts and roles are known, authorized, and have the correct permissions. Further, the DBA should audit accounts with null passwords. The users of such accounts should be required to protect those accounts with strong passwords. Also, as a general rule, accounts should be granted the lowest privileges possible.

Even the privileges for the DBA should be limited; this usually means that the DBA not have the privilege of processing the users' data. Of course, the DBA can always grant himself or herself privileges to process the data, but such a change from the default policy will leave an audit trail. Without such a limitation, the DBA could make unauthorized changes to data without any detection whatsoever.

Finally, the DBA should participate in security planning. Procedures both for preventing and detecting security problems should be developed. Furthermore, procedures should be developed for actions to be taken in case of a security breach. Such procedures should be practiced.

The Slammer worm attack in 2003 illustrated the importance of database security. Any installation that followed the guidelines in Figure 9-14 would have been protected from this attack. Follow those guidelines!.

Application Security

Although DBMS products such as Oracle and SQL Server do provide substantial database security capabilities, they are generic by their very nature. If the application requires specific security measures such as "No user can view a row of a table or of a join of a table that has an employee name other than his or her own," the DBMS facilities will not be adequate. In these cases, the security system must be augmented by features in the database application.

For example, as you will learn in Chapter 12, application security in Internet applications is often provided on the Web server computer. Executing application security on this server means that sensitive security data need not be transmitted over the network.

To understand this better, suppose that an application is written so that when users click a particular button on a browser page, the following query is sent to the Web server and then to the DBMS:

```
SELECT      *
FROM        EMPLOYEE;
```

This statement will, of course, return all EMPLOYEE rows. If the application security limits employees to access only their own data, a Web server could add the WHERE clause shown below to this query:

```
SELECT      *
FROM        EMPLOYEE
WHERE       EMPLOYEE.Name = '<%=SESSION("EmployeeName")%>';
```

As you will learn in Chapter 12, an expression like this will cause the Web server to fill the employee's name into the WHERE clause. For a user signed in under the name 'Benjamin Franklin,' the statement that results from this expression is:

```
SELECT      *
FROM        EMPLOYEE
WHERE       EMPLOYEE.Name = 'Benjamin Franklin';
```

Because the name is inserted by a program on the Web server, the browser user does not know that it is occurring and cannot interfere with it even if he or she did.

Such security processing can be done as shown here on a Web server, but it can also be done within the application programs themselves, or written as stored procedures or triggers to be executed by the DBMS at the appropriate times.

This idea can be extended by storing additional data in a security database that is accessed by the Web server, or by stored procedures and triggers. That security database could contain, for example, the identities of users paired with additional values of WHERE clauses. For example, suppose that the users in the personnel department can access more than just their own data. The predicates for appropriate WHERE clauses could be stored in the security database, read by the application program, and appended to SQL SELECT statements as necessary.

Many other possibilities exist for extending DBMS security with application processing. In general, however, you should use the DBMS security features first. Only if they are inadequate for the requirements should you add to them with application code. The closer the security enforcement is to the data, the less chance there is for infiltration. Also, using the DBMS security features is faster, cheaper, and probably results in higher-quality results than developing your own.

SQL Injection Attack

Whenever data from the user is used to modify a SQL statement, there is the possibility of what is termed a **SQL Injection Attack.** For example, in the prior section, if the value of EmployeeName used in the select statement is not obtained via a secure means such as from the operating system, but rather from a Web form, there is the chance that the user can inject SQL into the statement.

For this example, suppose users enter their names into a Web form textbox. Suppose that a user enters the value *Benjamin Franklin ' OR TRUE '* for his or her name. The SQL statement generated by the application will then be the following:

```
SELECT       *
FROM         EMPLOYEE
WHERE        EMPLOYEE.Name = 'Benjamin Franklin' OR TRUE;
```

Of course, the value TRUE is true for every row, so every row of the EMPLOYEE table will be returned!

Thus, any time user input is used to modify a SQL statement, that input must be carefully edited to ensure that only valid input has been received and that no additional SQL syntax has been entered.

▶ DATABASE RECOVERY

Computer systems can fail. Hardware breaks. Programs have bugs. Human procedures contain errors, and people make mistakes. All of these failures can and do occur in database applications. Because a database is shared by many people and because it often is a key element of an organization's operations, it is important to recover it as soon as possible.

Several problems must be addressed. First, from a business standpoint, business functions must continue. For example, customer orders, financial transactions, and packing lists must be completed manually. Later, when the database application is operational again, the new data can be entered. Second, computer operations personnel must restore the system to a usable state as quickly as possible and as close as possible to what it was when the system crashed. Third, users must know what to do when the system becomes available again. Some work may need to be re-entered, and users must know how far back they need to go.

When failures occur, it is impossible simply to fix the problem and resume processing. Even if no data are lost during a failure (which assumes that all types of memory are nonvolatile—an unrealistic assumption), the timing and scheduling of computer processing are too complex to be accurately recreated. Enormous amounts of overhead data and processing would be required for the operating system to be able to restart processing precisely where it was interrupted. It is simply not possible to roll back the clock and put all the electrons in the same configuration they were in at the time of the failure. Two other approaches are possible: recovery via reprocessing, and recovery via rollback/rollforward.

Recovery via Reprocessing Because processing cannot be resumed at a precise point, the next best alternative is to go back to a known point and reprocess the workload from there. The simplest form of this type of recovery is to make a copy periodically of the database (called a **database save**) and to keep a record of all transactions that have been processed since the save. Then, when there is a failure, the operations staff can restore the database from the save and then reprocess all the transactions.

Unfortunately, this simple strategy is normally infeasible. First, reprocessing transactions takes the same amount of time as processing them in the first place did. If the computer is heavily scheduled, the system may never catch up.

Second, when transactions are processed concurrently, events are asynchronous. Slight variations in human activity, such as a user inserting a floppy disk more slowly or a user reading an electronic mail message before responding to an application prompt, may change the order of the execution of concurrent transactions. Therefore, whereas Customer A got the last seat on a flight during the original processing, Customer B may get the last seat during reprocessing. For these reasons, reprocessing is normally not a viable form of recovery from failure in concurrent processing systems.

Recovery via Rollback/Rollforward A second approach is periodically to make a copy of the database (the database save) and to keep a log of the changes made by transactions against the database since the save. Then, when there is a failure, one of two methods can be used. Using the first method, called **rollforward,** the database is restored using the saved data, and all valid transactions since the save are reapplied. (We are not reprocessing the transactions because the application programs are not involved in the rollforward. Instead, the processed changes, as recorded in the log, are reapplied.)

The second method is **rollback,** in which we undo changes made by erroneous or partially processed transactions by undoing the changes they have made in the database. Then, the valid transactions that were in process at the time of the failure are restarted.

Both of these methods require that a **log** of the transaction results be kept. This log contains records of the data changes in chronological order. Transactions must be written to the log before they are applied to the database. That way, if the system crashes between the time a transaction is logged and the time it is applied, at worst there is a record of an unapplied transaction. If, on the other hand, the transactions were to be applied before they were logged, it would be possible (as well as undesirable) to change the database but have no record of the change. If this happened, an unwary user might reenter an already completed transaction.

In the event of a failure, the log is used both to undo and to redo transactions, as shown in Figure 9-15. To undo a transaction, the log must contain a copy of every database record (or page) before it was changed. Such records are called **before-images.** A transaction is undone by applying before-images of all its changes to the database.

To redo a transaction, the log must contain a copy of every database record (or page) after it was changed. These records are called **after-images.** A transaction is redone by applying after-images of all its changes to the database. Possible data items of a transaction log are shown in Figure 9-16.

For this example log, each transaction has a unique name for identification purposes. Furthermore, all images for a given transaction are linked together with pointers. One pointer points to the previous change made by this transaction (the reverse pointer), and the other points to the next change made by this transaction (the forward pointer). A zero in the pointer field means that this is the end of the list. The DBMS recovery subsystem uses these pointers to locate all records for a particular transaction. Figure 9-16 shows an example of the linking of log records.

Other data items in the log are the time of the action; the type of operation (START marks the beginning of a transaction and COMMIT terminates a transaction, releasing all locks that were in place); the object acted on, such as record type and identifier; and finally, the before-images and after-images.

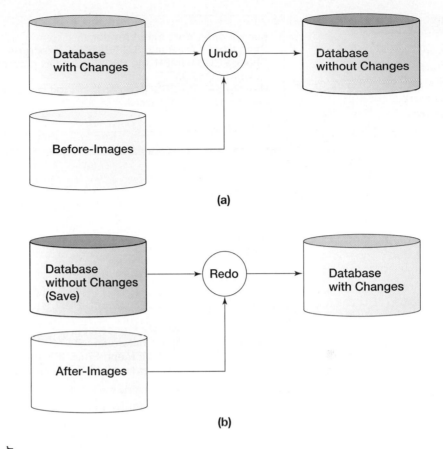

FIGURE 9–15

Undo and
RedoTransactions
(a) Rollback and
(b) Rollforward

FIGURE 9–16

Example Transaction
Log

Relative Record Number	Transaction ID	Reverse Pointer	Forward Pointer	Time	Type of Operation	Object	Before-Image	After-Image
1	OT1	0	2	11:42	START			
2	OT1	1	4	11:43	MODIFY	CUST 100	(old value)	(new value)
3	OT2	0	8	11:46	START			
4	OT1	2	5	11:47	MODIFY	SP AA	(old value)	(new value)
5	OT1	4	7	11:47	INSERT	ORDER 11		(value)
6	CT1	0	9	11:48	START			
7	OT1	5	0	11:49	COMMIT			
8	OT2	3	0	11:50	COMMIT			
9	CT1	6	10	11:51	MODIFY	SP BB	(old value)	(new value)
10	CT1	9	0	11:51	COMMIT			

Given a log with before-images and after-images, the undo and redo actions are straightforward, to describe, at least. To undo the transaction in Figure 9-17, the recovery processor simply replaces each changed record with its before-image. When all before-images have been restored, the transaction is undone. To redo a transaction, the recovery processor starts with the version of the database at the time the transaction

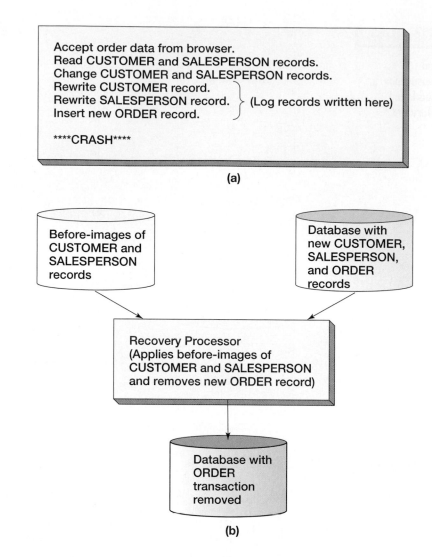

(a)

(b)

started and applies all after-images. As stated, this action assumes that an earlier version of the database is available from a database save.

Restoring a database to its most recent save and reapplying all transactions may require considerable processing. To reduce the delay, DBMS products sometimes use checkpoints. A **checkpoint** is a point of synchronization between the database and the transaction log. To perform a checkpoint, the DBMS refuses new requests, finishes processing outstanding requests, and writes its buffers to disk. The DBMS then waits until the operating system notifies it that all outstanding write requests to the database and to the log have been successfully completed. At this point, the log and the database are synchronized. A checkpoint record is then written to the log. Later, the database can be recovered from the checkpoint and only after-images for transactions that started after the checkpoint need be applied.

Checkpoints are inexpensive operations, and it is feasible to take three or four (or more) per hour. In this way, no more than 15 or 20 minutes of processing need to be recovered. Most DBMS products automatically checkpoint themselves, making human intervention unnecessary.

You will see specific examples of backup and recovery techniques for Oracle and SQL Server in the next two chapters. For now, you only need to understand the basic ideas and to realize that it is the responsibility of the DBA to ensure that adequate backup and recovery plans have been developed and that database saves and logs are generated as required.

Managing the DBMS

In addition to managing data activity and the database structure, the DBA must manage the DBMS itself. He or she should compile and analyze statistics concerning the system's performance and identify potential problem areas. Keep in mind that the database is serving many user groups. The DBA needs to investigate all complaints about the system's response time, accuracy of data, ease of use, and so forth. If changes are needed, the DBA must plan and implement them.

The DBA must periodically monitor the users' activity on the database. DBMS products include features that collect and report statistics. For example, some of these reports may indicate which users have been active, which files—and perhaps which data items—have been used, and which access methods have been employed. Error rates and types can also be captured and reported. The DBA analyzes these data to determine whether a change to the database design is needed to improve performance or to ease the users' tasks. If change is necessary, the DBA will ensure that it is accomplished.

The DBA should analyze run-time statistics on database activity and performance. When a performance problem is identified (by either a report or a user's complaint), the DBA must determine whether a modification of the database structure or system is appropriate. Examples of possible structure modifications are establishing new keys, purging data, deleting keys, and establishing new relationships among objects.

When the vendor of the DBMS being used announces new product features, the DBA must consider them in light of the overall needs of the user community. If she decides to incorporate the new DBMS features, the developers must be notified and trained in their use. Accordingly, the DBA must manage and control changes in the DBMS, as well as in the database structure.

Other changes in the system for which the DBA is responsible vary widely, depending on the DBMS product as well as on other software and hardware in use. For example, changes in other software (such as the operating system or the Web server) may mean that some DBMS features, functions, or parameters must be changed. The DBA must therefore also tune the DBMS product to other software in use.

The DBMS options (such as transaction isolation levels) are initially chosen when little is known about how the system will perform in the particular user environment. Consequently, operational experience and performance analysis over a period of time may reveal that changes are necessary. Even if the performance seems acceptable, the DBA may want to alter the options and observe the effect on performance. This process is referred to as *tuning,* or *optimizing,* the system. Figure 9-18 summarizes the DBA's responsibilities for managing the DBMS product.

FIGURE 9-18

Summary of the DBA's Responsibilities for Managing the DBMS

- Generate database application performance reports
- Investigate user performance complaints
- Assess need for changes in database structure or application design
- Modify database structure
- Evaluate and implement new DBMS features
- Tune the DBMS

Maintaining the Data Repository

Consider a large and active Internet database application like those used by e-commerce companies—for instance, an application that is used by a company that sells music over the Internet. Such a system may involve data from several different databases, dozens of different Web pages, and hundreds or even thousands of users.

Suppose that the company using this application decides to expand its product line to include the sale of sporting goods. Senior management of this company might ask the DBA to develop an estimate of the time and other resources required to modify the database application to support this new product line.

For the DBA to respond to this request, he or she needs accurate metadata about the database, about the database applications and application components, about the users and their rights and privileges, and about other system elements. The database does carry some of this metadata in system tables, but this metadata is inadequate to answer the questions senior management poses. The DBA needs additional metadata about COM and ActiveX objects, script procedures and functions, ASP pages, stylesheets, document type definitions, and the like. Furthermore, although DBMS security mechanisms do document users, groups, and privileges, they do so in a highly structured and often inconvenient form.

For all of these reasons, many organizations develop and maintain **data repositories,** which are collections of metadata about databases, database applications, Web pages, users, and other application components. The repository may be virtual in that it is composed of metadata from many different sources: the DBMS, version control software, code libraries, Web page generation and editing tools, and so forth. Or, the data repository may be an integrated product from a CASE tool vendor or from other companies such as Microsoft or Oracle.

Either way, the time for the DBA to think about constructing such a facility is long before senior management asks questions. In fact, the repository should be constructed as the system is developed and should be considered an important part of the system deliverables. If not, the DBA will always be playing catch-up: trying to maintain the existing applications, adapting them to new needs, and somehow gathering together the metadata to form a repository.

The best repositories are **active;** they are part of the system development process in such a way that metadata is created automatically as the system components are created. Less desirable, but still effective, are **passive repositories** that are filled only when someone takes the time to generate the needed metadata and place it in the repository.

The Internet has created enormous opportunities for businesses to expand their customer bases and increase their sales and profitability. The databases and database applications that support these companies are an essential element of that success. Unfortunately, there will be organizations whose growth is stymied for lack of ability to grow their applications or adapt them to changing needs. Often, building a new system is easier than adapting an existing one; certainly, building a new system that integrates with an old one while it replaces that old one can be very difficult.

SUMMARY

Multi-user databases pose difficult problems for the organizations that create and use them, and most organizations have created an office of database administration to ensure that such problems are solved. In this text, the term *database administrator* refers to the person or office that is concerned with a single database. The term *data administrator* is used to describe a similar function that is concerned with all of an organization's data assets. Data administration will be discussed in Chapter 15. Major functions of the database administrator are listed in Figure 9-1.

The DBA is concerned with the development of the initial database structures and with providing configuration control over them as requests for changes arise. Keeping accurate documentation of the structure and changes to it is an important DBA function.

The goal of concurrency control is to ensure that one user's work does not inappropriately influence another user's work. No single concurrency control technique is ideal for all circumstances. Trade-offs need to be made between level of protection and throughput. A transaction, or logical unit of work, is a series of actions taken against the database that occurs as an atomic unit; either all of them occur or none of them do. The activity of concurrent transactions is interleaved on the database server. In some cases, updates can be lost if concurrent transactions are not controlled. Another concurrency problem concerns inconsistent reads.

To avoid concurrency problems, database elements are locked. Implicit locks are placed by the DBMS; explicit locks are issued by the application program. The size of the locked resource is called lock granularity. An exclusive lock prohibits other users from reading the locked resource; a shared lock allows other users to read the locked resource, but they cannot update it.

Two transactions that run concurrently and generate results that are consistent with the results that would have occurred if they had run separately are referred to as serializable transactions. Two-phased locking, in which locks are acquired in a growing phase and released in a shrinking phase, is one scheme for serializability. A special case of two-phase locking is to acquire locks throughout the transaction, but not to free any lock until the transaction is finished.

Deadlock, or the deadly embrace, occurs when two transactions are each waiting on a resource that the other transaction holds. Deadlock can be prevented by requiring transactions to acquire all locks at the same time. Once it occurs, the only way to cure it is to abort one of the transactions (and back out partially completed work). Optimistic locking assumes that no transaction conflict will occur and deals with the consequences if it does. Pessimistic locking assumes that conflict will occur and so prevents it ahead of time with locks. In general, optimistic locking is preferred for the Internet and for many intranet applications.

Most application programs do not explicitly declare locks. Instead, they mark transaction boundaries with BEGIN, COMMIT, and ROLLBACK transaction statements; and declare the concurrent behavior they want. The DBMS then places locks for the application that will result in the desired behavior.

An ACID transaction is one that is atomic, consistent, isolated, and durable. Durable means that database changes are permanent. Consistency can mean either statement level or transaction level consistency. With transaction level consistency, a transaction may not see its own changes. The 1992 SQL standard defines four transaction isolation levels: read uncommitted, read committed, repeatable read, and serializable. The characteristics of each are summarized in Figure 9-10.

A cursor is a pointer into a set of records. Four cursor types are prevalent: forward only, static, keyset, and dynamic. Developers should select isolation levels and cursor types that are appropriate for their application workload and for the DBMS product in use.

The goal of database security is to ensure that only authorized users can perform authorized activities at authorized times. To develop effective database security, the processing rights and responsibilities of all users must be determined.

DBMS products provide security facilities. Most involve the declaration of users, groups, objects to be protected, and permissions or privileges on those objects. Almost all DBMS products use some form of user name and password security. Security guidelines are listed in Figure 9-14. DBMS security can be augmented by application security.

In the event of system failure, that database must be restored to a usable state as soon as possible. Transactions in process at the time of the failure must be reapplied or restarted. Although in some cases recovery can be done by reprocessing, the use of logs and rollback and rollforward is almost always preferred. Checkpoints can be taken to reduce the amount of work that needs to be done after a failure.

In addition to these tasks, the DBA manages the DBMS product itself, measuring database application performance, and assessing needs for changes in database structure or DBMS performance tuning. The DBA also ensures that new DBMS features are evaluated and used as appropriate. Finally, the DBA is responsible for maintaining the data repository.

GROUP I QUESTIONS

9.1 Briefly describe five difficult problems for organizations that create and use multi-user databases.

9.2 Explain the difference between a database administrator and a data administrator.

9.3 List seven important tasks for a DBA.

9.4 Summarize the DBA's responsibilities for managing database structure.

9.5 What is configuration control? Why is it necessary?

9.6 Explain the meaning of the word *inappropriately* in the phrase "one user's work does not inappropriately influence another user's work."

9.7 Explain the trade-off that exists in concurrency control.

9.8 Define an atomic transaction and explain why atomicity is important.

9.9 Explain the difference between concurrent transactions and simultaneous transactions. How many CPUs are required for simultaneous transactions?

9.10 Give an example, other than the one in this text, of the lost update problem.

9.11 Explain the difference between an explicit and an implicit lock.

9.12 What is lock granularity?

9.13 Explain the difference between an exclusive lock and a shared lock.

9.14 Explain two-phased locking.

9.15 How does releasing all locks at the end of the transaction relate to two-phase locking?

9.16 In general, how should the boundaries of a transaction be defined?

9.17 What is deadlock? How can it be avoided? How can it be resolved once it occurs?

9.18 Explain the difference between optimistic and pessimistic locking.

9.19 Explain the benefits of marking transaction boundaries, declaring lock characteristics, and letting the DBMS place locks.

9.20 Explain the use of BEGIN, COMMIT, and ROLLBACK TRANSACTION statements.

9.21 Explain the meaning of the expression *ACID transaction*.

9.22 Describe statement level consistency.

9.23 Describe transaction level consistency. What disadvantage can exist with it?

9.24 What is the purpose of transaction isolation levels?

9.25 Explain read uncommitted isolation level. Give an example of its use.

9.26 Explain read committed isolation level. Give an example of its use.

9.27 Explain repeatable read isolation level. Give an example of its use.

9.28 Explain serializable isolation level. Give an example of its use.

9.29 Explain the term *cursor*.

9.30 Explain why a transaction may have many cursors. Also, how is it possible that a transaction may have more than one cursor on a given table?

9.31 What is the advantage of using different types of cursors?

9.32 Explain forward only cursors. Give an example of their use.

9.33 Explain static cursors. Give an example of their use.

9.34 Explain keyset cursors. Give an example of their use.

9.35 Explain dynamic cursors. Give an example of their use.

9.36 What happens if you do not declare transaction isolation level and cursor type to the DBMS? Is this good or bad?

9.37 Explain the necessity of defining processing rights and responsibilities. How are such responsibilities enforced?

9.38 Explain the relationships of USERS, GROUPS, PERMISSION, and OBJECTS for a generic database security system.

9.39 Should the DBA assume a firewall when planning security?

9.40 What should be done with unused features and functions for the products' DBMS?

9.41 Explain how to protect the computer that runs the DBMS.

9.42 With regard to security, what actions should the DBA take on user accounts and passwords?

9.43 List two elements of a database security plan.

9.44 Describe the advantages and disadvantages of DBMS-provided and application-provided security.

9.45 What is a SQL injection attack and how can it be prevented?

9.46 Explain how a database could be recovered via reprocessing. Why is this generally not feasible?

9.47 Define *rollback* and *rollforward*.

9.48 Why is it important to write to the log before changing the database values?

9.49 Describe the rollback process. Under what conditions should it be used?

9.50 Describe the rollforward process. Under what conditions should it be used?

9.51 What is the advantage of taking frequent checkpoints of a database?

9.52 Summarize the DBA's responsibilities for managing the DBMS.

9.53 What is a data repository? A passive data repository? An active data repository?

9.54 Explain why a data repository is important. What is likely to happen if one is not available?

GROUP II QUESTIONS

9.55 Visit **www.msdn.microsoft.com** and search for *SQL Server Security Guidelines*. Read articles at three of the links that you find and summarize them. How does the information you find compare to that in Figure 9-14?

9.56 Visit **www.oracle.com** and search for *Oracle Security Guidelines*. Read articles at three of the links that you find and summarize them. How does the information you find compare to that in Figure 9-14?

9.57 Use **www.Google.com** to search for the topic *Database Security Guidelines*. Read articles at three of the links that you find and summarize them. How does the information you find compare to that in Figure 9-14?

Answer the following questions for the View Ridge database discussed in Chapter 7 with tables shown in Figures 7-4 and 7-5.

A. Suppose that you are developing a stored procedure to record an artist that has never been in the gallery before, along with a work for that artist, and a row in the transaction table to record the date acquired and acquisition price. How will you declare the boundaries of the transaction? What transaction isolation level will you use?

B. Suppose that you are writing a stored procedure to change values in the CUSTOMER table. What transaction isolation level will you use?

C. Suppose that you are writing a stored procedure to record a customer's purchase. Assume that the customer's data is new. How will you declare the boundaries of the transaction? What isolation level will you use?

D. Suppose that you are writing a stored procedure to check the validity of the intersection table. Specifically, for each customer, your procedure should read customers' transactions and determine the artist of that work. Given the artist, your procedure should then check to ensure that an interest has been declared for that artist in the intersection table. If there is no such intersection row, your procedure should create one. How will you set the boundaries of your transaction? What isolation level will you use? What cursor types (if any) will you use?

FIREDUP PROJECT QUESTIONS

A. Assume that FiredUp, Inc., has hired you as a database consultant to develop its operational database having the four tables described at the end of Chapter 6. Assume that FiredUp personnel are the two owners, an office administrator, a repair technician, and two employees in production. The office administrator processes all registration forms. The repair technician inputs repair data, and the production employees enter stove data on stoves they have produced. Prepare a three-to-five-page memo to FiredUp management that addresses the following issues:

1. The need for database administration at FiredUp.

2. Your recommendation for who should serve as database administrator. Assume that FiredUp is not sufficiently large to need or afford a full-time database administrator.

3. Using Figure 9-1 as a guide, describe the nature of database administration activities at FiredUp. As an aggressive consultant, keep in mind that you can recommend yourself for performing some of the DBA functions.

B. For the employees described in question A, define users, groups, and permissions on data in the four tables described at the end of Chapter 6. Use the security scheme shown in Figure 9-13 as an example. Again, don't forget to include yourself.

C. Suppose that you are writing a stored procedure to create new records in STOVE for a batch of stoves that have just been manufactured. Suppose that you know that while your procedure is running, another stored procedure that records new or modifies existing customer data and registrations can also be running.

Additionally, suppose that a third stored procedure that records stove repairs can also be running.

1. Give an example of a dirty read, a non-repeatable read, and a phantom read among this group of stored procedures.

2. What concurrency control measures are appropriate for the stored procedure that you are creating?

3. What concurrency control measures are appropriate for the two other stored procedures?

TWIGS TREE TRIMMING SERVICE PROJECT QUESTIONS

A. Assume that Twigs has hired you as a database consultant to develop its operational database having the three tables described at the end of Chapter 6. Assume that Twigs personnel are the owner, an office administrator, and two part-time gardener employees. The owner and the office administrator want to process data in all three tables. Additionally, the part-time employees enter data on services or deliveries they have made. Prepare a three-to-five-page memo to the Twigs owner that addresses the following issues:

1. The need for database administration at Twigs.

2. Your recommendation for who should serve as database administrator. Assume that Twigs is not sufficiently large that it needs or can afford a full-time database administrator.

3. Using Figure 9-1 as a guide, describe the nature of database administration activities at Twigs. As an aggressive consultant, keep in mind that you can recommend yourself for performing some of the DBA functions.

B. For the employees described in question A, define users, groups, and permissions on data in the four tables described at the end of Chapter 6. Use the security scheme shown in Figure 9-13 as an example. Again, don't forget to include yourself.

C. Suppose that you are writing a stored procedure to create new records in OWNER for a batch of new customers that Samantha has obtained. Suppose that you know that while your procedure is running, another stored procedure that records services can be running, and a third stored procedure that records chip deliveries can also be running. In fact, there can be two or three instances of either the service or chip delivery stored procedures running concurrently. This occurs when Samantha or the part-time gardeners are recording services and chip deliveries at the same time.

1. Give an example of a dirty read, a non-repeatable read, and a phantom read among this group of stored procedures.

2. What concurrency control measures are appropriate for the stored procedure that you are creating?

3. What concurrency control measures are appropriate for the two other stored procedures?

CHAPTER 10

Managing Databases with Oracle 9i

O racle is a powerful and robust DBMS that runs on many different operating systems, including Windows 2000, Windows XP, several variations of UNIX, several mainframe operating systems, and Linux. It is the world's most popular DBMS and has a long history of development and use. Oracle exposes much of its technology to the developer, and consequently can be tuned and tailored in many ways.

All of this means, however, that Oracle can be difficult to install and that there is a lot to learn. A gauge of Oracle's breadth is that one of the most popular references, *Oracle 9i, The Complete Reference* by Loney and Koch, is more than 1,300 pages long, but it does not contain everything. Moreover, techniques that work with a version of Oracle on one operating system may need to be altered when working with a version on a different operating system. You will need to be patient with Oracle and with yourself and not expect to master this subject overnight.

There are many configurations of the Oracle program suite. To start, there are two different versions of the Oracle DBMS engine: Personal Oracle and Enterprise Oracle. It addition, there are Forms and Reports and also Oracle Designer, and a host of tools for publishing Oracle databases on the Web. Add to this the need for these products to operate on many different operating systems and over networks using several different communication protocols, and you can see why there is considerable complexity to learn.

Oracle SQL*Plus is a utility for processing SQL and creating components like stored procedures and triggers. It is also one component that is constant through all of these product configurations. Consequently, we will begin by discussing it. SQL*Plus can be used to submit both SQL and PL/SQL statements to Oracle. The latter, PL/SQL, is a programming language that adds programming constructs to the SQL language. We will use PL/SQL to create tables, constraints, relationships, views, stored procedures, and triggers.

This chapter uses the View Ridge example from Chapter 7, and the discussion will roughly parallel the discussion of database administration in Chapter 9.

► INSTALLING ORACLE

The version of Oracle that you install depends on whether you will access databases created by someone else, or whether you will create databases on your own computer. If you will use a database created by someone else, you need only install Oracle 9i Client. You should obtain instructions on how to install and connect to the database from the person who created the database you will use.

If you will create your own databases, you should install Oracle 9i Personal Edition. See the Installation Guide link on **www.prenhall.com/Kroenke** for more information.

Creating an Oracle Database

There are three ways to create an Oracle database: via the Oracle Database Configuration Assistant, via the Oracle-supplied database creation procedures, or via the SQL CREATE DATABASE command. The Oracle Database Configuration Assistant is by far the easiest, and you should use it.

You can find the Database Configuration Assistant in one of the directories created when Oracle was installed. You will find it by clicking Start, Programs, Oracle-Oracle9i Home/Configuration and Migration Tools or something similar, depending on your operating system. Your directories may not be named exactly as these; search through the directories under Start, Programs to find Database Configuration Assistant.

Figure 10-1 will appear when you start the Configuration Assistant. Select Next, Create a database, General Purpose, and then type the name of your database for Global Database Name. This chapter uses the database named *VRG*. Next, select Dedicated Server Mode and Typical. At this point, you can click Finish and then OK, and Oracle will create your database with default file sizes and file locations. This process will take several minutes.

Once the database has been created, you will be asked to enter new passwords for the SYS and SYSTEM accounts. Select appropriate strong passwords that you will remember. You can also select Password Management to lock or unlock accounts. At this point, you need not perform any Password Management action, so click Exit in Password Management and your database will be ready for use.

FIGURE 10–1

Starting the Oracle Database Configuration Assistant

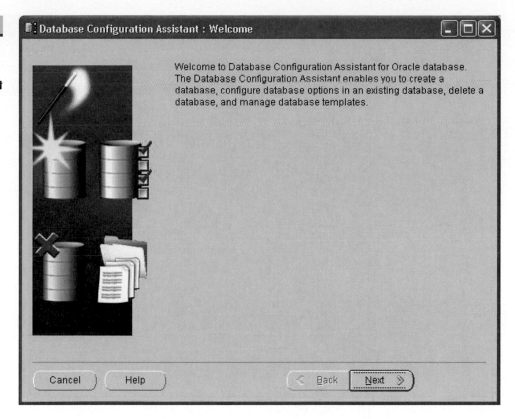

FIGURE 10–1

Starting the Oracle Database Configuration Assistant

You can manage an Oracle database using either the Oracle SQL*Plus command utility program, or you can use the Oracle Enterprise Manager Console. We will begin by using SQL*Plus because it is the classic way of creating and managing Oracle databases. It is also available with all installations of Oracle on all operating systems, so if you know how to use it, you know how to process an Oracle database on any operating system. After you have learned how to use SQL*Plus, we will discuss the Oracle Enterprise Manager.

Using SQL*Plus

To use SQL*Plus, find its icon under the Start/Programs/Oracle-Oracle 9i Home/Application Developed menu and click it. Sign on to your database using the SYSTEM account and enter the name of your database under Host String, as shown in Figure 10-2. (This procedure might be different if you are using a version of Oracle set

FIGURE 10–2

Logging on Using SQL*Plus

Log On

User Name:	SYSTEM
Password:	******
Host String:	VRG

OK   Cancel

FIGURE 10-3

SQL*Plus Prompt

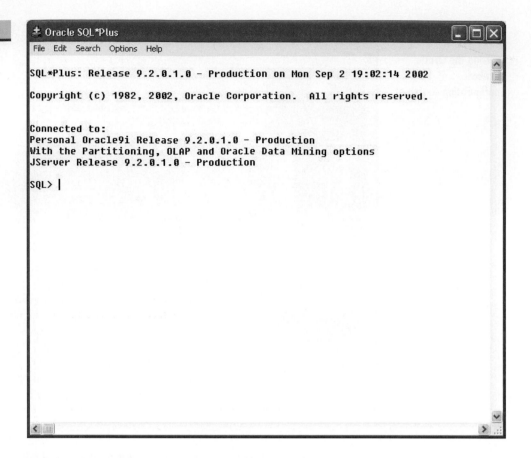

up by someone else. If this is the case, check with your database administrator.) Click OK and you should see a window similar to the one in Figure 10-3.

The SQL*Plus Buffer   Among its many functions, SQL*Plus is a text editor. Working with Oracle will be easier if you learn a bit about this editor. First, when you type into SQL*Plus, your keystrokes are placed into a buffer. When you press enter, SQL*Plus will save what you just typed into a line in the buffer, and go to a new line, but it will neither finish nor execute the statement.

For example, in Figure 10-4, the user has entered two lines of a SQL statement. The user can enter more lines if necessary. When the user types a semicolon and presses {Enter}, SQL*Plus will finish the statement and then execute it. Try this, but ignore the results—we'll worry about them later.

To see the contents of the buffer, type LIST, as shown near the bottom of Figure 10-5. The line shown with an asterisk (line 3, in this case) is the current line. You can change the current line by entering LIST followed by a line number, such as LIST 1. At that point, line 1 is the current line.

To change the contents of the current line, enter *change /astring/bstring/,* where astring is the string you want to change and bstring is what you want to change it to. In Figure 10-6, the user has entered the following:

change/Table_Name/*/

This expression will replace the string 'Table_Name' with the string '*'.

Now the expression in line 1 of the buffer has been changed from SELECT Table_Name to SELECT *. Type *LIST* to see the complete as shown in Figure 10-6. If you now enter the right-leaning slash (/) followed by {Enter}, the command in the buffer will be executed.

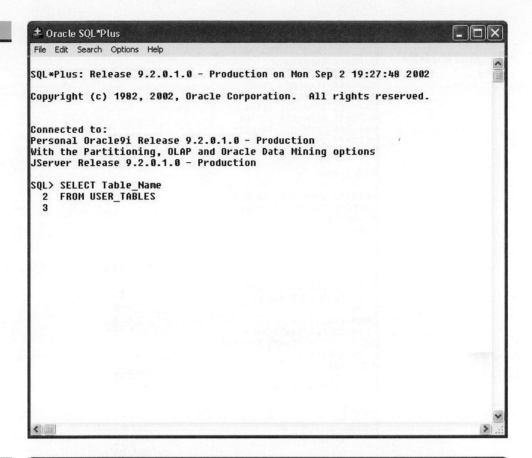

FIGURE 10–4

SQL*Plus Multi-line Buffer

FIGURE 10–5

Using the LIST Command

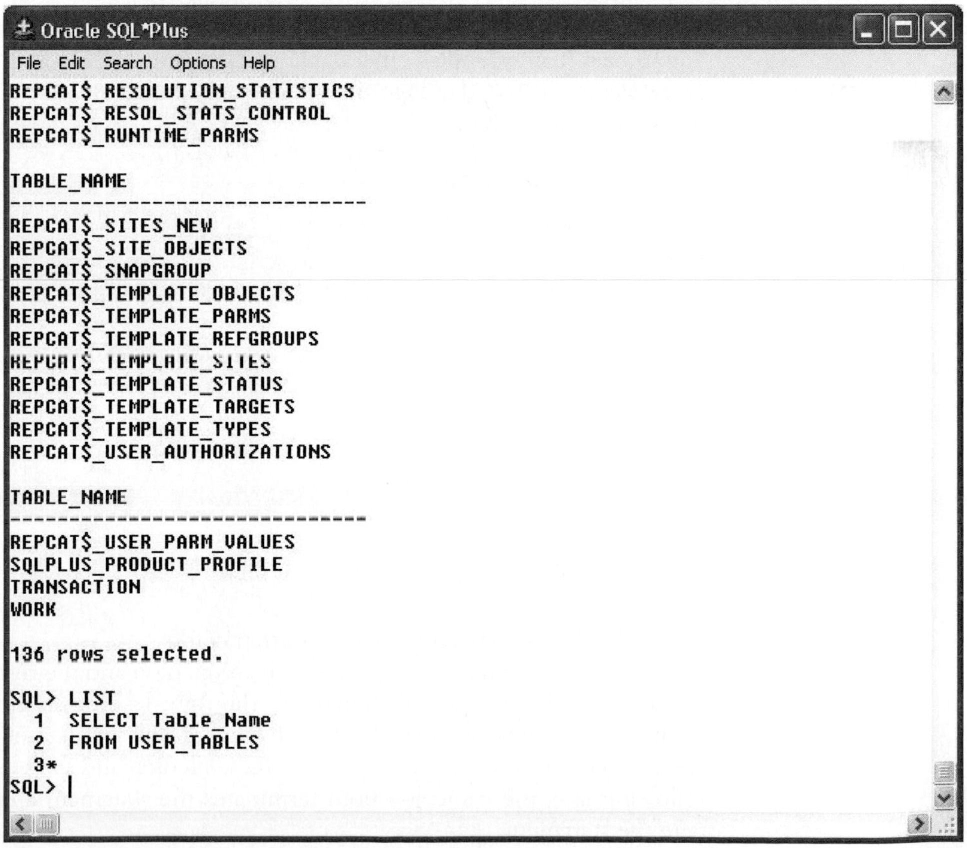

FIGURE 10-6

Changing a Line in the Buffer

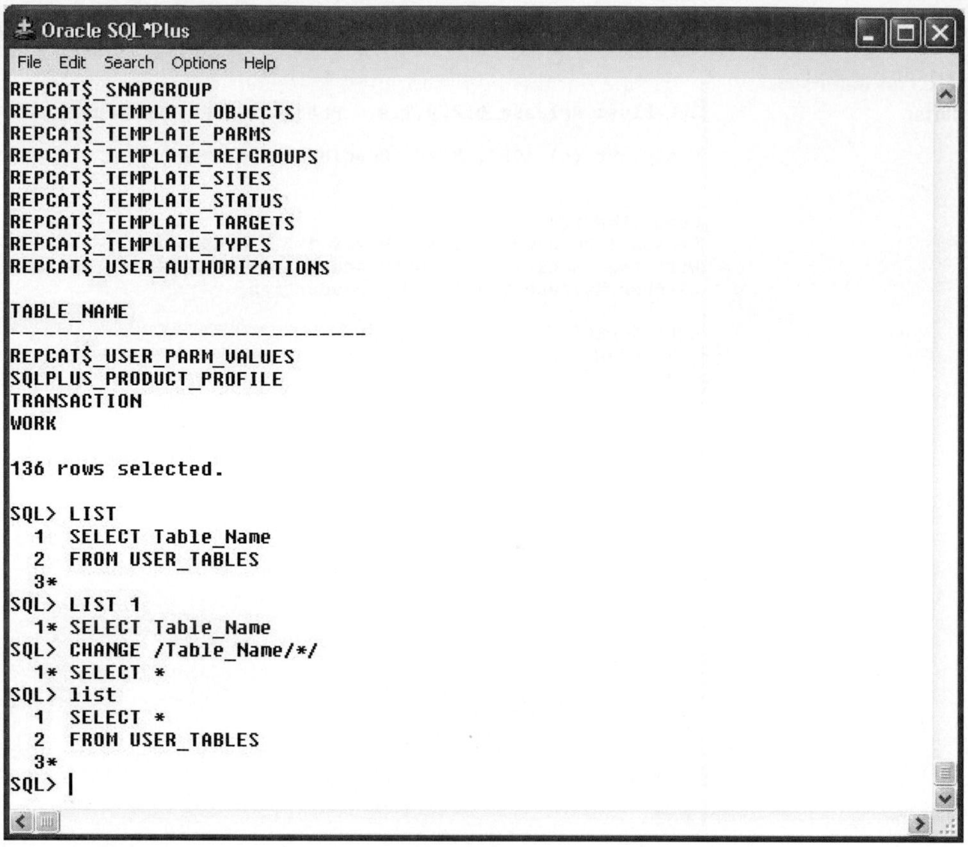

```
Oracle SQL*Plus
File  Edit  Search  Options  Help
REPCAT$_SNAPGROUP
REPCAT$_TEMPLATE_OBJECTS
REPCAT$_TEMPLATE_PARMS
REPCAT$_TEMPLATE_REFGROUPS
REPCAT$_TEMPLATE_SITES
REPCAT$_TEMPLATE_STATUS
REPCAT$_TEMPLATE_TARGETS
REPCAT$_TEMPLATE_TYPES
REPCAT$_USER_AUTHORIZATIONS

TABLE_NAME
------------------------------
REPCAT$_USER_PARM_VALUES
SQLPLUS_PRODUCT_PROFILE
TRANSACTION
WORK

136 rows selected.

SQL> LIST
  1  SELECT Table_Name
  2  FROM USER_TABLES
  3*
SQL> LIST 1
  1* SELECT Table_Name
SQL> CHANGE /Table_Name/*/
  1* SELECT *
SQL> list
  1  SELECT *
  2  FROM USER_TABLES
  3*
SQL>
```

Before going on, you should know that Oracle commands, column names, table names, view names, and all other database elements are case-insensitive. *LIST* is the same as *list* as demonstrated in Figure 10-6. The only time that case matters is inside quotation marks of strings. Thus,

SELECT * from ARTIST;

and

select * FROM artist;

are identical. But

SELECT * FROM ARTIST WHERE Name='Miro';

and

SELECT * FROM ARTIST WHERE Name='MIRO';

are different. Case matters inside quotation marks.

There is also a difference between the semicolon and the right-leaning slash (/). The semicolon terminates a SQL statement; the right-leaning slash tells Oracle to execute whatever statement is in the buffer. If there is only one statement and no ambiguity about what is wanted, Oracle will treat the semicolon and slash as the same. Thus, in the following line, the semicolon both terminates the statement and causes Oracle to execute the statement:

Select * from USER_TABLES;

Type / at this point, and that statement will be executed again.

Using a Text Editor   This facility is fine for making small changes, but it becomes unworkable for editing longer expressions such as stored procedures. For that purpose, you can set up SQL*Plus to connect to your text editor. Before doing this, however, you should create a directory for your code and point SQL*Plus to that directory.

First, exit SQL*Plus by typing exit at the SQL> prompt. Now, create a directory for your Oracle code: say, c:\MyDirectory\OracleCode. Find the SQL*Plus icon on your computer, right-click it to reveal properties, and enter the name of your new directory in the Start In text box. Click OK. Restart SQL*Plus.

Click the Edit item in the SQL*Plus window menu and then select Editor/Define Editor. You can enter the name of your editor here. Notepad is offered as the default and will be fine for our purposes, so click OK.

At this point, you've defined Notepad as your default editor to SQL*Plus and set it to point to your directory. Now, whenever you type *Edit,* SQL*Plus will invoke Notepad (or your editor, if you selected a different one). You can now create, save, and edit files of code in that directory. For example, re-enter the following statements:

SELECT Table_Name

FROM USER_TABLES;

After the results appear, type *Edit*. SQL*Plus will bring up Notepad with the contents of the buffer. Use Save As to give this file a new name, say EX1.txt. Close Notepad and you will return to SQL*Plus. To edit the file you just created, type *Edit EX1.txt* and you will enter your editor with that file. When you exit your editor and return to SQL*Plus, EX1.txt will be stored in the SQL*Plus buffer. To cause the buffer contents to execute, enter the right-leaning slash (/) key.

By the way, the default file extension for SQL*Plus is *.sql.* If you name a file *EX1.sql,* you can simply enter *Edit EX1* and SQL*Plus will add the extension for you.

Armed with this knowledge of SQL*Plus, we can now investigate some of the characteristics of Oracle. In the next section, we will use the View Ridge Gallery example introduced in Chapter 7 and create the surrogate key database schema shown in Figure 7-3.

Creating Tables

Oracle SQL CREATE TABLE statements for the View Ridge Gallery database shown in Figure 7-4 are shown in Figure 10-7. These statements were keyed into a text file named create_tables.sql and then executed from the SQL*Plus utility via the command start create_tables.

Several alterations to the SQL-92 statements shown in Figure 7-4 had to be made for Oracle. For one, Oracle does not support a CASCADE UPDATE constraint, and that constraint had to be removed. Additionally, the constraint on Birthdate and DeceasedDate was modified because Oracle does not interpret the constraint (Birthdate LIKE '([1-2], [0-9], [0-9], [0-9])) correctly. Here, these columns were changed to numeric (4,0) and constraints on data values imposed as shown. Other than these changes, the SQL in Figure 10-7 should be very familiar to you by now.

Once you have executed these statements, you can check on the status of the tables via the DESCRIBE command. Figure 10-8 shows the use of describe for the tables just defined. Notice that either DESCRIBE or DESC can be used. Also, notice that the SQL-

FIGURE 10-7

Oracle CREATE TABLE Statements for the View Ridge Schema

```
CREATE TABLE CUSTOMER(
        CustomerID          int             NOT NULL,
        Name                char(25)        NOT NULL,
        Street              char(30)        NULL,
        City                char(35)        NULL,
        State               char(2)         NULL,
        ZipPostalCode       char(5)         NULL,
        Country             varchar(50)     NULL,
        AreaCode            char(3)         NULL,
        PhoneNumber         char(8)         NULL,
        Email               varchar(100)    Null,
        CONSTRAINT          CustomerPK PRIMARY KEY (CustomerID)
        );


CREATE TABLE ARTIST(
        ArtistID            int             NOT NULL,
        Name                char(25)        NOT NULL,
        Nationality         varchar(30)     NULL,
        Birthdate           number (4,0)    NULL,
        DeceasedDate        number (4, 0)   NULL,
        CONSTRAINT          ArtistPK PRIMARY KEY (ArtistID),
        CONSTRAINT          ArtistAK1 UNIQUE (Name),
        CONSTRAINT          NationalityValues  CHECK (Nationality IN ('Canadian', 'English', 'French', 'German',
                            'Mexican', 'Russian', 'Spanish', 'US')),
        CONSTRAINT          BirthValuesCheck  CHECK (Birthdate < DeceasedDate),
        CONSTRAINT          ValidBirthYear    CHECK ((Birthdate > 1000) and (Birthdate < 2100)),
        CONSTRAINT          ValidDeathYear   CHECK ((DeceasedDate > 1000) and (DeceasedDate < 2100))
        );


CREATE TABLE CUSTOMER_ARTIST_INT(
        ArtistID            int             NOT NULL,
        CustomerID          int             NOT NULL,
        CONSTRAINT          CustomerArtistPK PRIMARY KEY (ArtistID, CustomerID),
        CONSTRAINT          Customer_Artist_Int_ArtistFK    FOREIGN KEY (ArtistID) REFERENCES ARTIST (ArtistID) ON
DELETE CASCADE,
        CONSTRAINT          Customer_Artist_Int_CustomerFK FOREIGN KEY (CustomerID) REFERENCES CUSTOMER
                            (CustomerID) ON DELETE CASCADE
        );


CREATE TABLE WORK (
        WorkID              int             NOT NULL,
        Title               varchar(25)     NOT NULL,
        Description         varchar(1000)   NULL,
        Copy                varchar(8)      NOT NULL,
        ArtistID            int             NOT NULL,
        CONSTRAINT          WorkPK PRIMARY KEY (WorkID),
        CONSTRAINT          WorkAK1 UNIQUE (Title, Copy),
        CONSTRAINT          ArtistFK FOREIGN KEY(ArtistID) REFERENCES ARTIST (ArtistID)
        );


CREATE TABLE TRANSACTION (
        TransactionID       int             NOT NULL,
        DateAcquired        Date            NOT NULL,
        AcquisitionPrice    Numeric (8,2)   NULL,
        PurchaseDate        Date            NULL,
        SalesPrice          Numeric (8,2)   NULL,
        AskingPrice         Numeric (8,2)   NULL,
        CustomerID          int             NULL,
        WorkID              int             NOT NULL,
        CONSTRAINT          TransactionPK PRIMARY KEY (TransactionID),
        CONSTRAINT          SalesPriceRange CHECK ((SalesPrice > 1000) AND (SalesPrice <=200000)),
        CONSTRAINT          ValidTransDate CHECK (DateAcquired <= PurchaseDate),
        CONSTRAINT          TransactionWorkFK FOREIGN KEY(WorkID) REFERENCES WORK (WorkID),
        CONSTRAINT          TransactionCustomerFK FOREIGN KEY(CustomerID) REFERENCES CUSTOMER
                            (CustomerID)
        );
```

FIGURE 10-8

Using the DESCRIBE Command

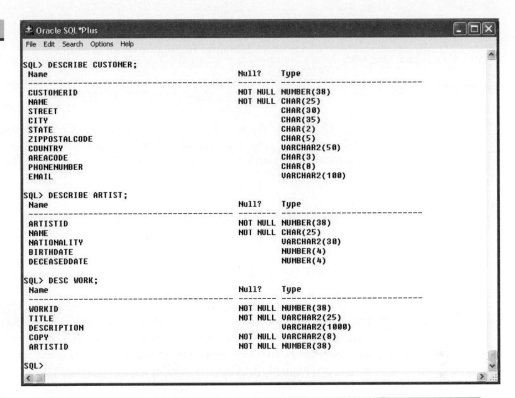

```
Oracle SQL*Plus
File  Edit  Search  Options  Help

SQL> DESCRIBE CUSTOMER;
 Name                                      Null?     Type
 ----------------------------------------- --------  -------------------
 CUSTOMERID                                NOT NULL  NUMBER(38)
 NAME                                      NOT NULL  CHAR(25)
 STREET                                              CHAR(30)
 CITY                                                CHAR(35)
 STATE                                               CHAR(2)
 ZIPPOSTALCODE                                       CHAR(5)
 COUNTRY                                             VARCHAR2(50)
 AREACODE                                            CHAR(3)
 PHONENUMBER                                         CHAR(8)
 EMAIL                                               VARCHAR2(100)

SQL> DESCRIBE ARTIST;
 Name                                      Null?     Type
 ----------------------------------------- --------  -------------------
 ARTISTID                                  NOT NULL  NUMBER(38)
 NAME                                      NOT NULL  CHAR(25)
 NATIONALITY                                         VARCHAR2(30)
 BIRTHDATE                                           NUMBER(4)
 DECEASEDDATE                                        NUMBER(4)

SQL> DESC WORK;
 Name                                      Null?     Type
 ----------------------------------------- --------  -------------------
 WORKID                                    NOT NULL  NUMBER(38)
 TITLE                                     NOT NULL  VARCHAR2(25)
 DESCRIPTION                                         VARCHAR2(1000)
 COPY                                      NOT NULL  VARCHAR2(8)
 ARTISTID                                  NOT NULL  NUMBER(38)

SQL>
```

FIGURE 10-9

Common Oracle Data Types

Data Type	Description
BLOB	Binary large object. Up to 4 gigabytes in length.
CHAR (n)	Fixed-length character field of length n. Maximum 2,000 characters.
DATE	7-byte field containing both date and time.
INT	Whole number of length 38.
NUMBER(n,d)	Numeric field of length n, d places to the right of the decimal
VARCHAR(n) or VARCHAR2(n)	Variable-length character field up to n characters long. Maximum value of n = 4,000

92 data type int is interpreted by Oracle as Number (38) and that the data type varchar is interpreted as an Oracle datatype VarChar2. Figure 10-9 summarizes basic Oracle data types. Observe that there is a Date data type, but there is no money or currency data type. Money or currency is defined in Oracle using the Numeric data type.

All of the View Ridge tables except CUSTOMER_ARTIST_WORK have surrogate keys. Unfortunately, Oracle does not directly support the definition of such keys. Instead, Oracle **sequences** must be used.

Surrogate Keys Using Sequences   A sequence is an object that generates a sequential series of unique numbers. The following statement defines a sequence called CustID that starts at 1000 and is incremented by 1 each time it is used.

Create Sequence CustID Increment by 1 start with 1000;

Two methods of sequences are important to us. The method NextVal provides the next value in a sequence and the method CurrVal provides the current value in a sequence. Thus, CustID.NextVal provides the next value of the CustID sequence. You can insert a row into CUSTOMER using a sequence as follows:

```
INSERT INTO CUSTOMER
        (CustomerID, Name, AreaCode, PhoneNumber)
        VALUES
        (CustID.NextVal, 'Mary Jones', '350', '555–1234');
```

A CUSTOMER row will be created with the next value in the sequence as the value for CustomerID. Once this statement has been executed, you can retrieve the row just created with the CurrVal method, as follows:

```
SELECT      *
FROM        CUSTOMER
WHERE       CustomerID = CustID.CurrVal
```

Here, CustID.CurrVal returns the current value of the sequence, which is the value just used.

Unfortunately, using sequences does not guarantee valid surrogate key values. For one, any developer can use a defined sequence for any purpose. If a sequence is used for purposes other than the surrogate key, some values will be missing. A second, more serious, problem is that there is nothing in the schema that prevents someone from issuing an insert statement that does not use the sequence. Thus, Oracle accepts the following:

```
INSERT INTO CUSTOMER
        (CustomerID, Name, Area_Code, Phone_Number)
        VALUES
        (350, 'Mary Jones', '350', '555–1234');
```

When this is done, it is possible that duplicate values of a surrogate could occur. In this case, Oracle will disallow the duplicate insertion because CustomerID is defined as a primary key. Still, however, this means code may need to be written to deal with this exception. Finally, it is possible that someone could accidentally use the wrong sequence when inserting into the table.

In spite of these possible problems, sequences are the best way to work with surrogate keys in Oracle.

We will use the following sequences in the View Ridge database. Create them now using SQL*Plus.

Create Sequence CustID Increment by 1 start with 1000;

Create Sequence ArtistID Increment by 1 start with 1;

Create Sequence WorkID Increment by 1 start with 500;

Create Sequence TransID Increment by 1 start with 100;

Entering Data   We can now use these sequences to add data. Figure 10-10 shows a file of insert statements created in Notepad. Type these in your editor, place a slash at the end of the file, and save the file using the name *ACIns.sql.* Enter the following and the statements in ACIns will be executed:

Start ACIns;

Your data should appear as shown in Figure 10-11.

FIGURE 10-10

Oracle INSERT Statements

```
INSERT INTO ARTIST VALUES (
ArtistID.Nextval, 'Miro', 'Spanish', 1870, 1950);
INSERT INTO ARTIST VALUES (
ArtistID.Nextval,'Kandinsky', 'Russian', 1854, 1900);
INSERT INTO ARTIST VALUES (
ArtistID.Nextval,'Frings', 'US', 1700, 1800);
INSERT INTO ARTIST (ArtistID, Name, Nationality, Birthdate) VALUES (
ArtistID.Nextval,'Klee', 'German', 1900);
INSERT INTO ARTIST (ArtistID, Name, Nationality) VALUES (
ArtistID.Nextval,'Moos', 'US');
INSERT INTO ARTIST (ArtistID, Name, Nationality) VALUES (
ArtistID.Nextval,'Tobey', 'US');
INSERT INTO ARTIST (ArtistID, Name, Nationality) VALUES (
ArtistID.Nextval,'Matisse, 'French');
INSERT INTO ARTIST (ArtistID, Name, Nationality) VALUES (
ArtistID.Nextval,'Chagall', 'French');


INSERT INTO CUSTOMER VALUES (
CustID.Nextval, 'Jeffrey Janes', '123 W. Elm St', 'Renton' , 'WA', '98123', 'USA', '206', '555-1345',
'Customer1000@somewhere.com');
INSERT INTO CUSTOMER VALUES (
CustID.Nextval, 'David Smith', '813 Tumbleweed Lane', 'Loveland', 'CO', '80345', 'USA', '303', '555-5434',
'Customer1001@somewhere.com');
INSERT INTO CUSTOMER VALUES (
CustID.Nextval, 'Tiffany Twilight', '88 - First Avenue', 'Langley', 'WA', '98114', 'USA', '206', '555-1000',
'Customer1015@somewhere.com');
INSERT INTO CUSTOMER VALUES (
CustID.Nextval, 'Fred Smathers', '10899 - 88th Ave', 'Bainbridge Island', 'WA', '98108', 'USA', '206', '555-1234',
'Customer1033@somewhere.com');
INSERT INTO CUSTOMER VALUES (
CustID.Nextval, 'Mary Beth Frederickson', '25 South Lafayette', 'Denver', 'CO', '80210', 'USA', '303', '555-1000',
'Customer1034@somewhere.com');
INSERT INTO CUSTOMER VALUES (
CustID.Nextval, 'Selma Warning', '205 Burnaby', 'Vancouver', 'BC', 'V0N 1B4', 'Canada', '253', '555-1234',
'Customer1036@somewhere.com');
INSERT INTO CUSTOMER VALUES (
CustID.Nextval, 'Susan Wu', '105 Locust Ave', 'Atlanta', 'GA', '23224', 'USA', '721', '555-1234',
'Customer1037@somewhere.com');
INSERT INTO CUSTOMER VALUES (
CustID.Nextval, 'Donald G. Gray', '55 Bodega Ave', 'Bodega Bay', 'CA', '92114', 'USA', '705', '555-1234',
'Customer1040@somewhere.com');
INSERT INTO CUSTOMER VALUES (
CustID.Nextval, 'Lynda Johnson', '117 C Street', 'Washington', 'DC', '11345', 'USA', '703', '555-1000','');
INSERT INTO CUSTOMER VALUES (
CustID.Nextval, 'Chris Wilkens' , '87 Highland Drive', 'Olympia', 'WA', '98008', 'USA', '206', '555-1234','');
```

DROP and ALTER Statements You can use the drop statement to remove structures from the database. For example, the following statements will drop the table MYTABLE and the sequence MySequence, respectively:

DROP TABLE MYTABLE;

DROP SEQUENCE MySequence;

FIGURE 10-11

Data After Inserts in Figure 10-10

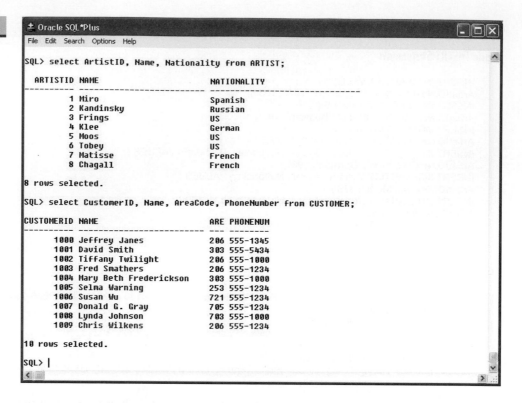

Any data in the MYTABLE table will be lost.

You can drop a column with the ALTER statement, as follows:

ALTER TABLE MYTABLE DROP COLUMN MyColumn;

Entering Sample Data   For consistency in illustration in chapters of this text, we will assume that the VRG database contains the data shown in Figure 7-5. We will also assume that the surrogate key values in that illustration resulted from the use of sequences and that the gaps in the sequence numbers resulted from inserts and deletions over time.

By the way, entering values for Date data types can be problematical when using Oracle. Oracle wants dates in a particular format, but it is sometimes difficult to determine which format it wants. The To_Date function can be advantageous in such circumstances. TO_DATE takes two parameters, as shown here:

TO_DATE('11/12/2002','MM/DD/YYYY')

The first parameter is the date value and the second is the pattern to be used when interpreting the date. In this example, the 11 is considered to be a month, and the 12 is considered to be the day of the month.

You can use the TO_DATE function with the INSERT statement to provide date values for new rows. For example, suppose that table T1 has two columns—A and B—where A is integer and B is date; the following insert statement can be used:

INSERT INTO T1 VALUES (100, TO_DATE ('01/05/02', 'DD/MM/YY'));

The result will be a new row with the values 100 and the Oracle internal format for May 1, 2002. TO_DATE can also be used with UPDATE statements.

Creating Indexes

Indexes are created to enforce uniqueness on columns, to facilitate sorting, and to enable fast retrieval by column values. Columns that are frequently used with equal conditions in WHERE clauses are good candidates for indexes. The equal clause can be either a simple condition in a WHERE clause or it can occur in a join. Both are shown in the following two statements:

```
SELECT      *
FROM        MYTABLE
WHERE       Column1=100;
```

and

```
SELECT      *
FROM        MYTABLE1, MYTABLE2
WHERE       MYTABLE1.Column1=MYTABLE2.Column2;
```

If statements like these are frequently executed, Column1 and Column2 are good candidates for indexes.

The following statement creates an index on the Name column of the CUSTOMER table:

```
CREATE INDEX CustNameIdx ON CUSTOMER(Name);
```

The index will be called CustNameIdx. Again, the name has no particular significance to Oracle. To create a unique index, add the keyword UNIQUE before the keyword INDEX. For example, to ensure that no work is added twice to the WORK table, we can create a unique index on (Title, Copy, ArtistID), as follows:

```
CREATE UNIQUE INDEX WorkUniqueIndex ON WORK(Title, Copy,
ArtistID);
```

Changing Table Structure

After a table has been created, its structure can be modified using the ALTER TABLE command. Be careful when you do this, however, because it is possible to lose data.

Adding or dropping a column is straightforward, as shown by the following:

```
ALTER TABLE MYTABLE ADD C1 NUMBER(4);
ALTER TABLE MYTABLE DROP COLUMN C1;
```

The first statement adds a new column named C1 and gives it a numeric data type with a length of four characters. The second statement drops the column just added. Note that the key word *column* is omitted when adding a new column.

When you issue these commands, you will receive the brief message "Table altered" in response. To ensure that the desired changes were made, use the DESCRIBE command to see the table's structure.

Restrictions on Table Column Modifications   You can drop a column at any time. All data will be lost when doing so, however. You can add a column at any time, as long as it is a NULL column.

To add a NOT NULL column, add it to the table as NULL, fill the new column in every row with data, and then change its structure to NOT NULL using the modify clause. For example, suppose that you have just added column C1 to table T1. After you have filled C1 in every row of T1, you can issue the following:

ALTER TABLE T1 MODIFY C1 NOT NULL;

Values will now be required for column C1.

When modifying a column, you can increase the number of characters in character columns or the number of digits in numeric columns. You can also increase or decrease the number of decimal places at any time. If the values of all rows of a given column are NULL, you can decrease the width of character and numeric data, and you can change the column's data type.

Creating Views

SQL views are created using the standard SQL-92 CREATE VIEW command in SQL*Plus. Oracle accepts all of the CREATE VIEW syntax described in Chapter 7. For example, the following statement creates the view named CustomerInterests:

CREATE VIEW CustomerInterests AS

SELECT   C.Name as Customer, A.Name as Artist

FROM   CUSTOMER C JOIN CUSTOMER_ARTIST_INT I

ON   C.CustomerID = I.CustomerID JOIN ARTIST A

ON   I.ArtistID = A.ArtistID;

The results of a query on this view for the data shown in Figure 7-5 are shown in Figure 10-12.[1]. Also, unlike the SQL-92 standard, Oracle allows the ORDER BY clause in view definitions.

▶ USING THE ORACLE ENTERPRISE MANAGER CONSOLE

In addition to SQL*Plus, Oracle databases can be managed using the Oracle Enterprise Manager Console as well. This tool provides graphical facilities for managing the database. To start it, click Programs, Oracle-Oracle9iHome, Enterprise Manager Console. Choose Launch standalone when the console application opens.

The left side of the console has a hierarchical list. Open the Network Node to display the databases on your computer. Figure 10-13 shows the results of clicking Network and then VRG. When VRG was clicked, Oracle required the user to log on. In the case, the user logged on using the SYSTEM account. Hence, Figure 10-13 shows the database as VRG–SYSTEM.

To view the tables that have been created in this database, click Schema and then the account whose tables you want to view. In this case, the tables were created under the SYSTEM account, so the user clicked SYSTEM, as shown in Figure 10-14.

To see the structure of a table, click its name. The list of columns, their data types, whether or not they can be null, and their default values will be shown in the right panel, as depicted in Figure 10-15. This display can be used to add and remove columns and to

---

[1] Oracle 9i supports the JOIN...ON syntax. If you are using Oracle 8i or earlier versions of Oracle, you will need to write this view using traditional join syntax. See page 210.

FIGURE 10-12

Using the
CustomerInterests
View

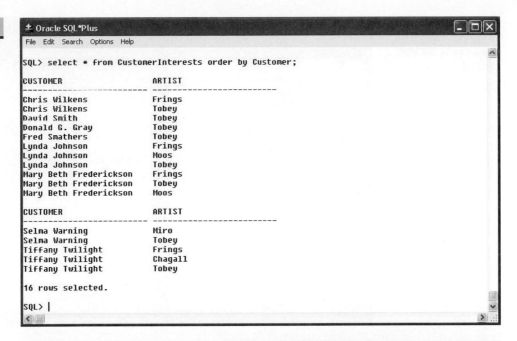

FIGURE 10-13

Opening the VRG
Database Using the
Enterprise Manager
Console

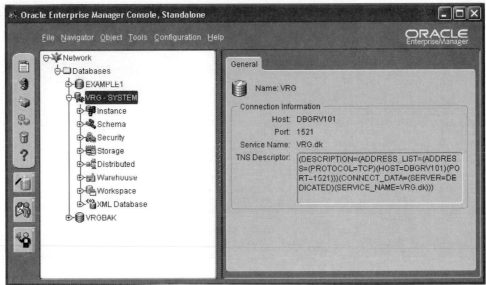

change column properties. For example, in Figure 10-16, the user has changed the length of the Name column to 35 characters and then clicked the Show SQL button. Oracle displays the SQL statement that will be executed when the user clicks Apply. This display is useful in more complicated cases in which the developer may need to know how Oracle is interpreting a change to the database structure. In this case, the change was cancelled by clicking Revert, thus leaving the length of Name at 25.

The Enterprise Manager Console can also be used to view constraints on the table by clicking the Constraint tab. Constraints for the ARTIST table are shown in Figure 10-17. This display can also be used to manage space allocations for the table and for other purposes. These topics are beyond the scope of this chapter, however.

The Enterprise Management Console can be used to create and drop tables as well as to view and edit them. In addition, you can use it to see, edit, add, and drop Views. Figure 10-18 shows the CustomerInterests view created earlier using SQL*Plus. The view can be modified by changing the SQL statements in this view.

FIGURE 10-14

Resources in the VRG
SYSTEM Account

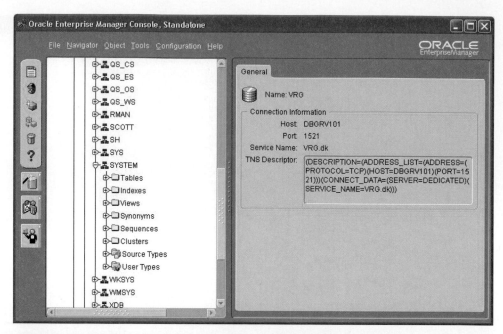

FIGURE 10-15

ARTIST Columns and
Properties

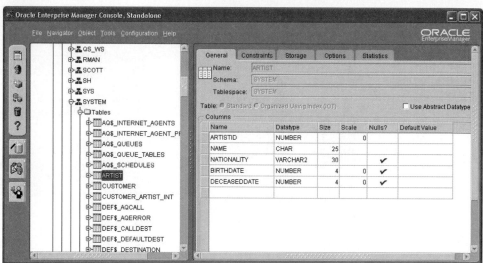

The Manager Console includes a SQL scratchpad for executing SQL statements. This scratchpad is especially useful during development and test. To access it, click the center tool in the left margin; when the tool expands, click the last element in the horizontal list, as shown in Figure 10-19(a). The scratchpad opens, as shown in Figure 10-19(b). You can key a SQL statement into the top area of the form and then click the lightning bolt button to cause the statement to be executed.

FIGURE 10–16

Changing a Column Property

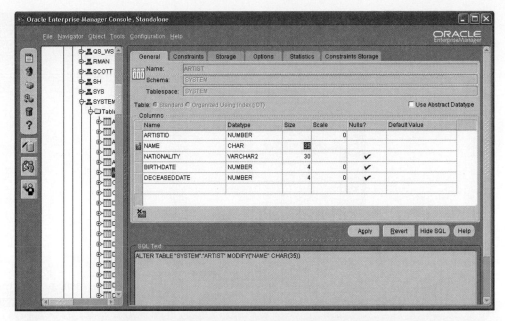

FIGURE 10–17

Constraints on the ARTIST Table

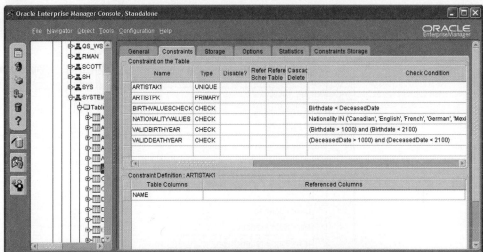

FIGURE 10–18

Displaying the CustomerInterests View

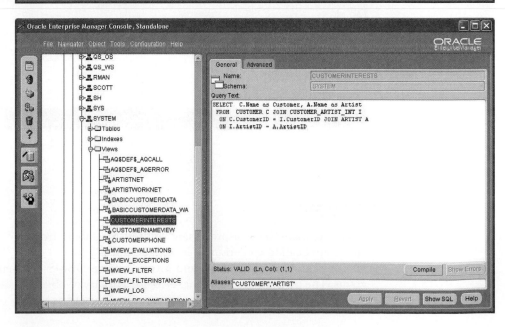

FIGURE 10-19

Using the SQL
Scratchpad (a) Starting
the SQL Scratchpad
and (b) Processing a
SELECT Statement in
the SQL Scratchpad

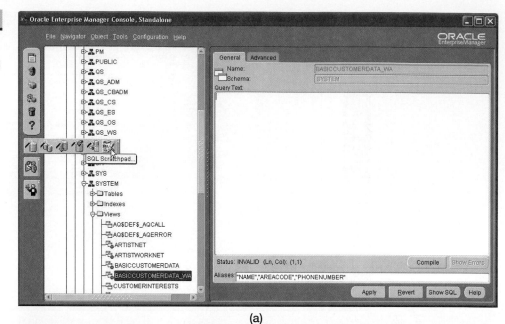

(a)

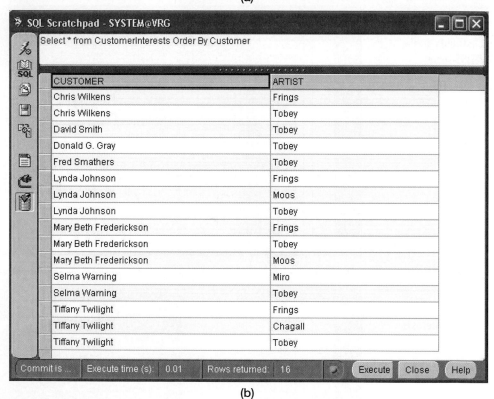

(b)

▶ APPLICATION LOGIC

There are many ways of processing an Oracle database from an application. One is to
create application code using a language such as Java, C#, C++, Visual Basic, or some
other programming language and invoke Oracle DBMS commands from those programs. The modern way to do that is to use a library of object classes, create objects that
accomplish database work, and process those objects by setting object properties and

invoking object methods. You will see examples of such processing when we discuss ADO in Chapter 12, ADO.NET in Chapter 13, and Java Server Pages in Chapter 14.

Another way of processing an Oracle database is to create stored procedures, as described in Chapter 7. These stored procedures can then be invoked from application programs or from Web pages using languages such as VBScript or JScript. Stored procedures can also be executed from SQL*Plus or from the SQL scratchpad in the management console. This should be done only when the procedures are being developed and tested, however. As described in Chapter 9, for security reasons no one other than authorized members of the DBA staff should be allowed to interactively process an operational database.

A third means of processing an Oracle database is to save groups of database commands in .sql files. Such files are then processed using the Start command, just as we did for creating the View Ridge database in the prior section. For security, such files should be used only during application development and test, never on an operational database.

Finally, application logic can be embedded in triggers. As you learned in Chapter 7, triggers can be used for validity checking, to set default values, to update views, and to implement referential integrity actions.

In this chapter, we will describe and illustrate two stored procedures. Here, we will test those procedures by invoking them from SQL*Plus. Again, this should be done only during development and test. You will learn how to invoke those stored procedures from application code in Chapters 12–14. We will also describe four triggers, one for each of the four trigger uses. These triggers are invoked by Oracle when the specified actions occur.

Stored Procedures

A stored procedure is a PL/SQL or Java program that is stored within the database. Stored procedures are programs; they can have parameters, they can invoke other procedures and functions, they can return values, and they can raise exceptions. Stored procedures can be invoked remotely. You will see examples of invoking stored procedures in Chapters 12–14. Here, we will consider two stored procedure examples.

Customer_Insert STORED PROCEDURE   Suppose that the View Ridge Gallery wants to be able to add a new customer to its database and record the customer's artist interests. In particular, the gallery wants to record the customer's name and phone data, and then to connect the customer to all artists of a specified nationality.

Figure 10-20 shows a stored procedure that accomplishes this task. The procedure, named Customer_Insert, receives four parameters: newname, newareacode, newphone, and artistnationality. The key word *IN* signifies that these are input parameters. *OUT* signifies an output parameter, and *IN OUT* signifies a parameter used for both input and output. Notice that the data type is given for the parameter, but not its length. Oracle will determine the length from the context.

Variables are declared after the keyword *AS*. A **cursor variable** named *artistcursor* is defined on the SELECT statement shown. This cursor will be used to process all of the rows for an artist of the input nationality.

The first section of the procedure checks to determine whether the customer data already exist. If so, nothing is done and an output message is printed using the Oracle package DBMS_OUTPUT. Note the syntax for printing a string and a variable value is

DBMS_OUTPUT.PUT_LINE ('string' || variable)

Before continuing with this procedure, note that this message can be seen only if the procedure is invoked from SQL*Plus. If the procedure were invoked differently—say, over the Internet using a browser—this message would not be seen. The developer would need to use an output parameter or raise an error exception. These topics are beyond the scope of the present discussion, however.

Additionally, to see such messages, execute the following:

FIGURE 10–20

Customer_Insert Stored Procedure

```
CREATE OR REPLACE PROCEDURE Customer_Insert
        (
        newname           IN        char,
        newareacode       IN        char,
        newphone          IN        char,
        artistnationality IN        char
        )

AS

        rowcount integer(2);

        CURSOR    artistcursor IS
                  SELECT ArtistID
                  FROM ARTIST
                  WHERE Nationality=ArtistNationality;

BEGIN
        SELECT    Count(*) INTO rowcount
        FROM      CUSTOMER
        WHERE     Name=newname AND AreaCode=newareacode AND PhoneNumber = newphone;

        IF    rowcount > 0 THEN
              BEGIN
                    DBMS_OUTPUT.PUT_LINE ('Customer Already Exists -- No Action Taken. Rowcount = 'll rowcount);
                    RETURN;
              END;
        END IF;

        INSERT INTO CUSTOMER
                  (CustomerID, Name, AreaCode, PhoneNumber)
                  VALUES (CustID.NextVal, NewName, NewAreaCode, NewPhone);

        FOR artist IN artistcursor
                  LOOP
                        INSERT INTO CUSTOMER_ARTIST_INT
                        (CustomerID, ArtistID)
                        VALUES (CustID.CurrVal, artist.ArtistID);
                  END LOOP;

        DBMS_OUTPUT.PUT_LINE ('New Customer Successfully Added');

END;
/
```

Set serveroutput on;

If you are not receiving output from your procedures when using SQL*Plus, it is likely you have not executed this statement.

The remainder of the procedure in Figure 10-20 inserts the new customer data and then loops through all artists of the given nationality. Observe the use of the special PL/SQL construct *FOR artist IN artistcursor*. This construct does several tasks. It opens the cursor and fetches the first row. Then, it iterates through all rows in the cursor; when there are no more rows, it transfers control to the next statement after the FOR. Also notice that the ArtistID value of the current cursor row can be accessed with the syntax artist.ArtistID, where artist is the name of the variable in the FOR statement and *not* the name of the cursor.

Once you have written this procedure, you must first compile and store it in the database. Code the procedure using your editor and save it under a name: say, SP_CI.sql. If you include a slash as your last line, the procedure will be compiled and stored when you enter the following command:

Start SP_CI

If you have made a mistake, you may have compile errors. Unfortunately, SQL*Plus does not automatically show them to you. Instead, it gives you the message "Warning: Procedure created with compilation errors." To see the errors, enter the following:

Show errors;

If there are no syntax errors, you receive the message "Procedure created." Now, you can invoke the procedure with the Execute or Exec command, as follows:

Exec Customer_Insert ('Michael Bench', '203', '555-2014', 'US');

After you execute this statement, you should query the CUSTOMER, ARTIST, and CUSTOMER_ARTIST_INT tables to ensure that the changes were made correctly.

If you have execution time errors, the line numbers reported differ from the line numbers you see in your text editor. You can adjust these line numbers to conform to yours, but the process is too complicated to describe here. For the simple procedures we will do, just work around the issue. Do not assume the line numbers match, however.

NewCustomerWithTransaction STORED PROCEDURE Figure 10-21 shows a second stored procedure for recording a new customer and the sale of a work to that customer. The logic of this procedure, named NewCustomerWithTransaction, is as follows. First, create new customer data and then search for TRANSACTION rows for the purchased work that have null values for CustomerID. That search involves the join of the ARTIST, WORK, and TRANSACTION tables because the Name of the artist is stored in ARTIST, and Title and Copy of the work are stored in WORK. If one, and only one, such row is found, update CustomerID, SalesPrice, and PurchaseDate in that row. Then, insert a row in the intersection table to record the customer's interest in this artist. Otherwise, make no changes to the database.

NewCustomerWithTransaction accepts parameters having customer and purchase data, as shown. Next, several variables and a cursor are declared. The cursor defines the join of the ARTIST, WORK, and TRANSACTION tables. It selects TransactionID and ARTIST.ArtistID of rows that match the input artist and work data, and that have a null value for CustomerID.

The procedure first checks to see whether the input customer data already exist in the database. If not, it inserts the new customer data. In PL/SQL, there is no BEGIN TRANSACTION[2] statement; the first database action automatically starts a transaction. Here, the customer data insert starts a new transaction.

Note, also, that comments are enclosed between /* and */. Such comments can extend over multiple lines, and if you begin a comment with /* and fail to terminate it with */, your entire program will be treated as a comment.

After the customer data are inserted, the TransCursor is processed. The variable *rowcount* is used to count the rows, the value of TransactionID is stored in *tid,* and the value of ArtistID is stored in *aid.* Observe that the assignment operator in Oracle is :=. Thus, tid := trans.TransactionID means to assign the value of trans.TransactionID to the variable tid.

According to this logic, if only one qualifying row is found, then *tid* and *aid* will have the values we need to continue. If zero or more than one qualifying rows are found, the transaction will be aborted, but neither *tid* nor *aid* will be used.

We could use Count(*) to count the qualifying rows, and if Count(*) = 1, execute another SQL statement to obtain the values of *tid* and *aid* we need. The logic in Figure 10-21 saves this second SQL statement.

---

[2] Watch out here! We are using the word TRANSACTION in two ways in this section: as the name of one of the View Ridge tables and as the name of a group of statements to be executed automatically. The context will make the usage clear, but be aware of the possible confusion.

FIGURE 10–21

NewCustomerWithTransaction Stored Procedure

```
CREATE OR REPLACE PROCEDURE NewCustomerWithTransaction
        (
        newname IN char,
        newareacode IN char,
        newphone IN char,
        artistname IN char,
        worktitle IN char,
        workcopy IN char,
        price IN number
        )

AS

        rowcount integer;
        tid        int;
        aid        int;

        CURSOR    transcursor IS
                SELECT            TransactionID, ARTIST.ArtistID
                FROM              ARTIST, WORK, TRANSACTION
                WHERE             Name=artistname AND Title=worktitle AND Copy=workcopy AND
                                  TRANSACTION.CustomerID IS NULL AND
                                  ARTIST.ArtistID = WORK.ArtistID AND
                                  WORK.WorkID = TRANSACTION.WorkID;

BEGIN

        /* Does Customer Already exist? */

        SELECT    Count(*) INTO rowcount
        FROM      CUSTOMER
        WHERE     Name=newname AND AreaCode=newareacode AND PhoneNumber = newphone;

        IF rowcount > 0 THEN
                BEGIN
                        DBMS_OUTPUT.PUT_LINE ('Customer Already Exists -- No Action Taken');
                        RETURN;
                END;

        END IF;


        /* Customer not exist, add new customer data */
        INSERT INTO CUSTOMER
                (CustomerID, Name, AreaCode, PhoneNumber)
                VALUES (CustID.NextVal, newname, newareacode, newphone);


        /* Look for one and only one available TRANSACTION row. */
        rowcount := 0;
        FOR trans In transcursor
                LOOP
                        tid := trans.TransactionID;
                        aid := trans.ArtistID;
                        rowcount := rowcount + 1;
                END LOOP;

        IF rowcount > 1 Then
                BEGIN
                        /* Too many available rows -- undo with message and return */
                        ROLLBACK;
                        DBMS_OUTPUT.PUT_LINE ('Invalid Artist/Work/Transaction data -- No Action Taken.  Rowcount = ' ||
                        rowcount);
                        RETURN;
                END;
        END IF;
```

FIGURE 10-21

(continued)

```
        IF rowcount = 0 Then

            BEGIN
                /* No available row exists -- undo with message and return */
                ROLLBACK;
                DBMS_OUTPUT.PUT_LINE ('No available transaction row -- No Action Taken');
                RETURN;

            END;

        END IF;

        /* Exactly one exists -- use it (tid obtained from transcursor above) */


        UPDATE TRANSACTION
                SET    CustomerID = CustID.Currval, Salesprice = price, PurchaseDate = SysDate
                WHERE   TransactionID = tid;
        DBMS_OUTPUT.PUT_LINE ('Customer created and transaction data updated');

        /* Now create interest in this artist for this customer */
        /* Use currval of sequence and aid from transcursor above */

        INSERT INTO CUSTOMER_ARTIST_INT (ArtistID, CustomerID)
                    VALUES (aid, CustID.CurrVal);

END;
/
```

If RowCount is greater than 1 or equal to zero, an error message is generated and the transaction is rolled back to remove the prior insert to CUSTOMER. If RowCount equals 1, the appropriate TRANSACTION row is updated. Note the use of the function SysDate to store the current date. Finally, an intersection row is inserted for this customer and the artist of the purchased work (*aid*).

This stored procedure can be invoked with a command like the following:

Exec NewCustomerWithTransaction ('Malinda Gliddens', '303', '555-6687','Chagall', 'Northwest by Night', '37/50', 27000);

To test this procedure, it is convenient to first define a view that shows customer purchases. Assume that the following view has been created:

```
CREATE VIEW WorkPurchase AS
        SELECT        C.Name as Customer, A.Name as Artist, W.Title, W.Copy,
                      T.PurchaseDate, T.SalesPrice
        FROM          CUSTOMER C JOIN TRANSACTION T
            ON    C.CustomerID = T.CustomerID
        JOIN WORK W
            ON    T.WorkID = W.WorkID
        JOIN ARTIST A
            ON    W.ArtistID = A.ArtistID;
```

Figure 10-22 shows SQL statements with queries of this view, the CustomerInterests view, and the CUSTOMER table. If you examine this figure, you will see that changes

FIGURE 10–22

Testing Results of the
Stored Procedure in
Figure 10-21

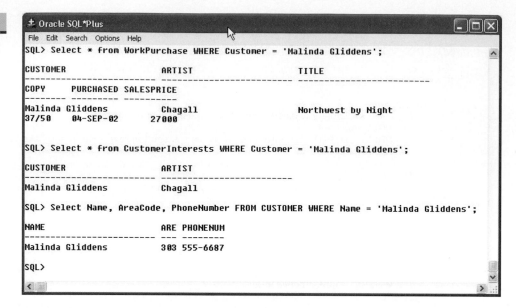

```
Oracle SQL*Plus
File  Edit  Search  Options  Help
SQL> Select * from WorkPurchase WHERE Customer = 'Malinda Gliddens';

CUSTOMER                       ARTIST                    TITLE
------------------------       -------------------       ------------------------
COPY      PURCHASED  SALESPRICE
--------  ---------  ----------
Malinda Gliddens               Chagall                   Northwest by Night
37/50     04-SEP-02  27000


SQL> Select * from CustomerInterests WHERE Customer = 'Malinda Gliddens';

CUSTOMER                       ARTIST
------------------------       -------------------
Malinda Gliddens               Chagall

SQL> Select Name, AreaCode, PhoneNumber FROM CUSTOMER WHERE Name = 'Malinda Gliddens';

NAME                           ARE PHONENUM
------------------------       --- --------
Malinda Gliddens               303 555-6687

SQL>
```

were made as required. Of course, to complete the testing of this stored procedure, it is necessary to test error conditions as well. We will omit that step here, however.

Triggers

Oracle triggers are PL/SQL or Java procedures that are invoked when specified database activity occurs. Oracle supports a variety of different types of triggers. Some triggers are invoked on SQL commands that create new tables, views, or other database triggers. Other triggers are invoked once per SQL command, and still others are invoked for each row that is involved in the processing of a SQL command.

To understand the difference between the latter two trigger types, consider the following SQL update statement:

UPDATE   CUSTOMER

SET   AreaCode = '425'

WHERE   ZipPostalCode = '98119';

A command trigger will be fired once when the statement is processed. A row trigger will be fired once for every row that is updated during the processing of this statement. Row triggers are the most common, and we will consider only that type of trigger in this chapter.

Oracle recognizes three types of row triggers: BEFORE, AFTER, and INSTEAD OF. BEFORE and AFTER triggers are placed on tables, and INSTEAD OF triggers are placed on views. Each trigger type can be fired on insert, update, or delete commands.

Because of the way that Oracle manages concurrency, AFTER triggers that update the table that caused the trigger to be fired can be problematic. For example, if table T1 has an AFTER update trigger, any code in the trigger that also attempts to process table T1 may not work correctly. When this occurs, Oracle issues a message like "Table T1 is mutating, trigger/function may not see it." For this reason, any actions that require processing the table that is firing the trigger are best done with BEFORE triggers.

AFTER triggers can be useful, however, when the action of the trigger applies to a table other than the one that fired the trigger. For example, if table T1 requires a child row in table T2, an AFTER trigger on T1 insert can be used to create the required T2 child. You will see an example of that use in Figure 10-27(a).

The values of columns of the table or view upon which the trigger is based are available to the trigger. For insert and update triggers, the new values of the table or view columns can be accessed with the prefix :new. Thus, if table T1 has two columns C1 and C2, when an insert or update trigger is fired on T1, the expression :new.C1 has the new value for the column C1 and the expression :new.C2 has the new value for the column C2.

For update and delete triggers, the old values of the table or view columns can be accessed with the prefix :old. Thus, :old.C1 will have the value of column C1 before the update or delete is processed.

In the next sections, we will discuss a trigger that enforces a business rule, one that computes an extended default value, one that updates a view, and finally, one that enforces a required child.

A Trigger for Enforcing a Business Rule   View Ridge Gallery keeps a list of customer problem accounts; these are customers who have either not paid promptly or who have presented other problems to the gallery. When a customer who is on the problem list is entered into the database, the gallery manager wants to know that this insert has occurred.

The AFTER trigger in Figure 10-23 provides such notification. The phrase "AFTER INSERT OR UPDATE OF Name ON CUSTOMER" is correct, but it contains an ambiguity. It means the trigger should fire after *any* insert on CUSTOMER or after an update of Name in CUSTOMER. Thus, any insert fires the trigger and an update of Name fires the trigger.

The statement FOR EACH ROW causes this trigger to be a row trigger that is fired once for every row that is inserted or for which Name is updated.

FIGURE 10-23

ValidateCustomer Trigger

```
CREATE OR REPLACE TRIGGER ValidateCustomer
AFTER INSERT OR UPDATE OF Name ON CUSTOMER

FOR EACH ROW

DECLARE

        rowCount integer;

BEGIN

/*  Look for the new customer in the Problem_Account Table.    */
        SELECT Count(*) INTO rowcount
        FROM PROBLEM_ACCOUNT PA
        WHERE :new.Name = PA.NAME
                AND :new.AreaCode = PA.AreaCode
                AND :new.PhoneNumber = PA.PhoneNumber;


/* If the customer exists in the problem table, then send warning message.  */

        If rowCount > 0 Then

                DBMS_OUTPUT.PUT_LINE ('A Customer with name 'll :new.Name ll ' and phone of ('ll
                :new.AreaCode ll ') ' ll:new.PhoneNumber ll ' has been a problem in the past.');

        End If;


END;
/
```

To create a trigger like this, write the code using a text editor and save it in a text file with a name having the suffix .sql—say, Trigger1.sql. Then, to create the trigger, open SQL*Plus and type *Start Trigger1*. In response, Oracle will compile your trigger. If you have syntax errors, type *Show Errors*, as described for stored procedures.

To test this trigger, first create a PROBLEM_ACCOUNT table with Name, AreaCode, and PhoneNumber columns that match those in CUSTOMER. Then, place rows into that table. Next, insert a new customer with values that match one of those in the PROBLEM_ACCOUNT trigger. Figure 10-24 shows the result for the customer 'Nichole Not Pay.' Notice that this trigger writes the notification message back to the SQL*Plus utility. More realistically, such a trigger would send an email to the gallery manager or take some other more obvious action.

Using a table of valid (or invalid) values is more flexible and dynamic than placing such values in a CHECK constraint. For example, consider the CHECK constraint on Nationality values in the ARTIST table. If the gallery manager wants to expand the nationality of allowed artists, he or she will have to change the CHECK constraint using the ALTER TABLE statement. In reality, the gallery manager will have to hire a consultant to change that constraint.

A better approach is to place the allowed values of Nationality in a table, say ALLOWED_NATIONALITY. Then, write a trigger like that shown in Figure 10-23 to enforce the constraint that new values of Nationality exist in ALLOWED_NATIONALITY. When the gallery owner wants to change the allowed artists, he or she would simply add or remove values in the ALLOWED_NATIONALITY table.

A Trigger for Setting Default Values   Triggers can be used to set default values that are more complex than those that can be set with the Default constraint on a column definition. For example, View Ridge has a pricing policy that says that the default AskingPrice of a work of art depends on whether the art has been in the gallery before. If not, the default AskingPrice is twice the AcquisitionPrice. If the work has been in the gallery before, the default price is the larger of twice the AcquisitionPrice or the AcquisitionPrice plus the average net gain of the work in the past.

The BEFORE trigger in Figure 10-25 implements this pricing policy. It is named SetAskingPrice and uses the view ArtistWorkNet, which was defined in Chapter 7 as follows:

CREATE VIEW ArtistWorkNet AS

SELECT	W.WorkID, Name, Title, Copy, AcquisitionPrice, SalesPrice,(SalesPrice - AcquisitionPrice) AS NetPrice
FROM	TRANSACTION T
JOIN	WORK W ON T.WorkID = W .WorkID JOIN ARTIST A
ON	W.ArtistID = A.ArtistID;

FIGURE 10–24

Execution of the ValidateCustomer Trigger

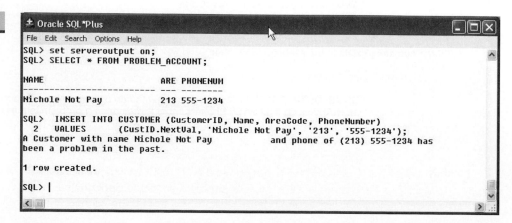

FIGURE 10–25

SetAskingPrice Trigger

```
CREATE OR REPLACE TRIGGER SetAskingPrice
        BEFORE INSERT ON TRANSACTION

FOR EACH ROW

DECLARE

        avgNetPrice numeric (8,2);
        newPrice numeric (8,2);
        rowCount integer;

BEGIN
        /* First find if work has been here before */


        SELECT  Count(*) INTO rowCount
        FROM    TRANSACTION
        WHERE   WorkID = :new.WorkID;

        IF rowcount = 0 Then
                /* This is first time work has been in gallery */

                :new.AskingPrice := 2*(:new.AcquisitionPrice);
        ELSE

                /* Work has been here before */
                SELECT          Avg(NetPrice) INTO avgNetPrice
                FROM            ArtistWorkNet AW
                WHERE           AW.WorkID = :new.WorkID
                GROUP BY        AW.WorkID;

                newPrice := avgNetPrice + :new.AcquisitionPrice;

                /*    */
                IF newPrice > 2 * :new.AcquisitionPrice Then
                        :new.AskingPrice := newPrice;
                ELSE
                        :new.Askingprice := 2 * :new.AcquisitionPrice;
                END IF;

        END IF;

END;
/
```

The trigger first counts the number of rows in TRANSACTION having the :new value of WorkID. Because this is a BEFORE trigger, the work has not yet been added to the database, and the count will be zero if the work has not been to the gallery before. If so, :new.AskingPrice is set to twice the AcquisitionPrice.

If the work has been to the gallery before, the average of NetPrice for this work is computed using ArtistWorkNet view. Then, the variable newPrice is computed as the sum of the average plus the acquisition price. Finally, :new.AskingPrice is set to the larger of newPrice or twice the AcquisitionPrice. Because this is a BEFORE trigger, the Avg built-in function can be used because the new row of WORK has not yet been added to the database and will not count in the average computation.

There may be a problem with the computations in this trigger, however, if either SalesPrice or AcquisitionPrice is null in any of the rows in the ArtistWorkView. The discussion of that problem, however, is beyond the scope of this chapter.

This trigger provides useful functionality for the gallery. It saves the gallery personnel considerable manual work in implementing their pricing policy and likely improves the accuracy of the results as well.

A Trigger for Updating a View   Chapter 7 discussed the problem of updating views. One such problem concerns updating views created via joins; it is normally not possible for the DBMS to know how to update the tables that underlie the join. However, there may be application-specific knowledge that can be used to determine how to interpret a request to update a joined view.

Consider the CustomerInterests view defined earlier in this chapter. It contains rows of CUSTOMER and ARTIST joined over their intersection table. CUSTOMER.Name is given the alias Customer, and ARTIST.Name is given the alias Artist.

A request to change the name of a customer in CustomerInterests can be interpreted as a request to change the name of the underlying CUSTOMER table. Such a request, however, can be processed only if the value of Name is unique in Customer. If not, the request cannot be processed.

Figure 10-26 shows an INSTEAD OF trigger that will update customer name only if the name is unique in the database. It conditions the update on the NOT EXISTS keyword rather than counting the number of rows with the given customer name and making the change only if there is one such row. Constructing the trigger with NOT EXISTS allows Oracle to optimize the SQL statement and will result in better performance.

A Trigger for Performing a Referential Integrity Action

According to the database design in Figure 7-4, the WORK table in the View Ridge database has a required TRANSACTION child. This means that whenever a WORK is inserted, a TRANSACTION child must be inserted as well.

Enforcing such referential integrity constraints is difficult. We want to create an AFTER trigger on WORK that ensures the application created the required TRANSACTION row. However, any such WORK trigger will be fired immediately after the WORK row is inserted, before the application has a chance to insert the new TRANSACTION row. Thus, the trigger will not be able to see the TRANSACTION row that the application is about to create.

Another alternative would be to require the application to create the TRANSACTION row before the WORK row. In this design, however, we have defined the relationship so that a TRANSACTION row requires a WORK row. The DBMS will therefore disallow any insert of a TRANSACTION row that does not have a parent, and it will do so before any trigger on TRANSACTION is invoked. Thus, a trigger on TRANSACTION never has a chance to create the necessary WORK row.

Although it is not aesthetically pleasing, one workable solution is to create a pair of triggers. The first creates a default TRANSACTION row when the WORK row is created. Then, the second trigger removes the default row when the application inserts a TRANSACTION. In this way, if the application does not create the required TRANSACTION row, the default row will be used. If the application does create a new TRANSACTION row, however, the default row is removed.

Figures 10-27(a) and 10-27(b) show this pair of triggers. The trigger in Figure 10-27(a) creates the default TRANSACTION row. It first checks to determine whether an appropriate TRANSACTION row exists; if not, it inserts a new row into

---

FIGURE 10-26

CustomerInterests Update Trigger

```
CREATE OR REPLACE TRIGGER CustomerInterests_Update
        INSTEAD OF UPDATE ON CustomerInterests

FOR EACH ROW

/* Update the name only if it is unique in the customer table   */

BEGIN
        UPDATE        CUSTOMER C1
        SET           C1.Name = :new.Customer
        WHERE         C1.Name = :old.Customer
              AND     NOT EXISTS
                      (Select *
                      FROM    CUSTOMER C2
                      WHERE   C2.Name = C1.Name
                      AND     c2.CustomerID <> C1.CustomerID);

        END;
        /
```

FIGURE 10-27

Triggers for Enforcing a
Required Child
Constraint
(a) EnforceTransChild
Trigger and
(b) RemoveDupTrans
Trigger

```
CREATE OR REPLACE TRIGGER EnforceTransChild
             AFTER INSERT ON WORK

FOR EACH ROW

DECLARE

        rowCount int;
        newID int;

BEGIN

        newID := :new.WorkID;
        SELECT  Count(*) INTO rowCount
        FROM    TRANSACTION
        WHERE   WorkID = newID
            AND  CustomerID IS Null;

        If rowCount = 0 then

        /* Insert new transaction row since none available */

                INSERT  INTO TRANSACTION
                (TransactionID, DateAcquired, WorkID) VALUES
                (TransID.NextVal, SysDate, newID);
        End If;

END;
/
```

(a)

```
CREATE OR REPLACE TRIGGER RemoveDupTrans
             BEFORE INSERT ON TRANSACTION

FOR EACH ROW


/* Clean up duplicate child if necessary */

BEGIN

        DELETE  FROM TRANSACTION
        WHERE   WorkID = :new.WorkID
            AND  CustomerID is Null
            AND  TransactionID <> :new.TransactionID;



END;
/
```

(b)

TRANSACTION. The trigger in Figure 10-27(b) then removes this default row when the user creates an appropriate TRANSACTION row.

Again, this solution is not satisfying. Another alternative, which is more complicated but more pleasing, is to require the application to create new works through a WORK/TRANSACTION view. The view would have the necessary values for WORK and TRANSACTION tables, and those values would be used to insert new WORK and TRANSACTION rows in the trigger. In that case, no direct insert of WORK or TRANS-ACTION should be allowed. See Project H.

Exception Handling   This discussion has omitted a discussion of PL/SQL exception handling. This is unfortunate because exception handling is both important and useful. There's just too much to do. If you program in PL/SQL in the future, however, be sure to learn about this important topic. It can be used in all types of PL/SQL programming, but it is especially useful in BEFORE and INSTEAD OF TRIGGERS for canceling pending updates. Exceptions are necessary because transactions in Oracle cannot be rolled back in triggers. Exceptions can be used instead to generate error and warning messages. They also keep users better informed about what the trigger has done.

▶ DATA DICTIONARY

Oracle maintains an extensive data dictionary of metadata. This dictionary describes the structures of tables, sequences, views, indexes, constraints, columns, stored procedures, and much more. It also contains the source code of procedures, functions, and triggers. And it contains much more.

The dictionary contains metadata about itself in the table DICT. You can query this table to learn more about the contents of the data dictionary, but be warned that it is a big table. For example, more than 800 rows will be returned if you query for the names of all tables in the data dictionary.

Suppose you want to know what tables the data dictionary contains about user or system tables. The following query obtains that result:

```
SELECT      Table_Name, Comments
FROM        DICT
WHERE       Table_Name LIKE ('%TABLES%');
```

Forty or so rows will be returned. One of those tables is named USER_TABLES. To display the columns of that table, enter the following:

```
DESC        USER_TABLES;
```

You can use this strategy of query and describe to obtain the dictionary's metadata for objects and structures you want. Figure 10-28 lists several of the tables and their pur-

FIGURE 10–28

Example Oracle Metadata

Table Name	Comments
DICT	Data dictionary metadata
USER_CATALOG	List of tables, views, sequences, and other structures owned by the user
USER_TABLES	User table structures
USER_TAB_COLUMNS	A child of USER_TABLES. Has data about table columns. Synonym is COLS.
USER_VIEWS	User views
USER_CONSTRAINTS	User constraints
USER_CONS_COLUMNS	A child of USER_CONSTRAINTS. Has columns in constraints
USER_TRIGGERS	Has trigger metadata. Query Trigger_Name, Trigger_Type, and Trigger_Event. Warning: Trigger_Body does not provide a useful listing.
USER_SOURCE	To obtain the text of procedure MY TRIGGER, SELECT Text FROM USER_SOURCE WHERE Name='MYTRIGGER' AND Type='PROCEDURE'

poses. The tables USER_SOURCE and USER_TRIGGERS are useful when you want to know what source code is currently stored in the database for procedures and triggers.

By now, you should know enough SQL to navigate your way around the dictionary. Be aware that Oracle stores all names in uppercase. If you're looking for a trigger named On_Customer_Insert, search for ON_CUSTOMER_INSERT.

▶ CONCURRENCY CONTROL

Oracle supports three different transaction isolation levels and also allows applications to place locks explicitly. Explicit locking is not recommended, however, because such locking can interfere with Oracle's default locking behavior and also because it increases the likelihood of transaction deadlock.

Before discussing transaction isolation levels, we need to summarize how Oracle processes database changes. Oracle maintains a **System Change Number (SCN),** which is a database-wide value that is incremented by Oracle whenever database changes are made. Whenever a row is changed, the before image of the row is placed in a **rollback segment,** which is a buffer maintained by Oracle. The before image includes the SCN that was in the row prior to the change. Then, after the row is changed, Oracle increments the SCN and places the new value in the changed row.

When an application issues a SQL statement like

```
UPDATE      MYTABLE
SET         MyColumn1='NewValue'
WHERE       MyColumn2='Something';
```

The value of SCN that was current at the time the statement started is recorded. Call this value the Statement SCN. While processing the query, in this case while looking for rows with MyColumn2 = 'Something,' Oracle selects only rows that have committed changes with an SCN value less than or equal to the Statement SCN. When it finds a row with a committed change and SCN value greater than the Statement SCN, it looks in the rollback segment to find an earlier version of the row. It searches the rollback segments until it finds a version of the row with a committed change having an SCN less than the Statement SCN.

In this way, SQL statements always read a consistent set of values—those that were committed at or before the time the statement was started. As you will see, this strategy is sometimes extended to apply to transactions. In that case, all of the statements in a transaction read rows having an SCN value less than the SCN that was current when the transaction started.

Because of this strategy, Oracle only reads committed changes. Hence, with Oracle, dirty reads are not possible.

Oracle supports Read Committed, Serializable, and Read Only transaction isolation levels. The first two are defined in the 1992 ANSI standard; Read Only is unique to Oracle. Figure 10-29 summarizes these isolation levels.

Read Committed Transaction Isolation Level

Recall from Chapter 9 that dirty reads are not allowed with Read Committed isolation, but reads may not be repeatable and phantoms are possible. Read Committed is Oracle's default transaction isolation level because Oracle never reads uncommitted data changes.

With Read Committed isolation, each statement is consistent, but two different statements in the same transaction may read inconsistent data. This is the same as statement level consistency, as defined in the last chapter. If transaction level consistency is required, Serializable isolation must be used. Do not confuse statement consistency with

FIGURE 10-29

Oracle Transaction
Isolation

Read Committed Transaction Isolation	The default Oracle isolation level. Dirty reads are not possible, but repeated reads may yield different data. Phantoms are possible.
	Each statement reads consistent data. When blocked for updates, statements are rolled back and restarted when necessary. Deadlock is detected and one of the blocking statements is rolled back.
Serializable Transaction Isolation	Dirty reads are not possible, repeated reads yield the same results, and phantoms are not possible.
	All statements in the transaction read consistent data. "Cannot serialize" error occurs when a transaction attempts to update or delete a row with a committed data change that occurred after the transaction started. Also occurs when blocking transactions or statements commit their changes or when the transaction is rolled back due to deadlock. Application programs need to be written to handle the "Cannot serialize" exception.
Read Only Transaction Isolation	All statements read consistent data. No inserts, updates, or deletions are possible.
Explicit Locks	Not recommended.

the lost update problem, however. Oracle prohibits lost updates because it never reads dirty data.

Because of the way it uses the SCN, Oracle never needs to place read locks. When a row is to be changed or deleted, however, Oracle places an exclusive lock on the row before making the change or deletion. If another transaction has an exclusive lock on the row, the statement waits. If the blocking transaction rolls back, the change or deletion proceeds.

If the blocking transaction commits, the new SCN value is given to the statement, and the statement (not the transaction) rolls back and starts over. When a statement is rolled back, changes already made by the statement are removed using the rollback segments.

Because exclusive locks are used, deadlock can occur. When that happens, Oracle detects the deadlock using a wait-for graph and rolls back one of the conflicting statements.

Serializable Transaction Isolation Level

As you learned in Chapter 9, with serializable transaction isolation, dirty reads are not possible, reads are always repeatable, and phantoms cannot occur. Oracle supports serializable transaction isolation, but the application program must play a role for it to work.

Use the Set command to change the transaction isolation level within a transaction. The following statement establishes serializable isolation for the duration of the transaction:

SET TRANSACTION ISOLATION LEVEL SERIALIZABLE;

To change the isolation level for all transactions in a session, use the ALTER command:

ALTER SESSION SET ISOLATION_LEVEL SERIALIZABLE;

When the isolation level is serializable, Oracle saves the SCN at the time the transaction started. Call this value the Transaction SCN. As the transaction proceeds, Oracle only reads committed changes that have an SCN value less than or equal to the Transaction SCN. Hence, reads are always repeatable and phantoms are not possible.

As long as the transaction does not attempt to update or delete any row having a committed change with an SCN greater than the Transaction SCN, the transaction proceeds normally. If, however, the transaction does attempt to update or delete such a row, Oracle issues a "Cannot serialize" error when the update or delete occurs. At that point, the application program must play a role. It can commit changes made to that point, roll back the entire transaction, or take some other action. Any program that executes under serializable isolation must include such exception handling code.

Also, when a transaction running under serializable isolation attempts to update or delete a row that has been locked exclusively by a different transaction or statement, the transaction waits. If the blocking transaction or statement later rolls back, the transaction can continue. If, however, the blocking transaction commits, Oracle generates the "Cannot serialize" error and the application needs to process that exception.

Similarly, if a serializable transaction is rolled back due to deadlock, the "Cannot serialize" error is also generated.

Read Only Transaction Isolation

With this isolation level, the transaction reads only rows having committed changes with an SCN value less than or equal to the Transaction SCN. If the transaction encounters rows with committed changes having an SCN value greater than the Transaction SCN, Oracle roots around in the rollback segments and reconstructs the row as it was prior to the Transaction SCN. With this level of transaction isolation, no inserting, updating, or deleting is allowed.

Additional Locking Comments

The application can invoke locks explicitly using the SELECT FOR UPDATE form of the select statement. This is not recommended and you should not use it until you have learned much more about Oracle locking than we have described here.

Behind the scenes, Oracle uses quite a wide variety of locks to provide isolation levels. There is a row share lock as well as several different types of table locks. There are other locks used internally within Oracle. You can learn more about these locks in the Oracle documentation.

To reduce the likelihood of lock conflict, Oracle does not promote locks from one level to another. Row locks remain row locks, even if there are hundreds of them on hundreds of rows of a table. This strategy is different from SQL Server, as you will learn in the next chapter. Oracle Corporation claims that not promoting locks is an advantage, and it probably is—especially given the rest of the Oracle lock architecture.

▶ SECURITY

Oracle provides robust and comprehensive security facilities. The relationships of the basic components of the Oracle security system are shown in Figure 10-30. The components are ACCOUNT, PROFILE, SYSTEM PRIVILEGE, and ROLE. An ACCOUNT is a user account such as SYSTEM, MaryJane, Fred, or some other user account[3]. A PROFILE is a set of system resource maximums that are assigned to an account. Figure

---

[3] Unfortunately, Oracle uses the word SYSTEM in two different ways here. There is an account named SYSTEM and there are SYSTEM PRIVILEGES. Figure 10-32 shows SYSTEM PRIVILEGES for the SYSTEM account.

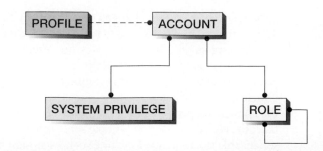

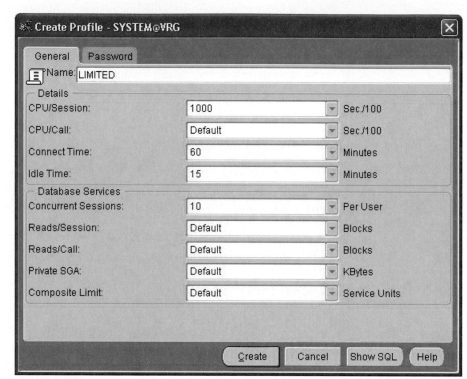

10-31 shows the definition of a typical PROFILE. Notice that the PROFILE limits both computer and database resources; it is also used for password management, as described in the next section. As shown in Figure 10-30, an ACCOUNT has exactly one PROFILE, but a PROFILE may be assigned to many accounts.

Account System Privileges

Each ACCOUNT can be allocated many SYSTEM PRIVILEGEs and many ROLEs. A SYSTEM PRIVILEGE is the right to perform some action on the database data; on a database structure such as a table, a view, or an index; or on one of the Oracle system resources such as a table space. Figure 10-32 shows the SYSTEM PRIVILEGEs for the SYSTEM account. Only one privilege is shown: UNLIMITED TABLESPACE. Other privileges that can be assigned to the SYSTEM account are shown in the panel in the upper-right portion of this figure.

A ROLE can have many SYSTEM PRIVILEGEs and it may also have a relationship to other ROLEs. As shown in Figure 10-33(a), three roles have been assigned to the SYSTEM account. The SYSTEM account inherits the ROLEs and PRIVILEGEs of each of the three ROLEs it has been granted. For example, SYSTEM has been granted the role SALES_HISTORY_ROLE. The SYSTEM PRIVILEGES of that ROLE are shown in Figure 10-33(b). Because the SYSTEM account has the ROLE SALES_HISTORY_ROLE, it obtains the four privileges shown in Figure 10-33(b).

FIGURE 10-32

Privileges Granted to
the SYSTEM Account

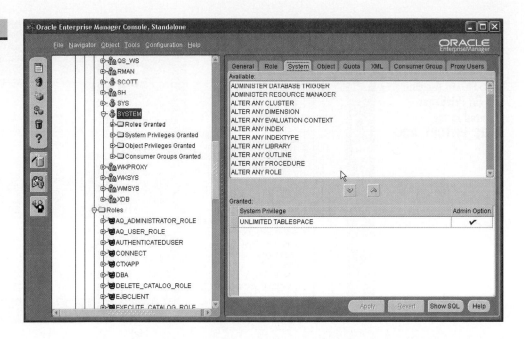

As shown in Figure 10-30, a ROLE may itself have other ROLEs assigned to it. If so, it inherits the ROLEs and PRIVILEGEs of those other ROLEs as well.

To summarize, the SYSTEM PRIVILEGEs of an account consist of all of the SYSTEM PRIVILEGEs that it has been granted directly, plus the SYSTEM PRIVILEGEs of all ROLEs that it has, plus the privileges of all ROLEs that those ROLEs have, and so forth through all the ROLEs. For our example, the SYSTEM account has been assigned the UNLIMITED TABLESPACE SYSTEM PRIVILEGE (shown in Figure 10-32), plus all of the SYSTEM PRIVILEGEs of the ROLEs AQ_ADMINISTRATOR_ROLE, DBA, and SALES_HISTORY_ROLE (shown in Figure 10 33(a)), plus all of the SYSTEM PRIVILEGEs that those roles inherit.

ROLEs simplify the administration of the database. Without ROLEs, each account would need to be assigned the privileges that it needs, one by one. This time-consuming process would need to be repeated every time a new account is created. Using ROLEs, a set of privileges can be assigned to a ROLE just once; and when a new account is given that ROLE, all PRIVILEGEs of the ROLE are given to the new account. Also, when a PRIVILEGE is removed from a ROLE, all accounts that have that ROLE automatically have that PRIVILEGE removed as well.

Account Authentication

Figure 10-34 shows the Oracle Enterprise Manager Console form that is used to create a new user account. The DBA enters the name of the account and specifies the profile to be used, the method used to authenticate that account, and other data. In Figure 10-34(a), a password is used to authenticate the account. A new password has been placed on the account, but the Expire Password Now option has also been checked. This means that the first time the user signs on using this account, he or she is told that the password has expired and they need to create a new one. This action will force the user to define their own password for the account before they can use the account.

Figure 10-34(b) shows an account that is to be authenticated externally to Oracle. This type of authentication means that the host operating system authenticates that the user is who they say they are and passes the necessary credentials to Oracle. By the way, if the operating system is authenticating the account, the Oracle account for that user must begin with the characters OPS$. In Figure 10-34(b), the operating system authenticates a user named MARY_JANE in the domain MYDOMAIN1. The OPS$ is not part

FIGURE 10–33

Account Role Example
(a) Roles Granted to
the SYSTEM Account
and (b) Privileges
Granted to the
SALES_HISTORY_ROLE

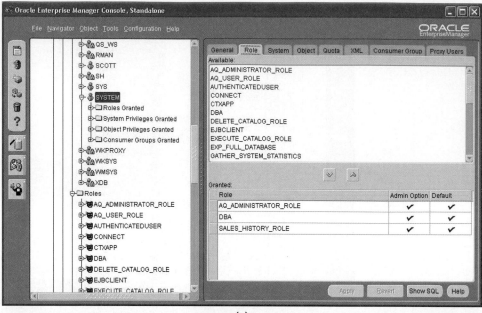

(a)

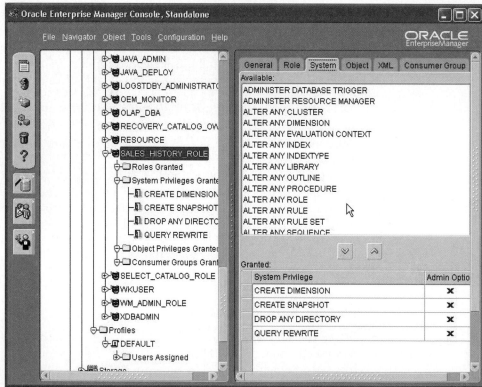

(b)

FIGURE 10-34

**Account Authentication
(a) Password
Authentication and
(b) External
Authentication**

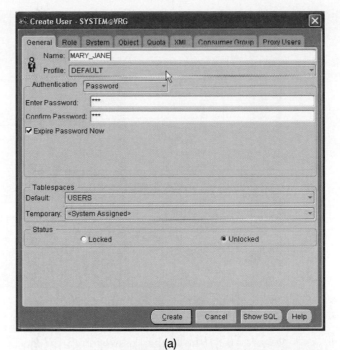

(a)

(b)

of the operating system user name; it is a prefix that is required by Oracle for such accounts. We will use operating system authentication in Chapters 12 and 13 when we show how to process an Oracle database using Integrated Security from ASP and ASP.NET.

FIGURE 10–35

Password Management via a Profile

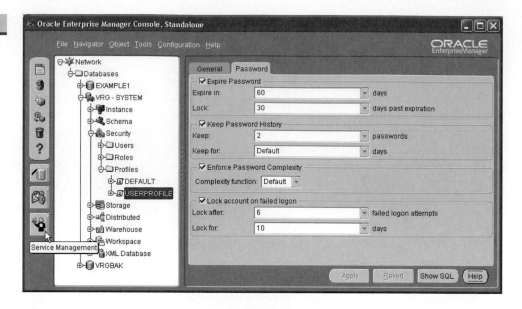

Oracle provides a number of useful functions and utilities for managing passwords. Figure 10-35 shows the Password tab for the PROFILE named USERPROFILE (a PROFILE that was previously created by the DBA).

The passwords for all user accounts that are based on this PROFILE are managed according to the choices in this form. Specifically, the passwords expire every 60 days, and if the user does not change the password for 30 days after that, the account is locked (made unusable). The second section of the form indicates that Oracle will store two generations of the user's passwords. This means that a user cannot reuse a password until he or she has used at least two other different passwords.

Password complexity concerns how strong a password must be in terms of the number of characters required, the use of upper- and lowercase and numbers, and the use of special characters. Default means that the default policy of the database is used. See the Oracle documentation for more information on this topic. Finally, if six or more attempts are made to enter a correct password, Oracle locks the account, and it will remain locked for 10 days.

This section has presented a quick summary of the security tools provided by Oracle. Of course, the tools by themselves do not make a secure database. Organizations that use databases need to develop security plans and policies that stipulate how these tools will be used. A discussion of such plans is beyond the scope of this text, but you should learn about them in your systems development class.

▶ BACKUP AND RECOVERY

Oracle provides a sophisticated set of facilities and utilities for backup and recovery processing. They can be used in many different ways to provide appropriate backup and recovery for databases, ranging from a small workgroup database that can be backed up when it is unused at night to large inter-organizational databases that must be operational 24 hours per day, 7 days per week (24/7), and can never be shut down.

Oracle Recovery Facilities

Oracle maintains three types of files that are important for backup and recovery. **Datafiles** contain user and system data. Because of the way that Oracle writes data buffers to disk, the datafiles may contain both committed and uncommitted changes at any arbitrary moment in time. Of course, Oracle processes transactions so that these uncommitted changes are eventually either committed or removed, but a snapshot of the datafiles at any arbitrary moment includes uncommitted changes. Thus, when Oracle shuts down or when certain types of backups are made, the datafiles must be cleaned up so that only committed changes remain in them.

ReDo files contain logs of database changes; they are backups of the rollback segments used for concurrent processing. **Control files** are small files that describe the name, contents, and locations of various files used by Oracle. Control files are frequently updated by Oracle and they must be available for a database to be operational.

There are two types of ReDo files. **OnLine ReDo** files are maintained on disk and contain the rollback segments from recent database changes. **Offline** or **Archive ReDo** files are backups of the OnLine ReDo files. They are stored separately from the OnLine ReDo files, and need not necessarily reside on disk media. Oracle can operate in either ARCHIVELOG or NOARCHIVELOG mode. If it is running in ARCHIVE mode, when the OnLine ReDo files fill up, they are copied to the Archive ReDo files.

Control files and OnLine ReDo files are so important that Oracle recommends that two active copies of them be kept, a process called **multiplexing** in Oracle terminology.

Types of Failure

Oracle recovery techniques depend on the type of failure. When an **application failure** occurs—because of application logic errors, for instance—Oracle simply rolls back uncommitted changes made by that application using the in-memory rollback segments and OnLine ReDo files as necessary.

Other types of failure recovery are more complicated and depend on the failure type. An **instance failure** occurs when Oracle itself fails due to an operating system or computer hardware failure. A **media failure** occurs when Oracle is unable to write to a physical file. This may occur because of a disk head crash or other disk failure, because needed devices are not powered on, or because a file is corrupt.

Instance Failure Recovery   When Oracle is restarted after an instance failure, it looks first to the control file to find out where all the other files are located. Then, it processes the OnLine ReDo logs against the datafiles. It rolls forward all changes in the ReDo log that were not yet written to the datafiles at the time of failure. In the process of rolling forward, rollback segments are filled with records of transactions in the ReDo log.

After rollforward, the datafiles may contain uncommitted changes. These uncommitted changes could have been in the datafiles at the time of the instance failure or they could have been introduced by rollforward. Either way, Oracle eliminates them by rolling back such uncommitted changes using the rollback segments that were created during rollforward. So that transactions do not need to wait for rollback to complete, all uncommitted transactions are marked as DEAD. If a new transaction is blocked by a change made by a DEAD transaction, the locking manager destroys the locks held by the DEAD transaction.

The Archive ReDo logs are not used for instance recovery. Accordingly, instance recovery can be done in either ARCHIVELOG or NOARCHIVELOG mode.

Media Failure Recovery   To recover from a media failure, the database is restored from a backup. If the database was running in NOARCHIVELOG, nothing else can be done. The OnLine ReDo log is not useful because it concerns changes made long after the backup was made. The organization must find another way to recover changes to the database. (This would be the wrong time to start thinking about this, by the way.)

If Oracle was operating in ARCHIVELOG mode, the OnLine ReDo logs will have been copied to the archive. To recover, the database is restored from a backup, and the database is rolled forward by applying Archive ReDo log files. After this rollforward finishes, changes made by uncommitted transactions are removed by rolling them back, as described previously.

Two kinds of backups are possible. A **consistent backup** is one in which all uncommitted changes have been removed from the datafiles. Database activity must be stopped, all buffers must be flushed to disk, and changes made by any uncommitted transactions removed. Clearly, this type of backup cannot be done if the database supports 24/7 operations.

An **inconsistent backup** may contain uncommitted changes. It is sort of flying backup, made while Oracle is processing the database. For recovery, such backups can be made consistent by applying the archive log records to commit or roll back all transactions that were in process when the backup was made. Inconsistent backups can be made on portions of the database. For example, in a 24/7 application, one-seventh of the database can be backed up every night. Over a week's time, a copy of the entire database will have been made.

The Oracle Recovery Manager (RMAN) is a utility program used to create backups and to perform recovery. RMAN can be instructed to create a special recovery database that contains data about recovery files and operations. The specifics of this program are beyond the scope of this discussion.

▶ TOPICS NOT DISCUSSED IN THIS CHAPTER

There are several important Oracle features that we have not discussed in this chapter. For one, Oracle supports object-oriented structures, and developers can use them to define their own abstract data types. Oracle can also be used to create and process databases that are hybrids of traditional databases and object databases. Such hybrids, called object-relational databases, will be described in Chapter 16.

Also, Enterprise Oracle supports distributed database processing, in which the database is stored on more than one computer. This topic will be introduced in Chapter 15. Additionally, there are quite a few Oracle utilities that we have not discussed. The Oracle Loader is a utility program for inputting bulk data into an Oracle database. Other utilities can be used to measure and tune Oracle performance.

We have, however, discussed the most important Oracle features and topics here. If you have understood these concepts, you are on your way to becoming a successful Oracle developer.

SUMMARY

Oracle is a powerful and robust DBMS that runs on many different operating systems and has many different products. This chapter addresses the use of the Oracle utility SQL*Plus, which can be used to create and process SQL and PL/SQL with all versions of Oracle. PL/SQL is a language that adds programming facilities to the SQL language.

You can create a database using the Database Configuration Assistant, using the Oracle-supplied database creation procedures and using the SQL CREATE DATABASE command. The Database Configuration Assistant creates default database and log files. SQL*Plus has a limited text editor that keeps the current statement in a multiline buffer. SQL*Plus can be configured to invoke text editors such as Notepad.

You can enter SQL statements directly into SQL*Plus, or you can create files of SQL and submit the files to Oracle via SQL*Plus. Any of the SQL statements discussed in Chapters 6–8 can be submitted to Oracle in this way.

The Oracle Enterprise Manager Console is a utility that provides graphical means for managing an Oracle database. The utility can be used to manage structures such as tables and views; and to manage user accounts, passwords, roles, and privileges.

PL/SQL statements and Java programs can be placed in the database as stored procedures and invoked from other PL/SQL programs or from application programs. Examples of stored procedures are shown in Figures 10-20 and 10-21. Oracle triggers are PL/SQL or Java programs that are invoked when specified database activity occurs.

Examples of BEFORE, AFTER, and INSTEAD OF TRIGGERS are shown in Figures 10-23 through 10-27, respectively. Oracle maintains a data dictionary of metadata. The metadata of the dictionary itself is stored in the table DICT. You can query this table to determine the dictionary's contents.

Oracle supports read committed, serializable, and read-only transaction isolation levels. Because of the way SCN values are processed, Oracle never reads dirty data. Serializable isolation is possible, but the application program must be written to process the "Cannot serialize" exception. Applications can place locks explicitly using SELECT FOR UPDATE commands, but this is not recommended.

Oracle security components include ACCOUNTs, PROFILEs, PRIVILEGEs, and ROLEs. An ACCOUNT has a PROFILE that specifies resource limits on the ACCOUNT as well as password management. A PRIVILEGE is the right to perform a task on an Oracle resource. ROLEs can be assigned to ACCOUNTs, and consist of groups of PRIVILEGEs and other ROLEs. An ACCOUNT has all the PRIVILEGEs that have been assigned directly, plus all the PRIVILEGEs of all of its ROLEs and all ROLEs that are inherited through ROLE connections. Passwords can be authenticated by password or by the host operating system. Password management can be specified via PROFILEs.

Three types of files are used in Oracle recovery: Datafiles, OnLine and OffLine ReDo log files, and Control files. If running in ARCHIVELOG mode, Oracle logs all changes to the database. Oracle can recover from application failure and instance failure without using the archived log file. Archive logs are required, however, to recover from media failure. Backups can be consistent or inconsistent. An inconsistent backup can be made consistent by processing an archive log file.

GROUP I QUESTIONS

10.1 Describe the general characteristics of Oracle and the Oracle suite of products. Explain why these characteristics mean there is considerable complexity to master.

10.2 What is SQL*Plus and what is its purpose?

10.3 Name three ways of creating an Oracle database. Which is the easiest?

10.4 Explain how to change a row in the SQL*Plus buffer. Assume that there are three statements in the buffer, the focus is on statement 3, and you want to change the second statement from CustID51000 to CustomerID51000.

10.5 How do you set the default directory for SQL*Plus to use?

10.6 Show the SQL statement necessary to create a table named T1 with columns C1, C2, and C3. Assume that C1 is a surrogate key. Assume that C2 has character data of maximum length 50 and that C3 contains a date.

10.7 Show the statement necessary to create a sequence starting at 50 and incremented by 2. Name your sequence T1Seq.

10.8 Show how to insert a row into table T1 (question 10.6) using the sequence created in question 10.7.

10.9 Show a SQL statement for querying the row created in question 10.8.

10.10 Explain the problems inherent in using sequences for surrogate key columns.

10.11 Show SQL statements for dropping table T1 and for dropping SeqT1.

10.12 Show SQL statements for dropping column C3 of table T1.

10.13 Show SQL statements for creating a relationship between table T2 and table T3. Assume that T3 has a foreign key column named FK1 that relates to T2 and that deletions in T2 should force deletions in T3.

10.14 Answer question 10.13, but do not force deletions.

10.15 Explain how to use the To_Date function.

10.16 Show SQL statements to create a unique index on columns C2 and C3 of table T1.

10.17 Under what circumstances should indexes be used?

10.18 Show SQL statements to add a new column C4 to table T1. Assume that table T1 will have currency values up to $1 million.

10.19 Under what conditions can you drop a column in an existing table?

10.20 Under what conditions can you add a column to an existing table?

10.21 Explain how to add a NOT NULL column to an existing table.

10.22 Under what conditions can you change the width of a character or numeric column?

10.23 Under what conditions can you change a column's data type?

10.24 Show how to add a constraint to specify that column C4 of table T1 cannot be less than 1,000.

10.25 Show how to add a constraint to specify that column C4 of table T1 cannot be less than column C5 of table T1.

10.26 For the View Ridge database discussed in this chapter, construct a view that contains Name, City, and State of a customer. Name your view CustView.

10.27 For the View Ridge database, construct a view that has customer name and artist name for all art that the customer has purchased.

10.28 For the View Ridge database, construct a view that has customer name and artist name for all artists in which the customer is interested. Explain the difference between this view and the view in question 10.27.

10.29 Can you combine the views in questions 10.27 and 10.28 into one view? Why or why not?

10.30 How can you update a join view using Oracle?

10.31 Create a file of PL/SQL statements that describes the structure of the CUSTOMER, ARTIST, WORK, TRANSACTION, and CUSTOMER_ARTIST_INT tables. Store the file with the name VRTabs.sql and show how to invoke the PL/SQL procedure using SQL*Plus.

10.32 In a PL/SQL procedure, what do the keywords IN, OUT, and IN OUT signify?

10.33 What must be done to be able to see output generated by the Oracle DBMS_OUTPUT package? What limits exist on such output?

10.34 Explain how the PL/SQL statement FOR *variable* IN *cursorname* work.

10.35 What statement is used to obtain errors when compiling stored procedures and triggers?

10.36 What is the syntax of the BEGIN TRANSACTION statement in PL/SQL? How is a transaction started?

10.37 In the stored procedure in Figure 10-20, how are the values of the variables tid and aid used if there are no suitable TRANSACTION rows in the database? How are they used if there is just one suitable TRANSACTION row in the database?

10.38 Explain the purpose of BEFORE, AFTER, and INSTEAD OF triggers.

10.39 When an update is in progress, how can the trigger code obtain the value of a column, say, C1, before the update began? How can the trigger code obtain the value that the column is being set to?

10.40 Explain why INSTEAD OF TRIGGERS are needed for join views.

10.41 Explain a limitation on the use of AFTER triggers.

10.42 Show a SQL statement to obtain the names of tables the data dictionary contains about triggers.

10.43 What three levels of transaction isolation are supported by Oracle?

10.44 Explain how Oracle uses the system change number to read data that are current at a particular point in time.

10.45 Under what circumstances does Oracle read dirty data?

10.46 Explain how conflicting locks are handled by Oracle when a transaction is operating in READ COMMITTED isolation mode.

10.47 Show the SQL statement necessary to set the transaction isolation level to SERIALIZABLE for an entire session.

10.48 What happens when a transaction in serializable mode tries to update data that have been updated by a different transaction? Assume that the SCN is less than the transaction's SCN. Assume the SCN is greater than the transaction's SCN.

10.49 Describe three circumstances under which a transaction could receive the "Cannot serialize" exception.

10.50 Explain how Oracle processes the read only transaction isolation level.

10.51 Explain the use of ACCOUNT, PRIVILEGE, and ROLE in Oracle security.

10.52 What three types of files are important for Oracle backup and recovery processing?

10.53 What is the difference between the OnLine ReDo logs and the OffLine or Archive ReDo logs? How is each type used?

10.54 What does multiplexing mean in the context of Oracle recovery?

10.55 Explain how Oracle recovers from application failure.

10.56 What is instance failure and how does Oracle recover from it?

10.57 What is media failure and how does Oracle recover from it?

PROJECT

For the following activities, use either SQL*Plus or the Oracle Enterprise Manager Console, whichever you prefer.

A. Install Oracle and create the View Ridge database.

B. Create the tables in Figure 10-7, but do not create the NationalityValues constraint.

C. Fill your database with sample data. Ensure that you have at least three customers, three artists, five works, and five transactions. Set the Nationality of ARTIST to one of 'German', 'French', or 'English'.

D. Write a stored procedure to read the ARTIST table and display the artist data using the DBMS_OUTPUT.PUT_LINE command.

E. Write a stored procedure to read the ARTIST and WORK tables. Your procedure should display an artist, then display all the works for that artist, then display the next artist, and so forth. Accept the name of the artist to display as an input parameter.

F. Write a stored procedure to update customer phone data. Assume that your stored procedure receives Name, priorAreaCode, newAreaCode, priorPhoneNumber, and newPhoneNumber. Your procedure should first ensure that there is only one customer with the values of (Name, priorAreaCode, priorPhoneNumber). If not, produce an error message and quit. Otherwise, update the customer data with the new phone number data.

G. Create a table named ALLOWED_NATIONALITY with one column called Nation. Place the values 'German', 'French', and 'English' into the table. Write a trigger that will check to determine whether a new or updated value of Nationality resides in this table. If not, write an error message using DBMS_OUT-PUT.PUT_LINE. Use SQL*Plus to demonstrate that your trigger works.

H. Create a view having all data from the WORK and TRANSACTION table. Write an insert INSTEAD OF trigger on this view that will create a new row in WORK and TRANSACTION. Use SQL*Plus to demonstrate that your trigger works.

FIREDUP PROJECT QUESTIONS

Use Oracle to create a database with the following four tables:

CUSTOMER (<u>CustomerID</u>, Name, Phone, EmailAddress)

STOVE (<u>SerialNumber</u>, Type, Version, DateOfManufacture)

REGISTRATION (<u>*CustomerID*</u>, <u>*SerialNumber*</u>, <u>RDate</u>)

STOVE-REPAIR (<u>RepairInvoiceNumber</u>, *SerialNumber*, RepairDate, Description, Cost, *CustomerID*)

Assume that the primary keys of CUSTOMER, STOVE, and STOVE-REPAIR are surrogate keys; and create sequences for each of them. Create relationships to enforce the following referential integrity constraints:

> CustomerID of REGISTRATION exists in CustomerID of CUSTOMER
> SerialNumber of REGISTRATION exists in SerialNumber of STOVE
> SerialNumber of STOVE-REPAIR exists in SerialNumber of STOVE
> CustomerID of STOVE-REPAIR exists in CustomerID of CUSTOMER

Do not cascade deletions.

A. Fill your tables with sample data and display them.

B. Create a stored procedure to register a stove. Assume that the procedure receives the customer's name, phone, email address, and stove serial number. If the customer already exists in the database (name, phone, and email match), use that customer's CustomerID for the REGISTRATION. Otherwise, create a new CUS-TOMER row for the customer. Assume that a stove with the input serial number already exists in the database. If not, print an error and roll back changes to the CUSTOMER table. Code and test your procedure.

C. Create a stored procedure to record a stove repair. Assume that the procedure receives customer's name, phone, email address, stove serial number, repair description, and cost. Assume that you are given a valid stove serial number; print an error message and make no database changes if not. Use an existing CUS-TOMER row if name, phone, and email match; otherwise, create a new CUS-

TOMER record. Assume that the STOVE_REPAIR row must be created. Register the stove if necessary.

D. Create a view named CustomerReg that contains all of the CUSTOMER, STOVE, and REGISTRATION data. Create an INSTEAD OF trigger for an insert of CustomerReg. Assume that the user will provide values for CustomerID, Name, Phone, EmailAddress, and SerialNumber. If the customer does not exist in the database, create a new row in CUSTOMER. Create a registration of the stove for this customer. If the SerialNumber does not exist in STOVE, write an error message and take no other action. Demonstrate that your trigger works.

TWIGS TREE TRIMMING SERVICE PROJECT QUESTIONS

Use Oracle to create a database with the following three tables:

OWNER (<u>OwnerName</u>, Phone, Street, City, State, Zip)

SERVICE (<u>DateOfService</u>, <u>OwnerName</u>, Description, AmountBilled, AmountPaid, DateOfPayment)

CHIP_DELIVERY (<u>CustomerName</u>, <u>DeliveryDate</u>, LoadSize, AmountBilled, AmountPaid, DateOfPayment)

Create relationships that will enforce the following referential integrity constraints:

> SERVICE.OwnerName exists in OWNER.OwnerName
> CHIP_DELIVERY.CustomerName exists in OWNER.OwnerName

Cascade deletions.

A. Fill your tables with sample data and display them.

B. Create a stored procedure to schedule a service. Assume that the procedure receives all owner data and DateOfService and Description. If the owner already exists in the database, use the existing owner data. Otherwise, create a new row in OWNER. Create the new SERVICE row. Code and test your procedure.

C. Create a stored procedure to schedule a chip delivery. Assume that the procedure receives all owner data and DeliveryDate, LoadSize, and Amount Billed. If the owner already exists in the database, use the existing owner data. Do not schedule the delivery if the owner has any unpaid SERVICE or CHIP_DELIVERY records. Write an error message using DBMS_OUTPUT.PUT_LINE instead. Unpaid means that there is a non-null value for AmountBilled, but a null value for AmountPaid.

D. Create a view named CustomerService that contains all of the OWNER and SERVICE data. Create an INSTEAD OF trigger for an insert of CustomerService. Assume that the user will provide values for all owner data and DateOfService and Description. If the owner does not exist in the database, create a new row in OWNER. Create a row in SERVICE for this service. Demonstrate that your trigger works.

CHAPTER 11

Managing Databases with SQL Server 2000

This chapter describes the basic features and functions of Microsoft SQL Server 2000. The discussion uses the example of View Ridge Gallery from Chapter 7 and it parallels the discussion of the database administration tasks in Chapter 9. The presentation is similar in scope and orientation to that for Oracle in the prior chapter.

SQL Server is a large and complicated product. In this one chapter, we will only be able to scratch the surface. Your goal should be to learn sufficient basics so that you can continue learning on your own or in other classes.

▶ INSTALLING SQL SERVER 2000

If you purchased the version of this book that has SQL Server, you should install it now. The SQL Server CD that comes with this text contains an evaluation copy that has a license valid for 120 days. It requires Windows NT with Service Pack 5 or later, or Windows 2000 Professional or Windows XP Professional. It also needs at least 64MB of RAM and about 250MB of disk space (less is possible, but not recommended).

To install this software, log in to your computer with Administrator privileges and insert the CD-ROM. The install program should start automatically. If not, double-click the autorun executable at the top level of the CD. Click on SQL Server Components and then click on Install Database Server. The rest of the installation process is a typical Windows program installation.

After you install the software, you can start to work with SQL Server by clicking Start, Programs, Microsoft SQL Server, Enterprise Manager. After you have done this, find the icon labeled Microsoft SQL Server in the left pane. Click the plus sign to open it and then open SQL Server Group the same way. You'll next see the name of your server followed by (Windows NT). Open this and you should see the display shown in Figure 11-1. In this figure, you see the name of the server used to make this figure, which is DBGRV101QA1.

FIGURE 11-1

Using Enterprise Manager to Display Databases on a Server

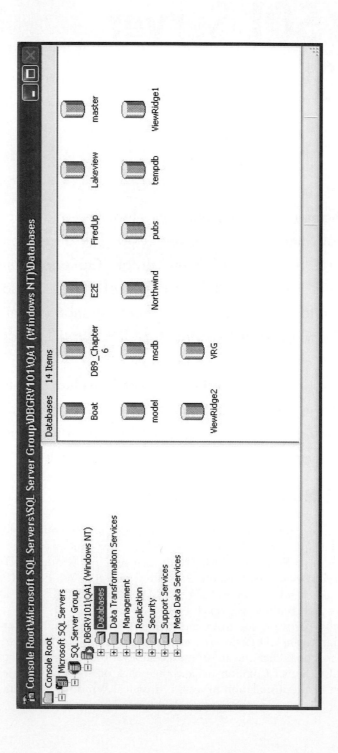

CREATING A SQL SERVER 2000 DATABASE

To create a new database, right-click Databases and select New Database. Type the name of your database (here, VRG) into the Name text box, as shown in Figure 11-2.

By default, SQL Server creates one data file and one log file for each database. You can create multiple files for both data and logs, and assign particular tables and logs to particular files and file groups. All of this is beyond the scope of this discussion, however. To learn more about it on your own, right-click Databases and select Help. In the left pane of the Help menu, search on *File Groups* in the Search text box to get started.

For now, take the default sizes and files that SQL Server offers. You can see what they are by clicking the Data Files and Transaction Log tabs.

After you create your database, open the Databases folder and then open the folder with the name of your database. Then, open Tables. Your screen should look like the one shown in Figure 11-3, but you will not yet have any user tables in it. All the tables listed in your display are system tables used by SQL Server 2000 to manage your database. By the way, *dbo* stands for database owner. That will be you if you installed SQL Server and created this database.

Creating Tables

There are two ways to create and modify tables and other SQL Server 2000 structures. The first is to write SQL code using either the CREATE or ALTER SQL statements, as we did in the last chapter for Oracle. The second is to use the graphical facilities of SQL Server Enterprise Manager. Although either method will work, CREATE statements are easier in that they do not require finding many windows and clicking and clicking. They can also be used to create database structures programmatically. Many professionals choose to create structures via SQL, but to modify them with the graphical tools.

FIGURE 11-2

Creating the VRG Database

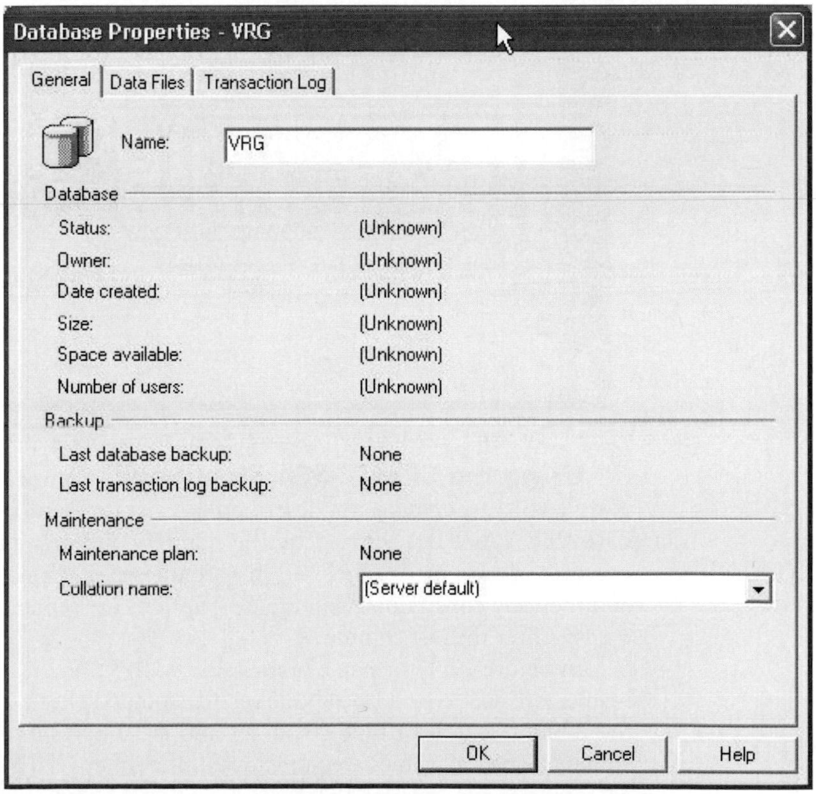

FIGURE 11–3

Tables in the VRG
Database

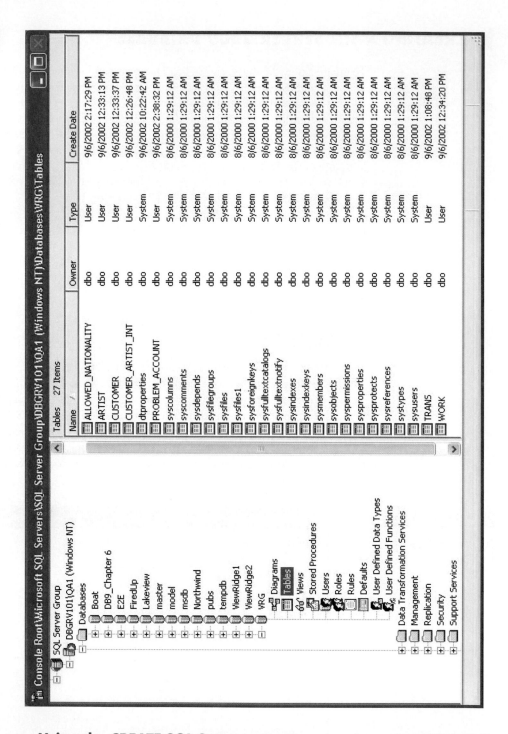

Using the CREATE SQL Statement   Figure 11-4 shows a typical SQL CRE-
ATE TABLE statement. As described in Chapter 7, such statements always begin with
CREATE TABLE, followed by the name of the new table. Next, a list of the table
columns is presented—enclosed in parentheses. Each column has a name, a data type,
and then any constraints. Column descriptions are separated by commas, but there is no
comma after the last column.

In Figure 11-4, the name of the table is CUST and it has four columns: CustomerID,
Name, AreaCode, and LocalNumber. CustomerID has type *int* and is the primary key of
the table. Name is of type character and is 30 bytes in length. Name is NOT NULL,
which means null values are not allowed. If neither NULL nor NOT NULL appears, the
column is assumed to be NULL.

FIGURE 11–4

Sample CREATE TABLE Statement for SQL Server

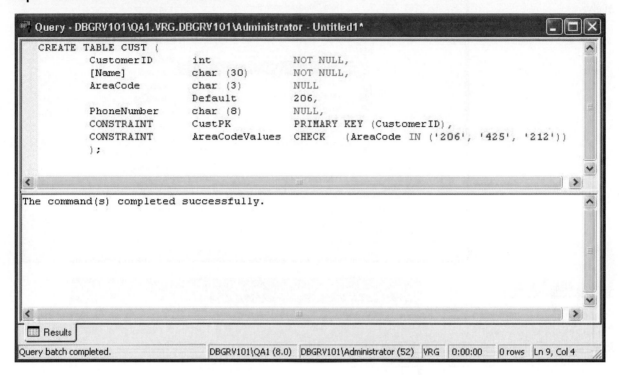

Name is enclosed in brackets as [Name]. This is necessary because *Name* is a SQL Server reserved word. If not placed in brackets, SQL Server will try to interpret *Name* as the name of one of its constructs. Hence, any time you are using a SQL Server reserved word as a user identifier, place the word in brackets. If you're not sure whether a word is reserved, place it in brackets. There is no harm in doing so.

In this example, the default value for AreaCode is defined as 206. Furthermore, the CHECK constraint limits the values of AreaCode to those listed. AreaCode values can be NULL. LocalNumber is defined as char(8) and because no indication is given about NULL or NOT NULL, the default of NULL will be used.

There are several ways to pass this CREATE statement to SQL Server. The simplest is to use the Query Analyzer. To do that, click Tools and then select the SQL Query Analyzer, as shown in Figure 11-5. Type the CREATE TABLE statement into the window and then click on the blue check mark. If your statement has syntax errors, they are reported in the pane underneath the statement. Once you have removed syntax errors, click the green right-pointing arrow and the table will be created.

To see that the table has been created, go back to the Enterprise Manager window, right-click Tables, and select Refresh. The new table should appear in the list in the right pane. Right-click the CUST table and select Design Table. You will see a display like that shown in Figure 11-6. Notice that the default of AreaCode is indeed 206 and that both AreaCode and LocalNumber are allowed to be null. Further, the primary key (denoted by the key symbol) of the table is CustomerID.

Creating the View Ridge Gallery Database

The graphical display shown in Figure 11-6 can be used to view and edit table structure. It can also be used to create tables from scratch. Just right-click Tables in the left pane of the Enterprise Manager window and select New Table. An empty grid with a format like

FIGURE 11-5

Starting the Query Analyzer

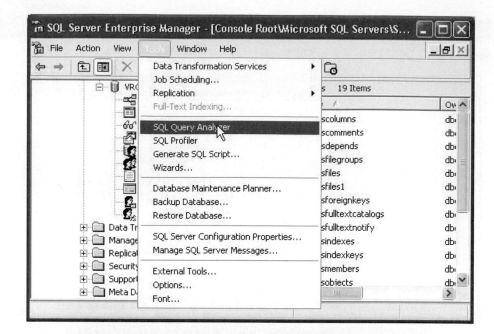

FIGURE 11-6

Columns and Properties of the CUST Table

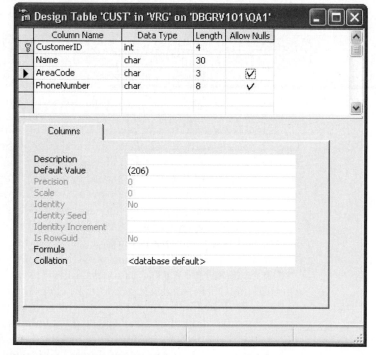

that in Figure 11-6 displays. You can define a new table by describing its columns in the rows of such a grid.

Use the Query Analyzer to Process CREATE TABLE Statements

For creating any but the simplest tables, however, the graphical tools are cumbersome. A better way to create the tables is to key CREATE TABLE statements into a text file and process that text file in the SQL Query Analyzer. Figure 11-7 shows CREATE TABLE statements for the View Ridge Gallery discussed in Chapter 7. They were keyed into a file named VRG_Create_Tables.sql and that file was opened in the Query Analyzer. In Figure 11-8, the developer has clicked the execute button, and the five tables were created.

The table name TRANSACTION was changed to TRANS in Figure 11-7. This was done because TRANSACTION is such a special word to SQL Server that even if you

FIGURE 11-7

CREATE TABLE Statements for the View Ridge Gallery

```
CREATE TABLE CUSTOMER(
        CustomerID      int             NOT NULL
                        IDENTITY (1000,1),
        Name            char(25)        NOT NULL,
        Street          char(30)        NULL,
        City            char(35)        NULL,
        State           char(2)         NULL,
        ZipPostalCode   char(9)         NULL,
        Country         char(50)        NULL,
        AreaCode        char(2)         NULL,
        PhoneNumber     char(8)         NULL,
        Email           char(100)       Null,
        CONSTRAINT      CustomerPK PRIMARY KEY (CustomerID),
        CONSTRAINT      CustomerAK1 UNIQUE (Name)
        );


CREATE TABLE ARTIST(
        ArtistID  int                   NOT NULL
                        IDENTITY (1,1),
        Name            char(25)        NOT NULL,
        Nationality     char(30)        NULL,
        Birthdate       numeric (4)     NULL,
        DeceasedDate    numeric (4)     NULL,
        CONSTRAINT      ArtistPK PRIMARY KEY (ArtistID),
        CONSTRAINT      ArtistAK1 UNIQUE (Name),
        CONSTRAINT      NationalityValues CHECK
        (Nationality IN ('Canadian', 'English', 'French', 'German', 'Mexican', 'Russian', 'Spanish', 'US')),
        CONSTRAINT      BirthValuesCheck CHECK (Birthdate < DeceasedDate),
        CONSTRAINT      ValidBirthYear CHECK (Birthdate LIKE '[1-2][0-9][0-9][0-9]'),
        CONSTRAINT      ValidDeathYear CHECK (DeceasedDate LIKE '[1-2][0-9][0-9][0-9]')
        );


CREATE TABLE CUSTOMER_ARTIST_INT(
        ArtistID  int                   NOT NULL,
        CustomerID      Int             NOT NULL,
        CONSTRAINT      CustomerArtistPK PRIMARY KEY (ArtistID, CustomerID),
        CONSTRAINT      Customer_Artist_Int_ArtistFK FOREIGN KEY (ArtistID)
                        REFERENCES ARTIST (ArtistID)
                        ON UPDATE CASCADE
                        ON DELETE CASCADE,
        CONSTRAINT      Customer_Artist_Int_CustomerFK FOREIGN KEY (CustomerID)
                        REFERENCES CUSTOMER (CustomerID)
                        on UPDATE CASCADE
                        ON DELETE CASCADE
        );


CREATE TABLE WORK (
        WorkID          int             NOT NULL
                        IDENTITY (500,1),
        Title           char(25)        NOT NULL,
        Description     varchar(1000)   NULL,
        Copy            char(8)         NOT NULL,
        ArtistID        int             NOT NULL,
        CONSTRAINT      WorkPK PRIMARY KEY (WorkID),
        CONSTRAINT      WorkAK1 UNIQUE (Title, Copy),
        CONSTRAINT      ArtistFK FOREIGN KEY(ArtistID) REFERENCES ARTIST (ArtistID)
        );
```

FIGURE 11-7

(continued)

```
CREATE TABLE TRANS (
        TransactionID     int               NOT NULL
                                            IDENTITY (100,1),
        DateAcquired      datetime          NOT NULL,
        AcquisitionPrice  Numeric (8,2)     NULL,
        PurchaseDate      datetime          NULL,
        SalesPrice        Numeric (8,2)     NULL,
        AskingPrice       Numeric (8,2)     NULL,
        CustomerID        int               NULL,
        WorkID            int               NOT NULL,
        CONSTRAINT        TransactionPK PRIMARY KEY (TransactionID),
        CONSTRAINT        SalesPriceRange CHECK ((SalesPrice > 1000) AND (SalesPrice <=200000)),
        CONSTRAINT        ValidTransDate CHECK (DateAcquired <= PurchaseDate),
        CONSTRAINT        TransactionWorkFK FOREIGN KEY(WorkID) REFERENCES WORK (WorkID),
        CONSTRAINT        TransactionCustomerFK FOREIGN KEY(CustomerID) REFERENCES CUSTOMER
                          (CustomerID)
);
```

FIGURE 11-8

Running the CREATE TABLE Statements in the Query Analyzer (Only Last Portion Visible)

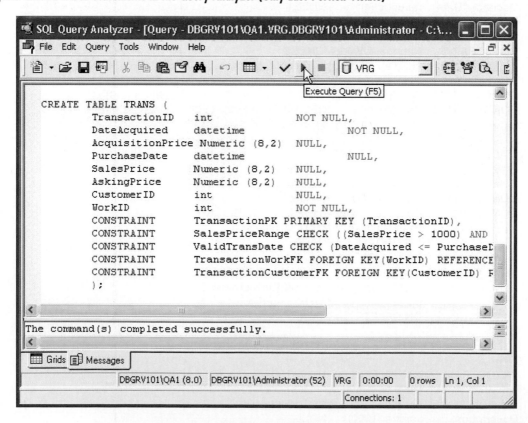

place its name in square brackets, like [TRANSACTION], SQL Server still becomes confused when executing the logic of stored procedures and triggers. Life became much simpler for this application when the table TRANSACTION was renamed to TRANS.

The SQL in Figure 11-7 has one new element: the IDENTITY constraint. This constraint is used to define a surrogate key to SQL Server. The syntax IDENTITY (m, n), means create a surrogate key with an Identity Seed of *m* and an Identity Increment of *n*. Thus, the column CustomerID will be a surrogate key with a starting value of 1000 and an increment of 1. By the way, if you are defining an IDENTITY property on an existing column in an existing table that already has data (using either the SQL ALTER command or the graphical interface), the Identity Seed will be set equal to the maximum of the seed (here *m*) and the largest column value already in that table. With this policy, SQL Server never creates a duplicate surrogate key value in a table that has existing data.

Review Database Structures in SQL Server Graphical Displays Figure 11-9 shows the structure of the ARTIST table after the CREATE TABLE statements have been processed. You can view Figure 11-9(a) by right-clicking the name ARTIST in the table list and selecting Design Table. Notice that ArtistID is an Identity column, as you would expect.

To see the constraints on the table, right-click anywhere in the white space in the table design window and select Check Constraints. Figure 11-9(b) shows the NationalityValues check constraint. Clearly, it is easier to key the constraint into SQL statements than it would be to type it as shown in this window!

Throughout this chapter, you will see dialog boxes, like the one shown in Figure 11-9(b), which have check boxes that reference something about replication. All such references refer to distributed SQL Server databases, in which data are placed in two or more databases and updates to them are coordinated in some fashion. We will not consider that topic here, so we ignore check boxes that refer to replication. You can learn more by searching on the Replication topic in the SQL Server documentation. We will also discuss it briefly in Chapter 15.

To ensure that the relationships were created correctly, click on Diagrams, New Database Diagram. A wizard appears to create a new diagram. Select the ARTIST, WORK, TRANS, CUSTOMER, and CUSTOMER_ARTIST_INT tables. The result is a diagram like that shown in Figure 11-10(a). To view the properties of a relationship, right-click the relationship line and select Properties. The properties of the TransactionWorkFK relationship are shown in Figure 11-10(b).

Entering Data You can enter data into SQL Server either by entering data into a table grid in Enterprise Manager or via INSERT statements submitted through the Query Analyzer. To do the former, right-click the table name and select Open Table, Return all rows. You can then add data by typing in the cells of the grid. To enter data via the Query Analyzer, just open it and type valid INSERT statements. For the examples in this chapter, all the data from Figure 7-5 were entered into SQL Sever using INSERT statements in the Query Analyzer.

Creating Views Figure 11-11(a) shows a CREATE VIEW statement for creating the CustomerInterests view discussed in Chapter 7. This statement was entered into the Query Analyzer window, and the view was created by clicking the green arrow. The view can be opened in Enterprise Manager by clicking views and right-clicking CustomerInterests, Design View. The graphical display shown in Figure 11-11(b) is shown. Observe that the aliases for the table names appear in the table design (top) pane. Also note that the aliases for the column names appear in the second column of the view definition rows in the middle pane of the form.

Views can be created using SQL syntax or they can be created using this form by right-clicking Views and selecting *New View*. Again, the best strategy is often to create the views using SQL, but to modify them, if necessary, by using the graphical tools.

Indexes

As stated, indexes are special data structures that are created to improve database performance (see Appendix A). SQL Server automatically creates an index on all primary and foreign keys. The developer can also direct SQL Server to create an index on other columns that are frequently used in WHERE clauses or on columns that are used for sorting data when sequentially processing a table for queries and reports.

FIGURE 11–9

The Resulting ARTIST Table (a) Columns and Properties and (b) Constraints

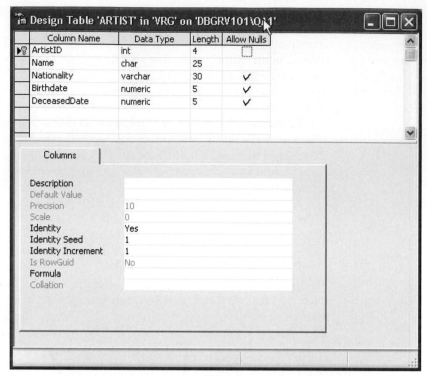

(a)

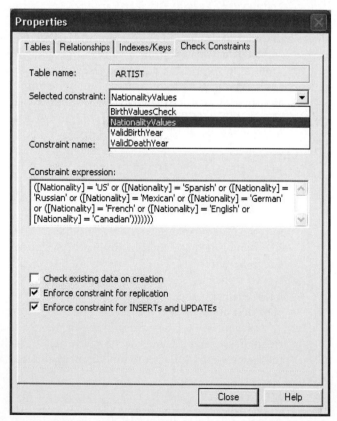

(b)

FIGURE 11-10

Relationship Diagram
(a) Table Relationships
and (b) Properties of
the TransactionWorkFK
Relationship

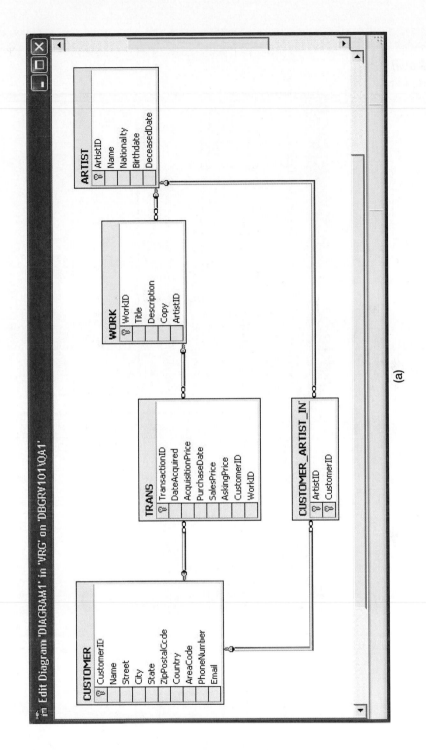

(a)

FIGURE 11-10

(continued)

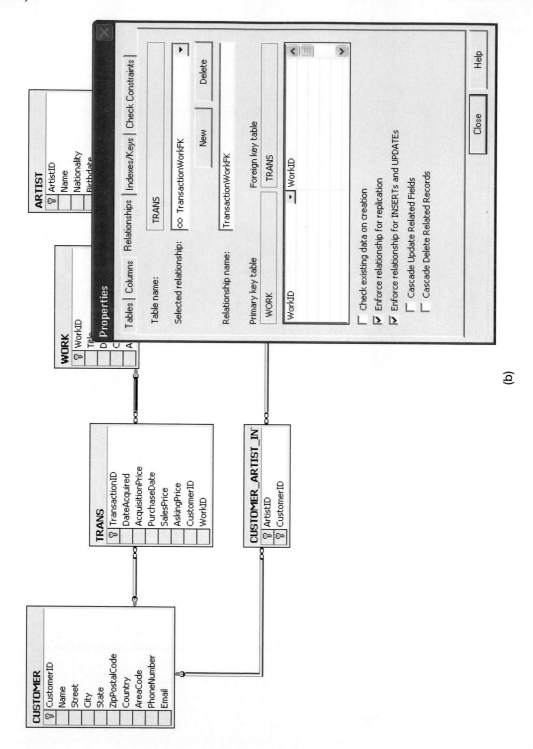

(b)

FIGURE 11–11

Creating a View (a) The **CREATE VIEW** Statement for CustomerInterests and (b) Graphical Display of CustomerInterests

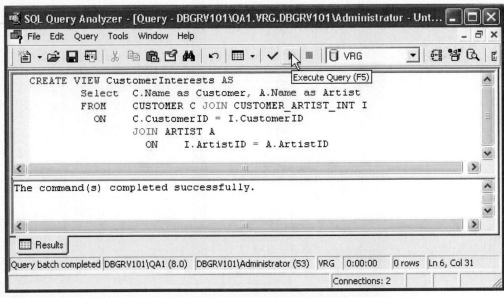

(a)

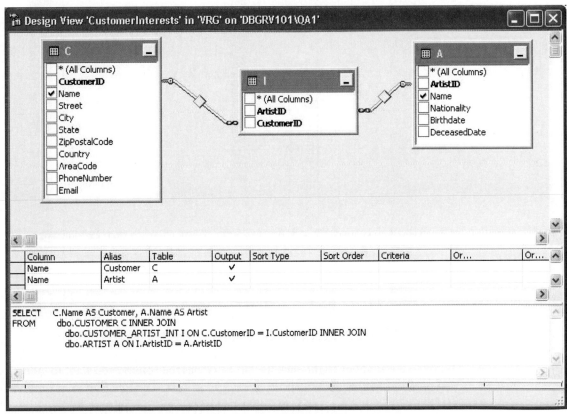

(b)

FIGURE 11-12

Creating an Index

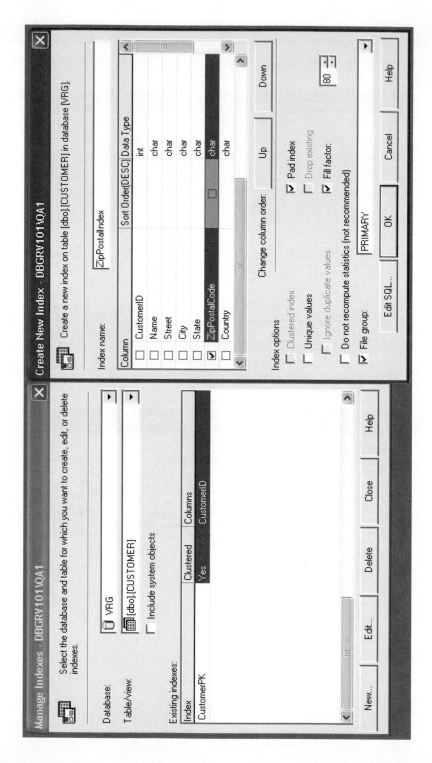

To create an index, right-click the table that has the column you want to index, click All Tasks, and then click Manage Indexes. You will see the dialog box shown in the left portion of Figure 11-12. Click New and you will be shown the dialog box in the right portion of this figure. The developer is creating an index on the ZipPostalCode column of the CUSTOMER table. The index, named ZipPostalIndex, is to be padded, filled to 80%, and assigned to the PRIMARY File Group. Padding causes space to be left open for inserts in all levels of the index except the bottom one. Filling refers to the amount of empty space left in the bottom level of the index. See Appendix A and the SQL Server documentation for more information about these choices.

FIGURE 11–13

SQL for Creating an
Index

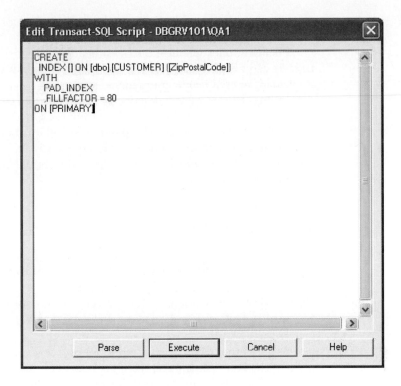

Click Edit SQL in this dialog box and you will see the dialog box shown in Figure 11-13. This shows the SQL statement that could be entered via the SQL Analyzer to create the index.

SQL Server supports two kinds of indexes: clustered and nonclustered. With a clustered index, the data are stored in the bottom level of the index and in the same order as that index. With a nonclustered index, the bottom level of an index does not contain data; it contains pointers to the data. Because rows can be sorted only in one physical order at a time, only one clustered index is allowed per table. Clustered indexes are faster than nonclustered indexes for retrieval. They are normally faster for updating as well, but not if there are many updates in the same spot in the middle of the relation. Again, see Appendix A and the SQL Server documentation for information about clustered and nonclustered indices.

▷ APPLICATION LOGIC

There are many ways of processing a SQL Server database from an application. One is to create application code using a language such as C#, C++, Visual Basic, Java, or some other programming language and invoke SQL Server DBMS commands from those programs. The modern way to do that is to use a library of object classes, create objects that access database structures, and process those objects by setting object properties and invoking object methods. You will see examples of such processing when we discuss ADO in Chapter 12, ADO.NET in Chapter 13, and Java Server Pages in Chapter 14.

Another way of processing a SQL Server database is to create stored procedures, as described in Chapter 7. These stored procedures can then be invoked from application programs or from Web pages using languages such as VBScript or JScript. Stored procedures can also be executed from the SQL Query Analyzer. This should be done only when the procedures are being developed and tested, however. As described in Chapter 9, for security reasons, no one other than authorized members of the DBA staff should be allowed to interactively process an operational database.

A third means of processing a SQL Server database is to save groups of database commands in text files. Such files are then processed from the SQL Query Analyzer. For security, such files should only be used during application development and test—never on an operational database.

Finally, application logic can be embedded in triggers. As you learned in Chapter 7, triggers can be used for validity checking, to set default values, to update views, and to implement referential integrity actions.

In this chapter, we will describe and illustrate two stored procedures. Here, we will test those procedures by invoking them from the Query Analyzer. Again, this should be done only during development and test. You will learn how to invoke those stored procedures from application code in Chapters 13–15. We will also describe four triggers, one for each of the four trigger uses. These triggers will be invoked by SQL Server when the specified actions occur.

Stored Procedures

With SQL Server 2000, stored procedures must be written in TRANSACT/SQL, or T/SQL as it is sometimes called. As of Fall, 2003, SQL Server stored procedures cannot be written in any of the .NET languages such as C# or VB.NET. Supposedly, this will change with future editions of SQL Server; such editions may be announced by the time you read this. If so, use a language such as C# or VB.Net. They are much better languages than T/SQL.

As with other database structures, you can write a stored procedure in a text file and process the commands using the Query Analyzer. There is one little gotcha to know, however. The first time you create a stored procedure in a text file, start the procedure with the words "CREATE PROCEDURE…" Subsequently, if you change the procedure, substitute the words "ALTER PROCEDURE…" Otherwise, you will get an error message saying that the procedure already exists when you execute the modified procedure code.

You can also create a stored procedure within the Enterprise Manager by right-clicking Stored Procedures and selecting New Stored Procedure. If you do this, SQL Server takes care of the CREATE/ALTER problem described previously. However, you cannot save your stored procedure until you have removed all of the syntax errors. This can be unhandy, so using a text file with the Query Analyzer is generally easier.

The Customer_Insert STORED PROCEDURE Figure 11-14 illustrates a stored procedure that stores data for a new customer and connects that customer to all artists having a particular nationality. Four parameters are input to the procedure: @NewName, @NewAreaCode, @NewPhone, and @Nationality. As you can see, parameters and variables in TRANSACT-SQL are preceded by @ signs. The first three parameters are the new customer data and the fourth one is the nationality of the artists for which the new customer has an interest.

The first task performed by this stored procedure is to determine whether the customer already exists. If the count of the first SELECT statement is greater than 0, a row for that customer already exists. In this case, nothing is done, and the stored procedure prints an error message and exits. This error message, by the way, is visible in the Query Analyzer, but it generally would not be visible to application programs that invoked this procedure. Instead, a parameter or other facility would need to be used to return the

FIGURE 11–14

Customer_Insert Stored Procedure

```
CREATE PROCEDURE Customer_Insert
                @NewName            char(50),
                @NewAreaCode        char (5),
                @NewPhone           char (8),
                @Nationality     char(25)
AS

DECLARE @Count      as smallint
DECLARE @Aid        as int
DECLARE @Cid        as int

/* Check to see if customer already exists */
SELECT          @Count = Count (*)
FROM            dbo.CUSTOMER
WHERE           [Name]=@NewName AND AreaCode=@NewAreaCode AND Pho

IF @Count > 0
        BEGIN
                PRINT 'Customer Already Exists -- No Action Taken'
                RETURN
        END

/* Add new Customer data */
INSERT INTO     dbo.CUSTOMER
                ([Name], AreaCode, PhoneNumber)
                VALUES
                (@NewName, @NewAreaCode, @NewPhone)

/* Get new surrogate key value  */
SELECT          @Cid = CustomerID
FROM            dbo.CUSTOMER
WHERE           [Name]=@NewName AND AreaCode=@NewAreaCode AND Pho

/* Now create intersection record for each appropriate artist */
DECLARE Artist_Cursor CURSOR FOR
        SELECT          ArtistID
        FROM            dbo.ARTIST
        WHERE           Nationality = @Nationality

/* process each Artist of specified nationality */
OPEN Artist_Cursor
FETCH NEXT FROM Artist_Cursor INTO @Aid
        WHILE @@FETCH_STATUS = 0
        BEGIN
                INSERT INTO dbo.[CUSTOMER_ARTIST_INT]
                        (ArtistID,CustomerID)
                        VALUES (@Aid, @Cid)
                FETCH NEXT FROM Artist_Cursor INTO @Aid
        END

CLOSE Artist_Cursor
DEALLOCATE Artist_Cursor
```

error message back to the user via the application program. We will consider this issue in later chapters.

Next, the procedure inserts the new data into dbo.CUSTOMER and then a new value of CustomerID is read into the variable @Cid.

To create the appropriate intersection table rows, a cursor is opened on a SQL Statement that obtains all ARTIST rows where Nationality equals the parameter @Nationality. The cursor is then processed in the WHILE loop and new values are inserted into the intersection table CUSTOMER_ARTIST_INT. The FETCH statement moves the cursor to the next row.

FIGURE 11-15

Running the
Customer_Insert
Stored Procedure from
the Query Analyzer

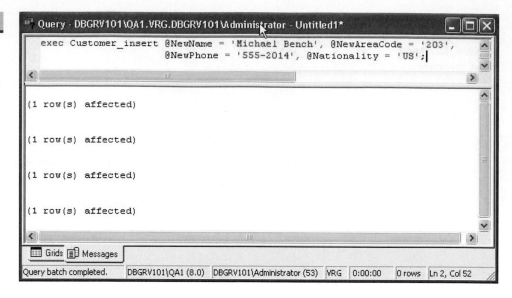

Figure 11-15 shows how to invoke this stored procedure using the SQL Query Analyzer to add a new customer having an interest in U.S. artists. Parameters are passed with the values shown. Figure 11-16 shows database data after the stored procedure has run. Customer Michael Bench has been added to the CUSTOMER table and assigned CustomerID 1058. Note that there are three U.S. artists, and that a row for each of them has been inserted into the CUSTOMER_ARTIST_INT table for CustomerID of 1058.

The NewCustomerWithTransaction STORED PROCEDURE A stored procedure that inserts data for a new customer and records a purchase is shown in Figure 11-17. This procedure receives seven parameters having data about the new customer and about the customer's purchase.

The first action is to see whether the customer already exists; if so, the procedure exits with an error message. If the customer does not exist, this procedure then starts a transaction. Recall from Chapter 9 that transactions ensure that all of the database activity is committed atomically; either all of the updates occur or none of them do. The transaction begins and the new customer row is inserted. The new value of CustomerID is obtained, as shown previously. Next, the procedure checks to determine whether the ArtistID, WorkID, and TransactionID are valid. If any of them are invalid, the transaction is rolled back.

If all of these are valid, an UPDATE statement updates PurchaseDate, Price, and CustomerID in the appropriate TRANS row. PurchaseDate is set to system date (via the system-supplied GETDATE() function), SalesPrice is set to the value of @Price, and CustomerID is set to the value of @Cid. Finally, a row is added to CUSTOMER_ARTIST_INT to record the customer's interest in this artist. If everything proceeds normally to this point, the transaction is committed.

FIGURE 11–16

Results from Figure 11-15

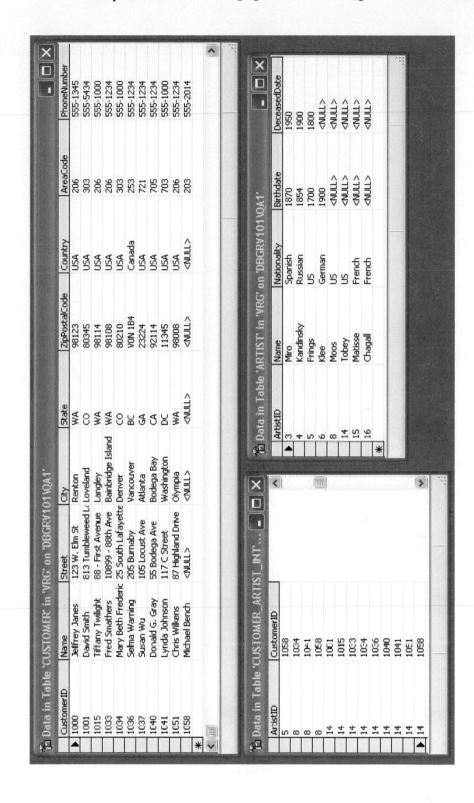

FIGURE 11–17

NewCustomerWithTransaction Stored Procedure

```
CREATE PROCEDURE dbo.NewCustomerWithTransaction
                @NewName char(50), @NewAreaCode char (3), @NewPhone char (8),
                @ArtistName char(50), @WorkTitle char(50), @WorkCopy char (10),
                @Price smallmoney
AS

DECLARE        @Count as smallint,
               @Aid as int,
               @Cid as int,
               @Wid as int,
               @Tid as int

SELECT         @Count = Count (*)
FROM           dbo.CUSTOMER
WHERE          [Name]=@NewName AND AreaCode=@NewAreaCode AND PhoneNumber=@NewPhone

IF @Count > 0
        BEGIN  PRINT 'Customer Already Exists -- No Action Taken'
               RETURN
        END

BEGIN TRANSACTION  /* Start transaction rollback everything if cannot complete it. */

INSERT INTO    dbo.CUSTOMER
               ([Name], AreaCode, PhoneNumber)
               VALUES (@NewName, @NewAreaCode, @NewPhone)

Select         @Cid = CustomerID
FROM           dbo.CUSTOMER
WHERE          [Name]=@NewName AND AreaCode=@NewAreaCode AND PhoneNumber=@NewPhone

SELECT         @Aid = ArtistID
FROM           dbo.ARTIST
WHERE          Name=@ArtistName
If @Aid IS NULL   /* Invalid Artist ID */
        BEGIN
               Print 'Artist ID not valid'
               ROLLBACK
               RETURN
        END

SELECT         @Wid = WorkID
FROM           dbo.[WORK]
WHERE          ArtistID = @Aid AND Title = @WorkTitle AND Copy = @WorkCopy
If @Wid IS NULL  /* Invalid Work ID */
        BEGIN
               Print 'Work ID not valid'
               ROLLBACK
               RETURN
        END

SELECT         @Tid = TransactionID
FROM           dbo.[TRANS]
WHERE          WorkID=@Wid AND SalesPrice IS NULL
If @Tid IS NULL /*Invalid Transaction ID */
        BEGIN
               Print 'No valid transaction record'
               ROLLBACK
               RETURN
        END

UPDATE         dbo.[TRANS] /* ALL is OK, update TRANS row */
SET            PurchaseDate = GETDATE(), SalesPrice = @Price, CustomerID = @Cid
WHERE          TransactionID=@Tid

INSERT INTO dbo.[CUSTOMER_ARTIST_INT] /* Create interest for this artist */
        (CustomerID, ArtistID)
        Values (@Cid, @Aid)
COMMIT
```

FIGURE 11–18

Running the NewCustomerWithTransaction Stored Procedure from the Query Analyzer

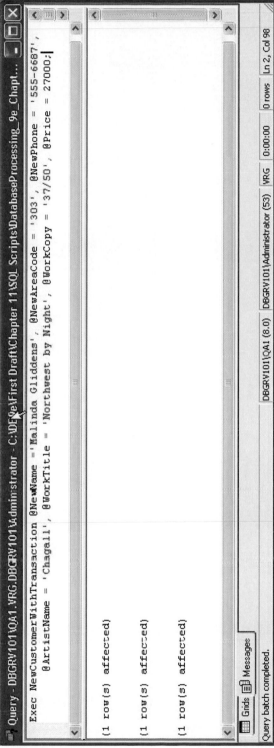

Figure 11-18 shows the invocation of this procedure using sample data, and Figure 11-19 shows the results in the database. The new customer was assigned CustomerID 1059, and this id was stored in the CustomerID foreign key column of TRANS, as required. PurchaseDate and SalesPrice were also set appropriately. Note the new row in the intersection table that records customer 1059's interest in artist 16, as required.

FIGURE 11–19

Results from Figure 11-18

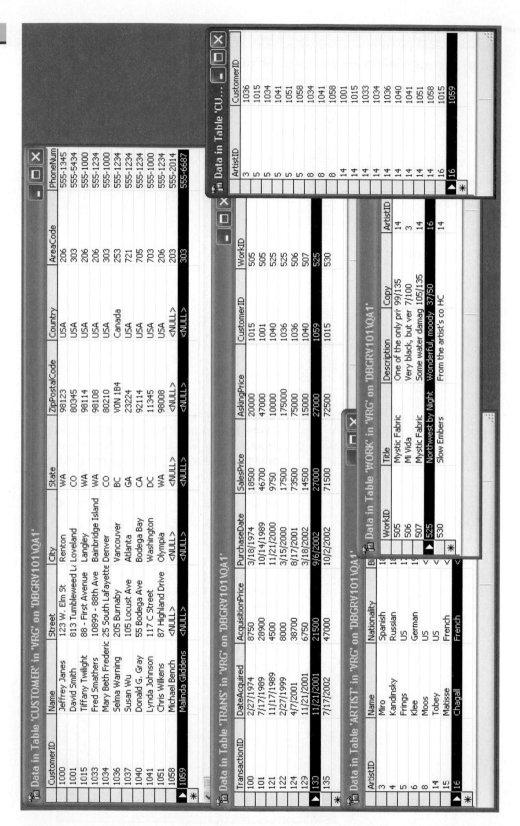

Triggers

SQL Server supports INSTEAD OF and AFTER triggers only. There is no SQL Server support for BEFORE triggers. A table may have one or more AFTER triggers for insert, update, and delete actions; AFTER triggers may not be assigned to views. A view or table may have at most one INSTEAD OF trigger for each triggering action of insert, update, or delete.

In SQL Server, triggers can roll back the transactions that caused them to be fired. When a trigger executes a ROLLBACK command, all work done by the transaction that caused the trigger to be fired will be rolled back. If the trigger contains instructions after the ROLLBACK command, those instructions will be executed. However, any instructions in the transaction after the statement that caused the trigger to be fired will not be executed.

For insert and update triggers, the new values for every column of the table being processed will be stored in a pseudo-table named *inserted*. If, for example, a new row is being added to the ARTIST table, the pseudo-table *inserted* will have four columns: Name, Nationality, Birthdate, and DeceasedDate. Similarly, for update and delete commands, the old values for every column of the table being updated or deleted will be stored in the pseudo-table named *deleted*. You will see how to use these pseudo-tables in the examples that follow.

The next four sections illustrate four triggers for each of the trigger functions described in Chapter 7. You can create these triggers by keying them into a text file (using CREATE TRIGGER or ALTER TRIGGER as the first statement) or by right-clicking the table name and selecting All Tasks/Manage Triggers. In the latter case, a window will appear, into which you can key the trigger. You cannot save your code in this window, however, until there are no syntax errors.

A Trigger for Enforcing a Business Rule   View Ridge Gallery keeps a list of customer problem accounts; these are customers who have either not paid promptly or who have presented other problems to the gallery. When a customer who is on the problem list is entered into the database, the gallery wants the insert or update of the customer data to be rolled back and a message displayed.

To enforce this policy, the gallery keeps the Name, AreaCode, and PhoneNumber of problem customers in a table named PROBLEM_ACCOUNT. When customer data are inserted or updated, a trigger determines whether the new or changed customer data reside in the PROBLEM_ACCOUNT table. If so, the insert or update is rolled back and a message is displayed.

The CheckForProblemAccount trigger in Figure 11-20 enforces this policy. Although this code does not directly specify that this is an AFTER trigger, we know that it is one because SQL Server does not have BEFORE triggers and because the phrase INSTEAD OF is not included in the trigger heading.

The code in Figure 11-20 tries to join the new values in the *inserted* table to any row in PROBLEM_ACCOUNT. If any results are returned from the join, the new or updated customer does exist in the PROBLEM_ACCOUNT table. In this case, the transaction should be rolled back and the warning message printed.

This trigger uses the system function @@rowCount, which contains the number of rows processed in the preceding T/SQL statement. Its value must be checked immediately after the statement is executed or saved in a variable to be checked later. Here, the trigger immediately checks the value of @@rowCount.

If @@RowCount is zero, the new or changed customer data is not in PROBLEM_ACCOUNT and nothing need be done. If, however, @@rowCount is positive, the inserted or changed data do reside in PROBLEM_ACCOUNT, and the change must be rolled back and the message displayed.

(By the way, in the prior two stored procedures, the @@rowCount function could have been used instead of counting rows into the variable @rowCount. This was not done so that you can learn alternative ways of obtaining row count data.)

To verify that this trigger works, the row 'Nichole Not Pay', '213', '555-1234' was inserted into the PROBLEM_ACCOUNT table. Then, the INSERT statement shown in Figure 11-21 was executed. As you can see, the proper message was printed. The customer table was also checked to ensure that the insert was not made (not shown here).

FIGURE 11–20

CheckForProblemAccount Trigger

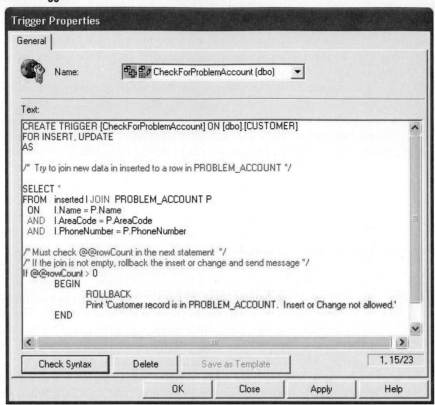

FIGURE 11–21

Testing the CheckForProblemAccount Trigger

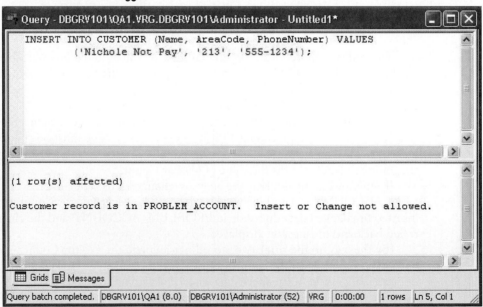

Using a table of valid or invalid values is more flexible and dynamic than placing such values in a CHECK constraint. For example, consider the CHECK constraint on Nationality values in the ARTIST table. If the gallery manager wants to expand the nationality of allowed artists, he or she will have to change the CHECK constraint using the ALTER TABLE statement. In reality, the gallery manager will have to hire a consultant to change that constraint.

A better approach is to place the allowed values of Nationality in a table, say ALLOWED_NATIONALITY. Then, write a trigger like that shown in Figure 11-20 to enforce the constraint that new values of Nationality exist in ALLOWED_NATIONALITY. When the gallery owner wants to change the allowed artists, he or she would simply add or remove values in the ALLOWED_NATIONALITY table.

A Trigger for Setting Default Values   Triggers can be used to set default values that are more complex than those that can be set with the Default constraint on a column definition. For example, View Ridge has a pricing policy that says that the default AskingPrice of a work of art depends on whether the art has been in the gallery before. If not, the default AskingPrice is twice the AcquisitionPrice. If the work has been in the gallery before, the default price is the larger of twice the AcquisitionPrice or the AcquisitionPrice plus the average net gain of the work in the past.

The AFTER trigger shown in Figure 11-22 implements this pricing policy. First, the new values of WorkID and AcquisitionPrice are obtained from *inserted*. Then, a SELECT FROM dbo.TRANS is executed to count the number of rows with the given WorkID. The variable @countPriorRows is set to @@rowCount minus one because this

FIGURE 11–22

SetAskingPrice Trigger

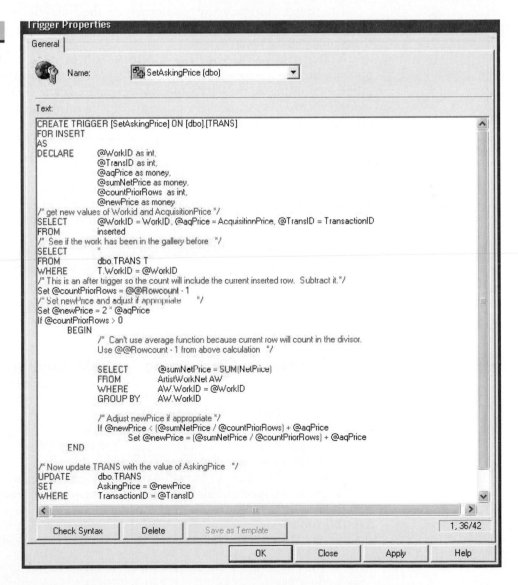

is an AFTER trigger, and the new row will already be in the database. Hence, the expression (@@rowCount-1) is the correct number of qualifying TRANS rows that were in the database prior to the insert.

@newPrice is then set to twice the AcquisitionPrice; it will be adjusted below, if necessary. If @countPriorRows is greater than zero, there were TRANS rows for this work in the database, and the ArtistWorkNet view (see page 241) is used to obtain the sum of the NetPrice. The average built-in function cannot be used because it will compute the average using @@rowCount rather than @countPriorRows. Next, the current value of @newPrice is compared to the average net gain plus the acquisition price. If less, @newPrice is recomputed to be the average net gain plus the acquisition price. Finally, an update is made to the just inserted row using the computed value of @newPrice for AskingPrice.

To test this trigger, we need to check the following three cases:

> The work has not been in the gallery before
> The work has been in the gallery before, but the average net plus acquisition price is less than or equal to twice the acquisition price
> The work has been in the gallery before but the average net plus acquisition price is greater than twice the acquisition price

This testing will be left as an exercise.

This trigger provides useful functionality for the gallery. It saves the gallery personnel considerable manual work in implementing their pricing policy and likely improves the accuracy of the results as well.

A Trigger for Updating a View   Chapter 7 discussed the problem of updating views. One such problem concerns updating views created via joins; it is normally not possible for the DBMS to know how to update tables that underlie the join. However, there is sometimes application-specific knowledge that can be used to determine how to interpret a request to update a joined view.

Consider the CustomerInterests view shown in Figure 11-11. It contains rows of CUSTOMER and ARTIST joined over their intersection table. CUSTOMER.Name is given the alias Customer, and ARTIST.Name is given the alias Artist.

A request to change the name of a customer in CustomerInterests can be interpreted as a request to change the name of the underlying CUSTOMER table. Such a request, however, can be processed only if the value of Name is unique in Customer. If not, the request cannot be processed.

The INSTEAD OF trigger shown in Figure 11-23 implements this logic. First, the new and old values of the Customer column in CustomerInterests are obtained. Then, a correlated subquery with EXISTS is used to determine whether the old value of CUSTOMER.Name was unique. If so, the name is changed; otherwise, no update is made.

This trigger needs to be tested against cases in which the name is unique and in which the name is not unique. Figure 11-24 shows the case in which the name was not unique; notice that no rows were updated in the Query Analyzer results pane.

A Trigger for Performing a Referential Integrity Action
According to the database design in Figure 7-4, the WORK table in the View Ridge database has a required TRANSACTION child. This means that whenever a WORK is inserted, a TRANSACTION child must be inserted as well.

Enforcing such referential integrity constraints is difficult. Please see the discussion about this topic in the Oracle chapter on pages 358 and 359. The remarks on those pages pertain to SQL Server as well as they do to Oracle.

Figures 11-25(a) and (b) show the pair of triggers to create the TRANS row on WORK insert and then to remove it when (if) the application creates the TRANS row after creating the WORK row. The trigger in Figure 11-25(a) creates the default TRANS row. It first obtains the new value of WorkID from *inserted*; then it checks for an available row in TRANS. There should be no such row because the transaction that created

FIGURE 11–23

CustomerNameUpdate Trigger

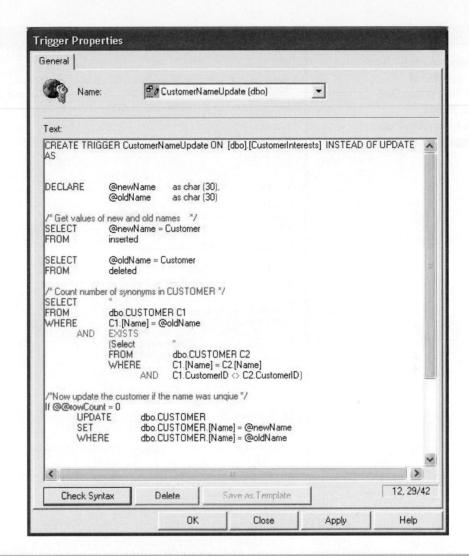

FIGURE 11–24

Testing the CustomerNameUpdate Trigger

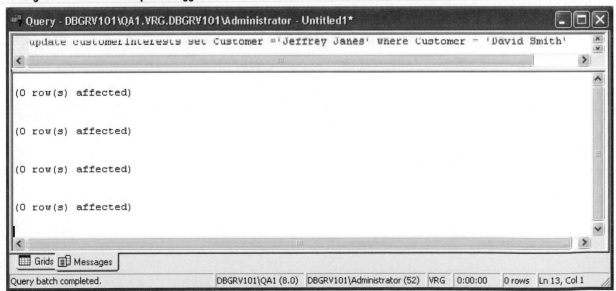

FIGURE 11–25

Triggers for Enforcing a
Required Child
(a) EnforceTransChild
Trigger and
(b) RemoveDupTrans
Trigger

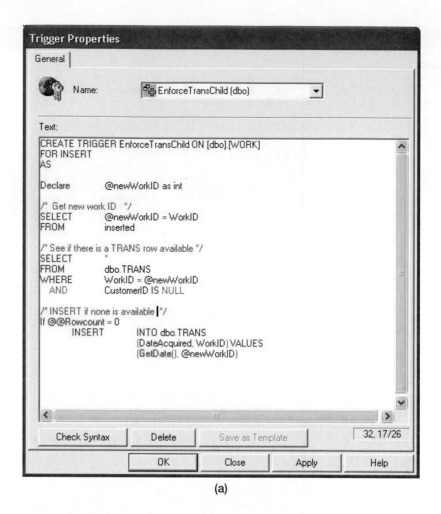

(a)

this WORK row has not yet had an opportunity to create the TRANS row. Then, assuming that @@rowCount is zero, it creates the default TRANS row.

The trigger in Figure 11-25(b) is based on insert of TRANS. The purpose of this trigger is to remove the default TRANS row when the application creates a TRANS row. If the application never creates such a row, this trigger will never be fired and the default row will be used to store transaction data for the inserted WORK.

Figures 11-26(a) and (b) show the results of the trigger on a WORK insertion. The new rows were added to WORK and TRANS, as you would expect. To complete the testing, it is necessary to verify that the TRANS trigger will remove this default row if a TRANS row is created for this work.

As mentioned in Chapter 10, another more pleasing solution for enforcing a required child constraint is to require the application to create new works through a WORK/TRANSACTION view. The view would have the necessary values for WORK and TRANSACTION tables, and those values would be used to insert new WORK and TRANSACTION rows in the trigger. In that case, no direct insert of WORK or TRANSACTION should be allowed. See Project H at the end of the chapter.

FIGURE 11-25

(continued)

(b)

FIGURE 11-26

Testing the Trigger in Figure 11-25(a) (a) Insert from the Query Analyzer and (b) Resulting WORK and TRANS Tables

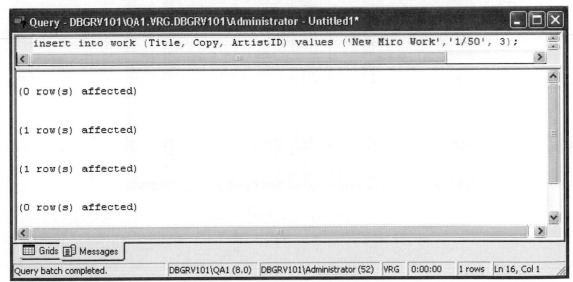

(a)

FIGURE 11-26

(continued)

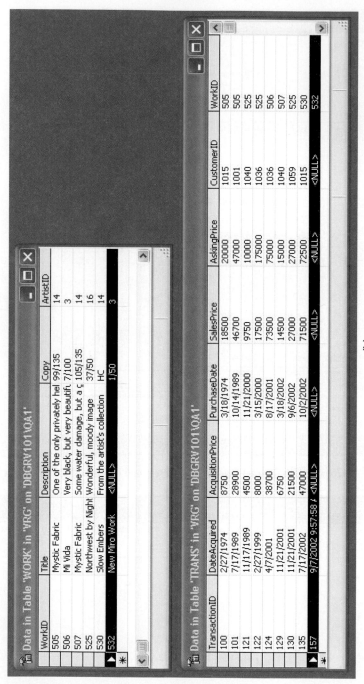

(b)

▶ CONCURRENCY CONTROL

SQL Server 2000 provides a comprehensive set of capabilities to control concurrent processing. There are many choices and options available, and the resulting behavior is determined by the interaction of three factors: transaction isolation level, cursor concurrency setting, and locking hints provided in the SELECT clause. Locking behavior is also dependent on whether the cursor is processed as part of a transaction, whether the SELECT statement is part of a cursor, and whether update commands occur inside of transactions or independently.

In this section, we will just describe the basics. See the SQL Server 2000 documentation for more information.

With SQL Server, developers do not place explicit locks. Instead, developers declare the concurrency control behavior they want, and SQL Server determines where to place the locks. Locks are applied on rows, pages, keys, indexes, tables, and even on the entire database. SQL Server determines what level of lock to use, and may promote or demote a lock level while processing. It also determines when to place the lock and when to release it, depending on the declarations made by the developer.

Transaction Isolation Level

Figure 11-27 summarizes the concurrency control options. The broadest level of settings is **transaction isolation level.** Options for it are listed in ascending level of restriction in the first row of Figure 11-27. These four options are the four you studied in Chapter 9; they are the SQL-92 standard levels. Note that with SQL Server, it is possible to make dirty reads by setting the isolation level to READ UNCOMMITTED. READ COMMITTED is the default isolation level.

The next most restrictive level is REPEATABLE READ, which means SQL Server places and holds locks on all rows that are read. This means that no other user can change or delete a row that has been read until the transaction commits or aborts. Rereading the cursor may, however, result in phantom reads.

The most strict isolation level is SERIALIZABLE. With it, SQL Server places a range lock on the rows that have been read. This ensures that no read data can be changed or deleted, and that no new rows can be inserted in the range to cause phantom reads. This level is the most expensive to enforce and should only be used when absolutely required.

FIGURE 11-27

Concurrency Options with SQL Server 2000

Type	Scope	Options
Transaction Isolation Level	Connection—all transactions	READ UNCOMMITTED READ COMMITTED (default) REPEATABLE READ SERIALIZABLE
Cursor Concurrency	Cursor	READ_ONLY OPTIMISTIC SCROLL_LOCK
Locking Hints	SELECT	READCOMMITTED READUNCOMMITTED REPEATABLEREAD SERIALIZABLE NOLOCK HOLDLOCK and others ...

An example TRANSACT-SQL statement to set the isolation level to, say, REPEAT-ABLE READ is the following:

SET TRANSACTION ISOLATION LEVEL REPEATABLE READ

This statement could be issued anyplace TRANSACT-SQL is allowed, prior to any other database activity.

Cursor Concurrency

The second way in which the developer can declare locking characteristics is with cursor concurrency. Possibilities are read-only, optimistic, and pessimistic—here called SCROLL_LOCK. As described in Chapter 9, with optimistic locking, no lock is obtained until the user updates the data. At that point, if the data have been changed since it was read, the update is refused. Of course, the application program must specify what to do when such a refusal occurs.

SCROLL_LOCK is a version of pessimistic locking. With it, an update lock is placed on a row when the row is read. If the cursor is opened within a transaction, the lock is held until the transaction commits or rolls back. If the cursor is outside of a transaction, the lock is dropped when the next row is read. Recall from Chapter 9 that an update lock blocks another update lock, but does not block a shared lock. Thus, other connections can read the row if they use shared locks.

The default cursor concurrency setting depends on the cursor type (see Chapter 9). It is read-only for static and forward only cursors, and is optimistic for dynamic and key-set cursors.

Cursor concurrency is set with the DECLARE CURSOR statement. An example to declare a dynamic, SCROLL_LOCK cursor on all rows of the TRANS table is as follows:

DECLARE   MY_CURSOR CURSOR DYNAMIC SCROLL_LOCKS

FOR

     SELECT   *

     FROM   dbo.TRANS

Locking Hints

Locking behavior can be further modified by providing locking hints in the WITH parameter of the FROM clause in SELECT statements. Figure 11-27 lists several of the locking hints available with SQL Server. The first four hints override transaction isolation level; the next two influence the type of lock issued.

Consider the following statements:

SET TRANSACTION ISOLATION LEVEL REPEATABLE READ

DECLARE MY_CURSOR CURSOR DYNAMIC SCROLL_LOCKS

FOR

     SELECT   *

     FROM   dbo.TRANS WITH READUNCOMMITTED NOLOCK

Without the locking hints, the cursor MY_CURSOR would have REPEATABLE READ isolation and would issue update locks on all rows read. The locks would be held until the transaction committed. With the locking hints, the isolation level for this cursor becomes READ UNCOMMITTED. Furthermore, the specification of NOLOCK changes this cursor from DYNAMIC to READ_ONLY.

Consider another example:

```
SET TRANSACTION ISOLATION LEVEL REPEATABLE READ
DECLARE MY_CURSOR CURSOR DYNAMIC SCROLL_LOCKS
FOR
      SELECT      *
      FROM        dbo.TRANS WITH HOLDLOCK
```

Here, the locking hint will cause SQL Server to hold update locks on all rows read until the transaction commits. The effect is to change the transaction isolation level for this cursor from REPEATABLE READ to SERIALIZABLE.

In general, the beginner is advised not to provide locking hints. Rather, until you have become an expert, set the isolation level and cursor concurrency to appropriate values for your transactions and cursors and leave it at that.

► SECURITY

We discussed security in general terms in Chapter 9. Here, we will summarize how those general ideas pertain to SQL Server security. You can find more information about securing SQL Server by searching on the term *SQL Server Security* at the Web address **msdn.microsoft.com**.

SQL Server Security Settings

Figure 11-28 shows the form that is used to define general SQL Server policies. You can access this form by right-clicking the name of your server in the Enterprise Manager. Select the Security tab, as has been done in Figure 11-28.

As shown, SQL Server provides two modes of authentication. With Windows only security, the authentication is provided by the Windows operating system. The user

FIGURE 11-28

SQL Server Security Properties

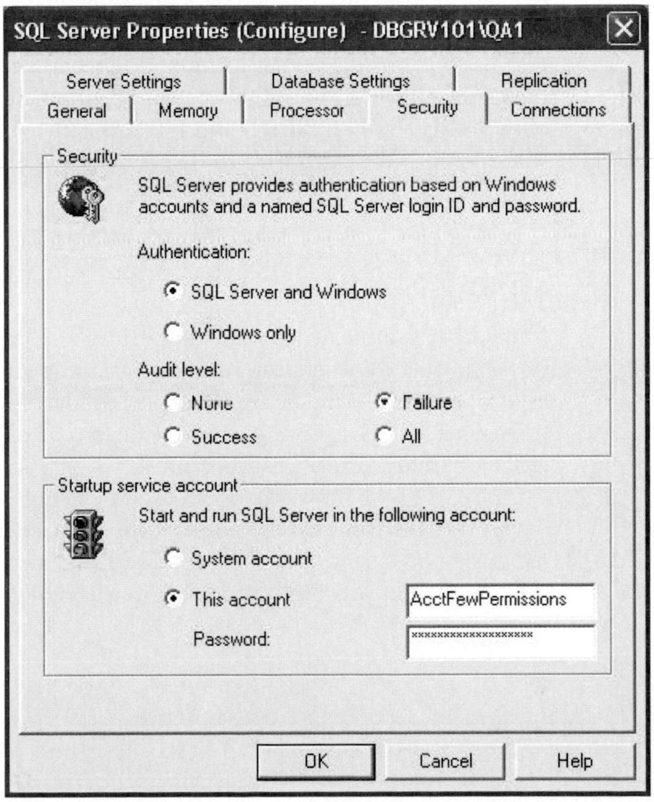

name used during sign on to Windows will be passed to SQL Server as the SQL Server user name. If both SQL Server and Windows security is selected, SQL Server will accept either the Windows-authenticated user name or it will perform its own authentication by presenting a sign-on dialog box to the user. This authentication mode is sometimes called *mixed security.*

Better security occurs if Windows only authentication is selected. There are, however, older programs such as ERWin that require SQL Server authentication. If SQL Server is to work with those programs, mixed security must be selected, as shown here.

Observe, too, that authentication failure attempts are to be logged. As stated in Chapter 9, DBA personnel should examine this log regularly for suspicious activity.

Finally, according to Figure 11-28, SQL Server is to be started in the windows account AcctFewPermissions. As the name of this account implies, this account was defined with the fewest operating system permissions needed to run SQL Server. By running SQL Server on such an account, if an intruder were to obtain control of SQL Server, he or she would have the least possible operating system authority. Never run an operational SQL Server on an account in the Windows Administrator group.

Security on Database Accounts

Figure 11-29 shows the forms used to set up security permissions for a SQL Server user account. You can access this form by right-clicking Security/Logins and selecting New Login. As shown in Figure 11-29(a), the account name is VRSalesperson in the Windows domain DBGRV101. The account is to be authenticated by Windows, and the default database is VRG.

Figure 11-29(b) shows the same form when the Database Access tab has been clicked. Here, the user is granted the authority to access the VRG database and will be given the role Public. A role is a group of predefined authorities, as discussed below. By default, the Public role has the authority only to connect to the database.

To enable the user of this account to do more than connect, additional authorities must be assigned. Figure 11-30 shows the forms used to do this. Access the User Properties form by clicking Users in the database to be processed; here, that database is named VRG. Right-click and select Properties to display the properties form. Click the Permissions button in that form, and the Permissions form shown on the right side of Figure 11-30 will display. In this example, the VRSalesperson has been granted the capability to SELECT, INSERT, and UPDATE the ARTIST and CUSTOMER tables. This user also has the authority to SELECT the view ArtistWorkNet and to execute the Customer_Insert stored procedure.

Security on Roles

In the last example, we granted authorities to a particular user login. The DBA can save work, however, by defining roles and granting authorities to those roles. Then, when a user login is given the defined role, it inherits all of the authorities granted to the role. Also, when an authority is removed from a role, all accounts that have that role automatically lose that authority as well.

Figure 11-31 shows the form used to define a role and allocation user accounts to that role. This form can be accessed by right clicking roles under the VRG (or other) database and selecting New Database Role. Permissions for the role are assigned by clicking the Permissions button, just as was done for an account in Figure 11-30.

FIGURE 11–29

**Creating a New Login
(a) Setting Login
Properties and
(b) Allocating
Databases to the Login**

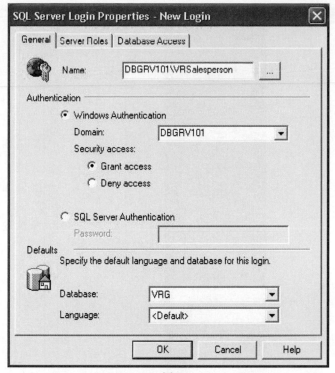

(a)

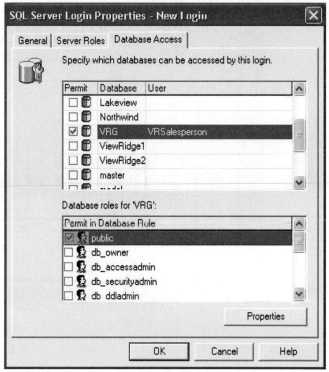

(b)

FIGURE 11–30

**Setting Login
Permissions**

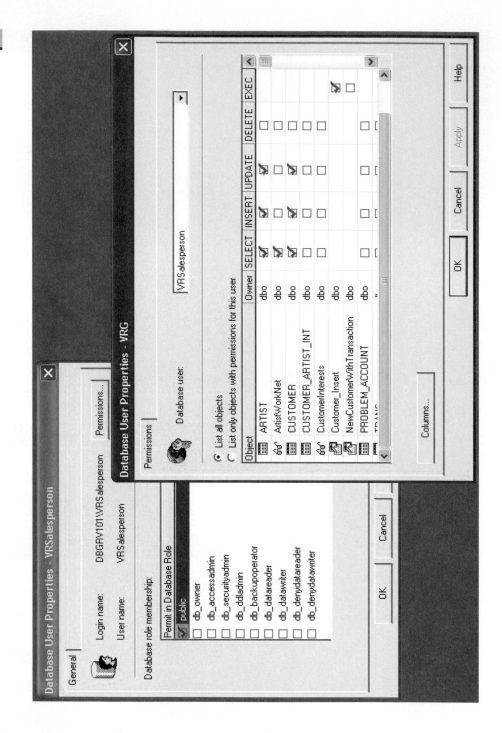

FIGURE 11-31

Allocating Users to Roles

BACKUP AND RECOVERY

When you create a SQL Server database, both data and log files are created. As explained in Chapter 9, these files should be backed up periodically. When this is done, it is possible to recover a failed database by restoring it from a prior database save and applying changes in the log.

To recover a database with SQL Server, the database is restored from a prior database backup and after images from the log are applied to the restored database. When the end of the log is reached, changes from any transaction that failed to commit are then rolled back.

It is also possible to process the log to a particular point in time or to a transaction mark. For example, the following statement causes a mark labeled NewCust to be placed into the log every time this transaction is run:

BEGIN TRANSACTION NewCust WITH MARK

If this is done, the log can be restored to a point either just before or just after the first NewCust mark or first NewCust mark after a particular point in time. The restored log can then be used to restore the database. Such marks consume log space, however, so they should not be used without good reason.

Types of Backup

SQL Server supports several types of backup. To see them, open the Enterprise Manager, open Databases, and right-click a database name. Select All Tasks and then select Backup Database. The dialog box shown in Figure 11-32 appears. At this point, you can create a complete or differential backup of the database, a transaction log backup, and a backup of particular files and file groups.

As the name implies, a complete backup makes a copy of the entire database. A **differential backup** makes a copy of the changes that have been made to the database

FIGURE 11–32

**Backing Up a SQL
Server Database**

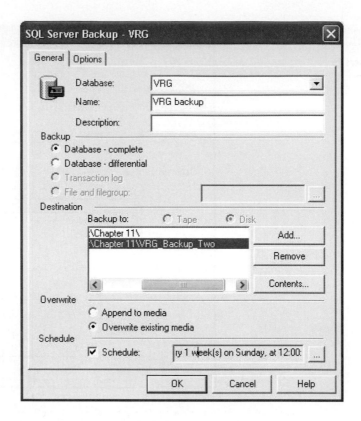

since the last complete backup. This means that a complete backup must be made before the first differential backup. Because differential backups are faster, they can be taken more frequently and the chance of data loss is reduced. On the other hand, complete backups take longer but they are slightly simpler to use for recovery, as you will see.

The transaction log also needs to be periodically backed up to ensure that its contents are preserved. Further, the transaction log must be backed up before it can be used to recover a database.

Backups can be made either to disk or tape. When possible, the backups should be made to devices other than those that store the operational database and log. Backing up to removable devices allows the backups to be stored in a location physically removed from the database data center. This is important for recovery in the event of disasters caused by flood, hurricanes, and the like.

SQL Server Recovery Models

SQL Server supports three recovery models: simple, full, and bulk-logged. You can set the recovery model by right-clicking a database name in the Enterprise Manager and selecting properties. The recovery model is specified under the Options tab. Figure 11-33 shows an example.

With the simple recovery model, no logging is done. The only way to recover a database is to restore the database to the last backup. Changes made since that last backup are lost. The simple recovery model can be used for a database that is never changed—one having the names and locations of the occupants of a full graveyard, for example. Or for one that is used for read-only analysis of data that is copied from some other transactional database.

With full recovery, all database changes are logged; and with bulk-logged database recovery, all changes are logged except those that cause large log entries. With bulk-logged recovery, changes to large text and graphic data items are not recorded to the log, actions like CREATE INDEX are not logged, and some other bulk-oriented actions are

FIGURE 11–33

Setting the Recovery
Model

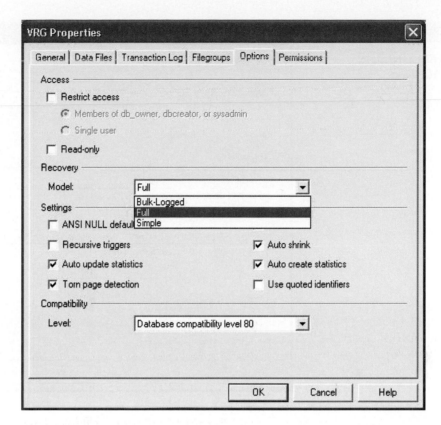

not logged. An organization uses bulk-logged recovery if conserving log space is important and if the data used in the bulk operations is saved in some other way.

Restoring a Database

If the database and log files have been properly backed up, restoring the database is straightforward. First, back up the current log so that changes in the most recent log will be available. Then, right-click the database name in the Enterprise Manager, select All Tasks and then select Restore Database. The dialog box shown in Figure 11-34 appears.

In this example, database VRG is being restored as database VRG Restore. It is not necessary to change the name of the database. Here, the thinking is to restore it under a different name, test the restored database, delete what's left of the old database, and then rename the recovered database VRG.

Database Maintenance Plan

You can create a database maintenance plan to facilitate the making of database and log backups, among other tasks. SQL Server provides a wizard for this task. To use it, right-click a database name, select All Tasks, and select Maintenance Plan. The wizard will guide you through the process of scheduling various tasks. Some of these tasks maintain the database by reorganizing indexes and other related activities. Of importance here, however, is that you can schedule the automatic backup of both database data and logs.

▶ TOPICS NOT DISCUSSED IN THIS CHAPTER

There are several important SQL Server topics that are beyond the scope of this discussion. For one, SQL Server provides utilities to measure database activity and performance. The DBA can use these utilities when tuning the database. Another facility not described here is connecting Access to SQL Server. You can check the Access documentation for more information about this topic.

FIGURE 11-34

**Restoring a Database
with SQL Server**

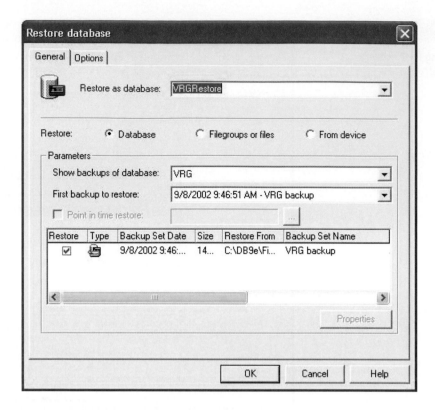

As stated, SQL Server 2000 provides facilities to support distributed database processing (called **replication** in SQL Server). These facilities use the publish-subscribe distributed model that we will discuss in Chapter 15. Although very important in its own right, distributed database processing is beyond the scope of this text. Microsoft provides an OLE DB server called the Distributed Transaction Manager that coordinates distributed transactions. Java supports Enterprise Java Beans for the same purpose. We will touch on these topics in Chapters 12 and 14.

Finally, SQL Server can produce the output of SELECT statements in the form of XML documents. We will discuss this feature in Chapter 13.

SUMMARY

SQL Server 2000 can be installed on Windows 2000 and Windows XP computers. There are two ways to create tables, views, indexes, and other database structures. One is to use the graphical design tools, which are similar to those in Microsoft Access. The other is to write SQL statements to create the structures and submit them to SQL Server via the SQL Query Analyzer utility.

SQL statements used with SQL Server are the same as those discussed in Chapters 6 through 8. The only new expression is IDENTITY (m, n). This expression causes SQL Server to create a surrogate key with a value starting at *m* and an increment of *n*.

Indexes are special data structures used to improve performance. SQL Server automatically creates an index on all primary and foreign keys. Additional views can be created using CREATE INDEX or the Manage Index graphical tool. SQL Server supports clustered and nonclustered indexes.

SQL Server supports a language called TRANSACT-SQL, which surrounds basic SQL statements with programming constructs such as parameters, variables, and logic structures such as IF, WHILE, and so forth.

SQL Server databases can be processed from application programs coded in standard programming languages such as Visual Basic or C#, or application logic can be placed in stored procedures and triggers. Stored procedures can be invoked from standard languages or from VBScript and JScript in Web pages. In this chapter, stored procedures were invoked from the SQL Server Query Analyzer. This technique should be used only during development and testing. For security reasons, no one should process a SQL Server operational database in interactive mode. This chapter demonstrated SQL Server triggers for checking validity, computing default values, updating a view, and implementing a referential integrity action.

Three factors determine the concurrency control behavior of SQL Server: transaction isolation level, cursor concurrency setting, and locking hints provided in the SELECT clause. These factors are summarized in Figure 13-31. Behavior also changes depending on whether actions occur in the context of transactions or cursors or independently. Given these behavior declarations, SQL Server places locks on behalf of the developer. Locks may be placed at many levels of granularity and may be promoted or demoted as work progresses.

SQL Server supports log backups and both complete and differential database backups. Three recovery models are available: simple, full, and, bulk-logged. With simple recovery, no logging is done nor log records applied. Full recovery logs all database operations and applies them for restoration. Bulk-logged recovery omits certain transactions that would otherwise consume large amounts of space in the log.

GROUP I QUESTIONS

11.1 Install SQL Server 2000 and create a database named MEDIA. Use the default settings for file sizes, names, and locations.

11.2 Write a SQL statement to create a table named PICTURE with columns Name, Description, DateTaken, and FileName. Assume that Name is char(20), Description is varchar(200), DateTaken is Smalldatetime, and FileName is char(45). Also assume that Name and DateTaken are required. Use Name is the primary key. Set the default value of Description to '(None).'

11.3 Use the SQL Query Analyzer to submit the SQL statement in question 11.2 to create the PICTURE table in the MEDIA database.

11.4 Open the MEDIA database using Enterprise Manager, and open the database design window for the PICTURE table. In this window, add a column PictureID, and set its identity seed to 300 and identity increment to 25. Change the primary key from Name to PictureID.

11.5 Using the graphical table design tool, set the default value of DateTaken to the system date.

11.6 Create a constraint called Valid_Description that defines the set of values {'Home', 'Office', 'Family', 'Recreation', 'Sports', 'Pets'}. Answer question 11.2, but use this constraint for the Description column.

11.7 Use the graphical tool to:
 A. Change the length of Name to 50.
 B. Delete the DateTaken column.
 C. Add column TakenBy as char(40).

11.8 Create table SLIDE_SHOW (ShowID, Name, Description, Purpose). Assume that ShowID is a surrogate key. Set the data type of Name and Description however you deem appropriate. Set the data type of Purpose to Subject. Use either a CREATE statement or the graphical table design tool.

11.9 Create table SHOW_PICTURE_INT as an intersection table between PICTURE and SLIDE_SHOW.

11.10 Create appropriate relationships between PICTURE and SHOW_PICTURE_INT and between SLIDE_SHOW and SHOW_PICTURE_INT. Set the referential integrity properties to disallow any deletion of a

SLIDE_SHOW row that has any SHOW_PICTURE_INT rows related to it. Set the referential integrity properties to cascade deletions when a PICTURE is deleted.

11.11 Explain how to set the Cascade Update property for the relationships in question 11.10.

11.12 Write a SQL statement to create a view name PopularShows that has SLIDE_SHOW.Name and PICTURE.Name for all slide shows that have a Purpose of either "Home" or "Pets." Execute this statement using the SQL Query Analyzer.

11.13 Open the view design tool and determine that PopularShows was constructed correctly. Modify this view to include Description and FileName.

11.14 Can the SQL DELETE statement be used with the PopularShows view? Why or why not?

11.15 Under what circumstances can PopularShows be used for inserts and modifications?

11.16 Create an index on the Purpose column. Use the Manage Index graphical design tool to do this.

11.17 In Figure 11-14, for what purpose is the @Count variable used?

11.18 Why is the SELECT statement that begins SELECT @Cid necessary?

11.19 Explain how you would change the stored procedure in Figure 11-14 to connect the customer to all artists who either (a) were born before 1900 or (b) had a null value Birthdate.

11.20 Explain the purpose of the transaction shown in Figure 11-17.

11.21 What happens if an incorrect value of Copy is input to the stored procedure in Figure 11-17?

11.22 In Figure 11-17, what happens if the ROLLBACK statement is executed?

11.23 Explain the use of the join statement in Figure 11-20.

11.24 In Figure 11-22, why is SUM used instead of AVG?

11.25 What are the three primary factors that influence SQL Server locking behavior?

11.26 Explain the meaning of each of the transaction isolation levels under Options shown in Figure 11-27.

11.27 Explain the meaning of each of the cursor concurrency settings listed in Figure 11-27.

11.28 What is the purpose of Locking Hints?

11.29 What is the difference between complete and differential backups? Under what conditions are complete backups preferred? Under what conditions are differential backups preferred?

11.30 Explain the differences between simple, full, and bulk-logged recovery models. Under what conditions would you choose each one?

11.31 When is point in time restore necessary?

PROJECT

For the following activities, use either the SQL Server Query Analyzer or the Enterprise Manager, whichever you prefer.

A. Install SQL Server and create the View Ridge database.

B. Create the tables shown in Figure 11-7, except do not create the NationalityValues constraint.

C. Fill your database with sample data. Ensure that you have at least three customers, three artists, five works, and five transactions. Set the Nationality of ARTIST to one of 'German', 'French', or 'English'.

D. Write a stored procedure to read the ARTIST table and display the artist data using Print.

E. Write a stored procedure to read the ARTIST and WORK tables. Your procedure should display an artist, then display all the works for that artist, then display the next artist, and so forth. Accept the name of the artist to display as an input parameter.

F. Write a stored procedure to update customer phone data. Assume that your stored procedure receives Name, priorAreaCode, newAreaCode, priorPhoneNumber, and newPhoneNumber. Your procedure should first ensure that there is only one customer with the values of (Name, priorAreaCode, priorPhoneNumber). If not, produce an error message and quit. Otherwise, update the customer data with the new phone number data.

G. Create a table named ALLOWED_NATIONALITY with one column, called Nation. Place the values 'German', 'French', and 'English' into the table. Write a trigger that will check to determine whether a new or updated value of Nationality resides in this table. If not, write an error message and roll back the insert or change. Use the Query Analyzer to demonstrate that your trigger works.

H. Create a view having all data from the WORK and TRANSACTION table. Write an insert INSTEAD OF trigger on this view that will create a new row in WORK and TRANSACTION. Use the Query Analyzer to demonstrate that your trigger

FIREDUP PROJECT QUESTIONS

Use SQL Server to create a database with the following four tables:

CUSTOMER (CustomerID, Name, Phone, EmailAddress)

STOVE (SerialNumber, Type, Version, DateOfManufacture)

REGISTRATION (*CustomerID*, *SerialNumber*, RDate)

STOVE_REPAIR (RepairInvoiceNumber, *SerialNumber*, RepairDate, Description, Cost, *CustomerID*)

Assume that the primary keys of CUSTOMER, STOVE, and STOVE_REPAIR are surrogate keys. Create relationships to enforce the following referential integrity constraints:

CustomerID of REGISTRATION is a subset of CustomerID of CUSTOMER

SerialNumber of REGISTRATION is a subset of SerialNumber of STOVE

SerialNumber of STOVE_REPAIR is a subset of SerialNumber of STOVE

CustomerID of STOVE_REPAIR is a subset of CustomerID of CUSTOMER

Do not cascade deletions.

A. Fill your tables with sample data and display them.

B. Create a stored procedure to register a stove. The procedure receives the customer's name, phone, email address, and stove serial number. If the customer already exists in the database (name, phone, and email match), use that customer's CustomerID for the REGISTRATION. Otherwise, create a new CUSTOMER row for the customer. Assume that a stove with the input serial number already exists in the database. If not, print an error message and rollback changes to the CUSTOMER table. Code and test your procedure.

C. Create a stored procedure to record a stove repair. The procedure receives the customer's name, phone, email address, stove serial number, repair description, and cost. Assume that you are given a valid stove serial number; print an error message and make no database changes if not. Use an existing CUSTOMER row if name, phone, and email match; otherwise, create a new CUSTOMER record. Assume that the STOVE-REPAIR row must be created. Register the stove, if necessary.

D. Create a view named CustomerReg that contains all of the CUSTOMER, STOVE, and REGISTRATION data. Create an INSTEAD OF trigger for an insert of CustomerReg. Assume that the user will provide values for CustomerID, Name, Phone, EmailAddress, and SerialNumber. If the customer does not exist in the database, create a new row in CUSTOMER. Create a registration of the stove for this customer. If the SerialNumber does not exist in STOVE, write an error message and take no other action. Demonstrate that your trigger works.

TWIGS TREE TRIMMING SERVICE PROJECT QUESTIONS

Use SQL Server to create a database with the following three tables:

OWNER (<u>OwnerName</u>, Phone, Street, City, State, Zip)

SERVICE (<u>DateOfService</u>, <u>OwnerName</u>, Description, AmountBilled, AmountPaid, DateOfPayment)

CHIP_DELIVERY (<u>CustomerName</u>, <u>DeliveryDate</u>, LoadSize, AmountBilled, AmountPaid, DateOfPayment)

Create relationships that will enforce the following referential integrity constraints:

SERVICE.OwnerName exists in OWNER.OwnerName
CHIP_DELIVERY.CustomerName exists in OWNER.OwnerName

Cascade both updates and deletions.

A. Fill your tables with sample data and display them.

B. Create a stored procedure to schedule a service. Assume that the procedure receives all owner data and DateOfService and Description. If the owner already exists in the database, use the existing owner data. Otherwise, create a new row in OWNER. Create the new SERVICE row. Code and test your procedure.

C. Create a stored procedure to schedule a chip delivery. Assume that the procedure receives all owner data and DeliveryDate, LoadSize, and Amount Billed. If the owner already exists in the database, use the existing owner data. Do not schedule the delivery if the owner has any unpaid SERVICE or CHIP_DELIVERY records.

Write an error message instead. Unpaid means that there is a non-null value for AmountBilled, but a null value for AmountPaid.

D.   Create a view named CustomerService that contains all of the OWNER and SER-VICE data. Create an INSTEAD OF trigger for an insert of CustomerService. Assume that the user will provide values for all owner data and DateOfService and Description. If the owner does not exist in the database, create a new row in OWNER. Create a row in SERVICE for this service. Demonstrate that your trigger works.

PART V

Database Access Standards

The three chapters in this section concern standards for database application processing. We begin in Chapter 12 by discussing older standards including ODBC, OLE DB, and ADO. Even though these standards are no longer on the leading edge of database processing, there are today many applications that use them, and you will likely encounter them in your career. Chapter 13 then discusses one of the most important developments in information technology today, the confluence of database processing and document processing. This chapter introduces you to XML and XML Schema and describes important features and functions of ADO.NET, especially those that concern ADO.NET datasets. Finally, Chapter 14 describes the use of the Java technologies JDBC and Java Server Pages. It also introduces MySQL, an open source DBMS product. In fact, all of the examples in Chapter 14 were developed using open source software.

CHAPTER 12

ODBC, OLE DB, ADO, and ASP

This chapter discusses traditional standard interfaces for accessing database servers. ODBC, or the Open Database Connectivity standard, was developed in the early 1990s to provide a DBMS-independent means for processing relational database data. In the mid-1990s, Microsoft announced OLE DB, which is an object-oriented interface that encapsulates data-server functionality. As you will learn, OLE DB was designed not just for relational databases, but for many other types of data as well. As a COM interface, OLE DB is readily accessible to C, C#, and Java programmers, but is not as accessible to Visual Basic and scripting developers. Therefore, Microsoft developed Active Data Objects (ADO), which is a set of objects for utilizing OLE DB that is designed for use by any language, including VB, VBScript, and JScript.

Before considering these standards, we need to gain a perspective on the data environment that surrounds the Web server in Internet technology database applications.

▶ THE WEB SERVER DATA ENVIRONMENT

The environment in which today's Internet technology database applications reside is rich and complicated. As shown in Figure 12-1, a typical Web server needs to publish applications that involve data of dozens of different data types. So far in this text, we have considered only relational databases, but as you can see from this figure, there are many other data types as well.

Consider the problems that the developer of Web server applications has when integrating this data. He or she may need to connect to an Oracle database, a DB2 mainframe database, a nonrelational database like IMS, file-processing data like VSAM and ISAM, email directories, and so forth. Each one of these products has a different programming interface that the developer must learn. Further, each of these products evolves, so new features and functions will be added over time that will increase the developer's challenge.

ODBC was created to address the part of this problem that concerns relational databases and data sources that are table-like, such as spreadsheets. As shown in Figure 12-2, ODBC is an interface between the Web server (or other database user) and the database server. It consists of a set of standards by which SQL statements can be issued, and results and error messages can be returned. Developers can call the DBMS using native DBMS interfaces if they want to (sometimes they do this to improve performance), but the developer who does not have the time or desire to learn many different DBMS native libraries can use the ODBC standard instead.

ODBC has been a tremendous success and has greatly simplified some database-development tasks. It is limited to table-like data sources, however, and to overcome that disadvantage (as well as others) Microsoft develped OLE DB. As shown in Figure 12-3 , OLE DB provides an object-oriented interface to data of almost any type. DBMS vendors can wrap portions of their native libraries in OLE DB objects to expose their product's functionality through this interface. OLE DB can also be used as an interface to ODBC data sources. Finally, OLE DB was developed to support the processing of non-relational data as well.

Because OLE DB is an object-oriented interface, it is particularly suited to object-oriented languages such as C++. Many database application developers, however, pro-

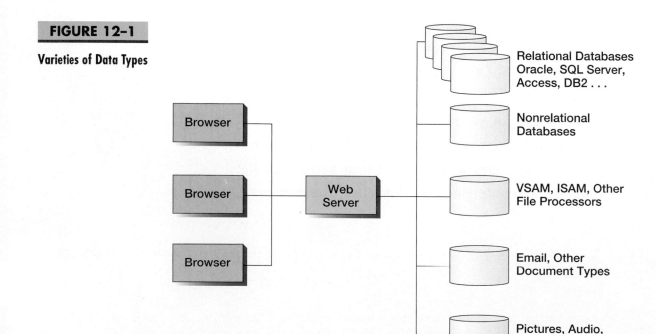

FIGURE 12-1

Varieties of Data Types

Browser

Browser

Browser

Web Server

Relational Databases
Oracle, SQL Server,
Access, DB2 . . .

Nonrelational
Databases

VSAM, ISAM, Other
File Processors

Email, Other
Document Types

Pictures, Audio,
Other????

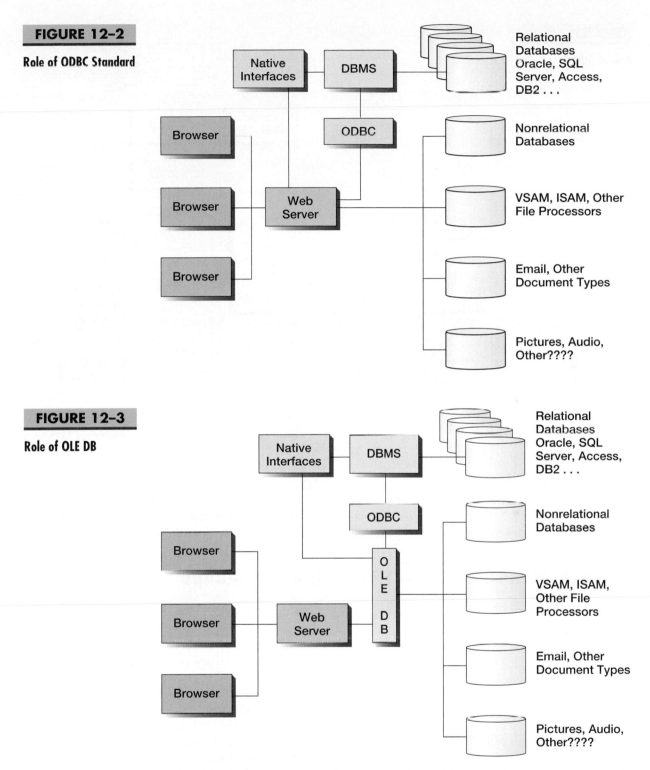

FIGURE 12-2

Role of ODBC Standard

FIGURE 12-3

Role of OLE DB

gram in Visual Basic or scripting languages such as VBScript and JScript. Consequently, Microsoft defined ADO as a cover over OLE DB objects (see Figure 12-4). ADO enables programmers in almost any language to be able to access OLE DB functionality.

You may feel uncomfortable with the strong Microsoft presence in this discussion. Both OLE DB and ADO were developed and popularized by Microsoft, and even ODBC received prominence in large measure because of support from Microsoft. In fact, other vendors and standards committees did propose alternatives to OLE DB and ADO, but because Microsoft Windows resides on nearly 90 percent of the world's desktops, it is difficult for others to promulgate opposing standards. Furthermore, in defense

FIGURE 12–4

Role of ADO

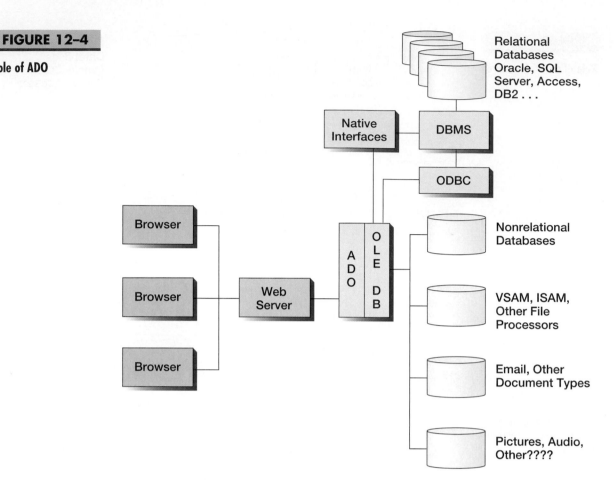

of Microsoft, both OLE DB and ADO are excellent. They simplify the job of the database developer, and they probably would have won out—even on a level playing field.

Our aims, here, however, are more pedestrian. You need to learn ADO so that you can build better database applications. To that end, we will now address each of these standards in more detail.

▶ OPEN DATABASE CONNECTIVITY (ODBC) STANDARD

The **open database connectivity (ODBC)** standard is an interface by which application programs can access and process SQL databases in a DBMS-independent manner. This means, for example, that an application that uses the ODBC interface could process an Oracle database, a DB2 database, a spreadsheet, and any other database that is ODBC-compliant without any program coding changes. The goal is to allow a developer to create a single application that can access databases supported by different DBMS products without needing to be changed or even recompiled.

ODBC was developed by a committee of industry experts from the X/Open and SQL Access Group committees. Several of such standards were proposed, but ODBC emerged as the winner, primarily because it has been implemented by Microsoft and is an important part of Windows. Microsoft's initial interest in support of such a standard was to allow products such as Microsoft Excel to access database data from a variety of DBMS products without having to be recompiled. Of course, Microsoft's interests have changed since the introduction of OLE DB and ADO.NET (see Chapter 13).

ODBC Architecture

Figure 12-5 shows the components of the ODBC standard. The application program, driver manager, and DBMS drivers all reside on the application server computer. The

FIGURE 12–5

ODBC Architecture

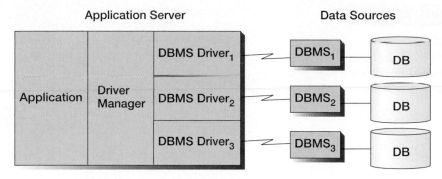

Application can process a database using any of the three DBMS products.

drivers send requests to data sources, which reside on the database server. According to the standard, a **data source** is the database, its associated DBMS, operating system, and network platform. An ODBC data source can be a relational database; it can also be a file server such as BTrieve, or it can be a spreadsheet or table-like text file.

The application issues requests to create a connection with a data source; to issue SQL statements and receive results; to process errors; and to start, commit, and roll back transactions. ODBC provides a standard means for each of these requests, and it defines a standard set of error codes and messages.

The **driver manager** serves as an intermediary between the application and the DBMS drivers. When the application requests a connection, the driver manager determines the type of DBMS that processes the given data source and loads that driver in memory (if it is not already loaded). The driver manager also processes certain initialization requests and validates the format and order of ODBC requests that it receives from the application. For Windows, the driver manager is provided by Microsoft.

A **driver** processes ODBC requests and submits specific SQL statements to a given type of data source. There is a different driver for each data source type. For example, there are drivers for DB2, for Oracle, for Access, and for all of the other products whose vendors have chosen to participate in the ODBC standard. Drivers are supplied by DBMS vendors and by independent software companies.

It is the responsibility of the driver to ensure that standard ODBC commands execute correctly. In some cases, if the data source is itself not SQL-compliant, the driver may need to perform considerable processing to fill in for a lack of capability at the data source. In other cases, where the data source supports full SQL, the driver need only pass the request through for processing by the data source. The driver also converts data source error codes and messages into the ODBC standard codes and messages.

ODBC identifies two types of drivers: single tier and multiple tier. A **single-tier** driver processes both ODBC calls and SQL statements. An example of a single-tier driver is shown in Figure 12-6(a). In this example, the data is stored in Xbase files (the format used by FoxPro, dBase, and others). Because Xbase file managers do not process SQL, it is the job of the driver to translate the SQL request into Xbase file-manipulation commands and to transform the results back into SQL form.

A **multiple-tier** driver processes ODBC calls, but passes the SQL requests directly to the database server. Although it may reformat an SQL request to conform to the dialect of a particular data source, it does not process the SQL. An example of the use of a multiple-tier driver is shown in Figure 12-6(b).

Conformance Levels

The creators of the ODBC standard faced a dilemma. If they chose to describe a standard for a minimal level of capability, many vendors would be able to comply. But if they

FIGURE 12–6

**ODBC Driver Types
(a) ODBC Single-Tier
Driver and (b) ODBC
Multiple-Tier Driver**

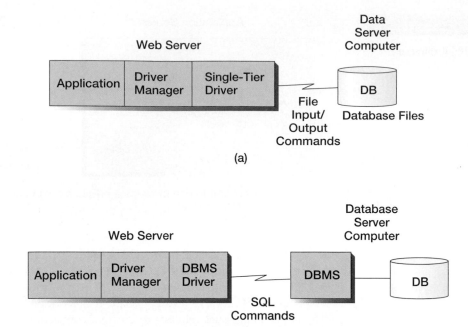

did so, the standard would represent only a small portion of the complete power and expressiveness of ODBC and SQL. On the other hand, if the standard addressed a very high level of capability, only a few vendors would be able to comply with the standard, and it would become unimportant. To deal with this dilemma, the committee wisely chose to define levels of conformance to the standard. There are two types: ODBC conformance and SQL conformance.

ODBC Conformance Level ODBC conformance levels concern the features and functions that are made available through the driver's application program interface (**API**). A driver API is a set of functions that the application can call to receive services. Figure 12-7 summarizes the three levels of ODBC conformance that are addressed in the standard. In practice, almost all drivers provide at least Level 1 API conformance, so the core API level is not too important.

An application can call a driver to determine which level of ODBC conformance it provides. If the application requires a level of conformance that is not present, it can terminate the session in an orderly fashion and generate appropriate messages to the user. Or the application can be written to use higher-level conformance features if they are available and to work around the missing functions if a higher level is not available.

For example, drivers at the Level 2 API must provide a scrollable cursor. Using conformance levels, an application could be written to use cursors if they are available; but if they are not, to work around the missing feature, selecting needed data using very restrictive WHERE clauses. Doing this would ensure that only a few rows were returned at a time to the application, and it would process those rows using a cursor that it maintained itself. Performance would likely be slower in the second case, but at least the application would be able to successfully execute.

SQL Conformance Level SQL conformance levels specify which SQL statements, expressions, and data types a driver can process. Three levels are defined, as summarized in Figure 12-8. The capability of the minimum SQL grammar is very limited, and most drivers support at least the core SQL grammar.

As with ODBC conformance levels, an application can call the driver to determine what level of SQL conformance it supports. With that information, the application can then determine which SQL statements can be issued. If necessary, the application can then terminate the session or use alternative, less-powerful means of obtaining the data.

FIGURE 12–7

Summary of ODBC
Conformance Levels

Core API
- Connect to data sources
- Prepare and execute SQL statements
- Retrieve data from a result set
- Commit or rollback transactions
- Retrieve error information

Level 1 API
- Core API
- Connect to data sources with driver-specific information
- Send and receive partial results
- Retrieve catalog information
- Retrieve information about driver options, capabilities, and functions

Level 2 API
- Core and Level 1 API
- Browse possible connections and data sources
- Retrieve native form of SQL
- Call a translation library
- Process a scrollable cursor

FIGURE 12–8

Summary of SQL
Conformance Levels

Minimum SQL Grammar
- CREATE TABLE, DROP TABLE
- Simple SELECT (does not include subqueries)
- INSERT, UPDATE, DELETE
- Simple expressions (A > B + C)
- CHAR, VARCHAR, LONGVARCHAR data types

Core SQL Grammar
- Minimum SQL Grammar
- ALTER TABLE, CREATE INDEX, DROP INDEX
- CREATE VIEW, DROP VIEW
- GRANT, REVOKE
- Full SELECT (includes subqueries)
- Aggregate functions such as SUM, COUNT, MAX, MIN, AVG
- DECIMAL, NUMERIC, SMALLINT, INTEGER, REAL, FLOAT, DOUBLE PRECISION data types

Extended SQL Grammar
- Core SQL Grammar
- Outer joins
- UPDATE and DELETE using cursor positions
- Scalar functions such as SUBSTRING, ABS
- Literals for date, time, and timestamp
- Batch SQL statements
- Stored Procedures

Establishing an ODBC Data Source Name

A **data source** is an ODBC data structure that identifies a database and the DBMS that processes it. Data sources identify other types of data, such as spreadsheets and other nondatabase data stores, but we are not concerned with that use here.

There are three types of data sources: file, system, and user. A **file data source** is a file that can be shared among database users. The only requirement is that the users have the same DBMS driver and privilege to access the database. The data source file can be emailed or otherwise distributed to possible users. A **system data source** is one that is local to a single computer. The operating system and any user on that system (with proper privileges) can use a system data source. A **user data source** is available only to the user who created it.

In general, the best choice for Web applications is to create a system data source on the Web server. Browser users then access the Web server, which in turn uses a system data source to set up a connection with the DBMS and the database.

Figure 12-9 shows the process of creating a system data source using the ODBC Data Source Administrator Service that can be found via the Windows Control Panel. In Figure 12-9(a), the user is selecting a driver for an Oracle database. Notice that there are two such drivers; one is provided by Microsoft and the other is provided by Oracle. The drivers may have different capabilities, and the user should check the documentation for each to determine which is most appropriate for his or her application. Other drivers shown in this figure are for Paradox, text files, and Visual FoxPro.

In Figure 12-9(b), the user is selecting the database. Here, it is VRG, the name given to the database created in Chapter 10. We will use this DSN, named ViewRidgeOracle2, later in this chapter to process that database. We will also use a second file DSN, named ViewRidgeSS, to process the SQL Server database created in Chapter 11.

▶ OLE DB

OLE DB is one of the foundations of data access in the Microsoft world. As such, it is important to understand the fundamental ideas of OLE DB, even if you will only work with the ADO interfaces that lie on top of it. In this section, we present essential OLE DB concepts.

OLE DB is an implementation of the Microsoft OLE object standard. OLE DB objects are COM objects and support all required interfaces for such objects. Fundamentally, OLE DB breaks the features and functions of a DBMS up into COM objects. There can be objects that support query operations; others that perform updates; others that support the creation of database schema constructs such as tables, indexes, and views; and still others that perform transaction management such as optimistic locking.

This characteristic overcomes a major disadvantage of ODBC. With ODBC, a vendor must create an ODBC driver for almost all DBMS features and functions in order to participate in ODBC at all. This is a large task that requires a substantial investment. With OLE DB, however, a DBMS vendor can implement portions of their product. One could, for example, implement only the query processor, participate in OLE DB, and hence be accessible to customers using ADO. Later, the vendor could add more objects and interfaces to increase their OLE DB functionality.

This text does not assume that you are an object-oriented programmer, so we need to develop a few concepts. In particular, you need to understand abstractions, methods, properties, and collections. An **abstraction** is a generalization of something. ODBC interfaces are abstractions of native DBMS access methods. When we abstract something, we lose detail, but we gain the ability to work with a broader range of types.

For example, a **recordset** is an abstraction of a relation. In this abstraction, a recordset is defined to have certain characteristics that will be common to all recordsets. Every recordset, for instance, has a set of columns, which in this abstraction are called Fields.

FIGURE 12–9

Creating a System
Data Source
(a) Selecting the Oracle
Driver and (b) Setting
Data Source Properties

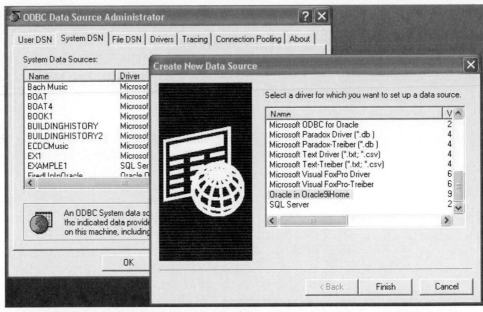

(a)

(b)

Now, the goal of abstraction is to capture everything important, but omit details that are not needed by users of the abstraction. Thus, Oracle relations may have some characteristic that is not represented in a recordset; the same might be true for relations in SQL Server, DB2, and in other DBMS products. These unique characteristics will be lost in the abstraction, but if the abstraction is a good one, no one will care.

Moving up a level, a **rowset** is the OLE DB abstraction of a recordset. Now, why does OLE DB need to define another abstraction? Because OLE DB addresses data sources that are not tables, but have *some of* the characteristics of tables. Consider all email addresses in your personal email file. Are those addresses the same as a relation? No, but they do share some of the characteristics that relations have. Each address is a semantically related group of data items. Like rows of a table, it is sensible to go to the first one, move to the next one, and so forth. But, unlike relations, they are not all of the same type. Some addresses are for individuals, and some are for mailing lists. Thus, any action on a recordset that depends on everything in the recordset being the same kind of thing cannot be used on a rowset.

Working from the top down, OLE DB defines a set of data properties and behaviors for rowsets. Every rowset has those properties and behaviors. Furthermore, OLE DB defines a recordset as a subtype of a rowset. Recordsets have all of the properties and behaviors that rowsets have, plus they have some that are uniquely characteristic of recordsets.

Abstraction is both common and useful. You will hear of abstractions of transaction management or abstractions of querying or abstractions of interfaces. This simply means that certain characteristics of a set of things are formally defined as a type.

An object-oriented programming object is an abstraction that is defined by its properties and methods. For example, a recordset object has an AllowEdits property and a RecordsetType property and an EOF property. These **properties** represent characteristics of the recordset abstraction. An object also has actions that it can perform that are called **methods.** A recordset has methods such as Open, MoveFirst, MoveNext, and Close.

Strictly speaking, the definition of an object abstraction is called an **object class,** or just class. An instance of an object class, such as a particular recordset, is called an object. All objects of a class have the same methods and the same properties, but the values of the properties vary from object to object.

The last term we need to address is collection. A **collection** is an object that contains a group of other objects. A recordset has a collection of other objects called Fields. The collection has properties and methods. One of the properties of all collections is Count, which is the number of objects in the collection. Thus, recordset.Fields.Count is the number of fields in the collection. In ADO and OLE DB, collections are named as the plural of the objects they collect. Thus, there is a Fields collection of Field objects, an Errors collection of Error objects, a Parameters collection of Parameters, and so forth. An important method of a collection is an iterator, which is a method that can be used to pass through or otherwise identify the items in the collection.

If you're getting frustrated with all these definitions, don't give up. You will see a practical use of these concepts before the end of this chapter!

Goals of OLE DB

The major goals for OLE DB are listed in Figure 12-10. First, as mentioned, OLE DB breaks DBMS functionality and services into object pieces. This partitioning means great flexibility for both **data consumers** (users of OLE DB functionality) and **data providers** (vendors of products that deliver OLE DB functionality). Data consumers take only the objects and functionality they need; a wireless device for reading a database can have a very slim footprint. Unlike with ODBC, data providers need only implement a portion of DBMS functionality. This partitioning also means that data providers can deliver capabilities in multiple interfaces.

This last point needs expansion. An object interface is a packaging of objects. An **interface** is specified by a set of objects and the properties and methods that they expose. An object need not expose all of its properties and methods in a given interface. Thus, a recordset object would expose only read methods in a query interface; but create, update, and delete methods in a modification interface.

How the object supports the interface, or the **implementation,** is completely hidden from the user. In fact, the developers of an object are free to change the implementation whenever they want. Who will know? But they may not ever change the interface without incurring the justifiable disdain of their users!

OLE DB defines standardized interfaces. Data providers, however, are free to add interfaces on top of the basic standards. Such extensibility is essential for the next goal,

FIGURE 12-10

OLE DB Goals

- Create object interfaces for DBMS functionality pieces
    Query
    Update
    Transaction management
    Etc.
- Increase flexibility
    Allow data consumers to use only the objects they need
    Allow data providers to expose pieces of DBMS functionality
    Providers can deliver functionality in multiple interfaces
    Interfaces are standardized and extensible
- Object interface over any type of data
    Relational database
    ODBC or native
    Nonrelational database
    VSAM and other files
    Email
    Other
- Do not force data to be converted or moved from where it is

which is to provide an object interface to any type of data. Relational databases can be processed through OLE DB objects that use ODBC or that use the native DBMS drivers. OLE DB includes support for the other types as indicated.

The net result of these design goals is that data need not be converted from one form to another, nor need it be moved from one data source to another. The Web server shown in Figure 12-1 can utilize OLE DB to process data in any of the formats, right where the data reside. This means that transactions may span multiple data sources and may be distributed on different computers. The OLE DB provision for this is the **Microsoft Transaction Manager** (**MTS**), but discussion of it is beyond the scope of this chapter.

OLE DB Basic Constructs

As shown in Figure 12-11, OLE DB has two types of data providers. **Tabular data providers** present their data via rowsets. Examples are DBMS products, spreadsheets, and ISAM file processors such as dbase and FoxPro. Additionally, other types of data like email can also be presented in rowsets. Tabular data providers bring data of some type into the OLE DB world.

A **service provider,** on the other hand, is a transformer of data. Service providers accept OLE DB data from an OLE DB tabular data provider and transform it some way. Service providers are both consumers and providers of transformed data. An example of a service provider is one that obtains data from a relational DBMS and transforms it into XML documents.

FIGURE 12-11

Two Types of OLE DB Data Providers

- Tabular data provider
    ◦ Exposes data via rowsets
    ◦ Examples: DBMS, spreadsheets, ISAMs, Email
- Service provider
    ◦ Transforms data through OLE DB interfaces
    ◦ Both a consumer and a provider of data
    ◦ Examples: query processors, XML document creator

The **rowset** object is fundamental to OLE DB; rowsets are equivalent to what we called **cursors** in Chapter 9, and in fact the two terms are used synonymously. Figure 12-12 lists the basic rowset interfaces that are supported. IRowSet provides object methods for forward-only sequential movement through a rowset. When you declare a forward-only cursor in OLE DB, you are invoking the IRowSet interface. The IAccessor interface is used to bind program variables to rowset fields. When using ADO, this interface is largely hidden because it is used behind the scenes in the scripting engine. If you work with type libraries in VB, however, you may use methods from this interface.

The IColumnsInfo interface has methods for obtaining information about the columns in a rowset. We will use this interface to advantage in two of the ADO examples at the end of this chapter. IRowSet, IAccessor, and IColumnsInfo are the basic rowset interfaces. Other interfaces are defined for more advanced operations such as scrollable cursors, update, direct access to particular rows, explicit locks, and so forth.

Consider these interfaces in the context of two rowsets—one a traditional relation and another that is a collection of email addresses. The first three interfaces readily pertain to either type of rowset. The last set of interfaces will likely be different in the features and functions between the two rowsets if they pertain at all. One final note—rowsets can contain pointers to objects so quite complicated structures can be created with them.

▶ ADO (ACTIVE DATA OBJECTS)

ADO is a simple object model that can be used by data consumers to process any OLE DB data. It can be called from scripting languages such as JScript and VBScript; and from Visual Basic, Java, C#, and C++.

Because of OLE DB abstractions and object structure, the ADO object model and interfaces are the same regardless of the type of data processed. Thus, a developer who learns ADO for processing a relational database can use that knowledge for processing an email directory as well. Characteristics of ADO are listed in Figure 12-13.

FIGURE 12-12

Rowset Interfaces

- IRowSet
    - Methods for sequential iteration through a rowset
- IAccessor
    - Methods for setting and determining bindings between rowset and client program variables
- IColumnsInfo
    - Methods for determining information about the columns in the rowset
- Other interfaces
    - Scrollable cursors
    - Create, update, delete rows
    - Directly access particular rows (bookmarks)
    - Explicitly set locks
    - And so on

FIGURE 12-13

Characteristics of ADO

- Simple object model for OLE DB data consumers
- Can be used from VBScript, JScript, Visual Basic, Java, C#, C++
- Single Microsoft data access standard
- Data access objects are the same for all types of OLE DB data

Invoking ADO from Active Server Pages

In this chapter, we will invoke ADO on a Web server using Active Server Pages. Such pages contain a mixture of HTML and program language statements expressed in either VBScript or JavaScript. In this chapter, we will use VBScript. ASPs can be written with any text editor, but they are easier to write with FrontPage or some similar Web page-authoring product.

Internet Information Server (IIS) is a Web server built into Windows XP and 2000 Professional. ASP is an ISAPI extension to IIS. As a practical matter, this simply means that whenever IIS receives a file with the extension .asp, it sends the file to the ASP program for processing.

Any program language statements enclosed within the characters <% . . . %> will be processed on the Web server computer. Other language statements will be sent to the user's browser for processing. In this chapter, all of our code will be processed on the Web server.

To invoke ASPs, place them in some directory, say, C:\MyDirectory. Then, open IIS and set up a virtual directory that points to the directory in which you have placed your ASPs. You can do this by opening Internet Information Services, and right-clicking Default Web Site. Choose New/Virtual Directory, and a wizard will start that asks you to name your virtual directory and the real directory (here, C:\MyDirectory) in which your ASP will reside. Select Read and Run Scripts on the third panel of the wizard. For the examples in this text, we will use the virtual directory name ViewRidgeExample1.

It is not necessary that the DBMS and the Web server be located on the same machine. When you create the ODBC DSN, you can point to a database on a different computer that is accessible from the Web server computer. This will be easier if that other computer runs a Windows operating system, but it can be done with other operating systems as well. Of course, the Web server and the DBMS can be on the same machine.

ADO Object Model

The ADO object model shown in Figure 12-14 is built on top of the OLE DB object model. The Connection object is the first ADO object to be created and is the basis for the others. From a connection, a developer can create one or more RecordSet objects and one or more Command objects. In the process of creating or working with any of these objects, ADO will place any errors that are generated in the Errors collection.

FIGURE 12-14

ADO Object Model

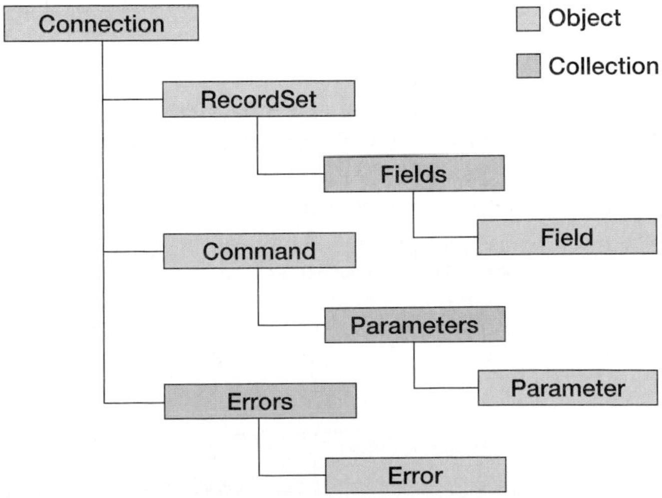

Each RecordSet object has a Fields collection; each Field element corresponds to a column in the recordset. In addition, each Command object has a Parameters Collection that contains objects for the parameters of the command.

Connection Object   The following VBScript code can be embedded in an ASP to create a connection object. After it runs, the variable objConn will point to an object that is connected to the ODBC data source ViewRidgeSS.

```
<%
    Dim objConn
    Set objConn = Server.CreateObject ("ADODB.connection")
    objConn.IsolationLevel = adXactReadCommitted ' use ADOVBS
    objConn.Open "ViewRidgeSS"
%>
```

In this code, the statement Server.CreateObject is invoking the CreateObject method of the ASP server object. The type of object, here ADODB.connection, is passed as a parameter. After this statement executes, the variable objConn points to the new connection object. Next, the isolation level of this connection is set using a constant from the file ADOVBS. That file can be made available to this script with the following include statement:

```
<!--#include virtual = "ADOExamples/ADOVBS.inc-->
```

This statement must be part of the ASP file, but **outside** of the <% . . . %>. For this to work, you must copy the file ADOVBS.inc into your directory (find it using Search). Also, substitute the name of your virtual directory if it is other than ADO Examples.

The names and values of important ADOVBS constants are listed in Figure 12-15. Using the names of the constants rather than their values makes your code more readable. It also makes it easier to adapt your code should Microsoft change the meanings of these values (doubtful, but it could happen).

In the last statement, the open method of the connection is used to open the ODBC data source. The name of the data source is passed to the open method. In this case, neither user ID nor password is being passed to the DBMS. Instead, the database will be opened using an authenticated name provided by the operating system. By default, ASP will use the name IUSR_*machine-name*, or in this case, IUSR_DBGRV101. This account must be set up in SQL Server with privileges to read and update the VRG user tables.

The Oracle ODBC driver that will be used in the figures that follow does not allow a null password to be passed. For that driver, we will need to provide a user ID and password. The examples use the user ID DK1 and the password Sesame. Again, the account DK1 must be set up in Oracle with privileges to read and update the VRG tables.

At this point, a connection has been established to the DBMS via the ODBC data source and the database is open. The objConn pointer can be used to refer to any other methods for a connection (see Figure 12-14), including the creation and use of RecordSet and Command objects. The Errors collection can be processed as well.

RecordSet Object   Given the connection with an open database, the following will create a RecordSet object (we omit the <% and %> from now on, but all of these code examples must be inserted between them or they will not be executed on the Web server):

FIGURE 12–15

ADO Constants

Isolation Level	Const Name	Value
Dirty reads	adXactReadUncommitted	256
Read committed	adXactReadCommitted	4096
Repeatable read	adXactRepeatableRead	65536
Serializable	adXactSerializable	1048576

(a) Isolation Levels

Cursor Type	Const Name	Value
Forward only	adOpenForwardOnly	0
Keyset	adOpenKeyset	1
Dynamic	adOpenDynamic	2
Static	adOpenStatic	3

(b) Cursor Types

Cursor Type	Const Name	Value
Read only	adLockReadOnly	1
Pessimistic locking	adLockPessimistic	2
Optimistic locking	adLockOptimistic	3
Optimistic with batch updates	adBatchOptimistic	4

(c) Lock Types

```
Dim  objRecordSet, varSql
varSQL = "SELECT * FROM ARTIST"
Set objRecordSet = Server.CreateObject ("ADODB.Recordset")
objRecordSet.CursorTye = adOpenStatic
objRecordSet.LockType = adLockReadOnly
objRecordSet.Open varSQL, objConn
```

CursorType and LockType could also be passed as parameters to the recordset open method, as follows:

```
Dim  objRecordSet, varSql

varSQL = "SELECT * FROM ARTIST"

Set objRecordSet = Server.CreateObject ("ADODB.Recordset")

objRecordSet.Open varSQL, objConn, adOpenStatic, adLockReadOnly
```

Either way, these statements cause the SQL statement in varSQL to be executed using a static, read-only cursor. All of the columns of the ARTIST table will be included as fields in the recordset. If the SELECT statement named only two columns—say, "SELECT ArtistID, Nationality FROM ARTIST"—only those two columns would be included as fields in the recordset.

By the way, there is a "gotcha" lurking here. With SQL Server, if a table name has spaces or odd characters or is a SQL Server reserved word, you enclose the name in brackets [ ]. To Oracle, however, a table name enclosed in brackets is illegal. For oddly named tables in Oracle, you enclose the name in quotes. Thus, if your database has such tables, you have to write different code, depending on whether you are using an Oracle or SQL Server database.

Fields Collection   After the recordset has been created, its Fields collection is instantiated. We can process that collection with the following:

```
Dim varI, varNumCols, objField

varNumCols = objRecordSet.Fields.Count

For varI = 0 to varNumCols - 1

        Set objField = objRecordSet.Fields(varI)

        ' objField.Name now has the name of the field

        ' objField.Value now has the value of the field

        ' can do something with them here

Next
```

In the second statement, varNumCols is set to the number of columns in the recordset by accessing the Count property of the Fields collection. Then a loop is executed to iterate over this collection. The property Fields(0) refers to the first column of the recordset, so the loop needs to run from 0 to Count − 1.

Nothing is done with the Fields objects in this example, but in an actual application, the developer could reference objField.Name to get the name of a column and objField.Value to obtain its value. You will see uses like this in the following examples.

Errors Collection   Whenever an error occurs, ADO instantiates an Errors collection. It must be a collection because more than one error can be generated by a single ADO statement. This collection can be processed in a manner similar to that for the Fields collection:

```
Dim varI, varErrorCount, objError

On Error Resume Next

varErrorCount = objConn.Errors.Count

If varErrorCount > 0 Then

        For varI = 0 to varErrorCount - 1
```

```
            Set objError = objConn.Errors(varI)
            ' objError.Description contains
            ' a description of the error
        Next
    End If
```

In the loop, objError is set to objConn.Errors(varI). Note that this collection belongs to objConn, not to objRecordSet. Also the Description property of objError can be used to display the error to the user.

Unfortunately, VBScript has quite limited error processing. The code for checking errors (starting with On Error Resume Next) must be placed after every ADO object statement that might cause an error. Because this can bulk up the code undesirably, it would be better to write an error-handling function and call it after every ADO object invocation.

Command Object   The ADO command object is used to execute queries and stored procedures that are stored with the database. The parameters collection of Command is used to pass parameters. For example, suppose that the database opened by objConn has a stored procedure called FindArtist that accepts one parameter, which is the nationality of artists to be retrieved. The following code invokes this stored procedure with the parameter value "Spanish" and creates a recordset named objRs that has the results of the stored procedure:

```
Dim  objCommand, objParam, objRs

'Create the Command object, connect it to objConn and set its format

Set objCommand = Server.CreateObject("ADODB.command")

Set objCommand.ActiveConnection = objConn

objCommand.CommandText="{call FindArtist (?)}"

'Set up the parameter with the necessary value

Set objParam = objCommand.CreateParameter ("Nationality", adChar,
adParamInput, 25)

objCommand.Parameters.Append objParam

objParam.Value = "Spanish"

'Fire the Stored Proc

Set objRs = objCommand.Execute
```

This example first creates an object of type ADODB.command and then sets the connection of that object to objConn. It then declares the format of the call to the stored procedure by setting the CommandText property. This property is used to pass the name of the stored procedure and the number of parameters it has. The question mark denotes a parameter. If there were three parameters, command text would be set to "{call FindArtist (?, ?, ?)}".

Next, an object is created for the parameter. The values adChar and adParamInput are from ADOVBS, and indicate that the parameter is of type char and is used as input to the stored procedure. The maximum length of the parameter value is 25. After the parameter has been created, it must be added to the command with the Append method. Finally, the stored procedure is invoked using the Execute method. At this point, a recordset named objRs has been created with the results from the stored procedure.

▶ **ADO EXAMPLES**

The following five examples show how to invoke ADO from VBScript using Active Server Pages. These examples focus on the use of ADO and not on the graphics, presentation, or workflow. If you want a flashy, better-behaving application, you should be able to modify these examples to obtain that result. Here, just learn how ADO is used.

All of these examples process the View Ridge database. In some of them, we connect to ViewRidgeSS, the SQL Server database. In others, we connect to the Oracle database ViewRidgeOracle2. In fact, in the last example, only one statement need be changed to switch from SQL Server to Oracle! That is amazing, and exactly what the originators of ODBC hoped for when they created the ODBC specification.

The ASP processor maintains transaction state. For each transaction, it keeps a set of session variables. In these examples, we will use session variables to preserve connection objects. The following statement creates a session variable named "abc" and gives it the string value "Wowzers":

Set Session("abc")="Wowzers"

More useful examples follow.

To run any of these pages, open your browser and enter the following URL if you are running on the same computer as is IIS:

http://localhost/ADOExamples/artist.asp

Otherwise, type the name or address of your server instead of "localhost."

Example 1—Reading a Table

Figure 12-16 shows an ASP that displays the contents of the ARTIST table. In this and the next several figures, statements included within <% %> are shown in red ink. Any code that will be passed to the browser—here, primarily HTML—is shown in blue ink. Any other statements are shown in gray.

The top of the page is standard HTML. The first section of the server code creates a connection object and then a recordset object that has the results of the SQL Statement:

SELECT   Name, Nationality
FROM   ARTIST

Because connection objects are expensive—both in terms of time to create them and memory used—this code preserves the connection object in the session variable _conn. The first time a user invokes this page, the connection object will not exist. In this case, the function call IsObject(Session("_conn")) will return false because _conn has not been set. The code after the Else will be executed to create the connection object. Next, the recordset is created for the SELECT statement in variable varSql.

The next section of the ASP contains HTML for the browser. It is followed by several snippets of server script code intermixed with HTML. The statement On Error Resume Next overrides the ASP script engine's error processing to continue the script. A better page would process the errors instead.

The last part of the page simply produces the HTML and fills in read values. The objRecordSet.MoveFirst . . . MoveNext loop is the logic for standard sequential processing of a file.

The result of this ASP is shown in Figure 12-17. There is nothing spectacular about this page or about this ASP file, except the following: If this were on the Internet, any of more than 250 million people worldwide would be able to view it! They would need no software other than what is already on their computer.

FIGURE 12–16

Artist.asp

```
<HTML>
<HEAD>
<META HTTP-EQUIV="Content-Type" CONTENT="text/html;charset=windows-1252">
<TITLE>Artist</TITLE>
</HEAD>
<!--#include virtual="ADOExamples/adovbs.inc"-->
<BODY>
<%
Dim objConn, objRecordSet, varSql

        If IsObject(Session("_conn")) Then ' if already have a connection, use it
            Set objConn = Session("_conn")
        Else
            Set objConn = Server.CreateObject("ADODB.connection") ' get connection
            objConn.open "ViewRidgeSS"  ' open VRG database using operating system authentication
            objConn.IsolationLevel = adXactReadCommitted ' avoid dirty reads
            Set Session("_conn") = objConn
        End If

        Set objRecordSet = Server.CreateObject("ADODB.Recordset") ' create the record set object

        varSql = "SELECT Name, Nationality FROM ARTIST" ' set up SQL command
        objRecordSet.Open varSql, objConn, adOpenStatic, adLockReadOnly ' static with no need to update
%>

<TABLE BORDER=1 BGCOLOR=#ffffff CELLSPACING=5><FONT FACE="Arial" COLOR=#000000><CAPTION><B>ARTIST
</B></CAPTION></FONT>
<THEAD>
<TR>
<TH BGCOLOR=#c0c0c0 BORDERCOLOR=#000000 ><FONT SIZE=2 FACE="Arial" COLOR=#000000>Name</FONT></TH>
<TH BGCOLOR=#c0c0c0 BORDERCOLOR=#000000 ><FONT SIZE=2 FACE="Arial" COLOR=#000000>Nationality</FONT>
</TH>

</TR>
</THEAD>
<TBODY>
<%
On Error Resume Next
objRecordSet.MoveFirst
do while Not objRecordSet.eof
  %>
<TR VALIGN=TOP>
<TD BORDERCOLOR=#c0c0c0 ><FONT SIZE=2 FACE="Arial" COLOR=#000000><%=Server.HTMLEncode(objRecordSet
("Name"))%><BR></FONT></TD>
<TD BORDERCOLOR=#c0c0c0 ><FONT SIZE=2 FACE="Arial" COLOR=#000000><%=Server.HTMLEncode(objRecordSet
("Nationality"))%><BR></FONT></TD>

</TR>
<%
objRecordSet.MoveNext
loop%>
</TBODY>
<TFOOT></TFOOT>
</TABLE>
</BODY>
</HTML>
```

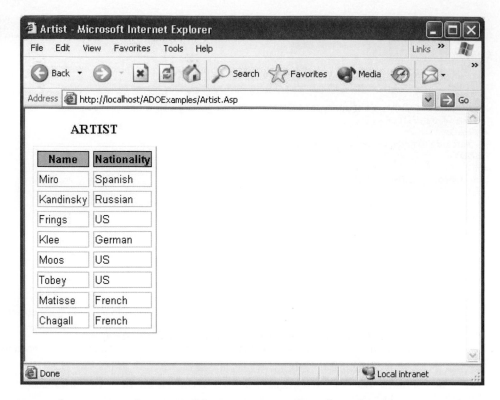

Example 2—Reading a Table in a Generalized Fashion

The first example made minimal use of objects in the ADO object model. We can extend this example by using the Fields collection. Suppose that we want to take the name of a table as input and display all of the columns in it except the surrogate key.

The ASP shown in Figure 12-18 accomplishes this task, except that the name of the table is set in the variable varTableName. We will show in the next example how to obtain a value for the desired table name using HTML form processing.

The first part of the server script has the same function as that shown in Figure 12-16. The only difference is that it opens the Oracle data source.

The varSql variable is set using the varTableName variable. The & is an operator that concatenates two strings together. The result of this expression is the following string:

SELECT * FROM CUSTOMER

Note, too, that the table name is included in the HTML table caption with the code `<CAPTION><B><%=varTableName%></B></CAPTION>`. The code inside the % will cause the value of varTableName to be placed in HTML for the caption.

The next set of server script statements processes the Fields collection. The variable varNumCols is set to the count property of the Fields collection and then the collection is iterated in the loop. Observe that HTML is interspersed in the server code (or server code is interspersed in the HTML, depending on your point of view). Previously, varKeyName has been set to the name of the surrogate key, so this loop checks to determine that the name of the current field object is not the name of the surrogate key. If not, HTML is generated to create the table header. A similar loop is used on the next page to populate the table with values from the recordset.

The advantage of this page is that it can process any table, not just a particular one. In fact, using terminology developed earlier, we can say the page in Figure 12-18 is an abstraction of that in Figure 12-16. The results of this page are shown in Figure 12-19. The CustomerID column is not displayed, as we expected.

FIGURE 12-18

CustomerOracle.asp

```
<HTML>
<HEAD>
<META HTTP-EQUIV="Content-Type" CONTENT="text/html;charset=windows-1252">
<TITLE>Table Display Page</TITLE></HEAD>
<BODY>
<!--#include virtual="ADOExamples/adovbs.inc"-->
<%
        Dim objConn, objRecordSet, objField
        Dim varNumCols, varI, varSql
        Dim varTableName, varKeyName

        varTablename = "CUSTOMER"
        varKeyName = "CUSTOMERID"

        If IsObject(Session("_conn")) Then ' if already have a connection, use it
                Set objConn = Session("_conn")
        Else
                Set objConn = Server.CreateObject("ADODB.connection") ' get connection

                ' open Oracle ODBC file using account DK1 with password
                objConn.open "DSN=ViewRidgeOracle2;UID=DK1;PWD=Sesame"
                objConn.IsolationLevel = adXactReadCommitted ' avoid dirty reads
                Set Session("_conn") = objConn
        End If

        Set objRecordSet = Server.CreateObject("ADODB.Recordset")

        varSQL = "SELECT * FROM " & varTableName
        objRecordSet.Open varSql, objConn   ' cursor type and lock type not supported by Oracle
%>
<TABLE BORDER=1 BGCOLOR=#ffffff CELLSPACING=5><FONT FACE="Arial" COLOR=#000000>
<CAPTION><B><%=varTableName%> (in Oracle database)</B></CAPTION></FONT>
<THEAD><TR>
<%
varNumCols = objRecordSet.Fields.Count
For varI = 0 to varNumCols - 1
Set objField = objRecordSet.Fields(varI)
If objField.Name <> varKeyName Then   ' omit surrogate key %>
<TH BGCOLOR=#c0c0c0 BORDERCOLOR=#000000 ><FONT SIZE=2 FACE="Arial" COLOR=#000000><%=objField.Name%>
</FONT> </TH>
<%
End If
Next%>
</TR></THEAD>
<TBODY>
<%
On Error Resume Next
objRecordSet.MoveFirst
do while Not objRecordSet.eof
%>
<TR VALIGN=TOP>
<%
varNumCols = objRecordSet.Fields.Count
For varI = 0 to varNumCols - 1
Set objField = objRecordSet.Fields(varI)
If objField.Name <> varKeyName Then   ' omit surrogate key%>
<TD BORDERCOLOR=#c0c0c0 ><FONT SIZE=2 FACE="Arial" COLOR=#000000><%=Server.HTMLEncode
(objField.Value)%><BR></FONT></TD>
<%
End If
Next%>
</TR>
<%
</FONT></TD>
<%
End If
Next %>
</TR>
<%
objRecordSet.MoveNext
loop%>
</TBODY>
</TABLE>
</BODY>
</HTML>
```

FIGURE 12–19

Result of CustomerOracle.asp

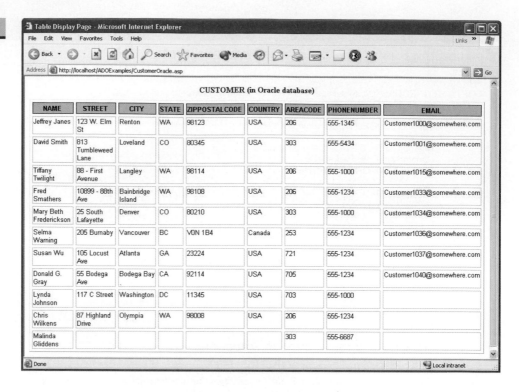

Example 3—Reading Any Table

Figure 12-20(a) shows a data entry form in which a customer can type the name of the table to be displayed. (A better design would be to use a drop-down list to display valid choices, but that discussion would take us away from the discussion of ADO.) The user of this form has typed *artist.* Assume now that when he or she clicks the Show Table button, the form is to cause script to be executed on the server that will display the ARTIST table in this same browser session. Also, assume that the surrogate key is not to be displayed. The desired results are shown in Figure 12-20(b).

This processing necessitates two ASP pages. The first, shown in Figure 12-21(a), is an HTML page that contains the FORM tag.

<FORM METHOD="post" ACTION="GeneralTable.asp">

This tag defines a form section on the page; the section will be set up to contain data entry values. In this form, there will be only one: the table name. The post METHOD refers to an HTML process that causes the data in the form (here, the table name *artist*) to be delivered to the ASP server in an object called Form. An alternative method is *get,* which would cause the data values to be delivered via parameters. This distinction is not too important to us here. The second parameter of the FORM tag is ACTION, which is set to GeneralTable.asp. This parameter tells IIS that when it receives the response from this form, it should pass the ASP file GeneralTable.asp to the ASP processor. The values from the form will be passed in an object called Form.

The rest of the page is standard HTML. Note that the name of the text input box is text1.

Figure 12-21(b) shows GeneralTable.asp, the page that will be invoked when the response is received from the form page in Figure 12-21(a). The first executable script statement is

varTableName = Request.Form("text1")

FIGURE 12–20

Displaying Any Table
(a) Entering the Name
of the Table to Display
and (b) Display of the
Artist Table

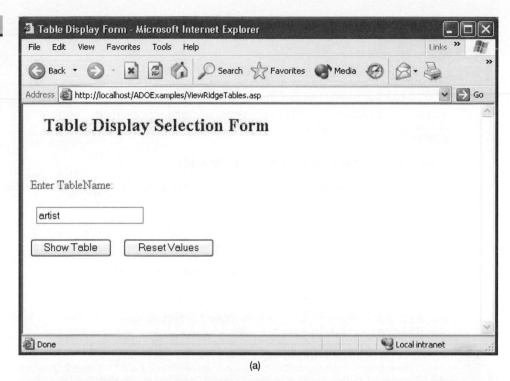

(a)

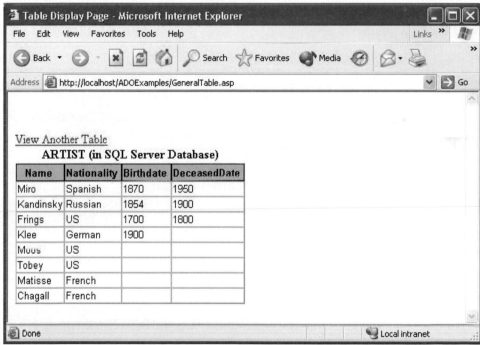

(b)

Request.Form is the name of the object that contains the values sent back from the
browser. In this case, text1 will be set to *artist*.

This version of GeneralTable processes the SQL Server View Ridge database. The
surrogate key names in SQL Server are in the form ArtistID, not ARTISTID. Because
VBScript comparisons are case-sensitive, we need to ensure that varKeyName has the
surrogate key name in the required format. The user might enter *ARTIST, artist, Artist,*
or aRtIsT, for that matter; so we cannot just append *ID* to the input table name. The

FIGURE 12-21

Pages to Display Any Table (a) ViewRidgeTables.asp and (b) GeneralTable.asp

```
<HTML>
<HEAD>
<META HTTP-EQUIV="Content-Type" CONTENT="text/html;charset=windows-1252">
<TITLE>Table Display Form</TITLE>
</HEAD>
<BODY>

<FORM METHOD="post" ACTION="GeneralTable.asp">

  <P><STRONG><FONT color=purple face="" size=5>   Table Display Selection Form</FONT>
</STRONG>
<P></P>
<P> </P>

<P><FONT style="BACKGROUND-COLOR: #ffffff"><FONT color=forestgreen face=""
style="BACKGROUND-COLOR: #ffffff">Enter
TableName:</FONT>     </FONT></P>

<P></P>

<P><FONT style="BACKGROUND-COLOR: #ffffff"></FONT> 
<INPUT id=text1 name=text1 size="20"></P>

<P><FONT style="BACKGROUND-COLOR: #ffffff">
<INPUT id=submit1 name=submit1 type=submit value="Show Table" >   
<INPUT id=reset1 name=reset1 type=reset value="Reset Values"></FONT></P>
</FORM>
</BODY>
</HTML>
```

(a)

three statements starting with varKeyNameFirst employ the UCase and LCase functions to set varKeyName correctly.

The remainder of this page is the same as the Customer.asp page shown in Figure 12-18. Note again that varKeyName will be set to ArtistID, which is the name of the surrogate key column that we do not wish to display.

Example 4—Updating a Table

The three previous examples all concern reading data. This next example shows how to update table data by adding a row with ADO. Figure 12-22(a) shows a data entry form that will capture artist name and nationality and create a new row. This form is similar to ViewRidgeTables.asp; it has two data entry fields rather than one. When the user clicks Save New Artist, the artist is added to the database; and if the results are successful, the form in Figure 12-22(b) is produced. The See New List reference will invoke Artist.asp, which will display the ARTIST table with the new row, as shown in Figure 12-22(c).

The ASPs are shown in Figure 12-23. The first page is a data entry form with two fields, one for artist name (named *Name*) and a second for artist nationality (named *Nation*). When the user clicks the submit button, these data are to be sent back to IIS, which in turn is to send it along with the page AddArtist.asp to the ASP processor.

FIGURE 12-21

(continued)

```
<HTML>
<HEAD>
<META HTTP-EQUIV="Content-Type" CONTENT="text/html;charset=windows-1252">
<TITLE>Table Display Page</TITLE>
</HEAD>
<BODY>
<!--#include virtual="ADOExamples/adovbs.inc"-->
<%

Dim objConn, objRecordSet, objField
Dim varNumCols, varI, varSql
Dim varTableName, varRecordSetName, varKeyName
Dim varTableNameFirst, varTableNameRest

varTablename = Request.Form("text1")

' set key name to upper first initial and lower remainder with ID, e.g., CustomerID
varTableNameFirst = UCase(Left(varTableName, 1))
varTableNameRest = LCase(Right(varTableName, Len(varTableName)-1))
varKeyName = varTableNameFirst & varTableNameRest &"ID"

varRecordSetName = "_rs_" & varTableName ' use for saving recordset object pointer

If IsObject(Session("_conn")) Then
        Set objConn = Session("_conn")
Else
        Set objConn = Server.CreateObject("ADODB.connection")
        objConn.IsolationLevel = adXactReadCommitted ' avoid dirty reads
        objConn.open "ViewRidgeSS" ' use operating system security
        Set Session("_conn") = objConn
End If

If IsObject(Session(varRecordSetName)) Then
        Set objRecordSet = Session(varRecordSetName) ' used saved recordset object if possible
        objRecordSet.Requery
Else
        varSql = "SELECT * FROM " & "[" & varTableName & "]" ' put brackets in case table name has spaces, etc.
        Set objRecordSet = Server.CreateObject("ADODB.Recordset")
        ' in the next statement, note use of cursor and lock types
        objRecordSet.Open varSql, objConn ', adOpenDynamic ',   adLockOptimistic ' allow for updates
        Set Session(varRecordSetName) = objRecordSet
 End If
%>
<TABLE BORDER=1 BGCOLOR=#ffffff CELLSPACING=0><FONT FACE="Arial" COLOR=#000000>
<CAPTION><B><%=UCase(varTableName)%> (in SQL Server Database)</B></CAPTION></FONT>
<THEAD><TR>
<%
varNumCols = objRecordSet.Fields.Count
For varI = 0 to varNumCols - 1
Set objField = objRecordSet.Fields(varI)
If objField.Name <> varKeyName Then %>
<TH BGCOLOR=#c0c0c0 BORDERCOLOR=#000000 ><FONT SIZE=2 FACE="Arial" COLOR=#000000><%=objField.Name%>
</FONT> </TH>
<%
End If
Next%>
</TH></THEAD>
<TBODY>
<%
On Error Resume Next
objRecordSet.MoveFirst
do while Not objRecordSet.eof
%>
<TR VALIGN=TOP>
<'%
varNumCols = objRecordSet.Fields.Count
For varI = 0 to varNumCols - 1
Set objField = objRecordSet.Fields(varI)
If objField.Name <> varKeyName Then %>
<TD BORDERCOLOR=#c0c0c0 ><FONT SIZE=2 FACE="Arial" COLOR=#000000><%=Server.HTMLEncode(objField.Value)%><BR></FONT></TD>
<%
End If
Next%>
</TR>

<%
objRecordSet.MoveNext
loop%>
<BR><BR><A HREF="ViewRidgeTables.asp">View Another Table</A>
</TBODY></TABLE>
</BODY>
</HTML>
```

(b)

FIGURE 12-22

Entering a New Artist (a) Form to Enter Artist Data; (b) Results of Add Operation and (c) Display of new Artist Table

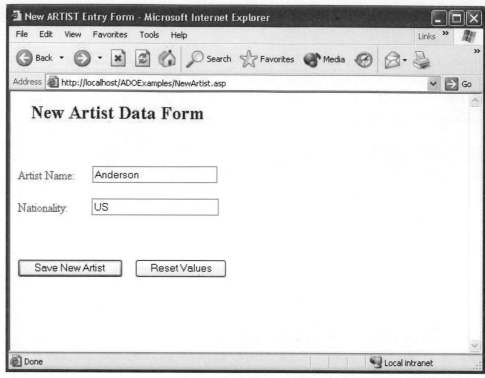

(a)

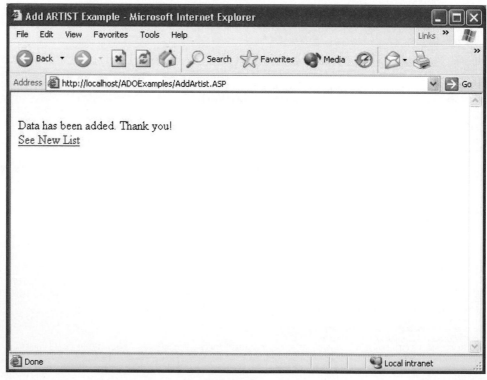

(b)

FIGURE 12-22

(continued)

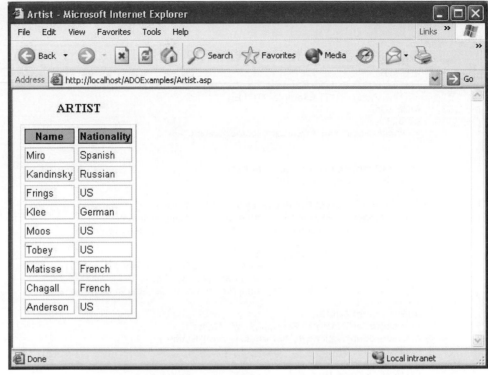

(c)

FIGURE 12–23

Pages to Enter New Artist Data (a) NewArtist.asp and (b) AddArtist.asp

```
<HTML>
<HEAD>
<META HTTP-EQUIV="Content-Type" CONTENT="text/html;charset=windows-1252">
<TITLE>New ARTIST Entry Form</TITLE>
</HEAD>
<BODY>

<FORM METHOD="post" ACTION="AddArtist.ASP">

 <P><STRONG><FONT color=purple face="" size=5>   New Artist Data Form</FONT></STRONG>
<P></P>
<P> </P>

<P><FONT style="BACKGROUND-COLOR: #ffffff"><FONT color=forestgreen face=""
style="BACKGROUND-COLOR: #ffffff">Artist Name:</FONT>     
<INPUT id=text1 name=Name style="HEIGHT: 22px; WIDTH: 164px" size="20"></FONT></P>

<P><FONT color=forestgreen face=""
style="BACKGROUND-COLOR: #ffffff">Nationality:       
<INPUT id=text2 name=Nation style="HEIGHT: 22px; WIDTH: 167px" size="20"></FONT></P>

<P> </P>

<P><FONT style="BACKGROUND-COLOR: #ffffff">
<INPUT id=submit1 name=submit1 type=submit value="Save New Artist">   
<INPUT Id=reset1 name=reset1 type=reset value="Reset Values"></FONT></P>
</FORM>
</BODY>
</HTML>
```

(a)

FIGURE 12-23

(continued)

```
<HTML>
<HEAD>
<META HTTP-EQUIV="Content-Type" CONTENT="text/html;charset=windows-1252">
<TITLE>Add ARTIST Example</TITLE>
</HEAD>
<BODY>
<!--#include virtual="ADOExamples/adovbs.inc"-->
<%

Dim objConn, objRecordSet, objField
Dim varNumCols, varl, varSql

Set objConn = Server.CreateObject("ADODB.connection")
objConn.open "ViewRidgeSS" ' open with operating system security
objConn.IsolationLevel = adXactReadCommitted ' avoid dirty reads

varSql = "SELECT * FROM [ARTIST]"
Set objRecordSet = Server.CreateObject("ADODB.Recordset")
' in the next statement, note use of cursor and lock types
objRecordSet.Open varSql, objConn, adOpenDynamic, adLockOptimistic

objRecordSet.AddNew
objRecordSet("Name")= Request.Form("Name")
objRecordSet("Nationality")= Request.Form("Nation")
objRecordSet.Update

On Error Resume Next
varErrorCount = objConn.Errors.Count
If varErrorCount > 0 Then
        For varl = 0 to varErrorCount - 1
                Response.Write "<BR><I>" & objConn.Errors(varl).Description & "</I><BR>"
        Next
End If

objRecordSet.Close
objConn.Close

Response.Write "<BR>Data has been added.  Thank you!<BR>"
Response.Write "<A HREF="& """" &"artist.asp" & """"& ">See New List</A>"

%>
<BR><BR>
</BODY>
</HTML>
```

(b)

AddArtist.asp [shown in Figure 12-23(b)] obtains connection and recordset objects. No attempt is made here to save connection and recordset object pointers in session variables. (The assumption is that only one artist will be added per session and saving them would be unnecessary.) If desired, code to save them could certainly be added as shown in the previous examples.

The key difference of this page is shown in the following statements:

```
objRecordSet.AddNew

objRecordSet("Name")= Request.Form("Name")

objRecordSet("Nationality")= Request.Form("Nation")

objRecordSet.Update
```

The first statement obtains a new row in the objRecordSet object and then values are obtained for the Name and Nationality columns from the Request.Form object. Note that there is no need for the column names and Request.Form names to be the same. Here, the second column name is Nationality, but the second value from the form is Nation. The objRecordSet.Update call causes the database update. Note the error-processing code that will cause error messages to be displayed via the Response.Write statement (this is a method available in the Response object of ASP). The page ends with two calls to send a confirmation message back to the user and to create a URL to Artist.asp if the user wants to see the table with the new values.

Example 5—Invoking a Stored Procedure

We created a stored procedure named Customer_Insert in both the Oracle and SQL Server databases (in Chapters 10 and 11, respectively). In both cases, the stored procedure accepts a new customer name, area code, local number, and nationality of all artists in whom the customer is interested. It then creates a new row in CUSTOMER and adds appropriate rows to the intersection table.

To invoke the stored procedure using an ASP page, we create a Web page to collect the necessary data, as shown in Figure 12-24(a). Now, when the user clicks Add Customer, we want to invoke an ASP that calls the stored procedure with the form data. So the user can verify that the new data has been entered correctly, the ASP then queries a view that joins customer names with artist names and nationalities. The result is shown in Figure 12-24(b).

FIGURE 12-24

Adding a New Customer via a Stored Procedure.
(a) Customer Data Entry Form and
(b) Display of Customer Interests View

(a)

FIGURE 12-24

(continued)

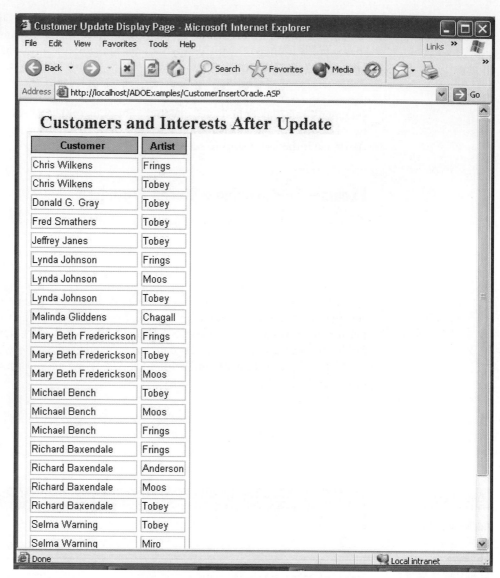

(b)

Figure 12-25(a) shows the code to generate the form to gather data. The parameter fields are named *text1* through *text4*. The form invokes the ASP CustomerInsertOracle in the FORM METHOD statement, so when the user clicks Add Customer, the data will be sent to CustomerInsertOracle, the page shown in Figure 12-25(b).

This page looks for a saved connection, and if one is not found, it obtains a new one, as shown earlier. Then, it creates a command object, *objCommand,* and associates it with objConn. It then sets up the call to the Customer_Insert stored procedure with CommandText= "{call Customer_Insert(?, ?, ?, ?)}." This pattern indicates that four parameters will be passed. The next sections of code create the parameters and append them to the command object. Finally, the command is executed, which causes the stored procedure to be invoked. No transaction isolation level or cursor properties are set because the stored procedure will set them for itself.

After the command is executed, a recordset is created on a select of all columns of the view CUSTOMERINTERESTS, and finally the columns are displayed in the browser using the techniques shown in earlier examples.

FIGURE 12–25

Pages to Invoke Stored Procedure (a) NewCustomerOracle.asp and (b) CustomerInsertOracle.asp

```
<HTML>
<HEAD>
<META HTTP-EQUIV="Content-Type" CONTENT="text/html;charset=windows-1252">
<TITLE>Table Display Form</TITLE>
</HEAD>
<BODY>

<FORM METHOD="post" ACTION="CustomerInsertOracle.ASP">

 <P><STRONG><FONT color=purple face="" size=5>   View Ridge Gallery</FONT></STRONG>

 <P>   <strong><font color="purple" face="5"> New Customer Form</font></strong>
<P><font style="background-color: #ffffff" color="forestgreen" face>   
 Name:   </font><FONT style="BACKGROUND-COLOR: #ffffff">     
               
  
 </FONT><INPUT id=text1 name=text1 size="20"></P>

 <P> <font style="background-color: #ffffff" color="forestgreen" face>   AreaCode
<font style="background-color: #ffffff">:   </font>      
           
 </font><INPUT id=text2 name=text2 size="6"></P>

 <P><font style="background-color: #ffffff" color="forestgreen" face>   
 Phone:              
           
 </font><INPUT id=text3 name=text3 size="20">        </P>

 <P>    <font style="background-color: #ffffff" color="forestgreen" face>Nationality
 of Artists:  </font>   <INPUT id=text4 name=text4 size="17"></P>

 <P> <FONT style="BACKGROUND-COLOR: #ffffff">
   </FONT>     <FONT style="BACKGROUND-COLOR: #ffffff">
<INPUT id=submit1 name=submit1 type=submit value="Add Customer" >   
<INPUT id=reset1 name=reset1 type=reset value="Reset Values"></FONT> </P>

</FORM>
</BODY>
</HTML>
```

(a)

In both the Oracle and SQL Server databases, this view was defined as the join of CUSTOMER and ARTIST over the intersection table. The syntax used for Oracle was

CREATE VIEW CUSTOMERINTERESTS AS

    SELECT CUSTOMER.NAME CUSTNAME, ARTIST.NAME

        ARTISTNAME, ARTIST.NATIONALITY

    FROM CUSTOMER, CUSTOMER_ARTIST_INT, ARTIST

    WHERE CUSTOMER.CUSTOMERID = CUSTOMER_ARTIST_

        INT.CUSTOMERID AND

    ARTIST.ARTISTID = CUSTOMER_ARTIST_INT.ARTISTID

One very interesting thing about this page is that the only difference between the Oracle version shown here and the SQL Server version is the name of the ODBC data source and the account name and password used. Note the comment line under the

FIGURE 12-25

(continued)

```
<HTML>
<HEAD>
<META HTTP-EQUIV="Content-Type" CONTENT="text/html;charset=windows-1252">
<TITLE>Customer Update Display Page</TITLE>
</HEAD>
<BODY>

<P><STRONG><FONT color=purple face="" size=5>   Customers and Interests After Update</FONT></STRONG>
<!--#include virtual="ADOExamples/adovbs.inc"-->
<%

        Dim objConn, objCommand, objParam, oRs
        Dim objRecordSet, objField
        Dim varl, varSql, varNumCols, varValue

        If IsObject(Session("_conn")) Then
                Set objConn = Session("_conn") ' use current session if available
        Else
                Set objConn = Server.CreateObject("ADODB.connection")
                ' stored procedure will set its own isolation level
                objConn.open "DSN=ViewRidgeOracle2;UID=DK1;PWD=Sesame"
                'objConn.open "ViewRidgeSS",  could use this to update via SQL Server
                Set Session("_conn") = objConn
        End If

        Set objCommand = Server.CreateObject("ADODB.Command") ' create a command object
        Set objCommand.ActiveConnection = objConn ' set the command objects connection

        objCommand.CommandText="{call Customer_Insert (?, ?, ?, ?)}" ' setup call to stored procedure

        ' Set up four parameters with necessary values
        Set objParam = objCommand.CreateParameter("NewName", adChar, adParamInput, 50)
        objCommand.Parameters.Append objParam
        objParam.Value = Request.Form("text1")

        Set objParam = objCommand.CreateParameter("AreaCode", adChar, adParamInput, 5)
        objCommand.Parameters.Append objParam
        objParam.Value = Request.Form("text2")

        Set objParam = objCommand.CreateParameter("PhoneNumber", adChar, adParamInput, 8)
        objCommand.Parameters.Append objParam
        objParam.Value = Request.Form("text3")

        Set objParam = objCommand.CreateParameter("Nationality", adChar, adParamInput, 25)
        objCommand.Parameters.Append objParam
        objParam.Value = Request.Form("text4")

' Fire the Stored Proc

        Set oRs = objCommand.Execute

        ' now read the data from a view having both CUSTOMER and ARTIST
        varSql = "SELECT * FROM CUSTOMERINTERESTS ORDER BY CUSTOMER" ' use that joins via the intersection table
        Set objRecordSet = Server.CreateObject("ADODB.Recordset")
        objRecordSet.Open varSql, objConn

%>
<TABLE BORDER=1 BGCOLOR=#ffffff CELLSPACING=5><FONT FACE="Arial" COLOR=#000000><CAPTION><B>
<CUSTOMERS AND INTERESTS</B></CAPTION></FONT>
<THEAD>
<TR>
<%
varNumCols = objRecordSet.Fields.Count
For varl = 0 to varNumCols - 1
Set objField = objRecordSet.Fields(varl)
%>
<TH BGCOLOR=#c0c0c0 BORDERCOLOR=#000000 ><FONT SIZE=2 FACE="Arial" COLOR=#000000><%=objField.Name%>
</FONT> </TH>
```

(b)

FIGURE 12-25

(continued)

```
<%
Next%>
</TR>
</THEAD>
<TBODY>
<%
On Error Resume Next
objRecordSet.MoveFirst
do while Not objRecordSet.eof
%>
<TR VALIGN=TOP>
<%
varNumCols = objRecordSet.Fields.Count
For varl = 0 to varNumCols - 1
Set objField = objRecordSet.Fields(varl)
If objRecordSet.Fields(varl).Type = adNumeric then
        varValue=CDbl(objField.Value)
        varValue = convert(char, varValue)
else
        varValue=Server.HTMLEncode(objField.Value)
End If
%>
<TD BORDERCOLOR=#c0c0c0 ><FONT SIZE=2 FACE="Arial" COLOR=#000000><%=(varValue)%><BR></FONT></TD>
<%
varValue=""
Next%>
</TR>

<%
objRecordSet.MoveNext
loop%>
</TBODY>
<TFOOT></TFOOT>
</TABLE>
</BODY>
</HTML>
```

(b) *continued*

objConn.open statement; all of the idiosyncrasies of the DBMS products are contained in the stored procedures and the ASP developer need know nothing about them.

These examples give you an idea of the use of ADO. The best way to learn more is to write some pages yourself. This chapter has shown all the basic techniques that you will need. You've worked hard to get to this point, and if you are able to understand enough to create some of your own pages, you have come very far indeed since Chapter 1!

SUMMARY

Database applications today reside in a rich and complicated environment. In addition to relational databases, there are nonrelational databases, VSAM and other file-processing data, email, and other types of data. To ease the job of the application programmer, various standards have been developed. The ODBC standard is for relational databases; the OLE DB standard is for relational and other datasources. ADO was developed to provide easier access to OLE DB data for the non-object-oriented programmer.

ODBC, or the open database connectivity standard, provides an interface by which database applications can access and process relational data sources in a DBMS-independent manner. ODBC was developed by an industry committee and has been implemented by Microsoft and many other vendors. ODBC involves applications program, driver manager, DBMS driver, and data source components. Single-tier and multiple-tier drivers are defined. There are three types of data source names: file, system, and user. System data sources are recommended for Web servers. The process of defining a system data source name involves specifying the type of driver and the identity of the database to be processed.

OLE DB is one of the foundations of the Microsoft data access world. It implements the Microsoft OLE and COM standards, and is accessible to object-oriented programs through those interfaces. OLE DB breaks the features and functions of a DBMS into objects, thus making it easier for vendors to implement portions of functionality. Key object terms are abstraction, methods, properties, and collections. A rowset is an abstraction of a recordset, which in turn is an abstraction of a relation. Objects are defined by properties that specify their characteristics and methods that are actions they can perform. A collection is an object that contains a group of other objects. The goals of OLE DB are listed in Figure 12-10. An interface is a set of objects and the properties and methods they expose in that interface. Objects may expose different properties and methods in different interfaces. An implementation is how an object accomplishes its tasks. Implementations are hidden from the outside world and may be changed without impacting the users of the objects. An interface ought not to be changed, ever.

Tabular data providers present data in the form of rowsets. Service providers transform data into another form; such providers are both consumers and providers of data. A rowset is equivalent to a cursor. Basic rowset interfaces are IRowSet, IAccessor, and IColumnsInfo. Other interfaces are defined for more advanced capability.

ADO is a simple object model used by OLE DB data consumers. It can be used from any language supported by Microsoft. The ADO object model has Connection, RecordSet, Command, and Errors collection objects. Recordsets have a Fields collection, and Commands have a Parameters collection.

A Connection object establishes a connection to a data provider and data source. Connections have an isolation mode. Once a connection is created, it can be used to create RecordSet and Command objects. RecordSet objects represent cursors; they have both CursorType and LockType properties. RecordSets can be created with SQL statements. The Fields collection of a RecordSet can be processed to individually manipulate fields.

The Errors collection contains one or more error messages that result from an ADO operation. The command object is used to execute stored parameterized queries or stored procedures. Input data can be sent to the correct ASP using the HTML FORM tag. Table updates are made using the RecordSet Update method.

GROUP I QUESTIONS

12.1 Describe why the data environment is complicated.

12.2 Explain the relationship of ODBC, OLE DB, and ADO.

12.3 Explain the author's justification for describing Microsoft standards. Do you agree?

12.4 Name the components of the ODBC standard.

12.5 What role does the driver manager serve? Who supplies it?

12.6 What role does the DBMS driver serve? Who supplies it?

12.7 What is a single-tier driver?

12.8 What is a multiple-tier driver?

12.9 Do the uses of the term *tier* in the three-tier architecture and its use in ODBC have anything to do with each other?

12.10 Why are conformance levels important?

12.11 Summarize the three ODBC API conformance levels.

12.12 Summarize the three SQL grammar conformance levels.

12.13 Explain the differences between the three types of data sources.

12.14 Which data source type is recommended for Web servers?

12.15 What are the two tasks to be accomplished when setting up an ODBC data source name?

12.16 Why is OLE DB important?

12.17 What disadvantage of ODBC does OLE DB overcome?

12.18 Define *abstraction* and explain how it relates to OLE DB.

12.19 Give an example of abstraction involving rowset.

12.20 Define object *properties* and *methods.*

12.21 What is the difference between an object class and an object?

12.22 Explain the role of data consumers and data providers.

12.23 What is an interface?

12.24 What is the difference between an interface and an implementation?

12.25 Explain why an implementation can be changed but an interface should not be changed.

12.26 Summarize the goals of OLE DB.

12.27 What is MTS, and what does it do?

12.28 Explain the difference between a tabular data provider and a service provider. Which type is a product that transforms OLE DB data into XML documents?

12.29 In the context of OLE DB, what is the difference between a rowset and a cursor?

12.30 What languages can use ADO?

12.31 List the objects in the ADO object model and explain their relationships.

12.32 What is the function of the Connection object?

12.33 Show a snippet of VBScript for creating a Connection object.

12.34 What is the function of the RecordSet object?

12.35 Show a snippet of VBScript for creating a RecordSet object.

12.36 What does the Fields collection contain? Explain a situation in which you would use it.

12.37 Show a snippet of VBScript for processing the Fields collection.

12.38 What does the Errors collection contain? Explain a situation in which you would use it.

12.39 Show a snippet of VBScript for processing the Errors collection.

12.40 What is the purpose of the Command object?

12.41 Show a snippet of VBScript for executing a stored parameterized query that has two parameters: A and B.

12.42 Explain the purpose of the <% and %> tags in ASP.

12.43 Explain the purpose of the _conn variable in Figure 12-16.

12.44 What is the reason for the code that creates varKeyName in Figure 12-21(b).

12.45 Explain the purpose of the ACTION parameter of the FORM tag in Figure 12-21(a).

12.46 Explain what happens when the following statement is executed in the ASP in Figure 12-21(b):

varTableName = Request.Form("text1")

12.47 Show a VBScript snippet for adding a new record to a recordset named objMyRecordSet. Assume that the fields are A and B and their values are to be "Avalue" and "Bvalue", respectively.

12.48 What purpose is served by the Response.Write statement?

GROUP II QUESTIONS

12.49 Microsoft expends much effort to promulgate the OLE DB and ADO standards. It does not directly receive revenue from these standards. IIS is free Windows XP and 2000. Its Web site has numerous examples of articles to help developers learn more, and all of it is free. Why do you think Microsoft does this? What goal is served?

12.50 In the code in Figure 12-23(b), the cursor type is set to dynamic. What effect does this have on the processing of this and the Customer.asp and Artist.asp pages? Explain how you think the isolation level, cursor type, and lock type parameters should be set for an application that involves all three of these pages.

12.51 Explain how to change the example ASP in Figure 12-16 to run with the DSN ViewRidgeOracle2. Explain how to change the ASP in Figure 12-18 to run with ViewRidgeSS. Although the ease of making these changes is interesting from a technology standpoint, does this capability have any importance in the world of commerce?

12.52 If you have installed Oracle, use your browser to execute the page shown in Figure 12-18. Now, open SQL Plus and delete two rows of CUSTOMER data using the SQL DELETE command. Go back to your browser and execute the page shown in Figure 12-18 again. Explain the results.

12.53 If you have installed SQL Server, use your browser to execute the page in Figure 12-16. Now, open SQL Query Analyzer and delete two rows of CUSTOMER data using the SQL DELETE command. Go back to your browser and execute the page in Figure 12-16 again. Explain the results. If you answered question 12.52, explain the difference in results you received, if any.

FIREDUP PROJECT QUESTIONS

Create the FiredUp database using either Oracle or SQL Server, if you have not already done so. Follow the instructions at the end of Chapters 10 or 11, respectively.

A. Code an ASP to display the STOVE table.

B. Code an ASP to display any table in the FiredUp database. Use Figure 12-21 as an example.

C. Code an ASP to enter new STOVE data. Justify your choice of transaction isolation.

D. Code an ASP to allow customers to register their own stoves. Assume that the customer and stove data already exist in the database. Justify your choice of transaction isolation.

E. Create a stored procedure to enter new stove repair data.

F. Code an ASP to invoke the stored procedure created in task E. Use Figure 12-25 as an example.

TWIGS TREE TRIMMING SERVICE PROJECT QUESTIONS

If you have not already done so, create the Twigs database using either Oracle or SQL Server. Follow the instructions at the end of Chapter 10 or 11, respectively.

A.   Code an ASP to display the OWNER table.

B.   Code an ASP to display any table in the Twigs database. Use Figure 12-21 as an example.

C.   Code an ASP to enter new OWNER data. Justify your choice of cursor isolation.

D.   Code an ASP to allow owners to schedule their own services. They should enter DateOfService and Description only. Assume that the customer data already exists in the database. Justify your choice of cursor isolation.

E.   Create a stored procedure to enter new OWNER data.

F.   Code an ASP to invoke the stored procedure created in task E. Use Figure 12-25 as an example.

CHAPTER 13

XML and ADO.NET

This chapter considers one of the most important, if not *the* most important, development in information systems technology today. It discusses the confluence of two information technology subject areas: database processing and document processing. For more than 20 years, these two subject areas developed independently of one another. With the advent of the Internet, however, they crashed together in what some industry pundits called a technology train wreck. The result is still being sorted out, with new products, product features, technology standards, and development practices emerging every month.

▶ THE IMPORTANCE OF XML

Database processing and document processing need each other. Database processing needs document processing for expressing database views; document processing needs database processing for storing and manipulating data. Even though these technologies need each other, however, it took the popularity of the Internet to make that need obvious. At first, Web sites did little more than display on-line brochures of fixed content. As Internet usage increased, however, organizations wanted to make their Web pages more functional by displaying (and later updating) data from organizational databases. At this point, Web developers began to take a serious interest in SQL, database performance, database security, and other aspects of database processing.

As the Web developers invaded the database community, database practitioners began to wonder, "Who are these people and what do they want?" Database practitioners began to learn about HTML, the language used to mark up documents for display by Web browsers. At first, the database community scoffed at HTML because of its limitations, but they soon learned that HTML was an application of a more robust document markup language called **SGML** or the **Standard Generalized Markup Language.**

SGML was clearly important, just as important to document processing as the relational model was important to database processing. Obviously, this powerful language had some role to play in the display of database data, but what role?

In the early 1990s, the two communities began to meet and the result of their work is a series of standards that concerns a language called **XML**, or **Extensible Markup Language**. XML is a subset of SGML, but additional standards and capabilities have been added to XML processing, and today XML technology is a hybrid of document processing and database processing. In fact, as the XML standards evolved, it became clear that the communities had been working on different aspects of the same problem for many years. They even used the same terms, but with different meanings. You will see later in this chapter how the term *schema* is used in XML for a concept that is completely different from the use of *schema* in the database world.

XML provides a standardized yet customizable way to describe the content of documents. As such, it can be used to describe any database view, but in a standardized way. As you will learn, unlike SQL views, XML views are not limited to one multivalued path.

In addition, when used with the XML Schema standard, XML documents can automatically be generated from database data. Further, database data can automatically be extracted from XML documents. Even more, there are standardized ways of defining how document components are mapped to database schema components and *vice-versa*.

Meanwhile, the rest of the computing community began to take notice of XML. **SOAP**, which originally meant **Simple Object Access Protocol**, was defined as an XML-based standard for providing remote procedure calls over the Internet. Initially, SOAP assumed the use of HTTP as a transport mechanism; but as Microsoft, IBM, Oracle, and other large companies joined forces in the support of the SOAP standard, this assumption was removed and SOAP was generalized to become a standard protocol for sending messages of any type, using any protocol. With this change, SOAP no longer meant simple object access protocol, so now SOAP is just a name, and not an acronym.

In any case, XML began to be used for many, many purposes in the computer profession. One of the most important is as a standardized means to define and communicate documents for processing over the Internet. XML plays a key role in Microsoft's .NET initiative; and Bill Gates called XML the "*lingua franca* of the Internet age" in 2001.

We will begin the discussion of XML by describing its use for materializing Web pages. As you will learn, however, XML uses go far beyond Web page materialization. In fact, Web page materialization may be the least important application of XML. We begin with page materialization only because it is an easy way to introduce XML documents. After that, we will explain the XML Schema standard and discuss its use for database processing. Finally, we will show examples of the integrated processing of database data and XML using Microsoft ADO.NET.

As you read this chapter, keep in mind that this area is the leading edge of database processing today. Standards, products, and product capabilities are changing frequently. You can keep abreast of these changes by checking the sites **www.w3c.org**, **www.xml.org**, **msdn.microsoft.com**, **www.oracle.com**, **www.ibm.com** and other vendor sites. Learning as much as you can about XML and database processing is one of the best ways you can prepare yourself for a successful career.

▶ XML AS A MARKUP LANGUAGE

As a markup language, XML is significantly better than HTML. There are several reasons for XML's superiority. For one, the designers of XML created a clear separation between document structure, content, and materialization. XML has facilities for dealing with each, and the nature of those facilities is such that they cannot be confounded as they can with HTML.

Additionally, XML is standardized, but as its name implies, the standards allow for extension by developers. With XML, you are not limited to a fixed set of elements like <TITLE>, <H1>, and <P>; but you can create your own.

One of the problems with HTML is that there is too much freedom. Consider the following HTML:

<h2>Hello World</h2>

Although the <h2> tag can be used to mark a level two heading in an outline, it can also be used simply to cause "Hello World" to be displayed with a particular style. Because of this characteristic, we cannot rely on tags to indicate the true structure of an HTML page. Tag use is too arbitrary; <h2> may mean a heading or it may mean nothing at all.

As you will see, the structure of the document is formally defined with XML. If we find the tag <street>, we know exactly where that tag belongs and how it relates in the document structure to other tags. Thus, XML documents are said to accurately represent the semantics of their data.

XML Document Type Declarations

Figure 13-1 shows a sample XML document. Notice that the document has two sections. The first section defines the structure of the document; it is referred to as the document type declaration, or **DTD.** The second part is the document data.

The DTD begins with the word DOCTYPE and specifies the name of this type of document, which is customer. Then, it calls out the content of the customer document. It consists of two groups: name and address. The name group consists of two elements: firstname and lastname. Firstname and lastname are defined as #PCDATA, which means that they are strings of character data. Next, the address element is defined to consist of

FIGURE 13-1

Customer XML Document with Internal DTD

```
<?xml version="1.0" encoding="UTF-8"?>
<!-- edited with XML Spy v3.5 NT (http://www.xmlspy.com) by David Kroenke (private) -->
<!DOCTYPE customer [
    <!ELEMENT customer (name, address)>
    <!ELEMENT name (firstname, lastname)>
    <!ELEMENT firstname (#PCDATA)>
    <!ELEMENT lastname (#PCDATA)>
    <!ELEMENT address (street+, city, state, zip)>
    <!ELEMENT street (#PCDATA)>
    <!ELEMENT city (#PCDATA)>
    <!ELEMENT state (#PCDATA)>
    <!ELEMENT zip (#PCDATA)>
]>
<customer>
    <name>
        <firstname>Michelle</firstname>
        <lastname>Correlli</lastname>
    </name>
    <address>
        <street>1824 East 7th Avenue</street>
        <street>Suite 700</street>
        <city>Memphis</city>
        <state>TN</state>
        <zip>32123-7788</zip>
    </address>
</customer>
```

four elements: street, city, state, and zip. Each of these is also defined as character data. The plus sign after street indicates that one value is required and that multiple values are possible.

The data instance of customer shown in Figure 13-1 conforms to the DTD; hence, this document is said to be a **type-valid** XML document. If it did not conform to the DTD it would be a **not-type-valid** document. Documents that are not-type-valid can still be perfectly good XML; they are just not valid instances of their type. For example, if the document in Figure 13-1 had two city elements, it could still be valid XML, but it would be not-type-valid.

Although DTDs are almost always desirable, they are not required in XML documents. Documents that have no DTD are by definition not-type-valid because there is no type to validate them against.

The DTD does not need to be contained inside the document. Figure 13-2 shows a customer document in which the DTD is obtained from the file C: \DB9e\First Draft\Chapter 13\XML Docs\Customer.dtd. The advantage of storing the DTD externally is that many documents can be validated against the same DTD.

The creator of a DTD is free to choose any elements he or she wants. Hence, XML documents can be extended, but in a standardized and controlled way.

Materializing XML Documents with XSLT

The XML document shown in Figure 13-1 shows both the document's structure and content. Nothing in the document, however, indicates how it is to be materialized. The designers of XML created a clean separation among structure, content, and format. The most popular way to materialize XML documents is to use XSLT, or the Extensible Style Language: Transformations. XSLT is a powerful and robust transformation language. It can be used to materialize XML documents into HTML, and it can be used for many other purposes as well. One common application of XSLT is to transform an XML document in one format into a second XML document in another format. A company can, for example, use XSLT to transform an XML order document in its own format into an equivalent XML order document in their customer's format. There are many features and functions of XSLT that we will be unable to discuss here. See **www.w3.org** for more information about it.

XSLT is a declarative transformation language. It is declarative because you create a set of rules that govern how the document is to be materialized instead of specifying a procedure for materializing document elements. It is transformational because it transforms the input document into another document.

FIGURE 13-2

Customer XML Document with External DTD

```
<?xml version="1.0" encoding="UTF-8"?>
<!DOCTYPE customer SYSTEM "C:\DB9e\First Draft\Chapter 13\XML Docs\customer.dtd">
<customer>
    <name>
       <firstname>Michelle</firstname>
       <lastname>Correlli</lastname>
    </name>
    <address>
       <street>1824 East 7th Avenue</street>
       <street>Suite 700</street>
       <city>Memphis</city>
       <state>TN</state>
       <zip>32123-7788</zip>
    </address>
</customer>
```

FIGURE 13-3

CustomerList XML Document (a) External DTD and (b) CustomerList with Data for Two Customers

```
<?xml version="1.0" encoding="UTF-8"?>
<!-- edited with XML Spy v3.5 NT (http://www.xmlspy.com) by David Kroenke (private) -->
<!ELEMENT customerlist (customer+)>
<!ELEMENT customer (name, address)>
<!ELEMENT name (firstname, lastname)>
<!ELEMENT firstname (#PCDATA)>
<!ELEMENT lastname (#PCDATA)>
<!ELEMENT address (street+, city, state, zip)>
<!ELEMENT street (#PCDATA)>
<!ELEMENT city (#PCDATA)>
<!ELEMENT state (#PCDATA)>
<!ELEMENT zip (#PCDATA)>
```

(a)

```
<?xml version="1.0" encoding="UTF-8"?>
<!-- edited with XML Spy v3.5 NT (http://www.xmlspy.com) by David Kroenke (private) -->
<!DOCTYPE customerlist SYSTEM "C:\DB9e\First Draft\Chapter 13\XML Docs\customerlist.dtd">
<?xml-stylesheet type="text/xsl" href="C:\DB9e\First Draft\Chapter 13\XML Docs\CustomerList.xsl"?>
<customerlist>
    <customer>
        <name>
            <firstname>Michelle</firstname>
            <lastname>Correlli</lastname>
        </name>
        <address>
            <street>1824 East 7th Avenue</street>
            <street>Suite 700</street>
            <city>Memphis</city>
            <state>TN</state>
            <zip>32123-7788</zip>
        </address>
    </customer>
    <customer>
        <name>
            <firstname>Lynda</firstname>
            <lastname>Jaynes</lastname>
        </name>
        <address>
            <street>2 Elm Street</street>
            <city>New York City</city>
            <state>NY</state>
            <zip>02123-7445</zip>
        </address>
    </customer>
</customerlist>
```

(b)

Figure 13-3 shows a DTD for a document that has a list of customers, and Figure 13-3(b) shows an XML document that is type-valid on that DTD. The DOCTYPE statement in Figure 13-3(b) points to a file that contains the DTD shown in Figure 13-3(a). The next statement in the XML document indicates the location of another document called a **stylesheet** (shown in Figure 13-4). Stylesheets are used by XSLT to indicate how to transform the elements of the XML document into another format; here, those elements will transform it into an HTML document that will be acceptable to a browser.

The XSLT processor copies the elements of the stylesheet until it finds a command in the format {*item, action*}. When it finds such a command, it searches for an instance of the indicated item; and when it finds one, it takes the indicated action. For example, when the XSLT processor encounters

```
<xsl:for-each select="customerlist/customer">
```

it starts a search in the document for an element named customerlist and when it finds such an element, is looks further, within the customerlist element, for an element named customer. If a match is found, it takes the actions indicated in the loop that ends with </xsl:for-each> (third from the bottom of the stylesheet).

FIGURE 13-4

XSL Document for CustomerList

```
<?xml version="1.0"?>
<HTML xmlns:xsl="http://www.w3.org/TR/WD-xsl">
 <BODY STYLE="font-family:Arial, helvetica, sans-serif; font-size:14pt;
    background-color:teal">
  <xsl:for-each select="customerlist/customer">
   <DIV STYLE="background-color:brown; color:white; padding:4px">
    <SPAN STYLE="font-weight:bold; color:white"><xsl:value-of select="name/lastname"/></SPAN>
    - <xsl:value-of select="name/firstname"/>
      </DIV>
   <xsl:for-each select="address/street">
    <DIV STYLE="margin-left:20px; margin-bottom:1em; font-size:10pt; font-style:bold; color:yellow">
      <xsl:value-of select="node()"/>
    </DIV>
   </xsl:for-each>
   <DIV STYLE="margin-left:20px; margin-bottom:1em; font-size:12pt; font-style:bold">
     <xsl:value-of select="address/city"/>, <xsl:value-of select="address/state"/>
     </DIV>

   <DIV STYLE="margin-left:20px; margin-bottom:1em; font-size:14pt; color:blue">
     <xsl:value-of select="address/zip"/>
   </DIV>

  </xsl:for-each>
 </BODY>
</HTML>
```

Within the loop, styles are set for each element in the customerlist document. The results of applying this stylesheet in Figure 13-4 to the document in Figure 13-3(b) are shown in Figure 13-5(a). Read through the document and the stylesheet, and see how the results are generated.

XSLT processors are context-oriented; each statement is evaluated in the context of the match that has been made. Thus, the following statement

<xsl:value-of select="name/lastname">

operates in the context of the customerlist/customer match that has been made. There is no need to code

<xsl:select="customerlist/customer/name/lastname">/

because the context has already been set to customerlist/customer. In fact, if the select were coded in this second way, nothing would be found. Similarly, <xsl:select "lastname"/> results in no match because lastname occurs only in the context customerlist/customer/name, and not in the context customerlist/customer.

This context orientation explains the need for the following statement (in the center of the style sheet):

<xsl:value-of select="node()"/>

The context at the location of this statement has been set to customerlist/customer/address/street. Hence, the current node is a street element, and this expression indicates that the value of that node is to be produced.

Observe, too, that a small transformation has been made by the stylesheet. The original document has firstname followed by lastname, but the output stream has lastname followed by firstname.

The document in Figure 13-5(a) is the XML document in Figure 13-3(b) with which we started, but transformed into HTML. When this transformed document is input to a browser, the browser will materialize it, as shown in Figure 13-5(b).

FIGURE 13–5

**Result of Applying XSL
(a) HTML Version and
(b) Browser Version**

```
<HTML xmlns:xsl="http://www.w3.org/TR/WD-xsl">
<BODY STYLE="font-family:Arial, helvetica, sans-serif; font-size:14pt;
    background-color:teal">
<DIV STYLE="background-color:brown; color:white; padding:4px">
<SPAN STYLE="font-weight:bold; color:white">Correlli</SPAN>
    - Michelle
</DIV>
<DIV STYLE="margin-left:20px; margin-bottom:1em; font-size:10pt; font-style:bold; color:yellow">
1824 East 7th Avenue
</DIV>
<DIV STYLE="margin-left:20px; margin-bottom:1em; font-size:10pt; font-style:bold; color:yellow">
Suite 700
</DIV>
<DIV STYLE="margin-left:20px; margin-bottom:1em; font-size:12pt; font-style:bold">
Memphis, TN
</DIV>
<DIV STYLE="margin-left:20px; margin-bottom:1em; font-size:14pt; color:blue">
32123-7788
</DIV>
<DIV STYLE="background-color:brown; color:white; padding:4px">
<SPAN STYLE="font-weight:bold; color:white">Jaynes</SPAN>
    - Lynda
</DIV>
<DIV STYLE="margin-left:20px; margin-bottom:1em; font-size:10pt; font-style:bold; color:yellow">
2 Elm Street
</DIV>
<DIV STYLE="margin-left:20px; margin-bottom:1em; font-size:12pt; font-style:bold">
New York City, NY
</DIV>
<DIV STYLE="margin-left:20px; margin-bottom:1em; font-size:14pt; color:blue">
02123-7445
</DIV>
</BODY>
</HTML>
```

(a)

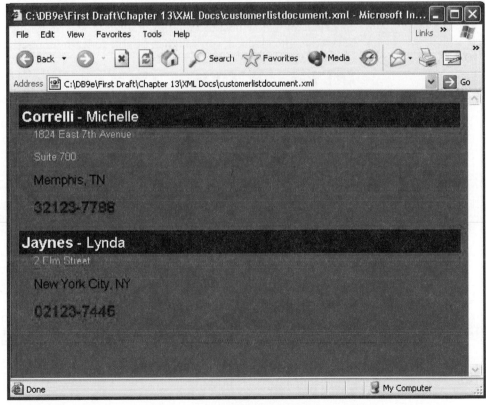

(b)

Most browsers today have a built-in XSLT processor. Thus, it is necessary to provide only the document and the stylesheet to the browser. It applies an XSLT transform using the stylesheet and automatically presents the results shown in Figure 13-5(b).

▶ **XML SCHEMA**

XML Schema is used to define the content and structure of documents, and in that respect, it serves a role similar to that of DTDs. XML Schema, however, improves upon and extends the DTD specification. XML Schema is used to define a set of symbols and the relationships of those symbols. Sometimes, this idea is expressed by saying that XML Schema provides a means to define custom vocabularies.

Earlier, you learned that an XML document that conforms to a DTD is called a type-valid document. Similarly, an XML document that conforms to an XML Schema is called a **schema-valid** document. An XML document can be well-formed and be neither type-valid nor schema-valid.

Unlike DTDs, which have syntax of their own, XML Schemas are themselves XML documents. This means that you use the same syntax to define an XML Schema as you do to define other XML documents. It also means that you can validate an XML Schema document against its schema, just as you would any other XML document. If you are following this discussion, you realize there is a chicken-and-the-egg problem here. If XML Schema documents are themselves XML documents, what document exists to be used as the schema of all schemas? In fact, there is such a document; the mother of all schemas is located at **www.w3.org**. All XML Schema documents are validated against that document.

XML Schema is a broad and complex topic. Dozens of sizable books have been written just on XML Schema alone. Clearly, we will not be able to discuss even the major topics of XML Schema in this chapter. Instead, we will focus on a few basic terms and concepts, and show how those terms and concepts are used with database processing. Given this introduction, you will then be able to learn more on your own.

XML Schema Validation

Figure 13-6(a) shows a simple XML Schema document that can be used to represent a single row from the ARTIST table at View Ridge Gallery. The first line indicates what schema is to be used to validate this document. Because this is an XML Schema document, it is to be validated against the mother of all schemas, the one at **www.w3.org**. This same reference will be used in all XML Schemas, in every company, worldwide. (By the way, this reference address is used only for identification purposes. Because this schema is so widely used, most schema validation programs have their own built-in copy of it.)

This first statement not only defines the document that is to be used for validation, it also establishes a labeled namespace. Namespaces are a complicated topic in their own right, and we will not discuss them in this chapter other than to explain the use of labels. In this first statement, *xsd* is defined by the expression: xmlns:xsd. The first part of that expression stands for **xml n**amespace, and the second part defines the label *xsd*. Notice that all the other lines in the document use the label xsd. The expression *xsd:complexType* simply tells the validating program to look into the namespace called xsd (here the one defined by **http://www.w3.org/2001/XMLSchema**) to find the definition of the term *complexType*.

Elements and Attributes

As you can tell from Figure 13-6(a), schemas consist of elements and attributes. There are two types of elements: simple and complex. Simple elements have a single data value. In Figure 13-6(a), the elements called "Name", "Nationality", "Birthdate", and "DeceasedDate" are all simple elements. By default, the cardinality of both simple and complex elements is 1.1, meaning that a single value is required and no more than a single value can be specified. For the schema in Figure 13-6(a), the minOccurs="0" expressions indicate that the defaults are being overridden for Birthdate and DeceasedDate so that they need not have a value. This is similar to NULL constraint in SQL schema definitions.

FIGURE 13-6

Using XML Schema
(a) Artist XML Schema
and (b) Schema-valid
Artist Document

```
<xsd:schema xmlns:xsd="http://www.w3.org/2001/XMLSchema">
    <xsd:element name="Artist">
        <xsd:complexType>
            <xsd:sequence>
                <xsd:element name="Name"/>
                <xsd:element name="Nationality"/>
                <xsd:element name="Birthdate" minOccurs="0"/>
                <xsd:element name="DeceasedDate" minOccurs="0"/>
            </xsd:sequence>
            <xsd:attribute name="ArtStyle"/>
        </xsd:complexType>
    </xsd:element>
</xsd:schema>
```

(a)

```
<Artist xmlns:xsi="http://www.w3.org/2001/XMLSchema-instance"
        xsi:noNamespaceSchemaLocation="C:\DB9e\First Draft\Chapter 13\XML Docs\Artist1.xsd"
        ArtStyle="Modern">
    <Name>Miro</Name>
    <Nationality>Spanish</Nationality>
    <Birthdate>1893</Birthdate>
    <DeceasedDate>1983</DeceasedDate>
</Artist>
```

(b)

Elements of complexType may contain one or more simple or complexType elements. Here, the complexType Artist contains all simple elements. As you will see, some complexType elements contain other complexTypes as well. Additionally, complexType elements can have attributes. In Figure 13-6(a), the Artist complexType has an attribute named ArtStyle. Note, too, that the schema in Figure 13-6(a) defines not only the list of contained elements, but the tags <xsd:sequence>...</xsd:sequence> specify that the elements must occur in the same order as they are listed in the schema.

You may be wondering what the difference is between an element and an attribute. For database/XML applications, a good rule of thumb is that elements are used to carry data and attributes are used to carry metadata. An ItemPrice element, for example, would carry a value of price such as 12.50; and it could have an attribute called Currency that defines what currency of the price, such as US$, Aus$, or Euros. In our example, the attribute ArtStyle carries data that describe a characteristic of the artist's work.

There is nothing in the XML standards that requires that elements and attributes be used in this way. It is a matter of style, and in subsequent sections we will show how it is possible to cause SQL Server to place all of the column values in attributes, to place all of them in elements, or to mix them up so that some columns are placed in attributes and others are placed in elements. Thus, these decisions are a matter of design choice rather than any XML standard. Most practitioners would agree with the rule of thumb mentioned previously.

Figure 13-6(b) shows an XML document that is valid on the schema shown in Figure 13-6(a). Observe that the value of the ArtStyle attribute is given with the heading of the Artist element. Also note that a namespace of *xsi* is defined. This namespace is used just once—for the noNamespaceSchemaLocation attribute. Do not be concerned about the name of this attribute; it is simply a means of telling the XML parser where to find the XML Schema for this document.

Flat vs. Structured Schemas

Figure 13-7 shows an XML Schema and XML document that represent the columns of the CUSTOMER table in the View Ridge database. As shown in Figure 13-7(a), Country and EmailAddress are optional, but all the other elements are required. The document in Figure 13-7(b) contains one of the rows of the CUSTOMER table.

FIGURE 13-7

Customer with Flat XML Schema (a) XML Schema Document; (b) Schema-valid Customer Document and (c) Graphical Display of Schema Structure Using XML Spy

```xml
<xsd:schema xmlns:xsd="http://www.w3.org/2001/XMLSchema">
    <xsd:element name="Customer">
        <xsd:complexType>
            <xsd:sequence>
                <xsd:element name="CustomerID" type="xsd:int"/>
                <xsd:element name="Name" type="xsd:string"/>
                <xsd:element name="Street" type="xsd:string"/>
                <xsd:element name="City" type="xsd:string"/>
                <xsd:element name="State" type="xsd:string"/>
                <xsd:element name="ZipPostalCode" type="xsd:string"/>
                <xsd:element name="Country" type="xsd:string" minOccurs="0"/>
                <xsd:element name="AreaCode" type="xsd:string"/>
                <xsd:element name="PhoneNumber" type="xsd:string"/>
                <xsd:element name="EmailAddress" type="xsd:string" minOccurs="0"/>
            </xsd:sequence>
        </xsd:complexType>
    </xsd:element>
</xsd:schema>
```

(a)

```xml
<Customer xmlns:xsi="http://www.w3.org/2001/XMLSchema-instance"
          xsi:noNamespaceSchemaLocation="C:\DB9e\First Draft\Chapter 13\XML Docs\FlatCustomer.xsd">
    <CustomerID>1000</CustomerID>
    <Name>Jeffrey Janes</Name>
    <Street>123 W. Elm St</Street>
    <City>Renton</City>
    <State>WA</State>
    <ZipPostalCode>98123</ZipPostalCode>
    <AreaCode>206</AreaCode>
    <PhoneNumber>555-1234</PhoneNumber>
    <EmailAddress>Customer1000@somewhere.com</EmailAddress>
</Customer>
```

(b)

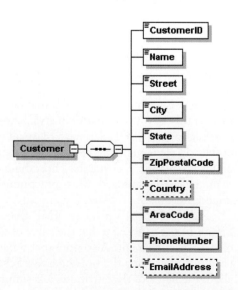

(c)

An XML Schema, such as the one shown in Figure 13-7, is sometimes called flat because all of the elements reside at the same level. Figure 13-7(c) is a diagram drawn by an XML editing tool called XML Spy. (You can find out more about this excellent product from a small company that is not yet owned by Microsoft or some other behemoth corporation, at the Web site **www.xmlspy.com**.) Anyway, Figure 13-7(c) graphically depicts why this schema is called flat. Also note that optional elements are shown in boxes drawn with dashed lines.

If you think about these elements for a moment, you will realize that something about the semantics of them has been left out. In particular, the group {Street, City, State, ZipPostalCode, Country} are all part of the Address theme. Also, the group {AreaCode, PhoneNumber} is part of the Phone theme. As you know, in the relational model, all columns are considered equal and there is no way to represent these themes.

With XML, however, there is a way of modeling such groups. The schema shown in Figure 13-8(a) structures the appropriate columns into an Address complexType and other columns into a Phone complexType. An XML document for one of the rows of CUSTOMER expressed in this format is shown in Figure 13-8(b). A graphical display of this schema is shown in Figure 13-8(c).

Schemas like this are sometimes called **structured schemas** because they add structure to table columns. A model like this captures additional user meaning, so it is superior to the relational model from a descriptive standpoint.

Global Elements

Suppose that we want to use XML Schema to represent a document that extends the customer data in Figure 13-8 to include the salesperson assigned to that customer. Further, suppose that both customers and salespeople have address and phone data. We can use the techniques shown so far to represent this new customer structure, but if we do so, we will duplicate the definition of phone and address.

In the relational world, we worry about duplication of data, not so much because of wasted file space, but more because there is always the chance of inconsistent data when one copy of the data is changed and the other copy is not changed. Similarly, in the document-processing world, people worry about duplicate definition of elements because there is always the chance that they become inconsistent when one is changed and the other is not.

To eliminate the definition duplication, elements can be declared globally and then reused. In Figure 13-9(a), for example, the address group is defined as a global element AddressType, and the phone group is defined as the global element PhoneType. According to the XML Schema standard, these are global elements because they reside at the top level of the schema.

If you examine Figure 13-9(a) further, you will see that both Customer and Salesperson within Customer use the AddressType and PhoneType global definitions. They are referenced by notations such as *type="AddressType."* By using these global definitions, if either PhoneType or AddressType is changed, the definition of Customer and Salesperson will inherit the change.

One other change in this figure is that the cardinality of the Phone group of Customer has been set to 1.3. This notation means that at least one Phone group is required and as many as three are allowed. As you learned in Chapter 2, representing such multi-valued attributes in the entity-relationship model requires the definition of an ID-dependent entity. That entity will later be transformed into a table in the relational model. We will ignore this issue here. This notation is shown only so that you can see how multi-valued elements are documented in an XML Schema.

Figure 13-9(b) shows how XML Spy graphically represents the PhoneType global element, and Figure 13-9(c) illustrates the way that the PhoneType reference is shown for Customer and Salesperson.

FIGURE 13-8

Customer with
Structured XML
Document (a) XML
Schema Document;
(b) XML Schema
Customer Document
and (c) Graphical
Display of Schema
Structure

```
<xsd:schema xmlns:xsd="http://www.w3.org/2001/XMLSchema" elementFormDefault="qualified">
    <xsd:element name="Customer">
        <xsd:complexType>
            <xsd:sequence>
                <xsd:element name="CustomerID" type="xsd:string"/>
                <xsd:element name="Name" type="xsd:string"/>
                <xsd:element name="Address" minOccurs="0">
                    <xsd:complexType>
                        <xsd:sequence>
                            <xsd:element name="Street" type="xsd:string"/>
                            <xsd:element name="City" type="xsd:normalizedString"/>
                            <xsd:element name="State" type="xsd:string"/>
                            <xsd:element name="ZipPostalCode" type="xsd:string"/>
                            <xsd:element name="Country" type="xsd:string" minOccurs="0"/>
                        </xsd:sequence>
                    </xsd:complexType>
                </xsd:element>
                <xsd:element name="Phone" minOccurs="0">
                    <xsd:complexType>
                        <xsd:sequence>
                            <xsd:element name="AreaCode" type="xsd:string"/>
                            <xsd:element name="PhoneNumber" type="xsd:string"/>
                        </xsd:sequence>
                    </xsd:complexType>
                </xsd:element>
                <xsd:element name="EmailAddress" type="xsd:string" minOccurs="0"/>
            </xsd:sequence>
        </xsd:complexType>
    </xsd:element>
</xsd:schema>
```

(a)

```
<Customer xmlns:xsi="http://www.w3.org/2001/XMLSchema-instance"
        xsi:noNamespaceSchemaLocation="C:\DB9e\First Draft\Chapter 13\XML Docs\CustomerWithGroups.xsd">
    <CustomerID>1000</CustomerID>
    <Name>Jeffrey Janes</Name>
    <Address>
        <Street>123 W. Elm St.</Street>
        <City>Renton</City>
        <State>WA</State>
        <ZipPostalCode>98123</ZipPostalCode>
    </Address>
    <Phone>
        <AreaCode>206</AreaCode>
        <PhoneNumber>555-1234</PhoneNumber>
    </Phone>
    <EmailAddress>Customer1000@somewhere.com</EmailAddress>
</Customer>
```

(b)

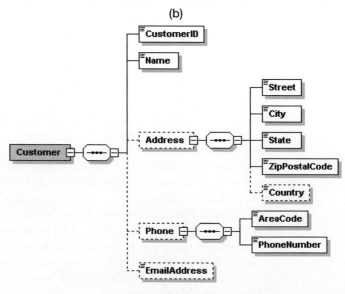

(c)

FIGURE 13–9

**Using Global Elements
(a) XML Schema
Document with Global
Elements;
(b) PhoneType Global
Element and (c) XML
Spy Display of
Elements Using Phone
Global Element**

```
<xsd:schema xmlns:xsd="http://www.w3.org/2001/XMLSchema" elementFormDefault="qualified">
    <xsd:complexType name="AddressType">
        <xsd:sequence>
            <xsd:element name="Street"/>
            <xsd:element name="City"/>
            <xsd:element name="State"/>
            <xsd:element name="ZipPostalCode"/>
            <xsd:element name="Country" minOccurs="0"/>
        </xsd:sequence>
    </xsd:complexType>
    <xsd:complexType name="PhoneType">
        <xsd:sequence>
            <xsd:element name="AreaCode"/>
            <xsd:element name="PhoneNumber"/>
        </xsd:sequence>
    </xsd:complexType>
    <xsd:element name="Customer">
        <xsd:complexType>
            <xsd:sequence>
                <xsd:element name="CustomerID" type="xsd:integer"/>
                <xsd:element name="Name"/>
                <xsd:element name="Address" type="AddressType"/>
                <xsd:element name="Phone" type="PhoneType" maxOccurs="3"/>
                <xsd:element name="EmailAddress" minOccurs="0"/>
                <xsd:element name="Salesperson">
                    <xsd:complexType>
                        <xsd:sequence>
                            <xsd:element name="Name"/>
                            <xsd:element name="Address" type="AddressType"/>
                            <xsd:element name="Phone" type="PhoneType"/>
                        </xsd:sequence>
                        <xsd:attribute name="SalespersonID" type="xsd:string"/>
                    </xsd:complexType>
                </xsd:element>
            </xsd:sequence>
        </xsd:complexType>
    </xsd:element>
</xsd:schema>
```

(a)

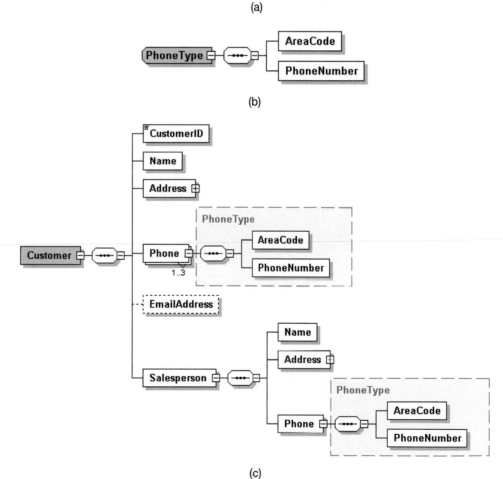

(b)

(c)

▶ CREATING XML DOCUMENTS FROM DATABASE DATA

Both Oracle and SQL Server have facilities for generating XML documents from database data. The Oracle XML features require the use of Java. Because we do not assume that you are a Java programmer, we will not discuss those features further in this chapter. If you are a Java programmer, you can learn more about Oracle's XML features at **http://www.Oracle.com/**. (Later in this chapter, we will illustrate how to generate XML documents from Oracle data using ADO.NET. In that case, however, Oracle is providing the data in non-XML format, and ADO.NET datasets are formatting that data in XML.)

The facilities in both Oracle and SQL Server are undergoing rapid development. In the case of SQL Server, version 7.0 added the expression FOR XML to SQL SELECT syntax. That expression was carried forward to SQL Sever 2000. In 2002, the SQL Server group extended the SQL Server capabilities with SQLXML, a class library that can be downloaded from **msdn.microsoft.com**. SQLXML, which was produced by the SQL Server group, is different from ADO.NET. Most likely the features and functions of SQLXML and ADO.NET will be merged in the future.

SELECT...FOR XML

Consider the following SQL statement:

```
SELECT       *
FROM         ARTIST
     FOR   XML RAW;
```

The expression FOR XML RAW tells SQL Server to place the values of the columns as attributes in the resulting XML document. Figure 13-10(a) shows an example of the results of this statement. As expected, each column is placed as an attribute of the element named ARTIST[1].

It is also possible to cause SQL Server to place the values of the columns into elements rather than attributes. The following statement produces a document like the one shown in Figure 13-10(b):

```
SELECT       *
FROM         ARTIST
     FOR   XML AUTO, ELEMENTS;
```

Using FOR XML EXPLICIT, the developer can also cause SQL Server to place some columns into elements and others into attributes. For example, a particular design might place all columns except surrogate key values into elements and all surrogate key values into attributes. The justification for this design is that surrogate key values have no meaning to the users, so they are more like metadata than data. The means by which this is done is beyond the scope of this discussion. See FOR XML EXPLICIT in the SQL Server documentation for information.

---

[1]In the interest of full disclosure, the figures in this section were produced by a VB.NET application that invoked the SQL...FOR XML statements via the SQLXML class SqlXMLCommand and saved them to a file using the ExecuteToStream method of that class. That application added the root element MyData. None of this is important for understanding the essential ideas in this section. Strive instead to understand how SQL statements can be mapped to XML documents. But if you want to produce them yourself, download SQLXML and read the tutorial documentation.

FIGURE 13-10

FOR XML Examples (a) FOR XML RAW Example and (b) FOR XML AUTO, ELEMENTS Example

```
<MyData>
    <ARTIST ArtistID="3" Name="Miro          " Nationality="Spanish          " Birthdate="1870" DeceasedDate="1950"/>
    <ARTIST ArtistID="4" Name="Kandinsky     " Nationality="Russian          " Birthdate="1854" DeceasedDate="1900"/>
    <ARTIST ArtistID="5" Name="Frings        " Nationality="US               " Birthdate="1700" DeceasedDate="1800"/>
    <ARTIST ArtistID="6" Name="Klee          " Nationality="German           " Birthdate="1900"/>
    <ARTIST ArtistID="8" Name="Moos          " Nationality="US               "/>
    <ARTIST ArtistID="14" Name="Tobey        " Nationality="US               "/>
    <ARTIST ArtistID="15" Name="Matisse      " Nationality="French           "/>
    <ARTIST ArtistID="16" Name="Chagall      " Nationality="French           "/>
</MyData>
```

(a)

```
<MyData>
    <ARTIST>
        <ArtistID>3</ArtistID>
        <Name>Miro          </Name>
        <Nationality>Spanish          </Nationality>
        <Birthdate>1870</Birthdate>
        <DeceasedDate>1950</DeceasedDate>
    </ARTIST>
    <ARTIST>
        <ArtistID>4</ArtistID>
        <Name>Kandinsky          </Name>
        <Nationality>Russian          </Nationality>
        <Birthdate>1854</Birthdate>
        <DeceasedDate>1900</DeceasedDate>
    </ARTIST>
    <ARTIST>
        <ArtistID>5</ArtistID>
        <Name>Frings          </Name>
        <Nationality>US          </Nationality>
        <Birthdate>1700</Birthdate>
        <DeceasedDate>1800</DeceasedDate>
    </ARTIST>
    <ARTIST>
        <ArtistID>6</ArtistID>
        <Name>Klee          </Name>
        <Nationality>German          </Nationality>
        <Birthdate>1900</Birthdate>
    </ARTIST>
    <ARTIST>
        <ArtistID>8</ArtistID>
        <Name>Moos          </Name>
        <Nationality>US          </Nationality>
    </ARTIST>
    <ARTIST>
        <ArtistID>14</ArtistID>
        <Name>Tobey          </Name>
        <Nationality>US          </Nationality>
    </ARTIST>
    <ARTIST>
        <ArtistID>15</ArtistID>
        <Name>Matisse          </Name>
        <Nationality>French          </Nationality>
    </ARTIST>
    <ARTIST>
        <ArtistID>16</ArtistID>
        <Name>Chagall          </Name>
        <Nationality>French          </Nationality>
    </ARTIST>
</MyData>
```

(b)

Multi-table SELECT with FOR XML

FOR XML SELECT statements are not limited to single-table SELECTs; they can be applied to joins as well. For example, the following join produced the XML document shown in Figure 13-11:

FIGURE 13–11

FOR XML AUTO, ELEMENTS Displaying Customer and Artist Interests

```
<MyData xmlns:xsi="http://www.w3.org/2000/10/XMLSchema-instance"
xsi:noNamespaceSchemaLocation="C:\DB9e\First Draft\Chapter 13\CustomerArtistInt.xsd">
        <CUSTOMER>
            <Name>Chris Wilkens                 </Name>
            <ARTIST>
                <Name>Frings                     </Name>
            </ARTIST>
            <ARTIST>
                <Name>Tobey                      </Name>
            </ARTIST>
        </CUSTOMER>
        <CUSTOMER>
            <Name>Donald G. Gray                 </Name>
            <ARTIST>
                <Name>Tobey                      </Name>
            </ARTIST>
        </CUSTOMER>
        <CUSTOMER>
            <Name>Fred Smathers                  </Name>
            <ARTIST>
                <Name>Tobey                      </Name>
            </ARTIST>
        </CUSTOMER>
        <CUSTOMER>
            <Name>Jeffrey Janes                  </Name>
            <ARTIST>
                <Name>Tobey                      </Name>
            </ARTIST>
        </CUSTOMER>
        <CUSTOMER>
            <Name>Lynda Johnson                  </Name>
            <ARTIST>
                <Name>Moos                       </Name>
            </ARTIST>
            <ARTIST>
                <Name>Tobey                      </Name>
            </ARTIST>
            <ARTIST>
                <Name>Frings                     </Name>
            </ARTIST>
        </CUSTOMER>
        <CUSTOMER>
            <Name>Malinda Gliddens               </Name>
            <ARTIST>
                <Name>Chagall                    </Name>
            </ARTIST>
        </CUSTOMER>
        <CUSTOMER>
            <Name>Mary Beth Frederickson         </Name>
            <ARTIST>
                <Name>Frings                     </Name>
            </ARTIST>
```

```
SELECT      CUSTOMER.Name, ARTIST.Name
FROM        CUSTOMER, CUSTOMER_ARTIST_INT, ARTIST
WHERE       CUSTOMER.CustomerID =
            CUSTOMER_ARTIST_INT.CustomerID
    AND     CUSTOMER_ARTIST_INT.ArtistID = ARTIST.ArtistID
ORDER BY    CUSTOMER.Name
FOR XML AUTO, ELEMENTS;
```

FIGURE 13-11

(continued)

```
        <ARTIST>
            <Name>Moos                    </Name>
        </ARTIST>
        <ARTIST>
            <Name>Tobey                   </Name>
        </ARTIST>
    </CUSTOMER>
    <CUSTOMER>
        <Name>Michael Bench               </Name>
        <ARTIST>
            <Name>Moos                    </Name>
        </ARTIST>
        <ARTIST>
            <Name>Frings                  </Name>
        </ARTIST>
        <ARTIST>
            <Name>Tobey                   </Name>
        </ARTIST>
    </CUSTOMER>
    <CUSTOMER>
        <Name>Selma Warning               </Name>
        <ARTIST>
            <Name>Miro                    </Name>
        </ARTIST>
        <ARTIST>
            <Name>Tobey                   </Name>
        </ARTIST>
    </CUSTOMER>
    <CUSTOMER>
        <Name>Tiffany Twilight            </Name>
        <ARTIST>
            <Name>Tobey                   </Name>
        </ARTIST>
        <ARTIST>
            <Name>Chagall                 </Name>
        </ARTIST>
        <ARTIST>
            <Name>Frings                  </Name>
        </ARTIST>
    </CUSTOMER>
</MyData>
```

SQL Server uses the order of the tables in the FROM clause to determine the hierarchical placement of the elements in the generated XML document. Here, the top-level element is CUSTOMER, and the next element is ARTIST. The CUSTOMER_ARTIST_INT table does not appear in the generated document because no column from that table appeared in the SELECT.

You can write the expression FOR XML AUTO, XMLDATA to cause SQL Server to produce an XML Schema statement in front of the XML document that it writes. The schema produced, however, involves topics that we will not cover in this chapter, so we will not do that. Another way to produce an XML Schema for an XML document is to have XML Spy generate one, using the document as an example. The schema in Figure 13-12(a) was produced in just this way. Observe that the MyData element can have an unbounded number of CUSTOMER elements, and each CUSTOMER can have an unbounded number of ARTIST elements, one for each artist interest. Figure 13-12(b) shows a graphical display of this same schema. In this figure, the notation $1..\infty$ means that at least one CUSTOMER is required and an unlimited number will be allowed.

FIGURE 13–12

XML Schema for
Document in Figure
13-11 (a) XML Schema
Inferred by XML Spy
and (b) Graphical
Display of Schema

```
<xsd:schema xmlns:xsd="http://www.w3.org/2001/XMLSchema"
            elementFormDefault="qualified">
    <xsd:element name="MyData">
        <xsd:complexType>
            <xsd:sequence>
                <xsd:element name="CUSTOMER" maxOccurs="unbounded">
                    <xsd:complexType>
                        <xsd:sequence>
                            <xsd:element ref="Name"/>
                            <xsd:element name="ARTIST" maxOccurs="unbounded">
                                <xsd:complexType>
                                    <xsd:sequence>
                                        <xsd:element ref="Name"/>
                                    </xsd:sequence>
                                </xsd:complexType>
                            </xsd:element>
                        </xsd:sequence>
                    </xsd:complexType>
                </xsd:element>
            </xsd:sequence>
        </xsd:complexType>
    </xsd:element>
    <xsd:element name="Name" type="xsd:string"/>
</xsd:schema>
```

(a)

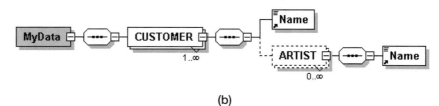

(b)

AN XML SCHEMA FOR ALL CUSTOMER PURCHASES

Suppose now that we want to produce a document that has all of the customer purchase data. To do that, we need to join CUSTOMER to TRANS to WORK to ARTIST, and select the appropriate data. The following SQL statement produces the required data:

```
SELECT      CUSTOMER.CustomerID, CUSTOMER.Name,
            TRANS.TransactionID, SalesPrice, [WORK].WorkID, Title,
            Copy, ARTIST.ArtistID, ARTIST.Name
FROM        CUSTOMER, TRANS, [WORK], ARTIST
WHERE       CUSTOMER.CustomerID = TRANS.CustomerID
    AND     TRANS.WorkID = [WORK].WorkID
    AND     [WORK].ArtistID = ARTIST.ArtistID
ORDER BY    CUSTOMER.Name
FOR XML AUTO, ELEMENTS;
```

Figure 13-13(a) shows an XML Schema document for this SQL statement. It was produced by having SQL Server create an XML document having all of the VRG data and then using XML Spy to generate this schema. A graphical view of it is shown in Figure 13-13(b).

FIGURE 13-13

Customer Purchase
View (a) XML Schema
Generated by XML
Spy; (b) Graphical
Display of Schema and
(c) Schema with
Correct Minimum
Cardinalities

```xml
<!-- edited with XML Spy v3.5 NT (http://www.xmlspy.com) by David Kroenke (private) -->
<!--W3C Schema generated by XML Spy v3.5 NT (http://www.xmlspy.com)-->
<xsd:schema xmlns:xsd="http://www.w3.org/2000/10/XMLSchema" elementFormDefault="qualified">
 <xsd:element name="MyData">
  <xsd:complexType>
   <xsd:sequence>
    <xsd:element name="CUSTOMER" maxOccurs="unbounded">
     <xsd:complexType>
      <xsd:sequence>
       <xsd:element ref="Name"/>
       <xsd:element name="TRANS" minOccurs="0" maxOccurs="unbounded">
        <xsd:complexType>
         <xsd:sequence>
          <xsd:element name="SalesPrice"/>
          <xsd:element name="WORK">
           <xsd:complexType>
            <xsd:sequence>
             <xsd:element name="Title" type="xsd:string"/>
             <xsd:element name="Copy" type="xsd:string"/>
             <xsd:element name="ARTIST">
              <xsd:complexType>
               <xsd:sequence>
                <xsd:element ref="Name"/>
               </xsd:sequence>
              </xsd:complexType>
             </xsd:element>
            </xsd:sequence>
           </xsd:complexType>
          </xsd:element>
         </xsd:sequence>
        </xsd:complexType>
       </xsd:element>
      </xsd:sequence>
     </xsd:complexType>
    </xsd:element>
   </xsd:sequence>
  </xsd:complexType>
 </xsd:element>
 <xsd:element name="Name" type="xsd:string"/>
</xsd:schema>
```

(a)

This schema is close, but not quite correct. According to the schema, MyData schema has at least one and an unlimited number of CUSTOMER elements, and CUSTOMER has at least one and an unlimited number of TRANS elements. That latter statement is not correct. According to our data model, each CUSTOMER should have from zero to many TRANS elements.

This error occurred because we constructed the schema from an existing XML document that was produced from an INNER join between CUSTOMER and TRANS. Because it was an inner join, only customers having a TRANS row appeared in the XML document. Thus, every CUSTOMER in the document had at least one TRANS row. Had we produced the XML document from an outer join that allowed customers to appear who have no transaction data, then there would have been instances of CUSTOMER without TRANS, and XML Spy would have created the correct cardinality on TRANS. Rather than do all that at this point, we can instead just use XML Spy to make the correction[2].

According to the corrected XML Schema in Figure 13-13(c), a CUSTOMER has from zero to unlimited TRANS elements. The cardinalities in the rest of the schema were correctly produced from our XML document. A TRANS element has exactly one WORK element, and a WORK element has exactly one ARTIST element.

---

[2]Actually, the same error occurred in the construction of the CUSTOMER/ARTIST schema shown in Figure 13-12(b). It, too, was corrected in XML Spy; only the corrected version is shown there.

FIGURE 13-13

(continued)

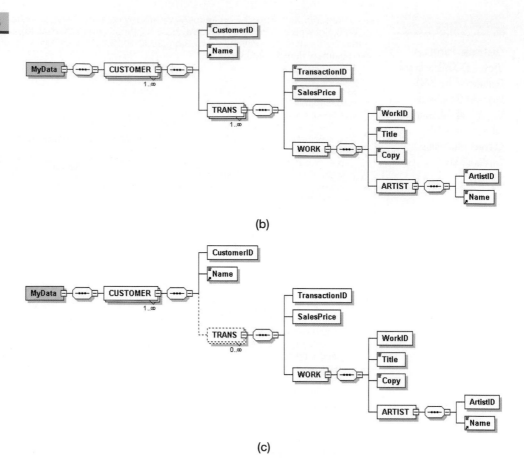

(b)

(c)

A Schema with Two Multi-value Paths

Suppose now that we want to construct an XML document that has all of the View Ridge customer data. We cannot construct such a view from a single SQL statement because it has two multi-valued paths. We need one SQL statement to obtain all customer purchase data and a second SQL statement to obtain all customer/artist interests.

There is no such limitation in XML Schema, however. An XML document may have as many multi-valued paths as the application requires. In our case, all we need to do is to combine the schemas in Figure 13-12(a) and Figure 13-13(a). While we're at it, we can also add the surrogate keys for each of the underlying tables.

The result of combining these results (using cut and paste in XML Spy!) is shown in Figure 13-14. Observe in Figure 13-14(b) that MyData may have from one to an unlimited number of CUSTOMER elements, and that each such element may have from zero to many TRANS and from zero to many ArtistInterests elements. All of the simple elements in this schema are required.

Why is XML Important?

At this point, you should have some idea of the nature of XML and the XML standards. You know that XML makes a clear separation between structure, content, and materialization. Structure is defined by either a DTD or an XML Schema document. Content is expressed in an XML document, and the materializations of a document are expressed in an XSL document. You also understand that SQL statements can be used to create XML documents, but only as long as those documents involve at most one multi-value path. If more than one such path exists in the document, multiple SQL statements need to be issued to fill the document in some fashion.

FIGURE 13-14

View Ridge Customer with Two Multi-value Paths (a) XML Schema and (b) Graphical Display of Schema

```
<xsd:schema xmlns:xsd="http://www.w3.org/2000/10/XMLSchema" elementFormDefault="qualified">
    <xsd:element name="MyData">
        <xsd:complexType>
            <xsd:sequence>
                <xsd:element name="CUSTOMER" maxOccurs="unbounded">
                    <xsd:complexType>
                        <xsd:sequence>
                            <xsd:element name="CustomerID" type="xsd:integer"/>
                            <xsd:element ref="Name"/>
                            <xsd:element name="TRANS" minOccurs="0" maxOccurs="unbounded">
                                <xsd:complexType>
                                    <xsd:sequence>
                                        <xsd:element name="TransactionID" type="xsd:integer"/>
                                        <xsd:element name="SalesPrice"/>
                                        <xsd:element name="WORK">
                                            <xsd:complexType>
                                                <xsd:sequence>
                                                    <xsd:element name="WorkID" type="xsd:integer"/>
                                                    <xsd:element name="Title" type="xsd:string"/>
                                                    <xsd:element name="Copy" type="xsd:string"/>
                                                    <xsd:element name="ARTIST">
                                                        <xsd:complexType>
                                                            <xsd:sequence>
                                                                <xsd:element name="ArtistID" type="xsd:integer"/>
                                                                <xsd:element ref="Name"/>
                                                            </xsd:sequence>
                                                        </xsd:complexType>
                                                    </xsd:element>
                                                </xsd:sequence>
                                            </xsd:complexType>
                                        </xsd:element>
                                    </xsd:sequence>
                                </xsd:complexType>
                            </xsd:element>
                            <xsd:element name="ArtistInterests" minOccurs="0" maxOccurs="unbounded">
                                <xsd:complexType>
                                    <xsd:sequence>
                                        <xsd:element name="ArtistID" type="xsd:integer"/>
                                        <xsd:element ref="Name"/>
                                        <xsd:element name="Nationality"/>
                                    </xsd:sequence>
                                </xsd:complexType>
                            </xsd:element>
                        </xsd:sequence>
                    </xsd:complexType>
                </xsd:element>
            </xsd:sequence>
        </xsd:complexType>
    </xsd:element>
    <xsd:element name="Name" type="xsd:string"/>
</xsd:schema>
```

(a)

Before we continue, you may be asking, "These are interesting ideas, but why do they matter? What's so important about all of this?" The answer to these questions is that XML processing provides a standardized facility to describe, validate, and material- ize any database view.

Consider the View Ridge Gallery. Suppose that the Gallery wants to share all of its customer data with another gallery, maybe because of a joint sales program. If both gal- leries agree on an XML Schema like that shown in Figure 13-14, they can prepare cus- tomer data documents in accordance with that schema. Before sending a document, they can run an automated process to validate the document against the schema. In this way, only correct data is transmitted. Of course, this process works in both directions. Not

FIGURE 13-14

(continued)

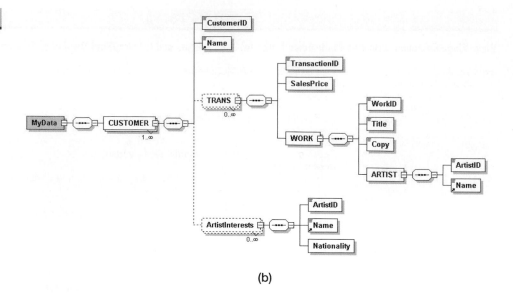

(b)

only can View Ridge ensure that it is sending only valid documents; by validating the documents it receives, it can ensure that it is receiving only valid documents.

Best of all, the programs for document validation are publicly available and free to the galleries. The galleries need write no program code for validation.

Additionally, each gallery can develop its own set of XSL documents to materialize the customer data documents in whatever ways they want. View Ridge can develop an XSL document to display the data on a customer's computer, another to display it on salespersons' computers, another to display it on mobile devices when art buyers are on the road, and so forth. Given these XSLs, customer data can be displayed regardless of whether it came from one gallery or the other.

Now, broaden this idea from two small businesses to an industry. Suppose, for example, that the real estate industry agrees on an XML Schema document for house property listings. Every real estate company that can produce data in the format of the schema can then exchange listings with every other such real estate company. Given the schema, each company can ensure that they are transmitting only valid documents, and they can also ensure that they are receiving only valid documents. Further, each company can develop its own set of XSL documents to materialize house listings in whatever way they want. Once the XSL documents have been prepared, any listing from any participating agent can be displayed in the local agency's materializations. Figure 13-15 lists some XML standards work that is under way in various industries.

For another example, consider the emerging trend of business-to-business e-commerce. Suppose that Wal-Mart wants to send orders to its vendors in a particular standardized format and that it wants to receive shipment responses to those orders in another particular standardized format. To do this, Wal-Mart can develop an XML Schema for Order documents and another for Shipment documents. It can then publish those XML schemas on a Web site accessible to its vendors. In this way, all vendors can determine how they will receive orders from Wal-Mart and how they should send their Shipment notifications back.

The schemas can be used by Wal-Mart and all of its vendors to ensure that they are sending and receiving only valid XML documents. Further, Wal-Mart can develop XSL documents to cause the Order and Shipment documents to be transformed into the specific formats needed by their own Accounting, Operations, Marketing, and General Management departments. These XSL documents work for any Order or Shipment from any of its vendors.

In all of these cases, once the XML Schema documents have been prepared and once the XSL documents have been written, all validation and materialization is done via

FIGURE 13–15

Example XML Industry Standards

Industry Type	Example Standards
Accounting	• American Institute of Certified Public Accountants (AICPA): Extensible Financial Reporting Markup Language (XFRML)[OASIS Cover page] • Open Applications Group, Inc (OAG)
Architecture and Construction	• Architecture, Engineering, and Construction XML Working Group (aecXML Working Group) • ConSource.com: Construction Manufacturing and Distribution Extensible Markup Language (cmdXML)
Automotive	• Automotive Industry Action Group (AIAG) • Global Automedia: • MSR: Standards for information exchange in the engineering process (MEDOC) • The Society of Automotive Engineers (SAE): XML for the Automotive Industry–SAE J2008[OASIS Cover page] • Open Applications Group, Inc (OAG)
Banking	• Banking Industry Technology Secretariat (BITS): [OASIS Cover page] • Financial Services Technology Consortium (FSTC): Bank Internet Payment System (BIPS)[OASIS Cover page] • Open Applications Group, Inc (OAG)
Electronic Data Interchange	• Data Interchange Standards Association (DISA): [OASIS Cover page] • EEMA EDI/EC Work Group[OASIS Cover page] • European Committee for Standardization/Information Society Standardization System (CEN/ISSS; The European XML/EDI Pilot Project[OASIS Cover page] • XML/EDI Group[OASIS Cover page]
Human Resources	• DataMain: Human Resources Markup Language (hrml) • HR-XML Consortium[OASIS Cover page]: JobPosting, CandidateProfile, Resume • Open Applications Group (OAG): Open Applications Group Interface Specification (OASIS)[OASIS Cover page] • Tapestry.Net: JOB markup language (JOB) • Open Applications Group, Inc (OAG)
Insurance	• ACORD: Property and Casualty[OASIS Cover page], Life (XMLife)[OASIS Cover page] • Lexica: iLingo

automated processes. There is no need for any human to touch the Order document between its origination at Wal-Mart and the picking of the inventory at the supplier.

So, the only challenge that remains is to populate the XML documents with database data in accordance with the relevant XML Schema. SQL can be used to populate schemas that only have one multi-value path, but this is too restrictive. There is a need for something more–some new technology to ease the transformation of database data into XML documents and to ease the transformation of XML documents to database data. That need brings us to ADO.NET.

FIGURE 13-15

(continued)

Industry Type	Example Standards
Real Estate	• <u>OpenMLS</u>: Real Estate Listing Management System (OpenMLS)[OASIS Cover page] • <u>Real Estate Transaction Standard working group (RETS)</u>: Real Estate Transaction Standard (RETS)[OASIS Cover page]
Software	• <u>IBM</u>: [OASIS Cover page] • <u>Flashline.com</u>: Software Component Documentation DTD • <u>Flashline.com</u>: • <u>INRIA</u>: Koala Bean Markup Language (KBML)[OASIS Cover page] • <u>Marimba and Microsoft</u>: Open Software Description Format (OSD)[OASIS Cover page] • <u>Object Management Group (OMG)</u>: [OASIS Cover page]
Workflow	• <u>Internet Engineering Task Force (IETF)</u>: Simple Workflow Access Protocol (SWAP)[OASIS Cover page] • <u>Workflow Management Coalition (MfMC)</u>: Wf-XML[OASIS Cover page]

▶ ADO.NET

ADO.NET is a new, improved, and greatly expanded version of ADO that was developed as part of Microsoft's .NET initiative. It incorporates the functionality of ADO and OLE DB discussed in Chapter 12, but adds much, much more. In particular, ADO.NET facilitates the transformation of XML documents to and from relational database constructs. ADO.NET also provides the ability to create and process in-memory databases called *datasets*.

Figure 13-16 shows the general role of ADO.NET As shown, it serves as an intermediary between all types of .NET applications and the DBMS and database. ADO.NET can work with any OLE DB-compliant DBMS, and there are special high-performance drivers for both SQL Server and Oracle.

An ADO.NET data provider is a class library that provides ADO.NET services. As shown in Figure 13-17, there are currently three Microsoft-supplied data providers. The OLE DB data provider can be used for ADO.NET processing of any OLE DB-compliant data source. The SQLClient data provider is purpose-built for processing SQL Server databases, and the OracleClient data provider is similarly purpose-built for processing Oracle databases.

All of these data providers were written by Microsoft. The information necessary for organizations to create data providers is publicly available, however. By the time you

FIGURE 13–16

Role of ADO.NET

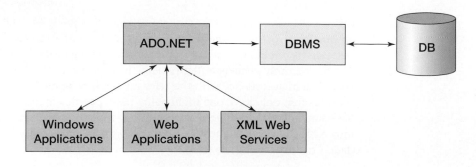

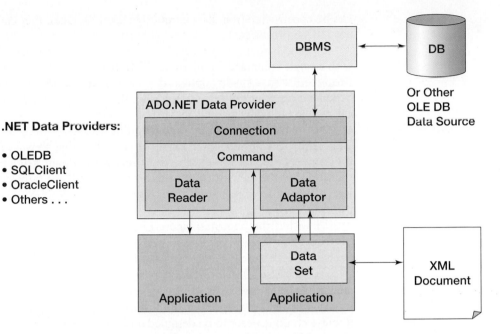

FIGURE 13-17

Components of an
ADO.NET Data
Provider

.NET Data Providers:

• OLEDB
• SQLClient
• OracleClient
• Others . . .

read this chapter, there will likely be data providers from the Oracle Corporation, from IBM, and from other companies.

Figure 13-17 depicts the major components of a .NET data provider. The connection object is similar to the connection object discussed in Chapter 12, except that ODBC is not used as a data source. The name of the data provider and the database is provided instead, as you will see.

Once a connection is established, a command object is created on that connection. A data reader provides read-only, forward-only, fast access to database data. Such readers are used for applications that need only to query the data in a forward direction. In addition to the data reader, an application can get and put data to and from the database using the command object similarly to that shown in Chapter 12. This facility is represented by the double headed arrow in the middle of the command object. Stored procedures can be executed in this way as well.

Although these capabilities of ADO.NET are important, they are just extensions and improvements on existing ADO features and functions. It is the next component, the dataset, which distinguishes ADO.NET from the data access technology of the past. It is also the dataset that provides the capabilities we need to process XML documents against database data.

The ADO.NET Dataset

A **dataset** is an in-memory database. Datasets have all the characteristics, features, and functions of a regular database. They can have multiple tables, and those tables can have relationships. The tables in a dataset can have foreign keys and referential integrity, and referential integrity actions can be defined on them as well. Tables in a dataset can have surrogate keys, meaning that new rows are given a value by ADO.NET rather than by the DBMS. Columns of dataset tables can be defined to be unique.

Relationships among dataset tables can be processed just as relationships in a database can be processed. You will see an example of using a relationship to compute the values of a column later in this chapter. Dataset tables can also have views.

The data in a dataset is disconnected from any regular database. Data can be created in a dataset without first being added to a database. Further, if the dataset's data was read from a database, no connection is maintained back to the source database for that data. A dataset is an independent, fully-functioned, in-memory database. Dataset data can be constructed from data in multiple databases, and they can be managed by different DBMS products.

Once a dataset is constructed, its contents can be formatted as an XML document with a single command. Similarly, an XML Schema document for the dataset can also be produced with a single command. This process works in reverse as well. An XML Schema document can be used to create the structure of a dataset, and the dataset data can then be filled by reading an XML document.

You may be wondering, "Why is all this necessary? Why do we need an in-memory database?" The answer lies in database views like that shown in Figure 13-14. There is no standardized way to describe and process such data structures. Because it involves two multi-value paths through the data, SQL cannot be used to describe the data. Instead, we must execute two SQL statements and somehow patch the results to obtain the view.

Views like that shown in Figure 13-14 have been processed for many years, but only by private proprietary means. Every time such a structure needs to be processed, a developer designs programs for creating and manipulating the data in memory and for saving it to the database. Object-oriented programmers define a class for this data structure and create methods to serialize objects of this class into the database. Other programmers use other means. But, the problem is that every time a different view is designed, a different technique needs to be designed and developed to process the new view.

As Microsoft developed .NET technology, it became clear that a generalized means needed to be developed to define and process such database views and related structures. Microsoft could have defined a new proprietary technology for this purpose, but thankfully they did not. Instead, they recognized that the concepts, techniques, and facilities used to manage regular databases can be used to manage in-memory databases as well. The benefit to you is that all of the concepts and techniques that you have learned to this point for processing regular databases can also be used to process datasets.

Datasets do have a downside, a serious one for some applications. Because dataset data are disconnected from the regular database, only optimistic locking can be used. The data are read from the database, placed into the dataset, and processed there. No attempt is made to propagate changes in the dataset back to the database. If, after processing, the application later wants to save all of the dataset data into a regular database, it needs to use optimistic locking. If some other application has changed the data, either the dataset will need to be reprocessed or the data change will be forced onto the database, causing the lost update problem.

Thus, datasets cannot be used for applications in which optimistic locking is problematical. For such applications, the ADO.NET command object should be used instead. But for applications in which conflict is rare or for those in which reprocessing after conflict can be accommodated, datasets provide significant value.

▶ USING ADO.NET TO PROCESS VIEW RIDGE CUSTOMER DATA

The remainder of this chapter discusses a Visual Basic.NET application that creates a dataset for the view shown in Figure 13-14. VB.NET is an object oriented programming language, and if you are not yet an object-oriented programmer, you will have to cope as best you can. Most of the examples can be understood intuitively, even if you do not understand the syntax.

(Note, however, that we said earlier that the only way to use Oracle's XML facilities is to write in Java, an object-oriented programming language. Further, the only way to process ADO.NET is from one of the .NET languages all of which, like VB.NET, are object-oriented languages. Thus, if you do not yet know object-oriented design and programming and if you want to work in the emerging world of database processing, you should run, not walk, to your nearest object-oriented design and programming class!)

Purpose of the Application

The purpose of this application is to demonstrate the creation and processing of a dataset. This application, which is an ASP.NET application, creates a Web page and, in the code behind file, constructs a dataset from the five View Ridge tables. The application reads all of the data for one customer (here, hard-coded as the customer with CustomerID = 1015).

Once the dataset is populated, the user of this application can display the contents of the datatables in the dataset; or the user can display the dataset as an XML document or display the structure of the dataset as an XML Schema document.

Additionally, the user can cause the application to examine all transactions for this customer; if any have a SalesPrice less than the AskingPrice, the user can set the SalesPrice equal to the AskingPrice. Finally, the changed dataset data are written back to the database. A log of the data activity is produced that we will examine to illustrate how the dataset tracks changes.

In the next sections, we will examine important portions of this code. The point, however, is not for you to understand this particular application; rather you should strive to understand the ideas behind datasets and the relationship between among datasets, the database, and XML.

Getting a Connection and Filling the Dataset

Figure 13-18 shows a code snippet that imports the necessary class libraries, defines variables used throughout the application, and initiates processing. This code was placed in a VB module named DataSetElements; this module contains subroutines used by the code that processes the Web page. Only the first subroutine in this module is shown in Figure 13-18. Other subroutines will be shown as we proceed.

The action starts in the subroutine ConstructDataSet. This routine is called when the Web page is loaded (not shown). It instantiates a new dataset in the dataset object variable dsCustomerView, and it obtains a connection object in the variable conViewRidge. The connection is to the Oracle database VRG using Integrated Security. The connection format shown here can be used when Oracle is running on the same machine as the Web server and when the database is also located on that same machine. Additionally, the use of Integrated Security means that the operating system (in this case,

FIGURE 13–18

"Creating the Dataset, Connection, and Data Adapter"

```
Imports System.Data
Imports System.Data.OracleClient ' use the Oracle client Data Provider

Module DataSetElements


    Public drcTransRows As DataRow()
    Public drTransRow As DataRow
    Public dtUpdatedRows As DataTable

    Public intCustomerID As Integer

    Public dsCustomerView As DataSet
    Public conViewRidge As OracleConnection
    Public daViewRidge As OracleDataAdapter

    Public Sub ConstructDataSet()

        ' Create data set and get connection to Oracle database
        dsCustomerView = New DataSet()
        conViewRidge = New OracleConnection("Data Source=VRG;Integrated Security = SSPI")
        ' instantiate the data adapter; set select command below
        daViewRidge = New OracleDataAdapter("", conViewRidge)

    End Sub
```

Windows XP Professional) provides the user's credentials[3]. The last statement in this subroutine instantiates a new data adapter object named daViewRidge. Note that the data adapter uses the connection, but not the dataset object. Thus, the same data adapter can be used for different datasets, if necessary. In this application, we will process only one dataset: dsCustomerView.

The Web page next calls the subroutine FillDataSet, shown in Figure 13-19. This routine uses the data adapter to fill the dataset tables. First, a string variable is set to the syntax of the appropriate SQL command. Then, the SelectCommand property of the data adapter is set to the SQL text. After that, the data adapter method FillSchema is invoked to obtain the schema metadata for the SelectCommand into a new table called CustomerAlias. Then, the data adapter Fill method is called to place the data results of the SelectCommand into the dataset.

FIGURE 13-19

Using the Data Adapter to Fill the Dataset Tables

```
Public Sub FillDataSet()
    Dim strSQLCommand As String

    'Fill the CustomerAlias table in the data set with qualifying CUSTOMER data from the database
    'First get schema info and then get data
    strSQLCommand = "Select * from SYSTEM.CUSTOMER where CustomerID = " & Str(intCustomerID)
    daViewRidge.SelectCommand.CommandText = strSQLCommand
    daViewRidge.FillSchema(dsCustomerView, SchemaType.Mapped, "CustomerAlias")
    daViewRidge.Fill(dsCustomerView, "CustomerAlias")

    'Fill the intersection table in the data set with CUSTOMER_ARTIST_INT data from the database
    strSQLCommand = "Select * from SYSTEM.CUSTOMER_ARTIST_INT where CustomerID = " & Str(intCustomerID)
    daViewRidge.SelectCommand.CommandText = strSQLCommand
    daViewRidge.FillSchema(dsCustomerView, SchemaType.Mapped, "IntersectionAlias")
    daViewRidge.Fill(dsCustomerView, "IntersectionAlias")

    'Fill the TransactionAlias table in the data set with TRANSACTION data from the database
    strSQLCommand = "Select * from SYSTEM.TRANSACTION where CustomerID = " & Str(intCustomerID)
    daViewRidge.SelectCommand.CommandText = strSQLCommand
    daViewRidge.FillSchema(dsCustomerView, SchemaType.Mapped, "TransactionAlias")
    daViewRidge.Fill(dsCustomerView, "TransactionAlias")

    ' Read Qualifying WORK table rows into the data set
    strSQLCommand = "Select * from SYSTEM.WORK where WorkID IN " _
        & "(Select WorkID from SYSTEM.TRANSACTION WHERE CustomerID = " & Str(intCustomerID) & ")"
    daViewRidge.SelectCommand.CommandText = strSQLCommand
    daViewRidge.FillSchema(dsCustomerView, SchemaType.Mapped, "WorkAlias")
    daViewRidge.Fill(dsCustomerView, "WorkAlias")

    ' Read qualifying ARTIST table rows into the data set via the interesection table
    strSQLCommand = "Select * from SYSTEM.ARTIST where ArtistID IN " _
        & "(Select ArtistID from SYSTEM.CUSTOMER_ARTIST_INT WHERE CustomerID = " & Str(intCustomerID) & "
    daViewRidge.SelectCommand.CommandText = strSQLCommand
    daViewRidge.FillSchema(dsCustomerView, SchemaType.Mapped, "ArtistAlias")
    daViewRidge.Fill(dsCustomerView, "ArtistAlias")

    ' Read any ARTIST table rows that weren't picked up from the intersection
    ' table
    strSQLCommand = "Select * from SYSTEM.ARTIST A where A.ArtistID IN " _
        & "(Select W.ArtistID from SYSTEM.WORK W Join SYSTEM.TRANSACTION T " _
        & "ON T.WorkID = W.WorkID Join SYSTEM.CUSTOMER C ON T.CustomerID = C.CustomerID " _
        & "AND C.CustomerID = " & Str(intCustomerID) & ") " _
        & "AND NOT EXISTS (Select * from SYSTEM.CUSTOMER_ARTIST_INT I " _
        & "WHERE I.ArtistID = A.ArtistID " _
        & "AND I.CustomerID = " & Str(intCustomerID) & ")"

    daViewRidge.SelectCommand.CommandText = strSQLCommand
    daViewRidge.FillSchema(dsCustomerView, SchemaType.Mapped, "ArtistAlias")
    daViewRidge.Fill(dsCustomerView, "ArtistAlias")

End Sub
```

[3]Small print: By default, ASP.NET connects to the DBMS using the user name ASPNET. As stated in Chapter 10, Oracle requires any user name that has operating system authentication to begin with the letters OPS$. Thus, for this application to run, there must be an account named OPS$ASPNET in the Oracle VRG database, and that account must have privileges necessary to read and update the View Ridge tables in VRG. Rather than using the default name ASPNET, you can cause ASP.NET to pass the user's credentials through to Oracle. That technique, however, is beyond the scope of this discussion.

The SELECT statement uses the value of the public integer variable intCustomerID to qualify the rows to be read. In this application, the form load routine sets intCustomerID to 1015 prior to calling this routine. Thus, only data for the customer with CustomerID = 1015 will be read into the dataset. Obviously, this variable can be changed to read data for other customers.

In this application, all SQL statements for Oracle must be preceded by the word SYSTEM. Thus, Select * from SYSTEM.Customer. This is necessary because the tables were created under the SYSTEM account and they will be processed by the OPS$ASP-NET account as explained. Also, with one exception, the tables in the dataset have the same name as the tables in the database, except that the word Alias is added. Thus, the CUSTOMER table in the database is called CustomerAlias in the dataset. The exception is that the intersection table is named IntersectionAlias.

The only notable characteristic of this routine is the SQL statements used to obtain the ARTIST data. First, all of the ARTIST data needed by the intersection table rows are selected. Then, any ARTIST data referenced by WORK that was not obtained from the intersection table is read.

At this point, all data for the customer having a CustomerID equal to the value of intCustomerID has been read into the dataset. All of the metadata that the OracleClient data provider obtained from Oracle about these tables has also been placed into the dataset.

Adding Structures to the Dataset

The next series of subroutines adds structure to the dataset. Figure 13-20 shows the BuildRelationships subroutine, which defines the relationships among the tables. The Add method of the Relations class of the dataset is used to do this. In each case, the Add method is passed the name of the relationship, the name of the key in the parent, and the name of the foreign key in the child. The relationships created here can be used to process tables in the dataset. Given a WorkAlias row, for example, it is possible to use the relationship to obtain the parent of the work. Similarly, given an ArtistAlias row, it is possible to use the relationship to obtain all related rows in WorkAlias.

The referential integrity constraints for the relationships are created in the subroutine shown in Figure 13-21. In each case, the parent and child tables are identified and then a

FIGURE 13-20

Building Relationships

```
Public Sub BuildRelationships()

    'Create the relationships

    dsCustomerView.Relations.Add("CustomerTransactionRel", _
        dsCustomerView.Tables("CustomerAlias").Columns("CustomerID"), _
        dsCustomerView.Tables("TransactionAlias").Columns("CustomerID"))

    dsCustomerView.Relations.Add("WorkTransRel", _
        dsCustomerView.Tables("WorkAlias").Columns("WorkID"), _
        dsCustomerView.Tables("TransactionAlias").Columns("WorkID"))

    dsCustomerView.Relations.Add("ArtistWorkRel", _
        dsCustomerView.Tables("ArtistAlias").Columns("ArtistID"), _
        dsCustomerView.Tables("WorkAlias").Columns("ArtistID"))

    dsCustomerView.Relations.Add("CustomerIntRel", _
        dsCustomerView.Tables("CustomerAlias").Columns("CustomerID"), _
        dsCustomerView.Tables("IntersectionAlias").Columns("CustomerID"))

    dsCustomerView.Relations.Add("ArtistIntRel", _
        dsCustomerView.Tables("ArtistAlias").Columns("ArtistID"), _
        dsCustomerView.Tables("IntersectionAlias").Columns("ArtistID"))

End Sub
```

<table>
<tr><td>

FIGURE 13–21

Creating Referential Integrity Constraints

</td><td>

```
Sub CreateRefIntegrityConstraints()

    'Create the constraints
    Dim dtParent As DataTable
    Dim dtChild As DataTable
    Dim fkConstraint As ForeignKeyConstraint

    dtParent = dsCustomerView.Tables("ArtistAlias")
    dtChild = dsCustomerView.Tables("WorkAlias")
    fkConstraint = New ForeignKeyConstraint _
        ("WorkFK", dtParent.Columns("ArtistID"), dtChild.Columns("ArtistID"))
    fkConstraint.DeleteRule = Rule.None
    fkConstraint.UpdateRule = Rule.None

    dtParent = dsCustomerView.Tables("WorkAlias")
    dtChild = dsCustomerView.Tables("TransactionAlias")
    fkConstraint = New ForeignKeyConstraint _
        ("WorkTransFK", dtParent.Columns("WorkID"), dtChild.Columns("WorkID"))
    fkConstraint.DeleteRule = Rule.None
    fkConstraint.UpdateRule = Rule.None

    dtParent = dsCustomerView.Tables("CustomerAlias")
    dtChild = dsCustomerView.Tables("TransactionAlias")
    fkConstraint = New ForeignKeyConstraint _
        ("CustomerTransFK", dtParent.Columns("CustomerID"), dtChild.Columns("CustomerID"))
    fkConstraint.DeleteRule = Rule.None
    fkConstraint.UpdateRule = Rule.None

    dtParent = dsCustomerView.Tables("CustomerAlias")
    dtChild = dsCustomerView.Tables("IntersectionAlias")
    fkConstraint = New ForeignKeyConstraint _
        ("CustomerArtistFK", dtParent.Columns("CustomerID"), dtChild.Columns("CustomerID"))
    fkConstraint.DeleteRule = Rule.Cascade
    fkConstraint.UpdateRule = Rule.Cascade

    dtParent = dsCustomerView.Tables("ArtistAlias")
    dtChild = dsCustomerView.Tables("IntersectionAlias")
    fkConstraint = New ForeignKeyConstraint _
        ("ArtistCustomerFK", dtParent.Columns("ArtistID"), dtChild.Columns("ArtistID"))
    fkConstraint.DeleteRule = Rule.Cascade
    fkConstraint.UpdateRule = Rule.Cascade

End Sub
```

</td></tr>
</table>

ForeignKeyConstraint object is created for each constraint. ForeignKeyConstraint objects have properties DeleteRule and UpdateRule. These properties can be set to specify foreign key behavior when the parents' keys are updated or deleted. Allowed values are {None, Cascade, Set Null, and Set Default}, the same choices as are available in the IDEF1X model discussed in Chapter 2. Here, we set the values to be consistent with the referential integrity constraints in the Oracle database.

Finally, the AddDataColumn subroutine in Figure 13-22 is called to create a new column in the CustomerAlias datatable. The new column will contain the sum of the SalesPrice columns in all TransactionAlias tables that are related to the CustomerAlias row. Notice how the CustomerTransactionRel relationship object is used to provide the TRANSACTION rows.

Keep in mind, the dataset and all of structures created here are in-memory. We have created a mini-database, but one that is in memory, not on disk. Furthermore, dataset data are disconnected from the database. We can close the connection object if we want, and process the dataset independently without problem.

<table>
<tr><td>

FIGURE 13–22

Adding a Computed Column to a DataTable

</td><td>

```
Sub AddDataColumn()
    Dim tCol As DataColumn

    ' Create new column Total Purchases and set to sum of child SalesPrice

    tCol = New DataColumn("Total Purchases", GetType(Int32))
    tCol.Expression = "Sum (Child(CustomerTransactionRel).SalesPrice)"
    dsCustomerView.Tables("CustomerAlias").Columns.Add(tCol)

End Sub
```

</td></tr>
</table>

Processing the Dataset

Datasets have built-in capabilities that make them very easy to process. Figure 13-23(a) shows the VB.NET code necessary to fill a data grid for display on the Web page. All that is required is to set the DataSource property of the grid to the dataset and the DataMember property to the name of the datatable that the grid is to contain. The grid's DataBind method can then be used to fill the grid with the datatable's data. Figure 13-23(b) shows the results of this binding.

FIGURE 13–23

Using Data Grids (a) Filling the Grids with Dataset Tables and (b) Grid Display in Browser

```
Private Sub FillGrids()

    ' bind data to grids
    grdCustomer.DataSource = dsCustomerView
    grdCustomer.DataMember = "CustomerAlias"
    grdCustomer.DataBind()

    grdTransaction.DataSource = dsCustomerView
    grdTransaction.DataMember = "TransactionAlias"
    grdTransaction.DataBind()

    grdWork.DataSource = dsCustomerView
    grdWork.DataMember = "WorkAlias"
    grdWork.DataBind()

    grdArtist.DataSource = dsCustomerView
    grdArtist.DataMember = "ArtistAlias"
    grdArtist.DataBind()

    grdIntersection.DataSource = dsCustomerView
    grdIntersection.DataMember = "IntersectionAlias"
    grdIntersection.DataBind()

End Sub
```

(a)

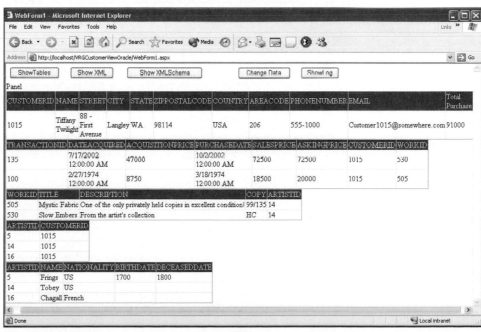

(b)

The data grids in this figure have a number of interesting characteristics. First, observe that the column names were obtained from Oracle. At no point did we code these names into the application. They were obtained when the data adapter FillSchema method read the metadata from the database. All of these names are shown in uppercase letters because Oracle stores them that way.

Also note that the TotalPurchases column has been added to the CustomerAlias datatable. Its value has been set correctly to 91000, which is the sum of SalesPrice for this customer's purchases. This means the relationship between CustomerAlias and TransactionAlias was correctly processed. All of the rest of the data for customer 1015 appear, as you would expect.

Although datasets can be accessed from a table perspective like that shown in Figure 13-23, they can also be processed from an XML perspective. The code in Figure 13-24(a) shows the use of the dataset method GetXml. Here, that method is used to place the XML version of this dataset into a string variable. The string variable is then displayed in a text box. The result is shown in Figure 13-24(b).

Without sounding like a shill for Microsoft, this is an amazing capability for very little work on our part. We can create a dataset and fill it with data for a database view of any level of complexity. After we have done so, we can readily process that dataset data either as tables or as XML. Furthermore, if we change the XML document, the changes will be updated in the dataset and hence in the tables. Similarly, if we change the dataset

---

FIGURE 13-24

Generating an XML Document from the Dataset (a) Code to Generate the XML Document and (b) Portion of Resulting XML Document

```
Private Sub btnShowXML_Click _
    (ByVal sender As System.Object, ByVal e As System.EventArgs) _
    Handles btnShowXML.Click

    'get the xml document for the dataset and place in the textbox
    strXml = dsCustomerView.GetXml()
    txtXMLShow.Text = strXml
    pnlTables.Visible = False
    txtXMLShow.Visible = True

End Sub
```

(a)

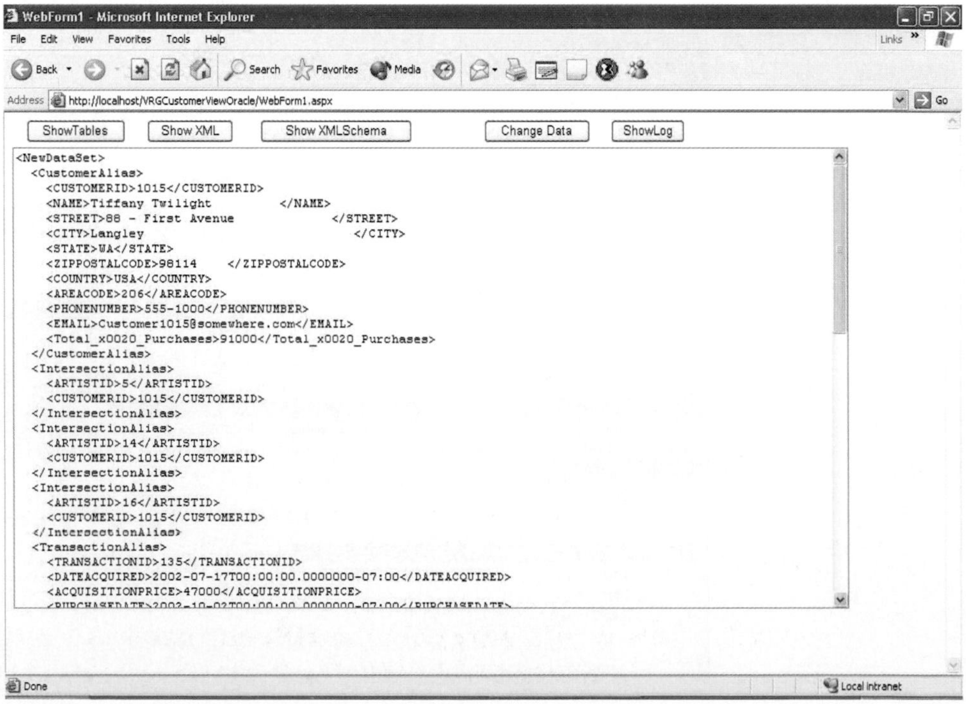

(b)

tables, those changes will automatically be reflected in the XML document produced. Thus, we can process the same data from either perspective.

Additionally, we can cause the dataset to produce the XML Schema for this dataset. To do this, we just call the dataset method GetXmlSchema and place the resulting string into our text box, as shown in Figure 13-25(a). The result is the XML Schema document for the XML document shown in Figure 13-24(b).

If we save the XML Schema document in a file, we can later use that file to re-create the dataset. All of the dataset tables, columns, and relationships will be restored correctly from the XML Schema document. Note, however, that there are some characteristics of the dataset that are not placed in the XML Schema. For example, although relationships are shown in the XML Schema, referential integrity is not. Referential integrity constraints have to be added to the dataset after it is constructed from the XML Schema.

Updating the Dataset Data and Updating the Database

Data in the dataset can be updated just like regular database data. The difference is that changes to the dataset are not necessarily propagated to the database. To illustrate how the dataset update process works, we will change some dataset data, examine the status of dataset rows, make database changes from the dataset, and then re-examine the status of the dataset rows. All of the action will be recorded in a textbox log for illustration.

FIGURE 13–25

Generating an XML Schema from the Dataset (a) Code to Generate the XML Schema and (b) Portion of Resulting XML Schema

```
Private Sub btnShowXMLSchema_Click _
    (ByVal sender As System.Object, ByVal e As System.EventArgs) _
    Handles btnShowXMLSchema.Click

    ' Get the xmlschema for the dataset and place in the textbox
    strXml = dsCustomerView.GetXmlSchema()
    txtXMLShow.Text = strXml
    pnlTables.Visible = False
    txtXMLShow.Visible = True

End Sub
```

(a)

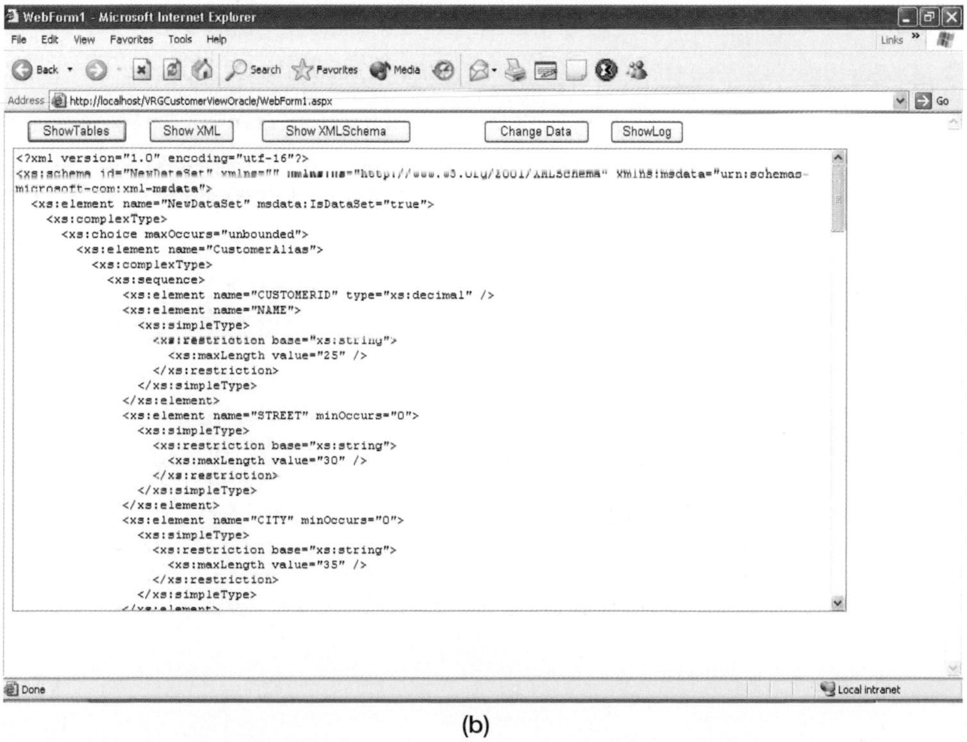

(b)

FIGURE 13–26

Updating a Dataset and Database
(a) Update Code;
(b) Trigger-like Event;
(c) Display RowVersion Code and
(d) Creating the UpdateCommand

```
Private Sub btnChangeData_Click(ByVal sender As System.Object, ByVal e As System.EventArgs) _
        Handles btnChangeData.Click
    txtBoxMessage.Visible = True ' make log visible
    txtBoxMessage.Text = "****   Start column change in TransactionAlias Table. ****" ' start log

    dtTrans = dsCustomerView.Tables("TransactionAlias") ' point dtTrans to proper dataset table
    drcTransRows = dtTrans.Select("(SalesPrice < AskingPrice) ") ' find qualifying rows
    For Each drTransRow In drcTransRows ' for each qualifying row
        drTransRow("SalesPrice") = drTransRow("AskingPrice") ' set salesprice to askingprice
    Next
    DisplayRowState() ' write to log

    dtUpdatedRows = dsCustomerView.Tables("TransactionAlias") ' make data table of updated rows
    dtUpdatedRows = dsCustomerView.Tables("TransactionAlias").GetChanges(DataRowState.Modified)

    BuildOracleUpdateCommand() ' Create updateCommand property for the Oracle Data Adapter
    daViewRidge.Update(dtUpdatedRows) ' Update database

    txtBoxMessage.Text = txtBoxMessage.Text & _
        "****           Oracle Updated From Data Set              **** "
    DisplayRowState() ' write to log

    dsCustomerView.AcceptChanges() ' accept changes into dataset
    txtBoxMessage.Text = txtBoxMessage.Text & _
        "****           Data Set Accept Changes Issued            **** "
    DisplayRowState() ' write to log last time
    FillGrids() 'fill grids with latest dataset data
End Sub
```

(a)

```
Private Sub dtTrans_ColumnChanging(ByVal sender As Object, _
            ByVal e As System.Data.DataColumnChangeEventArgs) _
            Handles dtTrans.ColumnChanging

    ' this is the dataset equivalent of a before trigger
    ' place before logic here; for example, could alter e.ProposedValue
    txtBoxMessage.Text = txtBoxMessage.Text & _
        "****    Column is changing.  Proposed value is: " & _
        e.ProposedValue & "       ****"

End Sub
```

(b)

```
Sub DisplayRowState()

    For Each drTransRow In dtTrans.Rows
        'show current version of SalesPrice in this row
        txtBoxMessage.Text = txtBoxMessage.Text & _
        " Transaction with TransactionID" & Str(drTransRow("TransactionID")) _
        & " Current Value Is " & drTransRow("SalesPrice", DataRowVersion.Current)

        'show original version of SalePrice in this row
        txtBoxMessage.Text = txtBoxMessage.Text & _
        " Transaction with TransactionID" & Str(drTransRow("TransactionID")) _
        & " Original Value Is " & drTransRow("SalesPrice", DataRowVersion.Original) & " "
    Next

End Sub
```

(c)

```
Sub BuildOracleUpdateCommand()
    Dim cmdUpdate As OracleCommand

    ' Create the UpdateCommand.
    cmdUpdate = New OracleCommand("UPDATE SYSTEM.Transaction SET SalesPrice = :pSalesPrice " & _
            "WHERE TransactionID = :pTransactionID", conViewRidge)
    cmdUpdate.Parameters.Add("pSalesPrice", OracleType.Number, 8, "SalesPrice")
    cmdUpdate.Parameters.Add("pTransactionID", OracleType.Int32, 0, "TransactionID")

    daViewRidge.UpdateCommand = cmdUpdate

End Sub
```

(d)

Figure 13-26(a) shows the code used. As you read this code, reference Figure 13-18 where the important object variables are declared. In particular, the variable drcTransRow (drc for *DataRowCollection*) is defined as an array of DataRow objects, and drTransRow is declared as a single DataRow object. dtUpdatedRows is a DataTable that contains the updated rows. Finally, dtTrans is defined as a DataTable object. For reasons unimportant to us here, that object is declared elsewhere in the code, but it is defined as a DataTable object.

As changes are made, the dataset keeps three versions of each column in each datatable. These versions are the *original* value, the *current* value, and the *proposed* value. The original value is the value of the column when first read from the database or the value of the column after changes have been committed in the dataset via the AcceptChanges method. The current value is the value after changes have been made, but before those changes have been committed to the dataset. If no changes have been made to a column value, the original and current values are the same. Finally, the proposed value is a value that exists during a modification. We will trap that value in the ADO.NET equivalent of a trigger.

Updating the Dataset When the user clicks the button Change Data, the procedure in Figure 13-26(a) is executed. First, it writes a start message to the textbox control txtBoxMessage. Then, dtTrans is set to the TransactionAlias table. Next, the drcTransRows is set equal to all of the rows in TransAlias for which SalesPrice is less than AskingPrice. After that, the SalesPrice of all the rows in the drcTransRow collection is set to AskingPrice. For the data in our dataset (see Figure 13-23(b)), there is one such row that will be updated.

When the change is made, the ColumnChanging event of dtTrans is invoked and the code in Figure 13-26(b) is executed. In this example, the code simply displays the proposed value in the textbox log. Of course, the application can place before trigger logic here, if appropriate. Note, too, that the proposed value can be changed here, prior to the dataset update.

After updating the SalesPrice column, the subroutine calls DisplayRowState. As shown in Figure 13-26(c), this routine adds a message to the textbox that shows the current and original values of SalesPrice for all rows in the TransactionAlias datatable.

As you can tell from the log shown in Figure 13-27, the change was trapped by the ColumnChanging event, and the proposed value of 20000 was displayed. Next, the DisplayRowState routine printed the current and original values for all the rows in dtTrans (there are two, as shown in Figure 13-23). Observe that the current and original

FIGURE 13-27

Log Showing Dataset Updates

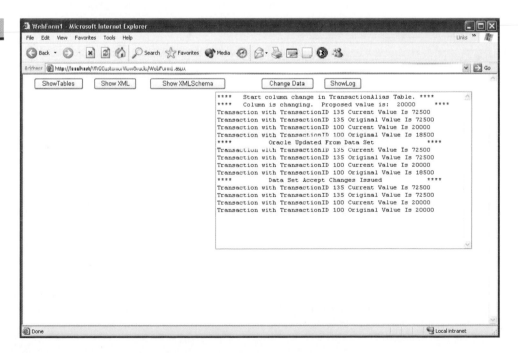

values of the first row are the same, but the current and original values for the second row differ because of the change to SalesPrice.

Updating the Oracle Database At this point, the dataset values have been altered in the dataset, but nothing has been changed in the database. The next statements, shown in Figure 13-26(a), propagate the dataset changes to the database. To do this, a datatable called dtUpdatedRows is created and the GetChanges method of a datatable is called to fill that datatable. GetChanges places all rows for which the current value is different from the original value into the dtUpdatedRows datatable.

The next statement calls a subroutine to build an Oracle update command. The code is shown in Figure 13-26(d). The purpose of this subroutine is to provide a value for the UpdateCommand property of the Oracle data adapter. Every data adapter has four such properties: SelectCommand, InsertCommand, UpdateCommand, and DeleteCommand. These commands are used to perform the indicated action. If, for example, a row needs to be updated, the data adapter calls the UpdateCommand to make the update in the database. Similarly, if a row needs to be deleted, the data adapter calls the DeleteCommand property to make the deletion. We used the SelectCommand of the data adapter in Figure 13-19 when we filled the dataset.

Any valid SQL command can be entered for these properties. Alternatively, these commands can invoke stored procedures to make the appropriate data changes. It is also possible to have VisualStudio.NET write these commands for you, but that option is beyond the scope of our present discussion. Instead, here we will create our own update command, as shown.

Before continuing, note that the ability to tailor how the data adapter makes insert, update, and delete commands gives tremendous flexibility to the developer. With ADO, the developer was stuck with ADO's particular implementation of these actions. By allowing the developer to specify his or her own commands, much more flexibility exists to build particular logic and functionality into the process of propagating dataset changes into the database.

There is one small point to note in Figure 13-26(d). As you know from Chapter 10, in PL/SQL stored procedures, variables are preceded by a colon. This means the parameters provided to the update command must also be preceded by a colon, as shown in Figure 13-26(d). The documentation of the Microsoft OracleClient data provider is unclear on this need.

After the UpdateCommand property has been set, the updates can be made. In Figure 13-26(a), this is done by invoking the Update method on the data adapter and passing it the datatable with the updated rows as a parameter. At this point, the Oracle database has been updated.

As the log in Figure 13-27 indicates, however, the changes have not yet been committed to the dataset. You can tell this from the log because after the Oracle update is issued, the Original and Current values of SalesPrice in the second dtTrans row are different.

The changes are committed in the dataset by invoking the dataset's AcceptChanges method. After that is done, the original and current values of all columns in all rows of tables in the dataset will be the same. This is demonstrated by the last four lines of the log shown in Figure 13-27.

The final values of all datatables in the dataset are shown in Figure 13-28. Observe that the computed value of TotalPurchases has been correctly updated as well.

We showed only a few of the features and functions of ADO.NET in this section. Although this discussion does not prepare you to write your own ADO.NET applications, it should give you the overall concept of datasets and how they can be processed. You also should be able to understand how the relational world and the document-processing world have been integrated into the idea of a dataset. This technology will be important for many, many years to come, and learning more about it would be an excellent investment of your time.

FIGURE 13-28

Dataset Tables after Update

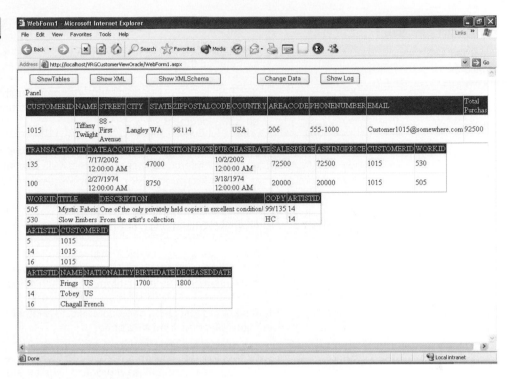

ADDITIONAL XML STANDARDS

As you know by now, XML was developed as a series of standards. So far, we have mentioned XML, XSL, XSLT, and XML Schema. There are a number of other XML standards that you will hear about. Figure 13-29 shows some that you may encounter. You can find the standards, documentation about them, and some tutorials for them on the **www.w3.org** and **www.xml.org** Web sites.

In addition to the four we have discussed, XPath is a standard for addressing elements within documents. In Figure 13-4, expressions like <xsl:value-of-select="name/lastname"> are using the XPath standard for locating a particular element in the document. XPath includes concepts from another standard XPointer, which was developed to provide a sophisticated means for documents to reference elements in other documents.

SAX and DOM refer to different methods of parsing XML documents. The process of parsing consists of reading a document, breaking it into components, and responding to those components in some way—perhaps storing them into a database. XML parsers also validate documents against the DTDs or Schemas.

To use the SAX API, a program that is working on an XML document—an XSLT processor, for example—invokes the SAX-compliant parser and passes it the name of the document to parse. The SAX parser processes the document and calls back objects within the XSLT processor whenever particular structures are encountered. A SAX parser, for example, calls the XSLT parser when it encounters a new element, passing the name of the element, its content, and other relevant items.

The DOM API works from a different paradigm. A DOM-compliant parser processes the entire XML document and creates a tree representation of it. Each element of the document is a node on the tree. The XSLT processor can then call the DOM parser to obtain particular elements using XPath or a similar addressing scheme. DOM requires the entire document to be processed at one time and may require an unreasonable amount of storage for very large documents. If so, SAX is a better choice. On the other hand, if all of the document contents need to be available for use at once, DOM is the only choice.

Standard	Description
XML	Extensible Markup Language. A document markup language that started the following:
XSL	XSLT Stylesheet. The document that provides the {match, action} pairs and other data for XSLT to use when transforming an XML document.
XSLT	A program (or process) that applies XSLT Stylesheets to an XML document to produce a transformed XML document.
XML Schema	An XML-compliant language for constraining the structure of an XML document. Extends and replaces DTDs. Under development and *very* important to database processing.
XPath	A sublanguage within XSLT that is used to identify parts of an XML document to be transformed. Can also be used for calculations and string manipulation. Comingled with XSLT.
XPointer	A standard for linking one document to another. XPath has many elements from XPointer.
SAX	Simple API (application program interface) for XML. An event-based parser that notifies a program when the elements of an XML document have been encountered during document parsing.
DOM	Document Object Model. An API that represents an XML document as a tree. Each node of the tree represents a piece of the XML document. A program can directly access and manipulate a node of the DOM representation.
XQuery	A standard for expressing database queries as XML documents. The structure of the query uses XPath facilities, and the result of the query is represented in an XML format. Under development and likely to be important in the future.
XML Namespaces	A standard for allocating terminology to defined collections. X:Name is interpreted as the element Name as defined in namespace X. Y:Name is interpreted as the element Name as defined in namespace Y. Useful for disambiguating terms.

XQuery is an emerging standard for expressing generalized queries on XML documents. You can think of XQuery as SQL for XML documents. When it becomes available, this standard will be very important to the database/XML world. Check **www.w3.org** because it is likely to have been finalized by the time you read this.

The last standard, XMLNamespaces, is very important because it is used to combine different vocabularies into the same XML Schema. It can be used to define and support domains and to disambiguate terms. The need for the latter occurs when a document contains synonyms—for example, suppose that it has two different uses for the term *Instrument*. Suppose that one use of this term refers to musical instruments and has subelements {Manufacturer, Model, Material} as in {Horner, Bflat Clarinet, Wood}; and a second use of this term refers to electronic instruments and has subelements {Manufacturer, Model, Voltage} as in {RadioShack, Ohm-meter, 12-volt}. The author of the XML Schema for such a document can define two different namespaces that each contains one of these definitions. Then, the complexType definition for each of these definitions of Instrument can be prefixed by the label of the namespace, as was done in our schema documents when we used the label xsd. There is more to XML Namespaces, and you will undoubtedly learn more as you work with XML.

The XML standards committee continues its important work, and more standards will be developed as the needs arise. At present (2003), work is underway for developing security standards. Other standards will be developed as well. Keep checking **www.w3.org** for more information.

SUMMARY

The confluence of the database-processing and document-processing technologies is one of the most important developments in information systems technology today. Database processing and document processing need each other. Database processing needs ideas from the document-processing world for the representation and materialization of database views. Document processing needs database processing for the permanent storage of data.

SGML is as important to the document-processing world as the relational model is to the database world. XML is a series of standards developed by the database-processing and document-processing communities, working together. XML provides a standardized, yet customizable way to describe the contents of documents. XML documents can automatically be generated from database data, and database data can be automatically extracted from XML documents.

Although XML can be used to materialize Web pages, this is one of its least important uses. More important, by far, is its use for describing, representing, and materializing database views. XML is on the leading edge of database processing; keep checking **www.w3.org** and **www.xml.org** for latest developments.

XML is a better markup language than HTML, primarily because XML provides a clear separation between document structure, content, and materialization. Symbols cannot be used ambiguously with XML.

Two means are used to describe the content of XML documents: Document Type Declarations (DTDs) and XML Schemas. An XML document that conforms to its DTD is called type-valid. A document can be well-formed and not be type-valid, either because it violates the structure of its DTD or because it has no DTD.

XML documents are transformed when an XSLT processor applies an XSL document to the XML document. A common transformation is to convert the XML document into HTML format. Other transformations will be more important in the future. For example, XSL documents can be written to transform the same Order document into different formats needed by different departments: say Sales, Accounting, and Production. XSLT processing is context-oriented; given a particular context, an action is taken when a particular item is located. Today, most browsers have built-in XSLT processors.

XML Schema is a standard for describing the content of an XML document. XML Schema can be used to define custom vocabularies. Documents that conform to an XML Schema are called schema-valid. Unlike DTDs, XML Schema documents are themselves XML documents that can be validated against their schema, one that is maintained by W3C.

Schemas consist of elements and attributes. There are two types of elements: simple and complex. Simple elements have one data value. ComplexType elements can have multiple elements nested within them. ComplexTypes may also have attributes. The elements contained in a complexType may be simple or other complexTypes. ComplexTypes may also define element sequences. A good rule of thumb is that elements represent data, and attributes represent metadata, although this rule of thumb is not part of any XML standard.

XML Schemas (and documents) may have more structure than the columns of a table. Groups such as Phone and Address can be defined. A schema that has all elements at the same level is a flat schema. Structured schemas are those that have defined sub-groups such as Phone and Address. To avoid definition duplication, elements can be defined globally. Duplication is undesirable because there is the risk that definitions will become inconsistent if a change is made to one definition and not the other.

Both Oracle and SQL Server can produce XML documents from database data. The Oracle facilities require the use of Java; see **www.Oracle.com** for more information. SQL Server supports an add-on expression to the SQL Select statement, the FOR XML expression. FOR XML can be used to produce XML documents in which all data are expressed as attributes; or alternatively, in which all data are expressed as elements. FOR XML can also write an XML Schema description as well as the XML document. Using FOR XML EXPLICIT, the developer can place some columns into elements and others into attributes.

When interpreting multi-table selects, the FOR XML processor uses the order of the tables to determine the hierarchical order of elements in the document. FOR XML can be used to produce XML documents with one multi-value path. Documents with more than one multi-value path must be patched together in the application by some means.

XML is important because it facilitates the sharing of XML documents (and hence database data) among organizations. After an XML Schema has been defined, organizations can ensure that they are receiving and sending only schema-valid documents. Additionally, XSL documents can be coded to transform any schema-valid XML document, from any source, into other standardized formats. These advantages become even more important as industry groups standardize on XML Schemas. XML also facilitates business-to-business processing.

ADO.NET is a new, improved, and greatly expanded version of ADO that was developed for the Microsoft .NET initiative. ADO.NET incorporates all of the functionality of ADO, but adds much more. In particular, ADO.NET facilitates the transformation of XML documents to and from database data. Most importantly, ADO.NET introduces the concept of datasets, which are in-memory, fully-functioned, independent databases.

A .NET data provider is a library of classes that provides ADO.NET services. Microsoft provides three data providers. The OLE DB data provider can be used to process any OLE DB-compliant data source. The SQLClient data provider is purpose-built for use with SQL Server, and the OracleClient data provider is purpose-built for use with Oracle. Data providers from companies other than Microsoft are likely in the near future.

A data provider data reader provides fast, forward-only access to data. A command object can be processed to execute SQL and also to invoke stored procedures in a manner similar to but improved from that in ADO. The major new concept of ADO.NET is the dataset.

A dataset in an in-memory database that is disconnected from any regular database, but has all the important characteristics of a regular database. Datasets can have multiple tables, relationships, referential integrity rules, referential integrity actions, views, and the equivalent of triggers. Dataset tables may have surrogate key columns (called auto increment columns), primary keys, and be declared as unique.

Datasets are disconnected from the database(s) from which they are constructed, and they may be constructed from several different databases, possibly managed by different DBMS products.

After a dataset is constructed, an XML document of its contents and an XML Schema of its structure are easily produced. Further, that process works in reverse as well. XML Schema documents can be read to create the structure of the dataset, and XML documents can be read to fill the dataset.

Datasets are needed to provide a standardized, non-proprietary means to process database views. They are especially important for the processing of views with multiple multi-value paths.

The potential downside of datasets is that because they are disconnected, any updates against the databases they access must be performed using optimistic locking. In the case of conflict, either the dataset must be reprocessed or the data change must be forced onto the database, causing the lost update problem.

Dataset concepts are illustrated by an ASP.NET application developed in VB.NET. The example processes a View Ridge Gallery view that has all customer data. A connection is established to an Oracle database, and a data adapter is defined that is used to read all five tables into the dataset. Then, relationships and referential integrity are defined, and a new data column that uses a relationship is created.

The dataset is then processed to show all tables, to produce an equivalent XML document and to produce the XML Schema document for the dataset. Finally, a row of the dataset is updated and written back to the Oracle database by appropriately setting the UpdateCommand property of the data adapter.

This chapter concludes with a brief description of additional XML standards: XPath, SAX, DOM, XQuery, and XMLNamespaces.

GROUP I QUESTIONS

13.1 Why do database processing and document processing need each other?

13.2 What is the relationship of HTML, SGML, and XML?

13.3 Explain the term *standardized but customizable.*

13.4 What is SOAP? What did it stand for originally? What does it stand for today?

13.5 What are the problems in interpreting a tag such as <h2> in HTML?

13.6 What is a DTD and what purpose does it serve?

13.7 What is the difference between a well-formed XML document and a type-valid XML document?

13.8 Why is it too limiting to say that XML is the next version of HTML?

13.9 What is the relationship between XML, XSL, and XSLT?

13.10 Explain the use of the pattern {item, action} in the processing of an XSL document.

13.11 What is the purpose of XML Schema?

13.12 How does XML Schema differ from DTD?

13.13 What is a schema-valid document?

13.14 Explain the chicken-and-egg problem concerning the validation of XML Schema documents.

13.15 Explain the difference between simple and complex elements.

13.16 Explain the difference between elements and attributes.

13.17 What is a good rule of thumb for using elements and attributes to represent database data?

13.18 Give an example, other than one in this text, of a flat XML Schema.

13.19 Give an example, other than one in this text, of a structured XML Schema.

13.20 What is the purpose of global elements?

13.21 What requirement is necessary for processing XML documents with Oracle?

13.22 Explain the difference between FOR XML RAW and FOR XML AUTO, ELEMENTS.

13.23 When would you use FOR XML EXPLICIT?

13.24 What is the importance of the order of tables in a SQL statement that uses FOR XML?

13.25 Explain why the schema in Figure 13-13(b) is incorrect. How did this come about?

13.26 Why would an outer join fix the problem in Figure 13.13(b)? Under what circumstances would it not fix that problem?

13.27 Explain, in your own words, why SQL with FOR XML cannot be used to construct an XML document having two multi-value paths.

13.28 Why is the limitation in question 13.27 important?

13.29 Explain, in your own words, why XML is important to database processing.

13.30 Why is XML Schema important for interorganizational document sharing?

13.31 What is ADO.NET?

13.32 What is a data provider?

13.33 What data providers are mentioned in the text?

13.34 What is a data reader?

13.35 How can ADO.NET be used to process a database without using data readers or datasets?

13.36 What is a dataset?

13.37 How do datasets differ conceptually from databases?

13.38 List the primary structures of a dataset, as described in this chapter.

13.39 How do datasets solve the problem of views with multi-value paths?

13.40 What is the chief disadvantage of datasets? When is this likely to be a problem?

13.41 Why, in database processing, is it important to become an object-oriented programmer?

13.42 What is an ADO.NET connection?

13.43 By default, what user account needs to exist in Oracle in order to use integrated security in an ASP.NET application?

13.44 What is a data adapter?

13.45 What is the purpose of the SelectCommand property of a data adapter?

13.46 Explain the difference between a data adapter's Fill and FillSchema methods.

13.47 How is a datatable relationship constructed in ADO.NET?

13.48 How is referential integrity defined in ADO.NET? What referential integrity actions are possible?

13.49 Explain how the TotalPurchases column of the CustomerAlias datatable gets its value.

13.50 Show the commands necessary to create an XML document from a dataset.

13.51 Show the commands necessary to create an XML Schema document from a dataset.

13.52 Explain the difference among original, current, and proposed values.

13.53 How does a dataset allow for trigger processing?

13.54 What is the purpose of the UpdateCommand property of a data adapter?

13.55 Describe the means by which parameters are created for the update command in Figure 13-26(d).

13.56 What are the purposes of the InsertCommand and DeleteCommand of a data adapter?

13.57 Explain the flexibility inherent in the use of the InsertCommand, UpdateCommand, and DeleteCommand properties.

13.58 What is XPath?

13.59 How does DOM differ from SAX?

13.60 What is XQuery? What is it used for?

13.61 What are XML Namespaces? What is their purpose?

GROUP II QUESTIONS

13.62 Create a DTD and XML document like that shown in Figure 13-1 to represent the first row in the ARTIST table (see Figure 7-5).

13.63 Using Figure 13-4 as an example, create an XSL document to materialize the document in your answer to question 13.62. Materialize your document using a browser.

13.64 Create an XML Schema document for a row of TRANSACTION. Place TransactionID as an attribute. Group acquisition data into a complexType, and group sales data into a second complexType. Use Figure 13-7 as an example.

13.65 Create an XML Schema for artists and the customers who are interested in them. Use Figure 13-12 as an example.

13.66 Create an XML Schema for artist, work, transaction, and customer data. Use Figure 13-13 as an example.

13.67 Create an XML Schema for all artist data. Use Figure 13-14 as an example.

FIREDUP PROJECT EXAMPLE

If you have not already done so, create the FiredUp database using either Oracle or SQL Server. Follow the instructions at the end of Chapter 10 or 11, respectively.

A. Using Figure 13-1 as an example, create an XML document with a DTD for a row of the CUSTOMER table.

B. Using Figure 13-4 as an example, create an XSL document to materialize the document you created in A. Show your document in a browser.

C. Create an XML Schema document for a join of CUSTOMER and STOVE_REPAIR data. Assume that the document has one customer and from zero to many repairs for that customer. Use Figure 13-12 as an example.

D. Code a SQL statement with FOR XML that will produce the document you created in C.

E. Create an XML Schema document that has all of the data for a given customer. How many multi-value paths does this schema have?

F. Explain how the Schema document you created in question E can be used to advantage by FiredUp.

G. Explain how a dataset can be used to create documents like that defined in your answer to question E.

If you have not already done so, create the Twigs database using either Oracle or SQL Server. Follow the instructions at the end of Chapter 10 or 11, respectively.

A. Using Figure 13-1 as an example, create an XML document with a DTD for a row of the OWNER table.

B. Using Figure 13-4 as an example, create an XSL document to materialize the document you created in question A. Show your document in a browser.

C. Create an XML Schema document for a join of OWNER and CHIP_DELIVERY data. Assume that the document has one customer and from zero to many repairs for that customer. Use Figure 13-12 as an example.

D. Code a SQL statement with FOR XML that will produce the document you created in question C.

E. Create an XML Schema document that has all of the data for a given owner. How many multi-value paths does this schema have?

F. Explain how the Schema document you created in E can be used to advantage by Twigs.

G. Explain how a dataset can be used to create documents like that defined in your answer to question E.

CHAPTER 14

JDBC, Java Server Pages, and MySQL

This chapter discusses alternatives to Microsoft's OLE DB, ADO, and .NET technology and products. In particular, we will discuss JDBC, Java Server Pages (JSP) using Apache/Tomcat, and the DBMS product MySQL. The open source movement has played a large role in the development of these technologies, and all of these are open source products. In fact, only open source software was used to develop all of the examples in this chapter.

Open source is not a requirement for use of JDBC, however. You can employ JDBC on Windows XP, 2000, and other operating systems to access SQL Server, Oracle, or other prominent DBMS products. You can run JSPs and Apache/Tomcat on Windows XP or 2000 as well. In this chapter, however, all of the examples were developed and run on Linux.

As you might guess, the one requirement for using JDBC is that programs be written in Java. Because this text does not assume that you are a Java programmer, we will explain examples at a high level. It will not be important to understand every line of code. Your goal should be to understand the nature and capability of the technologies presented here.

If you already program in Java, these examples should stimulate your thinking for more complex and realistic examples. In any case, after reading this chapter, you will be able to compare the capabilities of ODBC, ADO, and ASP to JDBC and JSP.

▶ JDBC

To begin, contrary to many sources, JDBC does *not* stand for Java Database Connectivity. According to Sun—the inventor of Java and the source of many Java-oriented products—JDBC is not an acronym; it just stands for JDBC. One can only imagine what legal or ego wrangles lie behind that assertion, but JDBC it is.

There are JDBC drivers for almost every conceivable DBMS product. Sun maintains a directory of them at **http://java.sun.com/products/jdbc**. Some of the drivers are free, and almost all of them have an evaluation edition that can be used free for a limited period of time. The JDBC drivers used for the preparation of this chapter are the MySQL open source drivers developed by Mark Mathews. They can be downloaded from **http://mmmysql.sourceforge.net**.

So that you do not develop unfortunate habits, we will correct one other possible mistake before we continue. The DBMS product MySQL is pronounced "my ess-queue-lll" and not "my see-quel." This is hardly important, but if you want to be cool, always say "my ess-queue-lll."

Driver Types

Sun defines four driver types. Type 1 drivers are JDBC-ODBC bridge drivers, which provide an interface between Java and regular ODBC drivers. Most ODBC drivers are written in C or C++. For reasons unimportant to us here, there are incompatibilities between Java and C/C++. Bridge drivers resolve these incompatibilities and allow access to ODBC data sources from Java. Because we described the use of ODBC in Chapter 12, we will not consider bridge drivers any further here.

Drivers of Types 2 to 4 are written entirely in Java; they differ only in how they connect to the DBMS. Type 2 drivers connect to the native API of the DBMS; they call Oracle, for example, using the standard (non-ODBC) programming interface to Oracle. Drivers of Types 3 and 4 are intended for use over communications networks. A Type 3 driver translates JDBC calls into a DBMS-independent network protocol. This protocol is then translated into the network protocol used by a particular DBMS. Finally, Type 4 drivers translate JDBC calls into DBMS-specific network protocols.

To understand the differences between the driver Types 2 to 4, you must first understand the difference between a **servlet** and an **applet.** As you probably know, Java was designed to be portable. To accomplish portability, Java programs are not compiled into a particular machine language, but instead are compiled into machine-independent bytecode. Sun, Microsoft, and others have written **bytecode interpreters** for each machine environment (Intel 386, Alpha, and so on). These interpreters are referred to as **Java virtual machines.**

To run a compiled Java program, the machine-independent bytecode is interpreted by the virtual machine at run-time. The cost of this, of course, is that bytecode interpretation constitutes an extra step, so such programs can never be as fast as programs that are compiled directly into machine code. This may or may not be a problem, depending on the application's workload.

An applet is a Java bytecode program that runs on the application user's computer. Applet bytecode is sent to the user via HTTP and is invoked using the HTTP protocol on the user's computer. The bytecode is interpreted by a virtual machine, usually part of the browser. Because of portability, the same bytecode can be sent to a Windows, UNIX, or Apple computer.

A servlet is a Java program that is invoked via HTTP on the Web server computer. It responds to requests from browser users. Servlets are interpreted and executed by a Java virtual machine running on the server.

Because they have a connection to a communications protocol, Type 3 and 4 drivers can be used in either applet or servlet code. Type 2 drivers can be used only in situations where the Java program and the DBMS reside on the same machine, or where the Type 2 driver connects to a DBMS program that handles the communications between the computer running the Java program and the computer running the DBMS.

Thus, if you write code that connects to a database from an applet (two-tier), only a Type 3 or Type 4 driver can be used. In these situations, if your DBMS product has a Type 4 driver, use it because it will be faster than a Type 3 driver.

In three-tier or *n*-tier architecture, if the Web server and the DBMS are running on the same machine, you can use a driver of any of the four types. If the Web server and the DBMS are running on different machines, Type 3 and Type 4 drivers can be used without a problem. Type 2 drivers can also be used if the DBMS vendor handles the communications between the Web server and the DBMS. Characteristics of JDBC driver types are summarized in Figure 14-1.

Using JDBC

Unlike ODBC, with JDBC there is no separate utility program for creating a JDBC data source. Instead, all of the work to define a connection is done in Java code via the JDBC driver. The coding pattern for using a JDBC driver is the following:

1. Load the driver.
2. Establish a connection to the database.
3. Create a statement.
4. Do something with the statement.

As you will see, the name of the DBMS product to be used and the name of the database are provided at step 2.

Loading the Driver   To load the driver, you must first obtain the driver library and install it in a directory. You need to ensure that the directory is named in the CLASSPATH for both the Java compiler and for the Java virtual machine. There are several ways to load the driver into program; the most reliable is

Class.forName(string).newInstance();

FIGURE 14–1

Summary of JDBC Driver Types

Driver Type	Characteristics
1	JDBC-ODBC bridge. Provides a Java API that interfaces to an ODBC driver. Enables processing of ODBC data sources from Java.
2	A Java API that connects to the native-library of a DBMS product. The Java program and the DBMS must reside on the same machine, or the DBMS must handle the intermachine communication, if not.
3	A JAVA API that connects to a DBMS-independent network protocol. Can be used for servlets and applets.
4	A JAVA API that connects to a DBMS-dependent network protocol. Can be used for servlets and applets.

The value of the string parameter depends on the driver you use. For the MM MySQL drivers, use

Class.forName("org.gjt.mm.mysql.Driver").newInstance();

This method will throw an exception, so you should write this code in a try:catch block. (If you're not a Java programmer, don't despair; just understand that these statements are making the JDBC classes available to the program.)

Establishing a Connection to the Database   After you have loaded the driver, the next step is to create an object that has a connection to your database. The format is

Connection conn = DriverManager.getConnection(string);

The DriverManager class is part of the JDBC library you loaded in step 1. It plays the same role as the ODBC driver manager. JDBC drivers register themselves with this class. On a given machine, there may be several drivers registered. When you call DriverManager.getConnection, it looks through its list of JDBC drivers for a suitable driver and uses it. It will pick the first suitable driver it finds, so if more than one driver can process your connection, you may not get the driver you expect.

The string parameter passed to getConnection has three parts, separated by colons. The first part is always "jdbc," the second is a keyword that identifies the DBMS you are using, and the third is a URL to the database you want to process, along with optional parameters such as user and password.

The following statement connects to a MySQL database named vr1 with user *dk1* and password *sesame*:

Connection conn = DriverManager.getConnection

("jdbc:mysql://localhost/vr1?user=dk1&password=sesame")

The content of the second and third part of this string depends on your JDBC driver. In fact, with some drivers, you specify the user name and password as separate parameters. Consult your driver's documentation to find out what to code.

By the way, most of this technology arose in the UNIX world. UNIX is case-sensitive, and almost everything you enter here is also case-sensitive. Thus, *jdbc* and *JDBC* are *not* the same. Enter everything in the case that is shown here. There are a few case-insensitive exceptions, but they're not worth mentioning or remembering. Just type the case as shown.

The getConnection method also throws an exception, so it too should appear in a try:catch block.

Creating a Statement   The next step is to create a new Statement object. This is similar to what we did in Chapter 12, when we created a command object with ADO. The syntax is

Statement stmt = conn.createStatement();

There are no parameters to pass to this method.

At this point, you can process the statement in various ways, as discussed next.

Processing the Statement   The Statement methods are standardized in the JDBC specification. Your driver will process any of the statements shown here (and many more as well). See your driver's API documentation for details. In our examples, we will use the executeQuery and executeUpdate methods, as follows:

ResultSet rs = stmt.executeQuery(querystring);

and

int result = stmt.executeUpdate(updatestring);

The first statement returns a result set that can be used in the same way we have used cursors in earlier chapters. The second statement returns an integer that indicates the number of rows updated. Specific examples are

ResultSet rs = stmt.executeQuery("SELECT * FROM CUSTOMER");

and

int result = stmt.executeUpdate("UPDATE ARTIST SET Nationality='English' WHERE Name='Foster'");

Note the use of single quotes to avoid problems with quoting inside quotation marks.

After the executeQuery method has run, the resultset object can be iterated to obtain all rows. The number of columns and the column names in the result set can be obtained from the getMetaData method. Its syntax is

ResultSetMetaData rsMeta = rs.getMetaData();

At this point, the getColumnCount and getColumnName methods can be invoked on rsMeta, as you will see in the examples that follow.

Prepared Statements and Callable Statements   Prepared Statement objects and Callable Statement objects can be used to invoke compiled queries and stored procedures in the database. Their use is similar to the use of the Command object discussed in Chapter 12. Because neither compiled queries nor stored procedures are supported by MySQL, we will not use them in the examples in this chapter.

To illustrate a callable statement, however, suppose that we are processing the View Ridge database created with Oracle in Chapter 10 and that we want to invoke the CustomerInsert stored procedure. Assume in the following that *conn* has been set to a connection to the Oracle View Ridge database:

CallableStatement cs = conn.prepareCall ("{call CustomerInsert(?, ?, ?, ?)}");

cs.setString (1, "Mary Johnson");

cs.setString (2, "212");

cs.setString (3, "555–1234");

cs.setString (4, "US");

cs.execute();

This sequence, which would invoke the CustomerInsert stored procedure with the data shown, is very similar to that shown for ODBC in Chapter 12. It is possible to receive values back from procedures as well, but that is beyond the scope of our discussion. See **http://java.sun.com/products/jdk/1.1/docs/guide/jdbc** for more information.

Figure 14-2 summarizes JDBC components. The application creates Connection, Statement, ResultSet, and ResultSetMetaData objects. Calls from these objects are routed via the DriverManager to the proper driver. Drivers then process their databases. Notice that the Oracle database in this figure could be processed via either a JDBC-ODBC bridge or via a pure JDBC driver.

FIGURE 14–2

JDBC Components

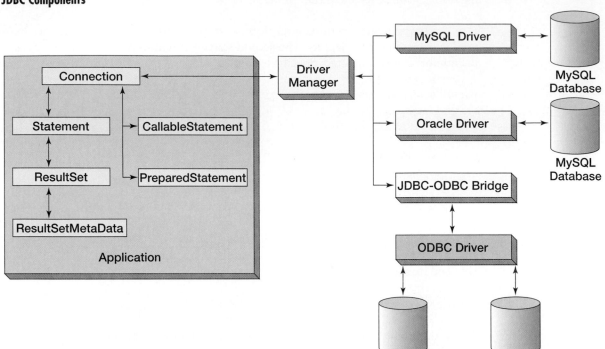

JDBC Examples

Figures 14-3 and 14-4 present two examples using the mm.mysql JDBC drivers and MySQL. Note that both of these programs import java.sql.*. Also, note that the JDBC drivers are not imported; they are loaded instead. If you try to import them, the result is a mess.

The database used in all of these examples is the View Ridge database shown in Figure 7-3(d). Tables in the database are

CUSTOMER(CustomerID, Name, AreaCode, PhoneNumber, Street, City, State, Zip)

ARTIST (ArtistID, Name, Nationality, Birthdate, DeceasedDate)

CUSTOMER_ARTIST_INT (*CustomerID, ArtistID*)

WORK (WorkID, Description, Title, Copy *ArtistID*)

TRANSACTION (TransactionID, DateAcquired, PurchasePrice, SalesPrice, *CustomerID, WorkID*)

Relationships and referential integrity are as described in Chapter 7.

The GeneralTable Class   Figure 14-3 shows the Java class GeneralTable. It accepts a single parameter that is the name of a table in the MySQL database vr1. MySQL is case-sensitive, and all table names in the database were created in uppercase letters. Thus, the code must convert the input table name to uppercase.

This example is a straightforward application of the concepts we just described. The GeneralTable class has a publicly accessible method that returns no parameters. (That's the meaning of "public static void main.") The program checks for at least one parameter, sets the variable varTableName to the input table name, and converts that name to uppercase. It then processes the database using the JDBC drivers in a try block. A try block is used because many of the methods throw exceptions; these exceptions will be caught in the catch block.

All exception handling is kept generic in these examples. If you program in Java, you will see many ways to improve exception handling from that shown here. We're after database concepts now, however.

If you do not program in Java, just assume that all statements that appear in the try block, denoted by "try { . . . . . }," are what happen under normal circumstances. All statements that appear in the catch block, denoted "catch { . . . }," are what happen when an error occurs. Also, like SQL, in Java a multiline comment is started with "/*" and terminated with "*/." A single line comment is started with "//."

The mm.mysql drivers are loaded as described previously and then a Connection object conn and a Statement object stmt are created. The database is vr1 and the user is

---

FIGURE 14–3

GeneralTable Class

```java
import java.io.*;
import java.sql.*;

public class GeneralTable {

    /** A Java program to present the contents of any table
     *  Call with one parameter which is table name --
     *  table name parameter will be converted to uppercase
     */

    public static void main(String[] args) {
        if (args.length <1) {
            System.out.println ("Insufficient data provided.");
            return;
        }

        String varTableName = args[0];
        varTableName = varTableName.toUpperCase();
        System.out.println ("Showing Table " + varTableName);
        try {

            // Load the MySQL JDBC classes from Mark Mathews
            //      mm.mysql.jdbc-1.2c

            Class.forName("org.gjt.mm.mysql.Driver").newInstance();

            // Set connect string to local MySQL database, user is dk1
            String connString = "jdbc:mysql://localhost/vr1?user=dk1";

            System.out.println (" Trying connection with " + connString);
            Connection conn = DriverManager.getConnection(connString);

            // Get result set
            Statement stmt = conn.createStatement();
            String varSQL = "SELECT * FROM " + varTableName;
            ResultSet rs = stmt.executeQuery(varSQL);

            // Get meta data on just opened result set
            ResultSetMetaData rsMeta = rs.getMetaData();
```

FIGURE 14-3

```
      // Display column names as string
      String varColNames ="";
      int varColCount = rsMeta.getColumnCount();
      for (int col =1; col <= varColCount; col++) {
           varColNames = varColNames + rsMeta.getColumnName(col) +" ";
      }
      System.out.println(varColNames);

      // Display column values
      while (rs.next()) {
           for (int col = 1; col <= varColCount; col++) {
                System.out.print(rs.getString(col) + "    ");
           }
           System.out.println();
      }

      // Clean up
      rs.close();
      stmt.close();
      conn.close();

}

catch (Exception e) {
     e.printStackTrace();
}
```

dk1. There is no password. (For this to work, user dk1 must have been defined in MySQL and granted permission to use database vr1 without a password. We will discuss these actions in the last section.)

A ResultSetMetaData named rsMeta is then created for the result set rs. After this has been done, the column names are obtained and printed in one long string (varColumnNames). Then rs is iterated, and each column in each row is displayed. The output is not pretty, but it works and gets us started.

A typical display is

Showing Table ARTIST

Trying connection with jdbc:mysql://localhost/vr1?user=dk1

Name Nationality Birthdate DeceasedDate ArtistID

Miro Spanish null null 1

Tobey US null null 2

Van Vronken US null null 3

Matisse French null null 4

Like I said, it's not pretty!

The CustomerInsert Class Figure 14-4 shows a second Java program that updates the vr1 database. This program implements the logic for the View Ridge CustomerInsert procedure, as described in Chapters 7, 10, 11, and 12. (Are you tired of it yet? At least the logic is familiar!)

As you recall, this procedure accepts four parameters: a new customer's Name, AreaCode, LocalNumber, and the Nationality of all artists in whom the customer maintains an interest. These parameters are received by the main procedure and passed to the method InsertData. The InsertData method is not necessary here; we could have a single method class, as shown in Figure 14-3. The logic is isolated in a separate method here because we will transform this method into a Java bean in the next section. That transformation will be easier if we isolate the code here.

The InsertData method first loads the drivers and then sets up a connection string to vr1 for user dk1. Next, it checks for duplicate data by querying vr1 for the input Name, AreaCode, and LocalNumber. If one is found, a message is printed; and the resultset, statement, and connection are closed. Otherwise, a new row is inserted in CUSTOMER.

FIGURE 14-4

CustomerInsert Class

```
import java.io.*;
import java.sql.*;

public class CustomerInsert {

    /** A Java implementation of the View Ridge Galleries CustomerInsert procedure.
     *  Receives values Customer Name, AreaCode, LocalNumber and Nationality
     *  Inserts the new customer if not already in the database and then
     *  connects that customer to Artists of the given nationality by
     *  adding appropriate rows to the intersection table.
     */

    public static void main(String[] args) {

        if (args.length < 4) {
            System.out.println ("Insufficient data provided");
            return;
        }

        String varName = args[0];
        String varAreaCode = args[1];
        String varLocalNumber = args[2];
        String varNationality = args[3];

        insertData(varName, varAreaCode, varLocalNumber, varNationality);

    }

    public static void insertData(String varName,
                        String varAreaCode,
                        String varLocalNumber,
                        String varNationality) {

        System.out.println ("Adding row for " + varName);
        try {

            // Load JDBC driver class from Mark Mathews
            // mm.mysql.jdbc-1.2c

            Class.forName("org.gjt.mm.mysql.Driver").newInstance();
```

FIGURE 14-4

(continued)

```
// Set up connection to db vr1 with user dk1, no password
String connString = "jdbc:mysql://localhost/" + "vr1" + "?user=dk1";
System.out.println (" Trying connection with " + connString);
Connection conn = DriverManager.getConnection(connString);


// If we get here, we have a connection.  Now check for duplicated data
Statement stmt = conn.createStatement();
String varSQL = "SELECT Name ";
String varWhere = "FROM CUSTOMER WHERE Name= '";
varWhere = varWhere + varName + "' AND AreaCode = '";
varWhere = varWhere + varAreaCode + "' AND PhoneNumber = '";
varWhere = varWhere + varLocalNumber + "'";
varSQL = varSQL + varWhere;

ResultSet rs = stmt.executeQuery(varSQL);
while (rs.next()) {
    // if get here, there is duplicate data
    System.out.println
    ("Data duplicates an existing customer.  No changes made.");
    rs.close();
    stmt.close();
    conn.close();
    return;
}

// OK to insert new data
varSQL = "INSERT INTO CUSTOMER (Name, AreaCode, PhoneNumber)";
varSQL = varSQL + " VALUES ('" + varName + "', '";
varSQL = varSQL + varAreaCode + "', '";
varSQL = varSQL + varLocalNumber + "')";

int result = stmt.executeUpdate(varSQL);
if (result == 0) {
    System.out.println ("Problem with insert");
    rs.close();
    stmt.close();
    conn.close();
    return;
}
```

CustomerID, which is the surrogate key column for CUSTOMER, has been defined as an AUTO_INCREMENT column in the database. Thus, no value need be provided for it. MySQL will set it.

If the insert is successful, the variable *result* should not equal zero; if it does, an error occurred during the update. In that case, a message is printed and the objects are cleaned up. Assuming that no error occurred, the value of CustomerID is read back from the database and then rows are inserted in the intersection table CUSTOMER_ARTIST_INT. This is very similar to the logic shown for the CustomerInsert stored procedures in Oracle and SQL Server.

In this code section, the variable *result* is not checked for zero; a better version of this program would do so. In fact, if you are a Java programmer, you know that all of these error messages and cleanup activities should be done using exceptions. We're stepping around those issues to focus on the database-only matters.

Given this quick introduction to JDBC, we will now discuss its use in Java Server Pages.

▶ JAVA SERVER PAGES

Java Server Pages (JSP) provide a means to create dynamic Web pages using HTML (and XML) and the Java programming language. Java Server Pages look very much like Active Server Pages, but this is deceptive because the underlying technology is quite different. JSP and ASP look similar because they both blend HTML with program code. The difference is that ASP are restricted to using scripting languages like VBScript or JScript. With JSP, however, the coding is done in Java, and only in Java—neither VBScript nor JScript is allowed. With Java, the capabilities of a complete object-oriented language are directly available to the Web page developer.

Because Java is machine-independent, JSPs are also machine-independent. With JSP, you are not locked into using Windows XP or 2000 and IIS. You can run the same JSP on a Linux server, on a Windows server, and on others as well.

The official specification for JSP can be found at **http://java.sun.com/products/jsp**.

JSP Pages and Servlets

JSPs are transformed into standard Java language and then compiled just like a regular program. In particular, they are transformed into Java servlets, which means that JSPs are transformed into subclasses of the HttpServlet class behind the scenes. JSP code thus has access to the HTTP request and response objects, and also to their methods and to other HTTP functionality.

Because JSP pages are converted into servlet subclasses, you do not need to code complete Java classes or methods in a JSP. You can insert snippets of Java code wherever you like and they will be placed correctly into a servlet subclass when the page is parsed. Thus, you can plop the following statements into a JSP without any other Java code and they execute just fine:

```
<% String partyName ="fiesta";

partyName = partyName.toUpperCase();

out.println ("Come to our " + partyName); %>
```

In this case, the string "Come to our FIESTA" would be displayed in the browser when this section of the JSP is processed. By the way, note that Java code is isolated between <% and %>, just as VBScript and JScript are in ASPs.

In order to use JSPs, your Web server must implement the Java servlet 2.1+ and the Java Server Pages 1.0+ specifications. You can check **http://java.sun.com /products/servlet/industry.html** for a list of servers that support these specifications. There are at least a half a dozen or so possibilities. For the rest of this chapter, we will use Apache Tomcat for this purpose.

Apache Tomcat

The Apache Web server does not support servlets. However, the Apache Foundation and Sun cosponsored the Jakarta Project that developed a servlet processor named Apache Tomcat. You can obtain the source and binary code of Tomcat from the Jakarta Project Web site at **http://jakarta.apache.org**.

Tomcat is a servlet processor that can work in conjunction with Apache or as a standalone Web server. Tomcat has limited Web server facilities, however, so it is normally used in standalone mode only for testing servlets and JSPs. For commercial production applications, Tomcat should be used in conjunction with Apache.

If you are running Tomcat and Apache separately on the same Web server, they need to use different ports. The default port for a Web server is 80 and normally Apache uses it. When used in standalone mode, Tomcat is usually configured to listen to port 8080, though this, of course, can be changed.

In the examples that follow, Tomcat is using port 8080. These examples were run on a private intranet in which the Tomcat server machine was assigned the IP address 10.0.0.3. Thus, to invoke the page *somepage.jsp*, we will use the string http:// 10.0.0.3:8080/somepage.jsp in the browser address field.

Setting Up Tomcat for JSP Processing

When you install Tomcat, it creates a directory structure into which you must place class libraries and Web pages. As of the 3.1 Tomcat release, place class libraries in the *install-dir*/lib directory, and place JSPs in the *install-dir*/webapps/ROOT/WEB-INF/classes directory. On Linux, the RPM utility installs Tomcat in the directory /usr/local/jakarta-tomcat/ by default. Hence, in this case, place the class libraries into /usr/local/jakarta-tomcat/lib and the JSPs into /usr/local/jakarta-tomcat/webapps/ROOT/WEB-INF/classes. If you are installing with other operating systems or installing a different servlet processor altogether, you should consult your documentation.

When installing new class files in the lib subdirectory, there is a small "gotcha." Tomcat creates its CLASSPATH when it is started. Therefore, after you have installed a new class file into the lib directory, you must stop and restart Tomcat before it will see your new file. If you just copy the new file into the lib subdirectory without restarting Tomcat, you will receive class not found exceptions. (Trust me, I know.)

The JSPs to follow all use the mm.mysql MySQL drivers. In order to work, the appropriate driver class library must be placed into the lib subdirectory. For these examples, the file "mm_uncomp.jar" was installed in that directory.

Figure 14-5 shows the process by which JSP pages are compiled. When a request for a JSP page is received, a Tomcat (or other) servlet processor finds the compiled version of the page and checks to determine whether it is current. It does this by looking for an uncompiled version of the page having a creation date and time later than the compiled page's creation date and time. If the page is not current, the new page is parsed and transformed into a Java source file and that source file is then compiled. The servlet is then loaded and executed. If the compiled JSP page is current, then it is loaded into memory if not already there and then executed. If it is in memory, it is simply executed.

(By the way, the downside of such automatic compilation is that if you make syntax errors and forget to test your pages, the first user to access your page will receive the compiler errors!)

Unlike CGI files and some other Web server programs, there is a maximum of one copy of a JSP in memory at a time. Further, pages are executed by one of Tomcat's threads; not by an independent process. This means that much less memory and processor time are required to execute a JSP than to execute a comparable CGI script.

JSP Examples

This section discusses two simple JSPs. The first is a JSP version of the GeneralTable class shown in Figure 14-3. The second encapsulates the logic in Figure 14-4 in a Java bean and then invokes that bean from a JSP.

GeneralTable.JSP   Figure 14-6 shows a JSP that displays the contents of any table in the MySQL database named vr1. The format and logic of this page is very simi-

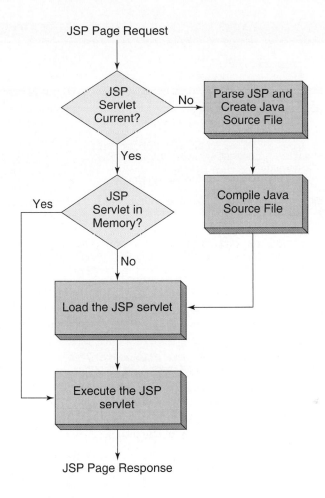

FIGURE 14-5

JSP Compilation Process

lar to that in GeneralTable.asp shown in Figure 15-21. Here, we assume that the user passes the name of the table to be displayed as a parameter to the page.

Figure 14-7 shows the results of invoking this page using Internet Explorer on a Windows 2000 computer. The page itself was processed by Tomcat on a Linux computer. Note the call to port 8080; in production, Tomcat would be running with Apache on default port 80 and this port specification would not be needed.

In Figure 14-6, all Java code is shown in red ink. The first line invokes a page directory, which imports the java.sql library. Then, the parameter having the table name is obtained using the HTTP request object method getParameter. The value is set to uppercase. Next, the JDBC classes are loaded, as was done in Figure 14-3, and a Connection is created to the vr1 database for user dk1. The rest of the code is the same as that shown in Figure 14-4—it is just spread among the HTML statements used for displaying results.

Again, this page appears deceptively similar to the ASP version of this page, GeneralTable.asp, shown in Chapter 13. The difference is not just that JDBC is used instead of ADO and ODBC. An even greater difference is that this page will be compiled into a Java program, and hence is portable and will be faster.

CustomerInsertUsingBean.JSP Because Java is used with JSPs, the full capabilities of an object-oriented program are available. This means that JSPs can invoke precompiled objects. Doing this is important and useful for a number of reasons. For one, it separates the tasks of writing program logic from generating HTML. Organizations can have different groups and people working on these two very different tasks. It also enables logic to be encapsulated into independent modules for reuse and the other benefits of encapsulation. Finally, it reduces the complexity of managing a Web site.

FIGURE 14-6

GeneralTable.jsp

```
<!DOCTYPE HTML PUBLIC "-//W3C//DTD HTML 4.0 Transitional//EN">
<!-- Example of Database Access from a JSP Page -->
<%@ page import="java.sql.*" %>
<HTML>
<HEAD>
<TITLE>Table Display Using JDBC and MySQL</TITLE>
<META NAME="author" CONTENT="David Kroenke">
<META NAME="keywords"
      CONTENT="JSP,JDBC,Database Access">
<META NAME="description"
      CONTENT="An example of displaying a table using JSP.">
<LINK REL=STYLESHEET HREF="JSP-Styles.css" TYPE="text/css">
</HEAD>
<BODY>
<H2>Database Access Example</H2>
<% String varTableName= request.getParameter("Table");
   varTableName = varTableName.toUpperCase(); %>
<H3>Showing Data from MySQL Database vr1</H3>
<%
try      {
      // Load the Mark Mathew MySQL JDBC Drivers
      Class.forName("org.gjt.mm.mysql.Driver").newInstance();

      // Connect to vr1 with user dk1
      String connString = "jdbc:mysql://localhost/" + "vr1" + "?user=dk1";
          Connection conn = DriverManager.getConnection(connString);

      // Get rs and rsMeta for the SELECT statement
      Statement stmt = conn.createStatement();
      String varSQL = "SELECT * FROM " + varTableName;
      ResultSet rs = stmt.executeQuery(varSQL);
      ResultSetMetaData rsMeta = rs.getMetaData();
%>
<TABLE BORDER=1 BGCOLOR=#ffffff CELLSPACING=5><FONT FACE="Arial" COLOR=#000000
><CAPTION><B><%=varTableName%></B></CAPTION></FONT>
<THEAD>
<TR><%
      String varColNames ="";
      int varColCount = rsMeta.getColumnCount();
      for (int col =1; col <= varColCount; col++) {
          %><TH BGCOLOR=#c0c0c0 BORDERCOLOR=#000000 ><FONT SIZE=2 FACE ="Arial" COLOR=#000000
          ><%=rsMeta.getColumnName(col)%></FONT> </TH>
<% }%>
</TR>
</THEAD>
<TBODY><%
      while (rs.next()) {
          %><TR VALIGN=TOP><%
              for (int col = 1; col <= varColCount; col++) {
          %><TD BORDERCOLOR=#C0C0C0 ><FONT SIZE=2 FACE="Arial" COLOR=#000000
              ><%=rs.getString(col)%><BR></FONT></TD>
<%      }
      }
      // Clean up
      rs.close();
      stmt.close();
      conn.close();
}
catch (ClassNotFoundException e) {
      out.println("Driver Exception   " + e);
}%>
</TR>
</TBODY>
<TFOOT</TFOOT>
</TABLE>
</BODY>
</HTML>
```

FIGURE 14–7

GeneralTable
ARTISTDisplay

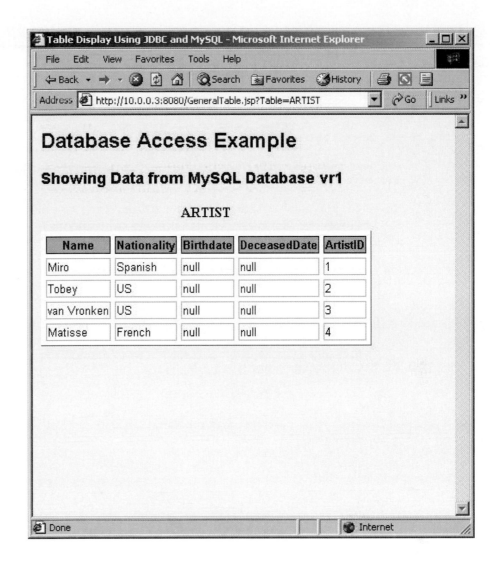

(If you are not a Java programmer, ignore the following paragraph. Think of a bean as a properly mannered Java class. One you could take home to meet Mother.)

In simple terms, a Java bean is a Java class that has three properties: First, there are no public instance variables. Second, all persistent values are accessed using methods named get*xxx* and set*xxx*. For example, a persistent value named myValue is obtained via a method named getmyValue() and is set by a method named setmyValue(). Finally, the bean class must either have no constructors or it must have one explicitly defined zero-argument constructor.

Figure 14-8 shows a Java bean named CustomerInsertUsingBean. This class has a method that implements the View Ridge Gallery CustomerInsert procedure (yes, it's BAAAACK!!! But this is the last time). This class has four persistent values: newName, newAreaCode, newLocalNumber, and newNationality. For each of these persistent values, get*xxx* and set*xxx* accessor methods are defined. There are no public persistent values and there is no constructor method. Hence, CustomerInsertUsingBean meets the requirements for a bean.

The actual update procedure is coded in a method named InsertData. This method is identical to the InsertData method shown in Figure 14-4.

FIGURE 14-8

CustomerInsertBean Class

```java
import java.io.*;
import java.sql.*;

public class CustomerInsertBean {

    /** A Java bean for the View Ridge Galleries CustomerInsert procedure.
     *  Persistent values obtained by accessors getxxx and setxxx
     *
     *  Inserts the new customer if not already in the database and then
     *  connects that customer to Artists of the given nationality by
     *  adding appropriate rows to the intersection table.
     */

    private String newName = "unknown";
    private String newAreaCode = "";
    private String newLocalNumber = "";
    private String newNationality = "";


    public String getnewName() {
        return(newName);
    }

    public void setnewName(String newName) {
        if (newName != null) {
            this.newName = newName;
        } else {

            this.newName = "unknown";
        }
    }

    public String getnewAreaCode() {
        return(newAreaCode);
    }

    public void setnewAreaCode(String newAreaCode) {
        if (newAreaCode != null) {
            this.newAreaCode = newAreaCode;
        } else {
            this.newName = "";
```

FIGURE 14-8

(continued)

```
public String getnewLocalNumber() {
      return(newLocalNumber);
}

public void setnewLocalNumber (String newLocalNumber) {
      if (newLocalNumber != null) {
            this.newLocalNumber = newLocalNumber;
      } else {
            this.newName = "";
      }
}

public String getnewNationality() {
      return(newNationality);
}

public void setnewNationality(String newNationality) {
      if (newNationality != null) {
            this.newNationality = newNationality;
      } else {
            this.newName = "";
      }
}


public String InsertData() {

      try {

            // Load JDBC driver class from Mark Mathews
            // mm.mysql.jdbc-1.2c

            Class.forName("org.gjt.mm.mysql.Driver").newInstance();

            // Set up connection to db vr1 with user dk1, no password
            String connString = "jdbc:mysql://localhost/" + "vr1" + "?user=dk1";
            Connection conn = DriverManager.getConnection(connString);

            // If we get here, we have a connection.  Now check for duplicated data
```

FIGURE 14-8

(continued)

```
Statement stmt = conn.createStatement();
String varSQL = "SELECT Name ";
String varWhere = "FROM CUSTOMER WHERE Name= '";
varWhere = varWhere + newName + "' AND AreaCode = '";
varWhere = varWhere + newAreaCode + "' AND PhoneNumber = '";
varWhere = varWhere + newLocalNumber + "'";
varSQL = varSQL + varWhere;
ResultSet rs = stmt.executeQuery(varSQL);
while (rs.next()) {
      // if get here, there is duplicate data
      rs.close();
      stmt.close();
      conn.close();
      return ("Duplicate data - no action taken");
}

// OK to insert new data
varSQL = "INSERT INTO CUSTOMER (Name, AreaCode, PhoneNumber)";
varSQL = varSQL + " VALUES ('" + newName + "', '";
varSQL = varSQL + newAreaCode + "', '";
varSQL = varSQL + newLocalNumber + "')";
int result = stmt.executeUpdate(varSQL);
if (result == 0) {
      // if get here, there is a problem with insert
      rs.close();
      stmt.close();
      conn.close();
      return ("Problem with insert");
}

// Update OK, add intersection rows - first get new ID
varSQL = "SELECT CustomerID " + varWhere;
rs = stmt.executeQuery(varSQL);
String varCid ="";
while (rs.next()) {
      varCid = rs.getString(1);
      if (varCid == "0" ) {
            // if get here, can't find new CustomerID
            rs.close();
            stmt.close();
            conn.close();
            return ("Can't find new customer after insert");
```

FIGURE 14-8

(continued)

```
        }
    }

    // Now add to intersection table
    varSQL = "SELECT ArtistID FROM ARTIST WHERE Nationality = '"
                                    + newNationality +"'";
    String varInsertStart = "INSERT INTO CUSTOMER_ARTIST_INT
                        (CustomerID, ArtistID) VALUES

            → (" + varCid +", ";
    String varInsertEnd = ")";
    rs = stmt.executeQuery(varSQL);
    while (rs.next()) {
        result = stmt.executeUpdate
            (varInsertStart + rs.getString(1) + varInsertEnd);
    }

    // Clean up
    rs.close();
    stmt.close();
    conn.close();
    return("Success");
    }

    catch (Exception e){
        return ("Exception: " + e );
    }
```

Figure 14-9(a) shows a data entry form to gather the new customer data. The HTML page for this form is shown in Figure 14-9(b). Note that the FORM ACTION value is CustomerInsertUsingBean.jsp. Also observe that the text boxes are named newName, NewAreaCode, NewLocalNumber, and newNationality. These names matter because when the Add Customer button is clicked, CustomerInsertUsingBean.jsp will be passed parameters with those names. JSP can match the input parameters with same-named object properties when told to do so, as you will see.

The JSP page CustomerInsertUsingBean.jsp is listed in Figure 14-10. The important statements in this page are the two jsp statements shown below:

<jsp:useBean id="insert" class="CustomerInsertBean" />

and

<jsp:setProperty name="insert" property="*" />

The first statement tells the JSP compiler to load the class CustomerInsertBean and to affiliate it with the name *insert*. For this to work with Tomcat 3.1, a compiled version of the bean, named CustomerInsertBean.class, must reside in the directory *install-dir*/webapps/ROOT/WEB-INF/classes. For the standard RPM install, this would be /usr/local/jakarta-tomcat/webapps/ROOT/WEB-INF/classes.

FIGURE 14-9

New Customer Data
Entry Form
(a) NewCustomer Form
and (b) HTML for
NewCustomer Form

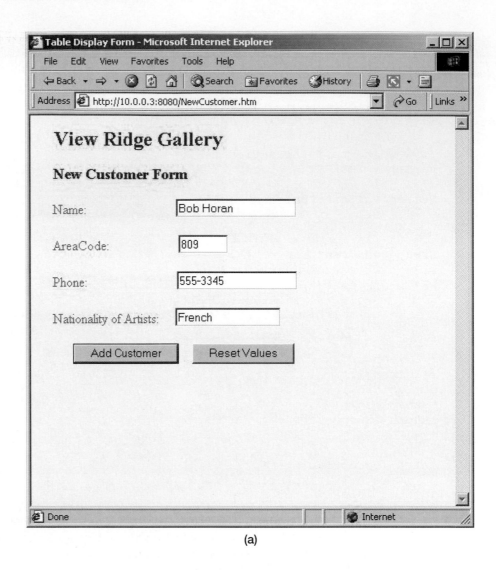

(a)

The second jsp: statement tells the JSP parser to set the class properties using form input parameters. The "*" signals that all properties should be matched with same-named parameters. This statement is a shorthand substitute for the following:

```
<jsp:setProperty name="insert"
        property="newName"
        value='<%= request.getParameter("newName") %>' />
<jsp:setProperty name="insert"
        property="newAreaCode"
        value='<%= request.getParameter("newAreaCode") %>' />
<jsp:setProperty name="insert"
        property="newLocalNumber"
        value='<%= request.getParameter("newLocalNumber") %>' />
<jsp:setProperty name="insert"
        property="newName"
        value='<%= request.getParameter("newNationality") %>' />
```

FIGURE 14-9

(continued)

```html
<HTML>
<HEAD>
<META HTTP-EQUIV="Content-Type" CONTENT="text/html">
<TITLE>Table Display Form</TITLE>
<LINK REL=STYLESHEET HREF="JSP-Styles.css" TYPE="text/css">
</HEAD>
<BODY>

<FORM METHOD="post" ACTION="CustomerInsertUsingBean.jsp">

 <P><STRONG><FONT color=purple face="" size=5>   View Ridge
Gallery</FONT></STRONG>

 <P>   <strong><font color="purple" face size="4"> New Customer
Form</font></strong><P><font style="background-color: #FDF5EC"
color="forestgreen" face>   
 Name:   </font><FONT style="BACKGROUND-COLOR:
#FDF5EC">           &nbs
p;         
 </FONT><INPUT id=newName name=newName></P>

 <P> <font style="background-color: #FDF5EC" color="forestgreen"
face>   AreaCode<font style="background-color:
#FDF5E6">:   </font>       &n
bsp;        
 </font><INPUT id=newAreaCode name=newAreaCode size="6"></P>

 <P><font style="background-color: #FDF5EC" color="forestgreen"
face>   

Phone:            &
nbsp;           &n
bsp;
 </font><INPUT id=newLocalNumber name=newLocalNumber
size="20">        </P>

 <P>    <font style="background-color: #FDF5EC"
color="forestgreen" face>Nationality
 of Artists:  </font>   <INPUT id=newNationality
name=newNationality size="17"></P>

 <P> <FONT style="BACKGROUND-COLOR: #FDF5EC">
   </FONT>     <FONT style="BACKGROUND-
COLOR: #FDF5EC">
<INPUT id=submit1 name=submit1 type=submit value="Add Customer"
>   
<INPUT id=reset1 name=reset1 type=reset value="Reset Values"></FONT></P>

</FORM>
</BODY>
</HTML>
```

(b)

FIGURE 14–10

Customer Insert Using Bean.jsp

```
<!DOCTYPE HTML PUBLIC "-//W3C//DTD HTML 4.0 Transitional//EN">
<!--
Example of Database Access from a JSP Page
-->
<%@ page import="java.sql.*" %>
<HTML>
<HEAD>
<TITLE>Updating Using a Java Bean</TITLE>
<META NAME="author" CONTENT="David Kroenke">
<META NAME="keywords"
     CONTENT="JSP,JDBC, Database Access">
<META NAME="description"
     CONTENT="An example of invoking a bean and displaying results.">
<LINK REL=STYLESHEET HREF="JSP-Styles.css" TYPE="text/css">
</HEAD>
<BODY>
<H2>Database Update Using JDBC from a Java Bean</H2>
<H3>Processing the View Ridge Customer Insert for MySQL Database vr1</H3>
<jsp:useBean id="insert" class="CustomerInsertBean" />
<jsp:setProperty name="insert" property="*" />
<%
// Bean properites were set in statement above, now call the
// bean for insert
String result=insert.InsertData();

if (result != "Success") {
    // print problem and return
    out.println("Problem" + result);
    return;
}
// Data was inserted successfully; now display the intersection table
try    {
    // Load the Mark Mathew MySQL JDBC drivers
    //

    Class.forName("org.gjt.mm.mysql.Driver").newInstance();
    String connString = "jdbc:mysql://localhost/" + "vr1" + "?user=dk1";

    Connection conn = DriverManager.getConnection(connString);

    // Join Customer to Artist via intersection table
    // Note synonyms for CUSTOMER.Name and ARTIST.Name
    Statement stmt = conn.createStatement();
    String varSQL = "SELECT CUSTOMER.Name Customer, ARTIST.Name  Artist, Nationality ";
    varSQL = varSQL + "FROM CUSTOMER, CUSTOMER_ARTIST_INT, ARTIST ";
    varSQL = varSQL + "WHERE CUSTOMER.CustomerID = CUSTOMER_ARTIST_INT.CustomerID AND ";
    varSQL = varSQL + "ARTIST.ArtistID = CUSTOMER_ARTIST_INT.ArtistID";
    ResultSet rs = stmt.executeQuery(varSQL);
    ResultSetMetaData rsMeta = rs.getMetaData();
%>
<TABLE BORDER=1 BGCOLOR=#ffffff CELLSPACING=5><FONT FACE="Arial" COLOR=#000000>
<CAPTION><B>Customers and Interests</B></CAPTION></FONT>
<THEAD>
<TR><%
    String varColNames ="";
    int varColCount = rsMeta.getColumnCount();
    for (int col =1; col <= varColCount; col++) {
        %><TH BGCOLOR=#c0c0c0 BORDERCOLOR=#000000 ><FONT SIZE=2 FACE ="Arial" COLOR=#000000
        ><%=rsMeta.getColumnName(col)%></FONT> </TH>
<% }%>
</TR>
</THEAD>
<TBODY><%
    while (rs.next()) {
        %><TR VALIGN=TOP><%
        for (int col = 1; col <= varColCount; col++) { %>
                <TD BORDERCOLOR=#C0C0C0 ><FONT SIZE=2 FACE="Arial" COLOR=#000000
                ><%=rs.getString(col)%><BR></FONT></TD><%
```

FIGURE 14-10

(continued)

```
=rs.getString(col)%><BR></FONT></TD><%
        }
    }
    // Clean up
    rs.close();
    stmt.close();
    conn.close();
}
catch (ClassNotFoundException e) {
    out.println("Driver Exception  " + e);
}%>
</TR>
</TBODY>
<TFOOT></TFOOT>
</TABLE>
</BODY>
</HTML>
```

Of course, either version can be used. In fact, the longer version is required if the names of the form parameters are different from the names of the object properties.

In Figure 14-10, the InsertData method is invoked by the following statement:

String result=insert.InsertData();

If the result is not "Success," the result message is printed. Otherwise, the join of the CUSTOMER, CUSTOMER_ARTIST_INT, ARTIST tables is displayed using code very similar to that shown in Figure 14-3. The result appears as shown in Figure 14-11.

This is a very short introduction to JSP development. There is much more to use and understand, but a longer discussion is beyond the scope of this text. An excellent reference on this topic is *Core Servlets and Java Server Pages* by Marty Hall.[1]

▶ MYSQL

MySQL is an open source DBMS product that runs on UNIX, Linux, and Windows. You can download MySQL source and binary code from the MySQL Web site: **http://www.mysql.com**. The examples in this text were run on MySQL on Linux, but the examples here work on MySQL on other operating systems as well. Currently, there is no license fee unless you build MySQL into a commercial application. See the license agreement on the MySQL site for more information.

MySQL is missing many of the capabilities of commercial DBMS products such as Oracle and SQL Server; and if you have access to one of those products, you probably should use it. If, however, you're working with a low budget or if you want to participate in the open source movement, MySQL can be a good choice. In the Linux/UNIX environment, MySQL is not only cheaper than Oracle and other commercial products; it is easier to install. A good reference for MySQL is *MySQL* by Paul DuBois.[2]

Ironically, because of its limited transaction management and logging capabilities, MySQL is very fast for pure query applications. There are Web-oriented data publishing companies that maintain their databases using Oracle, but download them to MySQL for query publishing on their Web servers.

---

[1]Marty Hall, *Core Servlets and Java Server Pages*. Upper Saddle River, NJ: Prentice Hall, 2000.
[2]Paul DuBois, *MySQL*. Indianapolis, IN: New Riders, 2000.

FIGURE 14–11

Result from CustomerInsertUsingBean.jsp

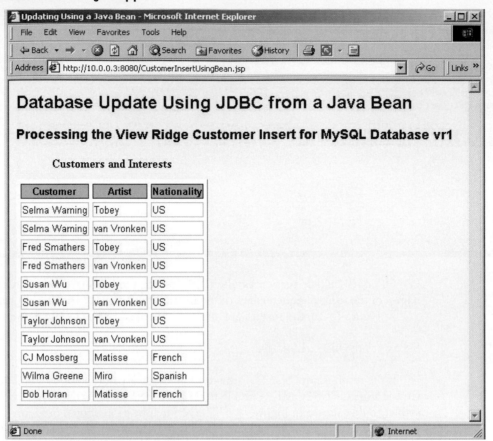

MySQL Limitations

As of release 3.x, MySQL does not support views, stored procedures, or triggers. All of these are on the MySQL to-do list, however, so check the latest documentation to determine whether some of these features have been added to the product in more recent releases.

In addition, although MySQL correctly parses foreign key (referential integrity) constraints, it does nothing with them. This means, for example, that it parses an ON DELETE CASCADE expression in a foreign key constraint, but it does not perform the cascading deletions that you might expect. In the View Ridge Gallery application, for example, MySQL parses the following constraint without a problem:

ALTER TABLE CUSTOMER_ARTIST_INT ADD CONSTRAINT CustomerIntFK

FOREIGN KEY(CustomerID) REFERENCES CUSTOMER ON DELETE

CASCADE;

When you delete a row in CUSTOMER, however, the cascading deletions are not made. You will need to make them yourself.

Using MySQL

To start MySQL from the command prompt, type

MySQL -u *username* -p

Fill in a valid user name; you will be prompted for a password. If you're using an account that does not have a password, you can enter

MySQL -u username

To see what databases have been created, type

Show databases;

Note that MySQL statements are terminated with a semicolon. Also, MySQL commands are case-insensitive, but names of developer-defined constructs such as table names and column names are case-sensitive.

Using an Existing Database   To use one of the existing databases, enter

Use *databasename*;

For example, enter

Use vr1;

To determine the tables in this database, enter

Show tables;

You can display the table metadata with the describe command:

Describe CUSTOMER;

At this point, any standard SQL statement can be used. SELECT, UPDATE, INSERT, and DELETE work as you would expect.

Creating a New Database   To create a new database, sign on to MySQL with the account that you want to own the new database. Then enter

Create Database *newdatabasename*;

For example, enter

Create Database vr2;

The database is created at that point and you can enter SQL create statements, as we have done before. Figure 14-12 shows the statements that you can use to create the View Ridge database. All surrogate keys are given the property AUTO_INCREMENT. This data type is a sequence maintained by MySQL that starts at 1 and increases by increments of 1. Note that MySQL supports a data type of Year. This data type, which is a four-digit integer, is used for the Birthdate and DeceasedDate columns in ARTIST. Also note that no foreign key constraints are defined. As stated earlier, MySQL parses them correctly, but does nothing with them.

The schema shown in Figure 14-12 creates a unique index on (Title, Copy, ArtistID) in WORK. This unique index prevents duplicate work rows from being inserted in the database. This means the logic in the Java programs shown earlier to prevent duplicate rows is unnecessary. It doesn't hurt anything, except perhaps performance just a bit. Still, as stated in Chapter 7, it is always better to enforce integrity rules in the database, if possible.

You can type all of these statements into MySQL. If you have them in a file, however, you can import them into MySQL. Suppose that the statements in Figure 14-12 are

MySQL uses read and write locks at the table level. When executing a SELECT statement, MySQL obtains read locks on all of the tables in the SELECT statement. Such a lock blocks other sessions from writing to any of those tables, but it does not block other reads. When executing an INSERT, UPDATE, or DELETE statement, MySQL obtains write looks on all of the tables involved. Such a lock blocks other sessions from either reading or writing. The result of this locking strategy is that consistent data is read or updated on a SQL statement-by-statement basis. All of the data read or written is desired.

A programmer can work around the lack of transactions by placing the LOCK TABLES/UNLOCK TABLES commands around transaction boundaries. Thus, the following keeps other users from reading or writing tables T1, T2, T3 while the transaction is processed:

LOCK TABLES T1, T2, T3 WRITE;

UPDATE TABLE T1 SET Col1="xzy" WHERE Col1="abc";

UPDATE TABLE T2 . . .

UPDATE TABLE T3 . . .

. . . do other transaction work on tables T1, T2, T3

UNLOCK TABLES;

All updates between the LOCK and UNLOCK statements are atomic because all of them are processed before any lock is released.

Unfortunately, when using locks in this manner, throughput will be zero for other users of the locked tables. While the transaction is underway, no one can read or write to T1, T2, T3. For the period of the lock, MySQL is a single user system of these tables. This is likely to be a serious problem if transactions are lengthy and if the application workload involves substantial updating.

A session must lock all tables at once. If it wants to lock more, it must release the lock it has and reacquire a new lock on that includes the additional tables. Thus, no session may have more than one LOCK TABLES statement open at one time. Recall from Chapter 9 that this strategy eliminates the possibility of deadlock.

Dirty reads may or may not be possible, depending on how the applications are written. MySQL does not roll back work, so dirty reads are not possible if no application performs its own rollback. If an application does perform its own rollback, and if it and the actions it is rolling back are placed between LOCK TABLES and UNLOCK TABLES statements, dirty reads are not possible. As mentioned, however, this strategy may result in unacceptable throughput. Finally, if an application performs rollback but does not use LOCK and UNLOCK statements, or does not appear in the same set of LOCK and UNLOCK statements as the statements that it is rolling back, dirty reads are possible.

Backup and Recovery

MySQL provides limited backup and recovery facilities. It provides a utility for saving the database and for saving individual tables within the database. In some cases, however, it is faster and just as easy to use the operating system copy commands to save the MySQL database files to back up mcdia.

MySQL maintains a log file of actions that it has processed. This log is one of commands and work, however, and not one of before and after images. To restore a database, an older version of the database is copied back, and the commands in the log are reapplied. Bulk changes are logged as commands; only the name of the file used as a source of data changes appears in the log. The individual changes do not appear.

By the way, if you're recovering a database because of a mistake such as an erroneous command like

DROP TABLE CUSTOMER;

be sure to remove this DROP statement from the log before you reprocess the log. Otherwise, the DROP TABLE will be processed by the log manager, and you will have recovered exactly to where you were when you started: without the CUSTOMER table.

MySQL Summary

As you can tell from this section, many features and functions of a modern DBMS product are missing from MySQL. You might be wondering why you should use it at all. As mentioned, it is free and it is also open source; if you want to participate in an open source project in the DBMS domain, this is a good one. Also, MySQL is easy and even fun to use. The features and functions that it does have work well. It would appear the community that is developing MySQL chooses to do only a few things, but to do them well. It is a pleasure to work with such a product.

SUMMARY

JDBC is an alternative to ODBC and ADO that provides database access to programs written in Java. There are JDBC drivers for almost every conceivable DBMS Product. Sun defines four driver types. Type 1 drivers provide a bridge between Java and ODBC. Types 2 through 4 drivers are written entirely in Java. Type 2 drivers rely on the DBMS product for inter-machine communication, if any. Type 3 drivers translate JDBC calls into a DBMS-independent network protocol. Type 4 drivers translate JDBC calls into DBMS-dependent network protocol.

An applet is a compiled Java bytecode program that is transmitted to a browser via HTTP and is invoked using the HTTP protocol. A servlet is a Java program that is invoked on the server to respond to HTTP requests. Type 3 and Type 4 drivers can be used for both applets and servlets. Type 2 drivers can be used only in servlets, and only then if the DBMS and Web server are on the same machine or if the DBMS vendor handles the inter-machine communication between the Web server and the database server.

There are four steps when using JDBC: (1) Load the driver. (2) Establish a connection to the database. (3) Create a statement. (4) Execute the statement. The driver class libraries need to be in the CLASSPATH for the Java compiler and for the Java virtual machine. They are loaded into a Java program with the forName method of Class. A connection is established using the getConnection method of DriverManager. A connection string includes the literal jdbc:, followed by the name of the driver and a URL to the database.

Statement objects are created using the createStatement method of a connection object. Statements can be processed with the executeQuery and executeUpdate methods of a Statement object. ResultSetMetaData objects are created using the getMetaData method of a ResultSet object. Both compiled queries and stored procedures can be processed via JDBC using PreparedStatement and CallableStatement objects.

Java Server Pages (JSP) provide a means to create dynamic Web pages using HTML (and XML) and Java. JSP pages provide the capabilities of a full object-oriented language to the page developer. Neither VBScript nor JavaScript can be used in a JSP. JSPs are compiled into machine-independent bytecode.

JSPs are compiled as subclasses of the HTTPServlet class. Consequently, small snippets of code can be placed in a JSP, as well as complete Java programs. To use JSPs, the Web server must implement the Java Servlet 2.1+ and Java Server Pages 1.0+ specifications. Apache Tomcat, an open source product from the Jakarta Project, implements these specifications. Tomcat can work in conjunction with Apache or can operate as a standalone Web server for testing purposes.

When using Tomcat (or any other JSP processor), the JDBC drivers and JSP pages must be located in specified directories. Any Java beans used by the JSP must also be stored in particular directories. When a JSP is requested, Tomcat ensures that the most recent page is used. If an uncompiled newer version is available, Tomcat will automatically cause it to be parsed and compiled. There is a maximum of one JSP in memory at a time, and JSP requests are executed as a thread of the servlet processor and not as a separate process. The Java code in a JSP can load invoke a compiled Java bean, if desired.

MySQL is an open source DBMS that runs on UNIX, Linux, and Windows. There is no license fee. MySQL can provide fast query processing, but it does not support views, stored procedures, or triggers. Referential integrity can be defined, but it is not enforced by MySQL. MySQL maintains a data dictionary in a database named *mysql*. The user and db tables can be queried to determine user permissions. To access MySQL from JDBC, the user account must be granted access to the database, either from any location or from a TCP/IP address that represents the local computer.

MySQL provides limited support for concurrent processing. There is no support for transactions, and thus there are no COMMIT or ROLL BACK statements or transaction isolation. MySQL locks at the table level. Shared read locks are obtained when processing SELECT statements, and exclusive locks are obtained when writing. Throughput can be a problem when locking at the table level. Users can surround transaction logic with LOCK TABLES and UNLOCK TABLES commands. Deadlock is prevented by allowing, at most, one lock statement to be open at a time. Dirty reads are possible if some applications roll back their own work and do not surround their activity with table locks.

MySQL provides limited backup and recovery facilities. There is a backup utility that augments the operating system copy utilities. MySQL maintains a log of commands processed. The log does not include before and after images, nor does it include data values from bulk updates or deletions. Even though it has many limitations, MySQL is easy to use, and the features and functions that it does have are well-implemented.

GROUP I QUESTIONS

14.1 What is the one major requirement for using JDBC?

14.2 What does JDBC stand for?

14.3 What are the four JDBC driver types?

14.4 Explain the purpose of Type 1 JDBC drivers.

14.5 Explain the purpose of Types 2 through 4 JDBC drivers.

14.6 Define *applet* and *servlet*.

14.7 Explain how Java accomplishes portability.

14.8 List the four steps of using a JDBC driver.

14.9 Show the Java statement for loading the mm.mysql drivers used in this chapter.

14.10 Show the Java statement for connecting to a database using the mm.mysql drivers. Assume that the database is named *CustData,* the user is *Lew,* and the password is *Secret*.

14.11 Show the Java statement for creating a Statement object.

14.12 Show the Java statement for creating a ResultSet object that will display the Name and Nationality of the ARTIST table using an already created Statement object named s.

14.13 Show Java statements for iterating the resultset created in Question 16.12.

14.14 Show the Java statement for executing an update to change the Nationality of an artist named "Jones" to "French." Use an already created Statement object named s.

14.15 In question 14.14, how can you determine if the update was successful?

14.16 Show a Java statement for creating an object referencing metadata for the resultset created in question 14.12.

14.17 Show the Java statements necessary to invoke a stored procedure named Customer_Delete. Assume that the procedure has three text parameters with values of customer name, area code, and phone number. Pass the values 'Mary Orange,' '206,' and '555-1234' to this procedure.

14.18 What is the purpose of Java Server Pages?

14.19 Describe the differences between ASP and JSP.

14.20 Explain how JSPs are portable.

14.21 How is it possible that small segments of Java can be coded in JSPs? Why are not complete Java programs required?

14.22 What is the purpose of Tomcat?

14.23 With the standard installation of Tomcat, what actions must be taken before using JSPs that load JDBC classes?

14.24 When adding new class libraries for Tomcat to use, what must you do to place the library in Tomcat's CLASSPATH?

14.25 Describe the process by which JSPs are compiled and executed. Can a user ever access an obsolete page? Why or why not?

14.26 Why are JSP programs preferable to CGI programs?

14.27 What conditions are necessary for a Java class to be a bean?

14.28 Show the JSP directive to access a bean named CustomerDeleteBean. Give this bean the identity *custdel*.

14.29 Show the JSP directives to set a bean property named *Prop1* to the value of a form parameter named *Param1*.

14.30 Why is it advantageous to give object properties and form parameters the same names? Show a JSP directive to associate properties and parameters when this is the case.

14.31 What is the difference between invoking a bean from a pure Java program and invoking a bean from Java code in a JSP?

14.32 Under what conditions would you choose to use MySQL?

14.33 For what type of workload does MySQL excel?

14.34 List the major limitations of MySQL.

14.35 How does MySQL 3.0 process referential integrity constraints?

14.36 What statement do you use for creating a new table using MySQL?

14.37 What issue must be addressed when connecting to MySQL using JDBC?

14.38 Show the MySQL command for giving the user *Lew* permission to access any table in the database in the CustData database. Assume that the password is *Secret*.

14.39 Describe transaction-management facilities in MySQL 3.0.

14.40 How does MySQL use read locks?

14.41 How does MySQL use write locks?

14.42 At what level does MySQL invoke locks? What are the advantages and disadvantages of this?

14.43 Show how an application could provide for transaction atomicity using LOCK TABLES and UNLOCK TABLES.

14.44 What is the disadvantage of the strategy used in your answer to question 14.43?

14.45 Why is deadlock not possible with MySQL?

14.46 Under what conditions are dirty reads possible with MySQL?

14.47 Describe the MySQL facilities for backup.

14.48 What are the limits on MySQL logging?

14.49 According to the author, why would one choose to use MySQL?

GROUP II QUESTIONS

14.50 Compare and contrast ASP and JSP. Describe the relative strengths and weaknesses of each. Under what circumstances would you recommend one over the other? How important is portability for Web servers? How much of a disadvantage is it to be Microsoft-dependent? Some people say preferring one over the other is more a matter of personal preference and values than anything else. Do you agree or disagree?

14.51 Rewrite the Java bean shown in Figure 14-8 to use exceptions rather than the *result* return parameter. Modify the JSP page to correctly process this bean. In what ways is your bean better than the one in Figure 14-8?

PROJECTS

A. Write a Java program to use MySQL and the mm.mysql drivers used in this chapter. Your program should implement the logic of the CustomerInsertWithTransaction stored procedure described for Oracle in Chapter 10 and for SQL Server in Chapter 11. Add logic to your program to display the same results as are displayed in the CustomerPurchasesView. Run your program as a standalone program.

B. Convert the program you wrote in project A to a Java bean. Write a JSP to invoke your bean.

C. Obtain a JDBC Oracle driver and write a Java program to connect to the Oracle version of the View Ridge database and display the contents of any table in the database. Write a Java program to invoke the CustomerInsert stored procedure. Use a JDBC CallableStatement object to invoke that procedure.

D. Convert the program you wrote in project C to a Java bean. Write a JSP to invoke your bean.

E. Obtain a JDBC SQL Server driver and write a Java program to connect to the SQL Server version of the View Ridge database and display the contents of any table in the database. Write a Java program to invoke the CustomerInsert stored procedure. Use a JDBC CallableStatement object to invoke that procedure.

F. Convert the program you wrote in project E to a Java bean. Write a JSP to invoke your bean.

FIREDUP PROJECT QUESTIONS

Create the FiredUp database using either MySQL or Oracle. If in MySQL, you will not be able to create the referential integrity constraints; otherwise, follow the instructions at the end of Chapter 10.

A. Code a JSP page to display the STOVE table.

B. Code a JSP page to display any table in the FiredUp database. Use Figure 14-3 as an example.

C. Code a JSP page to allow customers to register their own stoves.

D. Create a Java Bean to enter new stove repair data.

E. Code a JSP page to invoke the bean created in project question D. Use Figure 14-9 as an example.

TWIGS TREE TRIMMING SERVICE PROJECT QUESTIONS

Create the Twigs database using either MySQL or Oracle. If in MySQL, you cannot create the referential integrity constraints; otherwise, follow the instructions at the end of Chapter 10.

A. Code a JSP to display the OWNER table.

B. Code a JSP to display any table in the Twigs database. Use Figure 14-3 as an example.

C. Code a JSP to allow owners to schedule their own services. They should enter DateOfService and Description only. Assume that the owner data already exists in the database.

D. Create a Java Bean to enter new OWNER data.

E. Code a JSP to invoke the bean created in project question D. Use Figure 14-9 as an example.

CHAPTER 15

Sharing Enterprise Data

So far in this text, we have described database processing in the context of personal computing and in the context of Internet technology using a web server in conjunction with a database server. Enterprises also use several other older system types. Because you may encounter them, we will survey the characteristics of three such types in the first part of this chapter. A fourth type, distributed database processing, is beginning to be used for commercial database processing. Both Oracle and SQL Server provide support for it, and we will discuss it as well.

Data is an important organizational asset; an asset that can be used not only to facilitate the operations of a company, but also for management, planning, forecasting, strategic analysis, and the like. Unfortunately, although many organizations have found that their databases effectively support organizational operations, they know that their databases are ineffectively used for analysis, planning, and other management purposes. In this chapter, we address topics that are important in increasing the return of the investment on enterprise data in databases: downloading centralized data, OLAP, data warehousing, and data administration.

▶ ENTERPRISE DATABASE PROCESSING ARCHITECTURES

Several different system architectures are used for enterprise database processing. In the past, teleprocessing systems were the most common. But as microcomputers became common on the desktop and more powerful as data servers, new multi-user database architectures arose. In this section, we introduce teleprocessing, client-server, file-sharing, and distributed alternatives.

Teleprocessing Systems

The classic method of supporting a multi-user database system is teleprocessing, which uses one computer and one CPU. All processing is done by this single computer.

Figure 15-1 shows a typical teleprocessing system. Users operate dumb terminals (or microcomputers that emulate dumb terminals) that transmit transaction messages and data to the centralized computer. The communications control portion of the operating system receives the messages and data, and sends them to the appropriate application program. The program then calls on the DBMS for services, and the DBMS uses the data management portion of the operating system to process the database. When a transaction is completed, the results are returned to the users at the dumb terminals via the communications control portion of the operating system.

Figure 15-1 shows *n* users submitting transactions processed by three different application programs. Because there is little intelligence at the users' end (that is, the *terminals* are dumb), all commands for formatting the screen must be generated by the CPU and transmitted over the communication lines. This means that the users' interface is generally character-oriented and primitive. Systems like this are called teleprocessing systems because all inputs and outputs are communicated over a distance (*tele-* means "distance") to the centralized computer for processing.

Historically, teleprocessing systems were the most common alternative for multi-user database systems. But as the price–performance ratio of computers fell, and with the advent of the personal computer in particular, other alternatives that use multiple computers have supplanted it.

Client-Server Systems

Figure 15-2 is a schematic of one of these alternatives, called a **client-server system.** Unlike teleprocessing, which involves a single computer, client–server computing involves multiple computers connected in a network. Some of the computers process

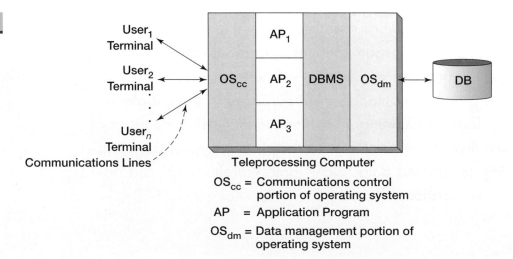

FIGURE 15–1

Relationships of Programs in a Teleprocessing System

OS_{cc} = Communications control portion of operating system

AP = Application Program

OS_{dm} = Data management portion of operating system

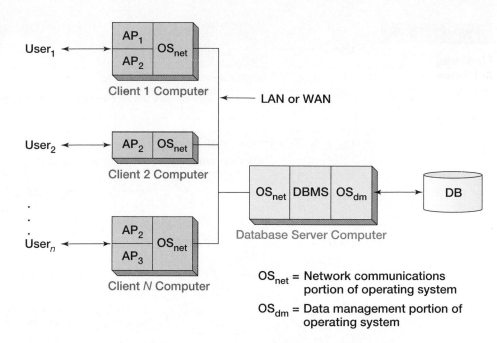

FIGURE 15-2

Client-Server
Architecture

OS_{net} = Network communications
portion of operating system

OS_{dm} = Data management portion of
operating system

application programs and are designated as *clients.* Another computer processes the database and is designated as the *server.*

Figure 15-2 shows an example in which each of *n* users has his or her own client (application processing) computer: $User_1$ processes AP_1 and AP_2 on Computer 1. $User_2$ processes AP_2 on Computer 2, and $User_n$ processes AP_2 and AP_3 on Computer *N.* Another computer is the database server.

There are many options regarding computer type. Theoretically, the client computers can be mainframes or microcomputers. Because of cost, however, in almost all cases the client computers are microcomputers. Similarly, any type of computer can be the server, but again, because of cost, the server is most often a microcomputer. The clients and server are connected using either a local area network (LAN) or wide area network (WAN).

Although it is rare for client computers to be anything other than micros, sometimes the server is a mainframe—especially when considerable power is required from the server or, for reasons of security and control, it is inappropriate to locate the database on a microcomputer.

The system in Figure 15-2 has a single server, although this need not always be the case. Multiple servers may process different databases or provide other services on behalf of the clients. For example, in an engineering-consulting firm, one server might process the database while a second server supports computer-assisted design applications.

If there are multiple database processing servers, each one must process a different database in order for the system to be considered a client-server system. When two servers process the same database, the system is no longer called a client-server system; rather, it is termed a distributed database system.

File-Sharing Systems

A second multi-user architecture is shown in Figure 15-3. This architecture, called **file-sharing,** distributes to the users' computers not only the application programs, but also the DBMS. In this case, the *server* is a file server and not a database server. Almost all file-sharing systems employ LANs of microcomputers.

The file-sharing architecture was developed before the client-server architecture, and in many ways it is more primitive. With file sharing, the DBMS on each user's computer sends requests to the data management portion of the operating system on the file

FIGURE 15-3

File-Sharing
Architecture

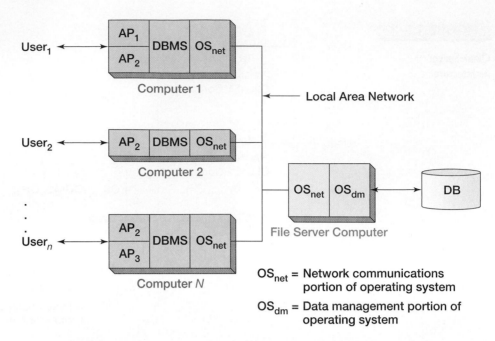

OS_{net} = Network communications portion of operating system

OS_{dm} = Data management portion of operating system

server for file-level processing. This means that considerably more traffic crosses the LAN than with the client-server architecture.

For example, consider the processing of a query to obtain the Name and Address of all rows in the CUSTOMER table where Zip equals 98033. In a client-server system, the application program would send the following SQL command:

```
SELECT      NAME, ADDRESS
FROM        CUSTOMER
WHERE       ZIP = 98033
```

The server would respond with all qualifying Names and Addresses.

In a file-sharing system, the DBMS is on the local computer, and therefore no program on the file server is capable of processing the SQL statement. All such processing must be done on the user computer, so the DBMS must ask the file server to transmit the entire CUSTOMER table. If that table has indexes or other overhead associated with it, the overhead structures must be transmitted as well. Clearly, with file sharing, much more data need be transmitted across the LAN.

Because of these problems, file-sharing systems are seldom used for high-volume, transaction-oriented processing. Too much data need to be locked and transmitted for each transaction, and this architecture results in very slow performance. There is, however, one database application for which this architecture makes sense: the query processing of downloaded, extracted data. If one or more users need access to large portions of the database in order to produce reports or answer queries, it can make sense to have a server that downloads large sections of data. In this case, the downloaded data are not updated and not returned to the database. We show examples of processing extracted data later in this chapter.

File-sharing systems are also used for nondatabase applications, such as those that require large fast disks to store large files such as large graphics, audio, and animations. They also are used to share expensive printers, plotters, and other peripheral equipment.

Distributed Database Systems

A fourth alternative, shown in Figure 15-4, is a distributed database system, in which the database itself is distributed. In Figure 15-4, the database (or a portion of it) is stored on

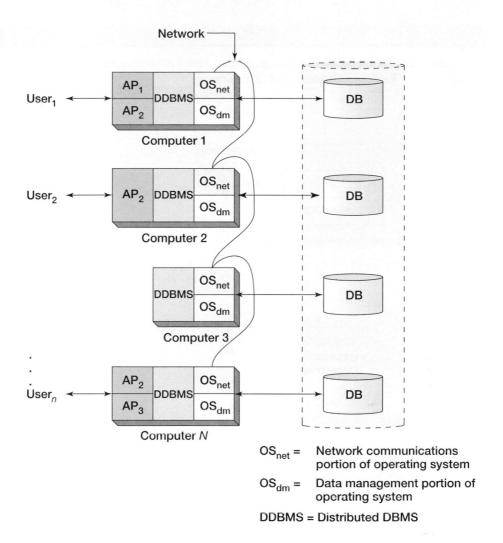

FIGURE 15–4

Distributed Database
Architecture

OS$_{net}$ = Network communications portion of operating system

OS$_{dm}$ = Data management portion of operating system

DDBMS = Distributed DBMS

all N computers. As shown, Computers 1, 2, and N process both the applications and the database, and Computer 3 processes only the database.

In Figure 15-4, the dashed line around the files indicates that the database is composed of all the segments of the database on all N computers. These computers may be physically located in the same facility, on different sides of the world, or somewhere in-between.

Distributed Processing Versus Distributed Database Processing

Consider Figures 15-1, 15-2, 15-3, and 15-4 again. The file-sharing, client-server, and distributed database alternatives all differ from teleprocessing in an important way: they all use multiple computers for applications or DBMS processing. Accordingly, most people would say that all three of these architectures are examples of **distributed systems** because applications processing has been distributed among several computers.

Observe, however, that the database itself is distributed only in the architecture shown in Figure 15-4. Neither the client-server nor the file-sharing architectures distribute the database to multiple computers. Consequently, most people would *not* refer to the file-sharing or client-server architectures as **distributed database systems.**

Types of Distributed Databases   There are several types of distributed database systems. First look at Figure 15-5(a), which shows a nondistributed database with four pieces: W, X, Y, and Z. All four pieces of these segments are located on a single database, and there is no data duplication.

Now, consider the distributed alternatives in Figure 15-5(b) through Figure 15-5(d). Figure 15-5(b) shows the first distributed alternative, in which the database has been

---

FIGURE 15-5

Types of Distributed Databases (a) Nonpartitioned, Nonreplicated Alternative; (b) Partitioned, Nonreplicated Alternative; (c) Nonpartitioned, Replicated Alternative and (d) Partitioned, Replicated Alternative

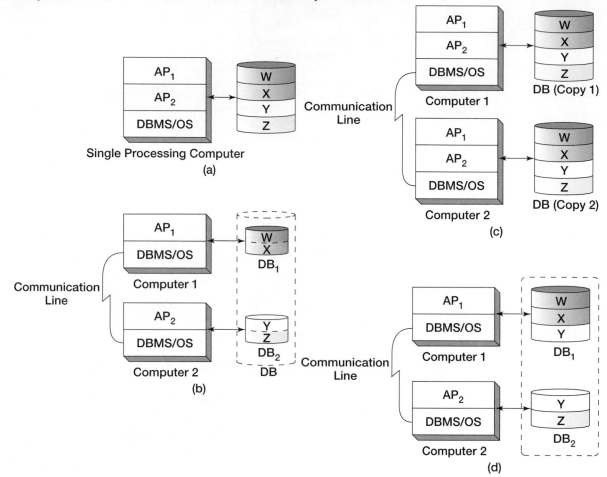

distributed to two computers; pieces W and X are stored on Computer 1, and pieces Y and Z are stored on Computer 2. In Figure 15-5(c), the entire database has been replicated on two computers. Finally, in Figure 15-5(d), the database has been partitioned, and a portion (Y) has been replicated.

Two terms are sometimes used with regard to the partitioning of databases. A vertical partition, or **vertical fragment**, refers to a table that is broken into two or more sets of columns. Thus, a table R(C1, C2, C3, C4) could be broken into two vertical partitions of P1(C1, C2) and P2(C3, C4). Depending on the application and the reason for creating the partitions, the key of R would most likely also be placed into P2 to form P2(C1, C3, C4). A horizontal partition, or **horizontal fragment**, refers to the rows of a table when they are divided into pieces. Thus, in the relation R, if the first 1,000 rows are placed into R1(C1, C2, C3, C4) and the remaining rows are placed into R2(C1, C2, C3, C4), two horizontal partitions will result. Sometimes, a database is broken into both horizontal and vertical partitions, and the result is sometimes called a mixed partition.

Comparison of Distributed Database Alternatives These alternatives are summarized on a continuum in Figure 15-6, arranged in increasing degree of distribution from left to right. The nondistributed database is on the leftmost point of the continuum, and the partitioned replicated database is on the rightmost point. In-

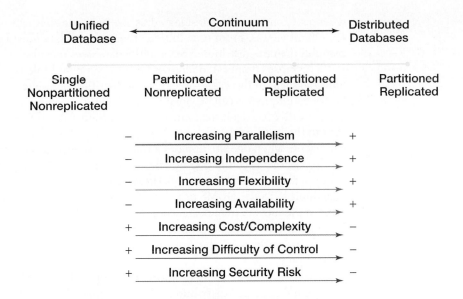

FIGURE 15-6

Continuum of Database Distribution Alternatives

between these extremes is a partitioned database. The partitions are allocated to two or more computers and a database that is not partitioned, but each entire database is replicated on two or more computers.

The characteristics of the alternatives on this continuum are listed in Figure 15-6. The alternatives toward the right increase parallelism, independence, flexibility, and availability; but they also mean greater expense, complexity, difficulty of control, and risk to security.

One of these advantages is particularly significant to business organizations. The alternatives on the right of Figure 15-6 provide greater flexibility and hence can be better tailored to the organizational structure and the organizational process. A highly decentralized manufacturing company, for example, in which plant managers have wide latitude in their planning, will never be satisfied with an organizational information system with the structure of Figure 15-5(a) because the structure of the information system architecture and the structure of the company fight with each other. Thus, the alternatives on the right side provide a better and more appropriate fit to that organization than do those on the left.

The greatest disadvantage is the difficulty of control and the resulting potential loss of data integrity. Consider the database architecture shown in Figure 15-5(d). A user connected to Computer 1 can read and update a data item in Partition Y on Computer 1 at the very same time that a different user connected to Computer 2 can read and update that data item in Partition Y on Computer 2.

Distributed Processing Techniques DBMS vendors provide several techniques for supporting distributed processing. Oracle and SQL Server provide similar types of support, but they use different names for the same things and the same name for different things. Other DBMS vendors use still other terminology. Here, we will focus on the basic ideas.

The simplest type of distributed database processing is the downloading of read-only data. In this case, only one computer updates any of the database data, but multiple computers (maybe even thousands) are sent copies to process in read-only mode. Oracle calls such read-only copies **materialized views.** SQL Server calls such read-only copies **snapshots.** We will address this type of distributed processing in the next section.

A more complex technique for distributed processing is to allow data update requests to originate on multiple computers, but to transmit those update requests to a designated computer for processing. Computer A, for example, could be designated as the only site that can update the EMPLOYEE table (and views based on EMPLOYEE), whereas Computer B is designated as the only site that can update the CUSTOMER table (and views). From time to time, the updated data must be transmitted back to all computers in the distributed net and the databases must be synchronized.

The most complicated alternative is to allow multiple updates on the same data at multiple sites. In this case, three types of **distributed update conflict** problem can occur. For one, uniqueness can be violated. At View Ridge Galley, two different sites might create a WORK row with the same Copy, Title, and ArtistID. Another possible problem is akin to the lost update problem. Two sites can each update the same row. A third problem occurs when one site updates a row that has been deleted by a second site.

To deal with conflicting updates, a single site is designated for conflict resolution. All updates are examined by this site, and conflicting updates are resolved using either logic built in to the DBMS or in application code that is similar to that written for triggers. In the most extreme case, conflicts are written to a log and resolved manually. This latter alternative is not recommended because many rows in operational databases can be left in limbo until the resolutions are resolved. This may unacceptably reduce throughput.

None of these techniques addresses the problem of providing atomic transactions when databases are distributed. This is especially problematical when conflicting updates may occur. At what point is a database action committed? If updates are subject to rollback during distributed update resolution, the distributed transaction cannot commit for potentially hours of days. This delay is clearly unacceptable.

Setting aside the issue of distributed update conflict, the coordination of distributed transactions is difficult. To be atomic, no update action in a distributed transaction can be committed until all are committed. This means a given site must provisionally commit its updates, pending notification from the distributed transaction manager that all other sites have committed. An algorithm called **two-phased commit** is used for this purpose. Microsoft an OLE service called the **Distributed Transaction Service (DTS)** that implements two-phased commit. In the Java world, **Enterprise Java Beans (EJB)** are used for this purpose. Both of these are beyond the scope of this text, but you should know that they exist. Search on the keyword *replication* in the Oracle and SQL Server documentation.

▶ DOWNLOADING DATA

With the advent of powerful personal computers, it has become feasible to download large quantities of enterprise data to departmental and user computers for local processing. Users can query these data using local DBMS products, and they can also import the data into spreadsheets, financial-analysis programs, graphics programs, and other tools with which they are familiar.

In general, downloaded data can be used for query and reporting purposes only. They cannot be updated because after the data are removed from the operational database, they are no longer subject to concurrency control. To understand more about the processing of downloaded data, consider a typical scenario.

Universal Equipment

The Universal Equipment Company manufactures and sells heavy equipment for the construction industry. Its products include bulldozers, graders, loaders, and drilling rigs. Every product is assigned to a product manager in the marketing department who is responsible for product planning, advertising, marketing support, development of sales support material, and so forth. Each product manager is assigned a group of two or three related products.

Advertising is the product managers' largest budget item, so managers want to be able to measure the effectiveness of the ads they run. Universal's ads always contain a mail-in card to request information. The cards have a preprinted number unique to each ad appearance so that this number can be used to identify the ad that generated a particular lead. To facilitate lead tracking, the marketing department has developed a microcomputer database application that the product managers can use.

Figure 15-7(a) shows a semantic object model (see Appendix B) for this application. AD represents an advertisement; AD-APPEARANCE is the occurrence of a particular ad in a particular publication; PRODUCT represents a particular product such as a bulldozer; and PRODUCT contains two repeating groups, one on quotas and one on sales. The groups are multi-value because sales quotas are assigned for each quarter and product sales are recorded on a weekly basis.

This view of PRODUCT is quite simple. The complete PRODUCT object actually contains more attributes. But because the other data are not needed for the product managers' application, we have omitted them. The database structure that supports these objects is shown in Figure 15-7(b).

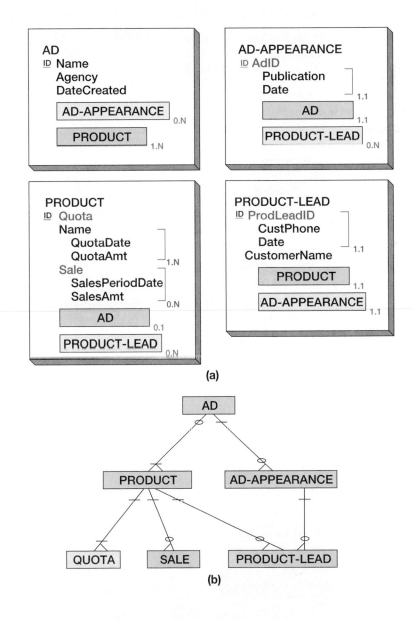

FIGURE 15-7

Objects and Relations Supporting Universal's Product-Marketing Database (a) Objects Processed by the Universal Product Managers and (b) Relational Structure Supporting These Objects

Download Process

The product managers are assigned a personal computer connected to other PCs through a LAN in Universal's marketing department. To obtain sales and product-lead data, the computers call on a file server that serves as a gateway to Universal's mainframe (transaction-processing computer). The architecture is similar to that shown in Figure 15-8.

Every Monday, a key user in the marketing department runs a program developed by Universal's MIS department that updates the SALES, QUOTA, and PRODUCT-LEAD tables on the file server's database with data from the corporation's mainframe database. This program adds to the database the data from the previous week and also makes corrections. Product and sales data are imported for all related products to enable product managers to do comparative studies. After the data have been downloaded to the file server, each product manager can obtain the data of interest to him or her from that server. Controls ensure that the product managers do not obtain data for which access has not been authorized.

Potential Problems in Processing Downloaded Databases

Downloading data moves the data closer to the user and increases the data's utility. Unfortunately, it may cause problems, including a lack of coordination, consistency, and access control, and also the possibility of computer crime.

FIGURE 15-8

Sharing of Downloaded Data with a Gateway Micro as the File Server

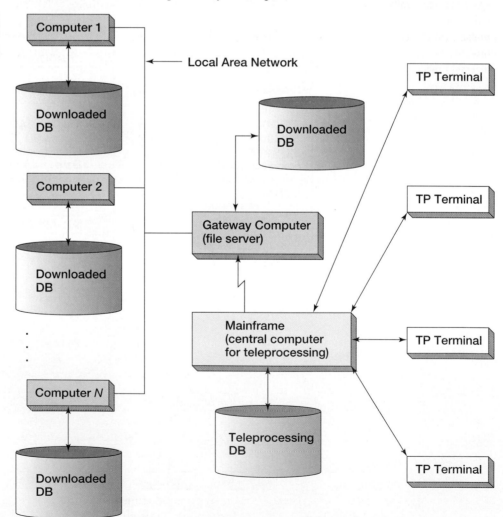

Coordination　First, consider coordination, using the PRODUCT-LEAD and AD-APPEARANCE tables for illustration. The PRODUCT-LEAD table is updated from data on the mainframe (leads are handled by sales personnel and are recorded on the mainframe). But the AD-APPEARANCE table is updated "locally" by the key user in the marketing department, who gets the data from reports prepared by the advertising manager and the advertising agency.

This situation could cause problems when an ad is run for the first time in a new issue or publication. For example, the ad could generate leads that are recorded on the mainframe database before the AD-APPEARANCE data is stored on the file server. Then, when those leads are downloaded, the program importing the data will have to reject the lead data because such data violate the constraint that a PRODUCT-LEAD must have an AD-APPEARANCE parent. Thus, the activities of local updating and downloading must be carefully coordinated: The key user needs to insert AD-APPEARANCE data before importing data from the mainframe. Similar coordination problems can occur when updating SALES and QUOTA data.

Consistency　The second problem with downloaded data concerns **consistency**. Each of the product managers receives downloaded SALES and QUOTA data that they are not supposed to change. But what would happen if a product manager did change the data? In this case, the data in that product manager's database might not match the data in the corporate database, the data in the file server, and possibly the data in other product managers' databases. The reports produced by that product manager could therefore disagree with other reports. And if several product managers update data, many inconsistent data could be generated.

Clearly, this situation calls for strict control. The database should be designed so that data cannot be updated. If this is not possible—suppose that the personal computer database product do not enforce such a restriction, and the costs of writing programs to enforce it are prohibitively high—the solution to this problem is education. Product managers should be aware of the problems that will ensue if they change data, and they should be directed not to do so.

Access Control　A third problem is access control. When data are transferred to several computer systems, access control becomes more difficult. At Universal, for example, SALES and QUOTA data may be sensitive. For example, the vice president of sales may not want the sales personnel to learn about upcoming sales quotas until the annual sales meeting. But if 15 product managers have copies of these data in their databases, it can be difficult to ensure that the data will be kept confidential until the appropriate time.

Furthermore, the file server receives all SALES and QUOTA data, which are supposed to be downloaded so that a product manager receives only the SALES and QUOTA data for the products that he or she manages. Product managers can be quite competitive, however, and they may want to find the data for one another's products. Making this data accessible on the file server in the marketing department may thus create management problems.

Computer Crime　The fourth problem, a greater possibility of computer crime, is closely allied to access control. Whereas access control concerns inappropriate but legal activity, crime concerns illegal actions. Data on the corporate mainframe can be very valuable. Universal Equipment's sales and quota data, for example, are of great interest to its competitors.

When data are downloaded in bulk to the file server and then to one or many personal computers, illegal copying becomes difficult to prevent. A diskette or CD-ROM is easily concealed, and employees sometimes have online connections with which they access work computers from off-site locations. In these situations, copying data is nearly impossible to detect or prevent. The risk of computer crime alone might prohibit such a system from being developed, even though it would otherwise be an excellent solution. The potential problems of downloaded databases are summarized in Figure 15-9.

FIGURE 15-9

Issues and Potential Problems Regarding Downloaded Data Applications

Coordination
- Downloaded data must conform to database constraints.
- Local updates must be coordinated with downloads.

Consistency
- In general, downloaded data should not be updated.
- Applications need features to prevent updating.
- Users should be made aware of possible problems.

Access Control
- Data may be replicated on many computers.
- Procedures to control data access are more complicated.

Potential for Computer Crime
- Illegal copying is difficult to prevent.
- Diskettes and illegal online access are easy to conceal.
- Risk may prevent the development of downloaded data applications.

FIGURE 15-10

Processing Downloaded Data with a Web Server

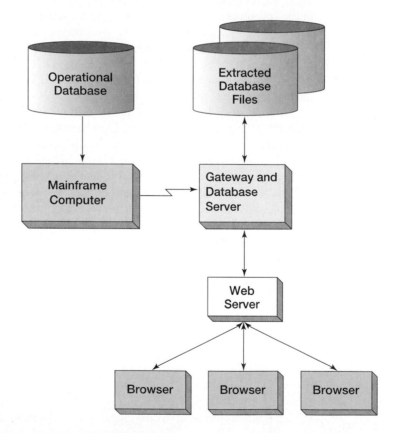

Using a Web Server to Publish Downloaded Data

Figure 15-10 shows one way to use a Web server to publish downloaded data. The gateway and database servers are shown here on one computer, but they could reside on two—one computer for the gateway and a second for the server. The Web server communicates with the database server to obtain downloaded data. This data is then published to browser users.

▶ ON LINE ANALYTIC PROCESSING (OLAP)

In recent years, a new way of presenting information has emerged that is called **On Line Analytical Processing**—or more frequently, **OLAP.** With OLAP, data is viewed in the frame of a table, or with three axes, in that of a **cube.** OLAP makes no limit on the number of axes, hence, you will sometimes hear the term **OLAP hypercube.** This term means a display with an unlimited number of axes. The term **OLAP cube** is used most frequently.

Consider the example relation shown in Figure 15-11. This data concerns the sales of single-family and condo housing properties in California and Nevada. As you can see from the data, the Sales Price and Asking Price for both new construction and existing properties are included.

OLAP Terminology An OLAP cube for this data is shown in Figure 15-12. This data has two **axes,** which are columns and rows. The row axis displays the Date **dimension,** and the columns axis displays both the Category and the Location dimensions. When two or more dimensions are shown on an axis, every combination of one is shown with every combination of the other. Thus, Existing Structures is shown for all locations, and New Construction is shown for all locations. The cells of the cube represent the **measures** of the cube, or the data that is to be displayed. In this cube, the measure is average Sales Price. Other measures concern Asking Price or even the difference between Sales Price and Asking Price.

Notice that all of the data in Figure 15-12 concern single-family dwellings. There is no condo data in this cube. In fact, there are two such cubes—one for single family and a second for condos. You could think of the two cubes as one behind the other, as

FIGURE 15-11

Relational Source Data for OLAP Cube

Category	Type	City	State	Date	Sales Price	Asking Price
New	Single Family	San Francisco	California	1/1/2000	679,000	685,000
Existing	Condo	Los Angeles	California	3/5/2001	327,989	350,000
Existing	Single Family	Elko	Nevada	7/17/2001	105,675	125,000
New	Condo	San Diego	California	12/22/2000	375,000	375,000
Existing	Single Family	Paradise	California	11/19/2001	425,000	449,000
Existing	Single Family	Las Vegas	Nevada	1/19/2001	317,000	325,000
New	Single Family	San Francisco	California	1/1/2000	679,000	685,000
Existing	Condo	Los Angeles	California	3/5/2001	327,989	350,000
Existing	Condo	Las Vegas	Nevada	6/19/2001	297,000	305,000
Existing	Single Family	Los Angeles	California	4/1/2000	579,000	625,000
New	Condo	Los Angeles	California	8/5/2001	321,000	320,000
Etc.						

FIGURE 15-12

Example OLAP Cube

Average Sales Price of Single-Family Dwellings ($thousands)									
			Existing Structures				New Construction			
			California			Nevada	California			Nevada
			San Francisco	Los Angeles	San Diego		San Francisco	Los Angeles	San Diego	
2000	Q1	Jan	408	465	375	179	418	468	371	190
		Feb	419	438	382	180	429	437	382	185
		Mar	427	477	380	195	426	471	387	198
	Q2		433	431	382	188	437	437	380	193
	Q3		437	437	380	190	438	439	382	190
	Q4		435	439	377	193	432	434	370	198
2001	Q1	Jan	452	454	368	198	450	457	367	197
		Feb	450	467	381	187	457	464	388	191
		Mar	432	444	373	188	436	446	371	201
	Q2		437	437	368	190	444	432	363	196
	Q3		436	452	388	196	447	455	385	199
	Q4		441	455	355	198	449	455	355	202

FIGURE 15-13

OLAP Cube Slice Dimensions

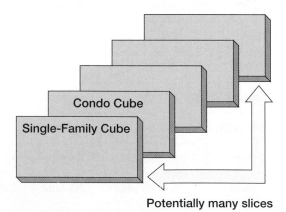

Potentially many slices

sketched in Figure 15-13. When viewed this way, these two cubes appear to be slices of data, and, in fact, the dimension(s) that are held constant in a cube are called **slices.** Thus, in this example, the cube is sliced on Type.

The values of a dimension are called **members.** The members of the Type dimension are {Single Family, Condo}, and the members of the Category dimension are {New,

Existing}. For this cube, the members of the State dimension are {California, Nevada}, but in general, there could be 50 such members for United States properties. Sometimes, there is a very large number of members in a dimension; consider all of the members for the combination {State, City}. Finally, in some cases, members are computed. Date and time are good examples. Given a date, we can compute the month, quarter, year, or century members for that date.

One last important OLAP term is **level.** The level of a dimension is its position in a hierarchy. For example, consider the Date dimension. Its levels are Year, Quarter, Month. The levels in the location dimension are State, City. OLAP terminology is summarized in Figure 15-14.

Cube and View Definitions OLAP terminology is evolving and is currently ambiguous in an important way. The term **cube** is used both to describe a semantic structure and also to describe materializations of that underlying structure. The cube shown in Figure 15-12 is one possible view or materialization of a semantic structure that has certain dimensions, levels, and measures. We could create a second cube on this data by exchanging the rows and columns; we could create a third cube on this data by showing Location at the top and then placing a New and Existing column for each Location member. So as you read OLAP documents, be careful to understand which meaning of *cube* is being used.

To illustrate this point further, consider the cube definition shown in Figure 15-15. The syntax used here is based on Microsoft's OLE DB for OLAP documentation, but it is similar to that used by other vendors as well. This Create Cube statement defines four dimensions and two levels in the logical structure. The Time and Location dimensions have levels, and the HousingCategory and HousingType dimensions do not. Although we do not show it here, it is possible for a dimension to have more than one set of Levels. In that case, two or more hierarchies are defined for that dimension.

The structure shown in Figure 15-15 is a definition of a way to interpret or comprehend housing data. It is not a presentation of data. To define a data presentation or materialization, the OLAP world has extended the syntax of SQL. Figure 15-16(a) shows the OLAP SQL to create the cube materialization shown in Figure 15-11. The only thing confusing about this statement is the CROSSJOIN term. A CROSSJOIN ({A,B}, {1,2}) results in the following display:

FIGURE 15-14	Term	Description	Example in Figure 15-12
OLAP Terminology	Axis	A coordinate of the hypercube	Rows, columns
	Dimension	A feature of the data to be placed on an axis	Time, Housing Type, Location
	Level	A (hierarchical) subset of a dimension	{California, Nevada} {San Francisco, Los Angeles, Other} {Q1, Q2, Q3, Q4}
	Member	A data value in a dimension	{New, Existing}, {Jan, Feb, Mar}
	Measure	The source data for the hypercube	Sales Price, Asking Price
	Slice	A dimension or measure held constant for the display	Housing Type—all shown are for Single Family—another cube exists for Condo

FIGURE 15–15

Extended SQL Used for OLAP (a) Example Create Cube Data Definition Statement and (b) Example Multidimensional SELECT Statement

```
CREATE CUBE HousingSalesCube (

       DIMENSION Time TYPE TIME,

              LEVEL Year TYPE YEAR,

              LEVEL Quarter TYPE QUARTER,

              LEVEL Month TYPE MONTH,

       DIMENSION Location,

              LEVEL USA TYPE ALL,

              LEVEL State,

              LEVEL City,

       DIMENSION HousingCategory,

       DIMENSION HousingType,

       MEASURE SalesPrice,

              FUNCTION AVG

       MEASURE AskingPrice,

              FUNCTION AVG

       )
```

(a)

```
SELECT    CROSSJOIN ({Existing Structure, New Construction}, {California.Children,

          Nevada})

          ON COLUMNS,

          {1998.Q1.Children, 1998.Q2, 1998.Q3, 1998.Q4,

          1999.Q1.Children, 1999.Q2, 1999.Q3, 1999.Q4}

          ON ROWS

FROM      HousingSalesCube

WHERE     (SalesPrice, HousingType = 'SingleFamily')
```

(b)

FIGURE 15-16

OLAP Schema Types (a) Example Star Schema and (b) Example Snowflake Schema

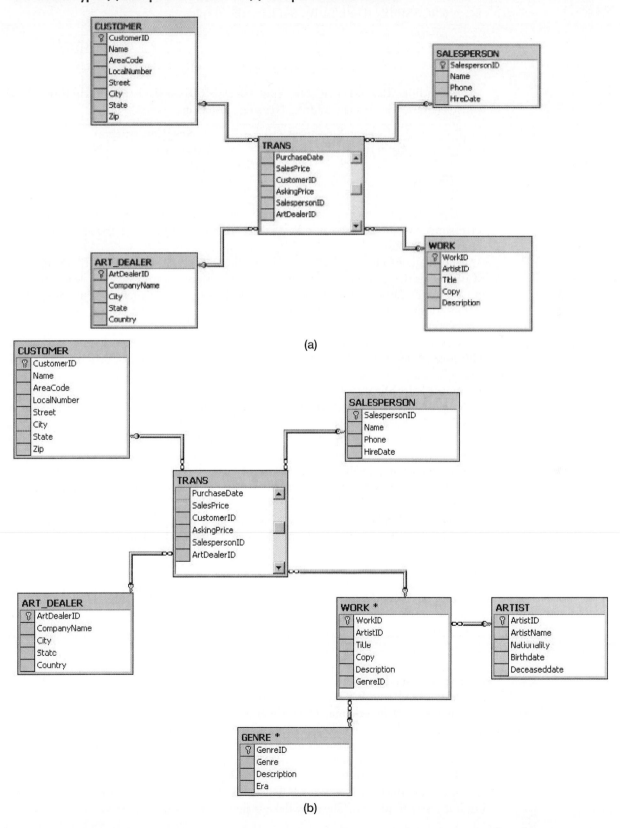

(a)

(b)

A		B	
1	2	1	2

A CROSSJOIN ({1,2}, {A,B}) results in this display:

1		2	
A	B	A	B

Extending this idea a bit, the CROSSJOIN ({Existing Structure, New Construction}, {California.Children, Nevada}) results in

Existing Structures			New Construction		
California		Nevada	California		Nevada
San Francisco	Los Angeles	San Diego	San Francisco	Los Angeles	San Diego

The only addition to this last statement was the expression California.Children. This term simply means to breakout all of the children for California for all of the levels defined in the cube.

The SQL in Figure 15-16(b) includes the expression ON COLUMNS and ON ROWS. This declares the axes on which the dimensions are to be placed. Note, too, that the WHERE clause is used to specify the slicers for the presentation. Only Sales Price and a HousingType of Single Family are to be shown. Note that both a measure and a dimension can serve as a slicer.

One of the key ideas of OLAP is that users be able to dynamically reformat a cube with ease while at their desks (hence the words *on line*). To do this, programs that process cube materializations need to be able dynamically to construct OLAP SQL like that in Figure 15-16(b).

OLAP Schema Structures All of the data for the OLAP example in Figures 15-11 and 15-12 arise from a single table. This is unusual; normally data for at least some of the dimensions are stored in a table other than the table having the measures. For example, Figure 15-16 shows sample OLAP table structures for View Ridge Gallery. The measure data, say SalesPrice, is stored in the TRANS table, but data about the dimensions are stored in parent tables that are connected via foreign keys to TRANS.

A cube based in the data in Figure 15-16(a) could have CUSTOMER, ART_DEALER, SALESPERSON, and WORK dimensions. The member data for those dimensions would be obtained from the related tables. The structure shown in Figure 15-16(a) occurs so frequently in OLAP processing that it has been given the name **star schema,** in reference to the pattern of the dimension tables around the table having the measure data.

Note that this figure does not include ARTIST Name. To include it, the OLAP designer has a choice to join Name of ARTIST to the WORK table via the ArtistID key. If that were done, WORK would not be in domain/key normal form, and consequently there would be duplicated data.

An alternative to storing such joins is shown in Figure 15-16(b). Here, the ARTIST table is not joined to WORK, but is kept in normalized form. Another table, GENRE, has been added as well. This table structure occurs frequently, too, and has been given the name **snowflake schema.** The difference between the star and the snowflake structures is that with the star, every dimension table is adjacent to the table storing the measure values. These tables may or may not be normalized. With the snowflake structure, there can be multilevels of tables, and each will be normalized.

The choice between these two structures depends on the size and nature of the data and also upon the OLAP workload. In general, the star schema requires greater storage, but it is faster to process. The snowflake is slower, but uses less storage.

OLAP Storage Alternatives (ROLAP, MOLAP, and HOLAP) No, we are not talking about a high-tech version of the seven dwarves. ROLAP, MOLAP, and HOLAP refer to different means for storing OLAP data. Basically, the question is this: In order to gain the best performance, should relational DBMS products be extended to include special facilities for OLAP, should a special-purpose processing engine be used, or should both be used?

ROLAP storage (relational OLAP) proponents claim that with preprocessing of certain queries and with other extensions, relational DBMS products are more than adequate. Proponents of MOLAP (multidimensional OLAP) storage believe that, although relational DBMS are fine for transaction processing and query and reporting, the processing requirements for OLAP are so specialized that no DBMS can produce acceptable OLAP performance. The third group, HOLAP (hybrid OLAP), believes that both DBMS products and specialized OLAP engines have a role and can be used to advantage.

Microsoft uses these terms more narrowly in the context of SQL Server OLAP. To Microsoft, ROLAP means that the source data and precomputed aggregations of data will be stored in a SQL Server database. With MOLAP, on the other hand, the data, cube structure, and precomputed aggregations of data will be stored in a special-purpose multidimensional data structure. With HOLAP, the data stay in the relational database, but data aggregations are stored in a multidimensional data structure.

MOLAP results in the best performance, but requires the most storage. ROLAP uses less storage, but will be slow. It is intended for large databases that are seldom queried. HOLAP is a compromise with fast performance for high-level OLAP activity, but will be slower for exploring fine levels of detail.

Figure 15-17 shows the OLAP architecture supported by SQL Server 2000 and Office 2000/XP. This HOLAP architecture involves OLAP processing on central data servers, on the Web server, and on client computers. Enterprise databases are processed by central data servers shown on the right-hand side of this diagram. The results of such processing are then made available to the Pivot Table Service on either a Web server or a client computer. Additionally, either the Web server or the client computer may have local versions of OLAP data.

There are several key elements of this architecture. First, the Pivot Table Service is an OLAP processor that is available as Windows 2000 and XP service. It is also available on other versions of windows that are running Office XP and 2000. In fact, the Pivot Table Service is invoked whenever creating data access pages in Access. This service is even more frequently used by Excel.

The Pivot Table Service is exposed through an extension to OLE DB called OLE DB for OLAP. This extension builds on the OLE DB that you learned in Chapter 12; basically, it extends the rowset abstraction to include not just recordsets, but also to include datasets (OLAP datasets; these are different from ADO.NET datasets), which are abstractions of cubes. The ADO extension for processing OLE DB for OLAP is called ADO MD (multidimensional). With ADO MD, Connection and Command objects can open datasets and process them dynamically, similarly to the way shown for recordsets in Chapter 12. Data can be both read and written.

This architecture moves as much OLAP processing as possible to the client because the processing requirements of OLAP can be great. There is no disadvantage to this when you process data that is stored locally, but when creating cubes that require data from a central enterprise server, considerable data transmission may occur. This may not be acceptable; certainly, such systems will need to be tuned as experience is gained.

As indicated in Figure 15-17, OLAP processing can be done on centralized, downloaded, or local data. As organizations disburse more of their data to the users, data management problems increase. Data warehousing is a possible solution to this problem, and we consider it next.

FIGURE 15–17

Microsoft OLAP Architecture

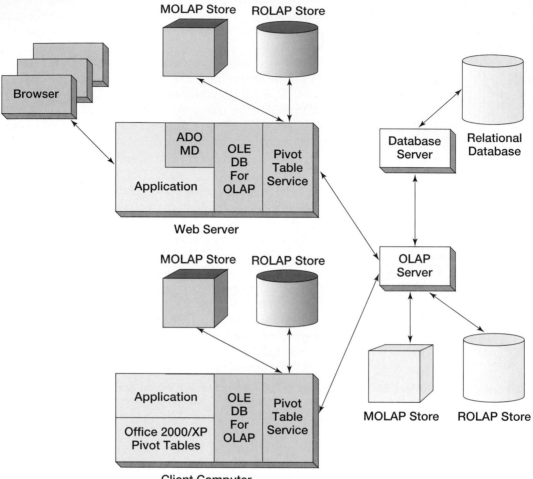

▶ DATA WAREHOUSES

Downloading does move the data closer to the user and thereby increase its potential utility. Unfortunately, although one or two download sites can be managed without a problem, the management problems become immense if every department wants to have its own source of downloaded data. Accordingly, organizations began to look for some means of providing a standardized service for moving data to the user and making them more useful. That service is called data warehousing.

A **data warehouse** is a store of enterprise data that is designed to facilitate management decision-making. A data warehouse includes not only data but also tools, procedures, training, personnel, and other resources that make access to the data easier and more relevant to decision makers. The goal of the data warehouse is to increase the value of the organization's data asset.

As shown in Figure 15-18, the role of the data warehouse is to store extracts from operational data and make those extracts available to users in a useful format. The data can be extracts from databases and files, but it can also be document images, recordings, photos, and other nonscalar data. The source data could also be purchased from other organizations. The data warehouse stores the extracted data and also combines it, aggregates it, transforms it, and makes it available to users via tools that are designed for analysis and decision-making, such as OLAP.

FIGURE 15–18

Data Warehouse

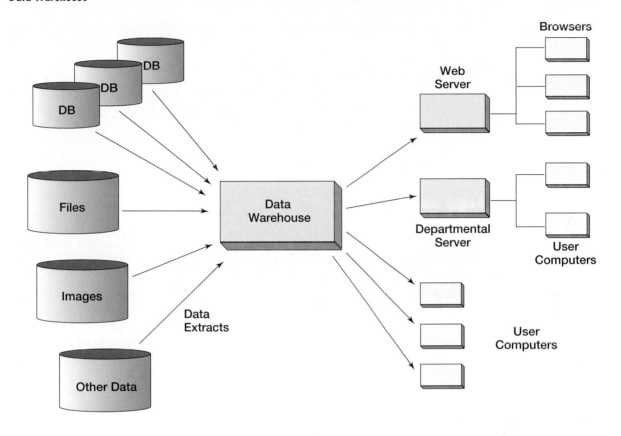

FIGURE 15–19

Components of a Data Warehouse

- Data extraction tools
- Extracted data
- Metadata of warehouse contents
- Warehouse DBMS(s) and OLAP servers
- Warehouse data management tools
- Data delivery programs
- End-user analysis tools
- User training courses and materials
- Warehouse consultants

Components of a Data Warehouse

The components of a data warehouse are listed in Figure 15-19. As stated, the source of the warehouse is operational data. Hence, the data warehouse needs tools for extracting the data and storing them. These data, however, are not useful without metadata that describe the nature of the data, their origins, their format, limits on their use, and other characteristics of the data that influence the way they can and should be used.

Potentially, the data warehouse contains billions of bytes of data in many different formats. Accordingly, it needs DBMS and OLAP servers of its own to store and process the data. In fact, several DBMS and OLAP products may be used, and the features and functions of these may be augmented by additional in-house developed software that reformats, aggregates, integrates, and transfers data from one processor to another within the data warehouse. Programs may also be needed to store and process nonscalar data such as graphics and animations.

Because the purpose of the data warehouse is to make organizational data more available, the warehouse must include tools not only to deliver the data to the users but also to transform the data for analysis, query, and reporting; and OLAP for user-specified aggregation and disaggregation.

The data warehouse provides an important but complicated set of resources and services. Hence, the warehouse needs to include training courses, training materials, on-line help utilities, and other similar training products to make it easy for users to take advantage of the warehouse resources. Finally, the data warehouse includes knowledge-able personnel who can serve as consultants.

Requirements for a Data Warehouse

The requirements for a data warehouse are different from the requirements for a traditional database application. For one, in a typical database application, the structure of reports and queries is standardized. Although the data in a report or query vary from month to month, for instance, the structure of the report or query stays the same. Data warehouse users, on the other hand, often need to change the structure of queries and reports.

Consider an example. Suppose that a company defines sales territories geographically—for simplicity, say that one salesperson is assigned to each state or province in North America. Now, assume that a user of a data warehouse wants to investigate the impact on sales commissions if staff are allocated to specific, named accounts instead of being allocated geographically. To compare these alternatives, sales must be grouped by company on the one hand and by state on another. Queries and reports with different structures need to be created for this purpose.

Another difference is that users want to do their own data aggregation. For example, a user who wants to investigate the impact of different marketing campaigns may want to aggregate product sales according to package color at one time, according to marketing program at another, according to package color within marketing program at a third, and according to marketing program with package color on a fourth. The analyst wants the same data in each report; she simply wants to *slice and dice it differently.*

Not only do data warehouse users want to aggregate data in their own terms; they may also want to disaggregate them in their own terms; or, as it is commonly called, such users want to **drill down** their data. For example, a user may be presented a screen that shows total product sales for a given year. The user may then want to be able to click the data and have them explode into sales by month; to click again and have the data explode into sales by product by month or sales by region by product by month. Although database applications can be written to meet this need for a specific set of drill-down requirements, more often, the requirements vary by user and task. In fact, sometimes the users do not know how they want to drill down until they see the data and start drilling down; hence, drill-down tools need to be flexible.

Graphical output is another common requirement. Users want to see the results of geographic data in geographic form. Sales by state and province should be shown on a map of North America. A reshuffling of employees and offices should be shown on a diagram of office space. Again, these requirements are more difficult because they vary from user to user and from task to task.

Finally, many users of data warehouse facilities want to import warehouse data into domain-specific programs. For example, financial analysts want to import data into their spreadsheet models and into more sophisticated financial-analysis programs. Portfolio managers want to import data into portfolio-management programs, and oil-drilling engineers want to import data into seismic-analysis programs. All of this importing usually means that the warehouse data needs to be formatted in specific ways. These requirements are summarized in Figure 15-20.

Challenges for Data Warehouses

So far, we've described data warehouses in an idealized way that makes them appear to be a panacea for management decision-making. In point of fact, delivering the capabilities we have described is very difficult. There are several important challenges that must be met and problems that must be solved.

Inconsistent Data   Obviously, the data warehouse is useless, if not downright harmful, if the data that it provides are inaccurate. The issue goes beyond the quality of the data that the warehouse extracts from its sources. The source data can be accurate as extracted, but inaccuracies can be introduced by unwittingly integrating data that are inconsistent in timing or domain.

Consider the example of extracted data shown in Figure 15-21. One table is an extract of order data, and the second is an extract of checks that were written as bonuses to salespeople. Suppose that a data warehouse user wants to investigate the relationship of sales performance to sales bonuses. At first glance, it would seem that all that needs to be done is to sum the order amounts for each salesperson and compare the total to the bonus. The following SQL code will accomplish that task:

```
SELECT      SPName, Sum(OrderAmount), Sum(BonusAmount)
FROM        ORDER, BONUS
WHERE       ORDER.SPNum = BONUS.SP#
GROUP BY    SpNum
```

(As an aside, the typical data warehouse user probably does not know sufficient SQL to write this code, so it needs to be written for him or her or provided indirectly through some type of graphical query interface.)

FIGURE 15-20

Categories of Requirements for a Data Warehouse

- Queries and reports with variable structure
- User-specified data aggregation
- User-specified drill down
- Graphical outputs
- Integration with domain-specific programs

FIGURE 15-21

Example Extracts of Order and Bonus Data

ORDER Table

SPNum	OrderNumber	OrderAmount
100	1000	$12,000
200	1200	$17,000
100	1400	$13,500
300	1600	$11,335

BONUS Table

SP#	SPName	BonusAmount
100	Mary Smith	$3,000
200	Fred Johnson	$2,500
300	Laura Jackson	$3,250

Now, suppose that these data were correct when extracted, and further suppose that they were obtained from two different information systems—order processing and accounts payable. Because they were obtained from two different systems, it is unknown whether the timing of the data is consistent. It might be that the order data were correct as of the last Friday of the month, but that the bonus check data were correct as of the last day of the month. There is nothing in the data to indicate that difference; in fact, no one may note that such a difference exists. It may have a substantial impact on the results of the analysis, however.

In addition to timing differences, there can also be differences in the underlying domains. Consider the SALESPERSON and REGION tables shown in Figure 15-22, and suppose that someone wants to produce a report of total sales for each region. To do that, the following SQL needs to be executed:

SELECT   SalesRegion, Sum(TotalSales)

FROM   REGION, SALESPERSON

WHERE   REGION.SalesRegion = SALESPERSON.Region

GROUP BY   SalesRegion

For the data shown, the result of this query will be a table having three rows; one each for the NW, NE, and SO sales regions. Because neither SE nor SW regions had a match in REGION, they were omitted from the join, and the sales from those regions will not appear in the result. This is most likely not what the user intended.

In actuality, between 2000 and 2001, this business changed its sales territories by merging the SE and SW sales regions into the SO region. Hence, all of the sales for salespeople in the SE and SW regions should have been added to the SO row in the query result. Put in database terms, the underlying domain of SalesRegion and Region are different. The domain of SalesRegion is the set of current regions; the domain of Region is the name of the region in which the sale occurred, at the time of the sale.

For the small amounts of data shown in Figures 15-21 and 15-22, these problems are obvious. If, however, there were thousands of rows of data, such problems could slip past the analyst, and incorrect information would be provided to the decision-making process.

FIGURE 15-22

Salesperson and Region Data for Two Years

SALESPERSON Table

SPName	Region	Year	TotalSales
Johnson	SO	2000	$175,998
Wu	NW	2000	$223,445
O'Connor	NE	2000	$337,665
Abernathy	SE	2000	$276,889
Lopez	SW	2000	$334,557
Johnson	SO	2001	$225,998
Wu	NW	2001	$276,445
O'Connor	NE	2001	$389,737
Abernathy	SO	2001	$362,768
Lopez	SO	2001	$419,334

REGION Table

SalesRegion	Manager
NW	Allen
NE	Brendlmann
SO	Currid

To solve this problem, metadata must be created that describe both the timing and the domains of the source data. These metadata must be made easily accessible to the users of the data warehouse, and those users need to be trained on the importance of considering such issues.

Tool Integration Another serious problem for data warehouses concerns the integration of various tools that the users need. The paradigms of different products in different product categories are usually different. DBMS products are table-oriented, OLAP products are cube-oriented; spreadsheets are spreadsheet-oriented, financial planning packages are plan-oriented, and so on. As a result, the user interfaces in the products are dissimilar. Users may need substantial training to learn how to use several products from several categories, and they often have neither the time nor the inclination to learn them.

Even more serious, the process for exporting and importing data across products from different categories may be difficult. Consider the spreadsheet shown in Figure 15-23(a). This spreadsheet contains data about three themes: Departments, Managers, and Employees. To import this spreadsheet into a normalized database, each of the themes will need to be allocated to separate tables like those shown in Figure 15-23(b). If the normalization is not done, considerable duplicated data will result, as described in Chapter 4. The typical data warehouse user, however, does not understand the need for normalization nor have any idea about how to do it.

Finally, when products are acquired from different vendors, it is often difficult to get to the source of problems when they occur. For example, the vendor of the product that is exporting data may believe that a problem in the export/import process is due to the product that is importing the data, and the vendor of the product that is importing the data may claim the opposite. Because vendors are not experienced in using one another's products, nor are they motivated to encourage the use of other companies' offerings, technical support can be a nightmare.

Missing Warehouse Data-Management Tools Although there are many products and tools for extracting data from data sources and many tools for end-user query/reporting and data analysis, at present there is a lack of tools for managing the data warehouse itself. If the data warehouse consisted only of extracts from relational databases, and if the problems of timing and domain differences could be solved with training and procedures, an off-the-shelf DBMS could be used to manage the data warehouse resources. In most instances, however, this is not the case.

Most data warehouses contain extracts from databases, files, spreadsheets, images, and external data sources. Because this is the case, these resources cannot be readily managed by a commercial DBMS, so the organization creating the data warehouse must write its own software. Usually, this software has a commercial DBMS at its core, and the

	FIGURE 15–23	

Example of Conceptual Difference Between Spreadsheet and Database Products

EmpNumber	EmpName	DeptNum	Manager	ManagerPhone	DeptCode
1000	Wu	10	Murphy	232-1000	A47
2000	O'Connor	20	Joplin	244-7788	D87
3000	Abernathy	10	Murphy	232-1000	A47
4000	Lopez	20	Joplin	244-7788	D87

(a)

EMPLOYEE(EmpNumber, EmpName, *DeptNum*)

DEPARTMENT(DeptNum, DeptCode, *Manager*)

MANAGER(Manager, ManagerPhone)

(b)

in-house data warehouse staff develops the additional features and functions necessary to manage the data warehouse resources.

The management of metadata presents another similar problem. Few DBMS data dictionaries have sufficient capability to meet the metadata needs of the data warehouse. As stated, users need to know not only what's in the data warehouse, but also where it came from, what its timing was, what the underlying domains of the data were, what assumptions were made when the data were extracted, and so forth. Data warehouse personnel need to write their own metadata-management software to augment the capabilities of the DBMS and other data dictionary products that they have.

Writing data-management software is difficult and expensive. After it is written, it must be supported. The vendors of the extraction programs and the data-analysis programs will change their products, and any in-house developed software that uses them will need to be altered to conform to new interfaces. Further, the users' requirements will change, and this will necessitate adding new programs that will then need to be integrated with the data warehouse-management software.

Ad Hoc Nature of Requirements Data warehouses exist to support management decision-making. Although a good portion of management decisions is regular and recurring, many other decisions are of an ad hoc nature. Questions such as the following are not regular and recurring: Should we combine sales territories? Sell a product line? Consolidate warehouses? Adopt new Internet-based sales and marketing strategies?

Computer systems, like bureaucracies, are slow and expensive to set up, are relatively inflexible, and work best with needs that follow a pattern. For that reason, such systems excel at tasks such as order entry and reservations processing. It is most difficult, however, to design systems that readily respond to changing needs and requirements on an ad hoc basis. Thus, data warehouses have the most success with applications in which the variance in requirements follows a pattern. If a new requirement is similar in structure to an earlier one—that is, "consolidating the northern sales region will be like the process we followed when consolidating the southern region"—the data warehouse probably can respond in a timely fashion. If not, considerable time, expense, and anguish probably need to be expended to meet the requirements.

Data Marts

Because of the challenges just described, some organizations have decided to limit the scope of the warehouse to more manageable chunks. A **data mart** is a facility akin to a data warehouse, but for a much smaller domain. Data marts can be restricted to a particular type of input data, to a particular business function, or to a particular business unit or geographic area.

Restricting a data mart to a particular type of data (for example, database and spreadsheets) makes the management of the data warehouse simpler, and probably means that an off-the-shelf DBMS product can be used to manage the data warehouse. Metadata are also simpler and easier to maintain.

A data mart that is restricted to a particular business function, such as marketing analysis, may have many types of data and metadata to maintain, but all of those data serve the same type of user. Tools for managing the data warehouse and for providing data to the users can be written with an eye toward the requirements that marketing analysts are likely to have.

Finally, a data mart that is restricted to a particular business unit or geographic area may have many types of input and many types of users, but the amount of data to be managed is less than for the entire company. There will also be fewer requests for service, so the data warehouse resources can be allocated to fewer users.

Figure 15-24 summarizes the scope of the alternatives for sharing data that we have addressed in this chapter. Data downloading is the smallest and easiest alternative. Data are extracted from operational systems and delivered to particular users for specific pur-

FIGURE 15–24

Continuum of Enterprise Data Sharing

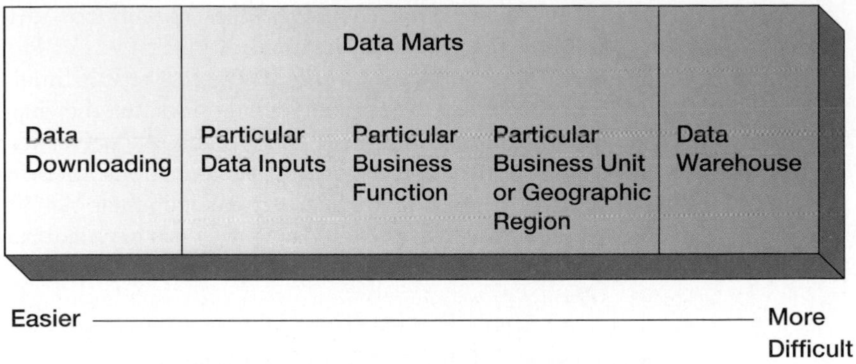

Data Downloading	Data Marts			Data Warehouse
	Particular Data Inputs	Particular Business Function	Particular Business Unit or Geographic Region	

Easier ———————————————————————— More Difficult

poses. The downloaded data are provided on a regular and recurring basis, so the structure of the application is fixed, the users are well trained, and problems such as timing and domain inconsistencies are unlikely to occur because users gain experience working with the same data. At the other extreme, a data warehouse provides extensive types of data and services for both recurring and ad hoc requests. Data marts fall in the middle. As we move from left to right in this figure, the alternatives become more powerful, but also more expensive and difficult to create.

▷ DATA ADMINISTRATION

An organization's data are as much a resource as are its plant, equipment, and financial assets. Data are time-consuming and expensive to acquire, and they have utility beyond operations. Information derived from data can be used to assess the effectiveness of personnel, products, and marketing programs; and to determine trends in customers' preferences, buying behavior, and so forth. It can be used to simulate the effect of changes in products, sales strategies, and territories. The list of potential applications is so long that, in fact, data often serve to establish and maintain the organization's competitive advantage. Unfortunately, however, as long as the data are locked in operational databases, their utility is limited.

Because of the potential value of the organizational data resource, many organizations have established offices of data administration. The purpose of these offices is not just to guard and protect the data, but also to ensure that they are used effectively.

In some ways, data administration is to data what the controller is to money. The responsibility of a controller is to ensure not only that financial assets are protected and accounted for, but also that they are effectively used. Storing an organization's money in a vault can protect it, but it will not be effectively used. Instead, it must be invested in ways that advance the organization's goals and objectives. Similarly, with data administration, simply protecting the data is not enough. Data administration must also try to increase the utility of the organization's data.

Need for Data Administration

To understand the need for data administration, consider the analogy of a university library. The typical university library contains hundreds of thousands of books, journals, magazines, government reports, and so forth; but they offer no utility while they are on the bookshelves. To be useful, they must be made available to people who have an interest in and need for them.

Clearly, the library must have some means of describing its collection so that potential users can determine what is available. At first glance, this might seem like a trivial problem. You might say, "Well, build a card catalog." But much work must be done to be able to do that. How should the library's works be identified? How should they be described? Even more basic, what constitutes a work? How can we accommodate different ways of identifying works (ISBN, Dewey Decimal System, government report number)? How do we help people find things that they may not know exist?

Other complications arise. Suppose that the university is so large that it has several libraries. In this case, how are the collections to be managed as one resource? Furthermore, some departments may maintain their own libraries. Are these to be made part of the university system? Many professors have extensive personal libraries. Should these be part of the system?

Challenges of Data Administration

The library analogy does not go far enough, however, because organizational data administration is considerably more difficult than library administration. First, it is not at all clear what constitutes a "work." Libraries contain books, periodicals, and so forth, but organizational data come in myriads of formats. Organizations have traditional data records, but they also have documents, spreadsheets, graphics and illustrations, technical drawings, and audio and video files. How should all of them be described? What are the basic categories of organizational data? These questions are important because their answers determine how the data will be organized, cataloged, managed, protected, and accessed.

Most organizations have many names for the same thing. For instance, a telephone number can be described as a PhoneNumber, Phone, TelephoneNumber, EmployeePhone, or DeptPhone. Which of these names is preferable? When a graphic designer places a telephone number on a new form, what label should he or she use? When a programmer writes a new program, what name should he or she use for the program variable that holds the telephone number? When a user wants to query for a customer area code while developing a buying trend analysis, which name should she use in her query?

There also are many ways of representing the data element. A phone number can be represented as a 10-digit integer, a 10-digit text field, a 13-digit text field in the form *(nnn)nnn-nnnn,* a 12-digit text field in the form *nnn-nnn-nnnn,* or in still other formats. Which of these should be allowed? Which, if any, should be the standard?

Such differences between organizational data and library materials are minuscule, however, when compared with the next difference: People must be able to change organizational data.

Consider what would happen at the library if people checked out books, wrote in them, tore out pages, added pages, and then put the books back on the shelves. Or, even worse, suppose that someone checked out three books, made changes in all three, checked them back in, and told the librarian, "Either change all of these or none of them."

Because data are a shared asset, limits must be placed on processing rights and responsibilities. For example, when an employee leaves the company, his or her records cannot be immediately deleted; they need to be maintained for several years for management reporting and tax purposes. Hence, one department cannot delete data from the database just because that department is finished with them. The office of data administration needs to help define users' processing rights and responsibilities. This role is similar to that described for database administration in Chapter 9; there, however, the scope was a particular database. Here, the scope is the entire organization.

In addition to all of these operationally oriented challenges, there are organizational issues. For example, data and processing rights can mean organizational power; hence, changes in data control can mean changes in power. Thus, behind the tasks of data administration lie all sorts of political issues. A discussion of these is beyond the scope of

FIGURE 15–25

Challenges of Data
Administration

- Many types of data exist.
- Basic categories of data are not obvious.
- The same data can have many names.
- The same data can have many descriptions and formats.
- Data are changed—often concurrently.
- Political-organizational issues complicate operational issues.

this text, but they are important nonetheless. The challenges for data administration are summarized in Figure 15-25.

Functions of Data Administration

Because of the challenges just described, data administration is complex. To protect the data asset while at the same time increasing its utility to the organization, several different functions or tasks must be performed. As shown in Figure 15-26, these activities can be grouped into several different categories.

Marketing   First and foremost, data administration is responsible for declaring its existence and selling its services to the rest of the organization. Employees need to know that data administration exists; they need to know that there are policies, standards, and guidelines that pertain to organizational data and the reasons for them; and they need to be given reasons for respecting and following data administration rules, guidelines, and restrictions.

FIGURE 15–26

Functions of Data
Administration

Marketing
- Communicate existence of data administration to organization.
- Explain reason for existence of standards, policies, and guidelines.
- Describe in a positive light the services provided.

Data Standards
- Establish standard means for describing data items. Standards include name, definition, description, processing restrictions, and so forth.
- Establish data proponents.

Data Policies
- Establish organizationwide data policy. Examples are security, data proponency, and distribution.

Forum for Data Conflict Resolution
- Establish procedures for reporting conflicts.
- Provide means for hearing all perspectives and views.
- Have authority to make decision to resolve conflict.

Return on Organization's Data Investment
- Focus attention on value of data investment.
- Investigate new methodologies and technologies.
- Take proactive attitude toward information management.

Data administration must be a service function, and the users must perceive it in that way. Thus, data administration activities must be communicated to the organization in a positive, service-providing light. Employees must believe that they have something to gain from data administration. Otherwise, the function becomes all cost and no benefit to the users, and it will be ignored.

Data Standards   For organizational data to be managed effectively, they must be organized coherently. If each department, function, or employee were to choose a different definition for a data item or for the means by which data items are to be named or described, the result would be chaos. It would be impossible even to compile an inventory of data, let alone manage it. Consequently, many organizations decide that important data items will be described in a standard way. For example, data administration may decide that every data item of importance to the organization will be described by a standard name, definition, description, set of processing restrictions, and the like. After this structure is determined, the next question is: Who will set the values of these standard descriptions? For example, who will decide the standard name or standard-processing restrictions?

In many organizations, the data administration group does not determine the standard descriptions. Instead, each item is assigned a **data proponent,** a department or other organizational unit in charge of managing that data item. The proponent is given the responsibility for establishing and maintaining the official organizational definitions for the data items assigned to it. Even though the data administration group may be the proponent of some data items, most proponents come from other departments.

You may encounter the term *data owner,* which is generally used in the same way that the term *data proponent* is used in this text. We avoid the term here because it implies a degree of propriety that does not exist. Both legally and practically, the organization is the one and only owner of the data. Although some group or groups have a legitimate claim to a greater degree of authority over particular data than others do, these groups do not own those data. Hence, we use the term *data proponent,* instead.

To summarize, the foundation of data administration is a system of data standards. The data administration group is responsible for working with users and management to develop a workable system of standards, which must be documented and communicated to the organization by some effective means. Procedures for assessing the employees' compliance with the standards also must be established.

Data Policies   Another group of data administration functions concerns data policies. To illustrate the need for such policies, first consider data security. Every organization has data that are proprietary or sensitive, and data administration is responsible for developing a security system to protect them. Questions such as the following need to be addressed: What security schemes should be put in place? Does the organization need a multilevel security system similar to that of the military? Or would a simpler system suffice? The security policy must also decide what is required for people to have access to sensitive data and what agreements they must sign to do so. What about employees of other organizations? Should sensitive data be copied? How should employees be trained with regard to security? What should be done when security procedures are violated?

A second type of data policy concerns data proponents and processing rights. What does being a data proponent mean? What rights does the proponent have that other groups do not? Who decides who will become a data proponent, and how can this be changed?

A third example of the need for data policy concerns the distribution of data, such as whether official data should be distributed on more than one computer; and if so, which—if any—should be the official copy? What processing should be allowed on distributed data? Should data that have been distributed be returned to the official data store? If so, what checks must there be to validate them before accepting them?

Forum for Data Conflict Resolution   To be effective, organizational data must be shared, but humans have difficulty sharing. Consequently, the organization must be prepared to address disputes regarding data proponents, processing restrictions, and other matters.

The first responsibility of data administration in this regard is to establish procedures for reporting conflicts. When one user's or group's needs conflict with another's, the groups need a way to make their conflict known in an orderly manner. After the conflict has been acknowledged, established procedures should allow all involved parties to present their case. Data administration staff, perhaps in conjunction with the data proponents involved, then must resolve the conflict. This scenario assumes that the organization has granted to data administration the authority to make and enforce the resulting decision.

Data administration provides a forum for resolving conflicts that apply to the entire organization. Database administration also provides a forum for resolving conflicts, but only those that pertain to a particular database.

Increasing the Return on the Organization's Data Investment
A final function for data administration is the need to increase the organization's return on its data investment. Data administration is the department that asks questions such as the following: Are we getting what we should be getting from our data resource? If so, can we get more? If not, why not? Is it all worthwhile? This function involves all of the others: It includes marketing, the establishment of standards or policies, conflict resolution, and so forth. Sometimes, this function also means investigating new techniques for storing, processing, or presenting data; new methodologies and technology; and the like.

The successful fulfillment of this role requires a *proactive* attitude toward information management. Relevant questions are whether we can use information to increase our market position, our economic competitiveness, and our overall net worth. Data administration must work closely with the organization's planning and development departments to anticipate rather than just react to the need for new information requirements.

Finally, data must be made available to their potential users. Availability means not only making it technically feasible for a highly motivated and skilled person to access data; it means that data must be provided to the users via processes that are easy for them to use and in formats that are directly applicable to the work that must be done.

SUMMARY

Teleprocessing is the classic architecture for multi-user database processing. With it, users operate dumb terminals or personal computers that emulate dumb terminals. The communications control program, application programs, DBMS, and operating system all are processed by a single centralized computer. Because all processing is done by a single computer, the user interface of a teleprocessing system is usually simple and primitive.

A client-server system consists of a network of computers, most often connected via a LAN. In nearly all cases, the user computers, called clients, are personal computers; and in most cases, the server computer is also a personal computer, although mainframes can be used. Application programs are processed on the client computer; the DBMS and the data-management portion of the operating system reside on a server.

File-sharing systems also involve networks of computers, and like client-server architectures, they usually consist of micros connected via LANs. The chief difference between file-sharing systems and client-server systems is that the server computer provides fewer services for the user computers. The server, which is called a *file* server and not a *database* server, provides access to files and other resources. Consequently, both the DBMS and the application programs must be distributed to the users' computers.

With a distributed database system, multiple computers process the same database. There are several types of distributed databases: partitioned, nonreplicated; nonpartitioned, replicated; and partitioned, replicated. In general, the greater the degree of partitioning and replication, the greater the flexibility, independence, and reliability will be. At the same time, expense, control difficulty, and security problems increase.

Three types of distributed database processing are the downloading of read-only data, the updating of database data by a designated computer, and the updating of database data by multiple computers. Three types of distributed update conflict can occur: loss of uniqueness, lost updates due to concurrent transactions, and updates of deleted data. If updating is allowed on more than one computer, such problems must be resolved.

Coordination of distributed atomic transactions is difficult and requires a two-phase commit. The OLE Distributed Transaction Server and Java Enterprise Beans are two technologies for dealing with these problems.

With the advent of powerful personal computers, it became possible to download substantial amounts of enterprise data to users for local processing. Users can query and report on downloaded data using DBMS products on their own machines. In most cases, users are not allowed to update and return data because doing so could create data integrity problems. Even when downloaded data are not updated and returned, problems of coordination, consistency, access control, and possible computer crime can occur. A Web server can be used to publish downloaded data.

On Line Analytical Processing (OLAP) is a new way of presenting information. With it, data is viewed in cubes that have axes, dimensions, measures, slices, and levels. Axes refer to the physical structure of the presentation like rows and columns. Dimensions are characteristics of the data that are placed on the axes. Measures are the data values to be displayed. Slices are the attributes of the cube (either dimensions or measures) that are to be held constant in the presentation. Level is an attribute of a dimension that describes its position in a hierarchy.

The term *cube* is used both to refer to the underlying semantic structure that is used to interpret data and to a particular materialization of data in such a semantic structure. Figure 15-15(a) shows one way to define the underlying structure, and Figure 15-15(b) shows one way to define a materialization of a cube structure.

ROLAP, MOLAP, and HOLAP are three of the seven dwarves in OLAP land. Proponents of ROLAP say that a relational DBMS with extensions is sufficient to meet OLAP requirements; proponents of MOLAP say a specialized multidimensional processor is necessary; and proponents of HOLAP want to use both.

Microsoft has extended OLE DB and ADO for OLAP. OLE DB for OLAP includes a dataset object; ADO MD has new objects for processing dataset objects in ways similar to recordset objects. The new Pivot Table Service has been added to Office 2000/XP and Windows 2000/XP. Microsoft's architecture moves much OLAP processing to client computers; whether this will be acceptable for the processing of data on enterprise servers is as yet unknown.

A data warehouse is a store of enterprise data that is designed to facilitate management decision-making. A data warehouse stores extracts of operational databases, files, images, recordings, photos, external data, and other data; and makes these data available to users in a format that is useful to them.

The components of a data warehouse are data-extraction tools, data extracts, metadata, one or more DBMS products, in-house-developed warehouse data-management tools, data delivery programs, user-analysis tools, user training, and warehouse consultants. Typical requirements for a data warehouse include variable-structure queries and reports; user-specified data aggregation; drill-down, graphical outputs; and integration with domain-specific programs.

Data warehouses must overcome several important challenges. For one, when data are integrated, inconsistencies can develop due to timing and domain differences. Also, because of the many tools required in a data warehouse, tools will have different user interfaces and inconsistent means of importing and exporting data, and it may be difficult to obtain technical support.

Another challenge is that there is a lack of tools for managing the data warehouse itself. The organization may have to develop its own tools for managing nonrelational data and for maintaining appropriate metadata. Such development is difficult and expensive. Finally, the nature of many requests on the data warehouse is ad hoc; such requests are difficult to satisfy. As a result, some organizations have developed limited-scope warehouses called data marts.

Data are an important organizational asset, one that can support both operations and management decision-making. The purpose of the office data administration is not just to guard and protect the data asset, but also to ensure that it is effectively used. One of the most important functions of data administration is to document the contents of the organization's data asset. This is a complicated task because data occur in many different formats in many different places in the organization. Data administration needs to help set organizational standards for names and formats of data items and also to define organizational processing rights and responsibilities. Finally, data are an asset, and their use can mean power; because of this, data administration must deal with organizational and political issues.

The specific functions of data administration include marketing its services, facilitating data standards and identifying data proponents, ensuring that appropriate data policies are established, and providing a forum for conflict resolution. All of these functions are aimed at the goal of increasing the return on the organization's data investment.

GROUP I QUESTIONS

15.1   List the architectures that are used to support multi-user databases.

15.2   Sketch the architecture of a teleprocessing system. Name and identify the computer(s) and programs involved, and explain which computer processes which programs.

15.3   Why is the users' interface on teleprocessing applications generally character-oriented and primitive?

15.4   Sketch the architecture of a client-server system. Name and identify the computer(s) and programs involved, and explain which computer processes which programs.

15.5   What types of processing hardware are used with client-server systems?

15.6   How many servers can a client-server system have? What restrictions apply to the servers?

15.7   Sketch the architecture of a file-sharing system. Name and identify the computer(s) and programs involved, and explain which computer processes which programs.

15.8   Explain how the processing of the following SQL query would differ in a client-server system and in a file-sharing system:

```
SELECT      StudentName, ClassName
FROM        STUDENT, GRADE
WHERE       STUDENT.StudentNumber = GRADE.StudentNumber
AND         GRADE.Grade = 'A'
```

Assume that the database contains two tables:

STUDENT (<u>StudentNumber</u>, StudentName, StudentPhone)

GRADE (<u>ClassNumber</u>, *StudentNumber*, Grade)

Also assume that the primary and foreign keys have indexes.

15.9 Explain why file-sharing systems are seldom used for high-volume, transaction-processing applications.

15.10 Define the terms *partitioned* and *replicated* as they pertain to distributed database applications.

15.11 Explain the difference between a vertical fragment and a horizontal fragment.

15.12 Explain the differences in the four types of distributed databases in Figure 15-5.

15.13 Name and describe three techniques for supporting distributed-database processing.

15.14 Describe three types of distributed update conflict.

15.15 What is the purpose of two-phase commit?

15.16 Summarize the coordination problem in processing downloaded databases.

15.17 Summarize the consistency problem in processing downloaded databases.

15.18 Summarize the access-control problem in processing downloaded databases.

15.19 Why is computer crime a risk when processing downloaded databases?

15.20 Sketch the components of a system that uses a Web server to publish downloaded data.

15.21 What is an OLAP cube? Give an example other than the one in Figure 15-12.

15.22 Explain the difference between an OLAP axis and an OLAP dimension.

15.23 What is the measure of an OLAP cube?

15.24 What does the term *slice* mean in reference to OLAP cubes?

15.25 What is a member of a dimension? Give examples for Time and Location dimensions.

15.26 Explain the use of levels in Figure 15-12.

15.27 Explain the ambiguity in the term *cube*.

15.28 What is the result of the expression CROSSJOIN ({Mary, Lynda}, {Sailing, Skiing})? Of CROSSJOIN ({Sailing, Skiing}, {Mary, Lynda})?

15.29 Give an SQL SELECT statement to produce a cube similar to that in Figure 15-12, except that the rows and columns are reversed and Location is presented before Category (when reading from left to right).

15.30 Explain the difference between the star and the snowflake schemas.

15.31 Define ROLAP, MOLAP, and HOLAP.

15.32 Considering the discussion in this text only, how has OLE been extended for OLAP?

15.33 What does ADO MD stand for, and what is its function?

15.34 Define *data warehouse*.

15.35 How does having a data warehouse compare to processing downloaded data?

15.36 List and describe the components of a data warehouse.

15.37 Explain what it means to change the structure of a query or report rather than change the data in a query or report.

15.38 Give an example, other than one in this book, of a user's need to aggregate data.

15.39 Give an example, other than one in this book, of a user's need to drill down data.

15.40 Explain two sources of data inconsistencies, and give an example of each, other than one in this book.

15.41 Summarize the problems of having tools that use different paradigms and are licensed by different vendors.

15.42 Explain which data warehouse tools must be written in-house.

15.43 Why does the ad hoc nature of data warehouse requests pose a problem?

15.44 What is a data mart, and why would a company develop one?

15.45 List and briefly explain three types of data marts.

15.46 Explain why data are an important organizational asset.

15.47 Describe several example uses of data besides operational systems.

15.48 How is data administration similar to the job of a controller?

15.49 Briefly summarize the necessity for data administration.

15.50 List and briefly explain the challenges of data administration.

15.51 Describe data administration's marketing function.

15.52 What role does data administration take with regard to data standards?

15.53 Define *data proponent*.

15.54 What is the difference between data proponent and data owner?

15.55 Summarize data administration's role in regard to data policy.

15.56 Explain what is involved in establishing a forum for conflict resolution.

15.57 How can data administration help increase the return on an organization's data asset?

GROUP II QUESTIONS

15.58 Consider a company that has a national sales manager and 15 regional salespeople. Each week, the salespeople download sales data from the mainframe and use it to update their sales projections for the next month. When they have done this, they connect via a modem to a server database and store their sales projections into that database. The manager then accumulates the sales data into a company-wide forecast. What problems, issues, and difficulties might exist in this situation in terms of coordination, consistency, access control, and computer crime?

15.59 Consider the enterprise data that exist at your college or university. Does it seem to you that your institution makes good use of its data asset? What ways can you identify that the data asset is used for more than operational processing? Describe ways in which you think your college or university could take advantage of its data asset in the areas of

Student recruitment
Fund-raising
Program planning
Student affairs
Alumni affairs
Other areas

PART VI

Object-Oriented Database Processing

This part consists of one chapter that addresses object-oriented programming and storage with ODBMS. It includes a brief tutorial on object-oriented programming and discussions on Oracle object-relational, on the object extensions to SQL called SQL3, and on an object data management standard called ODMG-93.

This part supplements the discussions of OLE DB, ADO, ADO.NET, and JDBC in Chapters 12-14. Whereas those chapters presented practical matters on using object interfaces to obtain database services, this chapter presents a more conceptual view on the rationale and purpose of object-oriented database processing.

CHAPTER 16

Object-Oriented Database Processing

This chapter addresses the persistent storage of objects created in programming languages such as Java, C#, and C++. As you know, relational databases store data in the form of tables, rows, and columns. As such, relational databases are not well-suited to store objects because objects can contain complex structures of data items and also pointers to other objects. Further, objects include executable statements, or methods; and to make objects persistent, some means must be provided to store those methods as well.

Special-purpose DBMS products called **Object-Oriented DBMS** (or **ODBMS** or sometimes **OODBMS**) were developed in the early 1990s to provide persistent object storage. These products have not been commercially successful, however, because they require that existing data be converted to ODBMS format. Organizations are reluctant to make that conversion because it is very expensive and the gain is not worth the expense.

Object-oriented programming is on the rise, however, and the need for persistent object storage has not disappeared. In response, the traditional DBMS vendors are augmenting the capabilities of their products to allow for object storage as well as traditional relational data storage. Such products are called **object-relational DBMS**, and they are likely to see increased use in the years to come. Oracle, in particular, has developed facilities for object modeling and storage.

Because we do not assume that you are an object-oriented programmer, this chapter begins with a sketch of object-oriented terms and concepts. Then, we will describe alternatives for providing persistent object storage and illustrate Oracle's support for object persistence. Finally, we will survey two important object standards: SQL3 and ODMG–93.

▶ A SKETCH OF OBJECT-ORIENTED PROGRAMMING

Object-oriented programming (**OOP**) is a way of designing and coding programs. OOP is substantially different from traditional programming because it entails a new way of thinking about programming structures. Instead of viewing programs as sequences of instructions to be processed, OOP views programs as sets of data structures that have both data elements and program instructions.

Another way to understand the difference between traditional programming and OOP is that traditional programming is organized around logic first and data second, whereas OOP is organized around data first and logic second. To design a traditional program to create an order, for example, we would first develop a flowchart or pseudo-code of the logic of the ordering process. The data to be processed would be documented as a part of the logic.

When developing an object-oriented program to create an order, we first identify the objects involved; say, ORDER, SALESPERSON, ITEM, and CUSTOMER. We then design those objects as data elements and programs that are shared or *exposed* to one another. Finally, we create a flowchart or pseudo-code of the behaviors of the objects.

OOP Terminology

An OOP object is an **encapsulated structure** having both **attributes** and **methods**. The term **encapsulated** means that it is complete in itself; programs external to an object know nothing of its structure and need to know nothing of its structure. The external appearance of an object is referred to as its **interface**. The interface consists of the attributes and methods that are visible to the outside world. The encapsulated internals of an object are referred to as its **implementation**. The *attributes* of OOP objects are arranged in a particular structure.[1]

OOP objects contain *methods,* or sequences of instructions that the object executes. For example, an OOP object may have a method to display itself, one to create itself, and one to modify a portion of itself. Consider a method that modifies a CUSTOMER object. This method, which is part of the OOP object, is a program; to modify the OOP object, this program contains instructions to obtain data from the user or other source.

---

[1]The term *properties* is sometimes used instead of *attribute*. In the ODMG-93 standard, the term property is used instead of attribute, and attribute is used in a more restricted sense, as you will see. When reading the terms *class*, *type*, *property*, and *attribute*, pay attention to the context because different authors use these terms slightly differently. Here, we will use the terms in a way that is consistent with the source of the topic.

OOP objects interact by calling each other's methods. The CUSTOMER Modify method, for example, invokes other objects' methods to obtain data, perform modifications on itself, and request services. These other objects' methods are called and may invoke yet other methods, and so forth. Because all the objects are encapsulated, none can or need know the structure of any other object. This reduces complexity and promotes effective cohesion.

Many objects have methods in common. To reduce the duplication in programming, objects are subclassed from more general classes. An object, say O_1, that is a subclass of another object, say O_2, **inherits** all the attributes and methods of O_2. For example, an application may have a general class EMPLOYEE with two subtypes: SALESPERSON and ENGINEER. Methods that are common to all three object classes, such as GetPhoneNumber, are made a part of the EMPLOYEE class. The SALESPERSON and ENGINEER subclasses inherit those methods. Hence, when a program issues a call to GetPhoneNumber on either a SALESPERSON or an ENGINEER, the GetPhoneNumber method in EMPLOYEE is invoked. If the application requirements are such that ENGINEERs have a different way of providing phone numbers than other employees, ENGINEER can have a special version of GetPhoneNumber as part of its class. That special version will be called when a program invokes GetPhoneNumber on ENGINEER. This characteristic is called **polymorphism.**

Several terms are commonly used in OOP discussions. The logical structure of an object—its name, attributes, and methods—is called an **object class.** A group of object classes is called an **object class library.** And instances of objects are called **object instances,** or simply **objects.**

Objects are created by calling object constructors—programs that obtain main memory and create the structures necessary to instantiate an object. Object destructors are programs that unbind objects and free memory. Objects can be **transient** or **persistent.** A transient object exists in volatile memory only during the execution of a program. When the program terminates, the object is lost. A persistent object is an object that has been saved to permanent storage, such as to disk. A persistent object survives the execution of a program and can be read back into memory from storage.

The purpose of an ODBMS is to provide persistent object storage. An object is both data and methods; this means that an ODBMS, unlike a traditional DBMS, should store object programs as well as data. Because each object of a given class has the same set of methods, the methods need be stored only once for the class; in contrast, data items must be stored once for each object instance. Figure 16-1 illustrates this point. In point of fact, few ODBMS today provide method persistence, but this is likely to change in the future.

<table>
<tr><td>**FIGURE 16–1**</td><td></td></tr>
<tr><td>**Sample of CUSTOMER Object**</td><td></td></tr>
</table>

CUSTOMER Object Class

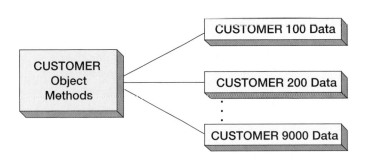

Object methods are stored once for each class
Object data are stored once for each object instance

▶ OOP EXAMPLE

Figures 16-2 and 16-3 present a portion of an object-oriented interface and a sample method. To avoid details unimportant to this discussion, the code is written in a generic form that is consistent with object programming but is not in any particular object-oriented language. Consider this code to be something like pseudo-code for an object program.

Figure 16-2 shows a portion of the interface of several objects used for order processing. Each object has a set of methods and attributes that it exposes. Every object has a constructor (Create) and a destructor (Destroy) method. Some of the methods take parameters; the Assign method of SALESPERSON, for example, takes a pointer to the ORDER object and a value of ZipCode as its parameters. Attributes that are marked with (R) may only be read; attributes marked (RW) may be read or written (changed).

The notation in Figure 16-3 needs explanation. First, the braces { } represent remarks. They are used here to describe the function of program code that needs to be written, but has been left out of this example for brevity or because it is unimportant to this discussion. The Dim statement is used to declare variables and their types, as it does in Basic. LineItem is declared as a structure having the data elements listed in the brackets [ ]. The exclamation point (!) is used as a separator between an object and one of its methods. Thus, CUSTOMER!Find refers to the Find method of the CUSTOMER object. This character is pronounced "bang." A period is used as a separator between an

---

FIGURE 16-2

Sample Objects, Methods, and Attributes

Object	Methods	Attributes
EMPLOYEE	Create Save Destroy ...	Number(R) Name(R) ...
SALESPERSON (subclass of EMPLOYEE)	Create Save Destroy Assign(ORDER, ZipCode) ...	TotalCommission(R) TotalOrders(RW) ...
CUSTOMER	Create Save Destroy Assign(ORDER) Find ...	Name(R) Phone(R) ZipCode(R) CurrentBalance(RW) ...
ITEM	Create Save Destroy Find(Number) Take(ORDER, Quantity) Put(ORDER, Quantity) Find ...	Number(R) Name(R) Description(R) Price ...
ORDER	Create Save Destroy Print ...	Number(R) Date(R) Total(R) CustomerName(R) SalespersonName(R) ...

FIGURE 16–3

Segment of an Object-Oriented Program

```
ORDER!Create method
Dim CustObj as object, SPObj as object, ItemObj as object
Dim OrderTotal as Currency, OrderDate as Date, OrderNumber as Number
Dim LineItem as Structure
         [
         ItemNumber as Number,
         ItemName as Text(25),
         ItemQuantity as Count,
         QuantityBackOrdered as Count,
         ExtendedPrice as Currency
         ]

         {Get CustomerName from some source}
         Set CustObj = CUSTOMER!Find (CustomerName)
         If CustObj = Nothing then
                  Set CustObj = CUSTOMER!Create(CustomerName)
         End If

         CustObj!Assign(Me)
         Set SPObj = SALESPERSON!Assign(Me, CustObj.ZipCode)

         {Get ItemNumber, Quantity of first ITEM from some source}
         Me.OrderTotal = 0
         While Not ItemNumber.EOF

                  Me.LineItem!Create
                  Me.LineItem.ItemNumber = ItemNumber

                  Set ItemObj = ITEM!Find (ItemNumber)
                  {process problem if ITEM not exist}

                  Me.LineItem.ItemName = ItemObj.Name
                  Me.LineItem.Quantity = ITEM!Take (Quantity)
                  If Me.LineItem.Quantity <> Quantity Then
                          Me.LineItem.QuantityBackOrdered = Quantity - Me.LineItem.Quantity
                  End If

                  Me.LineItem.ExtendedPrice = Me.LineItem.Quantity* ITEM.Price
                  Me.OrderTotal = Me.OrderTotal + Me.LineItem.ExtendedPrice

                  ItemObj!Save
                  Me.LineItem!Save
                  {Get ItemNumber, Quantity of next ITEM from some source
                  assume the source sets EOF to true when there are no more}
         While End

         SPObj.TotalOrders = SPObj.TotalOrders + Me.OrderTotal
         CustObj.CurrentBalance = CustObj.CurrentBalance + Me.OrderTotal

         SPObj!Save
         CustObj!Save
         ME!Save
End ORDER!Create
```

object and one of its attributes. Thus, CustObj.ZipCode refers to the ZipCode attribute of the object pointed to by CustObj.

Two keywords are also used in Figure 16-3. **Nothing** is a special value of an object pointer that is used to represent a null value. In this figure, the following expression means to compare the value of the object variable CustObj to the null object pointer:

If CustObj = Nothing

Me is an object pointer that references the object executing the code. When the code in Figure 16-3 is run, it will be run by an instance of the ORDER object because it is an ORDER method. Me refers to the particular ORDER object that is executing the code.

The ORDER!Create method begins by obtaining data about the name of the customer placing the order; it is unimportant to our purposes how this value is obtained—it might be from a text box on a form. The Find method of CUSTOMER is then invoked to find a customer having the given name and to set a pointer to the object that has been found. The particulars of how an instance is found are encapsulated in CUSTOMER!Find, and we do not know how the selection is made, what happens if there is more than one customer that has that name, or other details.

The result of this operation is to set CustObj to either the value of a valid pointer to a CUSTOMER object or to the special value Nothing, which is the null pointer. If CustObj is null, CustObj is set to a pointer to a new CUSTOMER object created by CUSTOMER!Create. As shown, the code assumes that a pointer to a valid customer object is returned at this point. In fact, CustObj should be checked again to see if it is null, but for brevity, we will omit all such checking in the rest of this program segment.

CUSTOMER exposes a method, Assign, which is to be called to assign a CUSTOMER to an ORDER. Because of encapsulation, we do not know what the Assign method does, but we do call it and pass Me, the pointer to the executing object. In fact, in this application, the Assign method is an example of what is called a **callback.** ORDER!Create is giving a pointer to itself to CUSTOMER so that CUSTOMER can keep track of which ORDERs it has. One reason for doing this is that when a CUSTOMER object is to be destroyed, it can call all ORDERs that are linked to it before it departs. In that way, ORDER can destroy its pointer to CUSTOMER when that pointer becomes invalid. There are many other uses for callbacks, as well.

Next, ORDER!Create sets SPObj to a SALESPERSON object. We are passing the value of the customer's ZipCode, so it would seem that ZipCode has something to do with how a salesperson is assigned to us. Again, because of encapsulation, we do not know how this is done, however. By hiding the allocation methodology, the SALESPERSON object is free to change its allocation method without disturbing this or any other program's logic. In fact, no code in Figure 16-3 would need to be changed if SALESPERSON.Assign started using phases of the moon to allocate salespeople!

The next section of code fills in line item values. Observe that the keyword Me is used to refer to local data items. (In fact, in most OO languages, Me would be assumed and would not be necessary; we put it here for explicitness.) At the start of each repetition of the While loop, storage is allocated for another line item in the method LineItem!Create.

The method ITEM!Take is used to withdraw items from inventory. Notice that the logic assumes that if a number of items less than the quantity requested were allocated, the balance of the items has been backordered. Also, observe that the changed ITEM is saved after each line item has been processed. Also, unlike with CUSTOMER or SALESPERSON, no callback is issued to ITEM. This means that the ITEM objects do not know which ORDERs are connected to them. Apparently, for this application, it is unimportant for the ITEM objects to know which ORDERs are using their data.

The loop continues until there are no more items to be placed on the order. At that point, totals are adjusted in the SALESPERSON and CUSTOMER objects, and both of those objects and Me are saved.

The segment of code in Figure 16-3 is typical of object-oriented code, and it brings to the surface several important issues for object-oriented database systems. In particular, how are the objects to be made persistent?

▶ OBJECT PERSISTENCE

Figure 16-4 summarizes the data structures that exist after an ORDER has been created. In the ORDER object, there are base order data, including ORDER.Number, ORDER.Date, and ORDER.Total; as well as a repeating group for line items that have ItemNumber, ItemName, Quantity, a QuantityBackordered, and Extended Price. In addition, the base order data have a pointer to the CUSTOMER object assigned, a pointer to the SALESPERSON object assigned, and a pointer to each ITEM for each line item. These pointers are part of the ORDER object's data. To make this object persistent, all of this data must be stored. Further, although we do not know their structure, every CUSTOMER, SALESPERSON, and ITEM object must also be stored. The CUSTOMER and SALESPERSON objects are also storing a pointer back to ORDER as a result of the callbacks (!Assign methods) that were issued.

The pointers pose a particular problem. In most object-oriented languages, pointers are some form of in-memory address. Such addresses are valid only during the execution of the program; if the program terminates and is later restarted, the addresses of the objects will be different. Hence, when storing an object, the in-memory pointers need to be transformed into a permanent unique identifier that will be valid for the lifetime of the object, whether it is in memory or not. The process of transforming permanent identifiers into in-memory addresses is called **swizzling.**

Finally, recall that an object is defined as data values plus methods. Thus, to make an object persistent, we must save both the methods and the object values. Unlike data values, however, every object in a given class has the same methods, so we need to store the methods only once for all object instances in the object class. The requirements for object persistence are listed in Figure 16-5.

Objects can be made persistent using traditional file storage, a relational DBMS, or an ODBMS. We now consider each of these.

FIGURE 16–4

Sample Object Data Structures

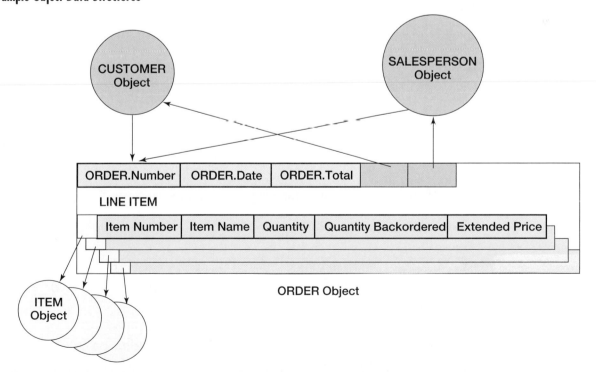

- Save object instance data values
- Convert in-memory object pointers
  to permanent, unique IDs (swizzling)
- Save object class methods

Object Persistence Using Traditional File Storage

Objects can be saved using traditional file storage, but doing so places a large burden on the programmer. Consider the data shown in Figure 16-4. The developer might decide to create one file to contain methods for all of the objects and a second file to contain the data for all of the objects. To do this, a generalized data structure needs to be developed to pack the methods and data into the files and to retrieve them when necessary. Figure 16-6 shows an example of such a file for storing just the data items. (Another needs to be developed to store the methods.)

To use such a file, the programmer writes code in the Save methods to pack and unpack object data in these records, to find objects on demand, to manage unused file space, and so forth. Also, the developer needs to devise and implement swizzling and deswizzling algorithms. Further, there is a bootstrap problem. All methods are stored in files, including the methods that store and read methods. How is the method that reads the first method to be obtained?

All of these problems are surmountable; they have been solved in operating system file-processing subsystems for many years. But, that is just the point. Such programming is slow, tedious, risky, and difficult; and it has already been done for traditional file processing. Why should such programming need to be done one more time?

Because of these problems, traditional file storage is viable for object persistence only when the application has a few simple objects whose structure does not change. Few business applications fall into this category.

Object Persistence Using Relational DBMS

Another approach to object persistence is to use commercial relational DBMS products. This approach places a smaller burden on the developer than traditional file processing because basic file management issues such as record allocation, indexing, space management, and so forth are handled by the DBMS. The data-management tasks left to the programmer include defining relational structures to represent the objects and writing the code to interface with the DBMS to get and put objects and to swizzle pointers.

Figure 16-7 shows the tables needed to store ORDER, LINEITEM, CUSTOMER, SALESPERSON, and ITEM objects. We've seen this design before. The only new element is a table to store object methods; this table contains a memo field that stores the method code.

Relational databases represent relationships via foreign keys. This means that the application programmer must devise some means to use foreign keys to make relationships persistent. The most common way of doing this is to code the creation of a unique

RecordNumber	RecordCode	Contents	Link
1	ORDER	ORDER 100 data	4
2	SALESPERSON	SALESPERSON Jones data	null
3	CUSTOMER	CUSTOMER 10000 data	null
4	LINEITEM	LineItem of ORDER 100 data	5
5	LINEITEM	LineItem of ORDER 100 DATA	null
...	...	...	...

EMPLOYEE (<u>Number</u>, Name,...)

SALESPERSON (<u>*Number*</u>, TotalCommission, TotalOrders,...)

CUSTOMER (<u>Name</u>, Phone, ZipCode, CurrentBalance,...)

ITEM (<u>Number</u>, Name, Description, Price,...)

ORDER (<u>Number</u>, Date, Total, *SALESPERSON.Number*, *CUSTOMER.Name*...)

LINEITEM (<u>*ORDER.Number*</u>, <u>*ITEM.Number*</u>, ItemName, ItemQuantity,
            QuantityBackOrdered, ExtendedPrice,...)

METHODS (<u>ObjectName</u>, <u>MethodName</u>, MethodCode)

ID in the object's constructor method. This ID can be stored in the object's base table and exposed as a read-only property. Objects that need to link to the object can save the ID value. This strategy creates the problem that when an object is destroyed, it must notify all objects that are linked to it so that they can remove the pointer to the soon-to-be-destroyed object and take other action as appropriate. This is one reason for having callbacks like those shown in the Assign methods in Figure 16-3.

Object-oriented thinking and design bury relationships in context. Thus, when an ORDER object assigns itself to a SALESPERSON, it is concerned only with its side of that relationship. If the ORDER wants to bind to many SALESPEOPLE, it does so. ORDER has no idea whether a SALESPERSON has a relationship to one or many ORDERs. Such knowledge is encapsulated in the SALESPERSON object and is no part of the ORDER logic.

This characteristic is either an advantage or a disadvantage, depending on how you think about it. Suppose that an ORDER can have several SALESPEOPLE and that a SALESPERSON can have many ORDERs. In database parlance, ORDER and SALESPERSON have an N:M relationship. Consequently, in the relational database world, an intersection table is defined to hold the identifiers of the ORDERs and SALESPEOPLE that are related to one another.

In the object world, SALESPERSON knows it has many ORDERs, and ORDER knows it has many SALESPEOPLE, but they do not know about each other. Hence, the data structures for carrying the relationship are separated. ORDER will contain storage for many links to SALESPERSON, and SALESPERSON will contain storage for many links to ORDER. The sets of links will be isolated from each other.

Does this matter? No, not as long as there are no errors in the object processing. But there is risk because the object links are separate but not independent. If ORDER 1000 is linked to SALESPERSON A, SALESPERSON A is linked to ORDER 1000 by definition. In the relational DBMS world, deleting the row from one side deletes it from the other side automatically because the relationship is carried in a row of an intersection table. But in the object world, the relationship could be deleted on one side but not on the other. Thus, ORDER 1000 might be linked to SALESPERSON A, but SALESPERSON A might not be linked to ORDER 1000. Clearly, this is an error and should not be allowed to occur, but it is possible if the relationships are defined from a purely object-oriented perspective.

Using a relational DBMS for object persistence is less work for the developer than using traditional file structures. There is still the need, however, for the developer to convert the objects into a relational design, to write SQL (or other code), to get and place the objects using the DBMS, and to swizzle. ODBMS are designed to accomplish these tasks.

Object Persistence Using ODBMS

The third alternative for object persistence is to use an ODBMS. Such products are purpose-built for object persistence and hence save the most work for the application programmer.

An ODBMS is designed to be integrated with an object-oriented language. Thus, no special structures, such as SQL, need be embedded in the application code. For the example in Figure 16-4, it is possible that the Save methods are, in fact, methods provided by the ODBMS. Hence, by invoking the Save method, the programmer has invoked the ODBMS.

Further, ODBMS products include a compiler (or are included with the compiler, depending on your point of view) that processes the source code and automatically creates data structures in the object database for storing objects. Hence, unlike with relational database or file processing, the object-oriented programmer need not transform objects into relation or file structures; the ODBMS does that automatically.

Finally, because ODBMSs are designed for object persistence, some form of swizzling is built in. Thus, code like that shown in Figure 16-3 is unaware of the problem. An object obtains a link to another object, and that link is a valid one for all time. If the link takes different forms, the program is unaware of it.

This leads to a characteristic of ODBMS that is called single-level memory. With certain ODBMS, the program (hence, the programmer) need not know whether an object is in memory or not. If ORDER 1000 has a link to SALESPERSON A, ORDER 1000 can use the exposed properties of SALESPERSON A without ever checking to see whether those data are in memory or issuing a read or SQL statement. If SALESPERSON A is in memory, the ODBMS makes the link; if not, the ODBMS reads SALESPERSON A into memory and then makes the link.

Figure 16-8 compares the work required for each of the three alternatives for object persistence. Clearly, an ODBMS provides substantial benefit to the object-oriented programmer, so what can be done to enable their use in a practical setting? We consider one answer to that question in the next section.

▶ OBJECT PERSISTENCE USING ORACLE

Oracle has extended the facilities of its database products to include support for object modeling and persistent object storage. As mentioned, such databases are sometimes called object-relational databases.

As you read this discussion, reflect about the ways that Oracle has grafted object-oriented thinking onto the relational model. Even though in some ways the graft is awkward, it does allow organizations to migrate gradually from relational data storage to object data storage. As mentioned earlier, pure object-oriented ODBMS, which required the abrupt shift from one paradigm to the other, were rejected. In many ways, Oracle has done a masterful job of supporting its current customer base while extending the product to the object world.

FIGURE 16-8

Application Development Work for Object Persistence for Three Alternatives

ODBMS	Relational DBMS	Traditional File Processing
• Invoke ODBMS Save methods	• Convert memory addresses to permanent ID and reverse (swizzling)	• Convert memory addresses to permanent ID and reverse (swizzling)
	• Define relational data structures	• Define file data structures
	• Create SQL (or other code)	• Create object persistence code
	• Embed SQL in program	• Invoke object persistence code
		• Pack and unpack objects into file structures
		• Find objects on demand
		• Manage file space
		• Other file management tasks

This discussion is based on Oracle version 9. These features and functions will certainly be expanded and improved, and you should review the Oracle documentation for newer releases for the latest object-storage features.

Object Types and Collections

To develop persistent storage for objects in Oracle, you first create a TYPE that represents the object. That type can then be used in a relation in any of four different ways. The simplest, called a **column object**, is to use the object type to define a table column. The other ways are to create one of three types of object collection: **variable length arrays**, **nested tables**, and **row objects**. We will consider each in turn.

Column Objects   The following statement defines an object type named *obj_Apartment:*

```
CREATE TYPE obj_Apartment AS OBJECT (
        BuildingName            VARCHAR2(25),
        ApartmentNumber         CHAR(4),
        NumberBedrooms          NUMBER)
/
```

This type has three columns that use built-in Oracle data types. (Recall that the slash tells SQL*Plus to execute the statement just entered. From now on, we will omit showing it at the end of each of these examples.)

The following CREATE statement defines a column object named Location that uses the obj_Apartment object type:

```
CREATE TABLE PERSON (
        Name                VARCHAR (50),
        Location            obj_Apartment)
```

This table can be queried and processed like any relational table. The syntax for insert and update commands is slightly different, however. The following SQL inserts a row into PERSON:

```
INSERT INTO PERSON (Name, Location) VALUES
('Selma Whitbread', obj_Apartment('Eastlake','206', 2));
```

Note the use of the data type name in the values clause. The following SQL updates a row:

```
UPDATE      PERSON
SET         Location=obj_Apartment('Eastlake', '444', 3)
WHERE       Name='Selma Whitebread';
```

Again, note the use of the data type name. Figure 16-9(a) shows the result of a query on this table.

Variable Length Arrays   Variable length arrays are one of three ways to create collections of object types. To understand the use of such arrays, suppose that we want to create a table that contains data for an apartment building. We want to store a surrogate key value, the name of the building, and a list of apartments in the building.

FIGURE 16-9

Example SELECTs for Object Structures (a) Selecting a Column Object; (b) Selecting a Vararray; (c) Selecting a Nested Table and (d) Selecting a Row Object

```
SQL> SELECT * FROM PERSON;

NAME
-,-------------------------------------------------
LOCATION(BUILDINGNAME, APARTMENTNUMBER, NUMBERBEDROOMS)
--------------------------------------------------------
Lynda James
OBJ_APARTMENT('Eastlake', '206 ', 2)

Selma Whitbread
OBJ_APARTMENT('Eastlake', '444 ', 3)
```

(a)

```
SQL> SELECT * FROM BUILDING1;

BUILDINGID NAME
---------- --------------------------------------------
UNITS(APARTMENTNUMBER, NUMBERBEDROOMS)
--------------------------------------------------------------------
        1 Eastlake
APARTMENT_LIST1(APT_UNIT('100 ', 1), APT_UNIT('200 ', 2), APT_UNIT('300 ', 1))

        2 Westview
APARTMENT_LIST1(APT_UNIT('101 ', 1), APT_UNIT('201 ', 2), APT_UNIT('301 ', 1))
```

(b)

```
SQL> SELECT * FROM BUILDING2;

BUILDINGID NAME
---------- --------------------------------------------
UNITS(APARTMENTNUMBER, NUMBERBEDROOMS)
--------------------------------------------------------------------
        1 Eastlake
APARTMENT_LIST2(APT_UNIT('100 ', 1), APT_UNIT('200 ', 2), APT_UNIT('300 ', 1))

        2 Westview
APARTMENT_LIST2(APT_UNIT('101 ', 1), APT_UNIT('201 ', 2), APT_UNIT('301 ', 1))
```

(c)

```
SQL> SELECT * FROM APARTMENTS;

BUILDINGNAME              APAR NUMBERBEDROOMS
------------------------- ---- --------------
Westview                  333               2
Westview                  235               2
```

(d)

To do this, we first create an object for apartment and then assign it to a variable length array, as follows:

```
CREATE TYPE Apt_Unit AS OBJECT (
        ApartmentNumber        char(5),
        NumberBedrooms         int);
CREATE TYPE APARTMENT_LIST1 AS VARRAY(50) OF Apt_Unit;
```

In this case, the type APARTMENT_LIST1 can have up to 50 elements of the Apt_Unit object type.

The following statement creates a table that uses this variable length array:

```
CREATE TABLE        BUILDING1 (
        BuildingID        NUMBER,
        Name              VARCHAR2(50),
        Units             APARTMENT_LIST1);
```

Now, we must use the name of both the array and the elements in the array to insert data into the table, as follows:

```
INSERT INTO BUILDING1 (BuildingID, Name, Units) VALUES
        (1, 'Eastlake',
        APARTMENT_LIST1    (Apt_Unit ('100', 1),
                            Apt_Unit ('200', 2),
                            Apt_Unit ('300', 1)));
```

A normal SELECT statement works to obtain the values of all columns, as long as the WHERE clause does not refer to elements in Apt_Unit. Figure 16-9(b) shows the results of a SELECT * for all rows.

If, however, you want to obtain only values from Apt_Unit, or if you want to use elements of Apt_Unit in a WHERE clause, you must turn the query inside out, as follows:

```
SELECT        ApartmentNumber
FROM          TABLE (
              SELECT UNITS
              FROM BUILDING1
              WHERE Name='Eastlake')
WHERE         ApartmentNumber>100;
```

This query selects ApartmentNumber from UNITS, which is the variable length array. The BUILDING table is processed like a subquery. The result will be a table with an ApartmentNumber column and two rows: 200 and 300.

You cannot update or delete individual rows within a variable array using UPDATE or DELETE statements. You must write a PL/SQL procedure to loop through the array. If you want to use UPDATE and DELETE for this purpose, you must create a nested table instead as shown next.

Nested Tables Nested tables are defined in almost the same way as variable length arrays. The difference between them is that whereas variable length array data are stored with the table in which they are defined, nested table data are stored in a separate table. To create the BUILDING table using nested arrays, use

```
CREATE TYPE APARTMENT_LIST2 AS TABLE OF Apt_Unit;
/
CREATE TABLE      BUILDING2 (
      BuildingID      NUMBER,
      Name            VARCHAR2(50),
      Units           APARTMENT_LIST2)
      NESTED TABLE Units STORE AS UNITS_TABLE;
```

The only difference from the vararray syntax is that the nested table must be named. Here, it is named UNITS_TABLE.

Figure 16-9(c) shows the result of a SELECT * on all rows of BUILDING2; note that it is identical to that from the vararray example. The INSERT and QUERY statements used with nested tables are also identical to those used for vararrays:

```
INSERT INTO BUILDING2 (BuildingID, Name, Units) VALUES
      (1, 'Eastlake',
      APARTMENT_LIST2   (Apt_Unit ('100', 1),
                         Apt_Unit ('200', 2),
                         Apt_Unit ('300', 1)));
```

and

```
SELECT ApartmentNumber
FROM TABLE (
      SELECT      Units
      FROM        BUILDING2
      WHERE       Name='Eastlake')
WHERE ApartmentNumber>100;
```

As promised, however, you can update and delete items in a nested table:

```
UPDATE TABLE (
              SELECT      Units
              FROM        BUILDING2
              WHERE       Name='Eastlake')
SET           NumberBedrooms=5
WHERE         ApartmentNumber=100;
```

and

DELETE FROM TABLE (

    SELECT   Units

    FROM   BUILDING2

    WHERE   Name='Eastlake')

WHERE ApartmentNumber=100;

As you can see, variable length arrays and nested tables are very similar, but there are also differences. For one, as stated, UPDATE and DELETE work only with nested tables. Additionally, variable length arrays have a maximum size, but nested tables do not. Also, Oracle stores variable length array data in line with the table, but nested table data are stored separately. Finally, the order of rows in a variable length array is maintained; with nested tables, the order of rows may change as new rows are added to the nested table.

Row Objects   Row objects are a fourth way to use object types in tables. A row object table is simply a table that contains only objects. For this example, define obj_Apartment as before:

CREATE TYPE obj_Apartment AS OBJECT (

    BuildingName   VARCHAR2(25),

    ApartmentNumber   CHAR(4),

    NumberBedrooms   NUMBER);

Then, the following creates a table of obj_Apartments:

CREATE TABLE APARTMENTS OF obj_Apartment;

Selects, inserts, updates, and deletions of rows in this table can be made using regular SQL syntax. Figure 16-9(d) shows a typical SELECT statement. To insert a new row, for example, use

INSERT INTO APARTMENTS (BuildingName, ApartmentNumber, NumberBedrooms)

VALUES ('Westview', '333',2);

The following updates a row in apartments:

UPDATE APARTMENTS

    Set NumberBedrooms=5

    Where ApartmentNumber='100';

Finally, to delete a row, use

DELETE FROM APARTMENTS

WHERE ApartmentNumber='100';

Oracle Objects

So far, we have shown how to define object types and use them as elements with tables. These techniques append object structures onto relations; the resulting relations can be processed using variations of SQL. Oracle provides another perspective, however—one that appends relational structures onto objects. SQL cannot be used with these structures. Instead, they are objects that will be stored in a database, but that must be manipulated by object-oriented programs.

Object Type Definition Figure 16-10 shows Oracle object definitions for the Order processing example illustrated in Figure 16-4. As shown before, the CREATE TYPE statement is used to define object structures and user-defined types. In this figure, the first two type definitions are used to declare a user-defined address type named obj_ADDRESS and a vararray type named obj_PHONE_LIST of maximum length 5. These two types can now be used in CREATE TYPE AS OBJECT statements in the same way that types were used with table-creation statements.

The next definitions in Figure 16-10 are of obj_SALESPERSON and obj_CUSTOMER. Both of these use the obj_ADDRESS and obj_PHONE_LIST user-defined types. This use means that both obj_SALESPERSON and obj_CUSTOMER objects have attributes named Street, City, State, Zip, and Country. They also each have a variable length array of phone numbers.

The next CREATE TYPE statement is an empty one; it is used to inform the Oracle type parser that there will be an obj_ITEM object defined subsequently. This statement allows a type definition like the next one for obj_LINEITEM to use the symbol obj_ITEM, even though obj_ITEM has not yet been defined.

The definition for obj_LINEITEM includes ItemNumber, Quantity, QuantityBackordered, and ExtendedPrice as shown in Figure 16-4. It also includes, however, a definition of a reference pointer attribute. ItemRef is defined as REF obj_ITEM. This means that this attribute will contain a system-supplied value that references a particular item object. This reference will be valid regardless of whether the referenced item object is in main memory or is on disk storage. If any swizzling is required, Oracle will do it behind the scenes.

Of course, the application program must assign a value to ItemRef. One way to do that is with a SQL statement like the following:

INSERT INTO ItemRef

SELECT REF(itemPtr) FROM obj_ITEM itemPtr

WHERE itemPtr.ItemNumber=10000

This assumes that only one item has an ItemNumber of 10000.

You may be wondering what the difference is between REF data types and foreign keys. The first difference is that REF values are hidden from the users and have no user meaning. Thus, like surrogate keys, such references have no need for cascading modifications. If, however, the referenced obj_ITEM is deleted, the value here will be invalid. It is up to the program to test it for validity before using it.

Second, such references point to objects, not to rows in tables. The referenced object may itself have a complex data structure and will have methods, as you will see. Also, Oracle supplied a class library that facilitates the manipulation of such references. A final difference is that such references are one-way. The obj_ITEM that is referenced may or may not have a pointer back to the obj_LINEITEM, and it does not in this example. This means we can navigate from obj_LINEITEM to obj_ITEM, but not the reverse.

In the next statement, list_LINEITEM is defined as a table of obj_LINEITEMs. This is similar to the earlier definition of APARTMENT_LIST2. The final type defini-

FIGURE 16–10

Oracle Object Definitions

```
CREATE TYPE obj_ADDRESS AS OBJECT (
      Street          VARCHAR2(50),
      City            VARCHAR2(50),
      State           VARCHAR2(2),
      Zip             VARCHAR2(10),
      Country         VARCHAR2(15)
)
/
CREATE TYPE obj_PHONE_LIST AS VARRAY(5) OF VARCHAR2(12)
/
CREATE TYPE obj_SALESPERSON AS OBJECT (
      SalespersonID NUMBER,
      Name            VARCHAR2(50),
      Address         obj_ADDRESS,
      PhoneNums       obj_PHONE_LIST
)
/
CREATE TYPE obj_CUSTOMER AS OBJECT (
      CustomerID    NUMBER,
      Name            VARCHAR2(50),
      Address         obj_ADDRESS,
      PhoneNums       obj_PHONE_LIST
)
/
CREATE TYPE obj_ITEM
/
CREATE TYPE obj_LINEITEM AS OBJECT (
      ItemNumber            NUMBER,
      ItemRef               REF obj_ITEM,
      Quantity              NUMBER,
      QuantityBackOrdered NUMBER,
      ExtendedPrice         NUMBER

)
/
CREATE TYPE list_LINEITEM AS TABLE OF obj_LINEITEM
/
CREATE TYPE obj_ITEM AS OBJECT (
      ItemNumber            NUMBER,
      ItemName              VARCHAR2(25),
      Price                 NUMBER
)
/
CREATE TYPE obj_ORDER AS OBJECT (
      OrderNumber           NUMBER,
      OrderDate             DATE,
      LineItems             list_LINEITEM,
      ShipToAddress         obj_ADDRESS,
      Customer              REF obj_CUSTOMER,
      Salesperson           REF obj_SALESPERSON,

MEMBER FUNCTION totalItems RETURN NUMBER
)
```

tion describes obj_ORDER. Unlike the definition of BUILDING2, which was a table, obj_ORDER is defined as an object. Because it is an object, the nested table attribute LineItems, which refers to the list_LINEITEM type, need not have a nested table defined for it.

As you examine Figure 16-10, keep in mind that we are defining the data members of an object, and not defining relational tables or anything like relational tables. The data structures in this object will be processed only by object methods.

The last section of the object type definition is to define the interface of this object's methods. In this case, the object has only one method, named totalItems, which returns a single parameter of type NUMBER. In a more realistic example, there would be many methods defined.

Object Method Definition   Figure 16-11 shows an example Oracle object method. The purpose of this method is to iterate through the LineItems and to total the extended price of each. The function begins by declaring three variables, and then starts a FOR loop over the set of LineItems. The following statement means to set the variable i to 1, to process the instructions through the block terminated by END LOOP, add 1 to i, and to iterate these statements until i is greater than the count of rows in the LineItems attribute.

FOR i in 1..SELF.LineItems.COUNT LOOP

The following statement invokes a class that is supplied in an Oracle class library:

UTL_REF.SELECT_OBJECT(LineItems(i).ItemRef, itemPtr)

The purpose of this function is to set the value of itemPtr to a valid object pointer to the obj_ITEM object that is referenced by ItemRef in the current row.

FIGURE 16–11

Example Oracle Method

```
CREATE OR REPLACE TYPE BODY obj_ORDER AS

  MEMBER FUNCTION totalItems RETURN NUMBER IS
      itemPtr              obj_ITEM;
      orderTotal           NUMBER :=0;
      i                    INTEGER;

      BEGIN

      FOR i in 1..SELF.LineItems.COUNT LOOP
          UTL_REF.SELECT_OBJECT(LineItems(i).ItemRef, itemPtr);
          orderTotal := orderTotal + SELF.LineItems(i).Quantity * itemPtr.Price;
      END LOOP;
      RETURN orderTotal;

      END;
  END;
```

After this statement has been executed, itemPtr can be used to refer to any of the properties of obj_ITEM. This is done in the next statement, in which itemPtr.Price has the value of Price in the obj_ITEM referenced by the current row.

Do not worry if not all of this makes sense. Strive to understand the role and purpose rather than the details of the statements in Figure 16-11. From this discussion, you should understand the general characteristics and nature of Oracle objects and realize how they move traditional relational database management a step or two in the direction of object-oriented programming.

▶ ODBMS STANDARDS

Several groups have been working toward the definition of an object-oriented database standard that can be used as a basis for the construction of ODBMS products. We survey the work of two of those groups here. The first group is a combination of ANSI and ISO (International Standards Organization) committees that has focused on extending the SQL-92 standard for object processing. The second group is a consortium of object database vendors and other interested parties that builds on another important standard in the industry, the Object Management Group's Common Object Model and Interface Design Language. As you might expect, the first standard begins with a database perspective and moves toward object thinking. The second standard begins with an object perspective and moves toward data management thinking. Both standards are important.

SQL3

SQL3 is an extension to the SQL-92 database standard that includes support for object-oriented database management. Both the ANSI X3H2 and the ISO/IEC JTC1/SC21/WG3 standardization committees have worked to develop the draft of the SQL3 standard that we will discuss here. This standard is very much a work in progress, and changes from this draft are likely. Furthermore, SQL3 is a standard for products; not a product itself. There are, at present, no commercial DBMS products that implement this standard. You should view this section more as a description of the likely evolution of relational DBMS products than as a description of specific product features.

SQL3 arises out of the tradition of database management; not out of the tradition of object thinking. The goal of the committees working on SQL3 has been to describe a standard that is upward-compatible with SQL-92. This means that all of the features and functions of SQL-92 would also work with SQL3. Consequently, SQL3 both looks like and is a relational database facility with object features added to it, as opposed to a new object-oriented database facility.

Three groups of new ideas are incorporated in SQL3: support for abstract data types, enhancements to the definitions of tables, and extensions to the language constructs to make SQL3 computationally complete.

Abstract Data Types   In SQL3, an **abstract data type (ADT)** is a user-defined structure that is equivalent to an OOP object. ADTs have methods, data items, and identifiers. ADTs can be subtypes of other ADTs; inheritance is supported. Either SQL (with the new language extensions) or external language—such as Java, C#, and C++—can be used to express the logic of ADT methods.

An ADT can be used in an SQL expression, it can be stored in a table, or both. If the ADT appears in one or more SQL expressions but is not stored in any table, the ADT is transient; otherwise, it is made persistent by its storage in a table.

Figure 16-12 shows the definition of a sample ADT for an employee object type. The current syntax of SQL3 is shown in capital letters, and the developer-supplied code is shown in small letters. This specific syntax is unimportant because it is likely to change. Instead, observe that this ADT, like an OOP object, has data items and

FIGURE 16-12

Sample ADT Definition in SQL3

```
CREATE OBJECT TYPE employee WITH OID VISIBLE
        (name VARCHAR NOT NULL,
        number CHAR(7)
        salary UPDATABLE VIRTUAL GET with get_salary SET WITH change_salary,
        PRIVATE
        hiredate DATE
        currentsalary CURRENCY
        PUBLIC
        ACTOR FUNCTION get_salary (:E employee) RETURNS CURRENCY
        {code to perform security processing
         and return value of currentsalary if appropriate}
        RETURN salary
        END FUNCTION,

        ACTOR FUNCTION change_salary (:E employee) RETURNS employee
        {code to perform security processing
         and compute and set new currentsalary, if appropriate}
        RETURN :E
        END FUNCTION,

        DESTRUCTOR FUNCTION remove_employee (:E employee)
                                            RETURNS NULL
        {code to get ready to delete employee data}
        DESTROY :E
        RETURN :E
        END FUNCTION,
```

functions (methods). The employee data items are name, number, hiredate, currentsalary, and salary, which is a virtual data item (one that exists only as the result of a computation in a function). The functions are get_salary, change_salary, and remove_employee.

SQL defines two kinds of ADT: OBJECT ADTs and VALUE ADTs. An OBJECT ADT is an identifiable, independent data structure that is assigned an identifier called an **OID.** This identifier is a unique value that persists for the life of the object. If the programmer wants to be able to use the value of the OID to pass to other functions or to store in other tables, the expression WITH OID VISIBLE must be added to the first line of the object definition. This has been done in Figure 16-12.

OID values are pointers to objects; saving an OID value in a table saves a pointer to the object. This can be convenient, but it also creates a problem. When an ADT is destroyed, its OID is invalid, but that particular OID value may have been stored in rows of tables that are not even in memory when the ADT is destroyed. The SQL3 standard does not indicate what is to happen in this case. Apparently, programs are to be written to test whether an OID is valid before attempting to use it.

The second kind of ADT is a VALUE ADT. VALUE ADTs are not assigned OIDs and cannot exist except in the context in which they are created. If a VALUE ADT is created as a column in a table, it will be saved with that table. It will not be possible to refer to that ADT except through the name of the table. If a VALUE ADT is created in a function, it will be transient and will be destroyed when memory for the function is released.

The code in Figure 16-12 defines the OBJECT ADT *employee* as a type. As such, the type name can be used in table definitions in the same way that SQL built-in data types can be used. In Figure 16-13, a table Dept is defined: It has a DeptName of type CHAR(10); a Manager of type employee; and an Admin, also of type employee. Thus, the ADT type is used as any other data type is used in a table definition.

When defining a column as having an ADT type, the keyword INSTANCE is used to indicate whether the object or a pointer to the object is to be stored. If INSTANCE is specified, the object data is stored in the column. If INSTANCE is omitted, a pointer to

FIGURE 16-13

Table Definition Using the Employee ADT

```
CREATE TABLE Dept
        ( DeptName           char(10),
          Manager            employee,
          Admin              employee INSTANCE
        )
```

the object is stored in the column. If the ADT is a VALUE ADT, INSTANCE is assumed.

In Figure 16-13, the Manager column does not specify INSTANCE, but the Admin column does. This means that each row of a Dept table contains a pointer to an employee in the Manager column and the actual data and methods for an employee in the Admin column.

The public data items of an object can be used in SQL statements, just like regular table columns can be used. For example, consider the table shown in Figure 16-13 and the following SQL code:

```
SELECT       DeptName, Manager.OID, Manager.Name, Admin.OID,
             Admin.Name

FROM         Dept
```

When this code is executed, the DeptName, Manager.OID, Admin.OID, and Admin.Name are extracted from the table. Behind the scenes, the DBMS uses the value of Manager.OID to find the instance of employee that it points to. The DBMS then extracts Manager.Name from that object and returns it as part of the response to this SQL statement. The result would be the same as if all of the Manager object were stored in the table. Clearly, if the OID that is stored in the table has become invalid because its object has been deleted, the DBMS needs to process this error in some fashion.

Consider the following SQL statement:

```
SELECT       DeptName, Manager.Name, Manager.Salary
FROM         Dept
```

To process this statement, the DBMS needs to access the Dept table, obtain the OID of the manager, obtain the instance of employee that is that manager, and then invoke the get_salary function in employee that materializes the virtual column salary. The get_salary function may perform security checking when it is executed, so the user may be asked to provide a name or password, or perform other tasks before the DBMS receives a response from get_salary. After get_salary has returned a value or an error code indicating that no value will be forthcoming, the DBMS can format the data for that Dept. Similar processing needs to be done for each row of the Dept table.

Private data items are private to the functions in the object. Hence, the following SQL is invalid:

```
SELECT       DeptName, Manager.currentsalary
FROM         Dept
```

The only way currentsalary data can be extracted from an Employee object is through the function get_salary.

Values can be assigned to columns, just like other SQL statements. Thus, the SQL expression sets the name of the Admin object that is instantiated in the Accounting department:

```
UPDATE        Dept
SET           Admin.Name = "Fred P. Johnson"
WHERE         DeptName = "Accounting"
```

Because some objects are represented by pointers and not by data values, some surprising results can occur. Consider the following SQL:

```
UPDATE        Dept
SET           Manager.Name = "Fred P. Johnson"
WHERE         DeptName = "Accounting"
```

This statement does not change the employee assignment so that a different employee whose name is "Fred P. Johnson" is assigned to Accounting. Instead, it changes the name of the employee who is currently the manager. The *employee* name is changed; this means that any other table that references this Employee object will also have its name changed. If no employee has yet been assigned to Manager in the Accounting row, this statement will generate an error.

In order to replace the manager of the Accounting department with a different employee whose name is "Fred P. Johnson," the Manager object needs to be set to the correct object instance. The following SQL will do this:

```
UPDATE        Dept
SET           Manager =
              SELECT        employee.OID
              FROM          employee
              WHERE         name = "Fred P. Johnson"
WHERE         DeptName = "Accounting"
```

Conceptually, this statement is correct. Whether or not it would actually work with a DBMS that implemented SQL3 would, of course, be up to the designers of the DBMS. As stated, because SQL3 is a work in progress and because no product yet implements it, consider the discussion here to indicate the direction of the industry—rather than a fixed, industry-accepted syntax.

The definition of ADTs gives SQL3 the capability to define, store, and manipulate objects. Two other changes to SQL are also proposed in SQL3. We consider them next.

SQL3 Table Extensions   SQL3 extends the definition of tables in several ways. First, SQL3 tables have a **row identifier,** which is a unique identifier for each row of a table. This identifier is the same as a *surrogate key,* the term we have used in prior discussions. Applications can use this identifier if it is made explicit by including the expression WITH IDENTITY in the table definition. Any table so defined is given an implicit column named IDENTITY. Values in the column can be used by the application, but it is not included in the results of a SELECT * expression.

Consider the table in Figure 16-14 and the next two SQL expressions:

FIGURE 16-14

Table Definition Using WITH IDENTITY

```
CREATE TABLE PROFESSOR WITH IDENTITY

        (ProfessorName        char(10),
         Phone                char(7),
         Office               char(5)
         )
```

SELECT   ProfessorName, Identity

FROM   PROFESSOR

SELECT   *

FROM   PROFESSOR

The result of the first SQL statement is a table with two columns; the first has the name of the professor, and the second has the value of the row identifier. The result of the second SQL expression is a table of three columns: ProfessorName, Phone, and Office.

The second extension to the table concept in SQL3 is the definition of three types of table: SET, MULTISET, and LIST. A SET table is a table with no duplicate rows; a MULTISET table may have duplicate rows and is equivalent to the table concept in SQL-92. (This definition, of course, ignores the IDENTITY column because no table has duplicate rows with the IDENTITY column.) Finally, a LIST table is a table that has an order defined by one or more columns.

A third extension to the table concept in SQL3 is the **subtable.** A subtable is a subset of another table, called the **supertable.** A subtable inherits all of the columns of its supertable and may also have columns of its own. A table that has a subtable or a supertable has a row identifier defined implicitly. Figure 16-15 defines two types of professor: TENURED-PROFESSOR and NONTENURED-PROFESSOR. The columns of TENURED-PROFESSOR are ProfessorName, Phone, Office, and DateTenureGranted. The columns of NONTENURED-PROFESSOR are ProfessorName, Phone, Office, and NextReviewDate. Even though WITH IDENTITY is not specified for TENURED-PROFESSOR or NONTENURED-PROFESSOR, both have an IDENTITY column because they are subtypes.

Reflect for a moment on the logical consequences of adding both ADTs and subtypes to the table construct. Both ADTs and tables can have subtypes, and the two are not the same. ADT subtypes define one generalization hierarchy, and table subtypes define another. One hierarchy may be nested in the other or the reverse, they may be disjoint, or they may partially overlap. SQL3 is open to the criticism of excessive complexity here, and it will be interesting to see how much of this complexity is actually implemented in DBMS products.

SQL Language Extensions   According to SQL3, ADT methods can be coded in the SQL language itself. To make this capability more robust, language elements are proposed that will make SQL computationally complete. The proposed additions are summarized in Figure 16-16.

To date, SQL has been a set-oriented language. SELECT statements identify a set of rows and operate upon them. The addition of the language statements in Figure 16-16

FIGURE 16–15

Subtable Definitions

CREATE TABLE PROFESSOR WITH IDENTITY

        (ProfessorName   char(10),
        Phone   char(7),
        Office   char(5)
)

CREATE TABLE TENURED-PROFESSOR UNDER PROFESSOR

        (DateTenureGranted   Date)

CREATE TABLE NON-TENURED-PROFESSOR UNDER PROFESSOR

        (NextReviewDate   Date)

FIGURE 16–16

Proposed SQL3
Language Extensions

Statement	Purpose
DESTROY	Destroy an object ADT; valid only in DESTRUCTOR functions
ASSIGNMENT	Allow the result of an SQL value expression to be assigned to a local variable, column, or ADT attribute
CALL	Invoke an SQL procedure
RETURN	Return a value from a value computation in a procedure or function
CASE	Select execution path on the basis of alternative values
IF THEN ELSE	Allow conditional logic
WHILE LOOP	Allow iterative logic

changes this characteristic. It is possible to develop row-at-a-time logic within SQL itself. This change makes SQL more and more like a traditional programming language. This is necessary if SQL is to be used as the language for logic in ADT methods, but it also represents a change in the fundamental character of SQL.

ODMG-93

The Object Data Management Group is a consortium of object database vendors and other interested industry experts that has applied the ideas of another group, the Object Management Group, to the problem of object databases. The first report on ODMG was produced in 1993 and is accordingly referred to as ODMG-93. This heritage of this standard is object programming and not traditional relational database management. Hence, it is based on the object as the fundamental construct, rather than on the table as the fundamental construct as we saw for SQL3.

ODMG-93 is a definition of interfaces for object data management products. The implementations of the ideas in ODMG-93 may be quite different. An ODMG-93 product that is designed for C++ object data storage and manipulation might have a completely different implementation from a product that is designed for Smalltalk object storage and manipulation. The two products can be very different and yet still both implement the ODMG-93 interfaces.

Because ODMG-93 arises out of the context of object programming, a detailed description of it requires substantial knowledge of OOP. Such a description is consequently beyond the scope of this text. Instead, we confine this discussion to fundamental ideas behind the ODMG-93 report. Figure 16-17 lists five core concepts, as described by Loomis.[2]

FIGURE 16–17

Key Elements of the
ODMG Object Model

- Objects are fundamental.
- Every object has a lifelong persistent, unique identifier.
- Objects can be arranged into types and subtypes.
- State is defined by data values and relationships.
- Behavior is defined by object operations.

---

[2]Loomis, Mary E. S. *Object Databases, the Essentials*. Reading, MA: Addison-Wesley, 1995, pp. 88–110.

Objects are Fundamental According to the ODMG Object Model, the object is the fundamental entity to be stored and manipulated. Unlike SQL3, in which the fundamental entity is a table and objects are stored in columns of tables, the object is the basic entity in ODMG-93. The ODMG concept is more like the one we described for the object program in Figure 16-3. That is, the application program defines objects in and of themselves, and it is up to the ODBMS to make those objects persistent. No other structure, such as a table, is required.

According to the ODMG model, objects can be **mutable** or **immutable.** Mutable objects can be changed; immutable objects are fixed, and no application is allowed to alter the state of any immutable object. The ODBMS is required to enforce immutability.

Every Object Has a Lifelong Persistent Identifier The second fundamental concept in the ODMG object model is that each object is given a unique identifier that is valid for the lifetime of the object. Further, the identifier must be valid, whether the object is stored externally or is in memory. The ODBMS is to perform swizzling transparently; the application program can use pointers to objects as if they are always valid.

The standard leaves the particular form of an object identifier open. Thus, different ODBMS vendors can use different means to specify object IDs. This means that object identifiers from different databases from different vendors are not necessarily compatible. For nondistributed databases, this is not likely to be a problem because all of the objects in a given object database will have been created and stored by the same ODBMS.

In a distributed environment, the object identification problem is more difficult for two reasons: First, because object IDs in different ODBMS may have different formats; and second, because object IDs are not necessarily unique across different databases. This issue is unaddressed by the ODMG-93 standard.

Objects Can be Arranged Into Types and Subtypes The ODMG standard object model specifies that objects be arranged into groups by type. Objects are created to be of a given type. All objects of a particular type have the same data characteristics and behavior. Objects can be defined as subtypes of other objects. In this case, they inherit all of the data characteristics and behavior of their parent type. According to the standard, an object is created as an instance of a given type, and that instance cannot change its type.

The terms *type* and *class* are often used synonymously. According to Loomis, this is incorrect. An object class is a logical group of objects, as defined in ODMG 93; such classes have subclasses that inherit from them. A type is the implementation of a class in a particular language. Thus, the class Employee is a logical definition of data and methods; it may have subclasses Salesperson and Accountant that inherit from Employee. An implementation of Employee in C++, for example, is called a type; implementations in C++ of Salesperson and Accountant are subtypes.[3] There may be another different implementation of Employee in Smalltalk, for example, and that implementation is a different Employee type. Distinguishing between *class* and *type* helps to delineate logical definitions from particular implementations of those logical structures.

Object classes (and hence types) can have properties. The ODMG standard specifies that each class has a name and uniqueness constraints as its properties. All of the instances of an object class are called the object's **extent.** Any attribute or combination of attributes can be declared to be unique over the extent. Thus, in Employee, EmployeeNumber can be defined to be unique, as can {FirstName, LastName}, and so on. Because uniqueness requirements apply to the entire extent and not to any given object instance, such requirements are class properties and not class instance properties. Thus, the name Employee and the requirement that EmployeeNumber be unique are class properties. EmployeeNumber itself, however, is a property of an Employee instance.

---

[3]Ibid., p. 96.

Because ODMG is a standard for an interface and not for an implementation, no attempt is made to describe how types and subtypes should be stored or manipulated. Rather, the interface simply indicates that objects should be stored and retrieved by class, and that inheritance should be provided.

State Is Defined by Data Values and Relationships   According to the ODMG standard, the state of any object is represented by its properties. Such properties can be either attributes or relationships. An attribute is a literal value or a set of literal values. DateOfHire and CurrentSalary are literal values. PastSalary is a set of literal values. A relationship is a property that indicates a connection between one object instance and one or more other object instances. Department is an example of a relationship property.

The ODMG specifies a set of operations that can be performed on relationships, which are listed in Figure 16-18. Operations are distinguished by the maximum cardinality of the relationship. This is done because in the case of a 1:1 relationship, the properties are single-value and no set of properties need be considered. In the case of a 1:N or N:M relationship, the number of elements in a property is plural; a set is created, and the program must be able to iterate over the elements of the set.

When objects have a relationship, the relationship must be made persistent when the object is made persistent. The standard does not specify how the relationship is to be represented and what means are to be used to swizzle the pointers among relationships. These issues must be solved when implementing an ODBMS, however.

Behavior Is Defined by Object Operations   The behavior of an object type is determined by its methods. All objects of a given type have the same methods, and objects of subtypes inherit those methods. If a subtype object redefines a method, the redefinition overrides the inherited method. If, for example, Employee has method Get_Salary, and if Salesperson, a subtype of Employee, also has a method called Get_Salary, the local method will be used for Salesperson!Get_Salary operations.

Objects interact by invoking one another's methods. Sometimes this is expressed by saying that objects pass messages to one another, where a message is a string such as Salesperson!Get_Salary that includes the name of the object type and the name of the method of that type. Messages can, of course, include parameters.

The purpose of an ODBMS is to make objects persistent. The ODMG standard indicates that objects include methods, so method storage and management would seem to be included in the functions of an ODMG-compliant ODBMS. In truth, current ODBMSs vary widely in their support for method storage. Some ODBMSs, in fact, provide no support whatsoever for method persistence. Others provide some support, but not support for versioning of objects.

Method persistence is important, and the capabilities of ODBMS in this area will probably be improved in the future. No application is static; requirements change, and

FIGURE 16–18
ODMG Relationship Operations

Operation	Function
Set	Create a 1:1 relationship
Clear	Destroy a 1:1 relationship
Insert_element	Add an element to the many side of a 1:N or N:M relationship
Remove_element	Remove an element from the many side of a 1:N or N:M relationship
Get	Return a reference to an object in a 1:1 relationship
Traverse	Return a reference to a set of objects on the many side of a 1:N or N:M relationship
Create_iterator	Create a structure to process the elements of a set of objects obtained by a Traverse operation

object behaviors must be adapted. Furthermore, methods can change without changing the underlying data properties of an object. Without method management, two instances of an object can be based on two different versions of methods.

Consider an example: Suppose that an instance of a Salesperson class—Salesperson A, for example—is created and stored using a version of the Set_Salary method. Now, suppose that the means of computing salesperson salaries change, and the Set_Salary method is altered accordingly. At this point, Salesperson B is created and stored. Now, Salesperson A and Salesperson B would appear to be equivalent in their data properties, but they are not. Without method management on the part of the ODBMS, there is no way to determine that Salespersons A and B represent different versions of the SALESPERSON object.

This situation is no different from what occurs today with application programs in non-ODBMS environments, so proponents of ODBMS would claim that ODBMS has not made the situation any worse. This, however, seems to be a cop-out. If objects are defined to include data properties and behavior properties, object persistence cannot be claimed to pertain to one and not to the other. Too much of the promise of object thinking is left on the table if ODBMS does not support method management as well as data management.

SUMMARY

Relational databases are not well-suited to store object-oriented programming objects because objects can contain complex structures that do not readily fit into a table. Also, objects include object methods that also need to be stored. Special-purpose, object-oriented DBMS products were developed to provide persistent object storage, but they have not been commercially successful because existing relational data must be converted into ODBMS format. The gain has not been worth the cost. Instead, DBMS products are beginning to support hybrids of object and relational storage called object-relational databases.

With object-oriented programming (OOP), programs are composed of objects that are encapsulated logical structures that have data elements and behaviors. An interface is the external appearance of an object; an implementation is the encapsulated interior of an object. Objects can be subclassed; a subclass inherits the attributes and methods of its superclass. Polymorphism allows several versions of the same method to exist; the compiler creates code to call the proper version, depending on the class of the object.

An object class is the logical structure of an object; a group of object classes is called an object class library. Instances of an object class are called object instances, or simply objects. Object constructors are methods that obtain memory and create object structures; object destructors unbind objects and free memory. Transient objects exist only during the execution of a program; persistent objects are saved to storage and survive the execution of a program.

Objects can be made persistent by using traditional file storage, relational DBMS, or ODBMS products. The use of traditional storage places considerable work on the application programmer, and is feasible only for applications having a few simple objects whose structure does not frequently change. Relational DBMS can be used for object persistence, but the application developer must convert object structures to relations, write SQL, and develop swizzling algorithms. Using an ODBMS is the most direct and easiest means of object persistence.

Oracle provides support for object persistence with object-relational database facilities. Object types can be defined and then used with table structures as column objects, as variable length arrays, as nested tables, and as row objects. Pure objects can also be defined; such objects can include variable length arrays and nested tables. They also may include object pointers as REF attributes. Finally, such objects include methods, which can use Oracle-supplied class libraries for processing.

SQL3 is an extension to SQL-92 that provides for abstract data types (ADTs), enhancements to tables, and new features in the SQL language. ADTs, which are made persistent by embedding in tables, can be object or value; object ADTs have identifiers called OIDs. In SQL3, tables have a row identifier and can have subtypes. Three types of tables are defined: SET, MULTISET, and LIST. Figure 16-13 shows extensions to the SQL language proposed in SQL3.

The five basic elements of the ODMG-93 standard are that objects are the fundamental data structure, objects are given a lifelong persistent identifier, objects can be arranged in types and subtypes, object state is carried by data values and relationships, and object behavior is defined by object operations.

GROUP I QUESTIONS

16.1 Explain how object-oriented programming differs from traditional programming.

16.2 Why are relational databases more popular than object databases today?

16.3 Define an OOP object.

16.4 Define the terms *encapsulated, attribute,* and *method.*

16.5 Explain the difference between an interface and an implementation.

16.6 What is inheritance?

16.7 What is polymorphism?

16.8 Define the terms *object class, object class library,* and *object instance.*

16.9 Explain the function of object constructors and object destructors.

16.10 Explain the difference between a transient object and a persistent object.

16.11 Explain the difference in the notation CUSTOMER!Find and CUSTOMER.ZipCode.

16.12 What is the function of the keyword *NOTHING* in Figure 16-3?

16.13 What is the function of the keyword *Me* in Figure 16-3?

16.14 What is a callback, and why is one used?

16.15 What does the term *swizzling* refer to?

16.16 Briefly explain what tasks are required to use traditional file storage for object persistence.

16.17 Briefly explain what tasks are required to use a relational DBMS for object persistence.

16.18 Summarize the advantages and disadvantages of using an ODBMS for object persistence.

16.19 Show the Oracle statements to define an object type named Pname having three attributes: FirstName, MiddleName, and LastName. Use this type as a column object in a table called PERSON.

16.20 Show Oracle statements to create a variable array of up to 100 Pnames. Show statements to create a table named CLUB1 with a surrogate key, a ClubName, and the variable array attribute of person names.

16.21 Show Oracle statements to create a CLUB2 table as in question 16.20, but use a nested table of person names instead of a variable array. Name the storage table Pname_Table.

16.22 Explain the differences between table CLUB1 and table CLUB2.

16.23 Show Oracle statements to create a table having Pname as a row object.

16.24 Explain the purpose of the REF attributes in Figure 16-10. How do these attributes differ from foreign keys?

16.25 Explain the purposes of the following two statements:

a.   FOR i in 1..SELF.Lineitems.COUNT LOOP

b.   UTI_REF.SELECT_OBJECT(LineItems(i).ItemRef, itemPtr)

16.26 What is SQL3?

16.27 What is an abstract data type (ADT)?

16.28 Explain the difference between an object ADT and a value ADT.

16.29 What is an OID? How can one be used?

16.30 Explain what the DBMS must do when executing the following SQL on the ADT in Figure 16-13:

SELECT   DeptName, Manager.Phone, Admin.Phone

FROM   Dept

16.31 What happens when the following SQL is executed on the ADT in Figure 16-13?

UPDATE   Dept

SET   Manager.Name = "John Jacob Astor"

16.32 Code SQL that would need to be executed to change the instance of the manager of a department for the ADT in Figure 16-13.

16.33 What is a row identifier in SQL3?

16.34 Explain the differences between a SET, MULTISET, and LIST in SQL3.

16.35 Explain the differences between a subtable, a supertable, and a table.

16.36 What is ODMG-93?

16.37 List the five core concepts in ODMG-93.

16.38 What is the difference between a type and a class in ODMG-93?

16.39 What is the difference between a property and an attribute in ODMG-93?

16.40 What is an extent?

16.41 What are the properties of a class in ODMG-93?

16.42 In the ODMG standard, what values can properties have?

16.43 In the ODMG standard, what values can attributes have?

16.44 In the ODMG standard, what values can relationship properties have?

16.45 Why is method persistence important? Give an example of a problem that can occur when such persistence is not provided.

16.46 Explain how semantic objects conform to the ODMG standard and how they do not.

GROUP II QUESTIONS

16.47 Review the requirements and relational design for View Ridge Gallery in Chapter 7. Consider the use of Oracle types and columns, vararrays, nested tables, and row objects in the context of View Ridge's needs. What changes would you make to the relational design? Would you recommend replacing TRANSACTION or WORK tables with vararrays or nested tables? If so, how? If not, why not? Show how you could use Oracle REF data types to eliminate the need for the intersection table. Would you recommend this course of action?

16.48 Consider Oracle types, vararrays, and nested tables in the context of the semantic object model described in Appendix B. Which elements of that model lend themselves to types? To vararrays? To nested tables? Show how you would use Oracle object-relational facilities to model each of the types of semantic objects described in Appendix B.

Appendix A

Data Structures for Database Processing

All operating systems provide data management services. These services, however, are generally not sufficient for the specialized needs of a DBMS. Therefore, to enhance performance, DBMS products build and maintain specialized data structures, which are the topics of this appendix.

We begin by discussing flat files and some of the problems that can occur when such files need to be processed in different orders. Then, we turn to three specialized data structures: sequential lists, linked lists, and indexes (or inverted lists). Next, we illustrate how each of three special structures—trees, simple networks, and complex networks—are represented using various data structures. Finally, we explore how to represent and process multiple keys.

Although a thorough knowledge of data structures is not required to use most DBMS products, this background is essential for database administrators and systems programmers working with a DBMS. Being familiar with the data structures also helps you evaluate and compare database products.

▶ FLAT FILES

A *flat file* is a file that has no repeating groups. Figure A-1(a) shows a flat file, and A-1(b) shows a file that is not flat because of the repeating field Item. A flat file can be stored in any common file organization—such as sequential, indexed sequential, or direct. Flat files have been used for many years in commercial processing. They are usually processed in some predetermined order—for example, in an ascending sequence on a key field.

FIGURE A-1

Examples of (a) a Flat and (b) a Nonflat File Enrollment Record

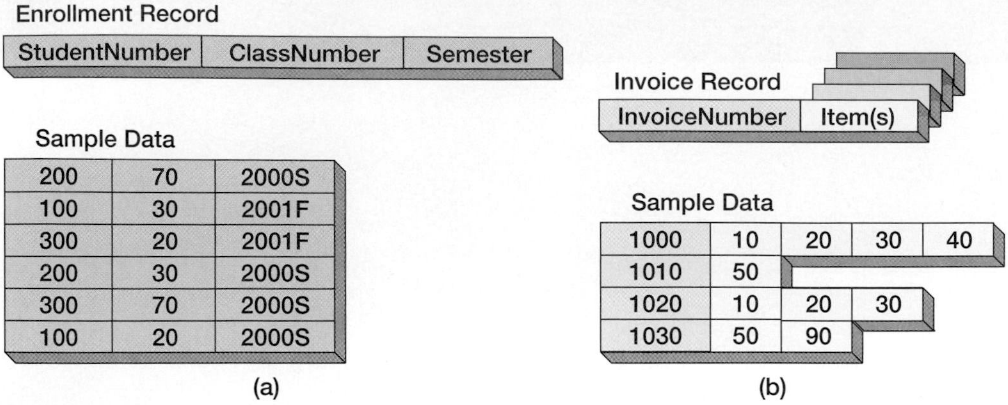

(a)

(b)

FIGURE A-2

ENROLLMENT Data Stored as Sequential Lists (a) Stored by StudentNumber and (b) Stored by ClassNumber

(a)

(b)

Processing Flat Files in Multiple Orders

Sometimes, users want to process flat files in ways that are not readily supported by the file organization. Consider, for example, the ENROLLMENT records shown in Figure A-1(a). To produce student schedules, they must be processed in StudentNumber sequence. But to produce class rosters, the records need to be processed in ClassNumber sequence. The records, of course, can be stored in only one physical sequence. For example, they can be in order on StudentNumber or on ClassNumber, but not on both at the same time. The traditional solution to the problem of processing records in different orders is to sort them in student order and process the student schedules; then sort the records in class order and produce class rosters.

For some applications, such as a batch-mode system, this solution is effective although cumbersome. But suppose that both orders need to exist simultaneously because two concurrent users have different views of the ENROLLMENT records. What do we do then?

One solution is to create two copies of the ENROLLMENT file and sort them, as shown in Figure A-2. Because the data are listed in sequential order, this data structure is sometimes called a *sequential list.* Sequential lists can be readily stored as sequential files. This solution, however, is not generally done by DBMS products because sequentially reading a file is a slow process. Further, sequential files cannot be updated in the middle without rewriting the entire file. Also, maintaining several orders by keeping multiple copies of the same sequential list is usually not effective because the duplicated sequential list can create data integrity problems. Fortunately, other data structures allow us to process records in different orders and do not require the duplication of data. These data structures include *linked lists* and *indexes.*

A Note on Record Addressing

Usually, the DBMS creates large physical records, or blocks, on its direct access files. These records are used as containers for logical records. Typically, there are many logical records per physical record. Here, we assume that each physical record is addressed by its relative record number (RRN). Thus, a logical record might be assigned to physical record number 7 or 77 or 10,000. The relative record number is thus the logical record's physical address. If there is more than one logical record per physical record, the address must also specify where the logical record is within the physical record. Thus, the complete address for a logical record might be relative record number 77, byte location 100. This means the record begins in byte 100 of physical record 77.

To simplify the illustrations in this text, we assume that there is only one logical record per physical record, so we need not be concerned with byte offsets within physical records. Although this is unrealistic, it simplifies our discussion to the essential points.

Maintaining Order with Linked Lists

Linked lists can be used to keep records in logical order that are not necessarily in physical order. To create a linked list, we add a field to each data record. The *link* field holds the address (in our illustrations, the relative record number) of the *next* record in logical sequence. For example, Figure A-3 shows the ENROLLMENT records expanded to include a linked list; this list maintains the records in StudentNumber order. Notice that the link for the numerically last student in the list is zero.

Figure A-4 shows ENROLLMENT records with two linked lists: One list maintains the StudentNumber order, and the other list maintains the ClassNumber order. Two link fields have been added to the records, one for each list.

When insertions and deletions are made, linked lists have a great advantage over sequential lists. For example, to insert the ENROLLMENT record for Student 200 and Class 45, both of the lists shown in Figure A-2 would need to be rewritten. For the linked lists in Figure A-4, however, the new record could be added to the physical end of the list, and only the values of two link fields would need to be changed to place the new record in the correct sequences. These changes are shown in Figure A-5.

FIGURE A-3

ENROLLMENT Data in StudentNumber Order Using a Linked List

Relative Record Number	Student-Number	Class-Number	Semester	Link
1	200	70	2000S	4
2	100	30	2001F	6
3	300	20	2001F	5
4	200	30	2000S	3
5	300	70	2000S	0
6	100	20	2000S	1

Start of list = 2

FIGURE A-4

ENROLLMENT Data in Two Orders Using Linked Lists

Relative Record Number	Student-Number	Class-Number	Semester	Student Link	Class Link
1	200	70	2000S	4	5
2	100	30	2001F	6	1
3	300	20	2001F	5	4
4	200	30	2000S	3	2
5	300	70	2000S	0	0
6	100	20	2000S	1	3

Start of student list = 2
Start of class list = 6

FIGURE A-5

ENROLLMENT Data After Inserting New Record (in Two Orders Using Linked Lists)

Relative Record Number	Student-Number	Class-Number	Semester	Student Link	Class Link
1	200	70	2000S	4	5
2	100	30	2001F	6	7
3	300	20	2001F	5	4
4	200	30	2000S	7	2
5	300	70	2000S	0	0
6	100	20	2000S	1	3
7	200	45	2000S	3	1

Start of student list = 2
Start of class list = 6

FIGURE A-6

ENROLLMENT Data After Deleting Student 200, Class 30 (in Two Orders Using Linked Lists)

Relative Record Number	Student-Number	Class-Number	Semester	Student Link	Class Link
1	200	70	2000S	7	5
2	100	30	2001F	6	7
3	300	20	2001F	5	2
4	200	30	2000S	7	2
5	300	70	2000S	0	0
6	100	20	2000S	1	3
7	200	45	2000S	3	1

Start of student list = 2
Start of class list = 6

When a record is deleted from a sequential list, a gap is created. But in a linked list, a record can be deleted simply by changing the values of the link, or the *pointer* fields. In Figure A-6, the ENROLLMENT record for Student 200, Class 30, has been logically deleted. No other record points to its address, so it has been effectively removed from the chain, even though it still exists physically.

There are many variations of linked lists. We can make the list into a *circular list,* or *ring,* by changing the link of the last record from zero to the address of the first record in the list. Now we can reach every item in the list starting at any item in the list. Figure A-7(a) shows a circular list for the StudentNumber order. A *two-way linked list* has links in both directions. In Figure A-7(b), a two-way linked list has been created for both ascending and descending student orders.

Records ordered using linked lists cannot be stored on a sequential file because some type of direct-access file organization is needed in order to use the link values. Thus, either indexed sequential or direct file organization is required for linked-list processing.

Maintaining Order with Indexes

A logical record order can also be maintained using *indexes*, or *inverted lists*, as they are sometimes called. An index is simply a table that cross-references record addresses with some field value. For example, Figure A-8(a) shows the ENROLLMENT records stored in no particular order, and Figure A-8(b) shows an index on StudentNumber. In this index, the StudentNumbers are arranged in sequence, with each entry in the list pointing to a corresponding record in the original data.

As you can see, the index is simply a sorted list of StudentNumbers. To process ENROLLMENT sequentially on StudentNumber, we simply process the index sequentially, obtaining ENROLLMENT data by reading the records indicated by the pointers. Figure A-8(c) shows another index for ENROLLMENT—one that maintains ClassNumber order.

FIGURE A-7

ENROLLMENT Data
Sorted by
StudentNumber Using
(a) a Circular and (b) a
Two-Way Linked List

Relative Record Number	Student-Number	Class-Number	Semester	Link
1	200	70	2000S	4
2	100	30	2001F	6
3	300	20	2001F	5
4	200	30	2000S	3
5	300	70	2000S	2
6	100	20	2000S	1

Start of list = 2

(a)

Relative Record Number	Student-Number	Class-Number	Semester	Ascending Link	Descending Link
1	200	70	2000S	4	6
2	100	30	2001F	6	0
3	300	20	2001F	5	4
4	200	30	2000S	3	1
5	300	70	2000S	0	3
6	100	20	2000S	1	2

Start of ascending list = 2
Start of descending list = 5

(b)

FIGURE A-8

ENROLLMENT Data and Corresponding Indexes (a) ENROLLMENT Data; (b) Index On StudentNumber and (c) Index On ClassNumber

Relative Record Number	Student-Number	Class-Number	Semester
1	200	70	2000S
2	100	30	2001F
3	300	20	2001F
4	200	30	2000S
5	300	70	2000S
6	100	20	2000S

(a)

Student-Number	Relative Record Number
100	2
100	6
200	1
200	4
300	3
300	5

(b)

Class-Number	Relative Record Number
20	3
20	6
30	2
30	4
70	1
70	5

(c)

To use an index, the data to be ordered (here, ENROLLMENT) must reside on an indexed sequential or direct file, although the indexes can reside on any type of file. In practice, almost all DBMS products keep both the data and the indexes on direct files.

If you compare the linked list with the index, you will notice the essential difference between them. In a linked list, the pointers are stored along with the data. Each record contains a link field containing a pointer to the address of the next related record. But in an index, the pointers are stored in indexes, separate from the data. Thus, the data records themselves contain no pointers. Both techniques are used by commercial DBMS products.

B-Trees

A special application of the concept of indexes, or inverted lists, is a *B-tree*: a multi-level index that allows both sequential and direct processing of data records. It also ensures a certain level of efficiency in processing because of the way that the indexes are structured.

A B-tree is an index that is made up of two parts: the sequence set and the index set. (These terms are used by IBM's VSAM file organization documentation. You may encounter other synonymous terms.) The *sequence set* is an index containing an entry for every record in the file. This index is in physical sequence, usually by primary key value. The sequence set can contain the record's data (called a clustered index in SQL Server), or it can contain a pointer to the record's data (called nonclustered index in SQL Server). Only one index per table can contain the record's data.

The *index set* is a hierarchical index to the sequence set. It is used to give rapid access to the sequence set.

An example of a B-tree appears in Figure A-9, and an occurrence of this structure can be seen in Figure A-10. Notice that the bottom row in Figure A-9, the sequence set, is simply an index. It contains an entry for every record in the file (although for brevity, both the data records and their addresses have been omitted). Also, notice that the sequence set entries are in groups of three. The entries in each group are physically in sequence, and each group is chained to the next one by means of a linked list, as can be seen in Figure A-10.

Examine the index set in Figure A-9. The top entry contains two values: 45 and 77. By following the leftmost link (to RRN2), we can access all the records whose key field values are less than or equal to 45; by following the middle pointer (to RRN3), we can access all the records whose key field values are greater than 45 and less than or equal to 77; and by following the rightmost pointer (to RRN4), we can access all the records whose key field values are greater than 77.

Similarly, at the next level there are two values and three pointers in each index entry. Each time we drop to another level, we narrow our search for a particular record. For example, if we continue to follow the leftmost pointer from the top entry and then follow the rightmost pointer from there, we can access all the records whose key field value is greater than 27 and less than or equal to 45. We have eliminated all that were greater than 45 at the first level.

B-trees are, by definition, balanced. That is, all the data records are exactly the same distance from the top entry in the index set. This aspect of B-trees ensures performance efficiency, although the algorithms for inserting and deleting records are more complex than those for ordinary trees (which can be unbalanced) because several index entries may need to be modified when records are added or deleted to keep all records the same distance from the top index entry.

Summary of Data Structures

Figure A-11 summarizes the techniques for maintaining ordered flat files. Three supporting data structures are possible. Sequential lists can be used, but the data must be duplicated in order to maintain several orders. Because sequential lists are not used in database processing, we will not consider them further. Both linked lists and indexes can be used without data duplication. B-trees are special applications of indexes.

As shown in Figure A-11, sequential lists can be stored using any of three file organizations. In practice, however, they are usually kept on sequential files. In addition, although both linked lists and indexes can be stored using either indexed sequential or direct files, DBMS products almost always store them on direct files.

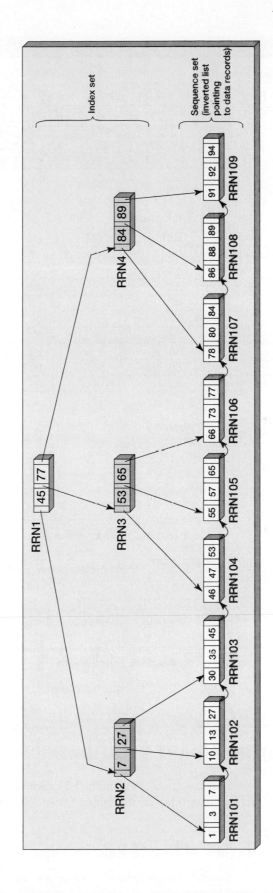

FIGURE A-9

General Structure of a
Simple B-Tree

FIGURE A-10

Occurrence of the B-Tree in Figure A-9

RRN	Link1	Value1	Link2	Value2	Link3
1	2	45	3	77	4
2	101	7	102	27	103
3	104	53	105	65	106
4	107	84	108	89	109

Index Set

.
.
.

	R1	Addr1	R2	Addr2	R3	Addr3	Link
101	1	Data or pointer	3	Data or pointer	7	Data or pointer	102
102	10	⋯	13	⋯	27	⋯	103
103	30	⋯	35	⋯	45	⋯	104
104	46	⋯	47	⋯	53	⋯	105
105	55	⋯	57	⋯	65	⋯	106
106	66	⋯	73	⋯	77	⋯	107
107	78	⋯	80	⋯	84	⋯	108
108	86	⋯	88	⋯	89	⋯	109
109	91	⋯	92	⋯	94	⋯	0

Sequence Set
(Addresses of
data records
are omitted)

FIGURE A-11

Summary of Data Structures and Data Organizations Used for Ordered Flat Files

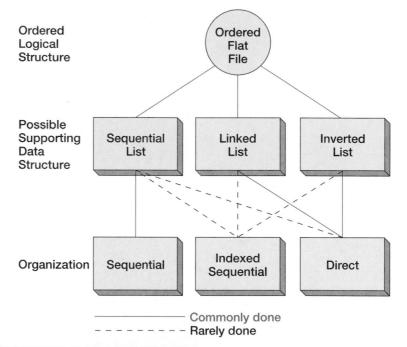

▶ REPRESENTING BINARY RELATIONSHIPS

In this section, we examine how each of the specialized record relationships—trees, simple networks, and complex networks—can be represented using linked lists and indexes.

Review of Record Relationships

Records can be related in three ways. A *tree* relationship has one or more one-to-many relationships, but each child record has at most one parent. The occurrence of faculty data shown in Figure A-12 illustrates a tree. There are several 1:N relationships, but any child record has only one parent, as shown in Figure A-13.

FIGURE A-12

Occurrence of a Faculty Member Record

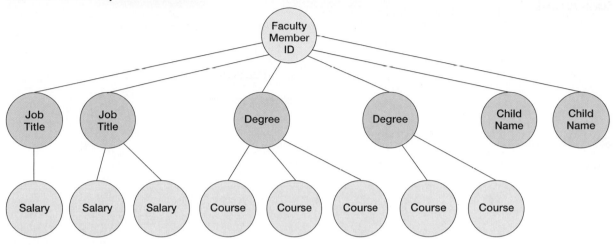

FIGURE A-13

Schematic of a Faculty Member Tree Structure

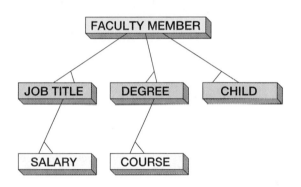

A *simple network* is a collection of records and the 1:N relationships among them. What distinguishes a simple network from a tree is the fact that in a simple network, a child can have more than one parent as long as the parents are different record types. The occurrence of a simple network of students, advisers, and major fields of study shown in Figure A-14 is represented schematically in Figure A-15.

A *complex network* is also a collection of records and relationships, but the relationships are many-to-many instead of one-to-many. The relationship between students and classes is a complex network. An occurrence of this relationship can be seen in Figure A-16, and the general schematic is in Figure A-17.

We saw earlier that we can use linked lists and indexes to process records in orders different from the one in which they are physically stored. We can also use those same data structures to store and process the relationships among records.

FIGURE A-14

Occurrence of a Simple Network

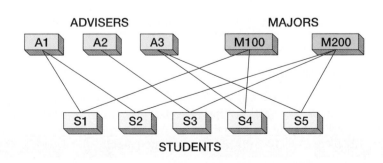

FIGURE –15

General Structure of a
Simple Network

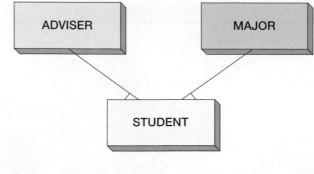

FIGURE A–16

Occurrence of a
Complex Network

FIGURE A–17

Schematic of a
Complex Network

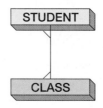

Representing Trees

We can use sequential lists, linked lists, and indexes to represent trees. When using sequential lists, we duplicate many data; and furthermore, sequential lists are not used by DBMS products to represent trees. Therefore, we describe only linked lists and indexes.

Linked-list Representation of Trees Figure A-18 shows a tree structure in which the VENDOR records are parents and the INVOICE records are children. Figure A-19 shows two occurrences of this structure, and all of the VENDOR and INVOICE records have been written to a direct access file in Figure A-20. VENDOR AA is in relative record number 1 (RRN1), and VENDOR BB is in relative record number 2. The INVOICE records have been stored in subsequent records, as illustrated. Note that these records are not stored in any particular order and that they do not need to be.

Our problem is that we cannot tell which invoices belong to which vendors from this file. To solve this problem with a linked list, we add a pointer field to every record.

FIGURE A–18

Sample Tree Relating
VENDOR and INVOICE
Records

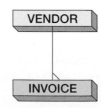

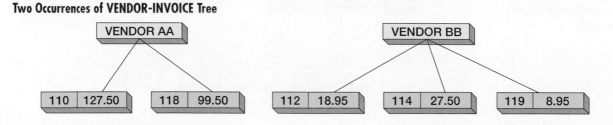

FIGURE A–19

Two Occurrences of VENDOR-INVOICE Tree

File Representation of the Trees in Figure A-19

Record Number	Record Contents	
1	VENDOR AA	
2	VENDOR BB	
3	118	99.50
4	119	8.95
5	112	18.95
6	114	27.50
7	110	127.50

In this field, we store the address of some other related record. For example, we place in VENDOR AA's link field the address of the first invoice belonging to it. This is RRN7, which is Invoice 110. Then, we make Invoice 110 point to the next invoice belonging to VENDOR AA, in this case RRN3. This slot holds Invoice 118. To indicate that there are no more children in the chain, we insert a 0 in the link field for RRN3.

This technique is shown in Figure A-21. If you examine the figure, you will see that a similar set of links has been used to represent the relationship between VENDOR BB and its invoices.

The structure in Figure A-21 is much easier to modify than is a sequential list of the records. For example, suppose that we add a new invoice, say number 111, to VENDOR AA. To do this, we just add the record to the file and insert it into the linked list. Physically, the record can be placed anywhere. But where should it be placed logically? Usually, the application will have a requirement; for example, children are to be kept in ascending order on invoice number. If so, we need to make Invoice 110 point to Invoice 111 (at RRN8), and we need to make Invoice 111, the new invoice, point to Invoice 118 (at RRN3). This modification is shown in Figure A-22.

Similarly, deleting an invoice is easy. If Invoice 114 is deleted, we simply modify the pointer in the invoice that is now pointing to Invoice 114. In this case, it is Invoice 112 at RRN5. We give Invoice 112 the pointer that Invoice 114 had before deletion. In this way, Invoice 112 points to Invoice 119 (see Figure A-23). We have effectively cut one link out of the chain and welded together the ones it once connected.

Tree Occurrences Represented by Linked Lists

Relative Record Number	Record Contents		Link Field
1	VENDOR AA		7
2	VENDOR BB		5
3	118	99.50	0
4	119	8.95	0
5	112	18.95	6
6	114	27.50	4
7	110	127.50	3

Inserting Invoice 111 into File in Figure A-21

Relative Record Number	Record Contents		Link Field
1	VENDOR AA		7
2	VENDOR BB		5
3	118	99.50	0
4	119	8.95	0
5	112	18.95	6
6	114	27.50	4
7	110	127.50	8
8	111	19.95	3

← Inserted Record

FIGURE A-23

Deleting Invoice 114 from File in Figure A-22

Relative Record Number	Record Contents		Link Field	
1	VENDOR AA		7	
2	VENDOR BB		5	
3	118	99.50	0	
4	119	8.95	0	
5	112	18.95	4	
6	114	27.50	4	← Deleted Record
7	110	127.50	8	
8	111	19.95	3	

Index Representation of Trees   A tree structure can readily be represented using indexes. The technique is to store each one-to-many relationship as an index. These lists are then used to match parents and children.

Using the VENDOR and INVOICE records in Figure A-21, we see that VENDOR AA (in RRN1) owns INVOICEs 110 (RRN7) and 118 (RRN3). Thus, RRN1 is the parent of RRN7 and RRN3. We can represent this fact with the index in Figure A-24. The list simply associates a parent's address with the addresses of each of its children.

If the tree has several 1:N relationships, several indexes will be required—one for each relationship. For the structure in Figure A-13, five indexes are needed.

Representing Simple Networks

As with trees, simple networks can also be represented using linked lists and indexes.

Linked-List Representation of Simple Networks   Consider the simple network shown in Figure A-25. It is a simple network because all the relationships are 1:N, and the SHIPMENT records have two parents of different types. Each SHIPMENT has a CUSTOMER parent and a TRUCK parent. The relationship between CUSTOMER and SHIPMENT is 1:N because a customer can have several shipments, and the relationship from TRUCK to SHIPMENT is 1:N because one truck can hold many shipments (assuming that the shipments are small enough to fit in one truck or less). An occurrence of this network is shown in Figure A-26.

In order to represent this simple network with linked lists, we need to establish one set of pointers for each 1:N relationship. In this example, that means one set of pointers to connect CUSTOMERs with their SHIPMENTs and another set of pointers to connect TRUCKs with their SHIPMENTs. Thus, a CUSTOMER record will contain one pointer (to the first SHIPMENT it owns); a TRUCK record will contain one pointer (to the first SHIPMENT it owns); and a SHIPMENT record will have two pointers, one for the next SHIPMENT owned by the same CUSTOMER and one for the next SHIPMENT owned by the same TRUCK. This scheme is illustrated in Figure A-27.

FIGURE A-24

Index Representation of VENDOR-INVOICE Relationship

FIGURE A-25

Simple Network Structure

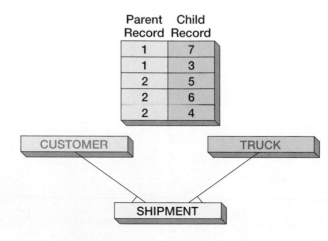

Parent Record	Child Record
1	7
1	3
2	5
2	6
2	4

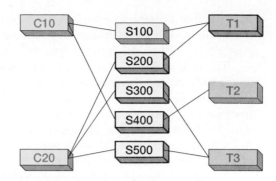

A simple network has at least two 1:N relationships, each of which can be represented using an index, as we explained in our discussion of trees. For example, consider the simple network shown in Figure A-25. It has two 1:N relationships, one between TRUCK and SHIPMENT and one between CUSTOMER and SHIPMENT. We can store each of these relationships in an index. Figure A-28 shows the two indexes needed to represent the example in Figure A-26. Assume that the records are located in the same positions as shown in Figure A-27.

Representing Complex Networks

Complex networks can be physically represented in a variety of ways. They can be decomposed into trees or simple networks, and these simpler structures can then be represented using one of the techniques we just described. Alternatively, they can be represented directly using indexes. Linked lists are not used by any DBMS product to represent complex networks directly. In practice, complex networks are nearly always decomposed into simpler structures, so we consider only those representations using decomposition.

A common approach to representing complex networks is to reduce them to simple networks and then to represent the simple networks with linked lists or indexes. Note,

Relative Record Number	Record Contents	Link Fields	
1	C10	6	
2	C20	7	
3	T1		6
4	T2		9
5	T3		8
6	S100	9	7
7	S200	8	0
8	S300	10	10
9	S400	0	0
10	S500	0	0

CUSTOMER Links   TRUCK Links

Customer Record	Shipment Record		Truck Record	Shipment Record
1	6		3	6
1	9		3	7
2	7		4	9
2	8		5	8
2	10		5	10

however, that a complex network involves a relationship between two records, whereas a simple network involves relationships among three records. Thus, in order to decompose a complex network into a simple one, we need to create a third record type.

The record that is created when a complex network is decomposed into a simple one is called an *intersection record.* Consider the StudentClass complex network. An intersection record contains a unique key from a STUDENT record and a unique key from a corresponding CLASS record. It will contain no other application data, although it might contain link fields. The general structure of this relationship is shown in Figure A-29. Assuming that the record names are unique (such as S1, S2, and C1), an instance of the STUDENT-CLASS relationship is illustrated in Figure A-30.

Notice that the relationship between STUDENT and the intersection record and that between CLASS and the intersection record both are 1:N. Thus, we have created a simple network that can now be represented with the linked-list or index techniques shown earlier. A file of this occurrence using the linked-list technique is shown in Figure A-31.

Summary of Relationship Representations

Figure A-32 summarizes the representations of record relationships. Trees can be represented using sequential lists (although we did not discuss this approach), linked lists, or indexes. Sequential lists are not used in DBMS products. A simple network can be decomposed into trees and then represented, or it can be represented directly using either linked lists or indexes. Finally, a complex network can be decomposed into a tree or a simple network (using intersection records), or it can be represented directly using indexes.

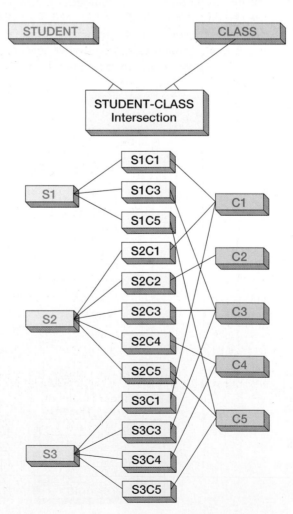

FIGURE A-29

Decomposition of Complex Network into Simple Network

FIGURE A-30

Instance of STUDENT-CLASS Relationship Showing Intersection Records

FIGURE A–31

Occurrence of Network
in Figure A-30

Relative Record Number	Record Contents	STUDENT Links	CLASS Links
1	S1	9	
2	S2	12	
3	S3	17	
4	C1		9
5	C2		13
6	C3		10
7	C4		15
8	C5		11
9	S1C1	10	12
10	S1C3	11	14
11	S1C5	0	16
12	S2C1	13	17
13	S2C2	14	0
14	S2C3	15	18
15	S2C4	16	19
16	S2C5	0	20
17	S3C1	18	0
18	S3C3	19	0
19	S3C4	20	0
20	S3C5	0	0

FIGURE A–32

Record Relationships,
Data Structures, and
File Organizations

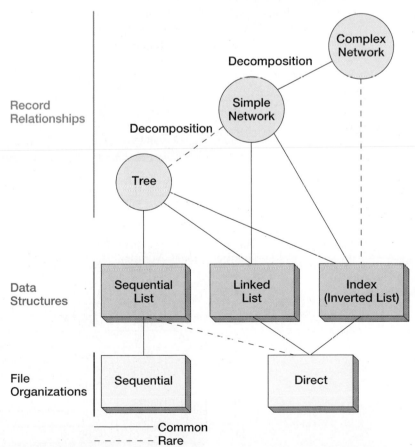

► SECONDARY-KEY REPRESENTATIONS

In many cases, the word *key* indicates a field (or fields) whose value uniquely identifies a record. This is usually called the *primary key*. Sometimes, however, applications need to access and process records by means of a *secondary key*, one that is different from the primary key. Secondary keys may be unique (such as a professor's name) or non-unique (such as a customer's Zip code). In this section, we use the term *set* to refer to all records having the same value of a non-unique secondary key; for example, a set of records having Zip code 98040.

Both linked lists and indexes are used to represent secondary keys, but linked lists are practical only for non-unique keys. Indexes, however, can be used for both unique and non-unique key representations.

Linked-List Representation of Secondary Keys

Consider the example of CUSTOMER records shown in Figure A-33. The primary key is AccountNumber, and there is a secondary key on CreditLimit. Possible CreditLimit values are 500, 700, and 1000. Thus, there will be a set of records for the limit of 500, a set for 700, and a set for 1000.

To represent this key using linked lists, we add a link field to the CUSTOMER records. Inside this link field, we create a linked list for each set of records. Figure A-34 shows a database of 11 customers; but, for brevity, only AccountNumber and CreditLimit are shown. A link field has been attached to the records. Assume that one database record occupies one physical record on a direct file using relative record addressing.

Three pointers need to be established so that we know where to begin each linked list. These pointers, called *heads*, are stored separately from the data. The head of the $500 linked list is RRN1. Record 1 links to record 2, which in turn links to record 7. Record 7 has a zero in the link position, indicating that it is the end of the list. Consequently, the $500 credit limit set consists of records 1, 2, and 7. Similarly, the $700 set contains records 3, 5, and 10; and the $1000 set contains relative records 4, 6, 8, 9, and 11.

FIGURE A-33

CUSTOMER Record

Account-Number	Name	Address	Credit-Limit	Account-Balance

Primary Key · · · · · · · · · · · · · · · Secondary Key

FIGURE A-34

Representing CreditLimit Secondary Key Using Linked List

Relative Record Number	Link	Account-Number	Credit-Limit	Other Data
1	2	101	500	
2	7	301	500	
3	5	203	700	
4	6	004	1000	
5	10	204	700	
6	8	905	1000	
7	0	705	500	
8	9	207	1000	
9	11	309	1000	
10	0	409	700	
11	0	210	1000	

HEAD-500 = 1
HEAD-700 = 3
HEAD-1000 = 4

To answer a query such as, How many accounts in the 1000 set have a balance in excess of 900?, the 1000-set linked list can be used. In this way, only those records in the 1000 set need to be read from the file and examined. Although the advantage of this approach is not readily apparent in this small example, suppose that there are 100,000 CUSTOMER records, and only 100 of them are in the 1000 set. If there is no linked list, all 100,000 records must be examined; but with the linked list, only 100 records need to be examined—namely, the ones in the 1000 set. Using the linked list, therefore, saves 99,900 reads.

Using linked lists is not an effective technique for every secondary-key application. In particular, if the records are processed non-sequentially in a set, linked lists are inefficient. For example, if it is often necessary to find the 10th or 120th or *n*th record in the 500 CreditLimit set, processing will be slow. Linked lists are inefficient for direct access.

In addition, if the application requires that secondary keys be created or destroyed dynamically, the linked-list approach is undesirable. Whenever a new key is created, a link field must be added to every record, which often requires reorganizing the database, which is a time-consuming and expensive process.

Finally, if the secondary keys are unique, each list will have a length of 1, and a separate linked list will exist for every record in the database. Because this situation is unworkable, linked lists cannot be used for unique keys. For example, suppose that the CUSTOMER records contain another unique field, say, Social Security Number. If we attempt to represent this unique secondary key using a linked list, every Social Security Number will be a separate linked list. Furthermore, each linked list will have just one item in it: the single record having the indicated Social Security Number.

Index Representation of Secondary Keys

A second technique for representing secondary keys uses an index; one is established for each secondary key. The approach varies, depending on whether the key values are unique or non-unique.

Unique Secondary Keys Suppose that the CUSTOMER records in Figure A-33 contain Social Security Numbers (SSN) as well as the fields shown. To provide key access to the CUSTOMER records using SSN, we simply build an index on the SSN field. Sample CUSTOMER data are shown in Figure A-35(a), and a corresponding index is illustrated in Figure A-35(b). This index uses relative record numbers as addresses. It is possible to use AccountNumbers instead, in which case the DBMS locates the desired SSN in the index, obtains the matching AccountNumber, and then converts the AccountNumber to a relative record address.

Non-Unique Secondary Keys Indexes can also be used to represent non-unique secondary keys, but because each set of related records can contain an unknown number of members, the entries in the index are of variable length. For example, Figure A-36 shows the index for the CreditLimit sets for the CUSTOMER data. The $500 set and the $700 set both have three members, so there are three account numbers in each entry. The $1000 set has five members, so there are five account numbers in that entry.

FIGURE A-35 **Representing a Unique Secondary Key with Indexes (a) Sample CUSTOMER Data (with SSN) and (b) Index for SSN Secondary Key**	Relative Record Number	Account-Number	Credit-Limit	Social Security Number (SSN)		SSN	Relative Record Number
	1	101	500	000-01-0001		000-01-0001	1
	2	301	500	000-01-0005		000-01-0003	4
	3	203	700	000-01-0009		000-01-0005	2
	4	004	1000	000-01-0003		000-01-0009	3
			(a)			(b)	

FIGURE A–36

Index for CreditLimit
Key in Figure A-33

CreditLimit	AccountNumber				
500	101	301	705		
700	203	204	409		
1000	004	905	207	309	210

In reality, representing and processing non-unique secondary keys are complex tasks. Several different schemes are used by commercial DBMS products. One common method uses a values table and an occurrence table. Each values table entry consists of two fields, the first of which has a key value. For the CUSTOMER CreditLimit key, the values are 500, 700, and 1000. The second field of the values table entry is a pointer into the occurrence table. The occurrence table contains record addresses, and those having a common value in the secondary-key field appear together in the table. Figure A-37 shows the values and occurrence tables for the CreditLimit key.

To locate records having a given value of the secondary key, the values table is searched for the desired value. After the given key value is located in the values table, the pointer is followed to the occurrence table to obtain the addresses of those records having that key value. These addresses are then used to obtain the desired records.

When a new record is inserted into the file, the DBMS must modify the indexes for each secondary-key field. For non-unique keys, it must make sure that the new record key value is in the values table; if it is, it adds the new record address to the appropriate entry in the occurrence table. If it is not, it must insert new entries in the values and occurrence tables.

When a record is deleted, its address must be removed from the occurrence table. If no addresses remain in the occurrence table entry, the corresponding values table entry must also be deleted.

When the secondary-key field of a record is modified, the record address must be removed from one occurrence table entry and inserted into another. If the modification is a new value for the key, an entry must be added to the values table.

The index approach to representing secondary keys overcomes the objections to the linked-list approach. Direct processing of sets is possible. For example, the third record in a set can be retrieved without processing the first or second one. Also, it is possible to dynamically create and delete secondary keys. No changes are made in the records themselves; the DBMS merely creates additional values and occurrence tables. Finally, unique keys can be processed efficiently.

The disadvantages of the index approach are that it requires more file space (the tables use more overhead than the pointers do) and that the DBMS programming task is more complex. Note that the *application programming* task is not necessarily any more or less difficult—but it is more complex to write DBMS software that processes indexes than it is to write software that processes linked lists. Finally, modifications are usually processed more slowly because of the reading and writing actions required to access and maintain the values in the occurrence tables.

FIGURE A–37

Values and Occurrence
Tables for CreditLimit
Key in Figure A-33

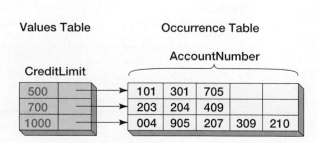

Values Table   Occurrence Table

SUMMARY

In this appendix, we surveyed data structures used for database processing. A flat file is a file that contains no repeating groups. Flat files can be ordered using sequential lists (physically placing the records in the sequence in which they will be processed), linked lists (attaching to each data record a pointer to another logically related record), and indexes (building a table, separate from the data records that contains pointers to related records). B-trees are special applications of indexes.

Sequential lists, linked lists, and indexes (or inverted lists) are fundamental data structures. (Sequential lists, however, are seldom used in database processing.) These data structures can be used to represent record relationships as well as secondary keys.

The three basic record structures—trees, simple networks, and complex networks—can be represented using linked lists and indexes. Simple networks can be decomposed into trees and then represented; complex networks can be decomposed into simple networks containing an intersection record and then represented.

Secondary keys are used to access the data on some field besides the primary key. Secondary keys can be unique or non-unique. Non-unique secondary keys can be represented with both linked lists and indexes. Unique secondary keys can be represented only with indexes.

GROUP I QUESTIONS

A.1 Define a flat file. Give an example (other than one in this text) of a flat file and an example of a file that is not flat.

A.2 Show how sequential lists can be used to maintain the file in question A.1 in two different orders simultaneously.

A.3 Show how linked lists can be used to maintain the file in question A.1 in two different orders simultaneously.

A.4 Show how inverted lists can be used to maintain the file in question A.1 in two different orders simultaneously.

A.5 Define a tree, and give an example structure.

A.6 Give an occurrence of the tree in question A.5.

A.7 Represent the occurrence in question A.6 using linked lists.

A.8 Represent the occurrence in question A.6 using indexes.

A.9 Define a simple network and give an example structure.

A.10 Give an occurrence of the simple network in question A.9.

A.11 Represent the occurrence in question A.10 using linked lists.

A.12 Represent the occurrence in question A.10 using indexes.

A.13 Define *complex network*, and give an example structure.

A.14 Give an occurrence of the complex network in question A.13.

A.15 Decompose the complex network in question A.14 into a simple network, and represent an occurrence of it using indexes.

A.16 Explain the difference between primary and secondary keys.

A.17 Explain the difference between unique and non-unique keys.

A.18 Define a file containing a unique secondary key. Represent an occurrence of that file using an index on the secondary key.

A.19 Define a nonunique secondary key for the file in question A.18. Represent an occurrence of that file using a linked list on the secondary key.

A.20 Perform the same task as in question A.19, but use an index to represent the secondary key.

A.21 Develop an algorithm to produce a report listing the IDs of students enrolled in each class, using the linked-list structure in Figure A-4.

A.22 Develop an algorithm to insert records into the structure in Figure A-4. The resulting structure should resemble the one shown in Figure A-5.

A.23 Develop an algorithm to produce a report listing the IDs of students enrolled in each class, using the index structure shown in Figures A-8(a), A-8(b), and A-8(c).

A.24 Develop an algorithm to insert a record into the structure shown in Figure A-8(a), being sure to modify both of the associated indexes shown in Figure A-8(b) and A-8(c).

A.25 Develop an algorithm to delete a record from the structure shown in Figure A-34, which shows a secondary key represented with a linked list. If all records for one of the credit-limit categories (say, $1000) are deleted, should the associated head pointer also be deleted? Why or why not?

A.26 Develop an algorithm to insert a record into the structure shown in Figure A-34. Suppose that the new record has a credit-limit value different from those already established. Should the record be inserted and a new linked list established? Or should the record be rejected? Who should make that decision?

Appendix B

The Semantic Object Model

This appendix discusses the semantic object model, which is used to create data models like the E-R model discussed in Chapters 2 and 3. As shown in Figure B-1, the development team interviews users; analyzes the users' reports, forms, and queries; and constructs a model of the users' data from them. This data model is later transformed into a database design.

The particular form of the data model depends on the constructs used to build it. If an E-R model is used, the model will have entities, relationships, and the like. If a semantic model is used, the model will have semantic objects and related constructs, which are discussed here.

The E-R model and the semantic object model are like lenses through which the database developers look when studying and documenting the users' data. Both lenses work, and they both ultimately result in a database design. They use different lenses to form that design, however; and because the lenses create different images, the designs they produce may not be exactly the same. When developing a database, you must decide which approach to use, just as a photographer needs to decide which lens to use. Each approach has strengths and weaknesses, which we discuss at the end of this chapter.

The semantic object model was first presented in 1988, in the third edition of this text. It is based on concepts that were developed and published by Codd and by Hammer and McLeod.[1] The semantic object model is a data model. It is different from **object-oriented database processing,** which was discussed in Chapter 16. Here you will learn how the purposes, features, and constructs of semantic object modeling differ from object-oriented database processing.

---

[1] E. F. Codd, "Extending the Relational Model to Capture More Meaning," *ACM Transactions on Database Systems,* December 1976, pp. 397–424; and Michael Hammer and Dennis McLeod, "Database Description with SDM: A Semantic Database Model," *ACM Transactions on Database Systems,* September 1981, pp. 351–386.

FIGURE B-1

Using Different Data Models for Database Designs

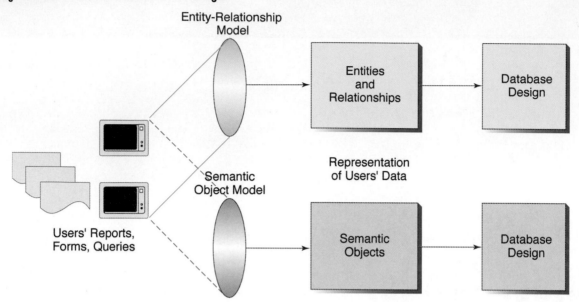

◢ SEMANTIC OBJECTS

The purpose of a database application is to provide forms, reports, and queries so that the users can track entities or objects important to their work. The goals of the early stages of database development are to determine the things to be represented in the database, to specify the characteristics of those things, and to establish the relationships among them.

In Chapters 2 and 3, we referred to these things as entities. In this appendix, we refer to them as **semantic objects,** or sometimes as just objects. The word *semantic* means meaning, and a semantic object is one that models, in part, the meaning of the users' data. Semantic objects model the users' perceptions more closely than does the E-R model. We use the adjective *semantic* with the word *object* to distinguish the objects discussed in this appendix from the objects defined in object-oriented programming (OOP) languages.

Defining Semantic Objects

Entities and objects are similar in some ways, and they are different in other ways. We begin with the similarities. A semantic object is a representation of some identifiable thing in the users' work environment. More formally, a semantic object is a *named collection of attributes that sufficiently describes a distinct identity.*

Like entities, semantic objects are grouped into classes. An object class has a *name* that distinguishes it from other classes and that corresponds to the names of the things it represents. Thus, a database that supports users who work with student records has an object class called STUDENT. Note that object class names, like entity class names, are spelled with capital letters. A particular semantic object is an instance of the class. Thus, 'William Jones' is an instance of the STUDENT class, and 'Accounting' is an instance of the DEPARTMENT class.

Like entities, an object has a *collection of attributes.* Each attribute represents a characteristic of the identity being represented. For instance, the STUDENT object can have attributes such as Name, HomeAddress, CampusAddress, DateOfBirth, DateOfGraduation, and Major. This collection of attributes also is a *sufficient descrip-*

tion, which means that the attributes represent all of the characteristics that the users need in order to do their work. As we stated in Chapter 3, things in the world have an infinite set of characteristics; we cannot represent all of them. Instead, we represent those necessary for the users to satisfy their information needs so that they can successfully perform their jobs. Sufficient description also means that the objects are complete in themselves. All of the data required about a CUSTOMER, for example, is located in the CUSTOMER object, so we need not look anywhere else to find data about CUSTOMERs.

Objects represent *distinct identities;* that is, they are something that users recognize as independent and separate and that users want to track and report. These identities are the nouns about which the information is to be produced. To understand better the term *distinct identity,* recall that there is a difference between objects and object instances. CUSTOMER is the name of an object, and 'CUSTOMER 12345' is the name of an instance of an object. When we say that an object represents a distinct identity, we mean that users consider each *instance* of an object to be unique and identifiable in its own right.

Finally, note that the identities that the objects represent may or may not have a physical existence. For example, EMPLOYEEs physically exist, but ORDERs do not. Orders are, themselves, models of a contractual agreement to provide certain goods or services under certain terms and conditions. They are not physical things but, rather, representations of agreements. Thus, something need not be physical in order to be considered an object; it need only be identifiable in its own right in the minds of the users.

Attributes

Semantic objects have attributes that define their characteristics. There are three types of attributes. **Simple attributes** have a single element. Examples are DateOfHire, InvoiceNumber, and SalesTotal. **Group attributes** are composites of other attributes. One example is Address, which contains the attributes {Street, City, State, Zip}; another example is FullName, which contains the attributes {FirstName, MiddleInitial, LastName}. **Semantic object attributes** are attributes that establish a relationship between one semantic object and another.

To understand these statements better, look at Figure B-2(a), which is an example of a **semantic object diagram**, or **object diagram.** Such diagrams are used by development teams to summarize the structures of objects and to present them visually. Objects are

FIGURE B-2

DEPARTMENT Object Diagram (a) DEPARTMENT Object and (b) DEPARTMENT Object with Cardinalities

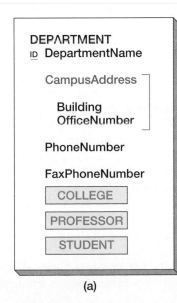
(a)

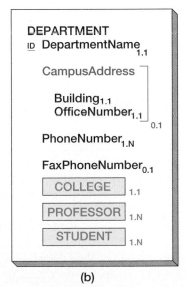
(b)

shown in portrait-oriented rectangles. The name of the object appears at the top, and attributes are written in order after the object name.

The DEPARTMENT object contains an example of each of the three types of attributes. DepartmentName, PhoneNumber, and FaxPhoneNumber are simple attributes, each of which represents a single data element. CampusAddress is a group attribute containing the simple attributes Building and OfficeNumber. Finally, COLLEGE, PROFESSOR, and STUDENT each are semantic object attributes, which means that those objects are connected to and logically contained in DEPARTMENT.

The object attributes, or **object links** as they are sometimes called, mean that when a user thinks about a DEPARTMENT, he or she thinks not only about DepartmentName, CampusAddress, PhoneNumber, and FaxPhoneNumber; but also about the COLLEGE, PROFESSORs, and STUDENTs who are related to that department. Because COLLEGE, PROFESSOR, and STUDENT also are objects, the complete data model contains object diagrams for them, too. The COLLEGE object contains attributes of the college; the PROFESSOR object contains attributes of the faculty; and the STUDENT object contains attributes of the students.

Attribute Cardinality   Each attribute in a semantic object has both a minimum cardinality and a maximum cardinality. The minimum cardinality indicates the number of instances of the attribute that must exist in order for the object to be valid. Usually, this number is either 0 or 1. If it is 0, the attribute is not required to have a value; if it is 1, it must have a value. Although it is unusual, the minimum cardinality can sometimes be larger than 1. For example, the attribute PLAYER in an object called BASKETBALL-TEAM might have a minimum cardinality of 5 because this is the smallest number of players required to make up a basketball team.

The maximum cardinality indicates the maximum number of instances of the attribute that the object may have. It is usually either 1 or N. If it is 1, the attribute can have no more than one instance; if it is N, the attribute can have many values, and the absolute number is not specified. Sometimes, the maximum cardinality is a specific number such as 5, meaning the object can contain no more than exactly five instances of the attribute. For example, the attribute PLAYER in BASKETBALL-TEAM might have a maximum cardinality of 15, which would indicate that no more than 15 players could be assigned to a team's roster.

Cardinalities are shown as subscripts of attributes in the format **n.m,** where n is the minimum cardinality and m is the maximum. In Figure B-2(b), the minimum cardinality of DepartmentName is 1 and the maximum is also 1, which means that exactly one value of DepartmentName is required. The cardinality of PhoneNumber is 1.N, meaning that a DEPARTMENT is required to have at least one PhoneNumber, but may have many. The cardinality of 0.1 in FaxPhoneNumber means that a DEPARTMENT may have either zero or one FaxPhoneNumber.

The cardinalities of groups and the attributes in groups can be subtle. Consider the attribute CampusAddress. Its cardinalities are 0.1, meaning that a DEPARTMENT need not have an address, and has at most one. Now, examine the attributes inside CampusAddress. Both Building and OfficeNumber have the cardinalities 1.1. You might be wondering how a group can be optional if the attributes in that group are required. The answer is that the cardinalities operate only between the attribute and the container of that attribute. The minimum cardinality of CampusAddress indicates that there need not be a value for address in DEPARTMENT. But the minimum cardinalities of Building and OfficeNumber indicate that both Building and OfficeNumber must exist in CampusAddress. Thus, a CampusAddress group need not appear; but if one does, it must have a value for both Building and OfficeNumber.

Object Instances   The object diagrams for DEPARTMENT shown in Figure B-2 are a format, or general structure, that can be used for any department. An instance of the DEPARTMENT object is shown in Figure B-3, with each attribute's value for a particular department. The DepartmentName is Information Systems, and it is located in

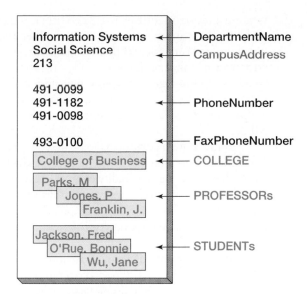

FIGURE B–3

An Instance of the DEPARTMENT Object in Figure B-2

Room 213 of the Social Science Building. Observe that there are three values for PhoneNumber—the Information Systems Department has three phone lines in its office. Other departments may have fewer or more, but every department has at least one.

Furthermore, there is one instance of COLLEGE—the College of Business, and there are multiple values for the PROFESSOR and STUDENT object attributes. Each of these object attributes is a complete object; each has all the attributes defined for an object of that type. To keep this diagram simple, only the identifying names are shown for each of the instances of object attribute.

An object diagram is a picture of the user's perception of an object in the work environment. Thus, in the user's mind, the DEPARTMENT object includes all of this data. A DEPARTMENT logically contains data about the COLLEGE in which it resides, as well as the PROFESSORs and STUDENTs who are related to that department.

Paired Attributes   The semantic object model has no one-way object relationships. If an object contains another object, the second object will contain the first. For example, if DEPARTMENT contains the object attribute COLLEGE, then COLLEGE will contain the matching object attribute DEPARTMENT. These object attributes are called **paired attributes** because they always occur as a pair.

Why must object attributes be paired? The answer lies in the way in which human beings think about relationships. If object A has a relationship with object B, then object B will have a relationship with object A. At the least, B is related to A in the relationship of "things that are related to B." If this argument seems obscure, try to envision a one-way relationship between two objects. It cannot be done.

Object Identifiers

An **object identifier** is one or more object attributes that the users employ to identify object instances. Such identifiers are potential names for a semantic object. In CUSTOMER, for example, possible identifiers are CustomerID and CustomerName. These are attributes that users consider to be valid names of CUSTOMER instances. Compare these identifiers with attributes such as DateOfFirstOrder, StockPrice, and NumberOfEmployees. Such attributes are not identifiers because the users do not think of them as names of CUSTOMER instances.

A **group identifier** is an identifier that has more than one attribute. Examples are {FirstName, LastName}, {FirstName, PhoneNumber}, and {State, License Number}.

Object identifiers may or may not be unique, depending on how the users view their data. For example, InvoiceNumber is a unique identifier for ORDER, but StudentName is not a unique identifier for STUDENT. There may, for example, be two students named "Mary Smith." If so, the users will employ StudentName to identify a group of one or more students and then, if necessary, use values of other attributes to identify a particular member of that set.

In semantic object diagrams, object identifiers are denoted by the letters *ID* in front of the attribute. If the identifier is unique, these letters will be underlined. In Figure B-2(b), for example, the attribute DepartmentName is a unique identifier of DEPART-MENT.

Normally, if an attribute is to be used as an identifier, its value is required. Also, generally there is no more than one value of an identifier attribute for a given object. In most cases, therefore, the cardinality of an ID attribute is 1.1, so we use this value as a default.

There are (relatively few) cases, however, in which the cardinality of an identifier is other than 1.1. Consider, for example, the attribute Alias in the semantic object PERSON. A person need not have an alias, or he or she may have several aliases. Hence, the cardinality of Alias is 0.N.

Showing the subscripts of all attributes clutters the semantic object diagram. To simplify, we will assume that the cardinalities of simple-value identifier attributes are 1.1 and the cardinalities of other simple-value attributes are 0.1. If the cardinality of the simple-value attribute is other than these assumptions, we will show it on the diagram. Otherwise, subscripts on simple-value attributes will be omitted.

Attribute Domains

The **domain** of an attribute is a description of an attribute's possible values. The characteristics of a domain depend on the type of the attribute. The domain of a simple attribute consists of both a physical and a semantic description. The physical description indicates the type of data (for example, numeric versus string), the length of the data, and other restrictions or constraints (for example, the first character must be alphabetic or the value must not exceed 9999.99). The semantic description indicates the function or purpose of the attribute—it distinguishes this attribute from other attributes that might have the same physical description.

For example, the domain of DepartmentName can be defined as "the set of strings of up to seven characters that represent names of departments at Highline University." The phrase *strings of up to seven characters* is the physical description of the domain, and the phrase *that represent names of departments at Highline University* is the semantic description. The semantic description differentiates strings of seven characters that represent names of departments from similar strings that represent names of courses, buildings, or some other attribute.

In some cases, the physical description of a simple attribute domain is an **enumerated list,** the set of an attribute's specific values. The domain of the attribute PartColor, for example, might be the enumerated list {'Blue', 'Yellow', 'Red'}.

The domain of a group attribute also has a physical and a semantic description. The physical description is a list of all of the attributes in the group and the order of those attributes. The semantic description is the function or purpose of the group. Thus, the physical domain description of CampusAddress (shown in Figure B-2) is the list {Building, OfficeNumber}; the semantic description is *the location of an office at Highline University.*

The domain of an object attribute is the set of object instances of that type. In Figure B-2, for example, the domain of the PROFESSOR object attribute is the set of all PROFESSOR object instances in the database. The domain of the COLLEGE object is the set of all COLLEGEs in the database. In a sense, the domain of an object attribute is a dynamically enumerated list; the list contains all of the object instances of a particular type.

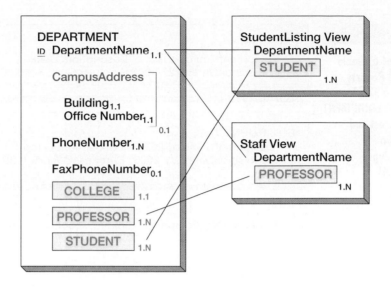

FIGURE B-4

StudentListings and Staff Views of the DEPARTMENT Semantic Object

Semantic Object Views

Users access the values of object attributes through database applications that provide data entry forms, reports, and queries. In most cases, such forms, reports, and queries do not require access to all of an object's attributes. For example, Figure B-4 shows two application views of DEPARTMENT. Some attributes of DEPARTMENT (its DepartmentName, for example) are visible in both application views. Other attributes are visible in only one. For example, STUDENT is seen only in the StudentListing View, but PROFESSOR is visible only in the Staff View.

The portion of an object that is visible to a particular application is called the **semantic object view**, or simply the **view.** A view consists of the name of the object plus a list of all of the attributes visible from that view.

Views are used in two ways. When you are developing a database, you can use them to develop the data model. Look at Figure 4-1 again. As shown, when developing the data model, the database and application developers work backward. That is, they begin with the forms, reports, and queries that the users say they need and then work backward to the database design. To do this, the team selects a required form, report, or query; and determines the view that must exist in order for the form, report, or query to be created. Then, the team selects the next form, report, or query; and does the same. These two views are then integrated. This process is repeated until the structure of the entire database has been created.

The second way in which views are used occurs after the database structure has been created. At this point, views are constructed to support new forms, reports, and queries based on the existing database structure. Examples of this second use were shown in Part IV, when we discussed SQL Server and Oracle.

▶ TYPES OF OBJECTS

This section describes and illustrates seven types of objects. For each type, we examine a report or form, and show how to model that report or form with an object. Then, we transform each of these types of objects into database designs.

Three new terms are used in this section: A **single-value attribute** is an attribute whose maximum cardinality is 1; a **multi-value attribute** is one whose maximum cardinality is greater than 1; and a **nonobject attribute** is a simple or group attribute.

FIGURE B-5

Example of a Simple
Object (a) Reports
Based on a Simple
Object; (b) EQUIPMENT
Simple Object and
(c) Relation
Representing
EQUIPMENT

EQUIPMENT TAG:
    EquipmentNumber: 100   Description: Desk
    AcquisitionDate: 2/27/2000 PurchaseCost: $350.00

EQUIPMENT TAG:
    EquipmentNumber: 200   Description: Lamp
    AcquisitionDate: 3/1/2000   PurchaseCost: $39.95

(a)

EQUIPMENT
ID EquipmentNumber
     Description
     AcquisitionDate
     PurchaseCost

(b)

EQUIPMENT (<u>EquipmentNumber</u>, Description, AcquisitionDate, PurchaseCost)

(c)

Simple Objects

A **simple object** is a semantic object that contains only single-value, simple, or group attributes. An example is shown in Figure B-5. Figure B-5(a) shows two instances of a report called an *Equipment Tag.* Such tags are applied to items of office equipment in order to help keep track of inventory. These tags can be considered a report.

Figure B-5(b) shows a simple object, EQUIPMENT, that models Equipment Tag. The attributes of the object include the items shown on the tag: EquipmentNumber, Description, AcquisitionDate, and PurchaseCost. Note that none of these attributes is multi-value, and none is an object attribute. Hence, EQUIPMENT is a simple object.

Figure B-5(b) is an example of a simple object, EQUIPMENT, which can be represented by a single relation, as shown in Figure B-5(c). Each attribute of the object is defined as an attribute of the relation; and the identifying attribute, EquipmentNumber, becomes the key attribute of the relation, denoted by underlining EquipmentNumber in Figure B-5(c).

The general transformation of simple objects is illustrated in Figure B-6. Object OBJECT1 is transformed into relation R1. The attribute that identifies OBJECT1 instances is O1; it becomes the key of relation R1. Nonkey data is represented in this and subsequent figures with ellipses (⪙).

Because a key is an attribute that uniquely identifies a row of a table, only unique identifiers—those with the ID underlined—can be transformed into keys. If there is no unique identifier in the object, one must be created by combining the existing attributes to form a unique identifier or by defining a surrogate key.

Composite Objects

A **composite object** is a semantic object that contains one or more multi-value, simple or group attributes but no object attributes. The hotel bill shown in Figure B-7(a) gives rise to the need for a composite object. The bill includes data that concerns the bill as a whole: InvoiceNumber, ArrivalDate, CustomerName, and TotalDue. It also con-

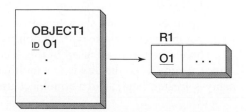

FIGURE B-7

Example of a Composite Object (a) Report Based on a Composite Object; (b) HOTEL-BILL Composite Object and (c) Relational Representation

GRANDVIEW HOTEL
Sea Bluffs, California

Invoice Number: 1234   Arrival Date: 10/12/2001
Customer Name: Mary Jones

10/12/2001	Room	$ 99.00
10/12/2001	Food	$ 37.55
10/12/2001	Phone	$ 2.50
10/12/2001	Tax	$ 15.00
10/13/2001	Room	$ 99.00
10/13/2001	Food	$ 47.90
10/13/2001	Tax	$ 15.00
	Total Due	$ 315.95

(a)

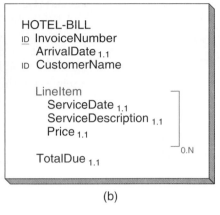

(b)

HOTEL-BILL (<u>InvoiceNumber</u>, ArrivalDate, CustomerName, TotalDue)

LINEITEM (*InvoiceNumber*, <u>ServiceDate</u>, ServiceDescription, Price)

Referential integrity constraint:

InvoiceNumber in LINEITEM must exist
in InvoiceNumber in HOTEL-BILL

(c)

tains a group of attributes that is repeated for services provided to the guest. Each group includes ServiceDate, ServiceDescription, and Price.

Figure B-7(b) shows an object diagram for the HOTEL-BILL object. The attribute LineItem is a group attribute having a maximum cardinality of N, which means that the group ServiceDate, ServiceDescription, Price can occur many times in an instance of the HOTEL-BILL semantic object.

LineItem is not modeled as an independent semantic object; instead, it is considered to be an attribute within a HOTEL-BILL. This design is appropriate because the hotel does not view one line of a guest's charges as a separate thing, so line items on the guest's bill do not have identifiers of their own. No employee attempts to enter a LineItem except in the context of a bill. The employee enters the data for bill number 1234 and then, in the context of that bill, enters the charges. Or the employee retrieves an existing bill and enters additional charges in the context of that bill.

The minimum cardinality of LineItem is 0, which means that a HOTEL-BILL object can exist without any LineItem data. This allows a bill to be started when the customer checks in and before there are any charges. If the minimum cardinality were 1, no HOTEL-BILL could be started until there was at least one charge. This design decision must be made in light of the business rules. It may be that the hotel's policy is not to start the bill until there has been a charge. If so, then the minimum cardinality of LineItem should be 1.

To represent this object, one relation is created for the base object, HOTEL-BILL, and an additional relation is created for the repeating group attribute, DailyCharge. This relational design is shown in Figure B-7(c).

In the key of DAILY-CHARGE, InvoiceNumber is underlined because it is part of the key of DAILY-CHARGE, and it is italicized because it is also a foreign key. (It is a key of HOTEL-BILL.) ChargeDate is underlined because it is part of the key of DAILY-CHARGE, but it is not italicized because it is not a foreign key.

In general, composite objects are transformed by defining one relation for the object itself and another relation for each multi-value attribute. In Figure B-8(a), object OBJECT1 contains two groups of multi-value attributes, each of which is represented by a relation in the database design. The key of each of these tables is the composite of the identifier of the object plus the identifier of the group. Thus, the representation of

<table>
<tr><td>

FIGURE B-8

General Transformation of Composite Objects (a) Composite Object with Separate Groups and (b) Composite Object with Nested Groups

</td><td>

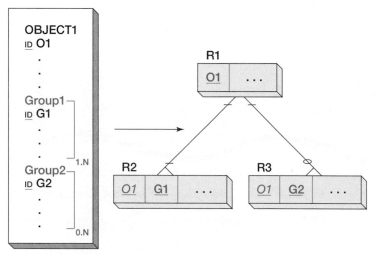

Referential integrity constraints:

O1 in R2 must exist in O1 in R1
O1 in R3 must exist in O1 in R1

(a)

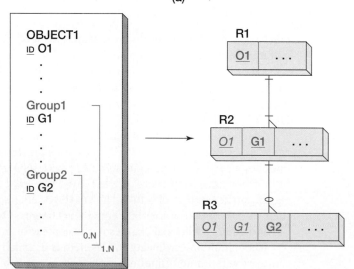

Referential integrity constraints:

O1 in R2 must exist in O1 in R1
(O1, G1) in R3 must exist in (O1, G1) in R2

(b)

</td></tr>
</table>

OBJECT1 is a relation R1 with key O1, a relation R2 with key (O1, G1), and a relation R3 with key (O1, G2).

The minimum cardinality from the object to the group is specified by the minimum cardinality of group attribute. In Figure B-8(a), the minimum cardinality of Group1 is 1 and that of Group2 is 0. These cardinalities are shown as a hash mark (on R2) and an oval (on R3) in the data structure diagram. The minimum cardinality from the group to the object is always 1 by default because a group cannot exist if the object that contains that group does not exist. These minimum cardinalities are shown by hash marks on the relationship lines into R1.

Groups can be nested. Figure B-8(b) shows an object in which Group2 is nested within Group1. When this occurs, the relation representing the nested group is made subordinate to the relation that represents its containing group. In Figure B-8(b), relation R3 is subordinate to relation R2. The key of R3 is the key of R2, which is (O1, G1) plus the identifier of Group2, which is G2; thus the key of R3 is (O1, G1, G2).

Make sure that you understand why the keys in Figure B-8(b) are constructed as they are. Also note that some attributes are underlined and italicized and some are simply underlined because some attributes are both local and foreign keys and some are just local keys.

Compound Objects

A **compound object** contains at least one object attribute. Figure B-9(a) shows two different data entry forms. One form, used by the company's motor pool, is used to keep track of the vehicles. The second form is used to maintain data about the employees. According to these forms, a vehicle is assigned to at most one employee, and an employee has at most one auto assigned.

FIGURE B-9

Compound Objects with 1:1 Paired Properties (a) Example Vehicle and Employee Data Entry Forms and (b) EMPLOYEE and VEHICLE Compound Objects

VEHICLE DATA			
License number	Serial number		
Make	Type	Year	Color
Employee assignment			

EMPLOYEE WORK DATA			
Employee name		Employee ID	
MailStop		Division	Phone
Pay code	Skill code	Hire date	Auto assigned

(a)

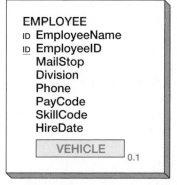 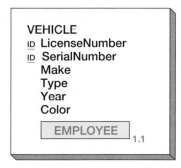

(b)

We cannot tell from these forms whether an auto must be assigned to an employee or whether every employee must have an auto. To obtain that information, we have to ask the users in the motor pool or human resources departments. Assume that we find out that an EMPLOYEE need not have a VEHICLE, but that a VEHICLE must be assigned to an employee.

Figure B-9(b) shows object diagrams for EMPLOYEE and VEHICLE. An EMPLOYEE contains VEHICLE as one of its attributes, and VEHICLE in turn contains EMPLOYEE as one of its attributes. Because both EMPLOYEE and VEHICLE contain object attributes, they both are compound objects. Furthermore, because neither attribute is multi-value, the relationship from EMPLOYEE to VEHICLE is one to one, or 1:1.

In Figure B-9(a), the Employee and Vehicle forms contain each other. That is, Vehicle Data has a field Employee assignment, and Employee Work Data has a field Auto assigned. But this is not always the case; sometimes, the relationship can appear in only one direction. Consider the report and form in Figure B-10(a), which concern two objects: DORMITORY and STUDENT. From the Dormitory Occupancy Report, we can see that users think of a dorm as having attributes regarding the dorm (Dormitory, ResidentAssistant, Phone) and also attributes regarding the students (StudentName, StudentNumber, Class) who live in the dorm.

On the other hand, the Student Data Form shows only student data; it does not include any dormitory data. (The campus address might contain a dorm address, but if it is true, it is apparently not important enough to document on the form. In a database development project, this possibility should be checked out with the users in an interview. Here, we will assume that the Student Data Form does not include dormitory data.)

As we stated earlier, object attributes always occur in pairs. Even if the forms, reports, and queries indicate that only one side of the relationship can be seen, both sides of the relationship always exist. By analogy, a bridge that connects two islands touches both islands and can be used in both directions, even if the bridge is, by custom or law, a one-way bridge.

When no form or report can be found to document one side of a relationship, the development team must ask the users about the cardinality of that relationship. In this case, the team needs to find out how many DORMITORY(ies) a STUDENT could have and whether a STUDENT must be related to a DORMITORY. Here, let us suppose that the answers to these questions are that a STUDENT is related to just one DORMITORY and may be related to no DORMITORY. Thus, in Figure B-10(b), DORMITORY contains multiple values of STUDENT, and STUDENT contains one value of DORMITORY. The relationship from DORMITORY to STUDENT is one to many, or 1:N.

A third illustration of compound objects appears in Figure B-11(a). From these two forms, we can deduce that one book can be written by many authors (from the Book Stock Data form) and that one author can write many books (from the Books in Stock, by Author form). Thus, in Figure B-11(b), the BOOK object contains many values of AUTHOR, and AUTHOR contains many values of BOOK. Hence the relationship from BOOK to AUTHOR is many to many, or N:M. Furthermore, a BOOK must have an AUTHOR, and an AUTHOR (to be an author) must have written at least one BOOK. Therefore, both of these objects have a minimum cardinality of one.

Figure B-12 summarizes the four types of compound objects. In general, OBJECT-1 can contain a maximum of one or many OBJECT-2s. Similarly, OBJECT-2 can contain one or many OBJECT-1s. All of these relationships involve some variation of one-to-one, one-to-many, or many-to-many relationships. Specifically, the relationship from OBJECT1 to OBJECT2 can be 1:1, 1:N, or N:M, whereas the relationship from OBJECT2 to OBJECT1 can be 1:1, 1:M, or M:N. To represent any of these, we need address only these three types of relationships.

FIGURE B–10

Compound Objects with 1:N Paired Properties (a) Example Dormitory Report and Student Data Form and (b) DORMITORY and STUDENT Compound Objects

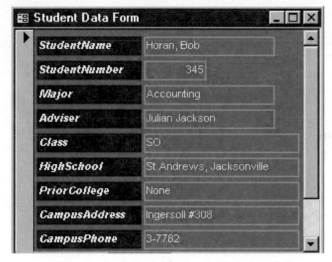

DORMITORY OCCUPANCY REPORT

Dormitory	Resident Assistant	Phone
Ingersoll	Sarah and Allen French	3-5567

Student name	Student Number	Class
Adams, Elizabeth	710	SO
Baker, Rex	104	FR
Baker, Brydie	744	JN
Charles, Stewart	319	SO
Scott, Sally	447	SO
Taylor, Lynne	810	FR

Student Data Form

StudentName	Horan, Bob
StudentNumber	345
Major	Accounting
Adviser	Julian Jackson
Class	SO
HighSchool	St Andrews, Jacksonville
PriorCollege	None
CampusAddress	Ingersoll #308
CampusPhone	3-7782

(a)

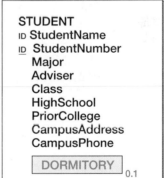

DORMITORY
ID DormName
ID ResidentAssistant
Phone
STUDENT 1.N

STUDENT
ID StudentName
ID StudentNumber
Major
Adviser
Class
HighSchool
PriorCollege
CampusAddress
CampusPhone
DORMITORY 0.1

(b)

FIGURE B–11

Compound Objects with N:M Paired Properties (a) Bookstore Data Entry Forms and (b) BOOK and AUTHOR Objects

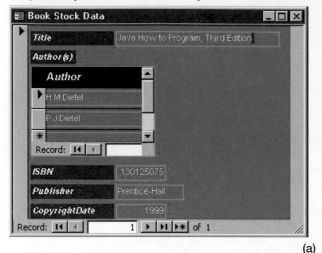 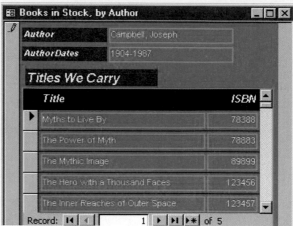

(a)

(b)

FIGURE B–12

Four Types of
Compound Objects

Object1 Can Contain		
Object2	One	Many
Can One	1:1	1:N
Contain Many	M:1	M:N

Representing One-to-One Compound Objects

Consider the assignment of a LOCKER to a health club MEMBER. A LOCKER is assigned to one MEMBER, and each MEMBER has one and only one LOCKER. Figure B-13(a) shows the object diagrams. To represent these objects with relations, we define a relation for each object; and, as with 1:1 entity relationships, we place the key of either relation in the other relation. That is, we can place the key of MEMBER in LOCKER or the key of LOCKER in MEMBER. Figure B-13(b) shows the placement of the key of LOCKER in MEMBER. Note that LockerNumber is underlined in LOCKER because it is the key of LOCKER and is italicized in MEMBER because it is a foreign key in MEMBER.

In general, for a 1:1 relationship between OBJECT1 and OBJECT2, we define one relation for each object, R1 and R2. Then, we place the key of either relation (O1 or O2) as a foreign key in the other relation, as shown in Figure B-14.

Representing One-to-Many and Many-to-One Relationships

Now, consider 1:N relationships and N:1 relationships. Figure B-15(a) shows an example of a 1:N object relationship between EQUIPMENT and REPAIR. An item of EQUIPMENT can have many REPAIRs, but a REPAIR can be related to only one item of EQUIPMENT.

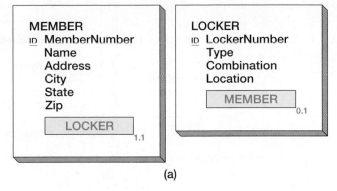

FIGURE B-13

Example Relational Representation of 1:1 Compound Objects (a) Example 1:1 Compound Objects and (b) Their Representation

(a)

MEMBER (<u>MemberNumber</u>, Name, Address, City, State, Zip, *LockerNumber*)

LOCKER (<u>LockerNumber</u>, Type, Combination, Location)

Referential integrity constraint:

LockerNumber in MEMBER must exist in
LockerNumber in LOCKER

(b)

FIGURE B-14

General Transformation of 1:1 Compound Objects

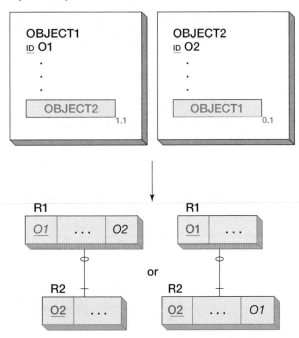

Referential integrity constraint:

O2 in R1 must exist in O2 in R2

Referential integrity constraint:

O1 in R2 must exist in O1 in R1

The objects in Figure B-15(a) are represented by the relations in Figure B-15(b). Observe that the key of the parent (the object on the one side of the relationship) is placed in the child (the object on the many side of the relationship).

Figure B-16 shows the general transformation of 1:N compound objects. Object OBJECT1 contains many OBJECT2s, and object OBJECT2 contains just one OBJECT1. To represent this structure by means of relations, we represent each object

FIGURE B–15

Example Relational Representation of 1:N Compound Objects (a) Example 1:N Compound Objects and (b) Their Representation

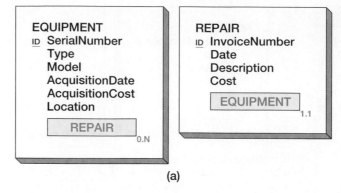

(a)

EQUIPMENT (<u>SerialNumber</u>, Type, Model, AcquisitionDate, AcquisitionCost, Location)

REPAIR (<u>InvoiceNumber</u>, Date, Description, Cost, *SerialNumber*)

Referential integrity constraint:

SerialNumber in REPAIR must exist in
SerialNumber in EQUIPMENT

(b)

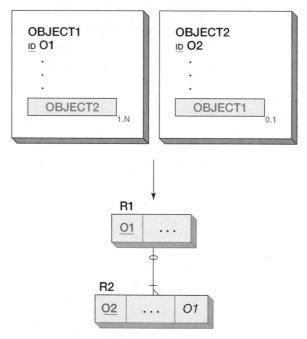

Referential integrity constraint:

O1 in R2 must exist in O1 of R1

with a relation and place the key of the parent in the child. Thus, in Figure B-16, the attribute O1 is placed in R2.

If OBJECT2 were to contain many OBJECT1s and OBJECT1 were to contain just one OBJECT2, we would use the same strategy, but reverse the role of R1 and R2. That is, we would place O2 in R1.

The minimum cardinalities in either case are determined by the minimum cardinalities of the object attributes. In Figure B-16, OBJECT1 requires at least one OBJECT2, but OBJECT2 does not necessarily require an OBJECT1. These cardinalities are shown in the data structure diagram as an oval on the R1 side of the relationship and as a hash mark on the R2 side of the relationship. These minimum cardinality values are simply examples; either or both objects can have a cardinality of 0, 1, or some other number.

Representing Many-to-Many Relationships

Finally, consider M:N relationships. As with M:N entity relationships, we define three relations: one for each of the objects and a third intersection relation. The intersection relation represents the relationship of the two objects and consists of the keys of both of its parents. Figure B-17(a) shows the M:N relationship between BOOK and AUTHOR. Figure B-17(b) depicts the three relations that represent these objects: BOOK; AUTHOR; and BOOK-AUTHOR-INT, the intersection relation. Notice that BOOK-AUTHOR-INT has no nonkey data. Both the attributes ISBN and SocialSecurityNumber are underlined and in italics because they are both local and foreign keys.

In general, for two objects that have an M:N relationship, we define a relation R1 for object OBJECT1, a relation R2 for object OBJECT2, and a relation R3 for the intersection relation. The general scheme is shown in Figure B-18. Note that the attributes of R3 are only O1 and O2. For M:N compound objects, R3 never contains nonkey data. The importance of this statement will become clear when we contrast M:N compound relationships with association relationships.

Considering minimum cardinality, the parents of the intersection relation are always required. The minimum cardinalities of the relationships into the intersection relation are determined by the minimum cardinalities of the object links. In Figure B-18, for example, a row in R1 requires a row in R3 because the minimum cardinality of OBJECT2 in OBJECT1 is 1. Similarly, a row in R2 does not require a row in R3 because the minimum cardinality of OBJECT1 in OBJECT2 is 0.

FIGURE B–17

Relational Representation of Example N:M Compound Objects (a) BOOK and AUTHOR Objects and (b) Their Relational Representation

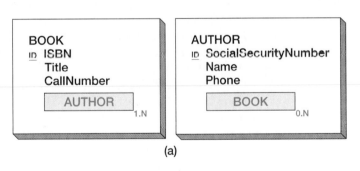

(a)

BOOK (<u>ISBN</u>, Title, CallNumber)

AUTHOR (<u>SocialSecurityNumber</u>, Name, Phone)

BOOK-AUTHOR-INT (<u>*ISBN*</u>, <u>*SocialSecurityNumber*</u>)

Referential integrity constraints:

ISBN in BOOK-AUTHOR-INT must exist in
ISBN in BOOK

SocialSecurityNumber in BOOK-AUTHOR-INT must exist in
SocialSecurityNumber in AUTHOR

(b)

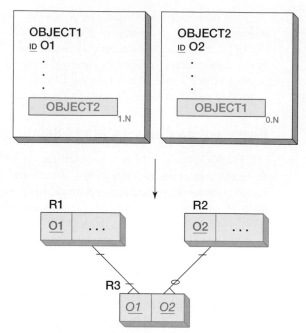

Hybrid Objects

Hybrid objects are combinations of composite and compound objects. In particular, a hybrid object is a semantic object with at least one multi-value group attribute that includes a semantic object attribute.

Figure B-19(a) is a second version of the report about dormitory occupancy shown in Figure B-10(a). The difference is that the third column of the student data contains Rent instead of Class. This is an important difference because Rent is not an attribute of STUDENT, but pertains to the combination of STUDENT and DORMITORY and is an attribute of DORMITORY.

Figure B-19(b) is an object diagram that models this form. DORMITORY contains a multi-value group having the object attribute STUDENT and the nonobject attribute Rent. This means that Rent is paired with STUDENT in the context of DORMITORY.

Now, examine the alternative DORMITORY object shown in Figure B-19(c). This is an *incorrect* model of the report in Figure B-19(a) because it shows that Rent and STUDENT are independently multi-value, which is incorrect because Rent and STUDENT are multi-value as a pair.

Figure B-20(a) shows a form based on another hybrid object. This Sales Order Form contains data about an order (Sales Order Number, Date, Subtotal, Tax, and Total), data about a CUSTOMER and a SALESPERSON, and a multi-value group that itself contains data about items on the order. Furthermore, ITEM data (Item Number, Description, and Unit Price) appear within the multi-value group.

Figure B-20(b) shows the SALES-ORDER semantic object. It contains the nonobject attributes SalesOrderNumber, Date, Subtotal, Tax, and Total. It also contains the CUSTOMER and SALESPERSON object attributes and a multi-value group that represents each line item on the sales order. The group contains nonobject attributes Quantity and ExtendedPrice, and the object attribute ITEM.

The object diagrams shown in Figure B-20(b) are ambiguous in one aspect that may or may not be important, depending on the application. According to the ITEM object

FIGURE B–19

DORMITORY Hybrid
Object (a) Dormitory
Report with Rent
Property; (b) Correct
DORMITORY and
STUDENT Objects and
(c) Incorrect
DORMITORY and
STUDENT Objects

diagram, an ITEM can be connected to more than one SALES-ORDER. But because the multi-value group LineItem is encapsulated (hidden within) SALES-ORDER, it is not clear from this diagram whether an ITEM can occur *once or many times* on the same SALES-ORDER.

In general, there are four interpretations of maximum cardinality for the paired attributes in the SALES-ORDER hybrid object:

1. An ITEM can appear on only one SALES-ORDER and in only one of the LineItems within that SALES-ORDER.
2. An ITEM can appear on only one SALES-ORDER, but in many different LineItems within that SALES-ORDER.
3. An ITEM can appear on many different SALES-ORDERs, but in only one LineItem within each of those SALES-ORDERs.
4. An ITEM can appear on many different SALES-ORDERs and in many different LineItems within those SALES-ORDERs.

FIGURE B–20

Hybrid SALES-ORDER and Related Objects (a) Sales Order Form and (b) Objects to Model Sales Order Form

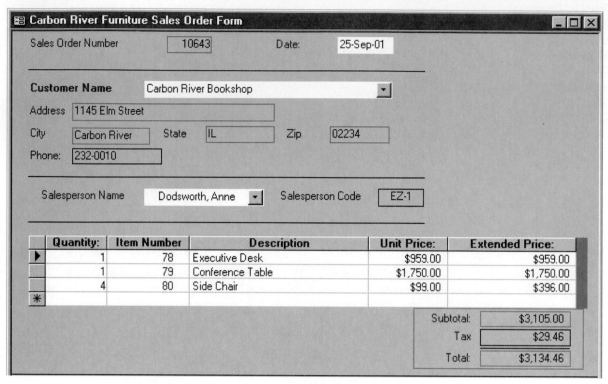

(a)

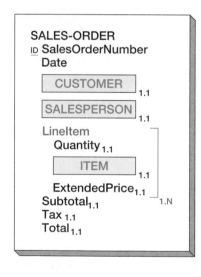
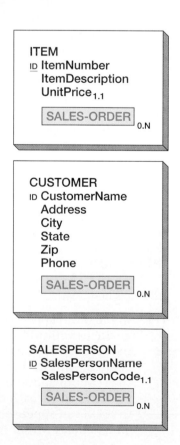

(b)

When it is important to distinguish between these cases, the following notation should be used: If either Case 1 or 2 is in force, the maximum cardinality of the hybrid object attribute should be set to 1. Thus, for this example, the maximum cardinality of SALES-ORDER in ITEM is set to 1. If an ITEM is to appear in only one LineItem of the SALES-ORDER (Case 1), it should be marked as having a unique ID in that group. Otherwise (Case 2), it need not be marked. These two cases are shown in Figures B-21(a) and B-21(b).

If either Case 3 or 4 is in force, the maximum cardinality of the hybrid object attribute is set to N. Thus, for this example, the maximum cardinality of SALES-ORDER in ITEM is set to N. Furthermore, if an ITEM is to appear in only one LineItem of a SALES-ORDER (Case 3), it should be marked as having a unique ID in that group. Otherwise (Case 4), it need not be marked. These two cases are shown in Figures B-21(c) and B-21(d).

Representing Hybrid Relationships

A general description of these four cases is shown in Figure B-22. Cases 3 and 4 are more common than Cases 1 and 2, so we consider them first. OBJECT1 in Figure B-23 shows two groups; Group1 illustrates Case 3 and Group2 illustrates Case 4.

Group1 has a maximum cardinality of N, which means that there can be many instances of Group1 within an OBJECT1. Furthermore, because OBJECT2 is marked as ID unique, this means that a particular OBJECT2 can appear in only one of the Group1 instances within an OBJECT1. Thus, OBJECT2 acts as an identifier for Group1 within OBJECT1.

Consider the relational representation of Group1 in Figure B-23. A relation, R1, is created for OBJECT1; and a relation, R2, is created for OBJECT2. In addition, a third relation, R-G1, is created for Group1. The relationship between R1 and R-G1 is 1:N, so we place the key of R1 (which is O1) into R-G1; the relationship between R2 and R-G1 is also 1:N, so we place the key of R2 (which is O2) in R-G1. Because an OBJECT2 can appear with a particular value of OBJECT1 only once, the composite (O1, O2) is unique to R-G1 and can be made the key of that relation.

Now, consider Group2. OBJECT3 does not identify Group2, so OBJECT3 can appear in many Group2 instances in the same OBJECT1. Because OBJECT3 is not the identifier of Group2, we assume that some other attribute, G2, is the identifier.

In Figure B-23, we create a relation R3 for OBJECT3 and another relation R-G2 for Group2. The relationship between R1 and R-G2 is 1:N, so place the key of R1 (which is O1) into R-G2. The relationship between R3 and R-G2 is also 1:N, so place the key of R3 (which is O3) into R-G2.

Unlike Group1, however, (O1, O3) cannot now be the key of R-G2 because an O3 can be paired with a given O1 many times. That is, the composite (O1, O3) is not unique to R-G2, so the key of R-G2 must be (O1, G2).

Case 1 is similar to Case 3, except for the restriction that an OBJECT2 can be related to only one OBJECT1. The relations in Figure B-23 still work, but we must add the key of R1 (which is O1) to R2 and establish the restriction that (O1, O2) of R-G1 must equal (O1, O2) of R2.

Case 2 is similar to Case 4, except for the restriction that an OBJECT3 can be related to only one OBJECT1. Again, the relations in Figure B-23 will work, but we must add the key of R1 (which is O1) to R3 and establish the restriction that (O1, O3) of R-G2 is a subset of (O1, O3) in R3 (see questions B.21 and B.22).

FIGURE B–21

Examples of the Four Cases of Maximum Cardinality in a Hybrid Object (a) ITEM in One ORDER; (b) ITEM in (Possibly) Many LineItems of One ORDER; (c) ITEM in One LineItem of (Possibly) Many ORDERs, and (d) ITEM in (Possibly) Many LineItems of (Possibly) Many ORDERs

FIGURE B–22

Four Cases of Hybrid Object Cardinality

Case	Description	Example
1	OBJECT2 relates to one instance of OBJECT1 and appears in only one group instance within that object.	ITEM relates to one ORDER and can appear on only one LineItem of that ORDER.
2	OBJECT2 relates to one instance of OBJECT1 and appears in possibly many group instances within that object.	ITEM relates to one ORDER and can appear on many LineItems of that ORDER.
3	OBJECT2 relates to possibly many instances of OBJECT1 and appears in only one group instance within each object.	ITEM relates to many ORDERs and can appear on only one LineItem of that ORDER.
4	OBJECT2 relates to possibly many instances of OBJECT1 and appears in possibly many group instances within those objects.	ITEM relates to many ORDERs and can appear on many LineItems of that ORDER.

FIGURE B–23

General Transformation of Hybrid Object into Relations

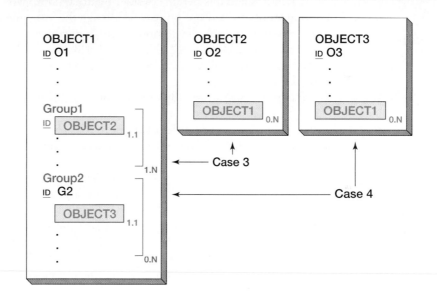

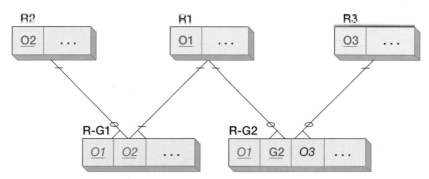

Referential integrity constraints:

O1 in R-G1 must exist in O1 in R1
O2 in R-G1 must exist in O2 in R2
O1 in R-G2 must exist in O1 in R1
O3 in R-G2 must exist in O3 of R3

Association Objects

An **association object** is an object that relates two (or more) objects and stores data that are peculiar to that relationship. Figure B-24(a) shows a report and two data entry screens that give rise to the need for an association object. The report contains data about an airline flight and data about the particular airplane and pilot assigned to that flight. The two data entry forms contain data about a pilot and an airplane.

In Figure B-24(b), the object FLIGHT is an association object that associates the two objects AIRPLANE and PILOT and stores data about their association. FLIGHT contains one each of AIRPLANE and PILOT, but both AIRPLANE and PILOT contain multiple values of FLIGHT. This particular pattern of associating two (or more) objects with data about the association occurs frequently, especially in applications that involve the assignment of two or more things. Other examples are a JOB that assigns an ARCHITECT to a CLIENT, a TASK that assigns an EMPLOYEE to a PROJECT, and a PURCHASE-ORDER that assigns a VENDOR to a SERVICE.

For the example shown in Figure B-24, the association object FLIGHT has an identifier of its own: the group {FlightNumber, Date}. Often, association objects do not have identifiers of their own, in which case the identifier is the combination of the identifiers of the objects that are associated.

To understand this better, consider Figure B-25(a), which shows a report about the assignment of architects to projects. Although the assignment has no obvious identifier, in fact the identifier is the combination {ProjectName, ArchitectName}. These attributes, however, belong to PROJECT and ARCHITECT, not to ASSIGNMENT. The identifier of ASSIGNMENT is thus the combination of those identifiers of the things that are assigned.

Figure B-25(b) shows the object diagrams for this situation. Both PROJECT and ARCHITECT are object attributes of ASSIGNMENT, and the group {PROJECT, ARCHITECT} is the identifier of ASSIGNMENT. This means that the combination of an instance of PROJECT and an instance of ARCHITECT identifies a particular ASSIGNMENT.

Note that the AssignmentID identifier shown in Figure B-25(b) is not unique, thereby indicating that an architect may be assigned to a project more than once. If this is not correct, the identifier should be declared to be unique. Also, if an employee may be assigned to a project more than once; and if for some reason it is important to have a unique identifier for an ASSIGNMENT, the attribute Date or some other time-indicating attribute (Week, Quarter, and so forth) should be added to the group.

In general, when transforming association object structures into relations, we define one relation for each of the objects participating in the relationship. In Figure B-26, OBJECT3 associates OBJECT1 and OBJECT2. In this case, we define R1, R2, and R3, as shown. The key of each of the parent relations, O1 and O2, appears as foreign key attributes in R3, the relation representing the association object. If the association object has no unique identifying attribute, the combination of the attributes of R1 and R2 is used to create a unique identifier.

Note the difference between the association relation shown in Figure B-26 and the intersection relation shown in Figure B-18. The principal distinction is that the association table carries data that represent some aspect of the combination of the objects. The intersection relation carries no data; its only reason for existence is to specify which objects have a relationship with one another.

FIGURE B-24

Examples of an Association Object (a) Example Flight Report and Forms and (b) FLIGHT, PILOT, AIRPLANE Objects

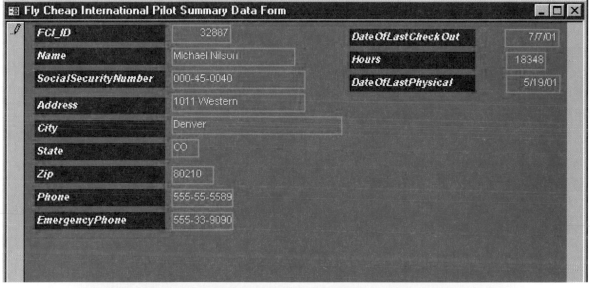

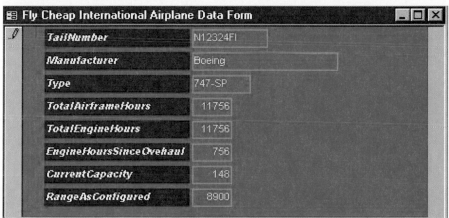

(a)

FIGURE B-24

(continued)

FLIGHT
ID FlightID
   FlightNumber
   Date
   OriginatingCity
   Destination
   FuelOnTakeOff
   WeightOnTakeOff
   | AIRPLANE |
           1.1
   | PILOT |
           1.1

AIRPLANE
ID TailNumber
   Manufacturer
   Type
   TotalAirframeHours
   TotalEngineHours
   EngHoursPastOH
   CurrentCapacity
   RangeAsConfig
   | FLIGHT |
           0.N

PILOT
ID FCI-ID
ID Name
ID SocialSecurityNumber
   Street
   City
   State
   Zip
   Phone
   EmergPhone
   DateOfLastCheckOut
   Hours
   DateOfLastPhysical
   | FLIGHT |
           0.N

(b)

FIGURE B–25

ASSIGNMENT
Association Object
(a) Example
Assignment Report and
(b) ASSIGNMENT
Object with Semantic
Object ID

Project Assignment Report

Project Name	Abernathy House	Architect Name	Jackson, B.
Project Manager	Smith, J	Phone	232-8878
Project Start	11/11/1999	Office Number	J-1133
Project End			

Assignment Starts	12/15/2001
Assignment Ends	3/15/2002
Maximum Budgeted Hours	345
Maximum Labor Cost	$27,500
Maximum Material Cost	$17,500

(a)

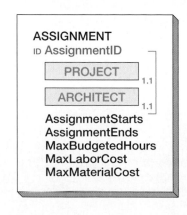

ASSIGNMENT
ID AssignmentID
   | PROJECT |
           1.1
   | ARCHITECT |
           1.1
   AssignmentStarts
   AssignmentEnds
   MaxBudgetedHours
   MaxLaborCost
   MaxMaterialCost

PROJECT
ID ProjectName
   ProjectManager
   ProjectStart
   ProjectEnd
   | ASSIGNMENT |
           1.N

ARCHITECT
ID ArchitectName
   Phone
   Office
   | ASSIGNMENT |
           1.N

(b)

FIGURE B–26

General
Transformation of
Association Objects
into Relations

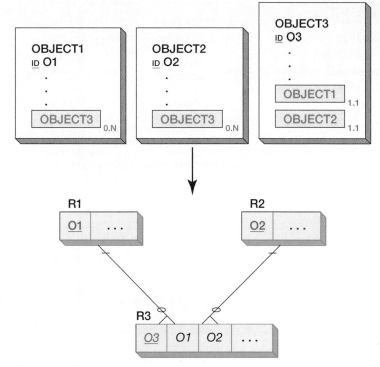

Referential integrity constraints:

O1 in R3 must exist in O1 in R1
O2 in R3 must exist in O2 in R2

Parent/Subtype Objects

To understand parent and subtype objects, consider the object EMPLOYEE shown in Figure B-27(a). Some of the attributes in EMPLOYEE pertain to all employees, and others pertain only to employees who are managers. The object in Figure B-27(a) is not very precise because the manager-oriented attributes are not suitable for nonmanager employees.

A better model is shown in Figure B-27(b), in which the EMPLOYEE object contains a subtype object: MANAGER. All of the manager-oriented attributes have been moved to the MANAGER object. Employees who are not managers have one EMPLOYEE object instance and no MANAGER object instances. Employees who are managers have both an EMPLOYEE instance and a MANAGER instance. In this example, the EMPLOYEE object is called a **parent object**, or **supertype object**; and the MANAGER object is called a **subtype object.**

The first attribute of a subtype, the parent attribute, is denoted by the subscript P. Parent attributes are always required. The identifiers of the subtype are the same as the identifiers of the parent. In Figure B-27(b), EmployeeNumber and EmployeeName are identifiers of both EMPLOYEE and MANAGER.

Subtype attributes are shown with the subscript 0.ST or 1.ST. The first digit (0 or 1) is the minimum cardinality of the subtype. If 0, the subtype is optional; if 1, the subtype is required. (A required subtype does not make sense for this example, but it will for the more complicated examples to follow.) The *ST* indicates that the attribute is a subtype, or IS-A attribute.

Parent/subtype objects have an important characteristic called inheritance. A subtype acquires, or *inherits,* all of the attributes of its parent; and therefore a MANAGER inherits all of the attributes of an EMPLOYEE. In addition, the parent acquires all of

FIGURE B–27

Need for MANAGER
Subtype (a) EMPLOYEE
without Subtype and
(b) EMPLOYEE with
MANAGER Subtype

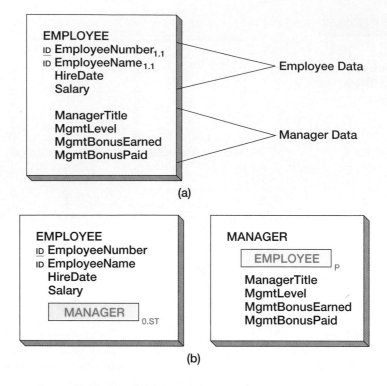

(a)

(b)

the attributes of its subtypes, and an EMPLOYEE who is a MANAGER acquires all of
the attributes of MANAGER.

A semantic object may contain more than one subtype attribute. Figure B-28 shows
a second EMPLOYEE object that has two subtype attributes: MANAGER and PRO-
GRAMMER. Because all of these attributes are optional, an EMPLOYEE can have neither, one, or both of these subtypes. This means that some employees are neither managers nor programmers, some are managers but not programmers, some are
programmers but not managers, and some are both programmers and managers.

Sometimes, subtypes exclude one another. That is, a VEHICLE can be an AUTO or
a TRUCK, but not both. A CLIENT can be an INDIVIDUAL, a PARTNERSHIP, or a
CORPORATION, but only one of these three types. When subtypes exclude one
another, they are placed into a subtype group, and the group is assigned a subscript of
the format $X.Y.Z$. X is the minimum cardinality and is 0 or 1, depending on whether or
not the subtype group is required. Y and Z are counts of the number of attributes in the

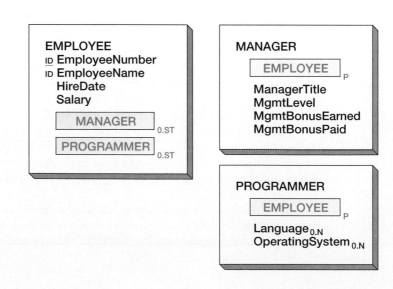

group that are allowed to have a value. Y is the minimum number required, and Z is the maximum number allowed.

Figure B-29(a) shows three types of CLIENT as a subtype group. The subscript of the group, 0.1.1, means that the subtype is not required; but if it exists, a minimum of one and a maximum of one (or exactly one) of the subtypes in the group must exist.

FIGURE B-29

Exclusive (a) and Nested (b) Subtypes

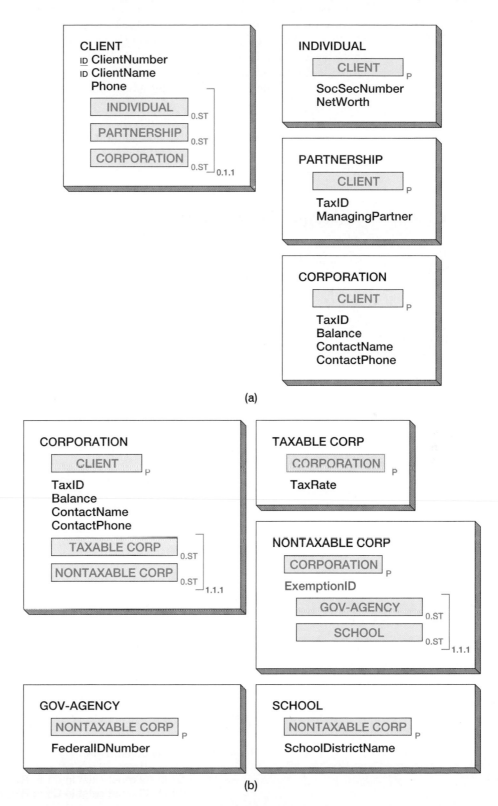

(a)

(b)

Note that each of the subtypes has the subscript 0.ST, meaning that they all are optional, as they must be. If they all were required, the maximum count would have to be three, not one. This notation is robust enough to allow for situations in which three out of five or seven out of 10 of a list of subtypes must be required.

Even more complex restrictions can be modeled when subtypes are nested. The subtype group in Figure B-29(b) models a situation in which the subtype CORPORA-TION must be either a TAXABLE-CORP or a NONTAXABLE-CORP. If it is a NONTAXABLE-CORP, it must be either GOV-AGENCY or a SCHOOL. Only a few nonobject attributes are shown in this example. In reality, if such a complex structure were required, there would likely be more attributes.

A general scheme for representing subtypes is shown in Figure B-30. One relation is created for the parent and one each for the subtypes. The key of all of the relations is the identifier of the parent. All relationships between the parent and the subtype are 1:1. Note the bar across the relationship lines and the presence of the subtype group's cardinality. The value shown, 0.1.1, means that no subtype is required, but, if present, at most one of the subtypes is allowed.

Archetype/Version Objects

The final type of object is the **archetype/version object.** An archetype object is a semantic object that produces other semantic objects that represent versions, releases, or editions of the archetype. For example, in Figure B-31, the archetype object TEXT-BOOK produces the version objects EDITIONs. According to this model, the attributes Title, Author, and Publisher belong to the object TEXTBOOK; and the attributes

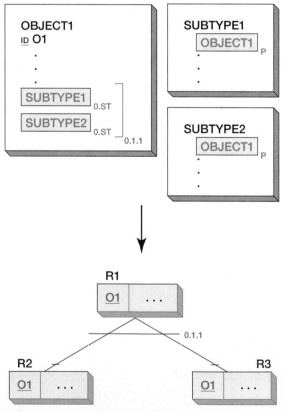

FIGURE B-30

General Transformation of Parent/Subtype Objects into Relations

Referential integrity constraints:

O1 in R2 must exist in O1 in R1
O1 in R3 must exist in O1 in R1

EditionNumber, PublicationDate, and NumberOfPages belong to the EDITION of the TEXTBOOK.

The ID group in EDITION has two portions: TEXTBOOK and EditionNumber; this is the typical pattern for an ID of a version object. One part of the ID contains the archetype object, and the second part is a simple attribute that identifies the version within the archetype. Figure B-32 shows another instance of archetype/version objects. Figure B-33 shows the general transformation of archetype/version objects. Attribute O1 of R2 is both a local and a foreign key, but O2 is only a local key.

FIGURE B-31

Example of an Archetype/Version Object

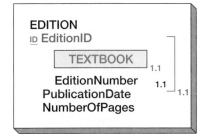

FIGURE B-32

Another Example of an Archetype/Version Object

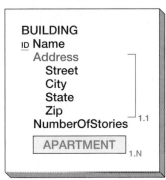
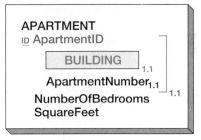

FIGURE B-33

General Transformation of Archetype/Version Objects and RELEASE Version Objects

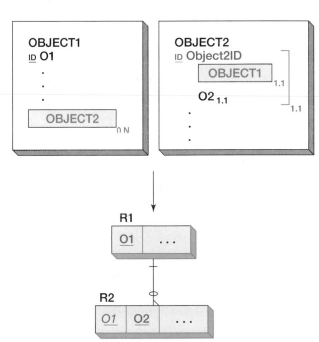

Referential integrity constraint:

O1 in R2 must exist in O1 in R1

▶ COMPARING THE SEMANTIC OBJECT AND THE E-R MODEL

The E-R model and the semantic object model have both similarities and differences. They are similar in that they both are tools for understanding and documenting the structure of the users' data. They both strive to model the structure of the things in the users' world and the relationships among them.

The principal difference between the two models is one of orientation. The E-R model sees the concept of *entity* as basic. Entities and their relationships are considered the atoms, if you will, of a data model. These atoms can be combined to form what the E-R model calls *user views,* which are combinations of entities whose structures are similar to those of semantic objects.

The semantic object model takes the concept of *semantic object* as basic. The set of semantic objects in a data model is a map of the essential structure of the things that the user considers important. These objects are the atoms of the users' world and are the smallest distinguishable units that the users want to process. They may be decomposed into smaller parts inside the DBMS (or application), but those smaller parts are of no interest or utility to the users.

According to the semantic object perspective, entities, as defined in the E-R model, do not exist. They are only pieces or chunks of the real entities. The only entities that have meaning to users are, in fact, semantic objects. Another way to state this is to say that semantic objects are *semantically self-contained* or *semantically complete.* Consider an example. Figure B-33 shows four semantic objects, SALES-ORDER, CUSTOMER, SALESPERSON, and ITEM. When a user says, "Show me sales order number 2000," he or she means show SALES-ORDER, as modeled in Figure B-34. That includes, among other attributes, CUSTOMER data. Because CUSTOMER is part of SALES-ORDER, the SALES-ORDER object includes CUSTOMER.

Figure B-35 is an E-R model of this same data and contains the SALES-ORDER, CUSTOMER, SALESPERSON, LINE-ITEM, and INVENTORY entities. The SALES-ORDER entity includes the attributes OrderNumber, Date, Subtotal, Tax, and Total. Now if a user were to say, "Show me sales order number 2000" and be given only the attributes Date, Subtotal, Tax, and Total, he or she would be disappointed. Most likely,

---

FIGURE B-34

SALES-ORDER and Related Semantic Objects

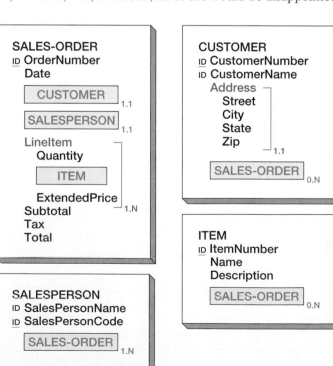

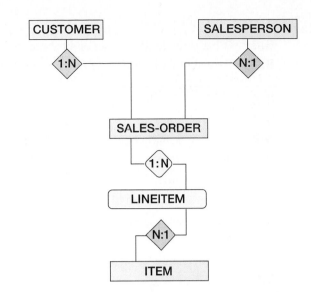

FIGURE B-35

Entity-Relationship
Model of SALES-
ORDER and
CUSTOMER

the user's response would be, "Where's the rest of the data?" That is, the entity SALES-ORDER does not represent the user's meaning of the distinct identity SALES-ORDER. The entity is only a part of SALES-ORDER.

At the same time, when a user (perhaps even the same user) says, "Show me customer 12345," he or she means to show all of the data modeled for CUSTOMER shown in Figure B-34—including CustomerName, all of the attributes of the group Address, and all of the SALES-ORDERs for that CUSTOMER. The entity CUSTOMER shown in Figure B-35 has only the attributes CustomerName, Street, City, State, Zip. If the user were to say, "Show me customer ABC," and be given only this data, he or she again would be disappointed: "No, that's only part of what I want."

According to the semantic object view, E-R entities are unnecessary. Semantic objects can be readily transformed into database designs without ever considering E-R model entities. They are halfway houses, so to speak, constructed in the process of moving away from the paradigm of computer data structures to the paradigm of the user.

Another difference is that the semantic objects contain more metadata than do the entities. In Figure B-34, the semantic object model records the fact that CustomerNumber is a unique identifier in the users' minds. It may or may not be used as an identifier for the underlying table, but that fact is not important to the data model. In addition, CustomerName is a nonunique identifier to the users. Furthermore, the semantic objects represent the fact that there is a semantic group of attributes called *Address*. This group contains other attributes that form the address. The fact that this group exists becomes important when forms and reports are designed. Finally, the semantic objects indicate that an ITEM may relate to more than one SALES-ORDER, but that it can relate to only one LineItem within that SALES-ORDER. This fact cannot be shown on the entity-relationship diagram.

In the final analysis, decide which of Figures B-34 and B-35 gives you a better idea of what the database should contain. Many people find that the boundaries drawn around the semantic objects and the brackets around the group attributes help them get a better idea of the overall picture of the data model.

GROUP I QUESTIONS

B.1 Explain why the E-R model and the semantic object model are like lenses.

B.2 Define *semantic object*.

B.3 Explain the difference between an object class name and an object instance name. Give an example of each.

B.4   What is required for a set of attributes to be a sufficient description?

B.5   Explain the words *distinct identity* as they pertain to the definition of a semantic object.

B.6   Explain why a line item of an order is not a semantic object.

B.7   List the three types of attributes.

B.8   Give an example of each of the following:

    A.   a simple, single-value attribute

    B.   a group, single-value attribute

    C.   a simple, multi-value attribute

    D.   a group, multi-value attribute

    E.   a simple object attribute

    F.   a multi-value object attribute

B.9   What is minimum cardinality? How is it used? Which types of attributes have minimum cardinality?

B.10   What is maximum cardinality? How is it used? Which types of attributes have maximum cardinality?

B.11   What are paired attributes? Why are they needed?

B.12   What is an object identifier? Give an example of a simple attribute object identifier and an example of a group attribute object identifier.

B.13   Define *attribute domain*. What are the types of attribute domain? Why is a semantic description necessary?

B.14   What is a semantic object view? Give an example of an object and two views other than those in this text.

B.15   Give an example of a simple object, other than one in this text. Show how to represent this object by means of a relation.

B.16   Give an example of a composite object, other than one in this text. Show how to represent this object by means of relations.

B.17   Give an example of a 1:1 compound object, other than one in this text. Show two ways to represent it by means of relations.

B.18   Give an example of a 1:N compound object, other than one in this text. Show how to represent it by means of relations.

B.19   Give an example of an M:1 compound object, other than one in this text. Show how to represent it by means of relations.

B.20   Give an example of an M:N compound object, other than one in this text. Show how to represent it by means of relations.

B.21   Give an example of a Case 1 (see Figure B-22) hybrid object. Show how to represent it by means of relations.

B.22   Give an example of a Case 2 (see Figure B-22) hybrid object. Show how to represent it by means of relations.

B.23   Give an example of an association and related objects, other than one in this text. Show how to represent these objects by means of relations. Assume that the association object has an identifier of its own.

B.24   Do the same as for question B.24, but assume that the association object does not have an identifier of its own.

B.25   Give an example of a parent object with at least two exclusive subtypes. Show how to represent these objects by means of relations. Use a type indicator attribute.

B.26 Give an example of a parent object with at least two nonexclusive subtypes. Show how to represent these objects by means of relations. Use a type indicator attribute.

B.27 Find an example of a form on your campus that would be appropriately modeled with a simple object. Show how to represent this object by means of a relation.

B.28 Find an example of a form on your campus that would be appropriately modeled with a composite object. Show how to represent this object by means of relations.

B.29 Find an example of a form on your campus that would be appropriately modeled with one of the types of a compound object. Show how to represent these objects by means of relations.

B.30 Find an example of a form on your campus that would be appropriately modeled with a hybrid object. Classify the object according to Figure B-22, and show how to represent these objects by means of relations.

B.31 Find an example of a form on your campus that would be appropriately modeled with an association and related objects. Show how to represent these objects by means of relations.

B.32 Find an example of a form on your campus that would be appropriately modeled with parent/subtypes objects. Show how to represent these objects by means of relations.

B.33 Find an example of a form on your campus that would be appropriately modeled with archetype/version objects. Show how to represent these objects by means of relations.

B.34 Explain the similarities between the E-R model and the semantic object model.

B.35 Explain the major differences between the E-R model and the semantic object model.

B.36 Explain the reasoning that entities, as defined in the E-R model, do not truly exist.

B.37 Show how both the E-R model and the semantic object model would represent the data underlying the SALES-ORDER form shown in Figure B-20(a), and explain the main differences.

FIREDUP PROJECT QUESTIONS

Consider the situation of FiredUp discussed at the end of Chapter 1. Assume that FiredUp has now developed a line of three different stoves: FiredNow, FiredAlways, and FiredAtCamp. Further, assume that the owners are selling spare parts for each of their stoves and they are also making stove repairs. Some repairs are at no charge because they are within the stove warranty period; other repairs are made at a charge for parts only; and still others are made for parts and labor. FiredUp wants to keep track of all of these data. When asked for further details, the owners made the following list:

CUSTOMER: Name, StreetAddress, ApartmentNumber, City, State/Province, Zip/PostalCode, Country, EmailAddress, PhoneNumber
STOVE: SerialNumber, Type, ManufactureDate, InspectorInitials
INVOICE: InvoiceNumber, Date, Customer, with a list of items and prices that were sold, TotalPrice
REPAIR: RepairNumber, Customer, Stove, Description, with a list of items that were used in the repair and the charge for them, if any, and TotalAmount of the repair
PART: Number, Description, Cost, SalesPrice

A. Create a set of semantic objects for a database at FiredUp. Set the minimum and maximum cardinality of all attributes as you think is appropriate. Explain your rationale for each cardinality value. Use as many types of semantic objects as you think appropriate, but do not use subtypes.

B. Transform the semantic object design from question A into a set of relations in domain/key normal form. For each relation, specify the primary key, candidate keys, if any, and foreign keys. Specify all referential integrity constraints. If necessary, make and justify assumptions regarding the underlying semantics of the application.

C. Adjust your answer to question A to allow un-normalized relations if you think just relations are appropriate. Justify any non-normalized relations you have. If necessary, make and justify assumptions regarding the underlying semantics of the application.

Glossary

Abstract Data Type: In SQL3, a user-defined structure having methods, data items, and identifiers; a version of an OOP object. Persistence is provided by binding the ADT to a column of a relation.

Abstraction: A generalization of something that hides some hopefully unimportant details, but enables work with a wider class of types. A recordset is an abstraction of a relation. A rowset is an abstraction of a recordset.

ACID transaction: ACID is an acronym that stands for atomic, consistent, isolated, and durable. An atomic transaction is one in which all of the database changes are committed as a unit; either all of them are done, or none of them is done. A consistent transaction is one in which all actions are taken against rows in the same logical state. An isolated transaction is one that is protected from changes by other users. A durable transaction is one that is permanent after it is committed to the database, regardless of subsequent failure. There are different levels of consistency and isolation. See Transaction level consistency and Statement level consistency. Also see Transaction isolation level.

Active Server Page: See ASP.

ActiveX control: An ActiveX object that supports interfaces that enable the control's properties and methods to be accessed in many different development environments.

ActiveX object: A COM object that supports a slimmed-down version of the OLE object specification.

ADO: Active data objects; an implementation of OLE DB that is accessible via both object and non-object-oriented languages; used primarily as a scripting language (JScript, VBScript) interface to OLE DB.

ADO.NET: Data access technology that is part of Microsoft's .NET initiative. ADO.NET provides the capabilities of ADO, but with a different object structure. ADO.NET also includes new capabilities for processing XML and for the processing of datasets. See Dataset for more information.

ADT: See Abstract Data Type.

After-image: A record of a database entity (normally a row or a page) after a change. Used in recovery to perform roll-forward.

Alternate keys: In IDEF1X logical models, a synonym for candidate key. In IDEF1X physical models, one or more columns that will be indexed.

Anomaly: An undesirable consequence of a data modification used primarily in discussions of normalization. With an insertion anomaly, facts about two or more different themes must be added to a single row of a relation. With a deletion anomaly, facts about two or more themes are lost when a single row is deleted.

API: See Application Program Interface.

Applet: A compiled, machine-independent Java bytecode program that is run by the Java virtual machine embedded in a browser.

Application: A business computer system that processes a portion of a database to meet a user's information needs. It consists of menus, forms, reports, queries, Web pages, and application programs.

Application design: The process of creating the structure of programs and data to meet the application's requirements; also the structure of the users' interface.

Application failure: A failure in the processing of a DBMS statement or in a transaction that is due to application logic errors.

Application metadata: Data dictionary; data concerning the structure and contents of application menus, forms, and reports.

Application program: A custom-developed program for processing a database. It can be written in a standard procedural language such as Java, C#, VB.NET, or C++; or in a language unique to the DBMS such as PL/SQL or T/SQL.

Application Program Interface (API): A set of program procedures or functions that can be called to invoke a set of services. The API includes the names of the procedures and functions; and a description of the name, purpose, and data type of parameters to be provided. For example, a DBMS product can provide a library of functions to call for database services. The names of procedures and their parameters constitute the API for that library.

Archetype/version object: A structure of two objects that represents multiple versions of a standardized item; for example, a SOFT-PRODUCT (the archetype) and PRODUCT-RELEASE (the version of the archetype). The identifier of the version always includes the archetype object.

ASP: Active Server Page. A file containing markup language, server script, and client script that is processed by the Active Server Processor in Microsoft IIS.

Association object: An object that represents the combination of at least two other objects and that contains data about that combination. It is often used in contracting and assignment applications.

Atomic: A set of actions that is completed as a unit. Either all actions are completed, or none of them is completed.

Atomic transaction: A group of logically related database operations that is performed as a unit. Either all of the operations are performed, or none of them is performed.

Attribute: (1) A column of a relation; also called a column, field, or data-item. (2) An element in an entity or semantic object. (3) A data or relationship property in an OOP object. (4) In the ODMG-93 model, an implementation of an object property in an OOP implementation such as C++ or Smalltalk.

Authorization rules: A set of processing permissions that describes which users or user groups can take particular actions against particular portions of the database.

Axis: In OLAP, a coordinate of a cube or hypercube.

Base domain: In IDEF1X, a domain definition that stands alone. Other domains may be defined as subsets of a base domain.

Before-image: A record of a database entity (normally a row or a page) before a change. Used in recovery to perform rollback.

Binary relationship: A relationship between exactly two entities or tables.

Bind: To connect a program variable or a GUI control to a column of a table or query.

Bottom-up database design: The design of a database that works from the detailed and specific to the general. Although this sort of design takes little time, it may result in a database that is too narrow in scope.

Boyce-Codd normal form: A relation in third normal form in which every determinant is a candidate key.

Branch: A subelement of a tree that consists of one or more nodes.

Buffer: An area of memory used to hold data. For a read, data is read from a storage device into a buffer; for a write, data are written from the buffer to storage.

Built-in function: In SQL, any of the functions COUNT, SUM, AVG, MAX, or MIN.

Callback: An OOP design practice by which an object passes its identity to another object with the expectation that the called object will notify the calling object when some event occurs. Often, the event is the destruction of the called object, but is used for other purposes as well.

Candidate key: An attribute or group of attributes that identifies a unique row in a relation. One of the candidate keys is chosen to be the primary key.

Cardinality: In a binary relationship, the maximum or minimum number of elements allowed on each side of the relationship. The maximum cardinality can be 1:1, 1:N, N:1, or N:M. The minimum cardinality can be optional-optional, optional-mandatory, mandatory-optional, or mandatory-mandatory.

Cartesian product: A relational operation on two relations, A and B, producing a third relation, C; with C containing the concatenation of every row in A with every row in B.

Cascading deletions: A referential integrity action specifying that when a parent row is deleted, related child rows should be deleted as well.

Cascading updates: A referential integrity action specifying that when the key of a parent row is updated, the matching foreign keys of child rows should be updated as well.

Categorization cluster: In IDEF1X, a group of mutually exclusive category entities. See also Complete category cluster and Incomplete category cluster.

Categorization relationships: In IDEF1X, a structured arrangement of subtypes. See Categorization cluster, Category entity, and Generic entity.

Category entity: In IDEF1X, a subtype that belongs to a category cluster.

Central Processing Unit: See CPU.

CGI: See Common Gateway Interface.

Check box: In a GUI environment, an element of the user interface in which a user can select one or more items from a list. Items are selected by clicking on them.

Checkpoint: The point of synchronization between a database and a transaction log. All buffers are force-written to external storage. This is the standard definition of checkpoint, but this term is sometimes used in other ways by DBMS vendors.

Child: A row, record, or node on the many side of a one-to-many relationship.

Class attributes: In the uniform modeling language (UML), attributes that pertain to the class of all entities of a given type.

Client computer: (1) A personal computer on a local area network with client-server architecture. In a database application, the client computer processes database application programs. Requests for actions on the database are sent to the database computer. (2) In the three-tier architecture, a computer that hosts a browser for accessing a Web server.

Client-server database architecture: The structure of a networked computing system in which one computer (usually a personal computer) performs services on behalf of other computers (usually personal computers). For a database system, the server computer, which is called a database server, processes the DBMS; and client computers process the application programs. All database activities are carried out by the database server.

Client-server system: A system of two or more computers in which at least one computer provides services for one or more other computers. The services can be database services, communication services, printer services, or some other function.

Collection: An object that contains a group of other objects. Examples are the ADO Names, Errors, and Parameters collections.

Column: A logical group of bytes in a row of a relation or a table. The meaning of a column is the same for every row of the relation.

Column object: In Oracle, an object structure that is stored in a table column.

COM: Component Object Model; a Microsoft specification for the development of object-oriented programs that enables such programs to work together readily.

COM object: An object that conforms to the COM standard.

Command: A statement input to a database application by which users specify the activity to be performed. Contrast this with menu.

Commit: A command issued to the DBMS to make database modifications permanent. After the command has been processed, the changes are written to the database and to a log in so that they will survive system crashes and other failures. A commit is usually used at the end of an atomic transaction. Contrast this with rollback.

Complete category cluster: A category cluster in which all possible category entities are defined. The generic entity must be one of the category entities.

Complex network: A collection of entities, objects, or relations and their relationships, of which at least one of the relationships is complex (many to many).

Component Object Model: See COM.

Composite group: A group of attributes in a semantic object that is multi-valued and contains no other object attributes.

Composite key: A key with more than one attribute.

Composite object: An object with at least one multi-value attribute or attribute group. It is called a composite object because the key of the relation that represents the multi-value attribute or group is a composite key.

Compound object: An object that contains at least one other object.

Computed value: A column of a table that is computed from other column values. Values are not stored, but are computed when they are to be displayed.

Conceptual schema: In the three-schema model, the complete logical view of the database.

Concurrency: A condition in which two or more transactions are processed against the database at the same time. In a single CPU system, the changes are interleaved; in a multi-CPU system, the transactions may be processed simultaneously, and the changes on the database server are interleaved.

Concurrent processing: The sharing of the CPU among several transactions. The CPU is allocated to each transaction in a round robin or in some other fashion for a certain period of time. Operations are performed so quickly that they appear to users to be simultaneous. In local area networks and other distributed applications, concurrent processing is used to refer to the (possibly simultaneous) processing of applications on multiple computers.

Concurrent update problem: An error condition in which one user's data changes are overwritten by another user's data changes. Same as lost update problem.

Conflict: Two operations conflict if they operate on the same data item and at least one of the operations is a write.

Connection relationship: In IDEF1X, a 1:1 or 1:N HAS-A relationship.

Consistency: Two or more concurrent transactions are consistent if the result of their processing is the same as it would have been if they had been processed in some serial order.

Consistent backup: A backup file from which all uncommitted changes have been removed.

Consistent schedule: An ordered list of transaction operations against a database in which the result of the processing is consistent.

Constraint: A rule concerning the allowed values of attributes whose truth can be evaluated. For the definition of domain/key normal form, a constraint does not include dynamic, time-related rules such as "SalesPersonPay can never decrease" or "Salary now must be greater than Salary last quarter."

Correlated subquery: A type of subquery in which an element in the subquery refers to an element in the containing query. Such subqueries require nested processing.

CPU: Central Processing Unit; the portion of the computer hardware that processes arithmetic and logic instructions. The term CPU usually includes main memory as well.

CRUD: An acronym representing create, read, update, delete—which are the four actions that can be performed on database data.

Cube: In OLAP, a presentation structure having axes upon which data dimensions are placed. Measures of the data are shown in the cells of the cube. Also called hypercube.

Cursor: An indicator of the current position or focus. (1) On a computer screen, a blinking box or underscore that indicates the position into which the next entry will be made. (2) In a file or embedded SQL SELECT, the identity of the next record or row to be processed.

Cursor type: A declaration on a cursor that determines how the DBMS places implicit locks. Four types of cursor discussed in this text are forward only, snapshot, keyset, and dynamic.

Data administration: The enterprise-wide function that concerns the effective use and control of the organization's data assets. It can be a person, but more often it is a group. Specific functions include setting data standards and policies and providing a forum for conflict resolution. See also Database administrator.

Database: A self-describing collection of integrated records.

Database administration: The function that concerns the effective use and control of a particular database and its related applications.

Database administrator: The person or group responsible for establishing policies and procedures to control and protect a database. He, she, or it works within guidelines set by data administration to control the database structure, manage data changes, and maintain DBMS programs.

Database data: The portion of a database that contains data of interest and use to the application end users.

Database Management System: See DBMS.

Database redesign: The process of changing database structure to adapt the database to changing requirements (or to fix it to have the structure it should have had in the first place).

Database save: A copy of database files that can be used to restore the database to some previous consistent state.

Database server: (1) On a local area network with client server database architecture, the computer that runs the DBMS and processes actions against the database on behalf of its client computers. (2) In the three-tier, multi-tier architecture, a computer that hosts a DBMS and responds to database requests from the Web server.

Data consumer: A user of OLE DB functionality.

Data Definition Language (DDL):   A language used to describe the structure of a database.

Data dictionary: A user-accessible catalog of both database and application metadata. An active data dictionary is a dictionary whose contents are automatically updated by the DBMS whenever changes are made in the database or application structure. A passive data dictionary is one whose contents must be updated manually when changes are made.

Data dictionary and database administration subsystem: A collection of programs in the DBMS used to access the data dictionary and to perform database administration functions such as maintaining passwords and performing backup and recovery.

Data integrity: The state of a database in which all constraints are fulfilled; usually refers to referential integrity constraints in which the value of a foreign key is required to be present in the table having that foreign key as its primary key.

Data-item: (1) A logical group of bytes in a record, usually used with file processing. (2) In the context of the relational model, a synonym for attribute.

Data Manipulation Language (DML):   A language used to describe the processing of a database.

Data mart: A facility similar to a data warehouse, but for a restricted domain. Often, the data are restricted to particular types, business functions, or business units.

Data model: (1) A model of the users' data requirements expressed in terms of either the entity-relationship model or the semantic-object model. It is sometimes called a users' data model. (2) A language for describing the structure and processing of a database.

Data owner: Same as data proponent.

Data proponent: In data administration, a department or other organizational unit in charge of managing a particular data item.

Data provider: A provider of OLE DB functionality. Examples are tabular data providers and service data providers.

Data replication: A term that indicates whether any portion or all of a database resides on more than one computer. If so, the data are said to be replicated.

Dataset: In ADO.NET, an in-memory collection of tables that is disconnected from any database. Datasets have relationships, referential integrity constraints, referential integrity actions, and other important database characteristics. They are processed by ADO.NET objects. A single dataset can materialize itself as tables, as an XML document, or as an XML Schema.

Data source: In the ODBC standard, a database together with its associated DBMS, operating system, and network platform.

Data structure diagram: A graphical display of tables (files) and their relationships. The tables are shown in rectangles, and the relationships are shown by lines. A many relationship is shown with a fork on the end of the line, an optional relationship is depicted by an oval, and a mandatory relationship is shown with hash marks.

Data sublanguage: A language for defining and processing a database intended to be embedded in programs written in another language—in most cases, a procedural language such as Java, C#, Visual Basic, or C++. A data sublanguage is an incomplete programming language because it contains only constructs for data access.

Data warehouse: A store of enterprise data that is designed to facilitate management decision-making. A data warehouse includes not only data, but also metadata, tools, procedures, training, personnel, and other resources that make access to the data easier and more relevant to decision makers.

DBA: See Database administrator.

DBMS: Database Management System; a set of programs used to define, administer, and process the database and its applications.

DBMS engine: A DBMS subsystem that processes logical I/O requests from other DBMS subsystems and submits physical I/O requests to the operating system.

DDBMS: See Distributed Database Management System.

DDL: See Data Definition Language.

Deadlock: A condition that can occur during concurrent processing in which each of two (or more) transactions is waiting to access data that the other transaction has locked. It is also called a deadly embrace.

Deadlock detection: The process of determining whether two or more transactions are in a state of deadlock.

Deadlock prevention: A way of managing transactions so that a deadlock cannot occur.

Deadly embrace: See Deadlock.

Decision Support System: See DSS.

Default namespace: In an XML schema document, the namespace that is used for all unlabeled elements.

Definition tools subsystem: The portion of the DBMS program used to define and change the database structure.

Degree: For relationships in the entity-relationship model, the number of entities participating in the relationship. In almost all cases, such relationships are of degree 2.

Deletion anomaly: In a relation, the situation in which the removal of one row of a table deletes facts about two or more themes.

Dependency graph: A network of nodes and lines that represents the logical dependencies among tables, views, triggers, stored procedures, indexes, and other database constructs.

Determinant: One or more attributes that functionally determine another attribute or attributes. In the functional dependency (A, B) → C, the attributes (A, B) are the determinant.

Differential backup: A backup file that contains only changes made since a prior backup.

Dimension: In OLAP, a feature of data that is placed on an axis.

Dirty read: Reading data that has been changed but not yet committed to the database. Such changes may later be rolled back and removed from the database.

Discriminator: In IDEF1X, an attribute of a generic entity that can be used to determine which category entity of a category cluster pertains to a given generic entity instance.

Distributed database: A database stored on two or more computers. Distributed data can be partitioned or not partitioned, replicated or not replicated.

Distributed database application: A business computer system in which the retrieval and updating of data occur across two or more independent and usually geographically separated computers.

Distributed Database Management System (DDBMS):   In a distributed database, the collection of distributed transaction and database managers on all computers.

Distributed database processing: Database processing in which transaction data are retrieved and updated across two or more independent and usually geographically separated computers.

Distributed database system: A distributed system in which a database or portions of a database are distributed across two or more computers.

Distributed system: A system in which the application programs of a database are processed on two or more computers.

Distributed Transaction Service (DTS):   An OLE service developed by Microsoft that supports distributed processing and implements two-phased commit in particular.

Distributed two-phase locking: Two-phase locking in a distributed environment, in which locks are obtained and released across all nodes on the network. See also Two-phase locking.

DK/NF: See Domain/Key Normal Form.

DML: See Data Manipulation Language.

Document Object Model (DOM):   An API that represents an XML document as a tree. Each node of the tree represents a piece of the XML document. A program can directly access and manipulate a node of the DOM representation.

Document Type Declaration (DTD):   A set of markup elements that defines the structure of an XML document.

DOM: See Document Object Model.

Domain: A named set of all possible values that an attribute can have. Domains can be defined by listing allowed values or by defining a rule for determining allowed values.

Domain/Key Normal Form (DK/NF):   A relation in which all constraints are logical consequences of domains and keys.

Download: Copying database data from one computer to another, usually from a mainframe or mini to a personal computer or LAN.

Drill down: User-directed disaggregation of data used to break higher-level totals into components.

Driver: In ODBC, a program that serves as an interface between the ODBC driver manager and a particular DBMS product. Runs on the client machines in a client-server architecture.

Driver manager: In ODBC, a program that serves as an interface between an application program and an ODBC driver. It determines the driver required, loads it into memory, and coordinates activity between the application and the driver. On Windows systems, it is provided by Microsoft.

DSD: See Data structure diagram.

DSS: Decision Support System; an interactive, computer-based facility for assisting decision making, especially for semistructured and unstructured problems. Such a system often includes a database and a query/update facility for processing ad hoc requests.

DTD: See Document Type Declaration.

DTS: See Distributed Transaction Service.

ECMAScript-262: The standard version of an easily learned interpreted language used for both Web server and Web client applications processing. The Microsoft version is called JScript, and the Netscape version is called JavaScript.

Encapsulated data: Properties or attributes contained in a program or object not visible or accessible to other programs or objects.

Encapsulated structure: A portion of an object that is not visible to other objects.

Enterprise Java Beans: A facility for managing distributed objects and distributed processing in the Java development world.

Entity: (1) Something of importance to a user that needs to be represented in a database. (2) In an entity-relationship model, entities are restricted to things that can be represented by a single table.

Entity class: A set of entities of the same type; for example, EMPLOYEE and DEPARTMENT.

Entity instance: A particular occurrence of an entity; for example, Employee 100 and the Accounting Department.

Entity-relationship diagram: A graphic used to represent entities and their relationships. In the traditional E-R model, entities are shown in squares or rectangles, and relationships are shown in diamonds. The cardinality of the relationship is shown inside the diamond. See also IDEF1X.

Entity-relationship model: The constructs and conventions used to create a model of the users' data (see also Data model). The things in the users' world are represented by entities, and the associations among those things are represented by relationships. The results are usually documented in an entity-relationship diagram.

Enumerated list: A list of allowed values for a domain, attribute, or column.

Equijoin: The process of joining relation A containing attribute A1 with B containing attribute B1 to form relation C, so that for each row in C, A1 = B1. Both A1 and B1 are represented in C.

E-R diagram: See Entity-relationship diagram.

Exclusive lock: A lock on a data resource that no other transaction can either read or update.

Existence-dependent entity: Same as a weak entity. An entity that cannot appear in the database unless an instance of one or more other entities also appears in the database. A subclass of existence-dependent entities is ID-dependent entities.

Explicit lock: A lock requested by a command from an application program.

Export: A service of a DBMS that extracts data from the database into a file. The file is intended to be read by another DBMS or program.

Extensible Markup Language: See XML.

Extensible Style Language: See XSLT.

Extent (of object): In the ODMG model, the union of all object instances. Attributes can be declared to be unique across an object's extent.

External schema: In the three-schema model, the subset of the database that is viewed by a user or group of users. Synonym of user view.

Extract: A portion of an operational database downloaded to a local area network or personal computer for local processing. Extracts are created to reduce communication cost and time when querying and creating reports from data created by transaction processing.

Failure transparency: In a distributed database system, the condition in which application programs are isolated from failure.

Field: (1) A logical group of bytes in a record used with file processing. (2) In the context of a relational model, a synonym for attribute.

File data source: An ODBC data source stored in a file that can be emailed or otherwise distributed among users.

First normal form: Any table that fits the definition of a relation.

Flat file: A file that has only a single value in each field. The meaning of the columns is the same in every row.

Force-write: A write of database data in which the DBMS waits for acknowledgment from the operating system that the data have been successfully written to the log.

Foreign key: An attribute that is a key of one or more relations other than the one in which it appears. Used to represent relationships.

Forward engineering: The automated process of using data model changes to drive changes in the database structure. Forward engineering is provided as a feature in data modeling tools such as ERWin and Visio.

Fourth normal form: A relation in third Boyce–Codd normal form, in which every multi-value dependency is a functional dependency.

Fragment: A row in a table (or record in a file) in which a required parent or child is not present. For example, a row in a LINE-ITEM table for which no ORDER row exists.

Functional dependency: A relationship between attributes in which one attribute or group of attributes determines the value of another. The expressions $X \rightarrow Y$, "X determines Y," and "Y is functionally dependent on X" mean that given a value of X, we can determine the value of Y.

Generalization hierarchy: A set of objects or entities of the same logical type that are arranged in a hierarchy of logical subtypes. For example, EMPLOYEE has the subtypes ENGINEER and ACCOUNTANT, and ENGINEER has the subtypes ELECTRICAL ENGINEER and MECHANICAL ENGINEER. Subtypes inherit characteristics of their supertypes.

Generalization object: An object that contains subtype objects. The generalization object and its subtypes all have the same key. Subtype objects inherit attributes from the generalization object. A generalization object is also called a supertype object.

Generic entity: In IDEF1X, an entity that has one or more category clusters. The generic entity takes the role of a supertype for the category entities in the category cluster.

Granularity: The size of database resource that can be locked. Locking the entire database is large granularity; locking a column of a particular row is small granularity.

Growing phase: The first stage in two-phase locking, in which locks are acquired but not released.

HAS-A relationship: A relationship between two entities or objects that are of different logical types, for example, EMPLOYEE HAS-A(n) AUTO. Contrast this with an IS-A relationship.

Hierarchical data model: A data model that represents all relationships using hierarchies or trees. Network structures must be decomposed into trees before they can be represented by a hierarchical data model. DL/I is the only surviving hierarchical data model.

HOLAP: Hybrid OLAP using a combination of ROLAP and MOLAP for supporting OLAP processing.

Horizontal partition: A subset of a table, consisting of complete rows of the table (for example, in a table with 10 rows, the first five rows).

Horizontal security: Limiting access to certain rows of a table or join.

Host variable: A variable in an application program into which a DBMS places a value from the database.

HTML: See Hypertext Markup Language.

HTTP: See Hypertext Transfer Protocol.

Hybrid object: An object containing a multi-value group that contains at least one object attribute.

Hypercube: In OLAP, a presentation structure having axes upon which data dimensions are placed. Measures of the data are shown in the cells of the hypercube. Also called cube.

Hypertext Markup Language (HTML): A standardized system of tagging text for formatting, locating images and other nontext files, and placing links or references to other documents.

Hypertext Transfer Protocol (HTTP): A standardized means for using TCP/IP for communicating HTML documents over networks.

ID-dependent entity: An entity that cannot logically exist without the existence of another entity. An APPOINTMENT, for example, cannot exist without a CLIENT to make the appointment. The identifier of the ID-dependent entity always contains the key of the entity on which it depends. Such entities are a subset of a weak entity. See also Strong entity, Weak entity, and Identifying connection relationship.

IDEF1X: A version of the entity-relationship model that was announced as a national standard in 1993.

Identifying connection relationship: In IDEF1X, a 1:1 or 1:N HAS-A relationship in which the child entity is ID-dependent on the parent.

IIS: Acronym for Internet Information Server; a Microsoft product that operates as an HTTP server. IIS is included as a part of Windows Professional.

Immutable object: In the ODMG standard, an object whose attributes cannot be changed.

Implementation: In OOP, a set of objects that instantiates a particular OOP interface.

Implicit lock: A lock that is automatically placed by the DBMS.

Import: A service of the DBMS which reads a file of data into the database.

Inconsistent backup: A backup file that contains uncommitted changes.

Inconsistent read problem: An anomaly that occurs in concurrent processing, in which transactions execute a series of reads that are inconsistent with one another. It can be prevented by two-phase locking and other strategies.

Index: Overhead data used to improve access and sorting performance. Indexes can be constructed for a single column or groups of columns. They are especially useful for columns used for control breaks in reports and to specify conditions in joins.

Information engineering: A version of the entity-relationship model developed by James Martin.

Inheritance: A characteristic of objected-oriented systems in which objects that are subtypes of other objects obtain attributes (data or methods) from their supertypes.

Inner join: Synonym for join. Contrast with outer join.

Insertion anomaly: In a relation, the condition that exists when, to add a complete row to a table, one must add facts about two or more logically different themes.

Instance failure: A failure in the operating system or hardware that causes the DBMS to fail.

Integrated definition 1, extended: Same as IDEF1X.

Integrated definition for information modeling: Same as IDEF1X.

Interface: (1) The means by which two or more programs call each other; the definition of the procedural calls between two or more programs. (2) In OOP, the design of a set of objects that includes the objects' names, methods, and properties.

Internal schema: In the three-schema model, a representation of a conceptual schema as physically stored using a particular product and/or technique.

Internet Information Server: See IIS.

Intersection relation: A relation used to represent a many-to-many relationship. It contains the keys of the relations in the relationship. An intersection relation transforms one N:M relationship into two 1:N relationships. In IDEF1X, an intersection relation is used to represent a non-specific relationship.

IS-A relationship: A relationship between two entities of the same logical type, in which one entity is a subtype of the other. For example, an ENGINEER is a subtype of EMPLOYEE and has an IS-A relationship to EMPLOYEE.

Isolation level: See Transaction isolation level.

IUnknown: An ActiveX interface in which one ActiveX program can call another, unknown ActiveX program. After a connection has been established, the first program can use the query interface to determine which objects, methods, and properties the second program supports.

Java: An object programming language that has better memory management and bounds checking than C++; used primarily for Internet applications, but also can be used as a general-purpose programming language. Java compilers generate Java byte code that is interpreted on client computers.

Java bean: A properly mannered Java class, suitable for taking home to Mother. Beans have no public instance variables; all of their persistent values are accessed via accessor methods, and they have either no constructors or only one explicitly defined zero-argument constructors.

JavaScript: A proprietary scripting language owned by Netscape. The Microsoft version is called JScript; the standard version is called ECMAScript-262. These are easily learned interpreted languages that are used for both Web server and Web-client applications processing. Sometimes written as Java Script.

Java Server Page (JSP): A combination of HTML and Java that is compiled into a Java servlet that is a subclass of the HttpServlet class. Java code embedded into a JSP has access to HTTP objects and methods. JSPs are used similarly to ASPs, but are compiled rather than interpreted.

Java servlet: See Servlet.

Java virtual machine: A Java bytecode interpreter that runs on a particular machine environment; for example, Intel 386 or Alpha. Such interpreters are usually embedded in browsers, included with the operating system, or included as part of a Java development environment.

JDBC: A standard interface by which application programs written in Java can access and process SQL databases (or table structures such as spreadsheets and text tables) in a DBMS-independent manner. It does not stand for Java Database Connectivity.

Join: A relational algebra operation on two relations, A and B, which produces a third relation, C. A row of A is concatenated with a row of B to form a new row in C if the rows in A and B meet restrictions concerning their values. For example, if A1 is an attribute in A and B1 is an attribute of B, then the join of A with B in which A1 < B1 will result in a relation, C, having the concatenation of rows in A and B in which the value of A1 is less than the value of B1. See also Equijoin and Natural join.

JScript: A proprietary scripting language owned by Microsoft. The Netscape version is called JavaScript; the standard version is called ECMAScript-262. These are easily learned interpreted languages used for both Web server and Web-client applications processing.

JSP: See Java Server Page.

Key: (1) A group of one or more attributes identifying a unique row in a relation. Because relations may not have duplicate rows, every relation must have at least one key, which is the composite of all of the attributes in the relation. A key is sometimes called a logical key. (2) With some relational DBMS products, an index on a column used to improve access and sorting speed. It is sometimes called a physical key.

Labeled namespace: In an XML schema document, a namespace that is given a name (label) within the document. All elements preceded by the name of the labeled namespace are assumed to be defined in that labeled namespace.

Level: In OLAP, a (possibly hierarchical) subset of a dimension.

Lock: The process of allocating a database resource to a particular transaction in a concurrent-processing system. The size of the resource locked is known as the lock granularity. With an exclusive lock, no other transaction may read or write the resource. With a shared lock, other transactions may read the resource, but no other transaction may write it.

Lock granularity: The size of a locked data element. The lock of a column value of a particular row is a small granularity lock, and the lock of an entire table is a large granularity lock.

Log: A file containing a record of database changes. The log contains before-images and after-images.

Lost update problem: Same as concurrent update problem.

Materialization: A database view as it appears in a form, report, or Web page.

Maximum cardinality: (1) In an E-R relationship, the maximum number of entities to which a given entity may be related. (2) In a relational design relationship, the maximum number of rows to which a given row may be related.

Me: In OOP, a special pointer to the current object instance. For example, Me.Name refers to the Name attribute of the current object.

Measure: In OLAP, the source data for the cube—data that are displayed in the cells. It may be raw data, or it may be functions of raw data such as SUM, AVG, or other computations.

Media failure: A failure that occurs when the DBMS is unable to write to a disk. Usually caused by a disk head crash or other disk failure.

Member: In OLAP, the value of a dimension.

Menu: A list of options presented to the user of a database (or other) application. The user selects the next action or activity from a list. Actions are restricted to those in the list. Contrast this with Command.

Metadata: Data concerning the structure of data in a database stored in the data dictionary. Metadata are used to describe tables, columns, constraints, indexes, and so forth. Compare this with Application metadata.

Method: A program attached to an object-oriented programming (OOP) object. A method can be inherited by lower-level OOP objects.

Minimum cardinality: (1) In an E-R relationship, the minimum number of entities to which a given entity must be related. (2) In a relational design relationship, the minimum number of rows to which a given row must be related.

Mixed partition: A combination of a horizontal and a vertical partition; for example, in a table with five columns and five rows, the first three columns of the first three rows.

Modification anomaly: The situation that exists when the insertion of a row into a table inserts facts about two or more themes, or when the deletion of a row removes facts about two or more themes.

MOLAP: Multidimensional OLAP using a purpose-built processor for supporting OLAP processing.

Multiple-tier driver: In ODBC, a two-part driver, usually for a client-server database system. One part of the driver resides on the client and interfaces with the application; the second part resides on the server and interfaces with the DBMS.

Multi-value attribute: The attribute of a semantic object that has a maximum cardinality greater than one.

Multi-value dependency: A condition in a relation with three or more attributes in which independent attributes appear to have relationships they do not have. Formally, in a relation R (A, B, C), having key (A, B, C) where A is matched with multiple values of B (or of C or both), B does not determine C, and C does not determine B. An example is the relation EMPLOYEE (EmpNumber, Emp-skill, Dependent-name), where an employee can have multiple values of Emp-skill and Dependent-name. Emp-skill and Dependent-name do not have any relationship, but they do appear to in the relation.

Mutable object: In the ODMG standard, an object whose attributes may be changed.

Natural join: A join of a relation A having attribute A1 with relation B having attribute B1, where A1 equals B1. The joined relation, C, contains either column A1 or B1, but not both. Contrast this with Equijoin.

Network: (1) A group of interconnected computers. (2) An intranet. (3) The Internet.

Network data model: A data model supporting at least simple network relationships. The CODASYL DBTG, which supports simple network relationships but not complex relationships, is the most important network data model.

N:M: An abbreviation for a many-to-many relationship between entities or between rows of a table.

Node: (1) An entity in a tree. (2) A computer in a distributed-processing system.

Non-identifying connection relationships: In IDEF1X, 1:1 and 1:N has-a relationships that do not involve ID-dependent entities.

Nonobject attribute: An attribute of a semantic object that is not an object.

Nonrepeatable reads: The situation that occurs when a transaction reads data it has previously read, and finds modifications or deletions caused by a committed transaction.

Non-specific relationships: In IDEF1X, an N:M relationship.

Normal form: A rule or set of rules governing the allowed structure of relations. The rules apply to attributes, functional dependencies, multi-value dependencies, domains, and constraints. The most important normal forms are 1NF, 2NF, 3NF, BoyceCodd NF, 4NF, 5NF, and domain/key normal form.

Normalization: The process of evaluating a relation to determine whether it is in a specified normal form and of converting it to relations in that specified normal form, if necessary.

Nothing: In OOP, a null object reference used to set an object pointer to null or test an object pointer to determine whether it is null.

Not-type-valid document: An XML document that either does not conform to its DTD or does not have a DTD; contrast with Type-valid document. See also Schema-valid document.

Null value: An attribute value that has never been supplied. Such values are ambiguous and can mean that (a) the value is unknown, (b) the value is not appropriate, or (c) the value is known to be blank.

Object: (1) A semantic object. (2) A structure in an object-oriented program that contains an encapsulated data structure and data methods. Such objects are arranged in a hierarchy so that objects can inherit methods from their parents. (3) In security systems, a unit of data protected by a password or other means.

Object attribute: An attribute of a semantic object that represents a link to an object.

Object class: In object-oriented programming, a set of objects with a common structure.

Object class library: In object-oriented programming, a collection of object classes, usually a collection that serves a particular purpose.

Object constructor: In object-oriented programming, a function that creates an object.

Object destructor: In object-oriented programming, a function that destroys an object.

Object diagram: A portrait-oriented rectangle that represents the structure of a semantic object.

Object identifier: An attribute that is used to specify an object instance. Object identifiers can be unique, meaning that they identify one (and only one) instance; or nonunique, meaning that they identify exactly one object instance.

Object instance: The occurrence of a particular semantic object; for example, the SALESPERSON semantic object having LastName equal to Jones.

Object-oriented programming: A style of computer programming in which programs are developed as sets of objects that have data members and methods. Objects interface with one another by calling each others' methods.

Object persistence: In object-oriented programming, the characteristic that an object can be saved to non-volatile memory such as a disk. Persistent objects exist between executions of a program.

Object-relational DBMS: DBMS products that support both relational and object-oriented programming data structures, such as Oracle.

Object view: The portion of a semantic object that is visible to a particular application. A view consists of the name of the semantic object plus a list of the attributes visible in that view.

ODBC: See Open Database Connectivity standard.

ODMG-93: A report issued by the Object Data Management Group, which is a consortium of object database vendors and other interested industry experts. The report applies the ideas of another group, the Object Management Group, to the problem of object databases. The first ODMG report was produced in 1993 and is accordingly referred to as ODMG-93.

OLAP: On-Line Analytical Processing; a form of data presentation in which data are summarized aggregated, de-aggregated, and viewed in the frame of a table or a cube.

OLE DB: The COM-based foundation of data access in the Microsoft world. OLE DB objects support the OLE object standard. ADO is based upon OLE DB.

OLE object: Object Linking and Embedding object; COM objects that support interfaces for embedding into other objects.

1:N: An abbreviation for a one-to-many relationship between entities or between rows of a table.

On-Line Analytical Processing: See OLAP.

OOP: See Object-oriented programming.

Open Database Connectivity standard (ODBC): A standard interface by which application programs can access and process SQL databases (or table structures such as spreadsheets and text tables) in a DBMS-independent manner. The driver manager portion of ODBC is incorporated into Windows. ODBC drivers are supplied by DBMS vendors, Microsoft, and by other third-party software developers.

Optimistic locking: A locking strategy that assumes no conflict will occur, processes a transaction, and then checks to determine whether conflict did occur. If so, the transaction is aborted. Also see pessimistic locking.

Option button: In a GUI environment, an element of the user interface in which the user can select an item from a list. Clicking one button deselects the button currently pressed, if any. It operates like the radio buttons on a car radio and is the same as a radio button (see Radio button), but was introduced under a different name to avoid litigation among vendors.

Orphan: Any row (record) that is missing its parent in a mandatory one-to-many relationship.

Outer join: A join in which all the rows of a table appear in the result relation, regardless of whether they have a match in the join condition. In a left outer join, all the rows in the left-hand relation appear; in a right outer join, all the rows in the right-hand relation appear.

Overhead data: Metadata created by the DBMS to improve performance; for example, indexes and linked lists.

Owner: In data administration, the department or other organizational unit in charge of the management of a particular data item. An owner can also be called a data proponent.

Paired attribute: In a semantic object, object attributes are paired. If object A has an object attribute of object B, object B will have an object attribute of object A; that is, the object attributes are paired with each other.

Parent: A row, record, or node on the one side of a one-to-many relationship.

Partition: (1) A portion of a distributed database. (2) The portion of a network that is separated from the rest of the network during a network failure.

Persistent object: An OOP object that has been written to persistent storage.

Pessimistic locking: A locking strategy that prevents conflict by placing locks before processing database read and write requests. See also Optimistic locking and Deadlock.

Phantom reads: The situation that occurs when a transaction reads data it has previously read and finds new rows that were inserted by a committed transaction.

Physical key: A column that has an index or other data structure created for it; a synonym for an index. Such structures are created to improve searching and sorting on the column values.

PL/SQL: Programming language for SQL. An Oracle-supplied language that augments SQL with programming language structures such as while loops, if-then-else blocks, and other such constructs. PL/SQL is used to create stored procedures and triggers.

Pointer: An address to an instance of a data item in a structure.

Polymorphism: In OOP, the situation in which one name can be used to invoke different functions. Polymorphism in which the functions are distinguished by having different parameter sequences is called parametric polymorphism. For it, names are resolved by the compiler at compile time. Polymorphism in which the functions are distinguished by object inheritance is called inheritance polymorphism. Such names are resolved at runtime by determining the type of object being invoked.

Primary key: A candidate key selected to be the key of a relation.

Processing-interface subsystem: The portion of the DBMS routines that executes commands for processing the database. It accepts input from interactive query programs and from application programs written in standard or DBMS-specific languages.

Processing rights and responsibilities: Organizational policies regarding which groups can take which actions on specified data-items or other collections of data.

Program/data independence: The condition existing when the structure of the data is not defined in application programs. Rather, it is defined in the database and then the application programs obtain it from the DBMS. In this way, changes can be made in the data structures that may not necessarily be made in the application programs.

Programming Language for SQL: See PL/SQL.

Property: Same as Attribute.

Proponent: See Data proponent.

Prototype: A quickly developed demonstration of an application or portion of an application.

QBE: Query By Example. A style of query interface, first developed by IBM but now used by other vendors, that enables users to express queries by providing examples of the results they seek.

Query By Example: See QBE.

Query Interface: An interface in Microsoft COM that can be used to determine the objects, methods, and properties supported by an ActiveX program.

Query/update language: A language that can be employed by end users to query the database and make changes in the database data.

RDS: See Remote Data Services.

Read committed: A level of transaction isolation that prohibits dirty reads, but allows nonrepeatable reads and phantom reads.

Read uncommitted: A level of transaction isolation that allows dirty reads, nonrepeatable reads, and phantom reads to occur.

Record: (1) A group of fields pertaining to the same entity; used in file-processing systems. (2) In a relational model, a synonym for row and tuple.

Recordset: An ADO object that represents a relation; created as the result of the execution of a SQL statement or a stored procedure.

Recursive relationship: A relationship among entities, objects, or rows of the same type. For example, if CUSTOMERs refer other CUSTOMERs, the relationship *refers* is recursive.

ReDo files: In Oracle, backups of rollback segments used for backup and recovery. There are online and offline ReDo files.

Referential integrity actions: Rules that specify the activities that should take place when insert, update, or delete actions occur on either the parent or child entities in a relationship. Possible actions are none, cascade, set default, set null, and restrict. Other actions can be defined as part of the database design.

Referential integrity constraint: A relationship constraint on foreign key values. A referential integrity constraint specifies that the values of a foreign key must be a proper subset of the values of the primary key to which it refers.

Relation: A two-dimensional array containing single-value entries and no duplicate rows. The meaning of the columns is the same in every row. The order of the rows and columns is immaterial.

Relational database: A database consisting of relations. In practice, relational databases contain relations with duplicate rows. Most DBMS products include a feature that removes duplicate rows when necessary and appropriate. Such a removal is not done as a matter of course because it can be time-consuming and expensive.

Relational data model: A data model in which data is stored in relations and relationships between rows are represented by data values.

Relational schema: A set of relations with referential integrity and other interrelation constraints.

Relationship: An association between two entities, objects, or rows of relations.

Relationship cardinality constraint: A constraint on the number of rows that can participate in a relationship. Minimum cardinality constraints determine the number of rows that must participate; maximum cardinality constraints specify the largest number of rows that can participate.

Relationship constraint: Either a referential integrity constraint or a relationship cardinality constraint.

Remote Data Services (RDS): A set of ActiveX controls and features that allow data to be cached on a client machine and formatted, sorted, and filtered without assistance from the Web server.

Repeatable read: A level of transaction isolation that disallows both dirty reads and nonrepeatable reads. Phantom reads can occur.

Replicated data: In a distributed database, data that are stored on two or more computers.

Replication: For both Oracle and SQL Server, a term that refers to databases that are distributed on more than one computer.

Replication transparency: In a distributed database system, the condition in which application programs do not know and do not need to know whether data are replicated. If data are replicated, the DDBMS will ensure that all copies are updated consistently, without the involvement of the application program.

Repository: A collection of metadata about database structure, applications, Web pages, users, and other application components. Active repositories are maintained automatically by tools in the application-development environment. Passive repositories must be maintained manually.

Resource locking: See Lock.

Resource-sharing architecture: The structure of a local area network in which one microcomputer performs file-processing services for other microcomputers. In a database application, each user computer contains a copy of the DBMS that forwards input/output requests to the file server. Only file I/O is processed by the file server; all database activities are processed by the DBMS on the user's computer.

Reverse engineered data model: The data model that results from reverse engineering. It is not a conceptual model because it includes physical structures such as intersection tables. It is, however, more conceptual that a database schema.

Reverse engineering: The process of reading the structure of an existing database and creating a reverse engineered data model from that schema.

ROLAP: Relational OLAP using a relational DBMS to support OLAP processing.

Rollback: The process of recovering a database in which before-images are applied to the database to return to an earlier checkpoint or other point at which the database is logically consistent.

Rollback segment: In Oracle, a buffer used to store before images for the purposes of concurrency control and transaction logging. Rollback segments can be archived and used subsequently for recovery.

Rollforward: The process of recovering a database by applying after-images to a saved copy of the database to bring it to a checkpoint or other point at which the database is logically consistent.

Root: The top record, row, or node in a tree. A root has no parent.

Row: A group of columns in a table. All the columns in a row pertain to the same entity. A row is the same as a tuple and a record.

Row identifier: In SQL3, a unique, system-supplied identifier; a surrogate key. The row identifier can be made visible by stating WITH IDENTITY in the table definition.

Row object: In Oracle, a table that contains objects as its rows.

Rowset: In OLE DB, an abstraction of data collections such as recordsets, email addresses, and nonrelational and other data.

SAX: Simple API (application program interface) for XML. An event-based parser that notifies a program when the elements of an XML document have been encountered during document parsing.

Schema: A complete logical view of the database.

SCN: See System Change Number.

Schema-valid document: An XML document that conforms to its XML Schema definition.

Scrollable cursor: A cursor type that enables forward and backward movement through a recordset. Three scrollable cursor types discussed in this text are snapshot, keyset, and dynamic.

Second normal form: A relation in first normal form in which all nonkey attributes are dependent on all of the key attributes.

Semantic object diagram: Same as Object diagram.

Semantic object model: The constructs and conventions used to create a model of the users' data. The things in the users' world are represented by semantic objects (sometimes called objects). Relationships are modeled in the objects, and the results are usually documented in object diagrams.

Semantic-object view: The portion of a semantic object that is visible in a form or report.

Serializable: A level of transaction isolation that disallows dirty reads, nonrepeatable reads, and phantom reads.

Service provider: An OLE DB data provider that transforms data. A service provider is both a data consumer and a data provider.

Servlet: A compiled, machine-independent Java bytecode program that is run by a Java virtual machine located on a Web server.

SGML: See Standard Generalized Markup Language.

Shared lock: A lock against a data resource in which only one transaction may update the data, but many transactions can concurrently read that data.

Shrinking phase: In two-phase locking, the stage at which locks are released but no lock is acquired.

Sibling: A record or node that has the same parent as another record or node.

Simple network: (1) A set of three relations and two relationships in which one of the relations, R, has a many-to-one relationship with the other two relations. The rows in R have two parents, and the parents are of different types. (2) Any set of tables and relationships containing the structure defined in (1).

Simple object: An object that contains no repeating attributes and no object attributes.

Simple Object Access Protocol: A standard used for remote procedure calls. It uses XML for definition of the data and HTTP for transport. Contrast with SOAP.

Single-tier driver: In ODBC, a database driver that accepts SQL statements from the driver manager and processes them without invoking another program or DBMS. A single-tier driver is both an ODBC driver and a DBMS; used for file-processing systems.

Single-value attribute: In a semantic object, an attribute having a maximum cardinality of one.

Slice: In OLAP, a dimension or measure held constant for a display.

Snowflake schema: In an OLAP database, the structure of tables such that dimension tables may be several levels away from the table storing the measure values. Such dimension tables are usually normalized. Contrast with Star schema.

SOAP: Originally, Simple Object Access Protocol. Today, it is a protocol for remote procedure calls that differs from the simple object access protocol because it involves transport protocols beyond HTTP.

SQL: Structured Query Language; a language for defining the structure and processing of a relational database. It can be used stand-alone or embedded in application code. The most common version is SQL92, a version adopted by the American National Standards Institute in 1992. It was originally developed by IBM.

SQL3: SQL3 is an extension to the SQL92 database standard that includes support for object-oriented database management. Developed by both the ANSI X3H2 and the ISO/IEC JTC1/SC21/WG3 standardization committees.

SQL view: A relation that is constructed from a single SQL SELECT statement. SQL views have at most one multi-valued path. The term *view* in most DBMS products, including Access, Oracle and SQL Server, means SQL view.

Standard Generalized Markup Language (SGML): A standard means for tagging and marking the format, structure, and content of documents. HTML is an application of SGML. XML is a subset of SGML.

Star schema: In an OLAP database, the structure of tables such that every dimension table is adjacent to the table storing the measure values. Contrast with snowflake schema. In the star schema, the dimension tables are often not normalized.

Statement level consistency: All rows impacted by a single SQL statement are protected from changes made by other users during the execution of the statement. Contrast with transaction level consistency.

Stored procedure: A collection of SQL statements stored as a file that can be invoked by a single command. Usually, DBMS products provide a language for creating stored procedures that augments SQL with programming language constructs. Oracle provides PL/SQL for this purpose; SQL Server provides TRANS-ACT/SQL. With some products, stored procedures can be written in a standard language such as Java. Stored procedures are stored within the database itself.

Strong entity: In an entity-relationship model, any entity whose existence in the database does not depend on the existence of any other entity. See also ID-dependent entity and Weak entity.

Structured Query Language: See SQL.

Structured schema: An XML schema that is not flat.

Subtable: In SQL3, a table that is a subtype of a second table called a supertable.

Subtype: In generalization hierarchies, an entity or object that is a subspecies or subcategory of a higher-level type. For example, ENGINEER is a subtype of EMPLOYEE.

Supertable: In SQL3, a table that has one or more subtables defined on it.

Supertype: In generalization hierarchies, an entity or object that logically contains subtypes. For example, EMPLOYEE is a supertype of ENGINEER, ACCOUNTANT, and MANAGER.

Surrogate key: A unique, system-supplied identifier used as the primary key of a relation. The values of a surrogate key have no meaning to the users and are usually hidden on forms and reports.

Swizzling: In OOP, the process of converting a permanent object identifier into an in-memory address and the reverse.

System Change Number (SCN): In Oracle, a database-wide value that is used to order changes made to database data. The SCN is incremented by whenever database changes are committed.

System data source: An ODBC data source that is local to a single computer and can be accessed by that computer's operating system and select users of that operating system.

Tabular data provider: An OLE DB data provider that presents data in the form of rowsets.

Target namespace: In an XML Schema document, the namespace that the schema is creating.

Third normal form: A relation in second normal form that has no transitive dependencies.

Three-tier architecture: A system of computers having a database server, a Web server, and one or more client computers. The database server hosts a DBMS, the Web server hosts an HTTP server, and the client computer hosts a browser. Each tier can run a different operating system.

Top-down database design: The design of a database that works from the general to the specific. The resulting database can serve an organization's overall needs; the danger is that it may never be completed. See also Bottom-up database design.

Transaction: (1) An atomic transaction. (2) The record of an event in the business world.

Transaction boundary: The group of database commands that must be committed or aborted as a unit.

Transaction isolation level: The degree to which a database transaction is protected from actions by other transactions. The 1992 SQL standard specified four isolation levels: Read Uncommitted, Read Committed, Repeatable Reads, and Serializable.

Transaction level consistency: All rows impacted by any of the SQL statements in a transaction are protected from changes during the entire transaction. This level of consistency is expensive to enforce and may (probably will) reduce throughput. It may also mean that a transaction cannot see its own changes. Contrast with Statement level consistency.

Transaction node: In a distributed database system, a computer that processes a distributed transaction manager.

TRANSACT-SQL: A Microsoft-supplied language that is part of SQL Server. It augments SQL with programming language structures such as while loops, if-then-else blocks, and other such constructs. TRANSACT/SQL is used to create stored procedures and triggers. Sometimes called T/SQL.

Transient object: In OOP, an object that has not been written to permanent storage. The object will be lost when the program terminates.

Transitive dependency: In a relation having at least three attributes: R (A, B, C), the situation in which A determines B, B determines C, but B does not determine A.

Tree: A collection of records, entities, or other data structures in which each element has at most one parent, except for the top element, which has no parent.

Trigger: A special type of stored procedure that is invoked by the DBMS when a specified condition occurs. BEFORE triggers are executed before a specified database action, AFTER triggers are executed after a specified database action, and INSTEAD OF triggers are executed in place of a specified database action. INSTEAD OF triggers are normally used to update data in SQL views.

T-SQL: See Transact-SQL.

Tuple: Same as Row.

Two-phase commitment: In a distributed database system, a process of commitment among nodes in which the nodes first vote on whether they can commit a transaction. If all the nodes vote yes, the transaction is committed. If any node votes no, the transaction is aborted. A two-phase commitment is required to prevent inconsistent processing in distributed databases.

Two-phase locking: The procedure by which locks are obtained and released in two phases. During the growing phase, the locks are obtained; and during the shrinking phase, the locks are released. After a lock is released, no other lock will be granted that transaction. Such a procedure ensures consistency in database updates in a concurrent-processing environment.

Type domain: In IDEF1X, a domain that is defined as a subset of a base domain or of another type domain.

Type-valid document: An XML document that conforms to its DTD; contrast with not-type-valid document.

UML: Unified Modeling Language; a set of structures and techniques for modeling and designing object-oriented programs and applications. It is both a methodology and a set of tools for such development. UML incorporates the entity-relationship model for data modeling.

Unified Modeling Language: See UML.

Updatable view: A SQL view that can be updated. Rules for determining whether or not a view can be updated are complex. See Figure 7-13. Non-updateable views can be made updateable by writing INSTEAD OF triggers.

User data source: An ODBC data source that is available only to the user who created it.

User view: In the three-schema model, the portion of the database that is viewed by a user or group of users. Synonym of external view.

VBScript: An easily learned, interpreted language used for both Web server and Web client applications processing; a subset of Microsoft Visual Basic.

Vertical partition: A subset of the columns of a table. For example, in a table with 10 columns, the first five columns.

Vertical security: Limiting access to certain columns of a table or join.

View: A structured list of data items from entities or semantic objects defined in the data model.

Weak entity: In an entity-relationship model, an entity whose logical existence in the database depends on the existence of another entity. See also ID-dependent entity, Strong entity, and Identifying connection relationship.

XML: Extensible Markup Language; a standard markup language that provides a clear separation between structure, content, and materialization; can represent arbitrary hierarchies and hence be used to transmit any database view.

XML Namespaces: A standard for assigning names to defined collections. X:Name is interpreted as the element Name as defined in namespace X. Y:Name is interpreted as the element Name as defined in namespace Y. Useful for disambiguating terms.

XML Schema: An XML-compliant language for constraining the structure of an XML document. Extends and replaces DTDs. Standards are evolving; very important to database processing.

XPath: A sublanguage within XSLT that is used to identify parts of an XML document to be processed. Can also be used for calculations and string manipulation. Co-mingled with XSLT.

XPointer: A standard for linking one document to another. XPath has many elements from XPointer.

XQuery: A standard for expressing database queries as XML documents. The structure of the query uses XPath facilities and the result of the query is represented in an XML format. Under development and likely to be important in the future.

XSL: XSLT Stylesheet. The document that provides the {match, action} pairs and other data for XSLT to use when transforming an XML document.

XSLT: Extensible Style Language: Transformations. A program (or process) that applies XSLT Stylesheets to an XML document to produce a transformed XML document.

Bibliography

▷ WEB RESOURCES

Check these sites for recent articles about database topics:
CNet—http://www.news.com
Advisor—http://www.advisor.com
Intelligent Enterprise—http://www.intelligententerprise.com
PCMagazine—http://www.pcmag.com
ZDNet—http://www.zdnet.com

▷ DBMS AND OTHER VENDORS

Java—http://java.sun.com
SQL Server—http://www.microsoft.com/sql
Oracle—http://www.oracle.com
MySQL—http://www.mysql.com
Tabledesigner—http://www.tabledesigner.com

▷ IDEF1X

http://www.idef.com/idef1x.html
http://www.idef.com/Downloads/pdf/Idef1x.pdf

▷ .NET

http://www.fawcette.com
http://www.microsoft.com/net
http://www.msdn.microsoft.com

▷ STANDARDS

JDBC—http://java.sun.com/products/jdbc and http://www.mysql.com/downloads/api-jdbc.html
ODBC—http://www.liv.ac.uk/middleware/html/odbc.html
ODMG—http://www.odmg.org
Worldwide Web Consortium—http://www.w3.org
XML—http://www.xml.org
XML and Web services—http://www.zapthink.com/

▷ BOOKS AND PUBLICATIONS

ANSI X3. *American National Standard for Information Systems—Database Language SQL*. ANSI, 1992.
Berson, Alex, and Stephen J. Smith. *Data Warehousing, Data Mining, and OLAP*. New York: McGraw-Hill, 1997.
Boumphrey, Frank. *Professional Stylesheets for HTML and XML*. Chicago: Wrox Press, 1998.

Bowen, Rich, and Ken Coar. *Apache Server Unleashed.* Indianapolis, IN: Sams, 2000.

Bruce, Thomas, and John A. Zachman. *Designing Quality Databases with IDEF1X Information Models.* New York: Dorset House, 1992.

Chamberlin, D. D., et al. "SEQUEL 2: A Unified Approach to Data Definition, Manipulation, and Control." *IBM Journal of Research and Development 20* (November 1976).

Chang, Ben, Mark Scardina, and Stefan Kiritzov. *Oracle 9i XML Handbook.* New York: McGraw-Hill Osborne Media, 2001.

Chen, Peter, Editor. *Entity-Relationship Approach to Information Modeling and Analysis—Proceedings*, Elsevier Science, 1984.

Chen, Peter. "The Entity-Relationship Model: Toward a Unified Model of Data." *ACM Transactions on Database Systems 1* (March 1976).

Coar, Ken A. L. *Apache Server for Dummies.* New York: John Wiley & Sons, 1997.

Codd, E. F. "Extending the Relational Model to Capture More Meaning." *Transactions on Database Systems 4* (December 1979).

Codd, E. F. "A Relational Model of Data for Large Shared Data Banks." *Communications of the ACM 25* (February 1970).

Coffee, Peter. "No-Sweat Database Design." *PC Week* (March 11, 1996).

Corning, Michael, Steve Elfanbaum, and David Melnick. *Working with Active Server Pages.* Indianapolis, IN: Que, 1997.

Deitel, Harvey M., and Paul J. Deitel. *Java: How to Program, 4th Edition.* Upper Saddle River, NJ: Prentice-Hall, 2002.

Embley, David W. "NFQL: The Natural Forms Query Language." *ACM Transactions on Database Systems 14* (June 1989).

Eswaran, K. P., et al. "The Notion of Consistency and Predicate Locks in a Database System." *Communications of the ACM 19* (November 1976).

Fagin, R. "Multivalued Dependencies and a New Normal Form for Relational Databases." *Transactions on Database Systems 2* (September 1977).

Fagin, R. "A Normal Form for Relational Databases that is Based on Domains and Keys." *Transactions on Database Systems 6* (September 1981).

Feuerstein, Steven and Bill Pribyl. *Oracle PL/SQL Programming, 3rd Edition.* Sebastopol, CA: O'Reilly, 2002.

Fields, Duane K., and Mark A Kolb. *Web Development with Java Server Pages.* Greenwich, CT: Manning Press, 2000.

Flanagan, David, et al. *Java Enterprise in a Nutshell, 2nd Edition.* Sebastapol, CA: O'Reilly, 2002.

Goldfarb, Charles F., and Paul Prescod. *The XML Handbook, 2nd Edition.* Upper Saddle River, NJ: Prentice Hall PTR, 2000.

Goodman, Danny. *Dynamic HTML: The Definitive Resource, 2nd Edition.* Sebastopol, CA: O'Reilly and Associates, 2002.

Hall, Marty. *Core Servlets and Java Server Pages.* Upper Saddle River, NJ: Prentice-Hall, 2000.

Hammer, M., and D. McLeod. "Database Description with SDM: A Semantic Database Model." *Transactions on Database Systems 6* (September 1981).

Halvorson, Michael. *Microsoft Visual Basic.Net Step by Step.* Redmond, WA: Microsoft Press, 2002.

Harold, Elliotte Rusty. *XML: Extensible Markup Language.* New York: John Wiley & Sons, 1998.

Kay, Michael H. *XSLT Programmer's Reference.* Birmingham, 2nd Edition. UK: WROX Press, 2001.

Keuffel, Warren. "Battle of the Modeling Techniques." *DBMS Magazine* (August 1996).

Kroenke, David. "Waxing Semantic: An Interview." *DBMS Magazine* (September 1994).

Loney, Kevin, and George Koch. *Oracle8i: The Complete Reference.* New York: McGraw-Hill Osborne Media, 2000.

Loney, Kevin, and Marlene Theriault. *Oracle9i DBA Handbook.* New York: McGraw-Hill Osborne Media, 2001.

Loomis, Mary E. S. *Object Databases: The Essentials*. Reading, MA: Addison-Wesley, 1994.

McLaughlin, Brett. *Java and XML, 2nd Edition: Solutions to Real-World Problems*. Sebastopol, CA: O'Reilly, 2001.

Meyers, Nathan. *Java Programming on Linux*. Indianapolis, IN: Waite Group Press, 1999.

Monson-Haefel, Richard. *Enterprise Java Beans, 2nd Edition*. Sebastopol, CA: O'Reilly, 2001.

Moriarty, T. "Business Rule Analysis." *Database Programming and Design* (April 1993).

Muench, Steve. *Building Oracle XML Applications*. Sebastapol, CA: O'Reilly, 2000.

Muller, Robert J. *Database Design for Smarties: Using UML for Data Modeling*. San Francisco: Morgan Kaufmann Publishers, 1999.

Nijssen, G. M., Nijssen, S., and T. A. Halpin. *Conceptual Schema and Relational Database Design: A Fact-Oriented Approach*. Englewood Cliffs, NJ: Prentice-Hall, 1989.

Nolan, Richard L. *Managing the Data Resource Function, 2nd Edition*. St. Paul: West Publishing, 1999.

Red Hat, Inc. *Linux 6.2 Getting Started Guide*. Durham, NC: Red Hat, Inc., 2000.

Ricart, Manuel Alberto. *The Complete Idiot's Guide to Linux, 2nd Edition*. Indianapolis, IN: Alpha Books, 1999.

Rogers, Dan. "Manage Data with Modeling Tools." *VB Tech Journal* (December 1996).

Sceppa, David. *Microsoft ADO.NET*. Redmond, WA: Microsoft Press, 2002.

Shumate, John. *A Practical Guide to Microsoft OLAP Server*. Reading, MA: Addison-Wesley, 2000.

Thakkar, Meghraj. *Teach Yourself Oracle 8i on Windows NT in 24 Hours*. Indianapolis, IN: Sams, 1999.

Theriault, Marlene and Aaron Newman. *Oracle Security Handbook*. New York: McGraw-Hill Osborne Media, 2001.

Thomsen, Erik. *OLAP Solutions: Building Multidimensional Information Systems, 2nd Edition*. New York: John Wiley & Sons, 2002.

Walther, Stephen. *ASP.NET Unleashed*. Indianapolis, IN: Sams, 2001.

Weissinger, A. Keyton. *ASP in a Nutshell: A Desktop Quick Reference, 2nd Edition*. Sebastopol, CA: O'Reilly, 2000.

Zloof, M. M. "Query by Example." *Proceedings of the National Computer Conference*, AFIPS 44 (May 1975).

Index

687